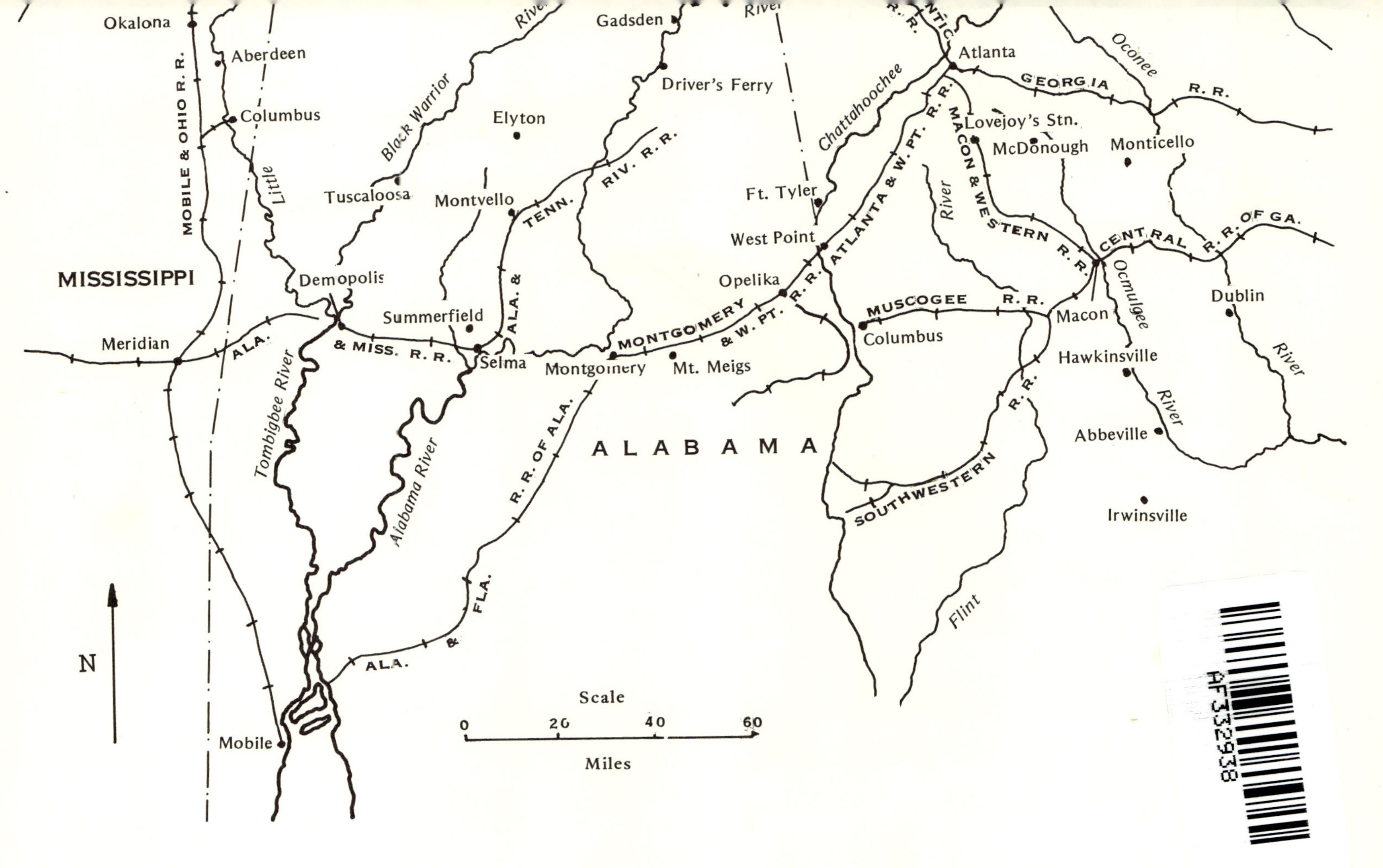

MISSISSIPPI
ALABAMA
GEORGIA
Okalona
Aberdeen
Columbus
Gadsden
Driver's Ferry
Atlanta
Lovejoy's Stn.
McDonough
Monticello
Elyton
Tuscaloosa
Montvello
Ft. Tyler
West Point
Opelika
Dublin
Meridian
Demopolis
Summerfield
Selma
Montgomery
Mt. Meigs
Columbus
Macon
Hawkinsville
Abbeville
Irwinsville
Mobile
Black Warrior
Little
Chattahoochee
River
Oconee
River
Tombigbee River
Alabama River
Flint
Ocmulgee
River
MOBILE & OHIO R. R.
TENN. RIV. R. R.
ATLANTA & W. PT. R. R.
MACON & WESTERN R. R.
CENTRAL R. R. OF GA.
ATLANTIC R. R.
ALA. & MISS. R. R.
MONTGOMERY & W. PT. R. R.
MUSCOGEE R. R.
SOUTHWESTERN R. R.
R. R. OF ALA.
ALA. & FLA.
N
Scale
0    20    40    60
Miles
AF332938

# THE DEPENDABLE GENERAL

General George H. Thomas, U. S. A.
Painted by Alden Finney Brooks in 1873.

# THE DEPENDABLE GENERAL

*Supreme in Tactics of
Strategy and Command*

*by Frank A. Palumbo*

*91 Illustrations*

Published 1983 by
MORNINGSIDE HOUSE, INC.
P. O. Box 1087, 260 Oak Street
Dayton, Ohio 45401

© by Frank A. Palumbo

Library of Congress Cataloging in Publication Data

Palumbo, Frank A.
George Henry Thomas, Major General, U. S. A.: the dependable general, supreme in tactics of strategy and command.

Bibliography: p.
Includes index.
1. Thomas, George Henry, 1816-1870. 2. United States—History—Civil War, 1861-1865—Campaigns. 3. Generals—United States—Biography. 4. United States. Army—Biography. I. Title.
E467.1.T4P34   1983        973.7'42'0924  [B]  83-17261
ISBN 0-89029-311-2 (alk. paper)

ISBN No. 0-89029-311-2



Library of Congress No. 83-17261

This book is printed on Gladfelter acid-free paper.

Composed, printed and bound in the United States of America.

Published by

MORNINGSIDE HOUSE, INC.
P. O. Box 1087, 260 Oak Street
Dayton, Ohio 45401

# TABLE OF CONTENTS

# *Maps*

Maps — Drawn by Dave Lilley

# *Acknowledgements*

No author labors alone who compiles a historical manuscript. A project of this kind requires the untiring generosity of able and knowledgeable persons from many walks of life and from many different places. Extensive research, though much of it must be performed by others, is the *sine qua non* of an authoritative work. For the invaluable assistance of friends and of strangers who, in the course of my writing this work, became friends, I am deeply indebted. To those myriad persons who have given me counsel, aid, and encouragement—historians, librarians, research assistants, scholars of the Civil War period, and others—I wish to extend my sincere gratitude and appreciation.

Deserving special mention are:

Dr. James I. Robertson, Jr., Professor of History and head of the Department of History, Virginia Polytechnic Institute and State Univerity, Blacksburg, to whom I am profoundly grateful for his reading and constructive criticism of the manuscript as well as for his gracious Foreword;

Joseph C. Wolf (Retired) Custodian of Local History and Genealogy of the Newberry Library, Chicago, at whose door I was constantly knocking for historical information, for the many long hours he spent in searching for reference material and placing it at my disposal;

The late E. B. "Pete" Long, Civil War historian and author, Associate Professor of American Studies, the University of Wyoming at Laramie, who also read the manuscript in preparation and who suggested many helpful changes of continuity; and his wife Barbara for her artistic touch-up of the rare print *Sherman's March to the Sea;*

Elmer C. Brinkman of Lake Forest, Illinois, a close friend and one of the most industrious scholars of the Civil War period, whose insights and opinions concerning the manuscript proved invaluable to me;

Alan C. Aimone, Military Librarian; Stanley P. Tozeski, Chief Archivist; and Kenneth W. Rapp, Assistant Archivist, United States Military Academy at West Point, New York, for their assistance in providing the academic and military records of General Thomas as well as copies of rare military documents;

Wilbur D. Thomas of Washington, D. C. (no relationship to General Thomas), author of *General George H. Thomas,* a biography, who furnished material for use in this text;

The Chicago Public Library (Central), which provided photographs of three illustrations from Volume One of Frank Leslie's *Pictorial History of the American Civil War* (N. Y., Frank Leslie, 1862): *Battle of Mill Spring; Death of the Rebel General Zollicoffer; and Battle of Mill*

*Spring — Conveying the dead body of General Zollicoffer,* and which
also granted permission to photograph as illustrations in this book a
painting of General Thomas, his belt, his sash cord, and the statuette
in the Civil War Museum of the G. A. R. Memorial Hall of the
Library. Miss Elda Colombo (Retired) Assistant Librarian, and Harold
Teitlebaum (Retired), Chief of the History and Travel Department,
were personally responsible for obtaining this permission. Also Donald
J. Schabel, Director of the Cultural Center; Walter J. Grantham,
Assistant Division Chief, Social Science and History; and Joseph C.
Lutz, Librarian, of the Library Staff, all of whom assisted in research-
ing material for this book;

Jack Harris, formerly Vice-President for Development, and Don L.
Moldenhauer, Director of Public Relations at Carthage College, Kenosha, Wisconsin, for assistance in photographing rare prints and personal effects of General Thomas in the author's Civil War Collection
currently on display at the college and for their helpful suggestions
after reading the manuscript;

Dr. Harold H. Lentz, President of Carthage College, (now retired)
a personal friend, for his continued inspiration and encouragement;

Richard Bennett, Exxon Company, U.S.A., Houston, Texas, for providing a copy of the illustration "Old Glory Rises Over Alaska," to be
used in the book;

Norm Flayderman (N. Flayderman & Co., Inc.), Purveyors of Military and Nautical Antiquities, New Milford, Connecticut, who furnished photographs of swords and medals of General Thomas; and

Staff members of the Library of Congress, Reference Department,
Prints and Photographs Division, and of the National Archives and
Records Service for their splendid cooperation.

Chicago, Illinois                                                        Frank A. Palumbo

# *About the Author*

Frank A. Palumbo first became actively interested in the American Civil War in the 1930s when, as a young man, he made the acquaintance of a veteran of that conflict, Joseph Pruitt, Sr., of Wellington, Illinois, who fought with Co. E, 135th Regiment, Indiana Infantry. The stories and anecdotes recounted by the old soldier inspired the author to pursue a serious study of the people and servants of this important chapter of our American heritage.

Mr. Palumbo's dedication to the study of the Civil War led him to collect and develop what is considered today to be one of the finest privately owned Civil War collections. Now on loan to Carthage College in Kenosha, Wisconsin, and on exhibit in the school's Lentz Hall, the Palumbo collection is highlighted by a complete 36-print series of the noted Kurz and Allison stone lithographs depicting famous Civil War battles—one of the few complete sets known to exist. The Palumbo collection was displayed in Chicago's City Hall in commemoration of the Civil War Centennial, where it was viewed by 82,976 persons from 42 states and 16 foreign countries. It was later placed on exhibit in the lobby of the Flick-Reedy Corporation, Bensenville, Illinois, and at Chicago's Museum of Science and Industry. It is now on exhibit at Carthage College, Kenosha, Wisconsin. By now, hundreds of thousands have viewed this impressive collection, always free to the public.

In 1961, Mr. Palumbo was the recipient of the annual Flick-Reedy Americanism Award for his remarkable achievement over the years in the collection of memorabilia of the American Civil War and for his dedication in preserving these rare artifacts. He brought together one of the most outstanding collections of the Civil War so that his fellow Americans could appreciate the principles and ideals which brought on this conflict, and so that the historical value of the artifacts might instill in all Americans a deep appreciation of their heritage.

As a serious student of the Civil War, Mr. Palumbo has been active in a number of organizations and societies devoted to the study of American history, including the Chicago Civil War Round Table, the Chicago Historical Society, the Kentucky Historical Society, and the Confederate Memorial Literary Society of Richmond, Virginia.

Professionally Mr. Palumbo is an Architect and Engineer. At present he is serving on the Chicago City Council, Committee on Local Transportation, as Transit and Traffic Engineer. While his study of the Civil War is a hobby, it has captured his full-time interest and efforts. Mr. Palumbo is an alumnus of the University of Illinois

(Architecture-Engineering). He also attended Northwestern University (Business Law and Insurance), and the State University of Iowa (Industrial-Engineering and Quality Control). He was born in New York City. Besides being a member of the Board of Associates at Carthage College, Kenosha, Wisconsin, he serves on the Board of Directors of the Museum of Surgical Science and Hall of Fame of the International College of Surgeons. He is also a member of The Executives Club of Chicago and of the Chicago Association of Commerce and Industry.

# *Was General Thomas Slow at Nashville?*

General Thomas was not "slow" at Nashville as we have been led to believe. The impatient General Grant was the first to make this charge. He withdrew this unfair insinuation in his official report when he realized that the delay by Thomas was necessary, and later said, ". . . his final defeat of Hood was so complete that it will be accepted as a vindication of that distinguished officer's judgment."

Thomas' determination in the reorganizing and re-equipping of his infantry forces and in the remounting of his cavalry under his able trusted Chief of Cavalry, Major General James H. Wilson, was the controlling factor for his success at Nashville. It was Wilson's dynamic and aggressive influence on other sources by which he was able to increase the necessary mounted force at Nashville from 5,500 to 13,500.

In General Sherman's preparation for the march to the sea, he made certain that all equipment and men were inspected. Why then was Sherman with a force of 62,000 well-equipped veterans and a large force of cavalry permitted to make his march to the sea leaving Thomas with a handful of men, most of whom were convalescents, including "those whose term of service were expiring"? As Sherman noted, every piece of equipment was examined, and if found not serviceable it was replaced by new. All other "trash" was "either destroyed or sent to Thomas." As Confederate General John Bell Hood began to make his move, Thomas lost the services of 15,000 men because their term of service were expiring. In their place he received 12,000 newly enlisted recruits, all of whom needed to be trained and equipped.

It was Thomas' careful efforts which perfected the essentials needed for this great Army of the Cumberland. When he requested that he keep his former corps that he had worked so diligently to organize, his request was refused. He had to do his best with two smaller corps assigned to him. In this account, we shall see that the assertion of General Thomas' slowness at Nashville was unfounded.

(Adapted from Henry V. Boynton, *Was General Thomas Slow at Nashville?* (New York: Harper, 1896, pp. 9-21.)

"It was at the day's turning-point, at the white-heat of that furnace-fire of battle which tries the soldier's soul, that he shone out most lustrous; and the very toils he most coveted, and out of which he alone gathered laurels, were those, as Pierrepont sings:

> *'Which meaner souls had quelled,*
> *But souls like his impelled*
> *To soar.'"*

(George W. Cullum, *Biographical Register of the Officers and Graduates of the U. S. Military Academy at West Point, N. Y.*
Boston and New York:
Houghton Mifflin, 1891, II, 40.)

# *Foreword*

"His is the history of the Army of the Ohio and the Cumberland. He organized and commanded the force that won our first important victory at Mill Spring[s]; and three years later, at Nashville, he destroyed the last armed opposition in the West. During those three years, men came and went, fields were lost and won, but he was always on duty, never made a mistake, and 'so ordered his command as to retrieve it from the mistakes of others.' He never sought a command and never shrank from responsibilities. He had confidence in himself, in his plans, and in his men. . . . His fixity of purpose and unbending will were stamped upon every line of his face. 'We will hold the place until we starve,' was his telegram from Chattanooga to Grant at Louisville. And yet this stern man of duty, who rarely smiled, was genial and humane, and from his great kindness of heart, from his ever-watchful care, was known to all his 'boys' as 'Pap' Thomas. Growing in strength as his burdens increased, he was at the close of the war everywhere recognized as one of our four great commanders."

So wrote in 1888 a soldier who served proudly under Major General George H. Thomas. Such pride, and such praise, of Thomas was universal among those thousands of Federal soldiers who followed him through the bloody campaigns of the Civil War's western theater. What makes this adoration strange, and what has dimmed Thomas' place in history, was the man himself. Thomas lacked the bull-like rushes of Grant, the fiery determination of Sherman, the flamboyance of Sheridan. He was an unassuming and unimpressive Virginian who did his duty fully but unspectacularly. A professionally trained soldier who worked his way slowly through the ranks, Thomas lacked a flair for the dramatic that brings lasting notoriety.

Not until late in the Civil War did his name make the headlines. Yet only twice in that terrible conflict was a Confederate army driven precipitately from its entrenchments . . . once at Chattanooga and once at Nashville. In command of the attacking Federal forces on each occasion was "Pap" Thomas.

His December, 1864, victory at Nashville was one of the decisive battles of the war. However, he is remembered more for a defensive stand he made on a September afternoon a year earlier. The place was Chickamauga Creek; a full-scale late morning attack by the Confederate Army of Tenessee shattered the center and right of the Union lines. By early afternoon full one-third of the Federal army was fleeing back to Chattanooga. But the Union left under Thomas, stood firm. Of

Thomas' conduct the remainder of that bloody day, Gen. James A. Garfield stated in 1870:

"While men shall read the history of battles, they will never fail to study and admire the work of Thomas during that afternoon. With but twenty-five thousand men, formed in a semi-circle of which he himself was the centre and soul, he successfully resisted for more than five hours the repeated assaults of an army of more than sixty-five thousand men, flushed with victory and bent on his annihilation. Toward the close of the day his ammunition began to fail. One by one his division commanders reported but ten rounds, five rounds, two rounds, left. The calm, quiet answer was returned: 'Save your fire for close quarters, and when the last shot is fired give them the bayonet.' . . . When night had closed over the combatants, the last sound of battle was the booming of Thomas' shells bursting among his baffled and retreating assailants. He was indeed the 'rock of Chickamauga,' against which the wild waves of battle dashed in vain."

Several biographies have been written of the "Rock of Chickamauga;" undoubtedly, more will follow in the years to come. This biographical tribute, however, is noteworthy for two reasons; it contains a number of illustrations never before published, and it is the work of a non-historian who loves history.

Frank A. Palumbo is best-known for the impressive Civil War museum he single-handedly established on the campus of Carthage College. It in itself is a testimonial to Mr. Palumbo's abiding interest in the Civil War period. His respectful enthusiam for history is an emotion more needed in our nation today. This book is but one expression of that enthusiam. Yet it is a simple memorial conceived with dedication and presented with sincerity.

It is . . . in short . . . precisely what "Pap" Thomas would have liked.

James I. Robertson, Jr.

# *Illustrations*

# CHAPTER ONE

# *Early Life*

The following pages detailing the life of Major General George
H. Thomas are set forth as a testimony to the author's enduring
admiration for one of the most successful of the Union generals
during the Civil War and one of the most admirable military men
ever produced in this country. He was, as General William T.
Sherman declared in the General Order announcing his death to
the reunited nation, a soldier who "never wavered in battle; who
was firm and full of faith in his cause; who never sought advancement of rank or honor at the expense of any one; who was the
very impersonation of honesty, integrity and honor; and who
stands as the beau ideal of the soldier and gentleman."[1]

On April 5, 1870, three days before Thomas was buried, the
Congress of the United States in a Joint Resolution expressed its
sympathy in the national bereavement and its conviction that
"his distinguished career in the defense of his country against
foreign and domestic enemies, his never-faltering faith and zeal
in the maintenance of the Union and the integrity of the Government, and his stern execution of every trust confided to him,
constitute a record in life made memorable in death."[2] He was
the dependable general, faithful to the end.

Death was to come to Thomas in a hotel room in San Fran-

---

1. Henry Coppée, *General Thomas* (New York: D. Appleton, 1893), p. 1.
2. George W. Cullum, *Biographical Register of the Officers and Graduates of
   the U. S. Military Academy at West Point, N. Y.* (Boston and New York:
   Houghton Mifflin, 1891), II, 40.

cisco, California, five years after the close of the Civil War. The record of his life began on a farm in Southampton County, Virginia, July 31, 1816. The family homestead, now known as "Thomaston,"[3] consisted of five to six hundred acres of good farm land, growing cotton, corn, and tobacco. The plain, white frame farmhouse still stands, "shaded by a magnificent oak tree."[4] It is the birthplace of one of the few Virginians who, unlike Robert E. Lee, chose country before state when the outbreak of war in April, 1861, required every soldier to declare his allegiance. Virginia, the "Mother of Presidents," soon became the mother of generals—and of countless common soldiers.

George Henry Thomas was one of nine children born to John C. Thomas and Elizabeth, nee Rochelle. The parents were married February 9, 1808, in Southampton County by Joseph Curley, an Episcopal clergyman. The father died April 20, 1829, at the early age of forty-five, the victim of a farm accident.[5] Mrs. Thomas lived for twenty-seven years following her husband's death. She managed the large farm as best she could, supporting her large family of six girls and three boys and discharging the responsibilities involved in working a considerable number of farmhands and slaves. Her death came on January 27, 1856, at the age of sixty-eight—curiously enough, it too caused by an accident.

After the death of Frances C. Thomas (the last of General Thomas' sisters), Mr. H. T. Miles of Newsoms, Southampton County, purchased "Thomaston" for a consideration of $4,000.00. The land consisted of 524½ acres.[6]

George Thomas' paternal forebears were Welsh and English, and his maternal ancestors were French Huguenot—"two of the best races for 'a combination and a form to give the world assurance of a man' of the highest physical, moral and mental development."[7]

3. Francis F. McKinney, *Education in Violence: The Life of George H. Thomas and the History of the Army of the Cumberland* (Detroit: Wayne State University Press, 1961), p. 3.
4. *Virginia: A Guide to the Old Dominion* (New York: Oxford, 1935), p. 473.
5. Coppée, p. 3.
6. Deed dated Sept. 22, 1903, recorded in Deed Book 59, p. 70, Southampton County Court House.
7. Cullum, II, p. 35.

His father's family, if originally Welsh, had lived in England for several generations before coming to America. Many members of the family died intestate, thereby providing no clues in tracing their ancestral lineage. His mother was descended from one of the Huguenot families who fled to America in 1690[8] to escape the persecution by Louis XIV of French Protestants as a result of the revocation of the Edict of Nantes in 1685.[9] Little is known of the Thomas family. Drawing upon what limited information is available, however, some authors have stated that the family inherited the traditions and the prestige of both the Cavaliers and the Huguenots, that they were "well-to-do" and eminently respectable, that his parents were members of the old first families of Virginia, and that their social position was all that could be desired.[10]

The untimely death of his father was but one of several distressing events in Thomas' early boyhood. Thomas was not quite thirteen years of age when his father died, and was thus compelled to face the world at an early age. He helped manage the family plantation, but farming never appealed to him. In his early years, Thomas lived a sheltered life in a quiet, refined home atmosphere. While he had very few playmates, he was always helpful in trying to teach the black children on the family plantation the lessons he had learned at church and at school. Although it was his intention to unfold the history of his youth, a wish expressed several days before his death, it was not accomplished and consequently little record of his early life is available.

It is known that Thomas was mechanically inclined and very skillful with the use of his hands. In his leisure time during his youth, he would frequently visit the saddlemaker's shop so that he might learn how to make his own saddles. He learned during his daily visits to the shop by his close observation of the saddler at work so that he finally succeeded in making a saddle for himself.[11] He became equally talented in the making of boots,

8. Wilbur Thomas, *General George H. Thomas, The Indomitable Warrior* (New York: Exposition Press, 1964), p. 47.

9. Coppée, p. 2.

10. *Ibid.*, p. 3.

11. Donn Piatt, *Memories of the Men Who Saved the Union* (New York and Chicago: Belford, Clarke, 1887), p. 174.

and was also interested in the making of furniture and would visit the cabinetmaker's shop daily to learn.[12] But he also attended school, and his early teachers praised him endlessly on his aptitude, ability, and eagerness to explore every possible subject. Then, too, his parents had a part in shaping his character, instilling a strong foundation based on truth and honor. He inherited from his father that solidity of judgment, devotion to duty, and lofty courage for which he was so well-known; and from his mother he inherited that kindly, unselfish, and cheerful disposition that made him so beloved by his friends. From his home training, Thomas was encouraged to be an independent thinker and self-reliant. He was "a boy of few words, but of an excellent spirit."[13] As a son of antebellum Virginia, Thomas was exposed to the plight of blacks at an early age. And he could not have escaped knowledge of slave unrest.

Surely the most disquieting experience of Thomas' youth was the slave revolt of Nat Turner. This uprising of blacks against their white masters, commonly called the Southampton Insurrection, was the greatest and bloodiest servile rebellion in United States history. And it took place in the neighborhood of the Thomas farm. Young George, fifteen years old at the time, must have known many of the whites murdered by Turner and his followers, and he may well have known as well some of the dozens of blacks whose lives were taken in reprisal.

Subject to strong religious feelings of a fanatical nature, Turner claimed he had an apparition in which Christ told him to "take up the yoke" which He had put down.[14] He felt a solar eclipse was the signal for him to start his mission, whose objective was to seize control of Southampton County, and annihilate all the white people in the area. The uprising started on the evening of August 21, 1831, and continued through the next day. Nat Turner and his band of fanatics began their campaign near Cross Keys,[15] seven miles southwest of Courtland (then known as Jerusalem).

12. Thomas B. Van Horne, *The Life of Major General George H. Thomas* (New York: Scribners, 1882), p. 4.
13. *Personal Recollections of the Rebellion* (New York: Military Order of the Loyal Legion, 1890), p. 287.
14. William Sidney Drewry, *The Southampton Insurrection* (Washington: Neale, 1900), p. 33.
15. *Ibid.*, p. 35.

They became wildly intoxicated by drinking a mixture of gunpowder and apple brandy.[16] Mrs. Thomas and her family were forewarned by a neighbor, James Gurley, of the approaching Turner and his murdering band, and fled from their home to safety at Jerusalem. Sam, the family's black overseer, assisted the Thomases in their escape.[17]

Soon after his capture, Nat Turner was arraigned and tried before a court and was convicted for his participation in the insurrection and was executed at Jerusalem on November 11, 1831.[18] Of the fifty-three blacks who participated and were arraigned, seventeen, including Turner, were executed. The others were discharged, with the exception of "four free Negroes" who were sent on to the Superior Court, three of the four later to be hanged.[19]

Thomas' early education was obtained in the local Southampton Academy. He began reading law under his uncle, James Rochelle, who was County Clerk of Southampton County. Three months after his uncle's death, August 17, 1835, Thomas became Deputy Clerk.[20]

16. *Ibid.*, p. 50.
17. *Ibid.*, p. 68.
18. Stephen B. Oates, *The Fires of Jubilee: Nat Turner's Fierce Rebellion* (New York: New American Library, 1976), p. 142.
19. Drewry, p. 101.
20. Thomas, p. 54.

# CHAPTER TWO

# Thomas' Cadetship at West Point

It was through the influence of his uncle, James Rochelle, that Thomas received an appointment from their Congressman John Young Mason as a candidate to the United States Military Academy at West Point, New York.

On March 1, 1836, Representative Mason addressed a letter announcing Thomas' appointment to Secretary of War Lewis Cass, as follows:

House of Representatives
March 1st, 1836.

Sir:

I have the honor to recommend George Thomas of Southampton County, Virginia, for admission into the Academy at West Point, as a Cadet. He is seventeen or eighteen years of age, of fine size and of excellent talents with a good preparatory education.

I have the honor to be,
Respectively your obedient servant,
(Signed)      J. Y. Mason[1]

---

1. Freeman Cleaves, *Rock of Chickamauga: The Life of General George H. Thomas* (Norman: University of Oklahoma Press, 1948), pp. 8-9; Thomas' ACP file, Adj. Gen. Office, RG 94, Old Military Records, National Archives, Washington, D. C.

Actually Thomas was 19 years and 11 months old when he was admitted to the Academy.

Shortly after Representative Mason's recommendation of Thomas' appointment, his mother gave her consent for her son to serve as a cadet at West Point:

> This is to certify that I give my consent for George Thomas to sign any articles, by which he will bind himself to serve five years as a Cadet in the United States Military Academy at West Point, unless sooner discharged.
>
> Given under my hand this 26th day of March, 1836.
> (Signed)      Elizabeth Thomas—Guardian.[2]

When Thomas thanked Representative Mason for his appointment, the Congressman replied very bluntly, "No cadet appointed from my district has ever graduated from the Military Academy; and if you do not, I never want to see your face again."[3]

Thomas did not need this word of caution. His strong character and determination to succeed in life were overwhelming factors in his favor, and failure never entered his mind.

George Thomas thought it would be advisable to arrive at West Point several weeks before the beginning of the school year so that he could brush up on some of the courses to better prepare himself for his entrance examinations. After he became settled at the Academy, Thomas addressed the following letter to the Secretary of War. In it he enclosed the written consent of his mother.

> West Point, April 25th, 1836.
>
> To the Honorable Lewis Cass,
> Secretary of War,
>
> I had the honor a short time since of receiving my conditional appointment as Cadet in this institution which, with the consent and approbation of my Guardian, I take great pleasure in accepting. The paper enclosed is the Certificate of my Guardian.
>
> Your most obedient servant,
> Geo. Thomas.[4]

2. *Ibid.*
3. Coppée, p. 5.
4. Thomas' ACP file, Adj. Gen. Office, RG 94, Old Military Records, National Archives.

The appointment was accepted and signed by President Andrew Jackson.[5]

Upon his admission into West Point on July 1, 1836, Thomas was approaching twenty years of age. He was two years older than the average age of the plebe cadet or the "fourth class" (freshman). He was a serious and an industrious student, mastering his subjects. Never hasty in his judgment or expression, he was always just and considerate of others. Conducting himself in such a mannerly way, his superiors at the Academy were certain that he could be molded into an able and faithful officer in the United States Army. His roommates were William Tecumseh Sherman of Ohio and Stewart Van Vliet of Vermont. Thomas and his roommates were assigned to a room in the Old South Barracks. "Cump" Sherman, as he was known, was a high-strung lad of sixteen, loquacious, and somewhat untidy in his dress. Van Vliet, a conscientious and hard-working student, was the oldest of the three, going on twenty-one years of age. During the Civil War, Van Vliet became an efficient supply officer. On Monday, March 13, 1865, he was commissioned Brevet Major General, U. S. Army, for faithful and distinguished services in the Quartermaster Department.

Thomas was a handsome, fair-complexioned youth with chestnut hair, deep blue eyes, and a square, impressive jaw. At first, suspicion was prevalent among some of the cadets from other sections of the country because of Thomas' Southern background, but when they were better acquainted with him they became his friends.

General Van Vliet in his reply to a request made by historian Henry Coppée on May 5, 1893, cited one of their experiences while the trio were cadets at West Point.

Washington, D. C.<br>May 10, 1893.

My Dear Coppée:
   . . . Sherman, George H. Thomas, and I arrived at West Point on the same day, and all three were assigned to the same room, on the south side of the old south barracks. A warm friendship commenced in that room, which continued, without a single break, during our lives. We were all three sturdy fellows, which

---

5. Cleaves, p. 9.

prevented our being annoyed by older cadets. They commenced to haze us, as was the fashion of those days, but Thomas put a stop to it. One evening a cadet came into our room and commenced to give us orders. He had said but a few words when Old Tom, as we always called him, stepped up to him and said, "Leave this room immediately, or I will throw you through the window." It is needless to say that the cadet lost no time in getting out of the room. There were no more attempts to haze us. When we graduated we consulted as to the regiments we should apply for. The Florida [Seminole] war was then going on, and we all concluded that we would apply for some regiment then in Florida, for we all wanted to see some actual fighting, and if we did not go to Florida we should never see any; so we all joined the Third Artillery. History shows how near we came to the facts in our reasoning.

Fifty-three years—over half a century—have passed since we separated at West Point, and, of course, one forgets many things in that time. . . .

Yours very truly,
Stewart Van Vliet, U.S.A.[6]

Cadet Samuel Gibbs French of New Jersey, Class of 1843, has provided an account of the first days at West Point after cadets had passed their entrance examinations. The cadets stood at rigid attention, shoulders squared, chin and stomach drawn in and chest out, elbows straight at the sides, and heels together with feet at an angle of forty-five degrees. "It was heads up, eyes to the front, and one seldom saw his boots,"[7] he remarked.

Cadet William Dutton of Connecticut, United States Military Academy, member of the Class of 1846, writing a letter to his brother, C. Dutton, on June 19, 1842, described cadet life at the academy before the Mexican War as follows:

> . . . we have five in our room, which you know is but about 10 by 12. At 5 A.M. which is ½ an hour after the morning gun, the drums are beat by the barracks, & the cry grows—"fall in there," when we all have to be in the ranks or be reported. The roll is then called, we go to our rooms & have 15 minutes to roll up our blankets, put them up, wash, clean the room etc., when everything must be in order. We have no mattresses &

6. Coppée, pp. 322-323.
7. Cleaves, p. 10.

only 2 blankets to lay on the floor and cover ourselves with, &
when we all five spread ourselves out we just cover the floor—
(In camp, we have no more.) We then remain in our rooms
until the drums beat for breakfast, again if missing we are
reported. We then march to the mess hall, & if one speaks,
raises his hand, looks to the right or left (which is the case
on all parade) we are reported for everything. I have been so
fortunate as to escape as yet. When we arrive at the tables, the
command is given "take seats," & then such a scrambling you
never saw. For breakfast we have the remains of the meat of
the former day's dinner, cut up with potato with considerable
gravy—& not more than two thirds of them get a bit.—bread
cut in chunks, butter and coffee. We have to eat fast as we
can, & before we get enough, the command is given "Squad
rise." At dinner we have "Roast Beef," & boiled potato, & bread
—no butter, at Tea, bread & butter & tea. We have to drill
twice a day, & a good many faint away. It is terrible, but I like
the whole of it, after we have marched from tea, we stay in
our room till ½ hour past 9 when we can go to bed if we choose,
& at taps at 10 every light must be out & after that the inspector happens in all times of night.[8]

In his first year (Fourth Class) at West Point, Thomas ranked
26th in a class of seventy-six; in his second year (Third Class)
he ranked 15th among fifty-eight as corporal; and in his third
year (Second Class) he stood 17th among forty-six as sergeant;
and in his fourth and final year (First Class) he ranked 12th in
a class of forty-two.[9]

In his final year, Thomas' standing in his respective studies
was 11th in Engineering, 10th in Ethics, 11th in Infantry Tactics, 7th in Artillery, and 9th in Mineralogy and Geology.[10]

Upon graduation from West Point on July 1, 1840, Thomas
was commissioned a Second Lieutenant in Company D, Third
Regiment of Artillery. In the same graduating Class of 1840,
Sherman ranked 6th and Van Vliet stood 9th. The outstanding
member of the 1840 class was Paul Octave Hébert who ranked
1st academically and enjoyed the distinction of being valedic-

8. United States Military Academy *Library Bulletin No. 1*, "*Barracks*," pp. 12-13.
9. *Official Register of the Cadets of West Point,* 1837 through 1840.
10. *Ibid.*

torian. Hébert resigned from the United States Army March 1, 1845, and, in 1852, became governor of Louisiana.[11] He was appointed a brigadier general in the Confederate Army on August 17, 1861. There were others of this class who became famous in the military history of our country. The Class of 1840 was one of unusual ability. That Thomas graduated 12th in his class shows him to have been not only a good student, but one of extraordinary capacity. He never forgot anything.

When Thomas graduated from West Point on July 1, 1840, he was placed on leave until September 30, 1840. Upon graduation many of the cadets were sent to Fort Columbus, New York Harbor, for their basic training in preparation for active duty in the field. Upon completion of their training and when they reached a certain proficiency, they were ordered to their duty stations.

11. Ezra J. Warner, *Generals in Gray* (Baton Rouge: Louisiana State University Press, 1959), pp. 131-132.

# CHAPTER THREE

# *The Second Seminole and Mexican Wars*

George H. Thomas served for a brief period in garrison duty at Fort Columbus on Governors Island until November 23, 1840, when his company was ordered to Florida for the duration of the Second Seminole War. Almost a year passed, however, before Thomas had a chance to personally participate in an expedition against the Seminoles. In early November 1841, Captain Richard D. A. Wade, commanding at Fort Lauderdale, was ordered to make a show of force at several Indian towns, with the mission of overawing the villagers. Thomas, as second in command of the combat patrol, was responsible for the day-to-day routine of 60 soldiers. Upon their return from a six-day sweep through the waterways and Everglades, Captain Wade submitted a report, detailing their activities.[1] It read:

> Fort Lauderdale, E. F., November 13, 1841.
> Sir,—In pursuance to the instructions contained in your [Major Thomas Childs'] communication of the 24th September, I set out on the morning of the 5th inst., accompanied by Lieutenant Thomas, Third Artillery, Assistant Surgeon [John] Emerson and sixty non-commissioned officers and privates,

1. Cleaves, p. 18; Thomas, p. 70.

13

embarked in twelve canoes and provisioned for fifteen days. We proceeded by the inland passage to the northward, coming out in the bay at the Hillsborough Inlet, and in such manner that our canoes were concealed from the view of an Indian whom I discovered fishing on the northern point of the inlet. I made the requisite dispositions immediately to land, and succeeded in surprising him. By operating on his hopes and fears, I induced him to lead us to his Indian village, fifteen miles distant in a westerly direction. This we reached on the morning of the 6th; surprised and captured twenty Indians, men, women, and children; took six rifles, destroyed fourteen canoes and much provisions of the usual variety. Of those who attempted to escape eight were killed by our troops. We returned to our boats the same forenoon with our prisoners, and proceeded up a small stream towards the Orange Grove haulover, where we encamped for the night.

On the morning of the 7th, after proceeding three miles farther north, the stream became too shallow for canoe navigation, and we made here a camp, leaving the prisoners, the boats, and a sufficient guard in charge of Dr. Emerson. Under the guidance of an old Indian found among our prisoners, who is called Chia-chee, I took up the line of march through nearly a mile of deep bog and saw-grass, then through the pine barren and some hummocks to a cypress swamp a distance of some thirty miles northward. Here (on the 8th inst.) we were conducted to another village, which we also surrounded, and surprised and captured twenty-seven Indians, took six rifles and one shot-gun and destroyed a large quantity of provisions and four canoes.

The next morning (November 9) we set out on our return to the boats, on a more easterly route than the former, which led us to the shores of Lake Worth, where we found and destroyed a canoe, a field of pumpkins, and an old hut. In the afternoon of this day one man came in and surrendered himself, thus making the whole number of our Indian prisoners forty-nine.

At 11 A.M. of the 10th we arrived at our boats and proceeded to the little Hillsborough bar by evening, and in the afternoon of the next day (November 11) we returned to Fort Lauderdale without any loss on our part, after an absence of six days. Having seen much in the old man Chia-chee to in-

14

spire my confidence in his integrity, I permitted him to go out from our camp (on the 10th November) to bring in other Indians, which he promised to do in three or four days. This promise he subsequently redeemed, having on the 14th inst. brought in six (four men and two boys) at Fort Lauderdale.

My warmest thanks are due to Dr. Emerson and Lieutenant Thomas for their valuable and efficient aid in carrying out my orders; and of the conduct of the troops likewise, without any exception, I can speak only in terms of the highest praise.

I have the honor to be, very respectfully,

> Your obedient servant,
> (Signed) R. D. A. Wade
> Captain Third Artillery,
> Commanding Expedition.[2]

Captain Wade's report was forwarded to the adjutant general by his commanding officer, Colonel William Worth, with this endorsement:

I have the satisfaction to forward the accompanying report of the successful operations of Captain Wade, Third Artillery, acting under the orders of his immediate commander, Major Childs. This very creditable affair will operate the most favorable influence upon the closing scenes of this protracted contest, and I but do equal justice to the distinguished merit and conduct of Captain Wade, and the expectations of the service, in respectfully asking that the special notice of the Department of War may be extended to him and his gallant, Second Lieutenant G. H. Thomas, of the same regiment.

> Respectfully, etc.
> (Signed) W. J. Worth,
> Colonel Commanding.[3]

Pursuant to Colonel Worth's recommendation, Lieutenant Thomas was made a brevet first lieutenant retroactive to November 8, 1841, "for gallantry and good conduct in the war against the Florida Indians."[4]

When a second combat patrol returned from another expedition, during which no Indians were seen, Thomas learned that Captain Erasmus D. Keyes had arrived at Fort Lauderdale, hav-

2. Richard W. Johnson, *A Soldier's Reminiscences* (Philadelphia: J. B. Lippincott Co., 1886), pp. 18-20.
3. *Ibid.,* pp. 20-21.
4. *Ibid.,* p. 21; Cullum, Vol. I, p. 600.

ing been named to replace Captain Wade as post commander. Keyes recalled that Thomas at this time was about 26 years old, six feet tall, his "form symmetrical, inclining to plumpness, complexion blond and his eyes large and deep blue."[5]

Successful patrols, such as Captain Wade's, caused the Seminoles to withdraw deeper into the Everglades, and, in December, the company to which Thomas was assigned boarded ship and was transferred to Tampa Bay, on the west side of the Florida peninsula. The stay at Fort Brooke was brief, and, in February 1842, the company was shifted to New Orleans to refit and recuperate.

Thomas was on garrison duty at New Orleans Barracks in Louisiana from February to June 30, 1842, when he was posted to Fort Moultrie in Charleston Harbor, South Carolina, where he pulled duty until December 5, 1843. From there he was assigned to Fort McHenry in Baltimore Harbor, Maryland, until October 19, 1844. Then he was on recruiting service at Charleston, South Carolina, until March 15, 1845, when he returned to Fort Moultrie for garrison duty with the regiment until June 26, 1845.

He received his commission as First Lieutenant, Third Artillery, on April 30, 1844, in recognition of his outstanding military service in the Second Seminole War.[6]

Thomas next saw service in the Military Occupation of the State of Texas and in the War with Mexico from April 24, 1846, to July 4, 1848.[7] On June 27, 1845, Company E, Third Artillery, left Fort Moultrie, boarding a New Orleans-bound ship. Commanding the company was Braxton Bragg, described by one of his brother officers as "ambitious and of a saturnine disposition and morbid temperament."[8] The company remained in New Orleans several days, before continuing on to Corpus Christi on the Texas frontier. There, the artillerists rendezvoused with Brigadier General Zachary Taylor and the 3d and 4th U. S. Infantry Regiments.

The annexation of Texas by the United States had been sanc-

<hr>

5. Erasmus D. Keyes, *Fifty Years' Observation of Men and Events* (New York: Charles Scribner's Sons, 1884), p. 166.
6. *Ibid.*, pp. 166-71.
7. Francis B. Heitman, *Historical Register and Dictionary of the United States Army* (Washington: Government Printing Office, 1903), II, 282.
8. Keyes, p. 173.

tioned by the Texas Congress and had been recently ratified by the citizens of the late republic. President James Knox Polk and his administration, in the months while Taylor's troops camped, drilled, and hunted near the mouth of the Nueces, laid claim to the vast territory extending southward from that river to the Rio Grande. Taylor was instructed that if Mexican armed forces crossed the Rio Grande, it would be deemed an act of war.[9]

Finally, in early February 1846, General Taylor was ordered by the War Department to march for the Rio Grande. On Sunday, March 8, Taylor's vanguard broke camp. The three infantry brigades followed on successive days. Among these units was Company E, Third U. S. Artillery, to which Lieutenant Thomas was assigned.

Arriving on the north bank of the Rio Grande on March 28, General Taylor turned his troops to throwing up a massive six-sided work, which was designated Fort Texas. Before the fort was finished, a force of Mexicans under Brigadier General Mariano Arista, on the Matamoros side of the river, erected and armed a number of batteries within easy range of the American stronghold.

Company E, Third Artillery, together with Company I, First Artillery, and the Seventh U. S. Infantry, all under Major Jacob Brown of the infantry regiment, were charged with the mission of holding Fort Texas. This occurred on May 1, when General Taylor, taking with him the rest of his army, headed for Point Isabel, where he had established his supply depot. Taylor's column reached Point Isabel at noon the next day without incident.[10]

While Fort Texas was strong enough to stand siege, no one knew how long General Taylor would be absent or how far supplies could be stretched. The garrison and Lieutenant Thomas would soon see, because at daybreak on the 3d the guns of Matamoros opened the bombardment of Fort Texas. During the cannonade, Captain Edgar S. Hawkins remarked to a young lieutenant sitting on a keg, with a calmness that contrasted with that of his comrades and the surroundings, "Well, Tom, what do you think of our service; good eh?" Lieutenant Thomas replied,

9. Cleaves, pp. 24-26; K. Jack Bauer, *The Mexican War: 1846-1848* (New York: MacMillan Publishing Co., 1974), pp. 32-36.
10. Bauer, pp. 38-39, 49-50; Cleaves, p. 26.

"Service excellent, but I am thinking you will need the ammunition you are throwing away." Thus was forecast a prophecy, realized the next day when ammunition began to run low.[11]

The story of the Fort Texas siege was chronicled in Captain Hawkins' report to General Taylor, which read:

Head Quarters, Fort Taylor,
Texas, May 10, 1846.

Sir:—I have the honor to report that on the morning of the 6th instant, during the third day of the bombardment of this fort its gallant commander, Major Brown, received a severe wound, which caused his death at 2 o'clock on the 9th instant. I immediately assumed command, and have the honor to report the result of the bombardment since 7 o'clock A.M., on the 4th, at which time Capt. [Samuel H.] Walker left with a report of the result up to that time.

At 9 o'clock P.M. on the 4th, firing of musketry was heard in our rear, about three or four hundred yards distant, and apparently extended a mile up the river; the firing was very irregular. This continued until half-past 11 o'clock P.M. The garrison was under arms, batteries and defences all manned, and continued so during the night. On the 5th instant, at 5 o'clock A.M., the fire was recommenced from the enemy's batteries, which was immediately returned from the eighteen-pounder battery [Capt. Allen Lowd's] and six-pounder howitzer, placed in embrasure on the southeast bastion. The firing was kept up one hour, receiving during that time about fifty round shot and shells from the enemy. The batteries on both sides ceased firing at the same time. Our expenditure of ammunition was thirty rounds of both calibre.

At 8 o'clock A.M., Valdez, a Mexican, came in and reported that a party of dragoons had been driven back from the prairie to the point, and also a party to the fort; that he had seen thirty deserters from Arista's army, who stated that the Mexicans were without subsistence-stores, that they were tired, and left for their homes; that it was stated in the Mexican camp that Arista had received an express from Mexico informing him that another revolution had broken out in Mexico, and that he could receive no support from the government. At 9 o'clock

11. Bauer, pp. 50-51; Donn Piatt, *General George H. Thomas* (Cincinnati, 1891), pp. 66-67.

A.M. it was reported that a reconnaissance of officers, escorted by mounted men of the enemy, was going on in rear, within eight hundred yards of the fort; and that other parties, mounted and infantry, were at the same distance, extending from the bend of the lagoon to the river. Lieut. [Charles] Hanson, Seventh Infantry, asked permission to take the dragoons and go and look at them. This was granted, and in an hour he returned, reporting that the enemy was establishing a battery at the cross roads; his appearance among them created great alarm, and they were soon concentrated at a distance under cover of their work. Every man at work to-day strengthening the defences. Several parties of cavalry and infantry seen to-day occupying our old encampment. At 11 o'clock P.M. musketry was heard in our rear, from bend of lagoon to the river. The troops all at their places in the bastions during the night.

*Wednesday, May 6*—At 5 o'clock A.M., the cannonade commenced from the lower fort and mortar battery. Many round shot and shells thrown until 6 o'clock, when there was a cessation of firing. During the last hour, the shot and shells were well directed, bursting in all directions in the interior of the fort, tearing our tents to pieces, and injuring several horses. At half past 6 o'clock the signal eighteen-pounders were fired, at which the enemy opened their batteries in our front and rear, and the cannonade continued from two mortars and a howitzer in front, and a mortar established at or near the cross roads in rear, until 10 o'clock A.M. when our gallant commander [Major Brown] received a mortal wound from a falling shell.

Large mounted parties and infantry were seen at this time in rear. At 7 o'clock one mortar was playing upon us from town, and two from the rear. At 10 o'clock a small party of infantry crept up in ravine, and fired musketry; but, being out of range, the fire was not returned. At half past 10 o'clock A.M., several parties of infantry and mounted men were seen surrounding us in rear. Several rounds of canister were fired from Lieut. Bragg's battery, which soon dispersed them. Several were afterwards heard to have been killed. Immediately afterwards, and until half past 12 o'clock P.M., we received a continual shower of shells from the enemy's batteries. At 2 o'clock five shells were thrown. At half past 4 o'clock

P.M., a white flag was shown at the old buildings in rear, and a parley sounded by the enemy. Two officers advanced, and were met by two officers of my command. . . .

The night was passed very quietly, but constant vigilance was exercised in the command; every man kept at his post, as an attack was confidently expected in the morning.

*Thursday, May 7*—At half past 5 o'clock A.M., the enemy's batteries opened with shells, and continued for about an hour and a half, and then ceased. At half past 7 A.M., several rounds of canister and grape were fired into the enemy's picket guards, at the houses in rear, and at the old guardhouse of the Second brigade, which caused them to abandon their positions. This was replied to by a discharge of some ten or twelve shells. At 9 o'clock A.M., we received a shower of some four or five shells, and then stopped. About this time the enemy commenced firing iron shells, having previously thrown composition shells, and it was discovered that one of the mortars had been removed from our rear, and returned to the city [of Matamoros]. At a quarter past 10 A.M., we received three shells; at 11 a.m., eight shells; at 12 P.M., six shells, by which four of Lieut. Bragg's horses were killed, and the wheel of one of his caissons disabled. At half past 12 the batteries were opened with round shot and shells, and continued for an hour and a half. By this time our bomb proofs were so far advanced, that our troops were comparatively protected. At 2 o'clock small parties of infantry commenced [firing] on us with random musketry, on the bank of the river, and from the ravine. At half past 2 P.M., a regular bombardment with shot and shells, from a howitzer and the mortars, was kept up with little intermission until sunset. At 5 o'clock, during this bombardment, a shell struck in a tent, almost entirely destroying the instruments of the Seventh infantry band, to the value of three hundred dollars. The accuracy of their firing now evidently increased, as at least one-half of the shells thrown fell in the fort. A sentinel [Private Moody] to-day lost his arm by a round shot from the enemy. As soon as it was dark enough, a party headed by our indefatigable engineer, Capt. [Joseph K. F.] Mansfield, was sent out to level the traverse thrown up by Gen. [William J.] Worth, and cutting down the chaparral, which served as a cover to the sharp shooters of the enemy. At 12 o'clock at night, a random fire of musketry commenced around us, followed by two bugles; this continued for about one hour, and from 3 A.M., was continued until near day-light.

*Friday, May 8*—At a quarter past 5 o'clock A.M., the enemy's batteries again opened with shells from the lower fort, from the sand-bag battery, and from our rear. The fire this morning was kept up until 8 o'clock A.M., without cessation. A party was sent out this morning, and burnt the old houses near the traverse, on the river bank. This drew from them [the Mexicans] several round shot and shells; from 12 to half past 2 P.M., a heavy bombardment of shells was kept up; at least fifty thrown at us during that time. At half past 3 they again opened their shells upon us, accompanied by round shot. At this time the enemy had established a mortar on the ridge of the chaparral across the river, and immediately west of us. Mortars were now playing upon us from the north, south, and west, four in number. The firing of round shot was kept up for two hours, and that of shells until half past 7 P.M. About half past 2 P.M., a heavy cannonading was heard, supposed to be a little north and east of us; it apparently approached until half past 4, when it became very distinct; it lasted until nearly 7 P.M. [This was from the battle of Palo Alto.] This we supposed to be an action between our forces and the enemy.

A little before sunset, a Mexican came running in with a white flag, from the direction of the Second brigade guard-house, claiming protection. He stated that our forces had come in contact with those of the enemy; had driven them back; that he was a prisoner in charge of the picket guards fired on by our batteries; that while they were burying the dead, and carrying off the wounded, he effected his escape. During the cannonade this afternoon, a small column of infantry from above, and one of cavalry from below, were seen advancing, supposed to be reinforcements to the enemy. The excitement in our command during this distant cannonading was intense. During the day we received from one hundred and fifty to two hundred shells, and from seventy-five to one hundred round shot, and not a man disabled. During the previous night the halliards of the flag on the outside had become unrigged; and as the firing had become too intense to re-establish them, a temporary staff was erected on the inside, and the national flag of the Seventh Infantry raised as a substitute. We passed a very quiet night—the men on the alert at their guns.

*Saturday, May 9*—An officer of the Seventh succeeded in

lowering the topmast of the flag-staff, and rigging the halliards, but found he could not raise it again without great labor and exposure; he therefore lashed it in position, and raised the national flag, after having stood a succession of round shot, canister, and shells from the enemy's batteries for fifteen or twenty minutes. At 10 o'clock, a sergeant and ten men fired the houses on the road which had been successively occupied by our own and the enemy's pickets. It brought a heavy discharge of shells, canister, and round shot from the enemy's batteries. Shells, with slight intervals, continued until half past 2 o'clock P.M.; the mortar on our west silent, and one firing from a position between us and the fort, at the upper ferry; it was much further off, but fired accurately.

Two P.M., Major Brown died, and in a short time we heard the re-engagement between the armies [the battle of Resaca de la Palma]. Quarter to six, quite a number of Mexican cavalry, and a few infantry, were seen in the retreat. At this time we received a heavy fire of round shot and shells. From the time the battle commenced, and continued to increase, an eighteen-pounder and six-pounder were fired in the direction of the upper ferry; when, finding it difficult to distinguish between friend and foe, the firing was discontinued. I cannot close this report, and pass in silence the gallant and laborious efforts of the soldiers and men of this command, to fulfil the high trust reposed in them by the commanding general. Under the most disadvantageous circumstances, labor was performed by the men with the greatest alacrity, and always in good cheer. The indefatigable engineer, Capt. Mansfield, is entitled to the highest praise. I have the honor to report a list of the killed and wounded during the seven days' bombardment of Fort Taylor, Texas.

I am, sir, respectfully, your obedient servant . . . .

Killed and Wounded during the Bombardment.

**KILLED**

May 3, 1846—Sergeant Weigart, B. co., Seventh Infantry.

**WOUNDED**

May 6, 1846—Major J. Brown, commanding post.

May 3, 1846—Private Lefear, E. co., Third Artillery, slight
   wound.

May 6, 1846—Private Thompson, E. co., Third Artillery, slight
   wound.

May 6, 1846—Private Thompson, D. co., Fifth Infantry, slight
wound.

May 6, 1846—Citizen J. Paugh, sutler's clerk, slight wound.

May 7, 1846—Mexican prisoner, slight wound.

May 7, 1846—Private Smith, C. co., Seventh Infantry, slight
wound.

May 7, 1846—Private Moody, H. co., Seventh Infantry, fracture
of arm.

May 8, 1846—Citizen Russell, discharged soldier, fracture of
leg.

May 8, 1846—Private Stewart, H. co., Seventh Infantry, slight
wound.

May 8, 1846—Private Ratcliff, H. co., Seventh Infantry, slight
wound.

May 8, 1846—Mexican prisoner, slight wound.

May 8, 1846—Recruit Cowan, Seventh Infantry, slight wound.

DIED

May 9, 1846—Major J. Brown, commanding post.

I am, sir, respectfully, your obedient servant.

E. S. HAWKINS,

*Capt. Seventh Infantry, commanding post.*

Capt. W. W. Bliss.

*Assistant Adjutant General, Army of Occupation, Texas.*[12]

On May 9, the fury of the bombardment had waned as much
of the investing force of Mexicans withdrew to reinforce General
Arista at Resaca de la Palma to where he had retired following
the battle of Palo Alto. The latter fight had erupted as General
Taylor's column was hastening to the relief of Fort Texas. On
the 9th, Arista was routed by Taylor's army at Resaca de la Palma,
and he and his troops fled across the Rio Grande. The Fort Texas
garrison had added to the Mexicans' discomforture by hammering
the retreating columns with shot and shell. Lieutenant Thomas,
who had a few rounds stashed away, deemed the opportunity
worth waiting for as he sped the Mexicans homeward.[13]

George Thomas learned an important lesson at the siege of
Fort Texas by reason of General Taylor's overextension of his

12. Thomas B. Thorpe, *Our Army on the Rio Grande* . . . (Philadelphia: Carey
& Hart, 1846), pp. 231-37.
13. Bauer, pp. 60-62; Cleaves, p. 27.

supply line, a move dictated by political and not military necessity. Taylor had been compelled to hasten off to Port Isabel for supplies before engaging the foe. This experience was etched in Thomas' mind because the importance of being "prepared for eventualities, come what may, was an outstanding characteristic throughout his career."[14]

The relief of Fort Texas (soon to be redesignated Fort Brown) led to the prompt evacuation of Matamoros by the Mexicans and its occupation by the Americans. On June 6, General Taylor organized a flying column to take possession of Reynosa. This force led by Lieutenant Colonel Henry Wilson, included four companies of the First Infantry, two 12-pounders under Lieutenant Thomas, and a company of Texas Rangers. The alcalde of Reynosa had appealed to General Taylor for protection against Comanches and a partisan band led by Brigadier General Antonio Canales.[15]

For the advance through Camargo and Cerralvo and beyond, Lieutenant Thomas' section rejoined Company E and Captain Bragg. It was early September, when the army's vanguard left Camargo en route to Monterrey. Two weeks on the road brought Taylor's columns in sight of Monterrey and its mountainous backdrop.

The bitter fight for the city began on Sunday, September 20, and ended on the 24th, when the Mexicans were granted an armistice and evacuated the city. Lieutenant Thomas, as at Fort Texas, commanded a section of guns in Captain Bragg's company, assigned to Lieutenant Colonel John Garland's 3d Brigade. Garland, in turn, reported to Brigadier General David E. Twiggs, the leader of the army's First Division.[16]

While events were fresh in their minds, Twiggs and Garland prepared their official reports of the battle. General Twiggs wrote:

*Camp near Monterey, Sept. 29, 1846.*
*Sir,*—For the information of the Major General [Taylor]

14. Cleaves, p. 28; W. S. Henry, *Campaign Sketches of the War With Mexico* (New York: Harper & Bros., 1847), p. 104.
15. Justin H. Smith, *The War With Mexico*, 2 vols. (New York: MacMillan & Co., 1918), Vol. I, pp. 209-10.
16. *Ibid.*, pp. 229, 236-37; Samuel G. French, *Two Wars* (Nashville: Confederate Veteran, 1901), p. 59.

commanding the Army of Occupation, I have the honor to
make the following report of the operations of the division of
the army under my command, against the enemy in position at
Monterey. On the morning of the 21 inst., my division advanced toward the city. Lieut. Col. J. Garland's brigade, composed of the Third and Fourth regiments of Regular Infantry,
and Capt. B. Bragg's Horse-Artillery, Lieut. Col. H. Wilson's
brigade, composed of the First regiment of Regular Infantry,
and the Washington and Baltimore battalion of Volunteers,
were ordered to the east and lower end of the city, to make
a diversion in favor of Brevet Brig. Gen. W. J. Worth's division,
which was operating against the west and upper part of the
city. It being deemed practicable, an assault was ordered
against two of the enemy's advanced works. The regular force
of my division was thrown to the right of the two works, with
orders to take possession of some houses in the city, on the
right and rear of the enemy's advanced position, with a view
of annoying him in flank and rear. The Washington and Baltimore battalion was ordered on the road leading directly to
the works. Under a most galling and destructive fire from
three batteries in front and one on the right, as well as from
that of small arms from all the adjacent houses and stone walls,
my division advanced as rapidly as the ground and the stern
opposition of the enemy would admit it. The First, Third, and
Fourth regiments of Infantry gained the position to which
they were ordered, and annoyed the enemy in flank and rear,
until he was obliged to evacuate his two advanced works,
which were hotly pressed by Gen. [William O.] Butler's Division of Volunteers, and the Washington and Baltimore battalion, under command of Lieut. Col. [W. H.] Watson.

The Third and Fourth [Infantry] advanced still further into
the city, but finding the streets strongly barricaded by heavy
masses of masonry, behind which batteries were placed, and
the houses filled with light troops, were obliged to retire to
the works first taken by the Volunteers. The position of the
enemy's batteries, and the arrangement of his defences, in
every street and corner, rendered it necessary for the regular
troops who advanced into the city to be separated, each company being led by its captain or immediate commander, and
for the time acting independently. After a most manly struggle
of some six hours, my men succeeded, after various repulses,

in driving the enemy from each and every of his position in the suburbs.

The Third Infantry, commanded by Major W. W. Lear, and part of the Fourth, all under the command of Lieut. Col. J. Garland, led off towards the right, and in the direction of one of the enemy's strongest works [Fort Diablo] in front of a bridge in the city. Capt. B. Bragg's battery accompanied the command, under a destructive fire, which killed and disabled several of his men and horses, until directed to retire beyond the range of small arms. In this desperate struggle, the Third Infantry had Captains N. L. Morris and G. P. Field, Brevet Major P. N. Barbour, First Lieut. and Adjt. D. S. Irvin, and Second Lieut. R. Hazlett, killed, together with several non-commissioned officers and men, and its commanding officer, Major W. W. Lear, and Capt. H. Bainbridge, wounded—the former dangerously, and the latter slightly; and the Fourth lost its adjutant, Lieut. C. Hoskins, and Brevet First Lieut. [G. W. F.] Woods, of the Second Infantry, serving with the Fourth. The number of killed and wounded amongst the officers, shows with what praiseworthy heroism each regiment and company was led against the intrenched enemy.

The First Infantry, commanded by Brevet Major J. J. Abercrombie, passing two of the enemy's advanced works, succeeded in gaining possession of some houses on the left of the position of the Third and Fourth. Captains E. Backus and J. M. Scott, of the First, with their companies, took an advantageous position in rear of the two works referred to, and by firing into the gorges, assisted the Volunteer force very materially in driving the enemy from them. Capt. J. H. Lamotte, of the First, with his company, was doing valuable service at this time, when he received two wounds, and was obliged to retire. The killed and wounded in these three companies, in this operation, number thirty-six. Lieut. R. Dilworth, of Capt. J. H. Lamotte's company, was mortally wounded by a twelve-pounder before entering the town. The remainder of Capt. J. H. Lamotte's company, being now without an officer, was incorporated with others of the regiment. Capt. A. S. Miller's company, First Infantry, was actively employed in driving the enemy from his hedges and stone-fences near the advanced work, and having succeeded, with considerable loss, took command of what remained of companies C, E, G, and K, First

Infantry, accompanied by Lieut. S. Hamilton, acting adjutant—Brevet Major J. J. Abercrombie, commanding the regiment, having been wounded and Lieut. J. C. Terrett, his adjutant—and moved to repel a threatened attack on Capt. B. Bragg's battery by a body of lancers; after which his command joined Gen. [Thomas L.] Hamer's brigade, operating in the suburbs, and there remained till the close of the day.

The Baltimore and Washington battalion, commanded by the gallant Lieut. Col. Wm. H. Watson, who was killed whilst advancing under a heavy fire, into the city, served in co-operation with the regular infantry. After their commander fell, the companies were detached and did good service till the close of the day.

The number of killed and wounded in this assault, shows with what obstinacy each position was defended by the enemy, as well as the gallantry and good conduct displayed by our officers and men.

Capt. B. Bragg's battery, having suffered severely, after advancing some distance into the city, was obliged to withdraw to a point out of range of the enemy's small arms.

Capt. R. Ridgely, with one section of his battery [Company C, Third U. S. Artillery], annoyed the enemy's advanced works for some time in the commencement of the assault, but was obliged to retire out of range of their batteries, that were playing on him. Having used a twelve-pounder taken from the first work, against the enemy, till the ammunition gave out, he was sent with one section of his own battery still further in advance; but being unable to accomplish much against the enemy's heavy breastworks, returned to, and occupied with his battery, the first work taken from the enemy.

Captains R. Ridgely and B. Bragg, and their subalterns W. H. Shover, G. H. Thomas, J. F. Reynolds, C. L. Kilburn, and S. G. French, deserve the highest praise for their skill and good conduct under the heaviest fire of the enemy, which, when an opportunity offered, was concentrated on them. In the advanced works [Fort de la Teneria] referred to were taken four officers and sixteen men, prisoners of war, together with five pieces of ordnance, some ammunition and small arms. Having thrown up some slight breastworks, the First, Third, and Fourth Infantry, and Capt. R. Ridgely's battery, occupied this position until the morning of the 22d.

Owing to the position of the enemy and the nature of the ground, the two squadrons of Second Dragoons, commanded by Lieut. Col. C. A. May, were not brought into action. They were, however, actively and usefully employed in collecting and conveying the wounded to our camp. On the 23d, the advance into the city was resumed—the infantry working their way from house to house, supported by Captains R. Ridgely and B. Bragg's . . . [batteries], driving the enemy before them. When night closed our operations on the 23d, our men had advanced to within two squares of the centre of the city.

A cessation of hostilities, on the morning of the 24th, stopped our further progress, and gave us time to collect the wounded and bury the dead. The operating strength of my command on the morning of the 21st, was sixty-three officers, and ten hundred and twenty-two men, and out of that number were killed and wounded fifteen officers, and one hundred and sixty-four men. I enclose, herewith a tabular statement of the killed, wounded, and missing. Of the field-officers, I take pleasure in noticing the conduct of the late and lamented Lieut. Col. W. H. Watson, of the Washington and Baltimore battalion of Volunteers, who fell at the head of his command, whilst gallantly leading it against the enemy's works; as also that of Major W. W. Lear, commanding Third Infantry, who was dangerously wounded in the same assault, for which good service, I present his name for praise and promotion. Lieutenants G. W. F. Wood, First Infantry, and W. T. H. Brooks, Third Infantry, were actively and usefully employed as acting Assistant Adjutant Generals—the former to Lieut. Col. H. Wilson, Fourth Brigade, and the latter to Lieut. Col. J. Garland, of the Third Brigade. They were both dismounted by the enemy's artillery.

My staff officers, Lieut. D. C. Buell, Third Infantry, acting assistant Adjutant General, and Lieut. P. W. McDonald, Second Dragoons, aide-de-camp, rendered me valuable and meritorious services, in exposed positions, during the time my division was engaged with the enemy.

I am, very respectfully, your obedient servant,

D. E. TWIGGS

*Brig. General U.S.A., Com. First Division,*

Major W. W. S. Bliss, *Asst. Adj't Gen. Army of Occupation.*

Note.—After Major W. W. Lear and Capt. H. Bainbridge left

the Third Infantry, wounded, that regiment was led and commanded by Capt. W. S. Henry, Third Infantry, until the close of the day.[17]

Coincidentally, Colonel Garland reported:

Head-quarters, Third Brigade,
*Camp at Walnut Springs, three miles from Monterey,*
*Sept. 29, 1846.*

General:—Pursuant to the order of the commanding general [Taylor] and yourself [Twiggs], given to me on the morning of the 21st inst., on the field, I moved to a safe position with the Third Infantry, two hundred and forty strong, and while awaiting a summons from the chief Engineer (Major Mansfield) to advance, Lieut. Col. Wilson, First Infantry, joined me with that regiment, and the Baltimore battalion—the former one hundred and thirty strong, and the latter two hundred and twenty-nine, making in all six hundred and forty-one bayonets. In a few minutes after this junction, the chief Engineer dispatched Lieut. [John] Pope for a Light Infantry company to support him in making his reconnoissance. The leading company of the Third Infantry, under Lieut. Hazlett, was immediately ordered forward. In a short time afterwards, another company was applied for, and Capt. Field, of the Third Infantry, was detached. They had proceeded about a quarter of a mile, when Major Mansfield sent a request for my whole command to advance in supporting distance. This was promptly done, and in a few minutes a request was followed for me to advance in line of battle. In moving forward in this order we soon encountered a direct fire of artillery from redoubt No. 1, and an enfilading fire from the citadel [the Black Fort]. I then ordered the command to quicken their pace; this soon brought us within the range of their musketry. The chief engineer then indicated a movement to the right, which would enable us to gain a position in the town and in rear of the first redoubt.

We soon found ourselves in narrow streets, where we received a most destructive fire from three directions. Near this point, Capt. Bragg came up with his battery and asked for orders. One gun was speedily placed in a position to rake a narrow street from the direction of which we had sustained

17. Thomas B. Thorpe, *Our Army at Monterey* . . . (Philadelphia: Carey & Hart, 1847), pp. 180-83.

29

some loss, but finding after several shots that but little impression could be made upon the barricade, I ordered the captain to retire with his battery to a place of greater security. The Infantry continued to press ahead until the chief Engineer, then wounded and seeming to have no care for himself, advised us to retire to another position, where, according to my understanding of the order, to support and consult with Major Mansfield. I yielded to his suggestion, and directed the command to retire in good order.

This was not done, however, until we had lost many men, and some of the most valuable and accomplished officers of the army. At this time Major Lear, whilst gallantly leading his regiment, (the Third Infantry,) was wounded and totally disabled; his high-toned adjutant (Lieut. Irwin) and the noble Barbour, were killed; and Capt. [William G.] Williams, of the Topographical Engineers, and Lieut. Terrett, of the First Infantry, mortally wounded. Brevet Major Abercrombie was also wounded at my side and thrown from his horse. Capt. Lamotte had been badly wounded more than a hundred yards in advance of this point and in the direction of the first redoubt, where Capt. Backus, with indomitable courage and perseverance, had succeeded with his company in gaining the roof of a stone building [Fort de la Teneria], and not hearing the order to retire, continued to pour a galling fire into the rear of the redoubt, until the Volunteers of Gen. [John A.] Quitman's brigade rushed in, took it, and kept it.

As soon as my command was reunited and put in order, having been joined by the Fourth Infantry, which had at this time suffered considerable loss, both in officers and men, the ever to be lamented Hoskins, and the distinguished Woods having been killed, and Lieut. [Richard H.] Graham badly wounded, in an assault upon the first redoubt, I was ordered to advance again, and if possible, carry the second redoubt at the point of the bayonet. In attempting the execution of this order, with not more than half my original force, I passed several barricaded streets, raked both by artillery and infantry, until I believed the command sufficiently advanced into the town to enable me to enter the rear of the redoubt. I then directed Capt. Morris, who headed the Third Infantry, to enter the back of a garden to his left, and press forward to the street nearest the rivulet [Rio de la Santa Catarina]. Brevet Major

[William M.] Graham, with the remnant of the Fourth Infantry, followed. These two commands, although few in number, sustained themselves in the most admirable manner, under the heaviest fire of the day; for instead of the second redoubt, of which we were in search, we unluckily ran afoul of a tête de pont, the strongest defence of the city, and from the opposite side of the bridge two pieces of artillery were brought to bear upon us at little more than a hundred yards distance.

Here the brave Morris fell, and also his friend Lieut. Hazlett, who had just placed him in a house. Capt. [William S.] Henry, who succeeded to the command of the Third Infantry, Capt. Bainbridge having been wounded and retired, and Brevet Major Graham, the senior officer at this point, with the Fourth, in their exposed situation, maintained their position against fearful odds, until their ammunition began to fail, when hearing nothing of the battery for which two staff officers had at different times been dispatched, I reluctantly ordered the truly Spartan band to retire, and I am proud to say, under all their afflictions, it was accomplished in good order. Lieut. Col. Wilson was with me during the greater part of this struggle, and displayed great personal courage. His command was, however, so much dispersed, that I saw but little of it. Brevet Major Allen was also by my side. Capt. Shivers, with his independent company of Volunteers, performed admirable service. They were with Bragg's battery during the greater part of the day.

It is impossible for me to speak of the many individual acts of gallantry, both of officers and men, during this day of trial. Their conduct was worthy of all praise. I cannot let the opportunity pass by to express my warmest thanks to Lieut. Brooks, acting assistant adjutant general, whose horse was killed under him; and to Capt. George Mason Graham, of the Louisiana Volunteers, my acting aid[e]-de-camp, for the efficient services they rendered me, in communicating orders throughout the day, incurring, as they did, the greatest personal danger. If it were not out of place, I would also mention the name of Lieut. Pope, of the Topographical Engineers, who deported himself as a gallant soldier, under the heaviest fire of the enemy.

I cannot trust myself to speak of the gallant Col. Watson, that sterling officer, Capt. Field, and the other distinguished dead. This must be done by others, whose grief is less profound.

I have the honor to be, very respectfully, your obedient servant, JNO. GARLAND,

*Lieut. Col. Fourth Infantry, Commanding*
*Third Brigade*[18]

Their gallantry at Monterrey made Braxton Bragg a major by brevet and George H. Thomas a brevet captain. Thomas likewise earned a nickname "Old Reliable," bestowed by the men of his section.[19]

The armistice remained in effect until November 13, when it was abrogated. Soon thereafter, General Taylor sent General Worth to occupy Satillo, 65 miles west, southwest of Monterrey on the far side of Rinconada Pass. Coincidentally, Brigadier, General John A. Quitman was selected to lead the advance aimed at Tampico on the Gulf Coast. Among the officers selected to accompany Quitman were Lieutenants George H. Thomas, John F. Reynolds, and Samuel G. French of Bragg's battery, with Thomas, the senior, in command. Quitman's intermediate objective was Victoria. He organized his volunteer infantry into two brigades and left Monterrey in mid-December, taking the road to Montemoralos.

Quitman's 2,000-man column entered Victoria on December 29. The general and his staff rode to the plaza, followed by Thomas' artillery and the footsoldiers. After the Mexican eagle was lowered, and the stars and stripes hoisted, the soldiers camped in fields outside the town. Northers buffeted the area, flattening the tents and filling the air with fine black dust.[20]

On January 4, 1847, General Taylor arrived with General Twiggs' division of regulars, and soon thereafter Major General Robert E. Patterson and 1,500 men showed up, having marched from near Matamoros. On January 12, with commissary supplies for the 5,000 soldiers being rapidly consumed, General Taylor ordered Twiggs and Patterson to continue on to Tampico with their commands. At Tampico, which they reached in late January, the troops boarded steamboats, preparatory to joining the force

18. *Ibid.*, pp. 187-88.
19. Cleaves, p. 34.
20. French, pp. 69-70; Smith, Vol. I, p. 365.

being assembled by Major General Winfield Scott for an amphibious landing at Veracruz.[21]

General Taylor, accompanied by Thomas' battery, two companies of dragoons, and several regiments of volunteer infantry, then returned to Monterrey. Thomas did not remain long at Monterrey, as early in February, General Taylor reinforced the Saltillo garrison. His army, some 4,600-strong, took position at Agua Nueva, 20 miles south of Saltillo. To take such a position was unnecessary and dangerous, and led to the battle of Buena Vista.[22]

In that terrible struggle, Taylor flirted with disaster, when assailed by 20,000 Mexican soldiers and 17 cannon led by General Antonio Lopez de Santa Ana. Only the light artillery, America's secret weapon in that conflict, saved Taylor's army from disaster.

General Taylor, in his official report, dated March 6, detailed the battle:

Head-quarters, Army of Occupation,<br>Agua Nueva, March 6, 1847

Sir: I have the honor to submit a detailed report of the operation of the forces under my command which resulted in the engagement of Buena Vista, the repulse of the Mexican army and the re-occupation of this position.

The . . . [information], which reached me of the advance and concentration of a heavy Mexican force in my front, had assumed such a probable form, as to induce a special examination far beyond the reach of our pickets, to ascertain its correctness. A small party of Texas spies, under Major [Ben] McCulloch, dispatched to the hacienda of Encarnacion, 30 miles from this, on the route to San Luis Potosi, had reported a cavalry force of unknown strength at that place. On the 20th of February a strong reconnaissance under Lieut. Col. [Charles A.] May was dispatched to the hacienda of Heclionda, while Major McCulloch made another examination of Encarnacion. The results of these expeditions left no doubt that the enemy was in large force at Encarnacion under the orders of General Santa Ana, and that he meditated a forward movement and attack upon our position.

---

21. Cleaves, p. 37.
22. *Ibid.*, p. 38.

As the camp of Agua Nueva could be turned on either flank, and as the enemy's force was greatly superior to our own, particularly in the arm of cavalry, I determined, after much consideration, to take up a position about eleven miles in rear, and there await the attack. The army broke up its camp and marched at noon on the 21st, encamping at the new position a little in front of the hacienda of Buena Vista. With a small force I proceeded to Saltillo to make some necessary arrangements for the defence of the town, leaving Brigadier General [John E.] Wool in the immediate command of the troops.

Before those arrangements were completed on the morning of the 22d, I was advised that the enemy was in sight, advancing. Upon reaching the ground it was found that his cavalry advance was in our front, having marched from Encarnacion, as we have since learned, at 11 o'clock on the day previous, and driving in a mounted force left at Agua Nueva to cover the removal of public stores. Our troops were in position occupying a line of remarkable strength. The road at this point becomes a narrow defile, the valley on its right being rendered quite impracticable for artillery by a system of deep and impassable gullies, while on the left a succession of rugged ridges and precipitous ravines extends far back towards the mountain which bounds the valley. The features of the ground were such as nearly to paralyze the artillery and cavalry of the enemy, while his infantry could not derive all the advantage of its numerical superiority.

In this position we prepared to receive him. Capt. [John M.] Washington's battery (4th artillery) was posted to command the road, while the 1st and 2d Illinois regiments, under Colonels [John J.] Hardin and [William H.] Bissell, each eight companies (to the latter of which was attached Capt. [A. Edward] Conner's company of Texas volunteers), and the 2d Kentucky under Col. [William R.] McKee, occupied the crests of the ridges on the left and in the rear. The Arkansas and Kentucky regiments of cavalry, commanded by Colonels [Archibald] Yell and H. Marshall, occupied the extreme left near the base of the mountain, while the Indiana brigade, under Brigadier General [Joseph] Lane, (composed of the 2d and 3d regiments under Cols. [William A.] Bowles and [James H.] Lane), the Mississippi riflemen under Col. [Jefferson] Davis, the squadrons of the 1st and 2d dragoons under Captain [Enoch] Steen, and Lieut. Col. May, and the light batteries of Captains [Thomas W.] Sherman and Bragg, 3d artillery, were held in reserve.

At 11 o'clock I received from General Santa Ana a summons to surrender at discretion, which, with a copy of my reply, I have already transmitted. The enemy still forbore his attack, evidently waiting for the arrival of his rear columns, which could be distinctly seen by our look-outs as they approached the field. A demonstration made on his left [by Brigadier General Francisco Mejía's brigade] caused me to detach the 2d Kentucky regiment and a section of artillery [from Bragg's company] to our right, in which position they bivouacked for the night. In the meantime the Mexican light troops had engaged ours on the extreme left (composed of parts of the Kentucky and Arkansas cavalry dismounted, and a rifle battalion from the Indiana brigade under Major [Willis A.] Gorman, the whole commanded by Col. Marshall), and kept up a sharp fire, climbing the mountain side, and apparently endeavoring to gain our flank. Three pieces of Capt. Washington's battery [under Captain John P. J. O'Brien] had been detached to the left, and were supported by the 2d Indiana regiment. An occasional shell was thrown by the enemy into this part of our line, but without effect. The skirmishing of the light troops was kept up with trifling loss on our part until dark, when I became convinced that no serious attack would be made before the morning, and returned with the Mississippi regiment and squadron of 2d dragoons to Saltillo. The troops bivouacked without fires, and laid upon their arms.

A body of cavalry, some 1,500 strong, had been visible all day in rear of the town, having entered the valley through a narrow pass east of the city. This cavalry, commanded by General [José V.] Miñon, had evidently been thrown in our rear to break up and harass our retreat, and perhaps make some attempt against the town if practicable. The city was occupied by four excellent companies of Illinois volunteers under Major [William B.] Warren of the 1st regiment. A field-work, which commanded most of the approaches, was garrisoned by Captain [Lucien B.] Webster's company, 1st artillery, and armed with two twenty-four-pound howitzers, while the train and head-quarter camp was guarded by two companies Mississippi riflemen under Captain [William P.]

Rogers, and a field-piece commanded by Captain [William H.] Shover, 3d artillery. Having made these dispositions for the protection of the rear, I proceeded on the morning of the 23d to Buena Vista, ordering forward all the other available troops. The action had commenced before my arrival on the field.

During the evening and night of the 22d the enemy had thrown a body of light troops [led by Major General Pedro de Ampudia] on the mountain side, with the purpose of out-flanking our left; and it was here that the action of the 23d commenced at an early hour. Our riflemen under Colonel Marshall, who had been reinforced by three companies under Major [Xerxes F.] Trail, 2d Illinois volunteers, maintained their ground handsomely against a greatly superior force, holding themselves under cover, and using their weapons with deadly effect. About 8 o'clock a strong demonstration was made against the centre of our position, a heavy column moving along the road. This force was soon dispersed by a few rapid and well-directed shots from Captain Washington's battery. In the meantime the enemy was concentrating a large force of infantry and cavalry [Major Generals Manuel M. Lombardini's and Francisco Pacheco's divisions] under cover of the ridges, with the obvious intention of forcing our left, which was posted on an extensive plateau. The 2d Indiana and 2d Illinois regiments formed this part of our line, the former covering three pieces of light artillery, under the orders of Captain [John P. J.] O'Brien—Brigadier General Lane being in the immediate command.

In order to bring his men within effective range, General Lane ordered the artillery and 2d Indiana regiment forward. The artillery advanced within musket range of a heavy body of Mexican infantry, and was served against it with great effect, but without being able to check its advance. The infantry ordered to its support had fallen back in disorder, being exposed, as well as the battery, not only to a severe fire of small arms from the front, but also to a murderous cross-fire of grape and canister from a Mexican battery on the left. Captain O'Brien found it impossible to retain his position without support, but was only able to withdraw two of his pieces, all the horses and cannoneers of the third piece being killed or disabled. The 2d Indiana regiment, which had fallen back as stated, could not be rallied, and took no further part in the action, except a handful of men, who, under its gallant colonel, Bowles, joined the Mississippi regiment, and did good service, and those fugitives who, at a later period in the day, assisted in defending the train and depot at Buena Vista. This portion of our line having given way, and the enemy appearing in overwhelming force against our left flank, the light troops which had rendered such good service on the mountain, were compelled to withdraw, which they did, for the most part, in good order. Many, however, were not rallied until they reached the depot at Buena Vista, to the defence of which they afterwards contributed.

Colonel Bissell's regiment (2d Illinois), which had been joined by a section [George H. Thomas'] of Captain Sherman's battery, had become completely outflanked, and was compelled to fall back, being entirely unsupported. The enemy was now pouring masses of infantry and cavalry along the base of the mountain on our left, and was gaining our rear in great force.

At this moment I arrived upon the field. The Mississippi regiment had been directed to the left before reaching the position, and immediately came into action against the Mexican infantry which had turned our flank. The 2nd Kentucky regiment and a section of artillery under Captain Bragg, had previously been ordered from the right to reinforce our left, and arrived at a most opportune moment. That regiment, and a portion of the 1st Illinois, under Colonel Hardin, gallantly drove the enemy, and recovered a portion of the ground we had lost. The batteries of Captains Sherman and Bragg [including Thomas' section] were in position on the plateau, and did much execution, not only in front, but particularly upon the masses which had gained our rear. Discovering that the enemy was heavily pressing upon the Mississippi regiment, the third Indiana regiment, under Colonel Lane, was dispatched to strengthen that part of our line, which formed a crotchet perpendicular to the first line of battle. At the same time Lieutenant [Charles L.] Kilburn, with a piece of Captain Bragg's battery, was directed to support the infantry there engaged.

The action was for a long time warmly sustained at that point—the enemy making several efforts both with infantry and cavalry against our line, and being always repulsed with heavy loss. I had placed all the regular cavalry and Captain

[Albert] Pike's squadron of Arkansas horse under the orders of Brevet Lieutenant Colonel May, with directions to hold in check the enemy's column, still advancing to the rear along the base of the mountain, which was done in conjunction with the Kentucky and Arkansas cavalry under Colonels Marshall and Yell.

In the meantime our left, which was still strongly threatened by a superior force, was further strengthened by the detachment of Captain Bragg's, and a portion of Captain Sherman's batteries, to that quarter. The concentration of artillery fire upon the masses of the enemy along the base of the mountain, and the determined resistance offered by the two regiments opposed to them, had created confusion in their ranks, and some of the corps attempted to effect a retreat upon their main line of battle. The squadron of the 1st dragoons, under Lieutenant [Daniel H.] Rucker, was now ordered up the deep ravine, which these retreating corps were endeavoring to cross, in order to charge and disperse them. The squadron proceeded to the point indicated, but could not accomplish the object, being exposed to a heavy fire from a battery established to cover the retreat of those corps. While the squadron was detached on this service, a large body of the enemy (cavalry led by Brigadier General Julián Juvera) was observed to concentrate on our extreme left, apparently with the view of making a descent upon the hacienda of Buena Vista, where our train and baggage were deposited. Lieutenant Colonel May was ordered to the support of that point, with two pieces of Captain Sherman's battery under Lieutenant Reynolds. In the meantime the scattered forces near the hacienda, composed in parts of Majors Trail and Gorman's commands, had been to some extent organized under the advice of Major [John] Munroe, chief of artillery, with the assistance of Major [James L. D.] Morrison, volunteer staff, and were posted to defend the position.

Before our cavalry had reached the hacienda, that of the enemy had made its attack, having been handsomely met by the Kentucky and Arkansas cavalry under Colonels Marshall and Yell. The Mexican column [Juvera's] immediately divided, one portion sweeping by the depot, where it received a destructive fire from the force which had collected there, and then gaining the mountain opposite, under a fire from Lieutenant Reynolds' section, the remaining portion regaining the base of the mountain on our left. In the charge at Buena Vista, Colonel Yell fell gallantly at the head of his regiment; we also lost Adjutant [Edward M.] Vaughn, of the Kentucky cavalry—a young officer of much promise. Lieutenant Colonel May, who had been rejoined by the squadron of the 1st dragoons and by portions of the Arkansas and Indiana troops under Lieutenant Colonel [John S.] Roane and Major Gorman, now approached the base of the mountain, holding in check the right flank of the enemy, upon whose masses, crowded in the narrow gorges and ravines, our artillery was doing fearful execution.

The position of that portion of the Mexican army which had gained our rear was now very critical, and it seemed doubtful whether it could regain the main body. At this moment I received from General Santa Ana a message by a staff officer, desiring to know what I wanted? I immediately dispatched Brigadier General Wool to the Mexican general-in-chief, and sent orders to cease firing. Upon reaching the Mexican lines, General Wool could not cause the enemy to cease their fire, and accordingly returned without having an interview. The extreme right of the enemy continued its retreat along the base of the mountain, and finally, in spite of all our efforts, effected a junction with the remainder of the army.

During the day, the cavalry of General Miñon had ascended the elevated plain above Saltillo, and occupied the road from the city, to the field of battle, where they intercepted several of our men. Approaching the town, they were fired upon by Captain Webster, from the redoubt occupied by his company, and then moved off towards the eastern side of the valley, and obliquely towards Buena Vista. At this time, Captain Shover moved rapidly forward with his piece, supported by a miscellaneous command of mounted volunteers, and fired several shots at the cavalry with great effect. They were driven into the ravines which lead to the lower valley, closely pursued by Captain Shover, who was further supported by a piece of Captain Webster's battery, under Lieutenant [James S.] Donaldson, which had advanced from the redoubt, supported by Captain [Erastus] Wheeler's company Illinois volunteers. The enemy made one or two efforts to charge the artillery, but was finally driven back in a confused mass, and did not again appear upon the plain.

In the meantime, the firing had partially ceased upon the principal field. The enemy seemed to confine his efforts to the protection of his artillery, and I had left the plateau for a moment, when I was recalled thither by a very heavy musketry fire. On regaining that position, I discovered that our infantry ([1st and 2d] Illinois and 2d Kentucky) had engaged a greatly superior force of the enemy [led by Brigadier General Francisco Pérez]—evidently his reserves—and that they had been overwhelmed by numbers. The moment was most critical. Captain O'Brien, with two pieces, had sustained this heavy charge to the very last, and was finally obliged to leave his guns on the field—his infantry support being entirely routed. Captain Bragg, who had just arrived from the left, was ordered at once into battery. Without any infantry to support him, and at the imminent risk of losing his guns, this officer came rapidly into action, the Mexican lines being but a few yards from the muzzle of his pieces. The first discharge of canister caused the enemy to hesitate; the second and third drove him back in disorder, and saved the day.

The 2d Kentucky regiment, which had advanced beyond supporting distance in this affair, was driven back and closely pressed by the enemy's cavalry. Taking a ravine which led in the direction of Captain Washington's battery, their pursuers [Brigadier General Anastasio Terrejón's cavalry] became exposed to his [Washington's] fire which soon checked and drove them back with loss. In the meantime, the rest of our artillery had taken position on the plateau, covered by the Mississippi and 3d Indiana regiments, the former of which had reached the ground in time to pour a fire into the right flank of the enemy, and thus contribute to his repulse. In this last conflict we had the misfortune to sustain a very heavy loss. Colonel Hardin, 1st Illinois, and Colonel McKee, and Lieutenant Colonel [Henry] Clay, 2d Kentucky regiments, fell at this time while gallantly heading their commands.

No further attempt was made by the enemy to force our position, and the approach of night gave an opportunity to pay proper attention to the wounded, and also to refresh the soldiers, who had been exhausted by incessant watchfulness and combat. Though the night was severely cold, the troops were compelled for the most to bivouack without fires, expecting that morning would renew the conflict. During the night the wounded were removed to Saltillo, and every preparation made to receive the enemy should he again attack our position. Seven fresh companies were drawn from the town, and Brigadier General [Thomas] Marshall, who had made a forced march from the Rinconada, with a reinforcement of Kentucky cavalry and four heavy guns, under Captain [James H.] Prentiss, 1st artillery, was near at hand, when it was discovered that the enemy had abandoned his position during the night. Our scouts soon ascertained that he had fallen back upon Agua Nueva. The great disparity of numbers, and the exhaustion of our troops, rendered it inexpedient and hazardous to attempt pursuit. A staff officer was dispatched to General Santa Ana to negotiate an exchange of prisoners, which was satisfactorily completed on the following day. Our own dead were collected and buried, and the Mexican wounded, of which a large number had been left upon the field, were removed to Saltillo, and rendered as comfortable as circumstances would permit.

On the evening of the 26th, a close reconnaissance was made of the enemy's position, which was found to be occupied only by a small body of cavalry, the infantry and artillery having retreated in the direction of San Luis Potosi. On the 27th, our troops resumed their former camp at Agua Nueva, the enemy's rear guard evacuating the place as we approached, leaving a considerable number of wounded. It was my purpose to beat up his quarters at Encarnacion early the next morning, but upon examination, the weak condition of the cavalry horses rendered it unadvisable to attempt so long a march without water. A command was finally dispatched to Encarnacion, on the 1st of March, under Col. [William G.] Belknap. Some two hundred wounded, and about sixty Mexican soldiers were found there, the army having passed on in the direction of Matehuala, with greatly reduced numbers, and suffering much from hunger. The dead and dying were strewed upon the road and crowded the buildings of the hacienda.

The American force engaged in the action of Buena Vista is shown, by the accompanying field report, to have been 334 officers, and 4,425 men, exclusive of the small command left in and near Saltillo. Of this number, two squadrons of cavalry, and three batteries of light artillery, making not more than 453 men, composed the only force of regular troops. The strength of the Mexican army is stated by Gen. Santa Ana, in his summons, to be 20,000; and that estimate is confirmed by all the information since obtained.—Our loss is 267 killed, 456 wounded, and 23 missing. Of the numerous wounded many did not require removal to the hospital, and it is hoped that a comparatively small number will be permanently disabled. The Mexican loss in killed and wounded may be fairly estimated at 1,500 and will probably reach 2,000. At least 500 of their killed were left upon the field of battle. We have no means of ascertaining the number of deserters and dispersed men from their ranks, but it is known to be very great.

Our loss has been especially severe in officers, twenty-eight having been killed upon the field. We have to lament the death of Captain George Lincoln, assistant adjutant general, serving on the staff of General Wool—a young officer of high bearing and approved gallantry, who fell early in the action. No loss falls more heavily upon the army in the field than that of Colonels Hardin and McKee, and Lieutenant Colonel Clay.

I perform a grateful duty in bringing to the notice of the government the general good conduct of the troops. Exposed for successive nights without fires to the severity of the weather, they were ever prompt and cheerful in the discharge of every duty, and finally displayed conspicuous steadiness and gallantry in repulsing at great odds a disciplined foe. While the brilliant success achieved by their arms releases me from the painful necessity of specifying many cases of bad conduct before the enemy, I feel an increased obligation to mention particular corps and officers, whose skill, coolness, and gallantry in trying situations and under a continued and heavy fire, seem to merit particular notice.

To Brigadier General Wool my obligations are specially due. The high state of discipline and instruction of several of the volunteer regiments was attained under his command, and to his vigilance and arduous services before the action, and his gallantry and activity on the field, a large share of our success may justly be attributed. During most of the engagement he was in immediate command of the troops thrown back on our left flank. I beg leave to recommend him to the favorable notice of the government. Brigadier General Lane (slightly wounded) was active and zealous throughout the day and displayed great coolness and gallantry before the enemy.

The services of the light artillery, always conspicuous, were more than usually distinguished. Moving rapidly over the roughest ground, it was always in action at the right place and the right time, and its well-directed fire dealt destruction in the masses of the enemy. While I recommend to particular favor the gallant conduct and valuable services of Major Munroe, chief of artillery, and Captains Washington, 4th artillery, and Sherman and Bragg, 3d artillery, commanding batteries, I deem it no more than just to mention all the subaltern officers. They were nearly all detached at different times, and in every situation exhibited conspicuous skill and gallantry. Captain O'Brien, Lieutenants [Thomas L.] Brent, [Henry M.] Whiting, and [Darius N.] Couch, 4th artillery, and [Francis T.] Bryan, topographical engineers (slightly wounded) were attached to Captain Washington's battery. Lieutenants Thomas, Reynolds, and French, 3d artillery [the latter] (severely wounded) to that of Captain Sherman; and Captain Shover and Lieutenant Kilburn, 3d artillery, to that of Captain Bragg, Captain Shover, in conjunction with Lieutenant Donaldson, 1st artillery, rendered gallant and important service in repulsing the cavalry of General Miñon. The regular cavalry, under Lieutenant Colonel May, with which was associated Captain Pike's squadron of Arkansas horse, rendered useful service in holding the enemy in check and in covering the batteries at several points. Captain Steen, 1st dragoons, was severely wounded early in the day, while gallantly endeavoring, with my authority, to rally the troops which were falling to the rear.

The Mississippi riflemen, under Colonel [Jefferson] Davis, were highly conspicuous for their gallantry and steadiness, and sustained throughout the engagement the reputation of veteran troops. Brought into action against an immensely superior force, they maintained themselves for a long time unsupported and with heavy loss, and held an important part of the field until reinforced. Colonel Davis, though severely wounded, remained in the saddle until the close of the action. His distinguished coolness and gallantry at the head of his regiment on this day entitle him to the particular notice of the government. The 3d Indiana regiment, under Colonel Lane, and a fragment of the 2d, under Colonel Bowles, were associated with the Mississippi regiment during the greater portion of the day, and acquitted themselves creditably in repulsing the attempts of the enemy to break that portion of our line.

The Kentucky cavalry, under Colonel Marshall, rendered good service dismounted, acting as light troops on our left, and afterwards, with a portion of the Arkansas regiment, in meeting and dispersing the column of cavalry at Buena Vista. The 1st and 2d Illinois, and the 2d Kentucky regiments, served immediately under my eye, and I bear a willing testimony to their excellent conduct throughout the day. The spirit and gallantry with which the 1st Illinois and 2d Kentucky engaged the enemy in the morning, restored confidence to that part of the field, while the list of casualties will show how much these three regiments suffered in sustaining the heavy charge of the enemy in the afternoon. Captain Conner's company of Texas volunteers, attached to the 2d Illinois regiment, fought bravely, its captain being wounded and two subalterns killed. Colonel Bissell, the only surviving colonel of these regiments, merits notice for his coolness and bravery on this occasion. After the fall of the field officers of the 1st Illinois and 2d Kentucky regiments, the command of the former devolved upon Lieutenant Colonel [William] Weatherford; that of the latter upon Major [Cary H.] Fry.

The medical staff, under the able direction of Assistant Surgeon [Charles M.] Hitchcock, were assiduous in attention to the wounded upon the field, and in their careful removal to the rear. Both in these respects and in the subsequent organization and service of the hospitals, the administration of this department was every thing that could be wished.

I am, sir, very respectfully, your obedient servant.

Z. Taylor,
*Major General U. S. A. Commanding.*[23]

General Wool reported that, "I also desire to express my high admiration and to offer my warmest thanks to Captains Washington, Sherman, and Bragg, and Lieutenants O'Brien and Thomas, and their batteries; to whose services at this point, and on every other part of the field, I think it but justice to say, we are mainly indebted for the great victory so successfully achieved by our arms over the great force opposed to us—more than 20,000 men and seventeen pieces of artillery. Without our artillery we

23. Zachary Taylor's report of the Battle of Buena Vista found in *Message from the President of the United States, to the Two Houses of Congress at the Commencement of the 1st Session of the 30th Congress, December 7, 1847* (Washington, 1848), pp. 132-43.

would not have maintained our position a single hour."[24]

And Thomas' company commander, Thomas W. Sherman wrote, "I was directed to take my battery back to the plateau, where I found Lieutenant Thomas, who had been constantly engaged during the forenoon in the preservation of that important position, and whom I found closely engaged with the enemy, and that, too, in a very advanced position . . . . Lieutenant Thomas more than sustained the reputation he has long enjoyed in his regiment as an accurate and scientific artillerist."[25]

Thomas, himself, left an account of the battle in a terse summary of his early military career, "The Battle of Buena Vista was fought on the 23 Feb. '47 and I was under fire from 6 o.c. until 4 P.M."[26]

The battle of Buena Vista ended active combat operations in northern Mexico with the Americans victorious. The services of the senior artillery officers were recognized by a grateful government with new brevet commissions. Braxton Bragg was named brevet lieutenant colonel, while Thomas W. Sherman, George H. Thomas, Samuel G. French, and John F. Reynolds were made brevet majors.[27]

24. John E. Wool's report of the Battle of Buena Vista found in *ibid.*, p. 150.
25. Thomas W. Sherman's report of the Battle of Buena Vista found in *ibid.*, p. 205.
26. Cleaves, p. 42.
27. *Ibid.*, p. 43.

# CHAPTER FOUR

# *The Years from the War With Mexico to the Civil War*

When news of Buena Vista, along with copies of the official reports, reached the citizens of Thomas' home village of Jerusalem in Southampton County, Virginia, they became very elated and excited about their young hero's distinguished conduct in the Mexican War. A special meeting was called by the citizens at their courthouse on Monday, July 19, 1847. Colonel William C. Parker, called upon to give the oration, rose, and, "in his natural eloquent and happy style, proceeded to deliver a spirit-stirring eulogy upon the character and conduct of our hero." He then proposed "the following resolutions, which were by acclamation adopted," and are so impressive that they are presented here in their entirety:

Resolved, That whilst we glory in the unfailing fame which our heroic army in Mexico has acquired for herself and country, our attention has been especially drawn to the military skill, bravery and noble deportment of our fellow countryman, George H. Thomas, exhibited in the campaign of Florida, at

Fort Brown [Texas], Monterey and Buena Vista, in which he has given ample proof of the best requisites of a soldier—patience, fortitude, firmness and daring intrepidity.

Resolved, That as a testimonial of our high appreciation of his character as a citizen and a soldier, we will present to him a sword, with suitable emblems and devices and that . . . a committee be appointed to collect by subscription a sum sufficient for the purpose and cause to be fabricated a sword to be presented to the said George H. Thomas, through the hands of his noble heroic commander, Major General Z. Taylor.[1]

A committee was appointed for the purpose of raising the necessary funds to cover the expenses of the sword, and the commission for sword and scabbard was given to the Wm. H. Horstman & Sons military store in Philadelphia. A motion was proposed and passed that a copy of the proceedings of the committee be published with a copy sent to the mother and brothers of Brevet Captain Thomas and a copy to be presented with the sword.[2] The Philadelphia *Evening Bulletin* gave the following description of the sword while it was on public exhibition:

The pattern of the sabre is that used by the United States Dragoons [formerly mounted infantrymen, now cavalrymen]. The blade is of the truest and prettiest steel, finished in a manner that would defy superiority of workmanship. The scabbard is of solid silver, standard value, beautifully enriched with engraved scroll work encircling military trophies, with the words: Florida, Fort Brown, Monterey, Buena Vista, and an engraved vignette of the Battle of Monterey. The hilt is of basket form, exquisitely chased. The grip is solid silver, also enriched with engraved scrolls. The pommel is of gold, grasping an amethyst, and the rings and band in bas-relief, and upon the grip an elephant is engraved.[3]

At the time the sword was awarded to Thomas, he was regarded as a true man and a brilliant officer by his relatives and admiring friends from Virginia. But after he had demonstrated his loyalty to the Union during the Civil War, there was a striking contrast of bitter animosity directed toward him by the

1. Van Horne, *Life,* pp. 7-8.
2. *Ibid.,* p. 8.
3. *Ibid.,* p. 9.

same people which lasted even after his death. The sword was in possession of General Thomas' sisters, Misses Judith Elvira and Frances C. Thomas. It has been said that Judith refused to return the sword to Thomas after the Civil War, and to have affirmed that she would only surrender it when the citizens of Southampton County, Virginia, demanded its return. Before the sisters' deaths, the sword was given to the Virginia Historical Society in Richmond, Virginia.[4] There is no doubt Thomas prized it above all other gifts and that the costly sword was too precious to be worn except on the occasion of his marriage.[5] The following letter of acknowledgment exemplifies his admiration of it:

March 31, 1848

Dear Sir:

Your letter of the 8th February transmitting the Resolutions of the citizens of Southampton at a meeting in their Court House on the 19th of July, 1847, was received by the last mail.

In accepting the Sword presented me by my fellow countrymen, and in acknowledging the very high compliment paid me in those resolutions, I beg you will present to the committee, and through them, to my old friends of Southampton my sincere and heartfelt thanks. Aware that the little service I have been able to render my country, although performed with cheerfulness, and to the utmost of my ability, does not in the least entitle me to this very high compliment from my old friends and fellow citizens, I shall always regard it as the result of kindness of heart and friendliness of feeling on their part, which renders the obligation doubly grateful, and as such will ever be a proud collection to the last hour of my life. "Next to the consciousness of having done his duty the sympathy of friends is the highest reward of a soldier."

In conclusion, I beg you will accept my hearty acknowledgements for the very flattering and friendly manner in which you have communicated, to me, these resolutions, and with every wish for long continued health, and happiness to yourself and family, I remain

Your friend and obedient Servant,<br>George H. Thomas

4. Thomas, p. 99.
5. Drewry, p. 22.

> To Captain James Maget
> Newsoms Depot
> Southampton County,
> Va.[6]

The battle of Buena Vista terminated major campaigning in northern Mexico. During the months immediately after the Mexican War, Thomas served and was in charge of the commissary depot at Brazos Santiago, Texas, from August 9, 1848, to February 1, 1849. He was granted a leave of absence to August 1, 1849, the second leave he had taken since his graduation from West Point in 1840. After his leave of absence he was assigned to Fort Adams, Rhode Island, on Brentons Point, near Newport. Subsequently, Thomas returned to Florida, as an officer of Company B, Third Artillery, where he served for 14 months, from mid-September 1849, until the autumn of 1850.

He pulled duty at Fort Independence, Massachusetts, on Castle Island in Boston Harbor, from January of 1851 to March 28, 1851, when he received an appointment to become an instructor at the U. S. Military Academy at West Point. Here he served as Instructor of Artillery and Cavalry from April 2, 1851, to May 1, 1854,[7] displaying the same qualities of service which had given him fame in the field. He was very popular with the cadets, not because he was lax in discipline, for he was quite the reverse, but for the reason that he was eminently just. In his memoirs of General Thomas, Major General Richard W. Johnson remarked, "It gave him great pain to be compelled to punish a cadet, and he never did so unless duty imperatively demanded it." Thomas' keen sense of justice prevented him from taking an undue advantage of anyone. He had a great compassion for others. This was the secret of his popularity. It was this that made his soldiers love him and made them willing to follow wherever he led the way.

During his first year as an instructor, Thomas had occasion to make frequent use of the Academy library. His selection of books borrowed from the library was initially professionally sober, but suddenly he became interested in romantic novels and poems.

6. Reproduced through courtesy of the Virginia Historical Society, Richmond.
7. Cullum, II, 33.

Still a bachelor at thirty-six, the record does not indicate that he had had any love affair up to this time to interest him in such literature. For several years, however, during the spring and summer seasons, Mrs. Abigail Kellogg, widow of Warren Kellogg, a prosperous merchant of Troy, New York, was a regular visitor at the West Point Hotel. She was accompanied by her two daughters, Frances Lucretia and Julia Augusta. Mrs. Kellogg had several interests at the Military Academy. One of them was her nephew, Cadet Lyman Mack Kellogg, class of 1852; another, less readily acknowledged but undeniable, was bringing her daughters into the society of eligible young men.

Inevitably, Thomas met Miss Frances L. Kellogg who was five years younger than he and in no time he was courting her. Miss Kellogg possessed a warm personality and was handsome in her appearance, possessing an uncommonly pleasing manner and a fluency in conversation. Her slim and attractive figure made her a woman of graceful appearance, and she was a lady of rare accomplishments. She had attended the best schools and had attained a reservoir of information drawn from her travels and the study of the best literary authors. It was not strange that they should be mutually fascinated with each other. "As he was the noblest type of manhood, so she was the purest and best type of womanhood," wrote General Johnson in his memoir of Thomas.[8] Frances' intellectual and literary interests impressed the enamored Thomas. On November 17, 1852, Brevet Major Thomas married Miss Frances Lucretia Kellogg, in St. Paul's Episcopal Church in Troy, New York. His fellow officers described her as a "noble lady, good natured and congenial." She provided a cheerful home for him when he was there. She participated in all of his interests and made them her own, and she cherished every happening of his famous career. Although they were separated for long periods of time by the Civil War, she kept abreast with his activities and purposes. She was greatly respected and admired by all Army people. No children were born of this marriage. "But," as an historian observed, "their lives—or rather their life—for it was one in both, proved prosperous in the tenderness, devotion, and confidence that gave a rest from turmoil of life

8. Johnson, p. 27.

to our hero and a home to both."[9]

Thomas' promotion to Captain, Third Artillery, on December 24, 1853, came during his tenure as instructor at West Point. Thomas was reassigned to the field in the spring of 1854, serving as company and battalion commander of the Third Artillery in California until the summer of 1855. On May 12, 1855, President Franklin Pierce appointed Thomas a major of the elite Second Regiment, U. S. Cavalry. The commission was also signed by Jefferson Davis, Secretary of War, who later became President of the Confederate States of America. (When Thomas acquired his captaincy in 1853, if the Regular Army had not been increased by the addition of four new regiments, two of which were cavalry and two of infantry, he would probably have been still a captain at the outbreak of the Civil War.)

Secretary of War Davis had secured the aid of the Adjutant-General, Colonel Samuel Cooper, a West Point graduate, in selecting from the Army the officers to be appointed to these regiments. When the list of these officers was presented to President Pierce, an objection was found to exist which Colonel Cooper and Secretary Davis did not expect. The selection of these officers solely on their military record did not constitute an allotment among the different States which for political reasons was advisable. The number of officers of Southern birth was found to be proportionately too high. Under instructions from President Pierce, the list was revised and modified to meet satisfactorily "this new element of geographical distribution."[10]

The number of Southern officers in the original list recommended for appointments is not on record. If, however, it surpassed the number of the revised list of appointments, the disproportion of Southern men must have been very great. When the officers were first appointed to the two cavalry regiments, forty-two of the seventy were of Southern birth; of the eight field officers—Braxton Bragg, William H. Emory, William J. Hardee, Albert Sidney Johnston, Joseph E. Johnston, Robert E. Lee, Ben McCulloch, and Edwin V. Sumner—only one was of Northern

9. Piatt, *Thomas*, p. 71.
10. Jefferson Davis, *The Rise and Fall of the Confederate Government* (New York: Appleton, 1881), I, 23-24.

birth, namely Colonel Sumner of the First Cavalry.[11] The number of Southern men in these regiments suggests the possibility that Secretary of War Davis may have foreseen the coming conflict and wanted to have Southern men in positions of power.

Whether or not Davis had motives other than the good of the service, he was desirous of seeing that officers with ability of the highest quality were placed in the cavalry arm. He intended that the personnel of the First and Second U. S. Cavalry would be the very best among all regiments constituted in the Army during his administration of the War Department.

Among the officers selected and billeted on March 26, 1855, to the First and Second U. S. Cavalry, Eugene Asa Carr, William H. Emory, Kenner Garrard, Richard W. Johnson, George B. McClellan, James Oakes, Innis N. Palmer, Delos B. Sacket, John Sedgwick, David S. Stanley, George Stoneman, Samuel D. Sturgis, Edwin Vose Sumner, George H. Thomas, Frank Wheaton, and Thomas J. Wood were commissioned as general officers in the Union Army during the Civil War; and George B. Anderson, William N. R. Beall, Braxton Bragg, George B. Cosby, Nathan G. Evans, Charles W. Field, Robert S. Garnett, William J. Hardee, John Bell Hood, Alfred Iverson, Jr., Albert Sidney Johnston, Joseph E. Johnston, Robert E. Lee, Ben McCulloch, James M. McIntosh, Robert Ransom, Jr., Edmund Kirby Smith, George H. Steuart, James Ewell Brown "Jeb" Stuart, Earl Van Dorn, and William S. Walker became general officers in the Confederate Army.[12]

Ben McCulloch of Texas, an enterprising leader of partisan troops, expected to be selected as colonel of the Second Regiment of Cavalry (which later became the Fifth Cavalry). He was disappointed when he was offered the commission as major, which he declined. Albert Sidney Johnston was appointed in his stead.[13] Captain Braxton Bragg of the artillery was also offered the commission of major, but he declined it because, as he said,

11. Official Army Register, August 1, 1855.
12. William H. Lambert, "George Henry Thomas," Oration given before the Society of the Army of the Cumberland, Rochester, N. Y., Sept. 17, 1884, p. 48.
13. William Preston Johnston, *Life of General Albert Sidney Johnston* (New York: Appleton, 1878), pp. 184-185.

"he did not know of a better man for the place than George H. Thomas," who had served with him as a lieutenant.[14]

On September 25, 1855, Major Thomas was assigned to Jefferson Barracks near St. Louis, Missouri, where he joined his regiment, the Second Cavalry, on October 27. After a period of training in the fundamentals of horsemanship, the regiment was ordered to Fort Mason, Texas, for further duty. For several months, Thomas was detached to Fort Washita, Indian Territory, upon court-martial duty, and subsequently was temporarily placed on recruiting service in New York City for the purpose of enlisting musicians for his regiment. Then on May 1, 1856, he rejoined his regiment and remained in Texas from then until November 12, 1860. During the period from 1856 until 1860, he served at various posts on the Indian frontier in Texas in command of units of his regiment at Fort Mason, San Antonio, Fort Belknap, and Camp Cooper. In 1859 and 1860, he was engaged in the western mountains in the exploration of the upper Red River country and the headwaters of the Colorado River. In this unknown region, he gathered scientific data of a geological and geographical nature. He was well adapted for this special service by his early training at West Point.

In August of 1860, Thomas participated in the Kiowa Expedition near the head of the Clear Fork of the Brazos River. During this expedition he and his troops engaged in a skirmish with the Indians on the Brazos River in the vicinity of the headwaters of the Concho and Colorado Rivers. It was then that, on August 26, Major Thomas received a painful wound when he was hit by an arrow which passed through his chin and entered his chest.[15] He removed the arrow from his breast and tossed it aside and continued his pursuit of the Indians.

Thomas, upon returning to camp, submitted an official report of the expedition. It read:

> I have the honor to submit for the information of the department commander, the following report of the operations of the expedition under my command, to the head waters of

14. George F. Price, *Across the Continent with the Fifth Cavalry* (New York: Van Nostrand, 1883), p. 28.
15. Coppée, p. 25.

the Concho and Colorado rivers, during the months of July and August . . . .

On the morning of the 25th inst. about fourteen miles east of the mountain pass, one of the Indian guides (Dloss) discovered a fresh horse trail crossing the road. As soon as the packs could be arranged and our wagons despatched with the remains of our baggage to the post, with the teams (two sick—the hospital steward and a private of the band—too sick to ride) I followed the trail with all the remainder of the detachment and three guides, in a west northwest direction for about forty miles, that day, traveling as long as we could see the trail after nightfall. On the 26th, about 7 A.M., the Delaware guide (Dloss) discovered the Indians, eleven in number, at camp. He and their spy discovered each other about the same time, and giving me the signal agreed upon, the party moved at once in a gallop for a mile and a half before coming in sight of their camp, which was located on the opposite side of a deep ravine, (running North, and I presume, into the Clear Fork), impassable except at a few points.

Here we lost considerable time searching for a crossing, and only succeeded, finally, in getting over by dismounting and leading our animals. In the meantime the Indians being already mounted and having their animals collected together, had increased their distance from us by at least half a mile. As soon as the crossing was effected and the men remounted, we pursued them at full speed for about three miles and a half further, pushing them so closely that they abandoned their loose animals, and continued their flight, effecting their escape solely from the fact that our animals had been completely exhausted by the fatiguing pace at which the pursuit had been kept up.

As we were gradually over-hauling them, one fellow, more persevering than the rest, suddenly dismounted and prepared to fight, and our men, in their eagerness to despatch him, hurried upon him so quickly that several of his arrows took effect, wounding myself in the chin and chest, also Private William Murphy, of Company "D", in the left shoulder, and Privates John Tile and Casper Siddle, of the band, each in the leg, before he fell, by twenty or more shots . . . . By this time the main body of the Indians, who were mounted on their best animals, were at least two miles from us, retiring at a rapid pace, and it being impossible to overtake them, on

account of the exhausted condition of our animals, the pursuit
was discontinued . . . .[16]

This was the first and only time Thomas was wounded during
his career, although he was exposed to great danger on numerous
occasions. Thomas' wound was not of a serious nature, but he
needed a rest which was richly deserved.

After his return from the Kiowa Expedition, Thomas applied
for a leave of absence, his third in twenty years. (He had been
granted his second leave of absence from February 1 to August
1, 1849, after nearly ten years of service.) He was granted his
third leave on November 12, 1860, and soon thereafter he left
his command at Camp Cooper, Texas.

"In returning from Texas," according to his devoted wife, "General Thomas met with a severe accident, which disabled him to
such an extent that it was supposed he would never again be
able to do any duty with his regiment, and was 'looking up some
means of support.' "[17] It was on his journey from Richmond to
Washington by way of Norfolk that he met with the following
accident near Norfolk, Virginia. When the train stopped to take
on water, he decided to get a breath of fresh air. Misled in the
moonlight shadows by what he thought to be the roadbed, he
stepped into a deep depression along the tracks and fell some
twenty feet or more.[18] In so doing he injured his spine but continued on his journey to Norfolk where he was met by Mrs.
Thomas. Although in severe pain, after six weeks' convalescence
under his wife's care, he was able to go to his family home in
Southampton County, Virginia, and rested there for several weeks.
He never entirely recovered from this accident. This spinal injury
was the cause of his slow riding and deliberate personal movements which were so noticeable during the war.

When he was able to travel again, he continued on his trip
to Washington, calling on General-in-Chief Winfield Scott to
press his reservation about the loyalty of Brigadier General David
E. Twiggs and some of his officers who were engaged in "meditated treachery" to the government.[19] While he was in Wash-

16. Van Horne, *Life,* pp. 14-15.
17. Cullum, II, 36.
18. Coppée, pp. 35-36.
19. Van Horne, *Life,* pp. 20-21.

ington, South Carolina seceded from the Union on the 20th of December, 1860. Then in January, 1861, the following states seceded: Mississippi on the 9th, Florida on the 10th, Alabama on the 11th, Georgia on the 19th, and Louisiana on the 26th.

Some time after his accident, he accompanied Mrs. Thomas to New York City, after stopping for a few days in Washington. They registered at the New York Hotel on Broadway near Tenth Street. While in New York City, Mrs. Thomas noticed an advertisement in the *Daily National Intelligencer* (a Washington newspaper):

To the Graduates of the U. S. Military Academy:
A Commandant of Cadets and Instructor of Tactics is wanted for the Virginia Military Institute. The situation is an eligible one, and should command the best talents and accomplishments. Address the undersigned, at Lexington, Virginia, until the 20th of January, 1861.

Francis H. Smith, Superintendent.[20]

Fearing that it would now be necessary for him "to be looking up some means of support," Major Thomas wrote to Colonel Smith on Friday, January 18, 1861, requesting information regarding the salary and allowances pertaining to the position:

New York Hotel, New York City,
January 18th, 1861.

Colonel Francis H. Smith,
Sup't. Virginia Military Institute,
Lexington, Va.

Dear Sir: In looking over the files of the National Intelligencer, this morning, I met with your advertisement for a commandant of cadets and instructor on tactics at the Institute. If not already filled, I will be under obligations if you will inform me what salary and allowances pertain to the situation, as from present appearances I fear it will soon be necessary for me to be looking up some means of support.

Very Respectfully, your obedient servant,
Geo. H. Thomas,
Major U. S. Army.[21]

<hr>

20. *Daily National Intelligencer,* Washington, D. C., Jan. 12, 1861.
21. Van Horne, *Life,* p. 22.

Thomas was informed that the vacancy had been filled. After his death the application for the position was unjustly construed by the authorities in Lexington. They felt Thomas was showing his intention of joining the Southern Army in the Civil War. "Why had not the enemies," wrote his wife, "the generosity to have made known their accusations during his life, so that he could have answered them?" In the conclusion of her letter dated December 31, 1875, she stated, in a most emphatic manner, that General Thomas "never applied for any commission in the service of his native State or in the Southern Army," and asserted also, "from the time the actual fact of war was upon us, General Thomas' course was clear before him," in spite of other assertions to the contrary, "without influence of any kind being brought to bear upon him."[22]

The following letter which was found among the archives at the Virginia State Capitol also clearly vindicated Thomas:

New York Hotel, March 12, 1861.

To His Excellency, Gov. John Letcher, Richmond, Va.

Dear Sir: I received yesterday a letter from Major William Gilham, of the Virginia Military Institute, dated the 9th inst., in reference to the position of Chief of Ordnance of the State, in which he informs me that you had requested him to ask me if I would resign from the service, and if so, whether that post would be acceptable to me. As he requested me to make my reply to you direct, I have the honor to state, after expressing my most sincere thanks for very kind offer, that it is not my wish to leave the service of the United States as long as it is honorable for me to remain in it, and, therefore, as long as my native State remains in the Union, it is my purpose to remain in the army, unless requested to perform duties alike repulsive to honor and humanity. I am very respectfully your obedient servant,

George H. Thomas,
Major United States Army.[23]

It must be remembered that the State of Virginia did not

22. Cullum, II, 36.
23. Calendar of Virginia State Papers and Other Manuscripts, January 1, 1836, to April 15, 1869; Preserved in the Capitol at Richmond (Richmond, 1893), II, 106; Piatt, *Thomas*, pp. 82-83.

approve the thoughtless haste in which South Carolina and the Cotton States seceded from the Union. Virginia did not pass her ordinance of secession until three months after the date of Thomas' application to be Commandant of Cadets in his native State.

As historian Donn Piatt commented, Thomas knew that "the scheme of secession, from its first inception to its final development, came not from the people, but from the hot-headed ambitious men chance and slavery had made leaders. The Virginia ordinance of secession was a fraud. It won its way with difficulty through a faithless legislature that knew that a fair submission to the people would have voted it down by an immense majority." And he added, "George H. Thomas could no more have clasped hands with these conspirators than Robert E. Lee could resist their appeals. The one followed his heart into an unholy cause, the other obeyed the dictates of reason and the high call of patriotic duty in remaining firm to the flag of the fathers, a soldier of the cross and a soldier of the great Republic."[24]

Thomas was extremely earnest with regard to the cause of the Union, and he felt that the majority of the people of the State of Virginia were in favor of "the Union, the Constitution, and the enforcement of the laws." He also felt that most of the people from his native State would have remained neutral and loyal if they had not been forced into disloyalty by their elected leaders. It was their maneuvering and manipulations which caused the dissolution of the people's bond to the United States Government.

Just before the secession crisis in 1860, there was a consensus of opinion shared by the majority of Virginia newspapers and of the upper South that the Union should be preserved and secession resisted. By the middle of April, 1860, the papers still favored support of the Union but at the same time were calling for the protection of Southern "rights." During the ensuing months, anti-Union sentiment crystallized and gathered such momentum that "one year later all but a handful of the same journals had endorsed the Confederacy."[25] Editorials became more militant and headlines cried for secession.

There were several reasons for this rather sudden shift in

24. Piatt, *Thomas*, pp. 81-82.
25. Donald E. Reynolds, *Editors Make War* (Nashville, Tenn.: Vanderbilt University Press, 1966), p. 210.

political temper. Certainly among them was the anticipated election of Abraham Lincoln as President of the United States. Southerners for the most part feared that Lincoln's election would mean the end of slavery which in the South had become a tradition.

Nor can one derogate the role of the press in creating and maintaining an atmosphere in which secessionist sentiment thrived and proliferated. Early in 1860, a Virginia newspaper claimed that responsibility for the impending crisis lay with the media, "Newspapers and Telegraphs have ruined the country. Suppress both and the country could be saved now." In *Editors Make War*, Dr. Donald E. Reynolds theorized that "perhaps a disruption of communications alone would not have saved the Union; the disagreement over slavery would have remained. But, without the press, the task of those who divided the Union would have been infinitely more difficult."[26]

A month after Lincoln was elected President, on November 6, 1860, he had made up his mind that the Union must be preserved, no matter what the cost. South Carolina had taken the bold step of seceding on December 20. By January 27, 1861, five other states—Mississippi, Florida, Alabama, Georgia, and Louisiana—all had renounced the Union. In February, Texas followed suit.

Certainly the slavery issue was a crucial factor in this divisiveness between North and South. Those states below the Mason-Dixon line bitterly resented the North's interfering with their way of life, a way of life that was rooted in slavery.

The South's economy was dependent upon a single crop, cotton, which was harvested by slave labor. From the South's point of view, cotton and slavery were an extremely successful combination. Cotton was very much in demand in the world market, as well as in the textile mills of the North. A good profit was guaranteed the plantation which need not rely on paid labor to pick its crop. During the mid-nineteenth century, about two and one-half million slaves worked the cotton fields of the South.

The variety of tasks necessary to the smooth operation of the plantation, however, demanded a reservoir of all types of skilled

26. *Ibid.*, p. 217.

and semi-skilled labor. In their study of the slave system in the United States entitled *Time on the Cross: The Economics of American Negro Slavery*, historians Robert W. Fogel and Stanley L. Engerman contest the wide-held myth that the slaves in the South were engaged only in cotton picking or in other menial occupations. During the thirty years immediately preceding the Civil War, "slaves were involved in virtually every aspect of Southern economic life, both rural and urban. They were not only tillers of the soil but were fairly well-represented in most of the skilled crafts. In the City of Charleston, for example, about 27 percent of the adult male slaves were skilled artisans."[27]

Male slaves often worked as carpenters, masons, blacksmiths, and coopers. Others were employed in and around the household as gardeners, servants, and coachmen, while the women served as maids, midwives, and seamstresses. Moreover, some slaves could and did work their way into managerial status, assuming responsibility for the functioning of certain aspects of plantation life.

During the later ante-bellum years, "over 25 percent of (male slaves) were managers, professionals, craftsmen, and semi-skilled workers," and of those slaves engaged mainly in field work, most were responsible as well for "the rearing of livestock (including the raising of feed), . . . land improvement, the construction of fences and buildings, the raising of other crops (oats, rye, wheat, potatoes, etc.), ... domestic duties, and home manufacturing. ..."[28]

It can clearly be seen from the foregoing that slavery and the Southern economy were almost inextricably interwoven. The Northern states, for their part, eschewed slavery as being "uneconomical." With the invention of Cyrus McCormick's mechanical reaper in 1834, the farmers in the Northern and Midwestern regions could now more efficiently produce grain in great abundance. An ample supply of cheap labor was furnished by the ever-increasing influx of European immigrants.

On December 14, 1860, Secretary of State Lewis Cass resigned from the Cabinet in disgust because the President, James Buc-

27. Robert William Fogel and Stanley L. Engerman, *Time on the Cross: The Economics of American Negro Slavery* (Boston: Little, Brown, 1974), pp. 38-39.
28. *Ibid.,* pp. 40-42.

chanan had failed to reinforce Major Robert Anderson at Fort Moultrie in Charleston Harbor, South Carolina. Buchanan similarly hesitated to take action when South Carolina seceded December 20. General Winfield Scott vainly endeavored to impress upon Buchanan that, as President, he possessed the same power to execute the laws of the nation, to defend federal property, and to collect federal taxes within the states of the Union that President Andrew Jackson had exercised in 1832.

Despite entreaties, during these last crucial months of his administration, Buchanan did nothing to forestall the threatening catastrophe. Although he dreaded seeing the Union disintegrate, he could not help but feel a great sympathy for the South's predicament.

On Friday, February 8, 1861, the Confederate Government was organized at Montgomery, Alabama. The following day, Jefferson Davis of Mississippi was elected provisional President of the Confederate States of America with Alexander H. Stephens as his Vice President.

One by one, it seemed, the Southern States were opting for secession. Already seven states had withdrawn from the Union. The state of Virginia was permanently split in two when its legislature voted for secession against the wishes of those citizens living in the western portion of the state. On Tuesday, June 11, 1861, delegates representing these pro-Union elements in the state met at Wheeling to organize a pro-Union government that eventually became the state of West Virginia.

Despite the inevitable internal friction, the states of Kentucky and Missouri continued to affirm their loyalty to the Union. The fate of Maryland, a vital crossroads, remained unsettled until President Lincoln took military control of the situation and the question was resolved in favor of solidarity.

# CHAPTER FIVE

# From Carlisle Barracks to Mill Springs

One must remember that an officer born in one of the Southern States and pledging himself to the Northern Army had to cut all family ties, severing all relationships and friendships so dear to every member of his family. For one to place himself in such a position required devotion and loyalty of the highest degree to his ultimate decision. Such was Thomas' devotion to his country when he said, "If these ties can only be preserved on the condition of my abandonment of the government for which my forefathers fought, bled, and died, then let them be severed." Thomas was presented with many offers of advancement from friends in the South if he would leave the United States Army and join the Confederacy. He refused them all.

When Major Thomas returned from the Kiowa Expedition, obtained a leave of absence, and left his regiment at Camp Cooper, Texas, Lieutenant Colonel Robert E. Lee, returning from a leave, was promoted and assigned to the command of the First U. S. Cavalry.[1] In February of 1861, after some of the Southern

1. Johnson, p. 35.

States had seceded, Colonel Lee was recalled from Texas to Washington, D. C., by General Scott for consultation with the possibility of promoting him in the event of war. General Scott, "Old Fuss and Feathers," was Commander-in-Chief of the United States Army. Promoting Lee threatened to leave Thomas' former regiment without a field officer. About this critical time, the fever of secession, having originated in South Carolina, was spreading "like wild-fire over the Southern States." The state of Texas, bound to the Federal Government when she was admitted into the Union (December 29, 1845) on the same basis of equality as was granted to other states, "should have been the last State in the Union to attempt to sever her connections, but when the treasonable tempest swept over the South, Texas was involved, and she drifted from her moorings into the deep sea of revolution and rebellion against the government."[2]

The case for secession, as expressed by historians Samuel Eliot Morison and Henry Steele Commager, was established on "the axiom that the Federal Constitution created a Confederacy, not a government, and did not impair state sovereignty." In 1800 the vast majority of American citizens felt more loyal to their respective states than to the Union. "In 1830 none but Virginians, Georgians, and South Carolinians would have followed their states out of the Union, on any possible issue. After 1844, with the growth of Southern self-consciousness, the phrase and the idea of state rights gave place in that section to 'Southern rights.' "[3]

When each state passed the ordinance of secession, the Southern people were under the impression that the way was clear to institute a Confederacy without any struggle. They were led to believe that the Federal Government would allow its dismemberment without any attempt to prevent it. At this time Sam Houston (a Jackson nationalist to the last) was Governor of Texas. He tried with all his conviction and power to restrain the people from passing the ordinance of secession but without success. Called upon to take the oath of allegiance to the Southern Confederacy, he declined and was deposed. In the meantime a com-

2. *Ibid.,* p. 36.

3. Samuel Eliot Morison and Henry Steele Commager, *The Growth of the American Republic,* 2 vols. (New York: Oxford University Press, 1962), I, 677.

mittee of safety was appointed to receive the surrender of the United States troops. General Twiggs, who commanded the Department of Texas in February of 1861 for the United States, yielded to the demands of the committee.[4] Captain George Stoneman (later a Union general) was in charge of Fort Brown, Texas (at Brownsville), when General Twiggs surrendered. Stoneman was fortunate to escape with part of his cavalry.

Twiggs, on surrendering the Texas garrisons, agreed to turn over all of the United States forces under his command, as well as government stores, arms, and ammunition to Colonel Ben McCulloch (who later became a brigadier general in the Provisional Confederate Army) and his Texas Rangers at San Antonio. Upon hearing of this, Thomas became indignant. He was disappointed that he was not on duty at the time. "I would have taken command of the men," he remarked, "marched them north until they reached the loyal states, and the rebels should have not taken a prisoner or captured a cannon or a flag."[5] At a time when the senior officers were away, Twiggs had surrendered the troops. In so doing, he dishonorably deserted the flag of his country. Because of these actions and for his Southern sympathies, he was dismissed from the United States service on Friday, March 1, 1861. Then on Wednesday, May 22, 1861, Twiggs was appointed a major general in the Provisional Army of the Confederacy and was assigned to the command of the District of Louisiana.[6]

On Friday, February 1, the 25th anniversary of the state's Declaration of Independence from Mexico, the state of Texas had seceded from the Union by an overwhelming vote of 166 to 7 in Austin at the Secession Convention.[7] It was after the secession of Texas that Lee was ordered to report to General Scott. After Lee relinquished the command of his regiment, he departed for Washington, D. C., arriving at Arlington House, Virginia, on Friday, March 1.

On Wednesday, April 17, Virginia seceded from the Union in

4. Johnson, p. 36.
5. McKinney, p. 87.
6. Warner, p. 312.
7. Ben La Bree and John S. Blay, *The Confederate Soldier in the Civil War* (Paterson, N. J.: Pageant Books, 1959), p. 12.

the convention held in the City of Richmond.[8] On the following day, Colonel Lee had a long discussion with General Scott regarding the possibility of promoting him in the event of war. On Scott's recommendation to President Lincoln, Lee was offered the command of the Federal armies.[9] The surprised Lee requested some time for deliberation at the family estate, Arlington House.

On a seemingly endless Friday evening, April 19, Lee spent many lonesome hours of anguish while walking around the family estate in meditation and in prayers hoping for the best before he made his final decision. What an agonizing experience it must have been for him to make this decision. He must have known that the time was approaching when he would be leaving forever the place he loved so much, "Arlington . . . where my affection and attachments are more strongly placed than at any other place in the world."

Lee did not believe in secession, nor did he approve of the Virginia Assembly's stand on this issue. He, however, was loyal to his native state.

On Saturday, Lee resigned his commission in the United States Army after giving about thirty-two years of dedicated service. On the same day, Lee wrote the following letter to General Scott:

Arlington, Washington City P. O.

20 April 1861

Lt. Genl Winfield Scott
    Command. the Army
    Genl

Since my interview with you on the 18th Inst. I have felt that I ought not longer to retain my commission in the Army. I therefore tender my resignation, which I request you will recommend for acceptance.

It would have been presented at once, but for the struggle it has cost me to separate myself from a service to which I have devoted all the best years of my life and all the ability I possessed.

During the whole of that time, more than 30 years, I have experienced nothing but kindness from my superiors and the

8. La Bree and Blay, p. 12.
9. Robert E. Lee, Jr., *Recollections and Letters of General Robert E. Lee,* 2 vols. (New York: Garden City, 1926), II, 24.

most cordial friendship from my companions. To no one Genl
have I been as much indebted as to yourself for uniform
kindness and consideration, and it has always been my ardent
desire to merit your approbation.

I shall carry with me to the grave the most grateful recollections of your kind consideration, and your name and fame
will always be dear to me. Save in the defense of my native
State, I never desire again to draw my sword.

Be pleased to accept my most earnest wishes for the continuance of your happiness and prosperity, and believe me
most truly yours

(Signed)<br>R. E. Lee.

The same day Lee wrote to the Secretary of War tendering his
resignation:

Arlington, Washington City P.O.<br>20 April 1861

Honorable Simon Cameron
    Sec. of War
        Sir:
I have the honour to tender the resignation of my commission as Colonel of the 1st Regt. of Cavalry.

Very Resply your obt servt<br>R. E. Lee<br>Col. 1st Cavalry[10]

While Major Thomas was on leave of absence, recovering from
his injuries, Fort Sumter in Charleston Harbor, South Carolina,
was fired upon on Friday, April 12, 1861, at 4:30 A.M., by the
Confederate forces under the command of Brigadier General
Pierre Gustave Toutant Beauregard. The fort was defended by
Major Robert Anderson of Kentucky. This was the day that sealed
the death warrants for more than 600,000 Americans.

Major Anderson had notified the War Department that his
supplies were giving out, and that new Confederate batteries
commanded his position. Fort Sumter had no strategic value in
case of Civil War. Why, then, risk war by holding it? The Confederacy made it clear that any attempt to reinforce or even to

10. *Ibid.*, pp. 24-25.

supply Sumter would be regarded as a hostile act, which would probably pull Virginia and other states of the Upper South into the Confederacy. If, however, the forts were tamely yielded, would not the principle of union be fatally compromised? Could a recognition of the Confederacy thereafter be avoided?

President Lincoln delayed decision, not from fear, but because he was watching Virginia. Jefferson Davis, too, was watching Virginia. The Old Dominion was a stake worth playing for. Although long since fallen from her primacy in wealth and statesmanship, some of her sons were among the ablest officers in the United States Army, and her soil was almost certain to be a major theater of any war between the sections. The "panhandle" of western Virginia thrust a salient between Pennsylvania and Ohio, to within 100 miles of Lake Erie. If Virginia seceded, she must carry North Carolina with her; and Maryland, Kentucky, Tennessee, Arkansas, and Missouri would probably follow.[11]

Major Anderson surrendered Fort Sumter on Saturday, April 13, to the Confederates after sustaining a thirty-four-hour bombardment which would have made continued resistance suicidal. On Sunday noon, April 14, he evacuated his garrison after saluting the United States flag with fifty guns. After lowering the huge garrison flag, Anderson and his command left Charleston Harbor on board the steamer *Isabel* furnished by General Beauregard to transport them to the United States fleet for passage to New York. Anderson was appointed brigadier general in the Regular Army by President Lincoln on May 15, 1861. Four years later, at the request of President Lincoln, Secretary of War Edwin M. Stanton issued an order that General Anderson be delegated to take the same United States flag he had lowered April 14, 1861, to be raised again over Fort Sumter on Good Friday, April 14, 1865. This was the day that President Lincoln was assassinated. General Sherman was to be present at the flag ceremony but, because of other pressing matters elsewhere, he could not attend and wrote to General Anderson, as follows:

11. Morison and Commager, I, 677.

Hdqrs. Military Division of the Mississippi,<br>
In the Field, Goldsborough, N. C., April 5, 1865.

Maj. Gen. Robert Anderson,

    Charleston, S. C.:

Dear General: I see in the papers that an order has been made by the War Department that on the 14th instant you are to raise the same flag over Sumter which you were compelled to lower four years ago, and that I am supposed to be present. I will be there in thought but not in person, and I am glad that it falls to the lot of one so pure and noble to represent our country in a drama so solemn, so majestic, and so just. It looks as a retribution decreed by Heaven itself. I doubt if we had fashioned events ourselves we could have produced a better conclusion. Four years of bitter war have tested our manhood, and dissipated the rude boastings of a class of men of which nothing but horrid war could have purged our country. But, alas! many of them have escaped punishment as yet, and have involved thousands and millions of innocents. But the end is not yet. The brain that first conceived the thought must burst in anguish, the heart that pulsated with hellish joy must cease to beat, and the hand that pulled the first lanyard must be palsied before the wicked act that began in Charleston on the 13th of April, 1861, is avenged. But "mine, not thine, is vengeance, saith the Lord," and we poor sinners, must let Him work out the drama to its close. I have not been in Charleston since we parted, then captain and lieutenant, in the spring of 1846, but I can see it in imagination almost as clearly as you behold it with your eyes, and though I may be far away, you may think of me as standing by your side, ready to aid you with labor to achieve the end I know you strive to attain, not to pull down the sacred fabric of our Government, but to improve and to strengthen it, so that the good and the brave will seek the shelter of its flag, and the evil and treacherous shall flee to other lands.

    Your lieutenant,

W. T. Sherman,<br>
Major General.[12]

12. *The War of the Rebellion: A Compilation of the Official Records of the Union and Confederate Armies* (73 vols. 128 parts; Washington, 1880-1901), Series I, Volume XLVII, Part III, pp. 107-108. Cited hereinafter as OR with appropriate specific references to series, volume, and page.

It had also been four years since George Henry Thomas had made his final decision to serve the Union because of his sense of duty to the flag that he loved and served so well. On April 13, 1861. Thomas made his decision while he was in Harrisburg, Pennsylvania, where news of the firing on Sumter reached him. He telegraphed his wife in New York to inform her of his decision to abide by the government. Several days later he announced his decision to his sisters in Virginia. The South had invaded every state of the Union when she fired on Fort Sumter. Fort Sumter was as much the soil of Maine as of South Carolina, when it was built to defend our nation. When Thomas informed his maiden sisters, Judith and Frances, they were reluctant to accept his decision because of their loyalty to the South. They destroyed most of his letters to them and decided he was never to hear from them again, except when they suggested that he change his name. Thomas made several attempts at reconciliation with his sisters, but his efforts were futile and he never went home again.

In his recollections, published in 1884, Major General Erasmus D. Keyes (who graduated from West Point in the Class of 1832 and died in Nice, France, on October 14, 1895) stated his belief that Mrs. Thomas was influential in keeping her husband in the Union ranks. Relative to this, Mrs. Thomas in her letter to a friend dated November 9, 1884, stated, "General Keyes' private opinion, that I was the cause of General Thomas remaining in the service, is decidedly a mistake. I do not think they met from the time General Thomas went to Kentucky to join that army until they met in San Francisco years after. There was never a word passed between General Thomas and myself, or any one of the family, upon the subject of his remaining loyal to the United States Government. We felt that, whatever his course, it would be from a conscientious sense of duty; that no one could persuade him to do what he felt was not right."[13]

On Sunday, April 14, Thomas, cutting his leave of absence short, was ordered to Carlisle Barracks, Pennsylvania, to await the arrival of what was left of his regiment from Texas. Thomas worked day and night from April 14 to May 27, 1861, to refit

13. Coppée, pp. 27-28.

his regiment in a condition to take the field. It required his individual attention for a thorough reorganization; horses and equipment had to be purchased, recruits had to be drilled and disciplined, and the regulars had to be re-clothed. These duties were enough to tax the capacity and industry of any ordinary man, but not Thomas. He became lieutenant colonel of his regiment at Carlisle Barracks on April 25, 1861. Shortly after, on Friday, May 3, Thomas was promoted colonel of his regiment, the Second U. S. Cavalry, becoming its commander when another Southerner, Albert Sidney Johnston, resigned his commission on May 3, 1861, Texas, Johnston's adopted state, having seceded from the Union. Thomas, with his regiment, subsequently joined Major General Robert Patterson in the Shenandoah Valley participating in several actions, among them an engagement at Falling Waters, Virginia, Tuesday, July 2, 1861, where he commanded a brigade. The Second Cavalry was re-designated the Fifth Cavalry by an Act of Congress on Saturday, August 3, 1861.

By the late summer of 1861, it was becoming obvious that the border state of Kentucky was going to be the scene of strife between the North and South. But the question remained, as Henry Coppée suggests, "Should it be swept into secession ranks, or should it remain with the Union?"[14] Governor Beriah Magoffin exhibited strong secessionist sympathies while the status of the legislature was questionable. A military force existed in the state, the State Guard, which was well armed and disciplined, but it was under the orders of the governor who had placed it under the immediate command of Adjutant General Simon B. Buckner, a graduate of West Point. Consisting of about four thousand men, its Union element was minimal. When the State Legislature met in January of 1861, it was about equally divided as to which direction the state should go. Many of the leading public men believed in compromise, naively hoping that some settlement would soon be reached and that Kentucky could keep out of the war altogether.

Consequently a position of neutrality was finally determined and formally declared by the governor's proclamation on May 20. The Union men, however, did make some gains. They agreed to

14. *Ibid.*, p. 37.

appropriations to arm the state forces, but only on the condition that the control of military affairs was to be taken from the governor and given to a military board of five members, the majority of whom were Union men. There was also a provision for the organizing and arming of the Home Guard, which were to be outside of the Militia force. And finally articles were passed directing all the members of the State Guard to take an oath required of officers which allowed Union members of that organization to free themselves of the stringent obligations of their enlistment. The neutrality stance also provided time. The secessionists believed that with time they could convince the people of Kentucky to accept the idea of separation. The Union men, on the other hand, wanted time to organize their forces, to elect a new, more favorable state legislature and to firmly put the state on the side of the Federal Government. And the Union men seemed to interpret matters correctly, for in a special congressional election on June 20, 1861, nine Union representatives were overwhelmingly elected to one pro-secessionist, and a state legislative election in August resulted in three-fourths of the members of both houses being Unionists.

When President Lincoln first called for troops, Kentucky was asked to supply four regiments. This Governor Magoffin refused to do, and he replied that Kentucky would "furnish no soldiers for the wicked purpose of subduing her sister Southern states." Then the Confederacy asked the state for a regiment, but the governor had to admit it was beyond his power to supply it. Blanton Duncan, however, had already obtained authority to recruit for the Confederacy, and by the end of April had raised a regiment that was ready to move to Harpers Ferry in Jefferson County, Virginia. As one company was leaving Cynthiana, Kentucky (in Harrison County), one of the privates told a friend, "be sure to vote for [John J.] Crittenden [then the Union candidate for delegate to the Border State Conference] and keep Kentucky out of the fuss. We are just going to Virginia on a little frolic and will be back in three months." This illustrates Kentucky's continued hope that it could stay out of the war.

After the governor's refusal to furnish troops, J. V. Guthrie, of Covington, traveled to Washington to obtain authority for himself and W. E. Woodruff of Louisville to raise two regiments. Establishing a camp above Cincinnati on the Ohio side of the river, two regiments were sent to take part in a western Virginia campaign early in July.

Another factor in rallying Union sentiment was a secret society called the Union Club which organized in Louisville in May. Within six weeks, it had six thousand members in Louisville alone and was rapidly spreading throughout the state. Members swore to be true to the flag and the United States government.

Further Union support also became evident in the state. Lieutenant William "Bull" Nelson of the U. S. Navy, a native of Kentucky and a friend of the Union, frequently visited his home state in the spring to observe how matters were progressing. He reported to President Lincoln that most of the arms of the state were in the hands of secessionists and the Union men could not maintain themselves unless also furnished weapons. Consequently he was given ten thousand rifle-muskets and the means of transporting them. Toward the end of April, Nelson met with the Kentucky anti-secessionists and helped organize the Union Home Guards. Later Nelson also obtained weapons for the Union men of East Tennessee. Nelson has the distinction of being the only naval officer to become a major general.

The secessionists also opened a recruiting center, close to Clarksville, Tennessee, a few miles from the state border, which was called Camp Boone. Thus, while the state was still a declared neutral, it was an active recruiting center for both sides. In fact in Louisville it was possible to see a squad of Northern recruits marching up one side of the street while a squad of Confederate recruits marched down the other.

After the August election, Nelson's recruits began to gather at Camp Dick Robinson, which was established by Nelson, and by the first of September he had four Kentucky regiments and 2,000 East Tennesseans. William T. Ward, a prominent Greensburg lawyer, began recruiting a brigade in August of 1861, and soon had twenty-two companies pledged to rendezvous when he had the necessary authority from Washington.

About this time, General Robert Anderson, a native of Kentucky and the defender of Fort Sumter, was given the command of the Department of Kentucky, making his headquarters in Louisville. In accepting this post, he made the stipulation that he would select four subordinate officers to serve under him as brigadier generals. He had in mind Don Carlos Buell, Ormsby M. Mitchel, and William T. Sherman. Anderson was somewhat skeptical of his fourth nominee, Simon B. Buckner, who was adjutant general in command of the Kentucky State Guard. Buckner had been given the responsibility of trying to maintain the neutrality of his native state. As late as August 17, President Lincoln wrote to Secretary of War Cameron to prepare a commission for Buckner as brigadier general of volunteers. General Anderson was to keep the commission in hand and employ it at his own discretion. Buckner's sympathies, however, became known after the Battle of Bull Run (Manassas). He declined the commission in the Union Army, and soon joined the Confederate ranks, taking charge of the Rebel forces based at Camp Boone, just south of the Kentucky line in Tennessee.

Colonel Thomas had also been recommended to General Anderson as his fourth choice as brigaider general by Anderson's nephew, Lieutenant Thomas M. Anderson, of the Fifth U. S. Cavalry. Anderson knew Thomas from the 1840s and of his reputation as a reliable and loyal officer and consequently submitted Thomas' name with the names of the other three. At first Lincoln was skeptical of an officer of Virginia birth, especially of one who had belonged to the Second U. S. Cavalry, the ranks of which had been depleted by resignations of those joining the Confederate forces. In his *Memoirs,* General Sherman stated that the President was unwilling to agree to the request for the appointment of Thomas, "because so many Southern officers had already played false,"[15] but yielded in favor of Thomas because of Anderson's insistence and sincerity and Sherman's emphatic assurance that Thomas could be depended upon. On Saturday, August 17, Lincoln appointed Colonel Thomas a brigadier general of U. S. Volunteers,[16] and on August 24 Thomas was assigned to the Department of the Cumberland, with which his services were to be identified until the end of the war. This

15. William T. Sherman, *Memoirs* (New York: Webster, 1891), I, 221.
16. Cullum, II, 33.

was Thomas' first step in the career which was unfolding before him. It was a test of his military judgment and his moral courage. From this time on he saw service in the western theatre of the war.

On September 3, Confederate forces under Major General Leonidas Polk crossed into Kentucky from Tennessee en route to Hickman and Columbus, on the Mississippi River. This act ended Kentucky's neutrality and soon resulted in a continuous war front from the Atlantic coast to the Indian Territory. Polk's move, which bolstered pro-Union sentiment in Kentucky, had been precipitated by Federal activities in the Belmont, Missouri, area across the river and erroneous reports of a Union build-up preparatory to a seizure of Columbus. News of the Confederate occupation of Columbus reached the Union commander at Cairo, Illinois, Brigadier General Ulysses S. Grant on the 5th. He appreciated the importance of Paducah, at the confluence of the Tennessee and Ohio Rivers. On September 6, troops from Grant's command landed at Paducah, forestalling a planned Confederate descent on this strategic Kentucky river town.

To counter Grant's move, General Albert Sidney Johnston, who had been named to command the Confederate forces in the West, took the offensive. General Buckner's forces broke camp. Marching northward from Camp Boone, they occupied Bowling Green, Kentucky, on the 18th, while patrols penetrated as far as Elizabethtown, 40 miles south of Louisville. Coincidentally, General Johnston sent Brigadier General Felix K. Zollicoffer with several thousand men through Cumberland Gap into eastern Kentucky. Zollicoffer's mission was to threaten Camp Dick Robinson. On September 19, Zollicoffer's vanguard clashed with the Home Guard at Barbourville Bridge. The Home Guard retreated to Rockcastle Hills, where they were reinforced by two Kentucky regiments rushed forward from Camp Dick Robinson under orders to obstruct the road and to delay the Rebel advance. Taking post at Camp Wildcat, the Federals were reinforced, and in the fourth week of October successfully repulsed several attacks on their breastworks by Zollicoffer's troops.

Meanwhile, General Anderson, apprised of Buckner's forward movement, had ordered General Sherman into the field. Sherman's 3,600-man force left Louisville aboard the cars of the

Louisville & Nashville Railroad. The locomotives and rolling stock were unable to proceed beyond the Rolling Fork of Salt River, 31 miles south of Louisville, the Confederates having burned the bridge. Detraining, the Yankees forded the river, and pressing on occupied the Muldraugh Hills with their two trestles and 1,500-foot tunnel. Confronted by Sherman's advance, General Buckner recalled his patrols, and turned his troops to fortifying Bowling Green.[17]

The people in Louisville were frightened, especially since General Anderson was virtually without trained troops, for all the surrounding camps were filled with raw recruits unprepared for the field. Fortunately Governor Oliver P. Morton of Indiana reserved a few regiments for Kentucky and rushed them to General Anderson.

In mid-September, Generals Robert Anderson and Thomas L. Crittenden of Kentucky, to cope with the Confederate threat, issued stirring proclamations addressed to the people of their state. They read:

> Louisville, Ky., September 21, 1861.
> Kentuckians: Called by the legislature of this, my native state, I hereby assume command of this department. I come to enforce, not to make laws, and, God willing, to protect your property and your lives.
> The enemies of the country have dared to invade our soil. Kentucky is in danger. She vainly strives to keep peace with her neighbors. Our state is now invaded by those who professed to be her friends, but who now seek to conquer her. No true son of Kentucky can longer hesitate as to his duty to his state and country. The invaders must, and, God willing, will be expelled. The leader of the hostile forces, who now approaches, is, I regret to say, a Kentuckian, making war on Kentucky and Kentuckians. Let all past differences of opinion be overlooked. Every one who now rallies to the support of our Union and our state, is a friend. Rally, then, my countrymen, around the flag our fathers loved, and which has shielded us so long. I call you to arms for self-defense, and

17. Henry M. Cist, *The Army of the Cumberland* (New York: Charles Scribner's Sons, 1882), pp. 1-4; Manning F. Force, *From Fort Henry to Corinth* (New York: Charles Scribner's Sons, 1882), pp. 17-19, 24-25.

for the protection of all that is dear to freemen. Let us trust in God and do our duty, as did our fathers.

Robert Anderson,<br>Brigadier-General U. S. A.[18]

*   *   *   *

To the Militia of Kentucky:

By the authority which you yourselves have appointed, you are called upon to defend your state. Misguided countrymen, whom you loved too well to fight, despite their wrongs to you, waging unnatural war, have tarnished the bright fame of Kentucky, and for the first time since your sires bequeathed to you this noble state, the soil is polluted by the tread of hostile armies.

I will not impugn the patriotism and courage of my countrymen by supposing that any appeal, however eloquent, could arouse them to energy and prompt action as this simple statement.

But to the State Guard I must add a word. Now is your opportunity to wipe out every reproach that has been put upon you. You owe it not only to your duty as men and citizens, but to that solemn obligation of soldiers which you can not forget without dishonor, to respond to this call.

The State Guard will rendezvous as soon as possible at Louisville, and report to me. The residue of the militia and such of the Home Guard as choose to volunteer, will rendezvous as soon as possible at Louisville, Frankfort, Camp Dick Robinson, General Sherman's Camp, New Haven, and Henderson.

Come in battalions, regiments, companies, or come as individuals, and you shall be mustered into the service under pay at once.

T. L. Crittenden,<br>Brigadier-General Kentucky State Guard.[19]

About this time, General Anderson's health began to fail, and he requested to be relieved of his command for a much needed rest.

On Sunday, October 6, General Anderson received the following communication from General Scott:

18. Thomas B. Van Horne, *History of the Army of the Cumberland,* 3 vols. (Cincinnati: Robert Clarke, 1875), I, 34.
19. Van Horne, *History,* I, 34-35.

77

Brigadier-General Anderson:

To give you rest necessary to restoration of health, call Brigadier-General Sherman to command the Department of the Cumberland. Turn over to him your instructions, and report here in person as soon as you may, without retarding your recovery.

Washington, D. C., October 6, 1861.

Winfield Scott.[20]

Anderson, complying with Scott's orders, relinquished his command to General Sherman, who assumed it on October 8. He was to hold it for five weeks, for Kentucky was soon absorbed into a larger administrative area conceived by higher headquarters in Washington. On November 15, General Buell succeeded Sherman by assuming the command of the Department of the Ohio (with headquarters in Louisville), which was organized by the consolidation of the Departments of the Ohio and of the Cumberland and consisted of the states of Ohio, Michigan, Indiana, and Tennessee, and that portion of Kentucky lying east of the Cumberland River. General Sherman was relieved from command at his request and sent to St. Louis, Missouri, to report to Major General Henry W. Halleck.

General Zollicoffer, unsuccessful in his efforts to drive the Federals from Camp Wildcat, retired to Cumberland Gap and, after strengthening the fortifications at that vital point, marched southwest to Jamestown, Tennessee, where he camped on November 22. Anxious to secure a good defensive position on the Cumberland River, Zollicoffer sent his engineers to make a reconnaisance. Coincidentally, he ordered a strong force forward to seize ferry boats at the various Cumberland crossings. The latter mission failed, when the Union commander at Somerset, divining the Rebels' intention, had a number of the boats destroyed. The engineers, returning to Jamestown, told Zollicoffer that there was a grist- and sawmill at Mill Springs and that that area would be a good location for winter quarters.

Zollicoffer accordingly put his column in motion and reached Mill Springs on November 29. He found the area defensible, commanding as it did the river, as well as the roads to Cumber-

20. *Ibid.*, I, 35.

land Gap and Jacksboro. The countryside was fertile and the farmers had a surplus of hogs, hominy, cattle, and hay. From this camp as a base of operations, Zollicoffer wrote General Johnston, "I hope in mild weather to penetrate the country toward London or Danville."[21]

In November, General Buell ordered General Thomas (then headquartered at Lebanon) to concentrate his command and be prepared for any movement Zollicoffer might undertake, and, if necessary, to attack the Confederates' camp. At this time, the commands in the field and reporting to Thomas were: Colonel Samuel Carter's brigade based at London, Colonel William Hoskins' post near Somerset, and Colonel Thomas E. Bramlette's combat team at Columbia.

To strengthen the units guarding the line of the Cumberland, Colonel Frank Wolford and 500 horse soldiers of the 1st Kentucky Cavalry were ordered from Columbia to reinforce Colonel Hoskins; while Brigadier General Albin F. Schoepf and two infantry regiments and a battery advanced and took position on the Cumberland River at Waitsborough, where he guarded the crossing.

General Schoepf's column reached Waitsborough from Lebanon on December 1. The next day, Zollicoffer, while building ferries to cross the Cumberland at Mill Springs, sent a battery to shell Schoepf's camp. That evening, Schoepf wrote General Thomas recounting the day's activities. His report read:

Camp Goggin, *December* 2, 1861.
General: I arrived here yesterday, reconnoitered same day and today. This morning the enemy opened fire from three pieces, one rifled, and infantry on Colonel Hoskins' camp subsequent to my order for the removal of the camp some distance back.

The strength of the enemy is estimated, by the best accounts we can get, of the following numbers: At Mill Springs, 2,000 infantry and 1,000 cavalry; at Captain West's farm, distant from Mill Springs 2 miles, 1,000 infantry; at Steubenville, 2 miles distant from West's, 2,000 infantry; and at Monticello, 5 miles from Steubenville, 3,000 infantry. Mill

21. Raymond E. Myers, *The Zollie Tree* (Louisville: The Filson Club Press, 1964), pp. 60-61.

Springs is distant from this point 12 miles, at which place they can cross the Cumberland with facility, and 2 miles below that point they can also cross.

Apprehending the probability of their crossing at Mill Springs, I detailed two companies of cavalry [under Captain Boston Dillon] to that place. I deem the position east of me safe, but west of me they may cross.

The river is high and not fordable, but by means of flats they can cross anywhere; the troops under my command are not sufficient to keep the river guarded as far as Mill Springs. Should they cross in the vicinity of my camp I can defend my position. The Thirty-eighth Ohio will be with me today. The Seventeenth [Ohio] will occupy a position on Fishing Creek, to defend against a flank movement should the enemy cross.

Very Respectfully, your obedient servant,<br>A. Schoepf,<br>Brigadier-General.

General George H. Thomas,
*Commanding Eastern Division.*
P. S.—The enemy have moved their artillery and opened fire again. I have hardly time to write.[22]

Writing General Thomas on the 3d, Schoepf reported:

Camp Goggin, December 3, 1861.

General: The enemy, after keeping up a brisk fire until 1 p. m., retired and took up march towards Mill Springs. I ordered Colonel [J. M.] Connell's Seventeenth Ohio Regiment from Somerset to that point; also three pieces of artillery and one company of cavalry. Should the enemy make an attempt to cross, we could be able to keep them in check.

Twenty reliable Union men crossed the river yesterday evening, and gave me information that Zollicoffer commands in person, and is at Mill Springs, with eight regiments of infantry, three of cavalry, and eight pieces of artillery.

My troops can be provided with beef and fresh pork; therefore I would suggest that only small stores and bread should be sent.

[Frederick E.] Prime [of the Corps of Engineers] arrived here today. We will go to work as soon as the tools arrive.[23]

22. OR, I, VII, 7-8.
23. *Ibid.,* p. 8.

Colonel Connell was incompetent, and failed to comply with his orders. He went into camp two miles in rear of where he was ordered, and failed to post men to guard the ford. Consequently, Zollicoffer crossed the Cumberland in force and occupied the north bank at Beech Grove without the Federals knowing that such a movement was under way. This was only discovered on the 4th, when the Rebels drove back the Federal cavalry and attacked Connell, who too late had finally bestirred himself to make a reconnaisance. Connell, unaware of the foe's movements, reached the area of the ford and found himself confronted by a host of Confederates, who had crossed the Cumberland. Covered by darkness, Connell extricated his command, withdrawing beyond Fishing Creek. Schoepf, satisfied that he was outnumbered, called on Colonel Carter at London for reinforcements. After ordering up the Thirty-third Indiana from Crab Orchard, Schoepf, on the 6th, took position three miles north of Somerset.[24]

From Somerset, on December 8, Schoepf wrote General Thomas:

> General: We met the enemy's scouts this evening about 3 miles to the west of the village; the collision took place between the Thirty-fifth Ohio and the enemy's cavalry. Our loss was 1 killed and 1 wounded; the enemy's, 1 officer killed and 3 men wounded. We captured 1 horse and killed 5. The cavalry under my command, as usual, behaved badly. They are a nuisance, and the sooner they are disbanded the better. They are scouring the country on their own account, lounging about the villages and drinking establishments, a nuisance and disturbance to the quiet citizens of the country. Captain [T. S.] Everett has just joined me, and reports a series of irregularities by stragglers of this regiment [1st Kentucky Cavalry] as having passed under his notice in the several villages through which he passed.
>
> Is there no such thing as obtaining a regiment of *reliable* cavalry? Such a regiment is indispensable with this brigade at this time. The absence of such troops has kept me in the saddle until I am nearly worn down with fatigue.
>
> I very much need a brigade commissary of subsistence, who could have the means to purchase such articles as it may become necessary to purchase. The system of making purchases by regimental commissaries and giving promise to

24. Cist, pp. 11-12.

pay is open to abuse, and has become a great annoyance.

The two Tennessee regiments (sent by Colonel Carter) will be here tomorrow. I shall, no doubt, need them by the time they arrive.

Very respectfully, your obedient servant,

A. Schoepf,
*Brigadier-General, Commanding.*

Brig. Gen. George H. Thomas.

P. S.—I regret to add that Major [Francis W.] Helveti, of the Kentucky Cavalry, and Captain Prime, Engineers, are both missing, and have been, I now learn, captured by the enemy. These officers left camp with me on Wednesday on a reconnaissance, but, taking a different road, fell into the hands of the enemy. An earlier report would have been made of this, but I had looked for their return until after the departure of the Saturday's mail, my last reliable means of communicating with you. I deem it useless now to send a dispatch by a cavalry express.[25]

The Confederate view of the crossing of the Cumberland and the establishment of a fortified camp and bridgehead was detailed by General Zollicoffer in his report of December 9 to General Johnston. He wrote:

Brigade Headquarters,
*Mill Springs, Ky., December 9, 1861.*

Sir: Having been disappointed in having ferry-boats captured by the force sent on in advance with that object, I have had to have boats built, and have been much delayed in crossing the Cumberland River. Five regiments, seven cavalry companies, and four pieces of artillery are now across. The position on both sides of the ferry is naturally strong, and I am rapidly strengthening the defenses on the right bank. The whole force with me is seven and one-half regiments, eighteen cavalry companies, and one 6-pounder battery of eight guns.

There is a force of the enemy at Columbia, the strength of which I am not able to ascertain. Three regiments of it were at Creelsborough, 18 miles above Burkesville, ten days ago. It is certain that there are now not less than five regiments at Somerset, possibly more.

25. OR, I, VII, 8-9.

82

On the 1st I reconnoitered from the left bank a camp of the enemy, a part of which was in view on the right bank of the river at Waitsborough. On the 2d I took up four pieces of artillery and shelled them out, compelling them to move their encampment hurriedly. They had but two pieces of artillery. On the 4th I threw over the first small cavalry picket at this place. They met a cavalry picket of the enemy a mile from the ferry and drove them back, capturing some trifling equipments. The Seventeenth Ohio Regiment, with orders to prevent our crossing, had advanced to within 2½ miles of the ferry. It fled precipitately to the neighborhood of Somerset.

On the 5th our cavalry pickets captured Major Helveti (supposed to be of General Buell's staff), Captain Prime, engineer officer, under orders from General Buell, and a corporal of Colonel Hoskins' regiment, after a chase of several miles, severely wounding the 2 officers.

Fishing Creek runs south into the Cumberland, 5 miles above here, and lies between our position and Somerset. There are two crossings from here to Somerset, 7 and 11 miles from here. The more distant, the enemy fortified on the eastern bank, and they had a force near the latter crossing. On the 7th our cavalry detachments crossed at both places, and found the enemy had fallen back to a camp 3 miles north of Somerset. They rode through their fortifications and returned. Yesterday our cavalry crossed at the upper (Fishing Creek) ford and reconnoitered the enemy's camp and the town of Somerset. In the fortifications at the creek they found an infantry picket and a cavalry picket in advance. They were also fired on from the bushes this side of the creek. They charged upon all they met, pursued the enemy 5 or 6 miles, killed 10, and captured 16, one of whom is badly wounded. All are of the Thirty-fifth Ohio Regiment, except one of Wolford's regiment. There were 2 of our horses killed and 1 more wounded. The prisoners say their regiment reached Somerset only the evening before, and they know but little of what regiments are there, except that four of them are from Ohio, the Thirty-fifth, Thirty-eighth, Seventeenth, and Thirty-first. Hoskins' Kentucky regiment is certainly there, perhaps others. Our cavalry are today picketing both towards Harrison and Somerset.[26]

26. *Ibid.*, pp. 10-11.

On December 2, 1861, General Buell issued an order constituting the Army of the Ohio and organizing it into brigades and divisions. Four days later, General Thomas formally assumed command of the First Division. The division consisted of four brigades commanded by Brigadier General Albin F. Schoepf, and Colonels Mahlon D. Manson, Robert L. McCook, and Samuel P. Carter, and a number of unbrigaded units.

General Schoepf with his reinforced brigade undertook a forced reconnaissance on December 18 to determine the position and purpose of the Rebel forces. Pushing forward in two columns, Schoepf drove in the enemy pickets and learned that Zollicoffer had entrenched his Beech Grove camp, the right flank of the breastworks anchored on Fishing Creek and the left on White Oak Creek, the Cumberland River to the Confederates' rear. Having accomplished his mission, Schoepf returned with his command to their encampment north of Somerset. The same day Colonel Hoskins made a patrol to Waitsborough, but found no enemy.[27]

General Buell, concluding that the only Rebel force currently operating in eastern Kentucky was Zollicoffer's and deeming it important that it be broken up, now modified his previous orders to General Thomas. On December 29, Buell directed Thomas to advance against Zollicoffer's left, from Columbia, and to cut off the Rebels' line of retreat. Schoepf was to make a frontal attack on the foe. To ensure that their movements were coordinated, Thomas was to communicate with Schoepf.[28]

On New Year's Day 1862, General Thomas took the field. Riding out of Lebanon, he was accompanied by Colonel Manson's brigade, two regiments of Colonel McCook's brigade, a battalion of the 1st Kentucky Cavalry, and Company C, 1st Ohio Light Artillery.

Eastern Kentucky roads, excepting the turnpikes, during the rainy season, were little more than ribbons of mud. When traveled, the clay subsoil of the roads become impassable, especially during the winter months. It was this type of road on which General Thomas' army marched beyond Columbia. He, however,

27. Cist, pp. 12-13; Van Horne, *History*, I, 48-53.
28. Van Horne, *History*, I, 53-54.

was able to use a turnpike from Lebanon to Columbia, over which his supplies had been advanced a few days previous to his departure.

The advance of General Thomas' column is best described in one of the general's communications to General Schoepf:

<blockquote>

Brigadier-General Schoepf,
           Commanding at Somerset:

General: I received yours of the 11th today, by Captain Hall. When I last wrote you I was in hopes of being near Somerset by this time, but the heavy rains have injured the roads so much that it will be impossible to say now when I can be in your vicinity. We have already been three days in making 16 miles, and our ammunition and provisions are far behind now—probably will not be up by tomorrow night. Should I ever succeed in getting near you, I will send a messenger to let you know. I wrote General Buell five days since, submitting your proposition of crossing the river and attacking from the bluffs of Meadow Creek, but have received no reply from him up to this time. As soon as I hear I will write you the result.

I have not had time to converse with the men you sent me fully, but if it be possible to approach the enemy by the way of White Oak Creek I should like to have them as guides.

          Respectfully, your obedient servant,
                   Geo. H. Thomas,
*Brigadier-General, U. S. Army, Commanding.*[29]

</blockquote>

It took eight days to march 40 miles. On Friday, January 17, the mud-spattered column reached Logan's Cross Roads, ten miles north of the Confederates' entrenched camp and about the same distance west of Somerset. Here, Thomas halted his vanguard and awaited the arrival of the Fourth and Tenth Kentucky, Fourteenth Ohio, and Eighteenth U. S. Infantry, bogged down to the rear by muddy roads. Thomas sent a message to General Schoepf, and before nightfall the latter reported in person. Thomas told Schoepf to reinforce him with Company B, First Ohio Light Artillery, the Twelfth Kentucky, and the First and Second East Tennessee Regiments. These units were to remain

29. OR, I, VII, 550-551.

with Thomas until his stragglers arrived.

After Schoepf departed, Thomas posted the Tenth Indiana, the First Kentucky Cavalry, and Company C, First Ohio Artillery, on the Mill Springs road. The Ninth Ohio and Second Minnesota were positioned three-quarters of a mile to the right on the Roberts Port road. Pickets were thrown forward, and during the evening they clashed with Confederate patrols. On the 18th, the Fourth Kentucky, a battalion of Michigan Engineers, and the Ninth Ohio Battery reported to Thomas.[30]

In November 1861, Major General George B. Crittenden of Kentucky and a veteran of long service in the "old army" had been named commander of all Confederate forces operating in Eastern Kentucky and East Tennessee. Then, in mid-December, Crittenden was ordered by President Jefferson Davis to proceed into Kentucky and assume command of all of Zollicoffer's forces, including Brigadier General William H. Carroll's brigade, and those Rebel troops at Cumberland Gap. Crittenden rode out of Knoxville on Christmas day and reached Mill Springs on January 3, 1862.[31]

Upon his arrival, Crittenden, finding Zollicoffer in the entrenched camp, gave orders for the construction of boats and rafts to facilitate the evacuation of the dangerously exposed position and the recrossing of the Cumberland by the division. But these had not been completed, when Confederate scouts reported that Thomas was approaching and had gone into camp at Logan's Cross Roads.

On the 18th, Crittenden wrote General Johnston that he was threatened by the enemy in superior force, and that as it was now impossible to recross the rain-swollen Cumberland, he would have to fight.

At midnight on January 18, in a cold rain, the Rebel column moved out screened by two companies of cavalry. Zollicoffer's brigade followed, trailed by Carroll's brigade.[32]

About daylight they encountered Colonel Wolford's pickets, which fell back on the reserves consisting of two companies of the

30. Van Horne, *History,* I, 54-55.
31. Johnston, p. 402; Myers, pp. 73-74.
32. Myers, p. 89; OR, I, VII, 103.

Tenth Indiana. Together they made a determined stand in which they were supported by Colonel Manson with the rest of the Tenth Indiana. Manson then called up the Fourth Kentucky and Kinney's and Standart's batteries and reported to General Thomas. As he rode through the camp of the Fourth Kentucky, Manson shouted for Colonel Speed S. Fry and warned of the attack. The men were responding to roll call at the time.

Colonel Fry quickly gathered his forces and led them in the direction of the firing. When he sighted the enemy, he positioned his soldiers along a fence on the edge of the woods with his right resting near the Mill Springs road. There was an open field in front of him across which the enemy was advancing. A ravine ran through the open field parallel to Fry's front heading near the road on his right with steep sides to his front but sloping gradually beyond his left. Before Fry's arrival, General Zollicoffer had deployed his brigade, forcing Colonel Wolford and the Tenth Indiana Regiment to fall back. Portions of Wolford's command and Captain James H. Vanarsdall's company of the Tenth Indiana rallied on the Fourth Kentucky when it appeared, while the rest fell back to reform their lines. Colonel Fry and his men were subjected to a severe attack. The enemy crawled up under the shelter of the ravine to within a short distance of Fry's lines before firing, and so had distinct advantage. Fry mounted the fence, defying them to stand up on their feet and come forward like men.

Confederate General Crittenden had warned his senior officers that there was danger of "firing into their friends," because some of the Southern soldiers were wearing blue uniforms. To avoid this hazard, a password "Kentucky" had been adopted. The morning of Sunday, January 19, was misty and dark. Visibility was poor, and it was hard to distinguish the opposing forces "except as a line of armed soldiers." Because of the gloom it was very difficult to distinguish between the Union and Confederate soldiers: many of the latter were wearing blue uniforms.

As General Zollicoffer oversaw the movements of the Nineteenth Tennessee Regiment of his command, he thought that the Fourth Kentucky (Union) to his front was part of his brigade, so he "ordered the Nineteenth Tennessee to cease firing, as they were firing upon their own troops." Zollicoffer, riding closer to the front, came upon Colonel Fry of the Fourth Kentucky. He convinced Fry that both commands belonged to the same army, and Zollicoffer said to Fry, "We must not shoot our own men." At the time Zollicoffer was wearing a "white gum overcoat," which covered up his uniform, and Colonel Fry, assuming him to be a Union officer, replied, "I would not, of course, do so intentionally."

General Zollicoffer, then pointing to the Nineteenth Tennessee, said, "Those are our men." Colonel Fry agreed to this and started toward his Fourth Kentucky and ordered them to cease firing. In the meantime, one of Zollicoffer's aides, Major H. M. R. Fogg, rode upon the scene and noticed that Fry was a Union officer. He drew his revolver and fired upon him, wounding Fry's horse. In the melee, Fry returned the fire as he rode away. "The ball passed through General Zollicoffer's heart, and he fell exactly where he had stood," being nearsighted, he "never knew that Fry was an enemy."[33]

Colonel Fry's account of the incident is of particular interest:

> In order to ascertain more certainly the exact state of affairs, the firing having nearly ceased, I rode from the right of my regiment some fifteen or twenty paces down to the fence behind which we had been fighting and, discovering no enemy in that direction, I turned my horse and rode slowly back to the place I had just left. As I neared the road I saw an officer riding slowly down the road on a white horse and within twenty paces of the right of my regiment. His uniform was concealed, except the extremities of his pantaloons, which I observed were of the color worn by Federal officers, by a long green overcoat. His near approach to my regiment, his calm manner, my close proximity to him, indeed everything I saw led me to believe he was a Federal officer belonging to one of the regiments just arriving. So thoroughly was I convinced that he was one of our men, I did not hesitate to ride up to his side so closely that our knees touched. He was calm, self-possessed and dignified in manner. He said to me, "We must not shoot our own men," to which I responded, "Of course not; I would not do so intentionally," then turning his eyes to his left and pointing in the same direction he said, "those are our men." I could not see the men from my position, but I now suppose they were there. I immediately

33. Johnston, p. 402; Myers, pp. 94-96.

moved off to the right of my regiment, perhaps some fifteen or twenty paces from the spot on which I met him. His language convinced me more than ever that he was a Federal officer. How it is that he did not discover that I was one I cannot tell, as my uniform was entirely exposed to view, having on nothing to conceal it.

As soon as I reached my regiment, I paused, turning my horse a little to the left, and across the road, looked back to see what was going on, when, to my great surprise, another officer whom I had not seen rode out from behind a large tree near the place of my meeting with the first officer, and, with pistol in hand, leveled it directly at me, fired, and paused for a moment, doubtless to observe the effect of his shot. Instead of striking the object at which it was aimed, the ball struck my horse just above the hip bone making a flesh wound. I immediately drew my Colt's revolver from the holster, and was about to fire, when he retreated behind a tree. Not until this time was I aware that I had been in conversation with an officer of the opposing army. In an instant the thought flashed across my mind that the officer with whom I had met and conversed had attempted to draw me into the snare of death or secure my capture by a false representation of his position, and, feeling thus, I aimed at him and fired.[34]

The Rebels continued to press the fight with only the fence separating the combatants. Since his left was not being assailed, Fry moved two of those companies to the right. General Thomas now appeared on the field and placed the Tenth Indiana in position to cover Fry's exposed flank. Zollicoffer's fall had caused the Confederates to recoil, so General Crittenden brought up reinforcements and ordered a general advance. The Federals, however, held and counterattacking gradually forced the Confederates back. The Ninth Ohio made a bayonet charge against the enemy's left, which broke up in confusion. The entire Rebel line then disintegrated, and a disorderly retreat began. Thomas ordered a pursuit, and the Yanks found hundreds of muskets abandoned, as well as haversacks filled with rations of corn pone and bacon. The Union soldiers had fought without breakfast but still were afraid to eat from these bags because the enemy was rumored to

34. W. H. Perrin, J. H. Battle, and G. C. Kniffin, *Kentucky: A History of the State* (Louisville and Chicago: Battey, 1887), p. 393.

have poisoned food. But, after finding so many, they finally determined it was safe to eat the Confederate rations.

On arriving near the enemy's entrenchments, Thomas deployed his troops in line of battle, and they advanced to the summit of the hill at Mouldens, which commanded the enemy's breastworks. From this point the batteries of Captains William B. Standart and Stephen R. Wetmore kept up a bombardment until dark, while Captain Dennis Kenny's on the left fired upon the ferry to keep the foe from crossing. The Fourteenth Ohio and Tenth Kentucky arrived during the pursuit, and General Schoepf approached with the Seventeenth, Thirty-First, and Thirty-Eighth Ohio. At daybreak, on the 20th, Wetmore's 10-pounder Parrott guns shelled a steamboat which was believed to have been used to cross troops, and the enemy burned her. On advancing, the Federals found the entrenchments abandoned, but near the ferry crossing they discovered eleven pieces of artillery with their caissons, battery wagons, and forges hitched and ready to roll. More than 150 wagons and over 1,000 horses and mules were also captured. The boats used to cross the Rebels had been destroyed, but later in the day the Fourteenth Ohio crossed the Cumberland for a reconnaissance and to secure abandoned property.[35]

Thomas, in his official report of this battle, wrote, "Their command was completely demoralized, and they retreated with great haste and in all directions, making their capture in any numbers quite doubtful if pursued. There is no doubt that the moral effect produced by their complete dispersion will have a more decided effect in re-establishing Union sentiments than though they had been captured."[36]

Some two weeks after the battle, General Thomas submitted to General Buell his "after action report" of the battle. It read:

> *Somerset, Ky., January 31, 1862.*
> Captain: I have the honor to report that in carrying out the instructions of the general [Buell] commanding the department, contained in his communication of the 29th of December, I reached Logan's Cross-Roads, about 10 miles north of the intrenched camp of the enemy on the Cumber-

35. E. G. Squire, ed., *Frank Leslie's Pictorial History of the American Civil War* (New York: Leslie, 1862), I, 279.
36. OR, I, VII, 81.

land River, on the 17th instant, with a portion of the Second and Third Brigades, Kenny's battery of artillery, and a battalion of Wolford's cavalry. The Fourth and Tenth Kentucky, Fourteenth Ohio, and the Eighteenth U. S. Infantry being still in rear, detained by the almost impassable condition of the roads, I determined to halt at this point, to await their arrival and to communicate with General Schoepf.

The Tenth Indiana, Wolford's cavalry, and Kenny's battery took position on the road leading to the enemy's camp. The Ninth Ohio and Second Minnesota (part of Colonel McCook's brigade) encamped three-fourths of a mile to the right, on the Roberts Port road. Strong pickets were thrown out in the direction of the enemy beyond where the Somerset and Mill Springs road comes into the main road from my camp to Mill Springs, and a picket of cavalry some distance in advance of the infantry.

General Schoepf visited me on the day of my arrival, and, after consultation, I directed him to send to my camp Standart's battery, the Twelfth Kentucky, and the First and Second Tennessee Regiments, to remain until the arrival of the regiments in rear.

Having received information on the evening of the 17th that a large train of wagons with its escort were encamped on the Roberts Port and Danville road, about 6 miles from Colonel [James B.] Steedman's camp, I sent an order to him to send his wagons forward under a strong guard, and to march with his regiment (the Fourteenth Ohio) and the Tenth Kentucky (Colonel [John M.] Harlan), with one day's rations in their haversacks, to the point where the enemy were said to be encamped, and either capture or disperse them.

Nothing of importance occurred from the time of our arrival until the morning of the 19th, except a picket skirmish on the night of the 17th. The Fourth Kentucky, the battalion of Michigan Engineers, and Wetmore's battery joined on the 18th.

About 6:30 o'clock on the morning of the 19th the pickets from Wolford's cavalry encountered the enemy advancing on our camp, retired slowly, and reported their advance to Col. M. D. Manson, commanding the Second Brigade. He immediately formed his regiment (the Tenth Indiana) and took a position on the road to await the attack, ordering the Fourth Kentucky (Col. S. S. Fry) to support him, and then informed me in person that the enemy were advancing in force and what disposition he had made to resist them. I directed him to join his brigade immediately and hold the enemy in check until I could order up the other troops, which were ordered to form immediately and were marching to the field in ten minutes afterwards. The battalion of Michigan Engineers and Company A, Thirty-eighth Ohio (Captain [Charles] Greenwood), were ordered to remain as guard to the camp.

Upon my arrival on the field soon afterwards I found the Tenth Indiana formed in front of their encampment, apparently awaiting orders, and ordered them forward to the support of the Fourth Kentucky, which was the only entire regiment then engaged. I then rode forward myself to see the enemy's position, so that I could determine what disposition to make of my troops as they arrived. On reaching the position held by the Fourth Kentucky, Tenth Indiana, and Wolford's cavalry, at a point where the roads fork leading to Somerset, I found the enemy advancing through a corn field and evidently endeavoring to gain the left of the Fourth Kentucky Regiment, which was maintaining its position in a most determined manner. I directed one of my aides to ride back and order up a section of artillery and the Tennessee brigade to advance on the enemy's right, and sent orders for Colonel McCook to advance with his two regiments (the Ninth Ohio and Second Minnesota) to the support of the Fourth Kentucky and Tenth Indiana.

A section of Captain Kenny's battery took a position on the edge of the field to the left of the Fourth Kentucky and opened an efficient fire on a regiment of Alabamians, which were advancing on the Fourth Kentucky. Soon afterwards the Second Minnesota (Col. H. P. Van Cleve) arrived, the colonel reporting to me for instructions. I directed him to take the position of the Fourth Kentucky and Tenth Indiana, which regiments were nearly out of ammunition. The Ninth Ohio, under the immediate command of Major [Gustave] Kammerling, came into position on the right of the road at the same time.

Immediately after these regiments had gained their position the enemy opened a most determined and galling fire, which was returned by our troops in the same spirit, and for nearly half an hour the contest was maintained on both sides in the most obstinate manner. At this time the Twelfth Kentucky (Col. W. A. Hoskins) and the Tennessee brigade reached the field to the left of the Minnesota regiment, and opened fire on the right flank of the enemy, who then began to fall back. The Second Minnesota kept up a most galling fire in front, and the Ninth Ohio charged the enemy on the right with bayonets fixed, turned their flank, and drove them from the field, the whole line giving way and retreating in the utmost disorder and confusion.

As soon as the regiments could be formed and refill their cartridge-boxes I ordered the whole force to advance. A few miles in rear of the battle-field a small force of cavalry was drawn up near the road, but a few shots from our artillery (a section of Standart's battery) dispersed them, and none of the enemy were seen again until we arrived in front of their [Mill Springs] intrenchments. As we approached their intrenchments the division was deployed in line of battle and steadily advanced to the summit of the hill at Moulden's. From this point I directed their intrenchments to be cannonaded, which was done until dark by Standart's and Wetmore's batteries. Kenny's battery was placed in position on the extreme left at Russell's house, from which point he was directed to fire on their ferry, to deter them from attempting to cross. On the following morning [the 20th] Captain Wetmore's battery was ordered to Russell's house, and assisted with his Parrott guns in firing upon the ferry. Colonel Manson's brigade took position on the left near Kenny's battery, and every preparation was made to assault their intrenchments on the following morning. The Fourteenth Ohio (Colonel Steedman) and the Tenth Kentucky (Colonel Harlan) having joined from detached service soon after the repulse of the enemy, continued with their brigade in the pursuit, although they could not get up in time to join in the fight. These two regiments were placed in front in my advance on the intrenchments the next morning and entered first. General Schoepf also joined me the evening of the 19th with the Seventeenth, Thirty-first, and Thirty-eighth Ohio. His entire brigade entered with the other troops.

On reaching the intrenchments we found the enemy had abandoned everything and retired during the night. Twelve pieces of artillery, with their caissons packed with ammunition; one battery wagon and two forges; a large amount of ammunition; a large number of small-arms, mostly the old flint-lock muskets; 150 or 160 wagons, and upwards of 1,000 horses and mules; a large amount of commissary stores, intrenching tools, and camp and garrison equipage, fell into our hands. A correct list of all the captured property will be forwarded as soon as it can be made up and the property secured.

The steam and ferry boats having been burned by the enemy in their retreat, it was found impossible to cross the river and pursue them . . .

It affords me much pleasure to be able to testify to the uniform steadiness and good conduct of both officers and men during the battle, and I respectfully refer to the accompanying reports of the different commanders for the names of those officers and men whose good conduct was particularly noticed by them.

I regret to have to report that Col. R. L. McCook, commanding the Third Brigade, and his aide, Lieut. A. S. Burt, Eighteenth U. S. Infantry, were both severely wounded in the first advance of the Ninth Ohio Regiment, but continued on duty until the return of the brigade to camp at Logan's Cross-Roads.

Col. S. S. Fry, Fourth Kentucky, was slightly wounded whilst his regiment was gallantly resisting the advance of the enemy, during which time General Zollicoffer fell from a shot from his (Colonel Fry's) pistol, which no doubt contributed materially to the discomfiture of the enemy.

Capt. G. E. Flynt, assistant adjutant-general; Capt. Alvan C. Gillem, division quartermaster; Lieut. Joseph C. Breckinridge, aide-de-camp; Lieut. S. E. Jones, acting assistant quartermaster; Mr. J. W. Scully, quartermaster's clerk; Privates Samuel Letcher, Twenty-first Regiment Kentucky Volunteers; [Joseph] Stitch, Fourth Regiment Kentucky Volunteers, rendered me valuable assistance in carrying orders and conducting the troops to their different positions.

Capt. George S. Roper deserves great credit for his perseverance and energy in forwarding commissary stores as far as the hill where our forces bivouacked.

In addition to the duties of guarding the camp, Lieut. Col. K. A. Hunton, commanding the Michigan Engineers, and Captain Greenwood, Company A, Thirty-eighth Regiment

Ohio Volunteers, with their commands, performed very efficient service in collecting and burying the dead on both sides and in moving the wounded to the hospitals near the battle-field.

A number of flags were taken on the field of battle and in the intrenchments. They will be forwarded to headquarters as soon as collected together.

The enemy's loss, as far as known, is a follows: Brigadier-General Zollicoffer, Lieutenant Bailie Peyton, and 190 officers, non-commissioned officers, and privates, killed; Lieut. Col. M. B. Carter, Twentieth Tennessee; Lieut. J. W. Allen, Fifteenth Mississippi; Lieut. Allen Morse, Sixteenth Alabama, and 5 officers of the medical staff and 81 non-commissioned officers and privates, taken prisoners; Lieut J. E. Patterson, Twentieth Tennessee, and A. J. Knapp, Fifteenth Mississippi, and 66 non-commissioned officers and privates, wounded; making 192 killed, 89 prisoners not wounded and 68 wounded; a total of killed, wounded, and prisoners of 349.

Our loss was as follows:

| Troops | Killed | | Wounded | |
| --- | --- | --- | --- | --- |
| | Officers | Men | Officers | Men |
| 10th Indiana | | 10 | 3 | 72 |
| 1st Kentucky (Cavalry) | 1 | 2 | .. | 19 |
| 4th Kentucky | | 8 | 4 | 48 |
| 2d Minnesota | | 12 | 2 | 31 |
| 9th Ohio | | 3 | 4 | 24 |
| Total | 1 | 38 | 13 | 194 |

A complete list of the names of our killed and wounded and of the prisoners is herewith attached.

I am, sir, very respectfully, your obedient servant,<br>
Geo. H. Thomas,<br>
Brigadier-General, U. S. Volunteers,<br>
Commanding.[37]

Colonel Manson reported from his headquarters that "the Federal force actually engaged did not exceed at any time over 2,500."[38] The entire command of General Thomas' forces on the

<hr>

37. *Ibid.*, pp. 79-82.
38. *Ibid.*, p. 86.

field during this battle probably numbered about 4,000 effectives.[39]

General Crittenden's report of Thursday, February 13, 1862, made from his headquarters at Camp Fogg, Tennessee, listed the Confederate losses as 125 killed, including General Zollicoffer, 309 wounded, and 99 missing or captured, for an aggregate of 529.[40] The Fifteenth Mississippi under the command of Lieutenant Colonel Edward C. Walthall of General Zollicoffer's brigade suffered the heaviest losses.

Historians have with difficulty sorted out what happened at Mill Springs. One reason for this difficulty is that there is too much information available. Many of the accounts found in *Frank Leslie's* are personal reminiscences which offer a great deal of conjecture and which, when seen together, are in conflict with one another. One northern recruit, for example, upon examining the provisions of Zollicoffer's encampment after the battle, comes to the conclusion that the Rebels lost the battle because they had too little whiskey. This sentiment may be a good example of northern prejudice, but it can hardly account for so significant a turn of events.

Perhaps too little attention has been paid to the matter from the southern perspective, and some recapitulation will here be necessary to make Zollicoffer's situation clear. It must be remembered that Zollicoffer had been at Mill Springs long enough to build a permanent encampment which included log cabins, and from a psychological standpoint Mill Springs must have represented a stronghold to the Confederates. It was, therefore, a location as well as an ideal that had to be defended, and when Thomas advanced to Logan's Cross Roads, Crittenden's hand was forced. This put him at a psychological, as well as a practical, disadvantage.

If he had been able to outguess Thomas, he might have used better judgment, but in this situation he had, roughly speaking, three alternatives. One was to retreat ingloriously, which would be hurtful to any Southerner's pride. The second was to wait for an attack by forces that were believed to be overwhelm-

<hr>

39. R. M. Kelly, "Holding Kentucky for the Union," *Battles and Leaders of the Civil War*, edited by Robert U. Johnson and C. C. Buel, 4 vols. (New York: Century, 1887), I, 392.
40. OR, I, VII, 108.

ing. It was at this point, if anywhere, that Crittenden's tragic flaw became manifest. It was incumbent upon him, in a position of responsibility such as this, to have all the information available from the best possible sources and to make a decision on the basis of that information. Personal accounts from Rebel soldiers make it clear that the information was conflicting and unreliable. Southern estimates of the number of troops under Thomas range from 8,000 to 25,000. Depending on which Crittenden believed and which his troops believed, anyone might be at a psychological advantage or disadvantage. It seems to be the case, however, that the number of troops under Thomas was grossly overestimated, and Crittenden was in fear of being forced back to the river, with no means of escape available, and slaughtered. This, again, seemed foolish.

The third alternative was to attack, a choice that might not have been unwise except for three reasons. First, Thomas had a reasonably accurate estimate of the number of Rebel troops. His figures added up to 9,000. Next, Thomas had had time to get acquainted with his territory, a consideration that proved to be decisive in terrain that included the wooded area and rough ground in which the battle was fought. Finally, the matter of terrain is compounded by the factor of the weather. Accounts from both Northern and Southern troops engaged in the battle testify to the ferocity of the storm that raged during the battle. This last factor might be considered accidental, but, whatever the case, the time chosen for the attack proved unfortunate for the Rebels. Some of the reports indicate that, because of the rain, the powder was so wet that one-third of their small-arms would not fire. Assuming this is an accurate estimate, this would have left Crittenden with about 6,000 effective troops against about 2,500 of Thomas'.

The final factor, the death of Zollicoffer, seems more like a cruel trick of fate than logic. Although Zollicoffer was nearsighted, the confusion of battle, the adverse weather, and gloom all conspired to prevent Zollicoffer from identifying Colonel Fry as a Union officer. His death probably contributed more than any logic to the defeat of the Rebels. Accounts in *Frank Leslie's* from Union men engaged in the battle testify to the fact that news of Zollicoffer's death spread rapidly among the troops, probably giving the Yanks a psychological advantage in the remainder of the battle. Reports also indicate that the battle continued to rage as fiercely as the weather for awhile after Zollicoffer was shot. Rebel accounts are less clear on the matter, but it seems likely that news of Zollicoffer's death would spread as rapidly among them as it did among the Federals, and that it would contribute significantly to the demoralization of the men under Zollicoffer's command. This, in fact, is what happened. If there is any agreement on both sides, it is that shortly after Zollicoffer fell, the troops under his command became demoralized and retreated in confusion. Contemporary understanding of mob psychology can perhaps best explain the behavior of Rebel troops who pillaged the countryside, taking what scattered farms and settlements could provide, because discipline had temporarily broken down and they had been left without cause or rations.

The death of Zollicoffer has been variously treated, and even romanticized, by history. Though he is described as clean shaven at the time of his death, possibly a precaution he took to avoid identification, he is represented in engravings of the time with a mustache. It is no wonder that reports differ too as to whether his death was eventual or immediate.

This much is certain: chivalry did not fail in the treatment of the fallen general's body. In response to a communication from General Crittenden, inquiring after Zollicoffer's body, the following note was sent:

Headquarters 2d Brigade, 1st Division,

Department of the Ohio<br>
*Mill Spring, January* 27, 1862.

General George B. Crittenden:

Sir,—Your note of the 25th inst., accompanying a flag of truce, has been received. In reply I will state that it would afford me great pleasure to comply with your request, but I am informed the body of General Zollicoffer was removed to Somerset, and has been from thence sent to his home in Tennessee in charge of one of your Surgeons who was taken prisoner by the United States forces in the engagement of the 19th inst.

For the satisfaction of the family and friends of the late General Zollicoffer, I will say that his body has been properly

98

cared for, decently clothed, and placed in a substantial
wooden box.

> Yours, etc.,
> M. D. Manson,
> *Commanding at Mill Spring.*[41]

So much, at least, can be said for chivalry in the Union's
treatment of the body of a man of rank.

After realizing the extent of the enemy's panic when they
entered the Rebels' entrenchments, Colonel Fry asked General
Thomas, "General, why didn't you send in a demand for surrender last night?" Thomas, looking at him for a moment as if
in thought, replied, "Hang it, Fry, I never once thought of it."

About this time there originated a story often repeated in the
Western armies. A lively young Confederate prisoner was permitted the freedom of the camp. When some of the Union soldiers
were kidding him in a good-natured way "about his army being
in such a hurry as even to throw away their haversacks," he
responded, "Well, we were doing pretty good fighting till old
man Thomas rose up in his stirrups, and we heard him holler
out: 'Attention, Creation! By kingdoms right wheel!' and then
we knew you had us, and it was no time to carry weight."[42]

General Thomas was honored by the men of the Fourth Kentucky Volunteer Infantry who presented him with a diamond-
and-emerald-studded sword and scabbard for his victory at
Mill Springs, the first major Union success in the West. Secretary
of War Edwin M. Stanton (who had replaced Simon Cameron)
was encouraged by the first sweeping victory scored by a Federal
general. Stanton accordingly issued the following order:

> A congratulatory order from President Lincoln to the
> United States forces for their victory at
> the battle of Mill Springs, Kentucky.
>
> > *War Department*, January 22, 1862.
> The President, Commander-in-Chief of the Army and Navy,
> has received information of a brilliant victory by the United
> States forces over a large body of armed traitors and Rebels
> at Mill Springs, in the State of Kentucky. He returns thanks
> to the gallant officers and soldiers who won that victory, and

41. *Frank Leslie's*, I, 279.
42. Kelly, "Holding Kentucky for the Union," *Battles and Leaders*, I, 391.

when the official reports shall be received the military and personal valor displayed in battle will be acknowledged and rewarded in a fitting manner.

The courage that encountered and vanquished the greatly superior numbers of the Rebel force, pursued and attacked them in their intrenchments, and paused not until the enemy was completely routed, merits and receives commendation.

The purpose of this war is to attack, pursue, and destroy a rebellious enemy, and to deliver the country from danger menaced by traitors. Alacrity, daring, courageous spirit, and patriotic zeal on all occasions and under every circumstance are expected from the Army of the United States. In the prompt and spirited movements and daring battle of Mill Springs the Nation will realize its hopes, and the people of the United States will rejoice to honor every soldier and officer who proves his courage by charging with the bayonet and storming the intrenchments, or in the blaze of the enemy's fire.

By order of the President:

Edwin M. Stanton,
*Secretary of War.*[43]

This message was more than a portion of triumph over a victory, more than an illustrious list of honors of the victors. It was an order by the Commander-in-Chief, an obligation which he could not pass on to another. It was a warning to those in the military service for them to get on with the job at hand. The principal object of the war was destruction of the enemy. It applied to the enemies of the country the names of "rebels" and "traitors" and held them up to the public execration, instead of treating them as misguided brethren with whom a conflict was to be avoided, in the hope of a peaceable compromise. It furnished the keynote of what the administration of the War Office would be; and finally, it was a warning to the Rebels that they need not count upon the Democratic antecedents of the Northern Union men to qualify their patriotism because of previous political affiliations.

Thomas also received a congratulatory letter from Congressman Horace Maynard of Tennessee, a vigorous advocate of the Union cause, which read:

43. OR, I, VII, 102.

Washington, February 4, 1862.

General George H. Thomas, Commanding:

Dear General: You will need no assurance that I was delighted at the intelligence conveyed by your letter of the 22d ultimo, more than confirming what had been matter of rumors. During a conference with the Secretary of War the morning after I received it I read it to him. At his request I left it in his hands and he has just returned it after retaining a copy. Hence my delay in replying.

You have undoubtedly fought the great battle of the war. The country is still reverberating the shout of victory. The more we hear of the engagement the greater its magnitude appears.

I was much gratified to learn to-night from Mr. [James] Speed, of Louisville, that you had sent Generals Schoepf and [Jeremiah T.] Boyle forward to Monticello with a large force, and that you were yourself actively engaged in pushing forward a column into Eastern Tennessee, for I know well enough that, winter though it is, rough as the ways are, you will not stop until Knoxville is in your possession and that line of railroad in your grip.

The advance into that region will necessarily involve some measures looking to the civil administration of the country. The mails should go simultaneously with the troops, and yet care should be taken that the Rebels should not be benefitted thereby. Trade, too, will naturally follow, to a limited extent at least; the Union people should as far as practicable be relieved from the inconveniences to which they have been subjected by the double rigors of external circumvallation by the Government and of domestic oppression by the secession . . . .

To look after these matters properly you might, I should think, employ with advantage some civilians, particularly some of the residents, being careful to select only persons both intelligent and reliable.

I am exceedingly anxious to be with you, but matters of great moment are just now before Congress, and seeing how partially our part of the country is represented in it, I dislike to leave.

101

Your own views on these matters would greatly interest me, and I beg you will favor me with them.

I am, very respectfully, your obedient servant,

Horace Maynard.

P. S.—Yesterday the Senate confirmed your nomination as brigadier-general.[44]

44. *Ibid.*, p. 582.

# CHAPTER SIX

# *From Mill Springs to Missionary Ridge with General Thomas*

General Thomas' Mill Springs victory was but the first in a series of Union successes in the West that staggered the Confederacy along a more than 700-mile front. Fort Henry on the Tennessee River surrendered on February 6; Springfield, Missouri, was occupied on February 13; Bowling Green was evacuated on the 14th; Fort Donelson and its more than 13,000 defenders were unconditionally surrendered to General Grant on the 16th; Nashville was entered by General Buell's vanguard on February 25; Columbus, Kentucky, the Gibraltar of the West, was abandoned without firing a shot on March 2; and, on March 6-8, Union forces under Brigadier General Samuel R. Curtis defeated Major General Earl Van Dorn and his Confederates at Pea Ridge.

In face of these sweeping Union victories, the Confederates abandoned southern Kentucky, much of Middle and West Tennessee, and northwest Arkansas. Calling up reinforcements from the Gulf Coast, General Johnston massed a formidable army at

Corinth, in northeast Mississippi. From mid-March until late May, this small Mississippi town, situated at the crossing of the Mobile & Ohio and Memphis & Charleston Railroads, became the most important point in the Confederacy.

Some two weeks after the capture of Fort Donelson, Union troops from General Grant's command began to ascend the Tennessee River in steamboats from their Fort Henry base. Savannah, Tennessee, on the east bank of the river was occupied and then Crumps Landing and Pittsburg Landing upstream and on the opposite side. Pittsburg Landing, where by Saturday, April 5, Grant had concentrated five of his six divisions, was 22 miles northeast of Corinth.

Meanwhile, General Thomas and his division had reported to General Buell at Nashville on March 2. To do so, Thomas had been recalled from Somerset on February 6 and, marching by way of Lebanon and Bardstown, had reached Louisville on the 25th. There, Thomas and his men had boarded steamboats for the trip down the Ohio and up the Cumberland to Nashville.[1]

From Nashville, Buell's columns were to march to Savannah. As soon as Buell's army had crossed the Tennessee, General Halleck, since March 13 the Union leader in the West, would come forward from his St. Louis headquarters, take field command of Grant's and Buell's armies, and advance on Corinth.

Buell's vanguard left Nashville on March 15, Thomas' division marching on the 20th. The army halted at Columbia for nine days, while Duck River was bridged. The lead division crossed the river on the morning of March 29, the other four divisions following. Thomas' division, the fifth in the march order, crossed on April 1, and camped on the night of the 5th east of Waynesboro, 40 miles east of Savannah. General Buell and his lead division, Brigadier General William Nelson's, had reached Savannah that afternoon.[2]

Apprised of Buell's approach, General Johnston determined to attack and defeat Grant's army before Buell's arrived on the west side of the Tennessee. Marching from Corinth on April 3, Johnston's 40,000 grim Confederates struck on Sunday morning, the

1. OR, I, VII, 658, 679.
2. Force, pp. 105-06.

6th. The Union soldiers, after a terrible struggle, were driven from their camps near Shiloh Church. Throughout the bloody day the Confederates edged closer to Pittsburg Landing. The fighting was desperate and General Johnston was among the slain.

General Nelson's vanguard crossed the Tennessee late in the day to bolster the line Grant had established to cover Pittsburg Landing. By the morning of April 7, three of Buell's divisions had reached the Tennessee's west bank, and the combined Union armies seized the initiative. The Confederates, now led by General Pierre G. T. Beauregard, fought doggedly as they slowly pulled back. By 2:30 P.M. the battle of Shiloh was history, as the Confederates retreated to their camps in and around Corinth. There was no pursuit by the Federals. Thomas and his division reached Savannah late on Monday, the 7th, but did not reach Pittsburg Landing until 11 A.M. on the 8th.[3]

In the weeks following the Shiloh holocaust, General Halleck arrived at the front and assumed field command. Major General John Pope's Army of the Mississippi, which had occupied New Madrid, Missouri, on March 14 and had captured 7,000 Confederates in a well-executed amphibious operation at Island No. 10 on April 8, was called over from the Mississippi River. The steamboats on which Pope's 18,000 soldiers made this move, ascended the Tennessee and, on April 21, the troops went ashore at Hamburg Landing, four miles upstream from Pittsburg Landing.

By April 29, Halleck was prepared to advance on Corinth. Before doing so, he organized his three armies into wings, designated the Right, Center, and Left, Reserves, and Cavalry, commanded respectively by Major Generals George H. Thomas, Don C. Buell, John Pope, and John A. McClernand, and Brigadier General Andrew J. Smith. General Grant, who had been savagely criticised by the press for allowing his troops at Shiloh to be surprised, was relegated by the pedantic Halleck to the innocuous position as second-in-command of the "army group." Thomas' wing included five divisions—four from the Army of the Tennessee and one from the Army of the Ohio. In the meantime, Thomas, on

3. Frederick W. Keil, *Thirty-fifth Ohio, A Narrative of Service from August, 1861, to 1864* (Fort Wayne: Archer, Housh & Co., 1894), pp. 60-61; James B. Shaw, *History of the Tenth Regiment Indiana Volunteer Infantry . . .* (Lafayette: Burt-Hayward Co., 1912), p. 165.

April 25, had been promoted to major general of United States Volunteers.[4]

General Halleck now put his 100,000-man army in motion. In the weeks since Shiloh, Beauregard's Confederate Army of the Mississippi had been reinforced, principally by General Van Dorn's Army of the West. The 50,000 Rebels had strongly fortified Corinth, throwing up extensive lines of rifle-pits and numerous batteries and by felling an abatis. The approaches to the Confederate right and center were covered by Bridge and Phillips Creeks, and to their left by Cane Creek.

General Thomas' Right Wing advanced via the Ridge Road and, by late afternoon on May 4, had halted and entrenched immediately beyond and to the west of Monterey. General Buell's wing, traveling the Hamburg Road, by the same date had taken post south and east of Monterey, on Thomas' left; and General Pope's columns, moving out from Hamburg Landing, had reached Sevenmile Creek on the 3d, while one of his divisions, crossing that stream, had occupied Farmington, four miles east of Corinth.

From then until the evening of May 29, General Halleck's host inched its way forward. Then, on the night of the 29th, Beauregard, having made preparations that enabled him to send off his sick and wounded and most of his supplies, stole a march on the cautious Halleck. Corinth was evacuated and the Confederate army retreated 50 miles down the Mobile & Ohio Railroad to Tupelo.[5]

General Thomas, in a report dated June 3, described the operations of his wing during the investment of Corinth. His report read:

> Hdqrs. Right Wing Army of the Tennessee,
> *Camp, near Corinth, Miss., June 3, 1862.*
> General: I have the honor to submit the following report of the operations of the right wing Army of the Tennessee before Corinth:
> On the 4th ultimo the right wing commenced its move upon Corinth, Maj. Gen. William T. Sherman's division taking up a position to the right of Monterey toward the Purdy and Corinth road, supported by Brigadier-General [Stephen A.]

4. Van Horne, *History,* I, 126-27.
5. Force, pp. 183-91.

Hurlbut's division on his left, Brig. Gen. T. W. Sherman's division taking position on the main road from Monterey to Corinth, with Generals [Thomas A.] Davies' and [Thomas J.] McKean's divisions in reserve. Major-General Sherman's right flank, being much exposed, was intrenched immediately.

On the 7th ultimo the right wing again moved forward, occupying the ground from the Monterey and Corinth to the Purdy and Farmington roads, intrenching the same day.

On the 16th the right wing was again advanced across Seven Mile Creek, occupying the ground in front of the Purdy and Farmington road, and extending from the Monterey and Corinth to the Purdy and Corinth roads. This advance was made in the face of a strong resistance from the enemy, who was in force in front of each of the wings of my command. The ground taken up was strongly intrenched the same day by all the troops. From this time until our next advance there was considerable skirmishing between our pickets and those of the enemy, our pickets cautiously but steadily advancing from day to day and always holding the ground they had gained.

On the 17th ultimo, Major General [W. T.] Sherman, with a regiment and a section of artillery from his division, drove in the enemy's pickets at the crossing of Phillips' Creek and occupied their position. The same day Brigadier Gen. T. W. Sherman drove a force of the enemy in his front across Bridge Creek, on the Monterey and Corinth road, and occupied with his pickets, supported by a strong reserve, all the ground in his front as far as the creek.

On the 21st ultimo Major General Sherman's division, supported by Brigadier-General Hurlbut, advanced to Russell's house, General Sherman taking up and fortifying a strong position, extending from Russell's house, on the Gravel Hill road, to the main road from Purdy to Corinth, refusing the right flank. General Hurlbut, connecting with Sherman's left, extended in a southerly direction along the main ridge between Phillips' Creek and Bridge Creek. Brigadier-General Davies, connecting with Hurlbut's left, extended along the same ridge to the position held by General [John] McArthur's brigade, of McKean's division, the latter connecting with General [Albin F.] Schoepf's brigade, which had moved forward from its last position, and stretching across Bridge Creek, nearly east, connected with the center of Brigadier-

General Sherman's division, which had advanced but little. The enemy made no serious opposition to this move, except in front of General Davies, who, in advancing his pickets before taking his position, encountered one brigade of the enemy posted on the Corinth side of Phillips' Creek. A few rounds from one of his field batteries dispersed them, and the different divisions intrenched their positions without further molestation.

About 10 o'clock a. m. that day our pickets reported that there appeared to be great commotion in Corinth, and there was every indication that the enemy would attack the right wing in force. I accordingly made all the dispositions necessary to receive them, but continued the work on the intrenchments until they were completed. Two days afterward we were informed by deserters that [Braxton] Bragg and [Earl] Van Dorn were to have attacked us that morning, but found on sending their scouts forward that we already held the position they intended to have taken up; consequently they withdrew.

On the 28th ultimo Major-General [W. T.] Sherman, with his division, supported by General Hurlbut and a part of General Davies' on the left, and General [John A.] Logan, of [Henry M.] Judah's division [of McClernand's Reserve], on his right, advanced along the main Corinth road and took up a strong position within a few hundred yards of the enemy's outer intrenchments. This advance was met with more determined opposition on the part of the enemy than any we had previously made. Every inch of ground was obstinately contested until we had gained our position, and soon after a strong effort was made by the enemy to drive us from it, which was met by our men with so much coolness and determination that it terminated in a complete withdrawal from our immediate front.

On the 29th there was comparative quiet all along the front of the right wing. Brigadier-General [T. W.] Sherman moved two brigades of his division across Bridge Creek, to fill up the gap between the left of General McKean's division and the right of General Buell's army corps, which had been advanced the day before.

About 5 a. m. on the 30th ultimo, several explosions being heard in the direction of Corinth, General Halleck telegraphed directly to Major-General [W. T.] Sherman to move forward his division, cautiously feel the enemy, and ascertain what they were doing, and sent me an order to support General Sherman's advance with as many troops as would be necessary. I immediately ordered one brigade from General Hurlbut's division to the support of Major-General Sherman, and directed Generals Davies and McKean to hold their divisions in readiness to move at a moment's notice. Major-General Sherman, anticipating General Halleck's order, was ready to move when the order was received, and moved forward, with his division in three columns, pursuing the enemy so closely that they barely had sufficient time to cross Tuscumbia Creek and destroy the bridge before the advance of General Sherman was upon their rear guard.

The cheerfulness with which labor in the trenches was performed by the officers and men, and their steady, energetic, and soldierly bearing on every advance evinces a state of discipline highly commendable, to which I take great pleasure in calling the attention of the general [Halleck] commanding the department. There were no casualties in the right wing on the 30th. Those occurring previously have been mentioned in the reports of the division commanders. Quite a number of prisoners were taken by Major-General Sherman's division during the pursuit on the 30th ultimo. Their number and rank will be reported to the provost-marshal by him.

Very respectfully, your obedient servant,

Geo. H. Thomas,

*Major-General, U. S. Volunteers, Commanding.*

Brig. Gen. G. W. Cullum,

*Chief of Staff, Hdqrs. Department of the Mississippi.*[6]

The evacuation and occupation of Corinth compelled the Confederates to abandon Fort Pillow on the Mississippi, on June 4. Two days later, the Mississippi squadron, descending the river, smashed the Confederates' River Defense Fleet as thousands watched from the Memphis bluffs. Memphis was surrendered and General Halleck detached W. T. Sherman's and Hurlbut's divisions from Thomas' wing and marched them west to strengthen the Union grip on that city. Meanwhile, Pope's wing, charged with the pursuit of Beauregard's army, had been recalled and went into camp near Rienzi.

6. OR, I, X, pt. 1, pp. 738-40.

On June 9, Halleck, in accordance with instructions from President Lincoln, ordered General Buell to turn his wing eastward toward Chattanooga. As he advanced, Buell was to repair the Memphis & Charleston Railroad. The next day, Halleck revoked the order by which the armies had been divided into a right wing, center, left wing and reserve, and Grant, Buell and Pope were ordered to respectively resume command of their armies of the Tennessee, the Ohio, and the Mississippi. Coincidentally, Thomas, who had not been happy as a wing commander, was placed in charge of the Corinth garrison. Thus was the mighty army group scattered and the initiative that seemingly had the Western Confederates on the ropes yielded by the Federals.[7]

Halleck remained at Corinth for another five weeks, before leaving for Washington, on July 16, to assume new duties as general-in-chief.

On June 11, General Buell had moved out and by the end of the month three of his six divisions were camped in and around Athens, Alabama, while Buell had established his headquarters at Huntsville. Meanwhile, Thomas had left Corinth, resumed command of the Army of the Ohio's First Division, and had deployed his regiments to repair and guard the Memphis & Charleston's bridges and trestles from Iuka, Mississippi, eastward to Decatur, Alabama. Thomas had his headquarters at Tuscumbia and posted a combat team at Eastport to protect that vital supply depot, with a strong cavalry picket at Russellville.

In mid-July, General Buell alerted Thomas to be ready to recall his scattered units and be prepared to join the advance divisions as they felt their way cautiously eastward toward Chattanooga. Upon being relieved from guarding the 66 miles of railroad by troops from the Army of the Mississippi, now led by Major General William S. Rosecrans, Thomas crossed the Tennessee on the 27th, at Florence. He marched along dusty roads through Athens and Huntsville, then veered northeast, crossed into Tennessee, and reached Decherd on the Nashville & Chattanooga Railroad, on August 5.[8]

7. Francis V. Greene, *The Mississippi* (New York: Charles Scribner's Sons, 1882), pp. 29-36.
8. Van Horne, *History*, I, 142-45.

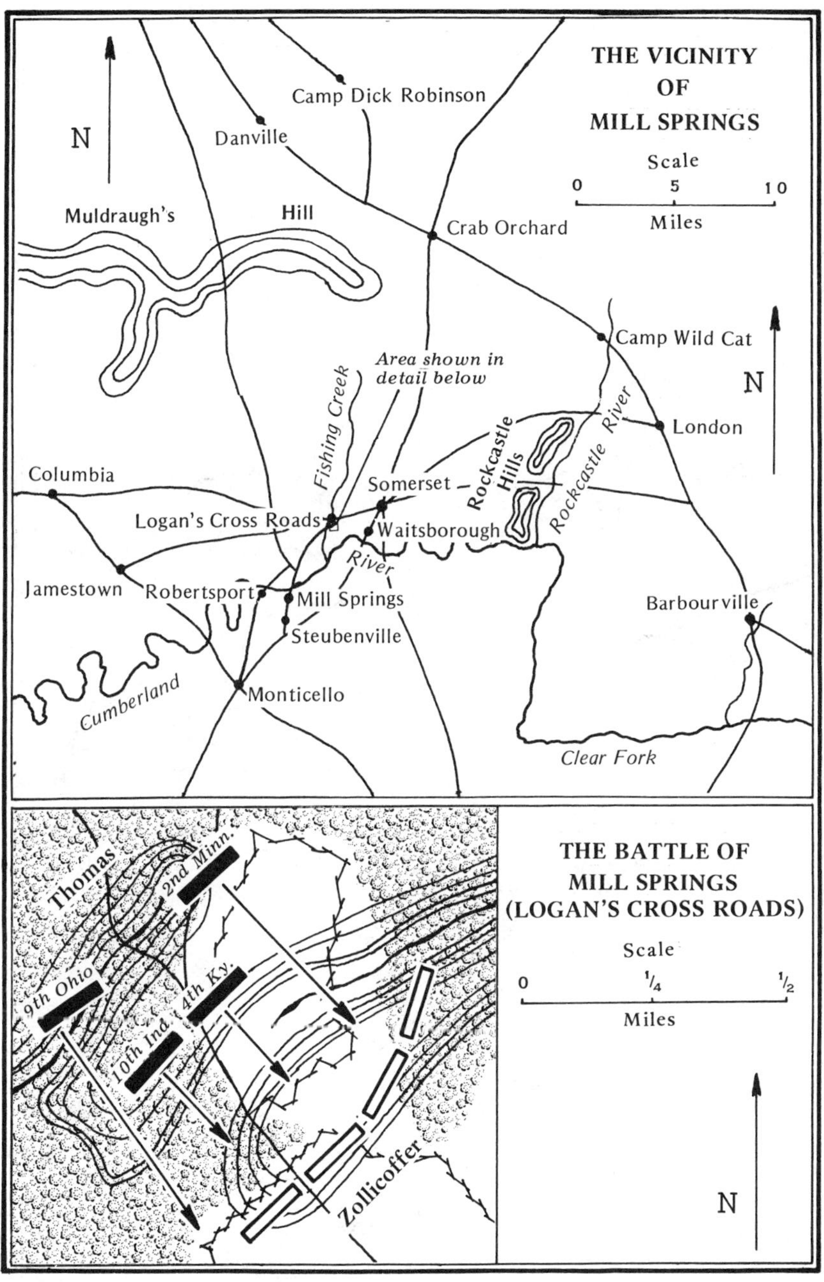

THE VICINITY
OF
MILL SPRINGS
Scale
0 5 10
Miles
N
Camp Dick Robinson
Danville
Muldraugh's Hill
Crab Orchard
Camp Wild Cat
N
London
Fishing Creek
Area shown in detail below
Rockcastle Hills
Rockcastle River
Columbia
Somerset
Logan's Cross Roads
Waitsborough
River
Jamestown
Robertsport
Mill Springs
Barbourville
Steubenville
Cumberland
Monticello
Clear Fork
THE BATTLE OF
MILL SPRINGS
(LOGAN'S CROSS ROADS)
Scale
0 1/4 1/2
Miles
N
Thomas
2nd Minn.
9th Ohio
10th Ind.
4th Ky.
Zollicoffer

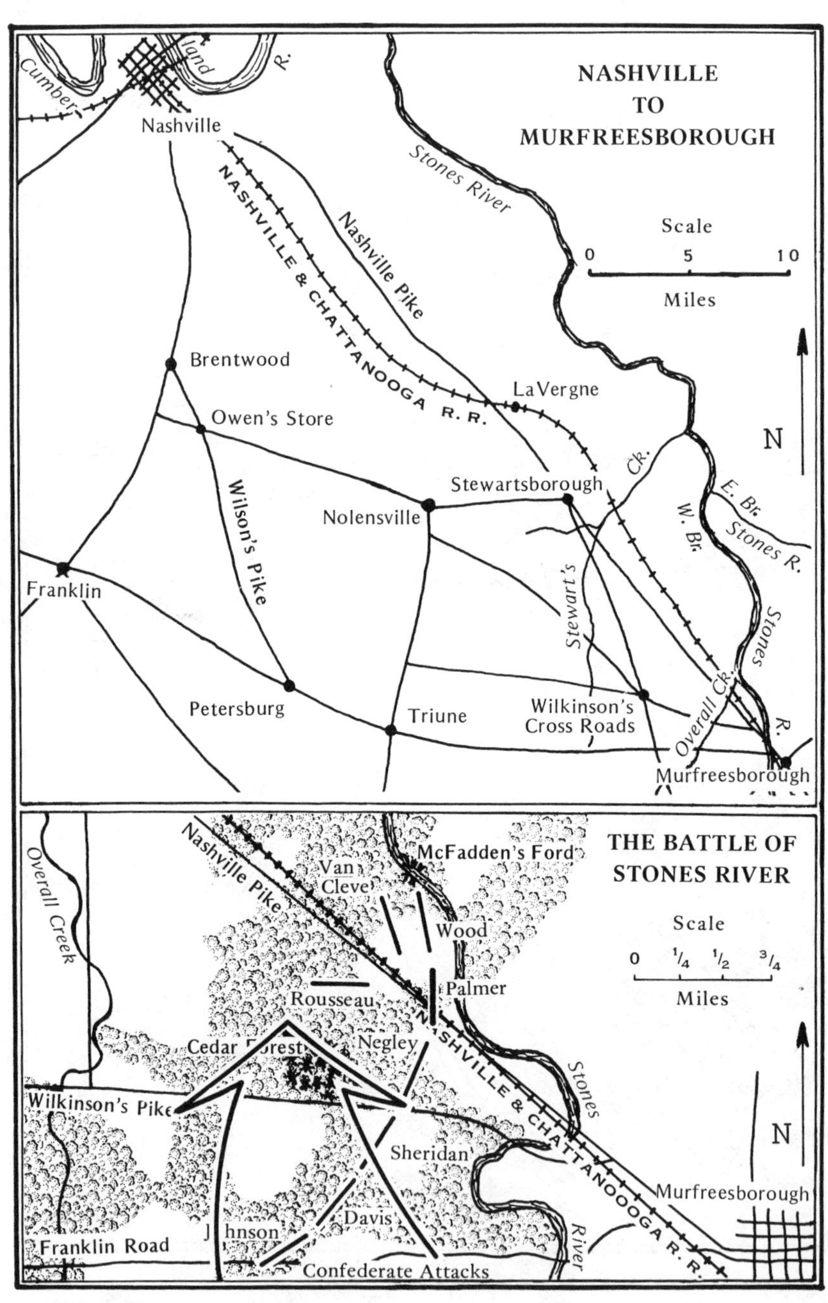
NASHVILLE
TO
MURFREESBOROUGH
Cumberland R.
Nashville
Stones River
Scale
0 5 10
Miles
N
NASHVILLE & CHATTANOOGA R. R.
Nashville Pike
Brentwood
Owen's Store
LaVergne
Wilson's Pike
Stewartsborough
Nolensville
Stewart's
Ck.
W. Br.
E. Br. Stones R.
Stones R.
Franklin
Petersburg
Triune
Wilkinson's
Cross Roads
Overall Ck.
Murfreesborough

THE BATTLE OF
STONES RIVER
Overall Creek
Nashville Pike
McFadden's Ford
Van
Cleve
Wood
Palmer
Rousseau
Negley
Cedar Forest
Scale
0 1/4 1/2 3/4
Miles
N
NASHVILLE & CHATTANOOGA R. R.
Stones
River
Wilkinson's Pike
Sheridan
Murfreesborough
Davis
Johnson
Franklin Road
Confederate Attacks

Meanwhile, General Braxton Bragg, Thomas' old comrade from the Third Artillery and General Taylor's Mexican War campaigns, had replaced General Beauregard as leader of the Confederate Army of the Mississippi. Bragg lost no time in employing the railroads to best Buell in the race for Chattanooga. Beginning on July 23, Bragg utilized the iron horse to shuttle his infantry and artillery from Tupelo by way of Mobile, Montgomery, and Atlanta to Chattanooga. His cavalry and trains, following roads well to the south of the Tennessee River, rejoined the army in the shadow of Lookout Mountain. The departure of Bragg left Major General Sterling Price's Army of the West to guard the Mobile & Ohio south of Corinth.

Bragg did not pause at Chattanooga but boldly took the offensive. On August 28, his divisions, organized into two corps, crossed the Tennessee River, snaked across Waldens Ridge, and up the Sequatchie Valley. Meanwhile, on August 14, Major General Edmund Kirby Smith's army had departed Knoxville, passed through Rogers' Gap 20 miles west of Cumberland Gap, and on August 30 routed a strong Union force near Richmond, Kentucky. Three days later, Smith's troops entered Lexington, in the heart of the Bluegrass Region.

Buell's Army of the Ohio was deployed to facilitate a rapid concentration against Bragg's columns, should they march from Chattanooga to the west or northwest. Generals Alexander M. McCook's and George Crittenden's divisions were at Battle Creek, William Nelson's at McMinnville, George H. Thomas' and Thomas J. Wood's along or near the Nashville & Chattanooga Railroad, and Lovell Rousseau's on the Central Alabama Railroad. But Buell, beset by the fog of war, hesitated at Decherd for several weeks as Bragg completed his build-up.[9]

Andrew Johnson, the hard-boiled Union governor of Tennessee, had already lost confidence in Buell. Johnson wrote Thomas, expressing grave concern over "dilatory steps," as he expressed it, to drive back the Rebels. The governor, putting it bluntly, hoped Thomas would be given the task of beating Bragg.[10] Thomas did

9. *Ibid.*, pp. 151-52. Rousseau commanded the division formerly led by Brigadier General Ormsby M. Mitchel. On August 16, General Nelson was relieved of command of the Fourth Division and ordered to Kentucky.
10. Cleaves, p. 108.

not agree. Loyal to his commander, in the face of what he perceived as a politician's interfering in army plans, Thomas answered the governor on August 16:

> Your favor of this day's date has just been handed me. I learned from it for the first time that you had urged me as the commander of the expedition to be sent into East Tennessee. Although I am under obligation to you for your favorable opinion, still I must earnestly hope that I may not be placed in the position for several reasons.
>
> One particular reason is that we have never yet had a commander of any expedition who has been allowed to work out his own policy, and it is entirely impossible for the most able general in the world to conduct a campaign with success when his hands are tied as it were by the constant apprehension that his plans may be interfered with at any moment, either by higher authority directly or through the influence of others who may have other plans or other motives of policy.
>
> I believe that the relief of East Tennessee has been entrusted to an able commander and that he will eventually give it sure and permanent relief. Our enemies are at this time fully aware of the desperate condition of their affairs and that the possession of both Tennessee and Kentucky is absolutely necessary to them or their cause is lost. . . .
>
> I am sure that I can confidently assure you that General Buell's dispositions will eventually free all Tennessee and go very far to crush the rebellion entirely. If our Army will not permit itself to degenerate with idleness the rebels will be crushed in 60 days, for the Confederacy cannot possibly subsist its troops a great while longer.[11]

Bragg's lean, hungry columns marched farther and faster than the Federals, while Buell had trouble making hard decisions during the feints and counter-feints that saw the armies head back toward Kentucky. Buell, compelled to shield Nashville, found himself outmaneuvered, as the Confederates tramped through Sparta, Cookville, Glasgow, and captured Munfordville, Kentucky, and its more than 4,000 defenders on September 17. Bragg now interposed between Buell and Louisville. To reach Louisville, Buell would have to attack Bragg's army strongly posted behind

11. Ltr., Thomas to Johnson, Aug. 16, 1862, Henry E. Huntington Library.

Green River. Bragg, who till now seemed destined to be a great captain, blundered. Abandoning his key position on the 21st, he turned his army east toward Frankfort, where he intended to inaugurate Richard Hawes as Confederate governor of Kentucky, and to rendezvous with Kirby Smith's army that had been threatening Cincinnati.

On the march up from Middle Tennessee, General Thomas had been rushed to Nashville to guard the city. There he remained from September 7 to the 15th, strengthening the defenses and endeavoring to pacify fire-breathing Governor Johnson. When he started for Kentucky to reinforce General Buell, Thomas left Brigadier General James S. Negley's 6,000-man division to garrison the city. Thomas reported to Buell at Prewitt's Knob on the 20th.[12]

Bragg, having moved aside, Buell's columns marched for Louisville, the vanguard entering the city on September 25. Thomas reached the city two days later.

On the 29th, orders arrived from Washington directing General Buell to turn over his command to George Thomas. Called to army headquarters from his command post outside Louisville, Thomas found the city agog with excitement over news that Brigadier General Jefferson C. Davis had shot and killed General Nelson in the lobby of the Galt House. Thomas walked to Buell's Galt House room and announced his decision to decline the command.[13]

"I answered," Buell recalled:
> that I could not consent to his doing so on any ground that was personal to me, and that if his determination was fixed, I must be allowed to see the message he prepared to send. He then prepared the following dispatch: "General Buell's preparations have been completed to move against the enemy and I respectfully ask that he may be retained in command. My position is very embarrassing, not being as well informed as I should be as the commander of this army and in the assumption of such responsibility."[14]

12. OR, I, XVI, pt. II, pp. 516, 522-23, 530-31.
13. Cleaves, p. 112.
14. Van Horne, *Thomas*, pp. 75-76; OR, I, XVI, pt. 1, pp. 544-55; Don Carlos Buell, "East Tennessee and the Campaign of Perryville," *Battles and Leaders of the Civil War*, III, 44.

At 11:45 A.M., Thomas telegraphed the War Department, asking General-in-Chief Halleck to reconsider the order for Buell's removal. He noted that Buell had completed preparations for going out in search of the enemy, and he should be permitted to implement his plans. Thomas reminded Halleck that, because he was not as well informed as he should be regarding Buell's dispositions, the subject was embarrassing. Upon receipt of Thomas' telegram, Halleck notified Buell and Thomas that the order for Buell's removal was suspended.[15]

Thomas' stance put a heavy burden on Buell; he must seek out and destroy Bragg's army. On Wednesday, October 1, the reorganized Army of the Ohio advanced from Louisville, so as to converge on units of General Bragg's army then in and around Bardstown. Buell marched with three corps, a force of about 60,000 troops. The "First" commanded by General Alexander M. McCook; the "Second" by General Thomas L. Crittenden; and the "Third" by Brigadier General Charles C. Gilbert. Thomas, serving as Buell's deputy, rode with Crittenden. Of Buell's 60,000 men, about 61 percent or 36,900 troops were engaged at the Battle of Perryville. On Tuesday afternoon, October 7, the Union forces under Buell sighted the enemy several miles west of Perryville. General Buell planned to attack the next morning. When the morning of the 8th came, Buell's forces, not yet in position, did not attack. Bragg's troops started the bloody battle which lasted throughout the day with the Union forces, except for McCook's corps, holding firm. Thomas himself, arriving on the battlefield with a part of Crittenden's corps, was directed by verbal orders delivered by Captain O. A. Mack of his staff, to the right and was told to await further instructions. No orders were forthcoming and Thomas did not engage because he had no knowledge of the battle that was raging on the far left against McCook. In fact, General Thomas received no word at all until 6:30 that evening when he was handed the following order:

October 8, 1862, 6: 30 p. m.

General Thomas, Second in Command:

The First Corps [McCook's], on our left, has been very

15. OR, I, XVI, pt. 1, pp. 554-55.

114

heavily engaged. The left and center of this corps gained ground, but the right of it yielded a little. Press your lines forward as far as possible to-night and get into position to make a vigorous attack in the morning at daylight. If you have got your troops into a position which you deem advantageous it will not be advisable to make a change for the purpose of complying with the general's [Buell's] instructions for you sent by Captain Mack. It may be as well to halt the division ordered to the center and let it wait where it is for further orders.

The general [Buell] desires to see you in person as soon tonight as your duties will permit you to come over.

Respectfully,

James B. Fry,
*Colonel and Chief of Staff.*[16]

General Buell, anticipating a renewal of the battle the next day, learned on the morning of the 9th that the Confederates had withdrawn during the night to Harrodsburg, which lay about 10 miles northeast of Perryville. Thus, there was no further activity until Buell ordered pursuit on Sunday, October 12.

The results of this battle proved less than the Union army and the Lincoln administration had anticipated. In addition, Federal losses were severe. Prominent among those killed were Brigadier Generals James S. Jackson, commander of the 10th Division of McCook's Corps, and William R. Terrill, leader of the 33d Brigade, and Jackson's senior brigade commander, both of whom fell while gallantly leading their men against the enemy.

Some two weeks after the Perryville battle, General Buell was sacked by the War Department. On October 24, General-in-Chief Halleck signed an order addressed to Buell, informing him that he was to turn over the command of the Department of the Cumberland, as the Department of the Ohio had been redesignated, to General Rosecrans. This order had been triggered by the Lincoln administration's continued disenchantment with Buell. Instead of hounding Bragg's weary columns as they abandoned the Bluegrass Region and recoiled into East Tennessee by way of Cumberland Gap, Buell had ordered his corps to concentrate at Bowling Green and Glasgow, preparatory to reopening the

16. OR, I, XVI, pt. II, p. 588.

railroad south from Bowling Green to Nashville.

Buell was at Louisville, to where he had returned for treatment of a leg injured by a fall from his horse, when he was relieved by General Rosecrans. Subsequently, Rosecrans likened his visit to Buell's headquarters "to that of a constable bearing a writ for ejection of a tenant than a general coming to relieve a brother officer in command of an army."[17]

News of Buell's replacement by Rosecrans distressed Thomas, who was supervising the massing of the army in and around Bowling Green. On October 30, Thomas protested to Halleck:

> On the 29th of last September I received an order . . . placing me in command of the Department of the Ohio and directing General Buell to turn over his troops to me. This order reached me just as General Buell had by most extraordinary exertions prepared his army to pursue and drive the rebels from Kentucky. Feeling convinced that great injustice would be done him if not permitted to carry out his plans, I requested that he might be retained in command. The order relieving him was suspended, but today I am officially informed that he is relieved by General Rosecrans, my junior. Although I do not claim for myself any superior ability, yet feeling conscious that no just cause exists for over-slaughing me by placing me under my junior, I feel deeply mortified and aggrieved at the action taken in this matter. . . .
>
> P.S. I do not desire the command of the Department of the . . . [Cumberland] but that an officer senior in rank should be sent here if I am retained on duty in it.[18]

Thomas did not personally object to Rosecrans, whom he deemed competent, however, he made no secret of his feelings, when he had a frank discussion with Rosecrans upon the latter's arrival at Bowling Green, on November 2. Thomas told Rosecrans of the reasons for his protest and coincidentally declared he would like to have a command in Texas, where he knew the country. Rosecrans would not hear of this, as he counted on Thomas for help. His new command, he continued, was all the more desirable, because Thomas was his senior major general. He assured Thomas that the command had not been solicited and shored up Thomas'

17. *Military Order of the Loyal Legion of the United States, District of Columbia Commandery, War Papers*, Vol. LXVIII, 5-6.
18. Piatt, *Thomas*, pp. 199-200.

ego, by remarking, "You and I have been friends for many years and I shall especially need your support and advice." Thomas was not disposed to sulk, and when offered his choice of commands in the new organization, Thomas announced he would prefer to have a corps rather than be deputy army commander.[19]

Consequently, on November 5, when Rosecrans reorganized the 14th Army Corps, as the troops in the field had been recently designated, into a Right Wing, Center, and Left Wing, he named Thomas to command the Center. General McCook was to lead the Right Wing and General Crittenden the Left. Five divisions were assigned to the Center and three to each wing. Rosecrans then told Thomas to advance two of his divisions to Gallatin, Tennessee, and hasten the repair of the Louisville & Nashville Railroad.[20]

By November 26, this task was completed and through locomotives and cars were again running between Bowling Green and Nashville, where Rosecrans was gathering his forces. During the next four weeks, a major effort was made to supply the troops for a winter campaign and to stockpile the Nashville magazines. All the while the War Department was pressuring Rosecrans to take the field and drive the Confederates out of Middle Tennessee.

General Bragg, upon reaching Knoxville, on his retreat from Kentucky, again employed the railroads to rapidly shift his divisions by way of Chattanooga to Middle Tennessee. There, he took position in and around Murfreesboro, 30 miles southeast of Nashville and prepared to place his troops in winter quarters.

On December 22, General Thomas transferred his headquarters from Gallatin to Nashville and these assembled for field service two of his five divisions (James S. Negley's and Lovell H. Rosseau's) and Moses B. Walker's brigade of Fry's division. Fry's other two brigades and Joseph J. Reynolds' division guarded the Louisville & Nashville Railroad and Robert B. Mitchell's division garrisoned Nashville. Four days later, on the 26th, Rosecrans put his 41,400 men in motion toward the foe. In contrast to his passive role at Perryville, Thomas saw savage combat at Stones River.

19. *Society of the Army of the Cumberland, Eighteenth Reunion, Washington, D. C. 1887* (Cincinnati, 1888), p. 48.
20. Van Horne, *History*, I, 207-08.

Indeed, his strategic sense and tactical grasp of the situation were important factors in Rosecrans' success in redeploying his forces and checking what for a number of hours on the last day of the year seemed to be an irresistible Confederate surge.

Rosecrans' intent was to attack Bragg's army on Wednesday, December 31, with Crittenden's Left Wing, while McCook's three divisions blunted the Confederate onset. This plan, however, miscarried when Bragg's forces struck first, assailing McCook's divisions. Two of McCook's divisions were quickly shattered, as McCook was caught off guard. This disaster forced Rosecrans to abandon his battle plan and to summon General Thomas to redeploy his troops to cover the retreat of McCook's people.

Under the cool and calm Thomas, the new Federal line repelled the Rebel onslaught, inflicting severe losses on the Confederates. The day's fighting ended with the Confederates unable to capitalize on their initial successes. The opposing armies watched and waited on January 1, 1863, and on the 2d a Rebel attack on the Union left was mauled. Then, on the night of January 3-4, General Bragg ordered his troops to retreat, because he felt his army could not withstand a Union attack. The way was clear for the Federals to march into Murfreesboro, where they remained for nearly six months. At the battle of Stones River, Thomas evinced to a marked degree the staying power which was to serve him so well at Chickamauga.

Some two weeks after the battle of Stones River, General Thomas filed his report of the recent campaign. It read:

Hdqrs. (Center) Fourteenth Army Corps,<br>
Department of the Cumberland<br>
*Murfreesborough, Tenn., January 15, 1863.*

Major: I have the honor to submit to the major-general commanding the Department of the Cumberland the following report of the operations of that part of my command which was engaged in the battle of Stone's River, in front of Murfreesborough:

It is proper to state here that two brigades of Fry's division and Reynolds' entire division were detained near Gallatin and along the Louisville and Nashville Railroad, to watch the movements of the rebel leader [John H.] Morgan, who had been, for a long time, on the watch for an opportunity to

118

destroy the railroad. Rousseau's, Negley's, and Mitchell's divisions, and Walker's brigade, of Fry's division, were concentrated at Nashville, but Mitchell's division being required to garrison Nashville, my only available force was Rousseau's and Negley's divisions, and Walker's brigade, of Fry's division, about 13,295 effective men.

December 26, Negley's division, followed by Rousseau's division and Walker's brigade, marched by the Franklin pike to Brentwood, at that point taking the Wilson's pike. Negley and Rousseau were to have encamped for the night at Owen's store.

On reaching the latter place, Negley, hearing heavy firing in the direction of Nolensville, left his train with a guard, to follow, and pushed forward with his troops to the support of Brig. Gen. [Jefferson] C. Davis, commanding the advanced division of McCook's corps, Davis having become hotly engaged with the enemy posted in Nolensville, and in the pass [Knob Gap] through the hills south of that village. Rousseau encamped with his division at Owen's store; Walker with his brigade at Brentwood.

During the night a very heavy rain fell, making the cross-roads almost impassable, and it was not until night of the 27th that Rousseau reached Nolensville with his troops and train. Negley remained at Nolensville until 10 a. m. on the 27th, when, having brought his train across from Wilson's pike, he moved to the east, over an exceedingly rough by-road, to the right of Crittenden, at Stewartsborough, on the Murfreesborough pike. Walker, by my orders, retraced his steps from Brentwood, and crossed over to the Nolensville pike.

December 28, Negley remained in camp at Stewartsborough, bringing his train from the rear. Rousseau reached Stewartsborough on the night of the 28th. His train arrived early next day.

December 29, Negley's division crossed Stewart's Creek, 2 miles southwest and above the turnpike bridge, and marched in support of the head and right flank of Crittenden's corps, which moved by the Murfreesborough pike to a point within 2 miles of Murfreesborough. The enemy fell back before our advance, contesting the ground obstinately with their cavalry rear guard. Rousseau remained in camp at Stewartsborough, detaching [John C.] Starkweather's brigade, with a section of artillery, to the Jefferson pike crossing of Stone's River, to observe the movements of the enemy in that direction. Walker reached Stewartsborough from the Nolensville pike about dark.

December 30, a cavalry force of the enemy [Joseph Wheeler's brigade], something over 400 strong, with two pieces of artillery, attacked Starkweather about 9 a. m., but was soon driven off. The enemy opened a brisk fire on Crittenden's advance, doing but little execution, however, about 7 a. m.

During the morning Negley's division was obliqued to the right, and took up a position on the right of [John M.] Palmer's division, of Crittenden's corps, and was then advanced through a dense cedar thicket, several hundred yards in width, to the Wilkinson Cross-Roads, driving the enemy's skirmishers steadily and with considerable loss. Our loss comparatively small.

About noon [Philip H.] Sheridan's division of McCook's corps, approached by the Wilkinson Cross-Roads, joined Negley's right, McCook's two other divisions coming up on Sheridan's right, [Rosecrans' army] thus forming a continuous line, the left resting on Stone's River, the right stretching in a westerly direction, and resting on high, wooded ground, a short distance to the south of the Wilkinson Cross-Roads, and, as has since been ascertained nearly parallel with the enemy's intrenchment thrown up on the sloping land bordering the northwest bank of Stone's River. Rousseau's division (with the exception of Starkweather's brigade), being ordered up from Stewartsborough, reached the position occupied by the army about 4 p. m., and bivouacked on the Murfreesborough pike in rear of the center.

During the night of the 30th I sent orders to Walker to take up a strong position near the turnpike bridge over Stewart's Creek, and defend the position against any attempts of the enemy's cavalry to destroy it. Rousseau was ordered to move by 6 a. m. on the 31st to a position in rear of Negley. This position placed his division with its left on the Murfreesborough pike, and its right extending into the cedar thicket through which Negley had marched on the 30th. In front of Negley's position, bordering a large open field, reaching to the Murfreesborough pike, a heavy growth of timber extended in a southerly direction toward the river. Across the field, running in an easterly direction, the enemy had thrown up rifle pits at intervals, from the timber to the river bank, to the east side of the turnpike. Along this line of intrenchments, on an eminence about 800 yards from Negley's position, and nearly in front of his left, some cannon had been placed, affording the enemy great advantage in covering an attack on our center. However, Palmer, Negley, and Sheridan held the position their troops had so manfully won the morning of the 30th against every attempt to drive them back, and remained in line of battle during the night.

December 31, between 6 and 7 a. m., the enemy, having massed a heavy force on McCook's right during the night of the 30th, attacked and drove it back, pushing his division[s] in pursuit *en echelon*, and in supporting distance, until he had gained sufficient ground to our rear to wheel his masses to the right and throw them upon the right flank of the center, at the same moment attacking Negley and Palmer in front with a greatly superior force. To counteract this movement, I had ordered Rousseau to place two brigades, with a battery, to the right and rear of Sheridan's division, facing toward the west, so as to support Sheridan, should he be able to hold his ground, or to cover him, should he be compelled to fall back.

About 11 o'clock General Sheridan reported to me that his ammunition was entirely out, and he would be compelled to fall back to get more. As it became necessary for General Sheridan to fall back, the enemy pressed on still farther to our rear, and soon took up a position which gave them a concentrated cross-fire of musketry and cannon on Negley's and Rousseau's troops at short range. This compelled me to fall back out of the cedar woods, and take up a line along a depression in the open ground, within good musket range of the edge of the woods, while the artillery was retired to the high ground to the right [north] of the [Nashville] turnpike. From this last position we were enabled to drive back the enemy, cover the formation of our troops, and secure the center on high ground. In the execution of this last movement, the regular brigade, under Lieutenant Colonel [Oliver L.] Shepherd, Eighteenth U. S. Infantry, came under a most murderous fire, losing 22 officers and 508 men in killed and wounded, but, with the co-operation of [Benjamin F.] Scribner's and [John] Beatty's brigades and [Francis L.] Guenther's and

[Cyrus O.] Loomis' batteries, gallantly held its ground against overwhelming odds. The center having succeeded in driving back the enemy from its front, and our artillery concentrating its fire on the cedar thicket on our right, drove him back far under cover, from which, though repeatedly attempting it, he could not make any advance.

January 1, 1863, repeated attempts were made by the enemy to advance on my position during the morning, but they were driven back before emerging from the woods. Colonel Starkweather's brigade of Rousseau's division and Walker's brigade of Fry's division having re-enforced us during the night, took post on the right of Rousseau and left of Sheridan, and bore their share in repelling the attempts of the enemy on the morning of the 1st instant.

For the details of the most valuable service rendered by these two brigades on December 30 and 31, 1862, and January 1, 2, and 3, 1863, I refer you to their reports. In this connection I also refer you to the report of Lieutenant Colonel [John G.] Parkhurst, commanding Ninth Michigan Infantry (on provost duty at my headquarters), for the details of most valuable services rendered by his command on December 31 and January 1 and 2. Negley's division was ordered early in the day to the support of McCook's right, and in which position it remained during the night.

January 2, about 7 a. m., the enemy opened a direct and cross fire from his batteries in our front, and from a position on the east bank of Stone's River to our left and front, at the same time making a strong demonstration with infantry, resulting, however, in no serious attack. Our artillery (Loomis', Guenther's, Stokes', and another battery, the commander's name I cannot now recall) soon drove back their infantry. Negley was withdrawn from the extreme right and placed in reserve behind Crittenden's right [near McFadden's Ford].

About 4 p. m. a division [Samuel Beatty's] of Crittenden's corps, which had crossed Stone's River to reconnoiter, was attacked by an overwhelming force of the enemy [John C. Breckinridge's reinforced division], and, after a gallant resistance, compelled to fall back. The movements of the enemy having been observed and reported by some of my troops in the center, I sent orders to Negley to advance to the support of Crittenden's troops, should they want help. This order was obeyed in most gallant style, and resulted in the complete annihilation of the Twenty-sixth Tennessee (rebel) Regiment and the capture of their flag; also in the capture of a battery [Byrne's Kentucky], which the enemy had been forced to abandon at the point of the bayonet.

January 3, soon after daylight, the Forty-second Indiana, on picket in a clump of woods about 800 yards in front of our lines, was attacked by a brigade of the enemy, evidently by superior numbers, and driven in with considerable loss. Lieutenant-Colonel [James M.] Shanklin, commanding the regiment, was surrounded and taken prisoner while gallantly endeavoring to draw off his men from under the fire of such superior numbers. From this woods the enemy's sharpshooters continued to fire occasionally during the day on our pickets.

About 6 p. m. two regiments from Col. John Beatty's brigade, Rousseau's division, co-operating with two regiments of [James G.] Spears' brigade, of Negley's division, covered by the skillful and well-directed fire of Guenther's Fifth U. S. Artillery and Loomis' First Michigan Batteries, advanced on the woods and drove the enemy not only from their cover, but from their intrenchments, a short distance beyond.

For the details of this gallant night attack, I refer you to the reports of Brigadier-General Spears, commanding Third Brigade of Negley's division, and Col. John Beatty, commanding Second Brigade of Rousseau's division. The enemy having retreated during the night of the 3d, our troops were occupied during the morning of the 4th in burying the dead left on the field. In the afternoon one brigade of Negley's division was advanced to the crossing of Stone's River, with a brigade of Rousseau's division in supporting distance, in reserve.

January 5, my entire command, preceded by [David S.] Stanley's cavalry marched into Murfreesborough and took up the position which we now hold. The enemy's rear guard of cavalry was overtaken on the Shelbyville and Manchester roads, about 5 miles from Murfreesborough, and, after sharp skirmishing for two or three hours, was driven from our immediate front.

The conduct of my command from the time the army left Nashville to its entry into Murfreesborough is deserving of the highest praise, both for their patient endurance of the fatigues and discomforts of a five days' battle, and for the manly spirit exhibited by them in the various phases in this memorable contest. I refer you to the detailed reports of the

Consolidated report of casualties of the Center, Fourteenth Army Corps, in the five days' battle before Murfreesborough, Tenn., commencing December 31, 1862, and ending January 4, 1863.

| | In action | | | | Lost in action | | | | | | | | | | |
| | | | | | Killed | | Wounded | | Missing | | Horses | | | Guns | |
| | Commissioned officers | Enlisted men | Horses | Guns (artillery) | Commissioned | Enlisted | Commissioned | Enlisted | Commissioned | Enlisted | Killed | Wounded | Missing | Lost | Disabled |
|---|---|---|---|---|---|---|---|---|---|---|---|---|---|---|---|
| First Division, Major-General Rousseau. | 303 | 5,883 | | 18 | 8 | 171 | 43 | 903 | 3 | 324 | 8 | 5 | | | |
| Second Division, Brigadier-General Negley. | 237 | 4,632 | 257 | 13 | 11 | 167 | 47 | 704 | 1 | 308 | 62 | 24 | 9 | 6 | 1 |
| First Brigade, Third Div., Col. M. B. Walker. | 97 | 2,243 | | 6 | | | 4 | 19 | | 1 | | | | | |
| | 637 | 12,758 | 257 | 37 | 19 | 338 | 94 | 1,626 | 4 | 633 | 70 | 29 | 9 | 6 | 1 |

division and brigade commanders, forwarded herewith, for special mention of those officers and men of their commands whose conduct they thought worthy of particular notice.

All the members of my staff, Maj. G. E. Flynt, assistant adjutant-general; Lieut. Col. A. Von Schrader, Seventy-fourth Ohio, acting inspector-general; Capt. O. A. Mack, Thirteenth U. S. Infantry, acting chief commissary, and Capt. A. J. Mackay, chief quartermaster, were actively employed in carrying my orders to various parts of my command and in the execution of the appropriate duties of their office. Capt. O. A. Mack was dangerously wounded in the right hip and abdomen while conveying orders from me to Major-General Rousseau.

The officers of the signal corps attached to my headquarters did excellent service in their appropriate sphere, when possible, and as aides-de-camp, carrying orders. My escort, composed of a select detail from the First Ohio Cavalry, commanded by First Lieut. J. D. Barker, of the same regiment, who have been on duty with me for nearly a year, deserve commendation for the faithful performance of their appropriate duties. Private [Fulton] Guiteau was killed by a cannon shot on the morning of January 2. Surg. G. D. Beebe, medical director, deserves special mention for his efficient arrangements for moving the wounded from the field and giving them immediate attention.

Annexed hereto is a consolidated return of the casualties of my command. The details will be seen in the accompanying reports of division and brigade commanders.

Very respectfully, your obedient servant,

Geo. H. Thomas,
*Major-General of Volunteers, Commanding.*

Maj. C. Goddard,

*Assistant Adjutant General and Chief of Staff.*[21]

The Confederate army, following its retreat from Stones River and evacuation of Murfreesboro, took position with its right under Lieutenant General William J. Hardee headquartered at Wartrace on the Nashville & Chattanooga Railroad. The troops were

21. OR, I, XX, pt. 1, pp. 371-74.
22. *Ibid.,* p. 375.

posted to cover the gaps by which the area's roads traversed the Knobs. General Polk's corps, based on Shelbyville, held the Rebel left, while General Bragg established his headquarters and principal magazines at Tullahoma. The Confederate cavalry, superior in both numbers and leadership to Rosecrans', extended their front east to McMinnville and west to Columbia.

In hopes of forcing the Federals to abandon Nashville, Bragg, both before and after Stones River, employed his mounted arm to raid the Louisville & Nashville Railroad and to attack shipping plying the Cumberland River. During the first few weeks, following the Union occupation of Murfreesboro, these efforts by the hard-riding horse soldiers came close to success, as the Union troops were placed on half rations, and the army was threatened by scurvy. The crisis was weathered and Rosecrans moved to strengthen his cavalry.

To boost morale and take advantage of the personal prestige accrued as a result of the Stones River victory, Rosecrans asked the War Department for authority to designate the three wings into which the Army of the Cumberland was organized as corps as in the Army of the Potomac. Secretary of War Stanton agreed, replying, "The order for army corps will be issued today. There is nothing within my power to grant to yourself or your command that will not be cheerfully given." Consequently, on January 9, the War Department by General Order No. 9 redesignated Thomas' Center the 14th Corps, McCook's Right Wing the 20th Corps, and Crittenden's Left Wing the 21st Corps.[23]

The winter and spring of 1863 found the Union troops camped in and around Murfreesboro. Besides furnishing large working parties for construction of extensive fortifications, to be known as Fortress Rosecrans, there were daily drills and occasional field exercises. Supplies were brought forward and stockpiled in the Murfreesboro and Fortress Rosecrans magazines. Large numbers of recruits reported and Reynolds' division, relieved of its railroad-guarding responsibilities, was brought forward, as were Fry's other two brigades. By late spring Thomas' 14th Corps numbered some 26,000 effectives.[24]

23. Cist, p. 139; Van Horne, *History*, I, 287-88.
24. Van Horne, *History*, I, 288; Cleaves, pp. 139-40.

As early as March 14, one of Thomas' brigade commanders, John Beatty, reported, "The roads are becoming good and everybody is on horseback. The Army . . . looks better than it ever did before." A careful observer, Beatty left us some candid impressions of the army's senior officers:

> Crittenden . . . is a good drinker, and the same can be said of Rousseau. Rosecrans is an educated officer who has rubbed much against the world and has had experience. Rousseau is brave, but knows little of military science. McCook is a chucklehead. Wood and Crittenden know how to blow their own horns exceedingly well. Major-General Thomas is tall, heavy, sedate; whiskers and head grayish. Puts on less style than any of those named and is a gentlemanly, modest, reliable soldier . . . shaves the upper lip.[25]

The Army of the Cumberland, in the months following Stones River, was generous in granting furloughs. Many officers and men were given leaves to return to their homes to cultivate their fields and to plant their spring crops. General Thomas obtained a leave to travel to Troy, New York, to see his wife, but soon reconsidered and remained at Murfreesboro. Explaining his position, he noted he could not risk being away while there was a possibility that the Confederates might take the offensive. Other soldiers saw the situation differently. One day, W. F. G. Shanks recalled, an enlisted man, whittling on a stick, personally presented his request for a leave to the general.

"I ain't seen my old woman, general, for four months," he declared as he whittled.

"And I have not seen mine for two years," Thomas replied. "If your general can submit to such privation, certainly a private can."

"Don't know about that, general, you see me and my wife ain't made that way," the soldier answered. Whereupon, Thomas and his staff roared with laughter.[26]

Starting in March, the War Department began pressuring General Rosecrans to pull his troops out of their winter quarters, where they had made themselves comfortable, and to drive Bragg's Confederates south of the Tennessee River. Rosecrans

---

25. John Beatty, *Memoirs of a Volunteer* (New York: W. W. Norton & Co., 1946), p. 172.
26. Piatt, *Thomas*, pp. 329-34; W. F. G. Shanks, *Personal Recollections of Distinguished Generals* (New York: Harper & Bros., 1866), p. 72.

refused to be goaded into undertaking what he deemed to be a hasty and ill-advised action. As the weeks stretched into months, the correspondence between the Washington authorities and Rosecrans became more acrimonious.

This was particularly true from mid-May through the third week of June, after the Confederate War Department had detached large numbers of troops from Bragg's army to help provide General Joseph E. Johnston with an army to raise the Vicksburg siege. Five infantry brigades and a cavalry division were rushed to Mississippi from Middle Tennessee. Satisfied that the Rebels were employing their interior lines to concentrate against General Grant at Vicksburg, the War Department urged Rosecrans to take the offensive. Rosecrans finally yielded and alerted his corps commanders to be ready to march on June 24. He planned a feint by Major General Gordon Granger's recently constituted Reserve Corps against Bragg's left at Shelbyville, while his other three corps massed against Bragg's right.[27]

Rain beat down as the Union troops broke camp on the 24th. General McCook's 20th Corps, advancing on Wartrace, penetrated Liberty Gap and, in the campaign's hardest fight against men of Pat Cleburne's division, compelled the Confederates to retire on Bellbuckle. Colonel John T. Wilder's Lightning Brigade, spearheading General Thomas' thrust toward Manchester, routed the Rebels from Hoover's Gap. General Crittenden's 21st Corps on the Union left and rear occupied Bradyville, while Granger's on the right felt its way toward Shelbyville.

Continuing downpours slowed the Federals' march, but on the 26th Thomas' columns pressed ahead and on the 27th occupied Manchester. Coincidentally, Union horse soldiers, screening Granger's corps, drove Confederate cavalry from Guy's Gap and into the entrenchments covering Shelbyville.

By seizing Manchester, Rosecrans flanked Bragg's Shelbyville-Wartrace line and the Confederates pulled back to Tullahoma. While his divisions converged on Manchester, Rosecrans sent a flying column, on June 28, to strike the railroad in Bragg's rear.

27. Cist, pp. 147-53. In early June, Rosecrans had organized a Reserve Corps, consisting of three divisions (Absolom Baird's, J. D. Morgan's, and R. S. Granger's), to be led by Gordon Granger.

Wilder's mounted brigade arrived too late to destroy the Elk River railroad bridge, but a supporting infantry brigade tore up several hundred yards of track at Decherd.

Satisfied that his Middle Tennessee position had become untenable, Bragg determined to abandon the region. When Rosecrans' soldiers resumed the advance, they entered Tullahoma on July 1, capturing a few prisoners. Pressing on, Thomas' corps overtook the Rebel rear guard at Bethpage bridge. Next day, the Federals reached the rain-swollen Elk River to find the bridge destroyed and Bragg's cavalry guarding the south bank. Though the Federals crossed the river on the 3d, this ended the pursuit and the Tullahoma Campaign. Bragg's army retreated across the Cumberland Plateau and took position behind the Tennessee River. Rosecrans now called a halt, sent his troops into camp, and began stockpiling supplies for a thrust across the Tennessee and on to Chattanooga.

During the campaign, Rosecrans' army, at a cost of 560 killed, wounded, and missing, had repeatedly outmaneuvered Bragg compelling him to withdraw 85 miles and to evacuate several formidable positions, with the loss of 1,634 prisoners, 11 cannon, and large quantities of supplies.[28]

General Thomas, as was his habit, lost no time in promptly complying with War Department regulations. He submitted his report on the Tullahoma Campaign on July 8. It read:

Hdqrs. 14th Army Corps, Dept. of the Cumberland,
*Camp Winford, Tenn., July 8, 1863.*

General: I have the honor to transmit the following report of the operations of the Fourteenth Army Corps from the 24th ultimo to the present time:

The Third Division, Brigadier-General [John M.] Brannan commanding, having in accordance with orders previously given, reached Salem from Triune on the 23d, received orders to march with McCook's corps in the direction of Fosterville on the 24th, and on the 25th to join the other divisions of the Fourteenth Army Corps on the Manchester pike. The First Division (Rousseau's), Second Division (Negley's), and the Fourth Division (Reynolds') marched from Murfrees-

28. *Ibid.,* pp. 154-71.

borough June 24, on the Manchester pike, Reynolds' division to advance, starting at 4 a. m., with orders, if possible, to seize and hold Hoover's Gap; Rousseau's division marching at 7 a. m., to move to the support of Reynolds, in case he called upon him for assistance. Negley's division marched at 10 a. m., in reserve. A few miles from our picket station, Wilder's brigade, mounted infantry, Reynolds' division, encountered the enemy's mounted vedettes, which he drove upon their reserve (Third Confederate Cavalry), and drove the whole through Hoover's Gap and beyond McBride's Creek. Colonel Wilder then observing that the enemy were in force in the direction of Fairfield, and preparing to attack him, took up a strong position on the hills at the southern terminus of Hoover's Gap. The other two brigades [Hall's and Crook's] of Reynolds moved into and occupied the gap in rear of Wilder's force, and prepared for an attack from the front, having marched 17 miles.

While the division was taking its position, the First Brigade [Wilder's] was attacked by a superior force. The attack was promptly accepted by Wilder's brigade, supported by the Second [A. S. Hall's] and Third [George Crook's] Brigades, which were immediately ordered to the front, and posted on the ridge of woods on the extreme right, to prevent the enemy turning our right flank, which was being heavily engaged by a superior force. As these re-enforcements arrived, the enemy was forced to fall back from the woods, and the right made secure by posting three regiments of Crook's brigade in the woods from which the enemy had just been so gallantly driven by the Seventeenth and Seventy-second Indiana Volunteers and Ninety-third Illinois Volunteers, and the position maintained. General Rousseau was ordered to send forward one brigade to re-enforce Reynolds, which was done. Major [Sidney] Coolidge, commanding brigade of Regulars, reported soon after dark, and every preparation was made for an attack on the following morning. The First [Scribner's] and Second [H. A. Hambright's] Brigades of Rousseau's division encamped in supporting distance, near the Widow Hoover's house, and Negley's division at Big Spring, in rear of Rousseau's division.

The disposition of General Reynolds' division remained unchanged on the morning of the 25th, with slight skirmishing with the enemy in front. Colonel Scribner's brigade, Second Division, having been ordered to the front in the early part of the day, was posted in position to support the batteries in front and to form picket line on the extreme left. General Brannan's division, arriving from Salem, was ordered to go into camp near Rousseau, at Hoover's Mill. Orders having been previously given from department headquarters, General Rousseau's division was moved immediately in rear of General Reynolds' division, on the night of the 25th, preparatory to an attack on the enemy's position at Beech Grove. General Brannan's division moved up at 4 a. m. to take part in the attack. General Negley's division moved up at 8 a. m. to support the attack of the other divisions. After carrying the position . . . [at] Beech Grove, Rousseau's (First) and Brannan's (Third) divisions were ordered to push the enemy in the direction of Fairfield, whilst Reynolds' division was to move along the Manchester pike, seize and hold Matt's Hollow, and push on to Manchester that night, if possible.

During the night of the 25th instant it rained so continuously that it became almost impossible for troops to move, but, with extraordinary exertions, the divisions were placed in their respective positions by 10:30 a. m. Immediately after, the advance was ordered, when the enemy were driven steadily and rapidly toward Fairfield; Rousseau and Brannan operating on his left flank from the hills on the north of the Fairfield road, while Reynolds advanced against his front and right. The enemy had evidently prepared for an obstinate resistance, and attempted to enfilade my troops from the high ground on our right, but were effectually prevented by a gallant charge of the First Brigade, Third Division, Colonel Walker, and the Fourth (Regular) Brigade, First Division, Major Coolidge commanding. The steady and rapid advance of my troops forced the enemy to retire in the direction of Fairfield very rapidly, covering his retreat with two batteries of artillery and occupying positions behind strong bodies of skirmishers, flanked by a large cavalry force. The behavior of our troops was admirable—everything that could be desired.

On the morning of the 27th, at 8 o'clock, Reynolds' advance brigade, Wilder's mounted infantry, took possession of Manchester, capturing a guard at the railroad depot and taking the town completely by surprise. Negley's division, marching in support of Rousseau's and Brannan's toward Fairfield, turned into the Manchester and Fairfield road by way of Noah's Fork, and reached Manchester at 8 p. m. Rousseau and Brannan pursued the enemy as far as Fairfield. Ascertaining at that place, from what they considered reliable sources, that the enemy had retreated entirely, these two divisions, in compliance with orders, turned into the Fairfield and Manchester road, Brannan's division reaching Manchester at 10 p. m. and Rousseau's division at 12 midnight. In compliance with department orders [from General Rosecrans], Colonel Wilder, with his mounted brigade, started at reveille on the morning of the 28th, by ways of Hillsborough, to break the Chattanooga Railroad at some point below Decherd. The First and Third Divisions started at 2 p. m. in the direction of Tullahoma, camping at Crumpton's Creek, Third Division throwing out a strong party 1½ or 2 miles to its front, toward Tullahoma.

On the morning of the 29th, headquarters and the Second and Fourth Divisions were moved to Crumpton's Creek, the Fourth Division camping at Concord Church, at the point where the road to Tullahoma leaves the Manchester and Winchester road, and relieved the two regiments of Brannan's division on outpost at Bobo's Cross-Roads. The Second Division camped at Bobo's Cross-Roads, where the road from Tullahoma to Hillsborough crosses the Manchester and Winchester road. General [John] Beatty, with his brigade, joining the Second Division at that point from Hillsborough, where he had taken position on the 28th, to support Colonel Wilder in his operations against the railroad. [Ferdinand] Van Derveer's brigade, from the Third Division (Brannan's), was thrown forward on Tullahoma road, and engaged the enemy's outposts and vedettes, driving them back toward Tullahoma, killing and wounding many; the rebel Colonel [James W.] Starnes [of Brigadier General Nathan B. Forrest's command] reported among the number killed. Our loss 2 men slightly wounded. Van Derveer's brigade was relieved about 6 p. m. by [James B.] Steedman's (Second) brigade. The road from Manchester to this point was rendered nearly impassable by one of the heaviest and most continuous rains ever experienced.

June 30, Steedman's (Second) brigade, Third Division, started at an early hour, supported by a brigade from General Sheridan's [20th Corps] division on the right and two regiments of Reynolds' division on the left, and pushed forward during the evening to within 1½ or 2 miles of Tullahoma with comparative ease, General Steedman reporting that he was opposed by two regiments of cavalry and one section of artillery, at the same time reporting a loss of 15 men in his command, also killing and wounding many of the enemy, but could not report the number, as they were carried from the field by the enemy. The two regiments of Reynolds' division also reached a point about 2 miles from Tullahoma, where they came upon a regiment of the enemy's cavalry, which retired after feeble resistance. The officer, believing it was intended to lead him into an ambuscade, did not pursue farther. Two regiments from Negley's division moved out on the Manchester road 4 or 5 miles without encountering or seeing the enemy. Colonel Wilder with his brigade returned today, having succeeded in striking the railroad and doing considerable damage near Decherd.

Early on the morning of July 1, having heard from a citizen that the enemy were evacuating Tullahoma, Steedman's brigade, Third Division, supported by two regiments of Reynolds' division on his left, were ordered to advance cautiously and ascertain if the report was true. Meeting with no opposition, he entered Tullahoma at 12 m., capturing a few prisoners; General Brannan, commanding Third Division, reporting that the last of the rebel infantry retired during the night, and their cavalry commenced evacuating at daylight. General Reynolds was accordingly ordered to Tullahoma with his division, and the two divisions (Reynolds' and Brannan's) ordered to rejoin the corps at Heffner's Mill on the following morning. General Negley was directed to march to Heffner's Mill, and take post there for the night, General Rousseau to support him. In executing this order, Negley came upon the enemy about 4 miles from Bobo's Cross-Roads, and drove them steadily until they retired just at nightfall beyond Heffner's Mill. He then went into camp for the night, throwing out strong pickets to the right and front. General Rousseau was instructed, after forming his camp, to throw pickets to the rear and left. The enemy made a stubborn resistance through the pass of Spring Creek, wounding a good many of our men, but were steadily driven back until darkness prevented farther pursuit through the thick brushwood bordering the hillsides of the pass.

On the 2d, the Third and Fourth Divisions joined on Spring Creek, and the enemy were followed to the Winchester road crossing of Elk River. The bridges having been burned by the rebels, and the river not fordable, the First, Third, and Fourth Divisions were moved up the river to Jones' Ford, and one brigade of Rousseau's division thrown across the stream, the remainder of the command camping on the north side. The ford being very deep, it was with great difficulty that the brigade effected a passage, damaging much of their ammunition by the water getting into their cartridge boxes. Colonel Hambright, commanding this brigade, reported that the enemy had left the vicinity of the ford, and was informed by rebel prisoners that their retreat was by way of Pelham and Cowan, and across the mountains.

On the morning of the 3d, Rousseau's and Brannan's troops crossed the [Elk] river at Jones' Ford, and took up a position on the Winchester and Hillsborough road, crossing their artillery and trains of both divisions. Negley's division and entire train crossed the ford on the Winchester and Manchester pike. The troops of Reynolds' division crossed at the same place, leaving his ordnance train on the north side of the river, to be crossed in the morning.

On the 4th, Rousseau's division marched to the Decherd and Pelham road, and took up a position at Featherstone's. Negley took up a position at Brakefield Point. Reynolds' division encamped at Pennington's, and Brannan's division at Taite's; the two latter positions on the Decherd, Winchester, and McMinnville road. The order to halt was received at 2 p. m. this day, and the details directed to be made for the repairs of roads were ordered. Location of corps headquarters on the Winchester and McMinnville road, half way between Taite's and Pennington's.

The positions of divisions of my corps are substantially the same to this date.

Without particularizing or referring to individual merit in any one division of my command, I can render willing testimony to the manly endurance and soldierly conduct of both officers and men composing my corps, marching day and night, through a most relentless rain, and over almost impassable roads, bivouacking by the roadside, ever ready and willing to "fall in" and pursue the enemy whenever ordered, with a cheerfulness and determination truly admirable, and no less commendable when confronting the enemy; fearless and undaunted, their columns never wavered, giving the highest proof of their veteran qualities, and showing what dependence can be placed upon them in time of peril.

For particulars, incidents, and the part taken by the different divisions, brigades, and regiments of my corps in the engagements mentioned in my report, I respectfully refer you to the accompanying reports of the division commanders.

I am, general, very respectfully, your obedient servant,

Geo. H. Thomas,

*Major-General U. S. Volunteers, Commanding.*

Brig. Gen. James A. Garfield,

*Chief of Staff, Department of the Cumberland.*

## CASUALTIES IN THE 14th CORPS (JUNE 24-JULY 4, 1863)

| Command | Officers | | | Enlisted Men | | | |
|---|---|---|---|---|---|---|---|
| | Killed | Wounded | Missing | Killed | Wounded | Missing | Aggregate |
| First Division | | 3 | | 4 | 39 | | 46 |
| Second Division | 1 | | | 1 | 5 | 2 | 9 |
| Third Division | | 1 | | 4 | 59 | 1 | 65 |
| Fourth Division | | | | 15 | 47 | | 62 |
| TOTAL | 1 | 4 | | 24 | 150 | 3 | 182 [29] |

Geography and the "iron horse" dictated that Chattanooga, only 2,545 inhabitants in 1860, play a key role in the Civil War. The town had grown up on the south bank of the Tennessee, where that great river cut its way through a formidable mountain barrier. Possession of Chattanooga, the "Gateway to the deep South," was vital to the Confederacy, and a strategic goal Union leaders could not ignore.

Railroads focused the armies' attention on Chattanooga. The city was the terminus of major railroads leading northeast to

29. OR, I, XXIII, pt. 1, pp. 430-33.

Knoxville and Richmond, southeast to Atlanta, and northwest to Nashville and Louisville. At Stevenson, Alabama, 40 miles to the southwest, the railroad to Memphis joined the tracks of the Nashville & Chattanooga.

Both North and South had recognized the strategic advantages imparted to the Chattanooga area by these railroads. In the summer of 1862, as we have seen, General Bragg employed these railroads to transfer his army from northeast Mississippi, to win the race to Chattanooga, and begin the sweep across Tennessee that carried his columns deep into Kentucky. President Lincoln had written General Rosecrans, "If we take and hold Chattanooga and East Tennessee, I think the rebellion must dwindle and die."

Regional topography was all important. The Appalachian Front, in its majestic sweep from northeast to southwest, consists of a series of bold continuous ridges, separated by valleys and coves. West of the Tennessee River, the Cumberland Plateau, Sequatchie Valley, and Waldens Ridge, guarded the approaches to Chattanooga. East of the river and west and southwest of the town, an advancing army was confronted by these successive barriers—Sand Mountain, Lookout Valley, Lookout Mountain, Chattanooga Valley, Missionary Ridge, Chickamauga Valley, Pigeon Mountain, and Taylor's Ridge.

This sterile, mountainous region was sparsely populated, and was traversed by few roads. The people, outside the towns and villages, cultivated small subsistence farms, separated by woods.

By mid-August 1863, General Rosecrans was ready to resume the offensive. The Army of the Cumberland, in the six weeks since the Tullahoma Campaign, had regrouped, and ripening corn promised forage for its thousands of horses and mules. Rosecrans' immediate objective was Chattanooga. As in his recent Tullahoma Campaign, he hoped to maneuver the Confederates out of their stronghold.

On August 16, Rosecrans put his army in motion. Columns crossed the Cumberland Plateau and approached the Tennessee River. General Crittenden's 21st Corps, on the left, traversed Waldens Ridge and boldly advanced on Chattanooga. Generals Thomas' and McCook's corps neared the river on a broad front, some 45 to 55 miles downstream from the "Gateway" city.

General Bragg, to cope with Rosecrans' columns, pending the arrival of reinforcements, massed his army in and around Chattanooga. Crittenden's artillery, north of the river, opened fire on the town. Bragg, to counter this threat, recalled most of his troops guarding the downstream crossings. Rosecrans took advantage of Bragg's miscalculation, and Thomas' and McCook's corps crossed the Tennessee.

Pressing rapidly forward, the two corps entered mountainous northwest Georgia. By September 10, McCook's corps was at Alpine, Thomas' vanguard in McLemore's Cove, and Crittenden's in Chattanooga. Some 45 miles of rugged country separated the wings of Rosecrans' army.

Meanwhile, General Bragg had been reinforced. Major General Simon B. Buckner's 8,000-man corps, threatened by the advance of Major General Ambrose E. Burnside's columns, had evacuated Knoxville and rejoined the Army of Tennessee, as the Army of the Mississippi had been redesignated. Some 11,500 troops arrived from central Mississippi. On September 6, Bragg had evacuated Chattanooga and had massed his army near LaFayette.

Bragg now took advantage of Rosecrans' blunder and sought to defeat the Yankees in detail. On September 10, he moved to crush Thomas' advance, and the week preceding the battle of Chickamauga was a critical and dangerous period for the Army of the Cumberland. Rosecrans' pursuit of Bragg's forces after they had evacuated Chattanooga, a move opposed by Thomas who objected to the unwarranted risk, proved an unwise decision.

Why an overconfident Rosecrans scattered his army in the presence of the enemy, and why Braxton Bragg failed to take advantage of so splendid an opportunity to attack the isolated Federal corps are questions that have never been satisfactorily resolved. Rosecrans acted in the belief that the Southerners were in wild retreat and so not incorrectly ordered his army to follow by the most rapid routes. Bragg, meanwhile, concentrated his forces east of Pigeon Mountain, awaiting further reinforcements before assuming the offensive.

It is true on September 10 and 11, while Rosecrans' army was perilously exposed, Bragg did issue orders to Major General Thomas C. Hindman and Lieutenant General Daniel H. Hill to strike units of Thomas' corps in such a way that they "would be hit in front, flank, and rear all at once and so of course would be overwhelmed."[30]

Twice Bragg gave the order to strike and both times his subordinates refused to obey, using various excuses until Thomas had pulled back into Stevens' Gap.

Incredibly, when Bragg turned his attention to Crittenden's corps and directed General Polk to attack on September 13, this order was also disregarded, Polk stubbornly assuming the defensive on his own initiative.

The Confederate army's unwarranted tardiness in attacking provided Rosecrans with an opportunity to recall his scattered columns when he realized their awkward situation. By the evening of Thursday, September 17, 1863, eight days after the occupation of Chattanooga, Rosecrans' forces were reunited and in position west of Chickamauga Creek. Here, the Union forces occupied a vantage point which enabled them to cover all roads leading into Chattanooga. A feeling of expectancy charged the atmosphere, for none could escape the knowledge that the great battle at hand would decide the result of the campaign.

Dismayed that he had lost his previous advantage over the Federals, Bragg revised his strategy. His new plan was to "cross the Chickamauga Creek to the western side, then attack with his right flank, envelop the northern end of the Union line, swing to the left and drive his enemy away from Chattanooga into the forbidding mountains to the south," severing all supply routes and lines of communication.[31]

It was unfortunate for Bragg that he did not begin his major attack on September 18 instead of the following day. Twenty-four hours made the critical difference, because, on the 18th, the Union left was anchored at Lee and Gordon's Mills, the center under Thomas at Crawfish Springs, and McCook's corps at Pond Springs. If Bragg could have forced his way across the Chickamauga early on the 18th, well downstream from Lee and Gordon's

30. Bruce Catton, *Never Call Retreat* (Garden City, N. Y.: Doubleday, 1965), p. 243.
31. Joseph B. Mitchell, "The Battle of Chickamauga," *Battles of the Civil War 1861-1865, A Pictorial Presentation* (Little Rock, Arkansas: Pioneer Press, 1960), opposite plate 17.

Mills, his plan would have probably succeeded.

But in war many things can go wrong and once again Bragg's plans were frustrated. This time several of his units marched too late and then too slow, and to cross the Chickamauga much hard fighting was necessary. On the late afternoon and evening of September 18, the Confederate vanguard, in face of dogged resistance by Union cavalry and mounted infantry, crossed the stream at various bridges and fords well downstream from where Rosecrans had positioned his army. Rosecrans used the time gained to shift Thomas' corps from the center at Crawfish Springs to the left. McCook's corps coincidentally closed to the left occupying the ground formerly held by Thomas. These movements were made on the night of the 18th, and on the part of Thomas' corps involved a particularly trying and fatiguing march. Thus, on the morning of the 19th, the Union left overlapped Bragg's right and Rosecrans had stolen a march on the Confederates.[32]

The region in which the two-day battle took place "lies between the river and Missionary Ridge, and was covered by woods of varying density, broken here and there by cleared fields. The Chickamauga . . . winding slowly through the forests of the region, flows into the Tennessee eight miles above Chattanooga."[33]

The battle opened shortly after daylight when Colonel Dan McCook's brigade of Granger's Reserve Corps, engaged on a reconnaissance, unexpectedly encountered Brigadier General Nathan B. Forrest's cavalry, advancing dismounted, near Reed's Bridge. Battle plans were hastily scuttled, both sides called up reinforcements, and the fight commenced in deadly earnest.

It was not surprising in view of the thickly-wooded terrain that "although the armies had been maneuvering in close proximity for twelve days, each army commander was ignorant of the special dispositions of the other, and a merely tentative advance became the initiative of one of the bloodiest battles of the war."[34]

The fighting was determined but disordered as each attack provoked a heavier counterattack. Rosecrans, early in the day, reinforced Thomas with a division (Palmer's) drawn from Crit-

32. Cist, pp. 188-92.
33. Emerson Opdycke, "Notes on the Chickamauga Campaign," *Battles and Leaders*, III, 670.
34. Van Horne, *History*, I, 333.

tenden's corps and Brigadier General Richard W. Johnson's division brought up from McCook. Crittenden's and McCook's other divisions closed to the left, as throughout the day Rosecrans' army "fought desperately to keep the Confederates away from the Lafayette Road, with Thomas' corps drawn up in a long shallow crescent and taking most of the pressure."[35]

In the first day's fighting, every division of the Army of the Cumberland, except for Granger's Reserve Corps, and all but two divisions of Bragg's Army of Tennessee were engaged. Losses on both sides were heavy.

By nightfall neither army had gained the advantage, and it was evident a still more furious encounter would occur in the morning. As the Union commanders met at Rosecrans' headquarters to assess the damage and to map the next day's strategy, Thomas advocated reinforcement of the Federal left. Pressure had been brought to bear all day long against the northern end of the line as the Confederates fiercely tried to separate the Union army from its Chattanooga base. Thomas predicted a renewed attack on the left in the morning. Rosecrans, however, merely advised McCook and Crittenden to be prepared to assist Thomas as needed.

In the Confederate camps, General Bragg undertook the reorganization of his army; General Polk assumed command of the Right Wing and Lieutenant General James Longstreet, who had arrived during the night from Virginia with two brigades to join the three brigades under Major General John B. Hood who had reported to Bragg on the 18th, was assigned to head the Left Wing. The coming day's battle would find the Confederates positioned for action according to Bragg's original plan along a north-south line west of the Chickamauga, roughly parallel with and facing the LaFayette-Chattanooga road.

Polk was instructed to begin the assault at dawn by striking Thomas' extreme left, the attacks to be taken up successively from right to left. Longstreet was to assail the Union right as soon as the fighting had progressed to that point.

Once again Bragg's orders went unheeded. Thus, "the attack on Thomas was badly delayed and the delay may have saved the

35. Catton, p. 246.

life of the Union Army, because when at last Polk's troops attacked they struck with enormous force and if they had come in before Rosecrans could send reinforcements from his right Thomas' corps would probably have been overpowered."[36]

With Brigadier General Absalom Baird's division as its northern anchor, the Federal line snaked in a half-circle from a point just east of the LaFayette Road, crossed the road to the south, and joined the Union center and right which prolonged the Union front west of and parallel to the roadway. It was almost 9:30 A.M. before the battle opened. John C. Breckinridge's and Pat Cleburne's divisions of Polk's wing struck the Union left in the overall plan to envelop it. Fighting raged fiercely and the casualties mounted alarmingly on both sides, but the two armies were equally determined. The Union left under Thomas, comprising more than half the Federal forces on the field, desperately held its ground, Baird on the left giving way slightly, and then in dire need calling on Rosecrans for more men.

"The unexpected result of this pressure on the Union left was that the Union Right collapsed. In the hot confusion of battle, army headquarters at last lost track of the shifting and countermarching that had been ordered, and Rosecrans finally pulled the division of [Brigadier] General Thomas J. Wood out of Crittenden's line and sent it off to the left. This left a big gap in the line and before anyone could fill it, Longstreet made his own attack, striking with . . . [three] divisions at the precise spot that had just been vacated."[37]

Through the Union center the Confederates poured, swinging to their right and attacking with such force and suddenness that the entire right flank and part of the center were driven from the battlefield. General Rosecrans, having been "swept off the field in the general rout," withdrew to Chattanooga, conceding the day and the battle to the Confederates. "Fugitives, wounded, caissons, escort, ambulances, thronged the narrow pathways. . . . McCook and Crittenden, caught in the same tide of retreat, shared the opinion of Rosecrans, and reported to him for instruc-

36. *Ibid.,* p. 248.
37. *Ibid.,* p. 249.

tions and cooperation."[38] Brigadier General James A. Garfield, Rosecrans' chief of staff, was not convinced that the battle was over and so made his way through retreating Union soldiers to the front, eventually reaching General Thomas by mid-afternoon.

Having met with such immediate and overwhelming success in his attack on the Union right, Longstreet, flushed with victory, disregarded earlier orders to keep to his left and now changed direction to strike the Federal left.

Thomas' forces, struck in flank and rear, hastily pulled back to the north and west and re-organized into an ell-shaped line of defense on Snodgrass Hill, "determined to hold on until dusk and make the final withdrawal an orderly one."[39]

Curled up upon themselves in an improvised horseshoe, the Federals were unyielding. "On the part of Thomas and his men, there was no thought but that of fighting. He was a soldier who had never retreated, who had never been defeated. He stood immovable, the 'Rock of Chickamauga.' Never had soldiers greater love for a commander. He imbued them with his spirit and their confidence in him was sublime."[40] But it was only a matter of hours before Longstreet's troops could extend their line behind Thomas and conmence an attack from the right and rear.

Here, on Snodgrass Hill, Thomas boldly withstood repeated assaults by the enemy, stubbornly maintaining the battle even when ammunition ran out and his men were reduced to fighting with bayonets and clubbed muskets.

All morning long, the sounds and smoke of battle had carried to General Granger's position at Rossville, about four miles northwest of the front where the fighting raged furiously along the Union left. Observing the distant movement of troops toward the battlefield, Granger grew increasingly restless under Rosecrans' orders to employ his Reserve Corps to cover the road to Chattanooga.

Time and again he paced fretfully in front of his headquarters, painfully aware that he was needed at the front, but still no

38. Gates P. Thruston, "The Crisis at Chickamauga," *Battles and Leaders*, III, 664.
39. Catton, p. 249.
40. J. S. Fullerton, "Reenforcing Thomas at Chickamauga," *Battles and Leaders*, III, 667.

orders came. Finally, his patience exhausted, Granger, "in a splendid example of battlefield initiative," declared to his aide, "I am going to Thomas, orders or no orders! Don't you see Bragg is piling his whole army on Thomas? I am going to his assistance."[41]

Knowing full well that his actions might endanger the army and leave him open to court-martial for disobedience, Granger, his decision made, immediately approached Brigadier General James B. Steedman, commander of his First Division, and directed him to take two of his brigades under Brigadier General Walter C. Whitaker and Colonel John G. Mitchell into battle. Colonel Dan McCook of the Second Division was to take position at McAfee's Church to guard the approach to Rossville Gap via the LaFayette road.

By now it was mid-afternoon and "Thomas was nearly four miles away. The day had now grown very warm . . . the troops marched rapidly over the narrow road, which was covered ankle-deep with dust that rose in suffocating clouds. [They] were met by a staff-officer sent by General Thomas to discover whether [they] were friends or enemies; he did not know whence friends could be coming, and the enemy appeared to be approaching from all directions."[42]

Granger rode directly to Thomas, shook hands with him, and asked him where his men could best be used against the Rebel assaults. None too soon had these two fresh brigades arrived, for Thomas was now almost outflanked, the forces of Longstreet storming his right, while Polk continued to pound away furiously on his left. Nevertheless, "from noon till night, the . . . [seven] divisions which had previously constituted Thomas' line, and such other troops as reached him from the right, under orders, or drifted to him after the disaster, and [Granger's] Reserve Corps, successfully resisted the whole Confederate Army."[43] Numbering only about 25,000 men, the Federals confronted at least twice that number of Confederates.[44]

Granger's chief of staff, Brevet Brigadier General J. S. Fullerton, wrote of Granger afterwards that he "was rough in manner

41. *Ibid.*, p. 666.
42. *Ibid.*, pp. 666-67.
43. Van Horne, *History,* I, 348.
44. Coppée, p. 151.

143

. . . [and] inclined to insubordination, especially when he knew his superior to be wrong. Otherwise he was a splendid soldier. Rosecrans named him well when he hailed him as 'Granger, great in battle.' "[45]

About five o'clock on the afternoon of the 20th, shortly before the battle ended, Rosecrans telegraphed General Halleck of the Union debacle:

> *Chattanooga, Tenn., September* 20, 1863, 5 P. M.
> (Received 8:40 P. M.)
> Major-General H. W. Halleck, General-in-Chief:
> We have met with a serious disaster; extent not yet ascertained. Enemy overwhelmed us, drove our right, pierced our center, and scattered troops there. Thomas, who had seven divisions, remained intact at last news. Granger, with two brigades, had gone to support Thomas on the left. Every available reserve was used when the men stampeded. Burnside will be notified of the state of things at once, and you will be informed. Troops from Charleston, Florida, Virginia and all along the seaboard are found among the prisoners. It seems that every available man was thrown against us.
> W. S. Rosecrans
> *Major-General, Commanding.*[46]

Sundown was fast approaching. Thomas, under orders from Rosecrans at Chattanooga, prepared to withdraw his troops to Rossville, which was midway between the battlefield and Chattanooga. As the army retreated, portions of the troops came under heavy attack as they left their positions, and additional losses were suffered before the retrograde could be completed.

That evening, at 8:40 p.m., General Garfield sent a telegram from his headquarters at Rossville to Rosecrans at Chattanooga reporting Thomas' success at the battle of Chickamauga:

> General Thomas has fought a most terrific battle and has damaged the enemy badly. General Granger's troops moved up just in time and fought magnificently. From the time I reached the battlefield, 3:45 p. m., till sunset, the fight was by far the fiercest I have ever seen; our men not only held their ground, but at many points drove the enemy splendidly. Longstreet's Virginians have got their bellies full. . . . On the

45. Fullerton, p. 667.
46. OR, I, XXX, pt. I, pp. 142-43.

whole, General Thomas and General Granger have done the enemy fully as much injury today as they have suffered from him, and they have successfully repelled the repeated combined attacks, most fiercely made, of the whole rebel army, frequently pressing the front and both our flanks at the same time.

Rosecrans was further advised that Thomas still had seven divisions intact, and Garfield expressed his belief that Thomas was now in a position to successfully resist any further assaults and possibly even turn the battle into a Federal victory.[47]

Rosecrans was so pleased with the news, he exclaimed, "Thank God!" Waving the communication above his head, he declared, "This is good enough, the day isn't lost yet." Turning to his corps commanders, Generals McCook and Crittenden, he reminded them, "Gentlemen, this is no place for you. Go at once to your command at the front."

Unfortunately, neither of these commanders was able to reach the battlefield before the fighting was over. Thomas reached Rossville on the night of the 20th and was joined there by Generals McCook and Crittenden who re-assumed command of their corps. Thus, the day after the battle, Rosecrans and his commanders, anticipating pursuit by the Confederate army, re-deployed their troops, brought up supplies, and braced themselves to meet a new attack. Rosecrans had communicated the precariousness of the Federal position in a dispatch to President Lincoln that morning:

*Chattanooga, Tenn., September* 21, 1863, 9 a. m.
(Received War Department 12:45 p. m.)

His Excellency Abraham Lincoln
President of the United States:

After two days of the severest fighting I ever witnessed our right and center were beaten. The left held its position until sunset; our loss is heavy and our troops worn down. The enemy received heavy reenforcements Saturday night. Every man of ours was in action Sunday and all but one brigade on Saturday. Our wounded large compared with that of the killed. We took prisoners from two divisions of Longstreet. We have no certainty of holding our position here.

47. Van Horne, *Life,* pp. 147-48.

If Burnside could come immediately it would be well; otherwise he may be unable to join us unless he comes on west
side of river.

W. S. Rosecrans
*Major-General, Commanding.*[48]

The decimated and exhausted soldiers of the Confederacy,
however, spent the day burying the dead, looking after the
wounded, and gathering together captured supplies. Though
General Forrest repeatedly urged Bragg to go after the Federals,
who had suffered the same terrible losses and were withdrawing
in defeat, Bragg failed to seize this last opportunity to get between Rosecrans and Chattanooga, and refused to give the order
to pursue. The view of many historians, aptly expressed by one
of Bragg's own men and critics, General Daniel H. Hill, is that
"whatever blunders each of us in authority committed before the
battles of the 19th and 20th, and during their progress, the great
blunder of all was that of not pursuing the enemy on the 21st."[49]
It was certainly the opinion of Bragg's corps commanders that
had a vigorous pursuit been made the Union Army of the Cumberland would have been destroyed. General Longstreet criti-
cized and derided Bragg's military strategy in a communication
to Secretary of War James A. Seddon on September 26, 1863,
written six days after the battle:

> . . . our chief has done but one thing that he ought to have
> done since I joined his army. That was to order the attack
> upon the 20th. All other things that he has done he ought
> not to have done. I am convinced that nothing but the hand
> of God can save us or help us as long as we have our present
> commander. . . . You will be surprised to learn that his army
> has neither organization nor mobility, and I have doubts if its
> commander can give it them. . . . When I came here I hoped
> to find our commander willing and anxious to do all things
> that would aid us in our great cause, and ready to receive
> what aid he could get from his subordinates. It seems that
> I was greatly mistaken. It seems that he cannot adopt and
> adhere to any plan or course whether of his own or of some-
> one else. I desire to impress upon your mind that there is

48. OR, I, XXX, pt. I, pp. 149-150.
49. Daniel H. Hill, "Chickamauga, the Great Battle of the West," *Battles and Leaders*, III, 662.

146

no exaggeration in these statements. On the contrary, I have failed to express my convictions to the fullest extent. All that I can add without making this letter exceedingly long is to pray you to help us, and speedily.

I remain, with the greatest respect, your obedient servant,

J. Longstreet,
*Lieutenant-General.*[50]

Union commanders, too, saw their military reputations either tarnished or destroyed in the crucible of Chickamauga. General Thomas was shortly thereafter placed in command of the Army of the Cumberland, while Gordon Granger also assumed greater responsibility. General Rosecrans and three of his lieutenants were relieved of their commands. Generals Alexander McCook, Thomas Crittenden, and James Negley (the latter early on the morning of the 20th had been ordered to reinforce Thomas but had unaccountably left the battlefield) were ordered North to await a "Court of Inquiry," "upon their conduct on September 19th and 20th."

Battle accounts of Chickamauga are replete with accolades for General Thomas. Brevet Brigadier General Henry M. Cist wrote, "There is nothing finer than Thomas at Chickamauga." Confederate General Thomas Hindman, who fought Thomas' right at Snodgrass Hill, reported that he had "never known Federal troops to fight so well."

Union General Richard W. Johnson, in his "Memoir of Major General George H. Thomas," was inspired to write of Thomas' feat:

Chickamauga! Who can tell of its horrors, or paint in words its deeds of "high surprise"? Who can portray the wonderful story of that Sabbath-day's valiant work, when Thomas held the outnumbering columns of the foe at bay with his encircled wall of steel?[51]

But perhaps the noblest tribute to the great general was that by Henry Coppée:

. . . everything went against Thomas, and yet we have the paradox that every adverse circumstance gave him an opportunity. His counsel was disregarded at the first. His corps

50. OR, I, XXX, pt. IV, pp. 705-06.
51. Johnson, p. 89.

was thrust single-handed into the jaws of disaster. . . .
His sublime valor and unequaled endurance received the
plaudits of the enemy. . . . His own men called him thence-
forth "The Rock of Chickamauga." He saved the army from
flight and utter ruin, for flight would have meant the scattering of the troops, the unrelenting pursuit by Bragg, his
occupation of Tennessee and Kentucky, and his seriously
threatening the line of [the] Ohio. . . . Thus the battle of
Chickamauga displays to us this heroic man, towering above
his colleagues by his cool and sensible judgment, his tenacity
of purpose and his splendid valor. His skill as a general was
tested and proved by his making . . . "his plans in the face
of the enemy"; changing and modifying them with the numerous and rapid changes of the field; assuming the command
and the responsibility with a clear grasp and a forecasting
intelligence not surpassed by any general in the history of
modern war. And his soldiers were worthy of such a general,
and were thoroughly infused with his spirit. It must [have
been] a glorious and invaluable retrospect to those brave
officers and men who [were] able to say, "I fought with
Thomas at Chickamauga."[52]

Chickamauga Creek, near the banks of which was waged this
fatal struggle, was prophetically named. An Indian term, Chickamauga means "River of Death."[53]

The battle itself, considering the forces engaged, was the Civil
War's bloodiest two-day battle. The Union lost approximately
16,000 men; the Confederates, 18,000. According to historian
Thomas Livermore, the casualties resulting from the battle were:

|  | Union | Confederate |
|---|---|---|
| Effectives | 58,222 | 66,326 |
| Killed | 1,657 | 2,312 |
| Wounded | 9,756 | 14,674 |
| Missing | 4,757 | 1,468 |
| Total Loss | 16,170 | 18,454 |

The loss to each army was a devastating 28 percent of the
forces engaged.

To the Confederates the fruits of this campaign proved to be
a victory barren in the sense of any "lasting benefits." The drain

52. Coppée, pp. 157-59.
53. Mitchell, opposite plate 17.

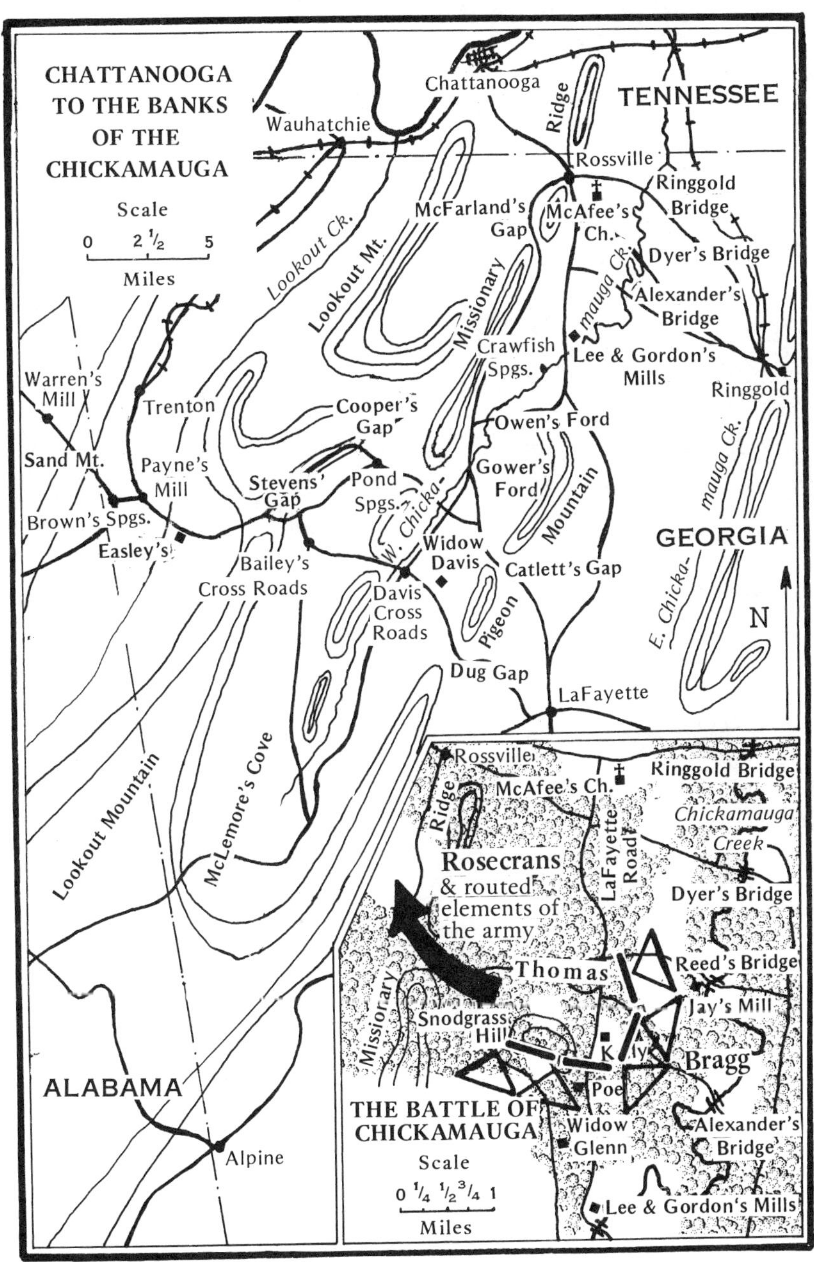
CHATTANOOGA
TO THE BANKS
OF THE
CHICKAMAUGA

Scale
0    2 1/2    5
Miles

TENNESSEE
GEORGIA
ALABAMA

Chattanooga
Wauhatchie
Ridge
Rossville
Ringgold Bridge
McFarland's Gap
McAfee's Ch.
Dyer's Bridge
Lookout Ck.
Lookout Mt.
mauga Ck.
Alexander's Bridge
Missionary
Crawfish Spgs.
Lee & Gordon's Mills
Ringgold
Warren's Mill
Trenton
Cooper's Gap
Owen's Ford
Sand Mt.
Payne's Mill
Stevens' Gap
Pond Spgs.
Gower's Ford
Mountain
Brown's Spgs.
Easley's
Bailey's Cross Roads
W. Chicka-
Widow Davis
Catlett's Gap
E. Chicka-
mauga Ck.
N
Davis Cross Roads
Pigeon
Dug Gap
LaFayette
Lookout Mountain
McLemore's Cove
Alpine

THE BATTLE OF CHICKAMAUGA

Scale
0  1/4  1/2 3/4  1
Miles

Rossville
McAfee's Ch.
Ringgold Bridge
Ridge
Chickamauga Creek
Rosecrans
& routed elements of the army
LaFayette Road
Dyer's Bridge
Thomas
Reed's Bridge
Missionary
Jay's Mill
Snodgrass Hill
Kelly
Bragg
Poe
Widow Glenn
Alexander's Bridge
Lee & Gordon's Mills

on the resources of Bragg's army, particularly in manpower, failed to produce results commensurate with the effort expended. His army was so disabled and disorganized that, when portions of his line were in need of reinforcements, he could not move his troops from one part of the field to another. Bragg paid a heavy price at Chickamauga, his success a victory in name only. His shattered corps could not follow up the retreating Union forces to claim possession of what, next to destruction of Rosecrans' army, was the principal objective of the campaign, Chattanooga.

When it became obvious that the Confederates had no plans to vigorously pursue the retreating corps of the Army of the Cumberland, Rosecrans, on the night of September 21-22, withdrew his army leisurely into Chattanooga, and thus ended the Chickamauga Campaign.

The Confederates held the battlefield, with the Union hospitals and a large number of prisoners, together with important and valuable captures of artillery and other materials of war, but the Army of the Cumberland had obtained possession of and held Chattanooga, a strategically located town 350 miles south of the Ohio River, and the gateway to the southeast.

In 1896, Joseph C. McElroy, a veteran of the war, wrote, "No men on any battlefield of the world ever exhibited greater personal daring and more steadfast courage than were displayed at Chickamauga by the rank and file of both armies, and while we may bitterly regret the carnage, grief and waste, which resulted from the conflict, we can not feel otherwise than proud of the stubborn valor manifested in this engagement by the American soldier, whether he wore the blue or the gray."[54]

On September 30, while events were fresh in his mind, General Thomas submitted a detailed report of his corps' actions in the Chickamauga Campaign. It read:

Headquarters Fourteenth Army Corps.

*Chattanooga, Tenn., September* 30, 1863.

General: I have the honor to report the operations of my corps from the 1st September up to date, as follows, viz:

54. Joseph C. McElroy, *Record of the Ohio Chickamauga and National Park Commission* (Cincinnati: Earhart and Richardson, 1896), p. 20.

General Brannan's division crossed the Tennessee River at Battle Creek, General Baird [Absalom Baird had replaced Rousseau on August 23 as leader of Thomas' First Division] was ordered to cross his division at Bridgeport, and to move to Taylor's Store; General Negley's division to cross the river at Caperton's Ferry, and to report at Taylor's Store also.

September 2.—General Baird's division moved to Widow's Creek. General Negley reports having arrived at Moore's Spring, 1¼ miles from Taylor's Store, and 2 miles from Bridgeport; he was ordered to cross . . . [Sand] mountain at that point, it being the most direct route to Trenton, in the vicinity of which place the corps was ordered to concentrate.

September 3.—Headquarters Fourteenth Army Corps moved from Bolivar Springs at 6 a.m. via Caperton's Ferry to Moore's Spring, on the road from Bridgeport to Trenton. Baird's division reached Bridgeport, but could not cross in consequence of damage to the bridge; Negley's division marched to Warren's Mill, on the top of Sand Mountain, on the road to Trenton: Brannan's division reached Graham's Store, on the road from Shellmound to Trenton; Reynolds' division marched 6 miles on the Trenton road from Shellmound.

September 4.—Negley's division camped at Brown's Spring, at the foot of Sand Mountain, in Lookout Valley; Brannan's division at Gordon's Mill, on Sand Mountain; Reynolds' division at foot of Sand Mountain, 2 miles from Trenton; Baird's division crossed the river at Bridgeport, and camped at that point; corps headquarters at Moore's Spring.

September 5.—Baird's division arrived at Moore's Spring; Negley's division still in camp at Brown's Spring. He reports having sent forward a reconnaissance of two regiments of infantry and a section of artillery to scour the country toward Chattanooga, and secure some captured stores near Macon Iron Works. They captured some Confederate army supplies. No report from Brannan's division; Reynolds' division in camp at Trenton; Brannan somewhere in the neighborhood; corps headquarters at Warren's Mill.

September 6.—Baird's division encamped at Warren's Mill; Negley's division reached Johnson's Crook; [John] Beatty's brigade was sent up the road [across Lookout Mountain] to seize Stevens' Gap; met the enemy's pickets, and, it being dark, did not proceed farther. The Eighteenth Ohio, of

Negley's division, went to the top of Lookout Mountain, beyond Payne's Mill; met the enemy's pickets and dispersed them. The head of Brannan's column reached Lookout Valley, 2 miles below Trenton. Reynolds' division in camp at Trenton. Rumors of the enemy's design to evacuate Chattanooga. Corps headquarters at Brown's Spring.

September 7.—Baird's division closed up with Negley's in the mouth of Johnson's Crook. Negley's gained possession of the top of the mountain [Lookout], and secured the forks of the road. Brannan's division reached Trenton; Reynolds' remained in camp at that place. Corps headquarters still at Brown's Spring.

September 8.—Baird's division remained in its camp of yesterday, at the junction of Hurricane and Lookout Creeks. Negley's division moved up to the top of Lookout Mountain, at the head of Johnson's Crook, one brigade occupying the pass; another brigade was sent forward and seized Cooper's Gap, sending one regiment to the foot of the gap to occupy and hold it; one regiment was also sent forward to seize Stevens' Gap, which was heavily obstructed with fallen trees. Brannan's division occupied the same position as last night. Reynolds' division headquarters at Trenton, with one brigade at Payne's Mill, 2 miles south of Trenton. Headquarters of the corps still at Brown's Spring.

September 9.—Baird's division moved across Lookout Mountain to the support of Negley. Negley's division moved across the mountain and took up a position in McLemore's Cove, near Rodgers' farm, throwing out his skirmishers as far as Bailey's Crossroads; saw the enemy's cavalry in front, drawn up in line; citizens reported a heavy force [Cleburne's] concentrated in his front at Dug Gap, consisting of infantry, cavalry, and artillery. Brannan's division in camp same as yesterday; Reynolds' division also. The Ninety-second Illinois (mounted infantry) [of Wilder's brigade] sent on a reconnaissance toward Chattanooga, along the ridge of Lookout Mountain. Colonel [Smith D.] Atkins, commanding Ninety-second Illinois, reports September 9, 11 a.m., entered Chattanooga as the rear of the enemy's column was evacuating the place; corps headquarters moved from Brown's Spring to Easley's farm, on Trenton and Lebanon road.

September 10.—General Negley's [division] in front of or 1

mile west of Dug Gap, which has been heavily obstructed by the enemy and occupied by a strong picket line [Cleburne's]. General Baird ordered to move up to-night to Negley's support. General Reynolds to move at daylight to support Baird's left, and General Brannan to move at 8 a.m. to-morrow morning to support Reynolds. Headquarters and General Reynolds' division camped at foot of the mountain; Brannan's division at Easley's.

September 11.—Baird's division closed up on Negley's at Widow Davis' house about 8 a.m. Soon afterward, Negley being satisfied, from his own observations and from the reports of officers sent out to reconnoiter, and also from loyal citizens, that the enemy [Hindman's and Cleburne's divisions] was advancing on him in very superior force, and that his train was in imminent danger of being cut off if he accepted battle at Davis' Cross-Roads, determined to fall back to a strong position in front of Stevens' Gap. This movement he immediately proceeded to put into execution, and by his untiring energy and skill, and with the prompt co-operation of Baird, succeeded in gaining possession of the hills in front of Stevens' Gap and securing his trains, without losing a single wagon. General [John] Turchin, commanding Third Brigade, Reynolds' division, was pushed forward, by way of Cooper's Gap, to Negley's support, on the left, reaching his position about 10 a.m. Orders were sent to General Brannan to close up as rapidly as possible. Corps headquarters at top of Cooper's Gap.

September 12.—Brannan's division reached Negley's position by 8 a.m., and took post next on the left of Baird. Reynolds' division was posted on the left of Brannan, one brigade covering Cooper's Gap. Reports from citizens go to confirm the impression that a large force of the enemy is concentrated at La Fayette. A report from General [Alexander] McCook confirms that fact. A later dispatch from the same source says it is reported that Bragg's whole army, with [General Joseph E.] Johnston's, is at La Fayette. Generals Brannan and Baird, with parts of their commands, went out on a reconnaissance toward Dug Gap at 1 p.m. to-day. General Brannan reports they advanced 2 miles beyond Davis' Cross-Roads without finding any enemy with the exception of a few mounted men. Corps headquarters encamped at top of Stevens' Gap.

September 13.—Negley's, Baird's and Brannan's divisions re-

mained in their camps of yesterday awaiting the arrival of Mc-
Cook's corps which had been ordered to close up to the left.
Reynolds concentrated his division on the road from Cooper's
Gap to Catlett's Gap. Two deserters from Eighteenth Tennes-
see state that they belong to [Simon B.] Buckner's corps. Buck-
ner's corps consists of eight [nine] brigades and two batteries
of six guns each; were in the fight with Negley [at Davis'
Cross-Roads]. Saw a brigade of Forrest's cavalry, commanded
by Forrest in person, pass toward the fight on the 11th. [D. H.]
Hill's and Buckner's corps were both engaged. Bragg's army
is concentrated at La Fayette. Headquarters moved by way of
Cooper's Gap to the foot of the mountain.

September 14.—General Reynolds took up a position at Pond
Spring with his two infantry brigades, and was joined by
Wilder at that place. Turchin's brigade, of Reynolds' division,
made a reconnaissance to the mouth of Catlett's Gap [across
Pigeon Mountain] with the Ninety-second Illinois (mounted
infantry). Was opposed by rebel mounted pickets from Chickamauga Creek to mouth of Catlett's Gap, at which place he
found their reserve drawn up, also a strong line of skirmishers
to the right of the road; but having received instructions to
avoid bringing on an engagement, he returned to camp with
the brigade, leaving two regiments on Chattanooga Valley road,
strongly posted on outposts. General Brannan advanced one
brigade of his division to Chickamauga Creek, east of Lee's
Mill, 1 mile to the right and south of Reynolds' position at Pond
Spring. A mounted reconnaissance was also pushed forward to
within a mile of Blue Bird Gap without encountering any of
the enemy. A negro who had been taken before General Buckner yesterday and released again reports that Buckner and his
corps are in Catlett's Gap preparing to defend that place. A
negro woman, lately from the neighborhood of Dug Gap, reports a large force of rebels between Dug Gap and La Fayette.

September 16.—Corps headquarters and First [Baird's] and
Second [Negley's] Divisions remained camped, as last reported,
at foot of Stevens' Gap. Turchin's brigade, of Reynolds' division, made a reconnaissance toward Catlett's Gap. The enemy
fell back as he advanced, until he came upon a force strongly
posted, with two pieces of artillery, in the road. He made a
second reconnaissance at 2 p.m. that day with but little further

result, as he could advance but a short distance farther, the enemy being in force in his front.

September 17.—First, Second, and Third Divisions changed their positions from their camps of yesterday; Baird's (First) division, with its right resting at Gower's Ford and extending along Chickamauga Creek to Bird's Mill; Negley's (Second) division, with its right at Bird's Mill and its left connecting with [Horatio H. P.] Van Cleve's [21st Corps] division at Owen's Ford; Brannan's (Third) division on the right of [21st Corps] the First, covering four fords between Gower's Ford and Pond Spring. One brigade of the Fourth Division (Reynolds') thrown out in front of Pond Spring, on the Catlett's Gap road, covering the pass through the . . . [Pigeon] mountains. Wilder's brigade detached and ordered to report to department head-quarters. The left of McCook's corps closed in; connected with our right near Pond Spring.

September 18.—At 4 p.m. the whole corps moved to the left along Chickamauga Creek to Crawfish Spring. On arriving at that place received orders to march on the cross-road leading by Widow Glenn's house to the Chattanooga and La Fayette road, and take up a position near Kelly's farm, on the La Fay-ette road, connecting with Crittenden on my right at [Lee and] Gordon's Mills. The head of the column reached Kelly's farm about daylight on the 19th, Baird's division in front, and took up a position at the forks of the road, facing toward Reed's and Alexander's Bridges over the Chickamauga. Colonel [John H.] Wilder, commanding the mounted brigade of Reynolds' division, informed me that the enemy had crossed the Chicka-mauga in force at those two bridges the evening [the 18th] before and drove his brigade across the State road, or Chatta-nooga and La Fayette road, to the heights east of Widow Glenn's house.

Kelly's house is situated in an opening about three-fourths of a mile long and one-fourth of a mile wide, on the east side of the State [La Fayette] road, and stretches along that road in a northerly direction, with a small field of perhaps 20 acres on the west side of the road, directly opposite to the house. From thence to the Chickamauga the surface of the country is undulating and covered with original forest timber, inter-spersed with undergrowth, in many places so dense that it is difficult to see 50 paces ahead. There is a cleared field near

Jay's Mill, and cleared land in the vicinity of Reed's and Alexander's Bridges. A narrow [Poe's] field commences at a point about a fourth of a mile south of Kelly's house, on the east side of the State [La Fayette] road, and extends, perhaps, for half a mile along the road toward [Lee and] Gordon's Mills. Between the State [La Fayette] road and the foot of Missionary Ridge there is a skirt of timber stretching from the vicinity of Widow Glenn's house, south of the forks of the road to McDonald's house, three-fourths of a mile north of Kelly's. The eastern slope of . . . Missionary Ridge, between Glenn's and McDonald's, is cleared and mostly under cultivation. This position of Baird's threw my right in close proximity to Wilder's brigade; the interval I intended to fill up with the two remaining brigades of Reynolds' division on their arrival. General Brannan, closely following Baird's division, was placed in position on his left, on the two roads leading from the State [La Fayette] road to Reed's and Alexander's Bridges.

Col. Dan. McCook, commanding a brigade of . . . [Granger's] Reserve Corps, met me at General Baird's headquarters, and reported to me that he had been stationed the previous night on the road leading to Reed's Bridge, and that he could discover no force of the enemy except one brigade, which had crossed to the west side of the Chickamauga at Reed's Bridge the day before; and he believed it could be cut off, because, after it had crossed, he had destroyed the bridge, the enemy having retired toward Alexander's Bridge. Upon this information I directed General Brannan to post a brigade [Croxton's] within supporting distance of Baird, on the road to Alexander's Bridge, and with his other two brigades to reconnoiter the road leading to Reed's Bridge to see if he could locate the brigade reported by Colonel McCook, and, if a favorable opportunity occurred, to capture it. His dispositions were made according to instructions by 9 a. m.

General Baird was directed to throw forward his right wing, so as to get more nearly in line with Brannan, but to watch well on his right flank. Soon after this disposition of those two divisions, a portion of [John M.] Palmer's division, of Crittenden's corps, took position to the right of General Baird's division. About 10 o'clock [John T.] Croxton's brigade of Brannan's division, posted on the road leading to Alexander's Bridge, became engaged with the enemy, and I rode forward to his position to ascertain the character of the attack.

Colonel Croxton reported to me that he had driven the enemy [Forrest's cavalry] nearly half a mile, but that he was then meeting with obstinate resistance. I then rode back to Baird's position, and directed him to advance to Croxton's support, which he did with his whole division, Starkweather's brigade in reserve, and drove the enemy steadily before him for some distance, taking many prisoners. Croxton's brigade, which had been heavily engaged for over an hour with greatly superior numbers of the enemy, and being nearly exhausted of ammunition, was then moved to the rear to enable the men to fill up their boxes; and Baird and Brannan, having united their forces, drove the enemy from their immediate front. General Baird then halted for the purpose of readjusting his line; and hearing from prisoners that the enemy [Liddell's Division] were in heavy force on his immediate right, he threw back his right wing in order to be ready for an attack from that quarter.

Before his dispositions could be completed, the enemy, in overwhelming numbers, furiously assaulted Scribner's and [John H.] King's brigades, and drove them in disorder. Fortunately, at this time [Richard W.] Johnson's division, of McCook's corps, and Reynolds' division, of my corps, arrived, and were immediately placed in position. Johnson preceded Reynolds, his left connecting with Baird's right, and Palmer being immediately on Johnson's right, Reynolds was placed on the right of Palmer, with one brigade of his division in reserve. As soon as formed they advanced upon the enemy, attacking him in flank and driving him in great disorder for a mile and a half, while Brannan's troops met him in front as he was pursuing Baird's retiring brigades, driving the head of his column back and retaking the artillery, which had been temporarily lost by Baird's brigades, the Ninth Ohio recovering Battery H, Fifth U. S. Artillery, at the point of the bayonet. The enemy, at this time being hardly pressed by Johnson, Palmer, and Reynolds in flank, fell back in confusion upon his reserves, posted in a strong position on the west side of Chickamauga Creek between Reed's and Alexander's Bridges.

Brannan and Baird were then ordered to reorganize their commands and take position on commanding ground on the road from McDonald's to Reed's Bridge, and hold it to the last extremity, as I expected the next effort of the enemy would be to gain that road and our rear. This was about 2 p. m. After a lull of about one hour, a furious attack [by B. Frank Cheatham's Tennessee Division and A. P. Stewart's Little Giant Division] was made upon Reynold's right, and he having called upon me for re-enforcements, I directed Brannan's division to move to his support, leaving King's brigade, of Baird's division, to hold the position at which Baird and Brannan had been posted, the balance of Baird's division closing up to the right on Johnson's division. It will be seen by General Reynolds' report, Croxton's brigade, of Brannan's division, reached his right just in time to defeat the enemy's efforts to turn Reynolds' right and rear.

About 5 p. m., my lines being at that time very much extended in pursuing the enemy, I determined to concentrate them on more commanding ground, as I felt confident that we should have a renewal of the battle in the morning. I rode forward to General Johnson's position and designated to him where to place his division; also to General Baird, who was present with Johnson. I then rode back to the cross-roads to locate Palmer and Reynolds on Johnson's right and on the crest of the ridge about 500 yards east of the State [La Fayette] road. Soon after Palmer and Reynolds got their positions and while Brannan was getting his on the ridge to the west of the State [La Fayette] road near Dyer's house, and to the rear and right of Reynolds, where I had ordered him as a reserve, the enemy [Cleburne] assaulted first Johnson and then Baird in a most furious manner, producing some confusion, but order was soon restored, and the enemy repulsed in fine style; after which these two divisions took up the positions assigned them for the night.

Before adjusting the line satisfactorily, I received an order to report to department headquarters at the [Widow Glenn's] immediately, and was absent from my command until near midnight. After my return from department headquarters, about 2 a. m. on the 20th, I received a report from General Baird that the left of his division did not rest on the Reed's Bridge road, as I had intended, and that he could not reach it without weakening his line too much. I immediately addressed a note to the general commanding [Rosecrans] requesting that General Negley be sent me to take position on Baird's left and rear, and thus secure our left from assault. During the night the troops threw up temporary breastworks of logs, and prepared for the encounter which all anticipated would come off the next day.

Although informed by note, from General Rosecrans' headquarters, that Negley's division would be sent immediately to take post on my left, it had not arrived at 7 a. m. on the 20th, and I sent Captain [J. P.] Willard, of my staff, to General Negley to urge him forward as rapidly as possible, and to point out his position to him. General Negley, in his official report, mentions that he received this order through Captain Willard at 8 a.m. on the 20th, and that he immediately commenced withdrawing his division for that purpose, when the enemy was reported to be massing a heavy force in his front, sharply engaging his skirmishers, and that he was directed by General Rosecrans to hold his position until relieved by some other command. General [John] Beatty's brigade, however, was sent under the guidance of Captain Willard, who took it to its position, and it went into action immediately. The enemy [Breckinridge's division] at that time commenced a furious assault on Baird's left, and partially succeeded in gaining his rear. Beatty, meeting with superior numbers, was compelled to fall back until relieved by the fire of several regiments of Palmer's reserve, which I had ordered to the support of the left, being placed in position by General Baird, and which regiments, with the co-operation of [Ferdinand] Van Derveer's brigade of Brannan's division and a portion of [Timothy R.] Stanley's brigade of Negley's division, drove the enemy entirely from Baird's left and rear. General Baird being still hardly pressed in front [by Cleburne's division], I ordered General [Thomas J.] Wood, who had just reported to me in person, to send one of the brigades of his division to General Baird. He replied that his division had been ordered by General Rosecrans to support Reynold's right, but that if I would take the responsibility of changing his orders, he would cheerfully obey them, and sent [Sidney M.] Barnes' brigade [of Van Cleve's division], the head of which had just reached my position. General Wood then left me to rejoin the remainder of his division, which was still coming up.

To prevent a repetition of this attack of the enemy on our left I directed Captain [W. B.] Gaw, chief topographical officer on my staff, to go to the commanding officer of the troops on the left and rear of Baird, and direct him to mass as much artillery on the slopes of Missionary Ridge, west of the State [La Fayette] road, as he could conveniently spare from his lines, supported strongly by infantry, so as to sweep the ground to the left and rear of Baird's position. This order General Negley, in his official report, mentions having received through Captain Gaw, but from his description of the position he assumed he must have misunderstood my order, and instead of massing the artillery near Baird's left, it was posted on the right of Brannan's division, nearly in rear of Reynolds' right.

At the time that the assault just described was made on Baird, the enemy [Cleburne and Cheatham] attacked Johnson, Palmer, and Reynolds, with equal fierceness, which was continued at least two hours, making assault after assault with fresh troops, which were met by my troops with a most determined coolness and deliberation. The enemy having exhausted his utmost energies to dislodge us, apparently fell back entirely from our front, and we were not disturbed again until near night, after the withdrawal of the troops to Rossville had commenced. Just before the repulse of the enemy on our left, General Beatty came to me for fresh troops, in person, stating that most of those I had sent to him had gone back to the rear and right, and he was anxious to get at least another brigade before they attacked him again. I immediately sent Captain [Sanford C.] Kellogg to hurry up General Sheridan [of McCook's corps], whose division I had been informed would be sent to me.

About 2 p.m., very soon after Captain Kellogg left me, hearing heavy firing [from Longstreet's attack] to my right and rear through the woods, I turned in that direction and was riding to the slope of the hill [Snodgrass] in my rear to ascertain the cause. Just as I passed out of the woods bordering the State [La Fayette] road, I met Captain Kellogg returning, who reported to me that in attempting to reach General Sheridan he had met a large force in an open corn-field to the rear of Reynolds' position, advancing cautiously, with a strong line of skirmishers thrown out to their front, and that they had fired on him and forced him to return. He had reported this to Colonel [Charles G.] Harker, commanding a brigade of Wood's division, posted on a ridge a short distance to the rear of Reynolds' position, who also saw this force [Longstreet's] advancing, but, with Captain Kellogg, was of the opinion that they might be Sheridan's troops coming to our assistance. I rode forward to Colonel

Harker's position, and told him that, although I was expecting Sheridan from that direction, if those troops fired on him, seeing his flag, he must return their fire and resist their farther advance. He immediately ordered his skirmishers to commence firing, and took up a position with his brigade on the crest of a . . . hill [Snodgrass] a short distance to his right and rear, plasing his right in connection with Brannan's division and portions of Beatty's and Stanley's brigades of Negley's division, which had been retired to that point from the left, as circumstantially narrated in the reports of General John Beatty and Colonel Stanley. I then rode to the crest of the hill referred to above. On my way I met General Wood, who confirmed me in the opinion that the troops advancing upon us were the enemy, although we were not then aware of the disaster to the right and center of our army. I then directed him to place his division on the prolongation of Brannan's, who I had ascertained from Wood, was on the top of the hill [Snodgrass] above referred to, and to resist the farther advance of the enemy as long as possible. I sent my aide, Captain Kellogg, to notify General Reynolds that our right had been turned, and that the enemy was in his rear in force.

General Wood barely had time to dispose his troops on the left of Brannan before another of those fierce assaults, similar to those made in the morning on my lines, was made on him and Brannan combined, and kept up by the enemy throwing fresh troops as fast as those in their front were driven back, until near nightfall. About the time that Wood took up his position, General Gordon Granger appeared on my left flank at the head of Steedman's division of his corps. I immediately dispatched a staff officer, Captain [Gilbert M.] Johnson, Second Indiana Cavalry, of Negley's division, to him with orders to push forward and take position on Brannan's right, which order was complied with the greatest promptness and alacrity. Steedman, moving his division into position with almost as much precision as if on drill, and fighting his way to the crest of the hill on Brannan's right, moved forward his artillery and drove the enemy down the southern slope, inflicting on him a most terrible loss in killed and wounded. This opportune arrival of fresh troops revived the flagging spirits of our men on the right, and inspired them with new ardor for the contest. Every assault of the enemy from that time until nightfall was repulsed in the most gallant style by the whole line.

By this time the ammunition in the boxes of the men was reduced, on an average, to 2 or 3 rounds per man, and my ammunition trains having been unfortunately ordered to the rear by some unauthorized person, we should have been entirely without ammunition in a very short time had not a small supply come up with General Steedman's command. This, being distributed among the troops, gave them about 10 rounds per man.

General [James A.] Garfield, chief of staff of General Rosecrans, reached this position about 4 p.m., in company with Lieutenant-Colonel [Gates P.] Thruston, of McCook's staff, and Captains Gaw and [J. D.] Barker, of my staff who had been sent to the rear to bring back the ammunition, if possible. General Garfield gave me the first reliable information that the right and center of our army had been driven, and of its condition at that time. I soon after received a dispatch from General Rosecrans, directing me to assume command of all the forces, and, with Crittenden and McCook, take a strong position and assume a threatening attitude at Rossville, sending the unorganized forces to Chattanooga for reorganization, stating that he would examine the ground at Chattanooga, and then join me; also that he had sent out rations and ammunition to meet me at Rossville.

I determined to hold the position until nightfall, if possible, in the meantime sending Captains Barker and Kellogg to distribute the ammunition, Major [W. E.] Lawrence, my chief of artillery, having been previously sent to notify the different commanders that ammunition would be supplied them shortly. As soon as they reported the distribution of the ammunition, I directed Captain Willard to inform the division commanders to prepare to withdraw their commands as soon as they received orders. At 5:30 p.m., Captain Barker, commanding my escort, was sent to notify General Reynolds to commence the movement, and I left the position behind General Wood's command to meet Reynolds and point out to him the position where I wished him to form line to cover the retirement of the other troops on the left.

In passing through an open woods bordering the State [La Fayette] road, and between my last and Reynolds' position, I was cautioned by a couple of soldiers, who had been to hunt water, that there was a large force of the rebels [Liddell's division] in these woods, drawn up in line and advancing toward me. Just at this time I saw the head of Reynolds' column approaching, and calling to the general himself, directed him to form line perpendicular to the State [La Fayette] road, changing the head of his column to the left, with his right resting on that road, and to charge the enemy, who were then in his immediate front. This movement was made with the utmost promptitude, and facing to the right while on the march. Turchin threw his brigade upon the rebel force, routing them and driving them in utter confusion entirely beyond Baird's left. In this splendid advance more than 200 prisoners were captured and sent to the rear.

Colonel [Milton S.] Robinson, commanding the Second Brigade, Reynolds' division, followed closely upon Turchin, and I posted him on the road leading through the ridge to hold the ground while the troops on our right and left passed by. In a few moments General [August] Willich, commanding a brigade of Johnson's division, reported to me that his brigade was in position on a commanding piece of ground to the right of the Ridge road. I directed him to report to General Reynolds, and assist in covering the retirement of the troops. Turchin's brigade, after driving the enemy a mile and a half, was reassembled, and took its position on the Ridge road, with Robinson and Willich.

These dispositions being made, I sent orders to Generals Wood, Brannan, and Granger to withdraw from their positions. Johnson's and Baird's divisions were attacked at the moment of retiring, but, by being prepared, retired without confusion or any serious losses. General Palmer was also attacked while retiring. [William] Grose's brigade was thrown into some confusion, but [Charles] Cruft's brigade came off in good style, both, however, with little loss. I then proceeded to Rossville, accompanied by Generals Garfield and Gordon Granger, and immediately prepared to place the troops in position at that point. One brigade of Negley's division was posted in . . . [Rossville] gap, on the Ringgold road, and two brigades on the top of the ridge to the right of the road, adjoining the brigade in the road; Reynolds' division on the right of Negley's and reaching to the Dry Valley road; Brannan's division in the rear of Reynolds' right, as a reserve; McCook's corps on the right of the Dry Valley road, and stretching toward the west, his right reaching nearly to Chattanooga Creek; Crittenden's entire corps was posted on the heights to the left of the Ringgold road, with Steedman's division of Granger's corps in reserve behind his left; Baird's division in reserve, and in supporting distance of the brigade in . . . [Rossville] gap; [Dan] McCook's brigade of Granger's corps was also posted as a reserve to the brigade of Negley on the top of the ridge to the right of the road; [Robert H. G.] Minty's brigade of cavalry was on the Ringgold road, about a mile and a half in advance of the gap.

About 10 a.m. of the 21st, receiving a message from Minty that the enemy were advancing on him with a strong force of cavalry and infantry, I directed him to retire through . . . [Rossville] gap and post his command on our left flank, and throw out strong reconnoitering parties across the ridge to observe and report any movements of the enemy on our left front. From information received from citizens, I was convinced that the position was untenable in the face of the odds we had opposed to us, as the enemy could easily concentrate upon our right flank, which, if driven, would expose our center and left to be entirely cut off from our communications. I therefore advised the commanding general [Rosecrans] to concentrate the troops at Chattanooga. About the time I made the suggestion to withdraw, the enemy made a demonstration on the direct road, but were soon repulsed. In anticipation of this order to concentrate at Chattanooga, I sent for the corps commanders, and gave such general instructions as would enable them to prepare their commands for making the movement without confusion. All wagons, ambulances, and surplus artillery carriages were sent to the rear before night.

The order for the withdrawal being received about 6 p.m. [on the 21st] the movement commenced at 9 p.m., in the following order: Strong skirmish lines, under the direction of judicious officers, were thrown out to the front of each division to cover this movement, with directions to retire at daylight, deployed and in supporting distance, the whole to be supported by the First Division, Fourteenth Army Corps, under the superintendence of Major-General Rousseau, assisted by Minty's brigade of cavalry, which was to follow after the skirmishers. Crittenden's corps was to move from the hill to the left of the road at 9 p.m., followed by Steedman's division. Next Negley's division was to withdraw at 10 p.m.; then Reynolds, McCook's corps, by divisions from left to right, moving within supporting distance one after the other; Brannan's division was posted at 6 p.m. on the road about half way between Rossville and Chattanooga to cover the movement. The troops were withdrawn in a quiet, orderly manner, without the loss of a single man, and by 7 a.m. on the 22d were in their positions in front of Chattanooga, which had been assigned to them previous to their arrival, and which they now occupy, covered by strong intrenchments thrown up on the day of our arrival, and strengthened from day to day until they were considered sufficiently strong for all defensive purposes.

I respectfully refer you to the reports of division, brigade, and regimental commanders for the names of those of their respective commands who distinguished themselves. Among them I am much gratified to find the names of Col. F. Van Derveer, Thirty-fifth Ohio, commanding Third Brigade, and Col. John T. Croxton, Fourth Kentucky, commanding Second Brigade, Brannan's division, both of whom I saw on Saturday [the 19th], and I can confirm the reports given of them by their division commander. Col. B. F. Scribner, Thirty-eighth Indiana, commanding First Brigade, Baird's division, was on the right of that division on Saturday morning, when it was attacked in flank by an overwhelming force of the enemy and driven back; yet Colonel Scribner was enabled to rally and reorganize it without the least difficulty, as soon as supported by Johnson's division.

All the troops under my immediate command fought most gallantly on both days, and were ably handled by their respective commanders, viz: Major-Generals Palmer and Reynolds, and Brigadier-Generals Brannan, Johnson, and Baird, on Saturday, and on Sunday, in the afternoon, in addition to the above, Maj. Gen. Gordon Granger, commanding Reserve Corps, and Brigadier-General Wood, commanding First Division, Twenty-first Army Corps, who, with two brigades of his division, under their brave commanders, Colonels Harker and [George P.] Buell, most nobly sustained Brannan's left, while Brigadier-General Steedman, commanding a division of the Reserve Corps, as valiantly maintained his right. Col. Dan. McCook, commanding a brigade of the Reserve Corps, and left by General Granger near McDonald's house, in a commanding position, kept a large force of the enemy's cavalry at bay while hovering on Baird's left, and with his battery materially aided Turchin's handsome charge on the enemy, who had closed in on our left. Brigadier-General Willich, commanding a brigade of Johnson's division, on Saturday, in the attack, and especially on Sunday, nobly sustained his reputation as a soldier. Brig. Gen. John Beatty and Col. T. R. Stanley, commanding brigades of Negley's division, bravely supported Baird's left in the morning of Sunday. Colonel Stanley being struck by the fragments of a shell and disabled in the afternoon, the brigade fought with Brannan's division under the command of Col. W. L. Stoughton, Eleventh Michigan. Col. J. G. Parkhurst, commanding Ninth Michigan Volunteers, and provost-marshal Fourteenth Army Corps, at the head of his regiment, did most valuable service on the 20th, in arresting stragglers and reorganizing the troops which had been driven from the field.

I also tender my thanks to the members of my staff for the services they rendered me. To Lieut. Col. G. E. Flynt, my assistant adjutant-general; Lieut. Col. A. J. Mackay, chief quartermaster; Lieut. Col. J. R. Paul, chief commissary of subsistence, who, although not present on the field of battle, were discharging their duties in their respective departments entirely to my satisfaction. Lieut. Col. A. von Schrader, Seventy-fourth Ohio, assistant inspector-general, who rendered most efficient service as aide-de-camp during the first day's fight, and who was taken prisoner on the afternoon of the . . . [20th] while in the discharge of his duty; Maj. W. F. Lawrence, First Ohio Artillery, my chief of artillery; Capts. J. P. Willard and S. C. Kellogg, aides-de-camp; Capt. J. D. Barker, First Ohio Cavalry, commanding my escort; Capt. W. B. Gaw, chief topographical officer Fourteenth Army Corps, as also the signal officers of the corps, who did duty on the field as aides, and were of great assistance in conducting the operations of my command. Surgs. F. H. Gross, medical director, and H. C. Barrell, medical purveyor, were untiring in their efforts to relieve the wants of the wounded. Dr. Gross was wounded early in the engagement Sunday, but continued in the discharge of his duties. Capt. G. C. Moody, Nineteenth U. S. Infantry, commissary of musters, also rendered efficient service as aide-de-camp. Captain Johnson, Second Indiana Cavalry, of General Negley's staff, and Capt. T. C. Williams, Nineteenth U. S.

Infantry, of General Baird's staff, having been cut off from their respective commanders, reported to me for duty, and were of great assistance as aides.

I submit herewith annexed a consolidated report of the casualties of the Fourteenth Army Corps.

Very respectfully, your obedient servant,

GEO. H. THOMAS,
*Major-General U. S. Volunteers, Commanding.*

Brig. Gen. James A. Garfield,
*Chief of Staff, Department of the Cumberland.*[55]

Upon reviewing Thomas' report, General Rosecrans took exception to one of the statements. In calling this to Thomas' attention, Rosecrans wrote:

[Chattanooga, Tenn., *September* 30, 1863.]

General Thomas:

Your report says you received my dispatch of 12.15 p.m., directing you to retire on Rossville. This is an error in the hour of the dispatch. I did not leave the battlefield until after that hour, nor reach Chattanooga before 3.40 p.m.

Please have the error corrected. The first dispatch to you must have been written as late as 4.15.

W. S. ROSECRANS.[56]

Whereupon Thomas replied:

Headquarters Fourteenth Army Corps,
*Chattanooga, October* 3, 1863.

Major-General Rosecrans,
*Commanding Department:*

General: Your dispatch just received. I made mention of the time of receiving your dispatch on the battle-field to call attention to the fact, believing it to have been an error. I will make the correction in my forthcoming report, or in my fair copy.

Very respectfully, your obedient servant,

GEO. H. THOMAS,
*Major-General U. S. Volunteers, Commanding.*[57]

Ironically, the battle that gave Thomas his greatest distinction was one that Smith D. Atkins believed should never have been

55. OR, I, XXX, pt. I, pp. 245-56.
56. *Ibid.,* p. 256.
57. *Ibid.,* p. 257.

fought. Atkins, who commanded the 92d Illinois Mounted Infantry of Wilder's Brigade, 14th Corps, Army of the Cumberland, reviewed his thesis in an address before the Women's Relief Corps of the Grand Army of the Republic at Mendota, Illinois, February 22, 1907. He held that faulty Union generalship imperiled a position that ought never have been risked in the first place. According to Atkins:

On Friday, September 4, 1863, my regiment was ordered to join [Colonel John H.] Wilder, north of Chattanooga, and on reporting to Wilder I found that my regiment was . . . to report to General Thomas to be used by General Rosecrans for scouting purposes, and immediately ascended to the top of Walden's Ridge, a continuation of Lookout Mountain, on the north side of the Tennessee River, and from that elevation I looked for hours with my field glass into the deserted streets of Chattanooga, and became convinced that Bragg had evacuated that Confederate stronghold.

Crossing the Tennessee River on the pontoons at Bridgeport, I reported to General Thomas, and in person to General Rosecrans at Trenton, twenty miles from Chattanooga, on the west side of Lookout Mountain, on the forenoon of Tuesday, September 8th, 1863, and gave General Rosecrans my reason for believing that Chattanooga had been evacuated by Bragg, and nothing left there but his cavalry to curtain his movements. I told General Rosecrans I had found a cow-path on the west side of Lookout Mountain, four miles from its head, that cattle could go up onto the mountain, and offered to send a body of Ninety-Second men onto the mountain by that cow-path, and drive the enemy's cavalry from off the mountain, demonstrating that Chattanooga was evacuated, and by the order of General Rosecrans I did so, and again reported to him in person at Trenton [Georgia] about 9 o'clock on the evening of September 8th, 1863, and was ordered by him to take the advance into Chattanooga on the morning of the 9th of September, 1863.

Crossing the nose of the mountain on the Nashville road early on the morning of September 9th, I found the enemy's cavalry holding the road, and my regiment was driving them over the mountain when Wilder's Brigade battery [Captain Eli Lilly's 18th Indiana Battery] from Moccasin Point on the north side of the Tennessee began throwing its shells onto the mountain, enfilading my line of skirmishers, and I was compelled to fall back. It was decidedly disagreeable to be fired upon by the artillery of the brigade to which my regiment belonged. How to communicate with Wilder and stop that firing was a difficult problem, and I thought the only way to do so would be to have some one swim the river; but that would occasion a long delay. A little boy, a stranger to me, said he had served in the signal corps, and could send a message by tying his handkerchief to two hazel sticks, and when he was ready, standing on a jutting rock where he could be seen by Wilder's men across the river, he inquired what message, and I said, "Ninety-Second Illinois," and he had not long been waving his flag, spelling out the words, when Wilder's men on the north side of the river set up a great cheer, and, knowing they would no longer fire upon us, we pressed forward, driving the Confederates before us and off the mountain, and at 10 o'clock a.m. the flag of the Ninety-Second Illinois Volunteers was floating from the top of the Crutchfield House, the first Union flag to float in Chattanooga since Bragg's army occupied that place.

I had brought to me every person I could find, and sent word back to Rosecrans that Bragg had evacuated the city and fallen back beyond Chickamauga with the intention of giving battle as soon as his reinforcements [two divisions of Longstreet's corps] came from Lee's army in Virginia.

Now, keep this date carefully in mind, September 9, 1863, while the battle of Chickamauga was not begun until ten days after that, on September 19, 1863. I believed then, and I believe now, that General Rosecrans could have put the Army of the Cumberland into Chattanooga by the evening of September 10th, 1863, without the loss of a man or a wheel. I know that he could have done that, and the battle of Chickamauga, with its awful loss of life, have been wholly avoided. It was a useless battle, and because it was useless and disastrous, Rosecrans was relieved from the command of the Army of the Cumberland, and was never again restored to favor as an army commander. These views are not new; they were entertained and expressed by me at that time, and I have entertained them ever since, and never hesitated to express them. The battle of Chickamauga was a useless battle, the broken and shattered Army of the Cumberland [was] driven from the field and cooped up and nearly starved to death in

Chattanooga, that Rosecrans was in full possession of on September 9, 1863, and which might have been held by him with his full army intact, with abundant force to protect his line of supplies, and where he never could have been or would have been assaulted by the Confederate army. That was my deliberate judgment at that time, and, it will be, in my opinion, the deliberate judgment of history. . . .

Common sense is often quite as valuable as technical military knowledge, and by every rule of common sense, Rosecrans should have occupied the evacuated city of Chattanooga when he became in full possession of it on September 9, 1863, and have avoided entirely the bloody and disastrous battle of Chickamauga.

My orders from General Rosecrans were to enter the city of Chattanooga, obtain all the information possible concerning the evacuation by Bragg, and to return to him with my regiment. When I was ready to start back the road was filled with Crittenden's corps of the Army of the Cumberland that followed me into Chattanooga, and when just ready to return I was ordered by General Crittenden to go up the Tennessee River to Fire Island, ten miles, and enable Wilder with his brigade to cross. I told Crittenden of my order to return to General Rosecrans, but he gave me positive orders, and I obeyed, driving small parties of the Confederate cavalry before me until I reached a famous grape plantation eight miles north of Chattanooga, where I learned that Wilder's Brigade was already crossing the river[.] Putting my regiment into camp I rode forward to communicate with Wilder, and was by him positively ordered to march with his brigade the next day, which I did, camping at night at Graysville, almost directly east of Chattanooga, and during the night I received positive orders to report with my regiment to General Rosecrans at La Fayette, Georgia, and moving before daylight on September 11, I struck the Confederate pickets about two miles north of Ringgold.

Sending word back to Wilder I dismounted my regiment, when the enemy [Forrest's cavalry] mounted and moved out to charge my line—waiting until they were close upon me[,] my repeating Spencer rifles halted their charge and turned it back. Then they formed in two lines to renew the charge when Wilder came up with a section of 10-pound [er] rifled cannon, and opened immediately. Instantly the artillery fire was answered, but not a shot came near us; firing again with our artillery, instantly came the response. We did not know it then, but Crittenden's troops were approaching Ringgold from the west and we from the north, and it was Crittenden's guns we heard, while Forrest retreated through Ringgold gap. Had Crittenden's troops and Wilder's Brigade been acting in concert, General Forrest and his cavalry would have been captured at Ringgold. Sending out a company on the La Fayette road, the enemy was found in strong force at the Chickamauga . . . , and my regiment marched to Rossville, reaching there after dark.

Confident that Rosecrans was in Chattanooga, and not in La Fayette, I sent officers to Chattanooga before daylight on the 12th of September, but they did not return to me, and an hour after daylight I tock the road to La Fayette, striking the enemy in strong force at [Lee and] Gordon's Mill[s] on the Chickamauga. I was without corn for my animals, and finding a cornfield I fed my horses and filled the nose-bags with corn, and was just about to cross the . . . [Chickamauga] with my regiment when I received a written order from General Rosecrans to send my regiment to the foot of Lookout Mountain and report in person to General Rosecrans at Chattanooga, which I did, and was ordered to find Thomas somewhere on Lookout Mountain, and marching all night down the mountain I communicated with Thomas at daylight on September 13, and sent word to General Rosecrans at Chattanooga.

During the day my regiment followed General Thomas down the mountain on its east side at . . . [Stevens'] Gap. On the 14th, 15th, 16th, and 17th of September with my regiment I scouted the country between . . . [Stevens'] Gap and [Lee and] Gordon's Mill[s], finding the crossings of the Chickamauga always heavily guarded by the enemy.

I was never ordered to scout south and east of the Chickamauga. . . . I never knew why. No Union soldiers ever were sent by Rosecrans . . . [east] of that river so far as I know. The woods were full of Rebel spies pretending to be deserters, and by the order of General Rosecrans none of them were arrested or interfered with in any way, as Rosecrans believed that Bragg's army was disintegrating and going home, and General Rosecrans thought that the Rebel spies were deserters from Bragg's army. They were not. They were well and strong, and well clothed, and such men seldom desert from any army. I never could understand the infatuation of a Union General who by his own official orders filled his camps with spies from the forces opposing him.

Early on the morning of September 19, 1863, the Army of the Cumberland began its race for Chattanooga, where that army might have been and should have been safely placed ten days before that time. In that race the Army of the Cumberland was attacked in flank by Bragg's army. The Army of the Cumberland would repulse the enemy at some point and immediately move on toward Chattanooga. All day long it was a continuous race. At about 10 a. m. my regiment was ordered by General Rosecrans to take position and rest in a field southeast of Widow Glenn's house, and putting my regiment in the field, I sent out a skirmish line into the woods in my front, and captured a prisoner from the Confederate skirmish line that was found west of the La Fayette road. The prisoner was brought immediately to me. He was a Virginia boy, badly frightened at first, but he soon told me that he belonged to Longstreet's corps from the Virginia Army, and detailed to me how he came by cars, where they disembarked, and how they marched to the battlefield. I took the prisoner, the first one captured from Longstreet's corps, to General Rosecrans at his then headquarters at Widow Glenn's house, and told him I had a prisoner from Longstreet's corps, when Rosecrans flew into a passion, denounced the little boy as a liar, declared that Longstreet's corps was not there. The little boy prisoner was so frightened that he would not speak a word. In sorrow I turned away, and joined my regiment. Rosecrans [soon] found out that Longstreet's corps was there. . . .

Atkins continued by speaking highly of the role played by General Thomas in the battle:

The heroic conduct of Thomas on Snodgrass Hill saved the Army of the Cumberland from total rout and defeat, but that gallant soldier with his jaded but brave troops sought safety in flight to Rossville Gap under the cover of the friendly darkness of the night.

The useless battle had been fought, the useless sacrifice of thousands of brave men of the Army of the Cumberland had been made, and the shattered remnant of the Army of the Cumberland in Chattanooga, where the entire army might have been and ought to have been on the evening of September 10th, 1863, without the loss of a man or a wheel.[58]

The Army of the Cumberland, having taken position at Chattanooga, found itself with Bragg's troops to its front and to its rear a sterile and inhospitable region north of the Tennessee River. Union soldiers threw up and occupied formidable lines of rifle-pits, covering the approaches to Chattanooga. Bragg's army advanced on the morning of September 22. Missionary Ridge was occupied, and, taking advantage of a blunder by Rosecrans, Longstreet's corps took possession of Lookout Mountain and blocked the direct road and railroad to Bridgeport. Pressing forward on their right, the Confederates established two advance lines of rifle-pits—the first at the foot of Missionary Ridge and the second nearly a mile forward of the ridge and within one-third of a mile of the Union entrenchments. A key position on Bragg's forward line was Orchard Knob. To connect his left on Lookout Mountain and his right on and in front of Missionary Ridge, Bragg's center occupied Chattanooga Valley.

Rosecrans, his 40,000-man army partially invested and his back to the Tennessee River, was confronted by a desperate situation. To supply his army, Rosecrans was compelled to rely upon a tortuous 60-mile mountainous road linking Chattanooga with Bridgeport. After crossing the Tennessee on a pontoon bridge, the trace snaked its way over Waldens Ridge, crossed the Sequatchie Valley, and then negotiated the Cumberland Plateau to the railroad.

General Bragg sent his cavalry under Major General Joseph Wheeler to raid this supply line. On October 2, the Confederate horsemen swept down on a wagon train as it passed Anderson's Cross Roads. Scores of wagons were burned and hundreds of horses and mules shot or stampeded. Union cavalry coming upon the scene broke the Rebel roadblock, and Wheeler's men retreated westward, finally recrossing the Tennessee on October 9 at Muscle Shoals.[59]

58. Smith D. Atkins, *Chickamauga, Useless, Disastrous Battle, Talk by Smith D. Atkins* (GAR, 1907, Mendota, Ill.).
59. Cist, pp. 230-32; Van Horne, *History*, I, pp. 386-91; John P. Dyer, *From Shiloh to San Juan: The Life of "Fighting Joe" Wheeler* (Baton Rouge: Louisiana University Press, 1961), pp. 99-107.

Although the Confederate cavalry had failed to seriously interrupt traffic over the supply route, torrential rains pelting the region turned the road into a ribbon of mud. Supplying the army quickly became a critical problem for the Union quartermasters. Forage for the animals was slashed and large numbers of artillery horses starved to death. The soldiers were put on reduced rations. Corn and hardtack dropped in unloading the wagons was "eagerly seized and eaten to stay the demands of hunger, and still the pressure was growing daily, and no one knew how it would ultimately end."[60]

As soon as news reached Washington of the Chickamauga debacle, the War Department extended itself to retrieve the situation. Two corps, the 11th and 12th, from the Army of the Potomac under Major General Joseph Hooker were rushed from near Warrenton, Virginia, to Middle Tennessee. Hooker reached Nashville on October 2, while his vanguard had detrained at Bridgeport on the previous afternoon. General Grant, under orders to send reinforcements from central Mississippi, embarked General William T. Sherman and four Army of the Tennessee divisions aboard steamboats at Vicksburg. Disembarking at Memphis, Sherman and his men started for Bridgeport riding cars of the Memphis & Charleston to a short distance beyond Corinth, and then taking up the march.[61]

Coincident with the sacking of Generals Crittenden and McCook and the reorganization of their 20th and 21st Corps into the newly constituted 4th Corps, to be led by General Gordon Granger, General Rosecrans had come under increasing fire from Washington. Particularly hurtful to Rosecrans' cause were the confidential reports forwarded to Secretary of War Stanton by his assistant and resident spy, Charles A. Dana. On October 12, Dana wrote Stanton:

> I have never seen a public man possessing talent with less administrative power, less clearness and steadiness in difficulty, and greater practical incapacity than General Rosecrans. He has inventive fertility and knowledge, but he has no strength of will and no concentration of purpose. His mind

60. Cist, p. 232.
61. *Ibid;* Van Horne, *History,* I, pp. 392-93, 405-06.

scatters; there is no system in the use of his busy days and restless nights, no courage against individual in his composition, and, with great love of command, he is a feeble commander. He is conscientious and honest, just as he is imperious and disputatious; always with a stray vein of caprice and an overweening passion for the approbation of his personal friends and the public outside.

Under the present circumstances I consider this army to be very unsafe in his hands; but do know of no man except Thomas who could now be safely put in his place. Weather pleasant but cloudy.[62]

Some of Rosecrans' senior officers likewise threw darts at their superior. Division commander Major General John M. Palmer believed Rosecrans drank and swore too much, although his headquarters "was the resort of priests." Palmer wrote his wife that "self-indulgence and unmanly desire to escape personal damage and responsibility drove several officers of the highest rank into Chattanooga [where] they told horrible tales of rout and disaster."[63]

General Thomas, learning that Rosecrans was being savaged in Washington, supported his chief. Satisfied that Dana was a meddlesome busybody and apprised of the tenor of the Stanton dispatches by a telegraph office clerk, Thomas sent General Garfield to caution Rosecrans that "spies from Washington now in camp are working for your removal." Thomas, as heretofore, separated himself from any actions that might be interpreted that he was campaigning to replace Rosecrans.[64]

It was at this time that Dana called on Thomas and read the general a telegram received from Stanton contending that the Secretary was not responsible for Thomas not being placed in command of the army "months ago." Thomas, Dana recalled, appeared "much too affected" to reply for several minutes. Then, possibly recalling Camp Dick Robinson, Thomas answered that he would have desired the command of an army organized and disciplined by himself, but added, I did not wish to accept any


62. OR, I, XXX, pt. I, p. 215.
63. George T. Palmer, *A Conscientious Turncoat* (New Haven, 1941), p. 117.
64. *Society of the Army of the Cumberland, Eleventh Reunion, Washington, D. C.* (Cincinnati, 1880), p. 179.

command if exposed to the imputation of having intrigued to replace my superior. When camp rumors spread that Thomas was about to relieve Rosecrans, Thomas asked Garfield to tell Dana that he would never consent to become Rosecrans' successor.[65]

This question, however, would be decided by the Lincoln administration and not by General Thomas. On October 16, as the supply situation became daily more bleak and rations were further pared, Dana telegraphed the Secretary of War, "The incapacity of the commander is astonishing . . . his imbecility . . . contagious."[66]

Galvanized into action by such messages, the War Department finally acted. By orders, dated the 16th, the Departments of the Ohio, Cumberland, and the Tennessee were merged and constituted as "The Military Division of the Mississippi" to be commanded by General Ulysses S. Grant. General Burnside was retained as leader of the Army of the Ohio, Sherman replaced Grant as head of the Army of the Tennessee, while the appointment of Thomas to lead the Army of the Cumberland was mentioned, but left to Grant's judgment.

Grant did not hesitate and, in accordance with his recommendation, the War Department directed Thomas to relieve Rosecrans as commander of the Army of the Cumberland.[67]

On the evening of October 19, Rosecrans returned to his Chattanooga headquarters from Brown's Ferry, where he had spent the day, with William F. "Baldy" Smith, his chief engineer, perfecting plans for opening a new route to supply the army. There, he was handed the orders relieving him of command. Departing for Stevenson that night, Rosecrans left a farewell order, to be published and issued the next morning.[68]

One of Grant's first acts on taking command of the Division of the Mississippi was to telegraph Thomas from Louisville, ordering him to "Hold Chattanooga at all hazards." Thomas replied, "We will hold the town till we starve," and Thomas' men

65. Charles A. Dana, *Recollections of the Civil War* (New York: 1913), p. 125.
66. OR, I, XXX, pt. I, p. 221.
67. Cist, p. 234; Van Horne, *History*, I, 394-95.
68. Cist, pp. 234-36; Van Horne, *History*, I, 403-04.

"cheerfully agreed to starve a while longer."[69] Thomas was confident his troops would endure hardships and accept death rather than abandon all their successes of the Tullahoma and Chickamauga campaigns.

On Tuesday, October 20, General Thomas issued his first General Order to his newly assigned command:

Hdqrs. Dept. of the Cumberland,
*Chattanooga, Tenn., October* 20, 1863.

General Orders,
   No. 243.

In obedience to the orders of the President of the United States, the undersigned hereby assumes command of the Department and Army of the Cumberland.

In assuming the control of this army, so long and ably commanded by Major-General Rosecrans, the undersigned confidently relies upon the hearty co-operation of every officer and soldier of the Army of the Cumberland to enable him to perform the arduous duties devolved upon him.

The officers on duty in the various departments of the staff at these headquarters will continue in their respective places.

All orders heretofore published for the government of this army will remain in force until further orders.

Geo. H. Thomas,
*Major-General, U. S. Volunteers.*[70]

General Grant, having reached Bridgeport by rail from Louisville, continued on by horseback to Chattanooga and a meeting with General Thomas. Grant reached Thomas' headquarters on the evening of October 23. Staff officer James H. Wilson, who had preceded Grant by several hours, recalled that Thomas sat on one side of the fire and Grant on the other. John A. Rawlins, Grant's chief-of-staff, and other officers either stood or sat. Rawlins looked angry, while Thomas seemed preoccupied. Wilson gave Thomas a cue, remarking, "General Grant is wet and in pain." At that Thomas turned to his aides, dry clothing was found and a hot supper served. The embarrassment soon passed. After the meal,

69. Henry Steele Commager, ed., *The Blue and the Gray,* 2 Vols. (Indianapolis: Bobbs-Merrill, 1950), II, 896.
70. OR, I, XXXI, pt. I, p. 669.

conversation "became carefree, if not hilarious."[71]

The next day, Grant, accompanied by Generals Thomas and Smith, personally reconnoitered the Tennessee River below Chattanooga, with reference to carrying out Rosecrans' plan for opening a cracker route for supply of the Army of the Cumberland by way of Brown's and Kelley's ferries. Grant approved the plan, directing Thomas to proceed to its execution, whereupon Grant and his staff returned to Bridgeport.[72]

General Thomas sketched the opening of the "Cracker Line," in which the Army of the Cumberland was given a big assist by General Hooker and the 11th and 12th Corps, in a report dated November 7, 1863:

Headquarters Department of the Cumberland,
*Chattanooga, November 7, 1863.*

General: I have the honor to forward herewith the official reports of Major-General Hooker, commanding Eleventh and Twelfth Corps, and of Brig. Gen. W. F. Smith, chief engineer, Department of the Cumberland, commanding the expedition composed of Turchin's brigade, Baird's division, Fourteenth Army Corps, and [William B.] Hazen's brigade, Wood's division, Fourth Army Corps, and detachments of the Eighteenth Ohio Infantry, under command of Col. T. R. Stanley, and of the First Michigan Engineers, under command of Capt. P. V. Fox, of the operations of their respective commands between the 26th and 28th ultimo, to gain possession of the south bank of the Tennessee River and to open the road for a depot of supplies at Bridgeport.

Preliminary steps had already been taken to execute this vitally important movement before the command of the department devolved on me. The bridge, which it was necessary to throw across the river at Brown's Ferry to gain possession of the northern end of Lookout Valley and open communication with Bridgeport by road and river, was nearly completed.

On the 23d, orders were sent to General Hooker to concentrate the Eleventh Corps and one division of the Twelfth at Bridgeport, informing him at the same time what his force was expected to accomplish, and that a force from this place

71. James H. Wilson, *Under the Old Flag,* 2 vols. (New York: D. Appleton & Co., 1912), I, 272; —————, *Life of Charles A. Dana* (New York, 1907), pp. 280-81.
72. Cist, pp. 237-38.

would co-operate with him by establishing a bridge across the river at Brown's Ferry and seize the heights on the south, or Lookout Valley side, thus giving him an open road to Chattanooga when his forces should arrive in Lookout Valley. The force to throw the bridge was organized by Saturday, the 24th, and the boats and bridge completed, giving General Smith two days to examine the ground with the two brigade

(Inclosure)

## Consolidated Return of Casualties.

| Troops | Killed | | | Wounded | | | Missing | | | Aggregate |
|---|---|---|---|---|---|---|---|---|---|---|
| | Officers | Men | Total | Officers | Men | Total | Officers | Men | Total | |
| Maj.-Gen. Hooker's Command, 11th Corps. | 5 | 23 | 38 | 13 | 135 | 148 | .... | 14 | 14 | 200 |
| 2nd Division, 12th Corps. | 4 | 30 | 34 | 15 | 159 | 174 | .... | 8 | 8 | 216 |
| Brig.-Gen. Smith's Command | .... | 4 | 4 | 2 | 15 | 17 | .... | .... | .... | 21 |
| Total | 9 | 67 | 76 | 30 | 309 | 339 | .... | 22 | 22 | 437[73] |

commanders, and to give all the necessary detailed instructions to insure success. General Hooker reported on the 26th that he would be ready to move on the 27th at daylight.

He was instructed to move at the appointed time, with full instructions how to provide for the defense of his flank, and to cover the approaches to the road from the direction of Trenton. The bridge was successfully thrown across the river on the night of the 26th, and General Hooker reached Lookout Valley and communicated with this place on the 28th. The enemy [Longstreet's Corps] attempted to surprise him the night after reaching his position in Lookout Valley, and, after an obstinate contest [the battle of Wauhatchie] of two hours duration, was completely repulsed, with a loss of upward of

73. OR, I, XXXI, pt. I, pp. 42-3.

1,500 killed and wounded, over 100 prisoners, and several hundred stand of arms. I refer you to the reports of Generals Hooker and Smith for the details of the operations of their commands, commending to favorable consideration the names of those officers specially mentioned by them for gallant and meritorious conduct. The skillful execution by General Smith of the work assigned him, and the promptness with which General Hooker, with his troops, met and repulsed the enemy on the night of the 28th, reflects the greatest credit on both of those officers and their entire commands. I herewith annex consolidated returns of casualties.

I am, general, very respectfully, your obedient servant,

GEO. H. THOMAS,

*Major-General, U. S. Volunteers, Commanding.*

Brig. Gen. Lorenzo Thomas,
*Adjutant-General U. S. Army, Washington, D. C.*

During the first two weeks of November, as Sherman and his four divisions approached Bridgeport, General Bragg weakened his army by detaching Longstreet's Corps and Wheeler's cavalry and sending them to attack General Burnside at Knoxville. Sherman, having ridden ahead, joined Grant and Thomas in beleagured Chattanooga on November 15. As the first order of business, General Grant, accompanied by Thomas and Sherman, rode out of the town to reconnoiter the Rebel lines and to make plans for raising the siege. Grant bit down on a cigar; Sherman looked fit and alert, gesturing nervously as he spoke; and Thomas was grave and silent.

As the officers and their staffs returned to Chattanooga, Thomas pointed toward Missionary Ridge, where Bragg had his headquarters. Speculating about their old messmates from the Third Artillery and their Fort Moultrie days, Sherman asked, "Tom, have you seen Bragg or had any communication with him?" Thomas' temper flared as he retorted, "Damn him, I'll be even with him yet!" "What's the matter now?" Sherman interrupted.

Thomas then explained that several months ago an unsealed letter had arrived from the north addressed to a person in the Confederacy with a request that it be forwarded under a flag of truce. Thomas had attached a note asking Bragg to send it on to the addressee. The letter bounced back with a Bragg endorsement reading, "Respectfully returned to Genl. Thomas. Genl. Bragg declines to have any intercourse with a man who has betrayed his state." Because nothing could hurt Thomas more deeply than an imputation upon his loyalty, as Sherman recalled the incident, Thomas muttered about what would happen to Bragg, when a reckoning came.[74]

Before Sherman returned to Bridgeport, Grant had perfected his plans. The principal attack was to be made on the 21st at daylight. To accomplish this Sherman with his four divisions was to cross the Tennessee River at Brown's Ferry and march behind Stringer's Ridge, concealed from the eyes of the Confederates, and take position near the North Chickamauga Creek. Then Sherman was to recross the river by pontoon bridge at the mouth of the South Chickamauga Creek, strike the north end of Missionary Ridge, and occupy it as far as the railroad tunnel. Thomas was to move his Army of the Cumberland to the left, and connect with Sherman. This united force was to sweep the Confederates southward off Missionary Ridge and away from their base of supplies at Chickamauga Station. Major General Oliver O. Howard's 11th Corps was to act as a general reserve for this force. Hooker, with the 12th Corps and Brigadier General Charles Cruft's division (4th Corps), was to hold Lookout Valley. Colonel Eli Long's cavalry was to cover Sherman's left and, when no longer needed for this task, was to strike Bragg's communications. This original plan, however, was changed several times to fit the situation.

The rains that hampered movement of Union supplies also delayed Sherman's march and the crossing of the Tennessee. High water broke the bridge at Brown's Ferry and Brigadier General Peter J. Osterhaus' division could not cross the river. Subsequently it received orders to join Hooker in Lookout Valley.

On November 22, Grant received word that Bragg was withdrawing his army; actually the movement reported was General Buckner leaving to reinforce Longstreet near Knoxville. To "test the truth" of the report, Grant changed his plans and ordered Thomas to make a demonstration to his front on the 23d. This began the battles for Chattanooga.

74. Lloyd Lewis, *Sherman: Fighting Prophet* (New York: Harcourt, Brace & Co., 1932), p. 317; Sherman to Garfield, July 28, 1870, Sherman Papers, Library of Congress; *North American Review*, April 1877, 377.

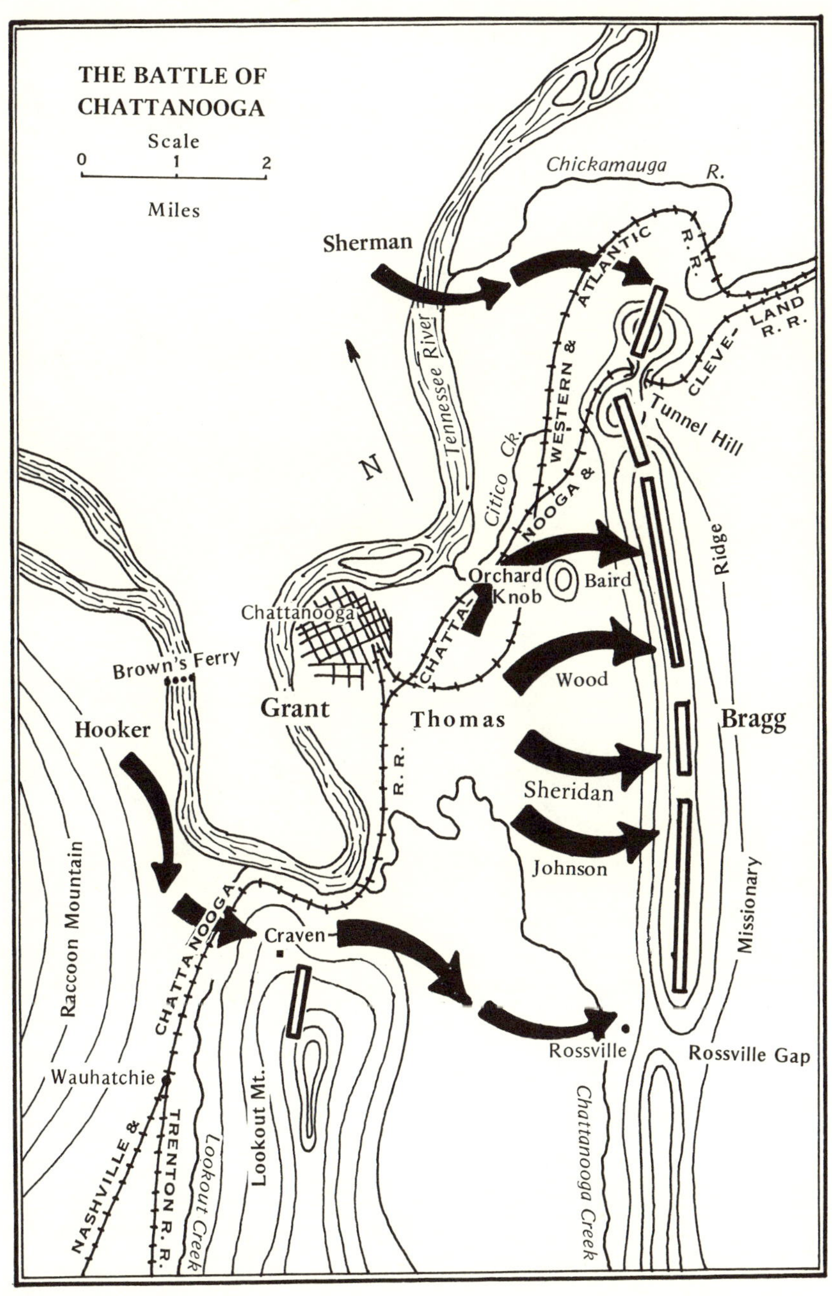

THE BATTLE OF
CHATTANOOGA
Scale
0
1
2
Miles
Sherman
Chickamauga
R.
WESTERN & ATLANTIC
R. R.
CLEVE-
LAND
R. R.
Tunnel Hill
Ridge
Tennessee River
Citico Ck.
NOOGA &
Orchard
Knob
Baird
N
Chattanooga
Brown's Ferry
CHATTA-
Wood
Grant
Thomas
Bragg
R. R.
Sheridan
Hooker
Johnson
Missionary
Raccoon Mountain
CHATTANOOGA
Craven
Rossville
Rossville Gap
Wauhatchie
NASHVILLE &
TRENTON R. R.
Lookout Creek
Lookout Mt.
Chattanooga Creek

Thomas' army had made its positions very strong during the nine weeks it was besieged by Bragg's soldiers. One of its strong points was Fort Wood on an elevated point east of the town. Thomas, according to instructions, sent General Sheridan's and General Wood's divisions to the level, open ground at Fort Wood and there formed them in line—Wood on the left, Sheridan on the right, with General Baird supporting Sheridan. General Johnson's troops held the rifle-pits, and Howard's corps, which had crossed from the north bank of the river, acted as the reserve.

At 2 p. m. on November 23, the lines in blue moved forward, driving the Confederate outposts and their supports back to the base of Missionary Ridge, and captured Orchard Knob, a low hill a little more than a mile in front of the ridge. The Union forces occupied the captured entrenchments and emplaced a battery on Orchard Knob. Except for occasional artillery firing, the fighting ended for the day. General Grant apprised the War Department of this success, telegraphing:

*Chattanooga, Tenn., November 23, 1863, 3 p. m.*
(Received 6:40 p. m.)

General Thomas' troops attacked the enemy's left at 2 p. m. today, carried the first line of rifle-pits running over the knoll, 1,200 yards in front of Fort Wood, and low ridge to the right of it, taking about 200 prisoners, besides killed and wounded. Our loss small. The troops moved under fire with all the precision of veterans on parade. Thomas' troops will intrench themselves, and hold their position until daylight, when Sherman will join the attack from the mouth of the Chickamauga, and a decisive battle will be fought.

U. S. Grant,
*Major-General.*[75]

Then, on the night of the 23d, General Sherman put his troops in motion. A brigade crossed the Tennessee near the mouth of Chickamauga Creek and established a bridgehead. By early afternoon on the 24th, a pontoon bridge had been positioned, and Sherman's troops were across and ready to attack. They were reinforced by General Jefferson C. Davis' 14th Corps division.

Sherman advanced and seized the northeastern end of Missionary Ridge, overrunning a line of Confederate outposts. To his

75. OR, I, XXXI, pt. II, p. 24.

chagrin, Sherman encountered a saddle separating the section of ridge occupied from Tunnel Hill immediately southwestward. Bold fighters from Cleburne's division rushed to Tunnel Hill caused Sherman to pause, and soldiers in blue and gray entrenched and grimly awaited the dawn.

Coincidentally, General Hooker's three divisions assailed the Confederate left anchored on Lookout Mountain. The Federals crossed Lookout Creek, worked their way up onto the shoulder of the mountain, and drove the Confederates from their stronghold at the Cravens' farm. By mid-afternoon, the fog put a stop to the fighting, and on the evening of the 24th the Confederates withdrew from Lookout Mountain to reinforce the divisions defending Missionary Ridge.

On the 25th, the Federal strength was directed toward Missionary Ridge, the last stronghold of General Bragg and his Rebel forces. With Sherman on the left and Hooker advancing but not yet in sight on the right, General Grant gave Thomas the order to attack Missionary Ridge, defended by the center of Bragg's army. The order, however, was for the troops to go only as far as the rifle-pits at the base of the ridge, then reform, and await further instructions. This having been accomplished, Thomas' troops found themselves under heavy fire from the heights above with no order either to go forward or to retire. Therefore, they had the choice of whether to stand still and die or to go forward without orders and take the crest. The men and their immediate commanders chose the latter, and what followed proved to be one of the brilliant assaults of American military history.

In his official report, General Grant described what happened on Wednesday, November 25:

> Early in the morning of the twenty-fifth the remainder of Howard's corps reported to Sherman and constituted a part of his forces during the day's battle, the pursuit and subsequent advance for the relief of Knoxville.
>
> Sherman's position not only threatened the right flank of the enemy, but from his occupying a line across the mountain and to the railroad bridge across Chickamauga Creek, [threatened] his rear and stores at Chickamauga Station. This caused the enemy to move heavily against him. This movement of his [the foe] being plainly seen from the position I

occupied on Orchard Knob, Baird's division of the Fourteenth corps was ordered to Sherman's support, but receiving a note from Sherman informing me that he had all the force necessary, Baird was put in position on Thomas' left.

The appearance of Hooker's column was at this time anxiously looked for and momentarily expected, moving north on the ridge with his left in Chattanooga Valley and his right east of the ridge. His approach was intended as the signal for storming the ridge in the centre with strong columns, but the length of time necessarily consumed in the construction of a bridge near Chattanooga Creek [actually the bridge was over Chattanooga Creek] detained him to a later hour than was expected. Being satisfied from the latest information from him, that he must by this time be on his way from Rossville [Georgia], though not yet in sight, and discovering that the enemy, in his desperation to defeat or resist the progress of Sherman, was weakening his centre on Missionary Ridge, determined me to order the advance at once. Thomas was accordingly directed to move forward his troops constituting our centre—Baird's division (Fourteenth corps), Wood's and Sheridan's divisions (Fourth corps), and Johnson's division (Fourteenth corps) with a double line of skirmishers thrown out, followed in easy supporting distance by the whole force, and carry the rifle-pits at the foot of Missionary Ridge, and when carried to re-form his lines with a view of carrying the top of the ridge.

These troops moved forward, drove the enemy from the rifle-pits at the base of the ridge like bees from a hive; stopped but a moment until the whole were in line, and commenced ascent of the mountain from right to left almost simultaneously, following closely the retreating enemy without further orders. They encountered a fearful volley of grape and canister from near thirty pieces of artillery, and musketry from still well filled rifle-pits on the summit of the ridge. Not a waver, however, was seen in all that long line of brave men; their progress was steadily onward until the summit was in their possession.[76]

On December 1, six days after his soldiers routed Bragg's army from the seemingly impregnable crest of Missionary Ridge, General Thomas, while events were vivid, drafted and forwarded his

76. Van Horne, *Life,* pp. 192-93.

"after action report" for the preceding month to the War Department. It read:

Headquarters Department of the Cumberland,<br>
Chattanooga, December 1, 1863.

General: The following operations of the Army of the Cumberland since October 31 are respectfully submitted to the General-in-Chief:

As soon as communications with Bridgeport had been made secure, and the question of supplying the army at this point rendered certain, preparations were at once commenced for driving the enemy from his position in our immediate front on Lookout Mountain and Missionary Ridge, and, if possible, to send a force to the refief of [General Burnside at] Knoxville. To enable me to dislodge the enemy from the threatening position he had assumed in our front guns of a heavier caliber than those with the army were needed, also additional means for crossing the Tennessee River. Brigadier-General Brannan, chief of artillery [Brannan, in the army's October reorganization, had been named chief of artillery and General Baird had been assigned to lead the Third Division], was directed to send for the necesssary number of guns and ammunition, and after consulting with Brig. Gen. W. F. Smith, chief engineer, to prepare the batteries for the guns on their arrival. While awaiting the arrival of the guns and ammunition, work was prosecuted on the fortifications around the town. In addition to his duties of superintending the work on the fortifications, General Smith pushed vigorously the construction of two pontoon bridges, to be used in the execution of the movements which were determined upon as necessary to a successful dislodgment of the enemy.

Guerrillas having become somewhat troublesome to the northeast of McMinnville and east of the Caney Fork of the Cumberland, Brigadier-General [Washington L.] Elliott, chief of cavalry, was ordered, November 14, to establish his headquarters with the First Division of Cavalry at or near Alexandria, and employ the division in hunting up and exterminating these marauders. Elliott reached Alexandria on the 18th, and on the 27th reports that his scouts met those of [General] Burnside on Flint Ridge, east of Sparta, and that Lieutenant-Colonel [James P.] Brownlow, with detachments from the First East Tennessee and Ninth Pennsylvania Cavalry, attacked the rebel Colonel [Thomas B.] Murray on the 26th at Sparta, killing 1,

184

wounding 2, and capturing 10 of the enemy, including a lieutenant of Champ. Ferguson's; he also captured a few horses and some ammunition, and destroyed extensive salt-works used by the rebels. A company of scouts, under Captain [Calvin] Brixey, also encountered a party of guerrillas near Beersheba Springs, capturing 15 or 20, and dispersing the rest.

Brig. Gen. R. S. Granger reports from Nashville, November 2, that—

> A mixed command, under Lieutenant-Colonel James [W.] Scully, First Middle Tennessee Infantry, sent out from Nashville, attacked and defeated [William S.] Hawkins and other guerrilla chiefs, and pursued them to Centerville, Hickman County, where Hawkins made another stand, attacking our forces while crossing the river. Hawkins was again routed, and pursued until his forces dispersed. Rebel loss from 15 to 20 killed and 6 prisoners; our loss 1 severely and several slightly wounded.

Again, on November 4, that—

> Major [Thomas C.] Fitz Gibbon, Fourteenth Michigan Infantry, came upon the combined forces of [Albert G.] Cooper, [L. M.] Kirk, Williams, and [F. P.] Scott (guerrillas), at Lawrenceburg, 35 miles from Columbia, and after a severe hand-to-hand fight defeated them, killing 8, wounding 7, and capturing 24 prisoners; among the latter, 1 captain and 2 lieutenants. Major Fitz Gibbon's loss, 3 men slightly wounded and 8 horses killed. He reports the enemy 400 strong, and his force 120.

November 13:

> Captain Cutler, with one company of mounted infantry and a portion of Whittemore's battery [H, 2d Illinois] (mounted) belonging to the garrison of Clarksville, had a fight near Palmyra with Captain Grey's company of guerrillas, killing 2, wounding 5, and taking 1 prisoner; Cutler's loss, 1 lieutenant and 1 man wounded.

November 16:

> Scout organized by Brigadier-General [Eleazer A.] Paine, and sent out from Gallatin and La Vergne, returned, and reports having killed 5 and captured 26 guerrillas, with horses, sheep, cattle, and hogs in their possession, collected for the use of the rebel army.

Brigadier-General Crook, commanding Second Division of Cavalry, was ordered, November 17, to concentrate his division at or near Huntsville, Ala., and to patrol the north side of the Tennessee from Decatur to Bridgeport, and to hunt up bands of guerrillas reported to be roaming about in that region, arresting and robbing Union citizens. General Crook reports on the 21st that an expedition sent down the Tennessee had destroyed nine boats between Whitesburg and Decatur, some of them 60 feet long. The expedition crossed the river and drove off the rebels, taking their boats. From the best information to be obtained, there were two small regiments of cavalry and one battery on the other side doing picket duty. Confederate Generals [S. D.] Lee and [Philip D.] Roddey reported as having gone to Mississippi. Major-General Sherman, commanding Army of the Tennessee, having been ordered with the Fifteenth Corps to this point to participate in the operations against the enemy, reached Bridgeport with two divisions on the 15th.

He [Sherman] came to the front himself, and having examined the ground, expressed himself confident of his ability to execute his share of the work. The plan of operations was then written out substantally as follows: Sherman, with the Fifteenth Corps, strengthened with one division from my command, was to effect a crossing of the Tennessee River just below the mouth of the South Chickamauga, on Saturday, November 21, at daylight; his crossing to be protected by artillery planted on the heights on the north bank of the river. After crossing his force, he was to carry the heights of Missionary Ridge from their northern extremity to about the railroad tunnel before the enemy could concentrate a force against him.

I was to co-operate with Sherman by concentrating my troops in Chattanooga Valley, on my left flank, leaving only the necessary force to defend the fortifications on the right and center, with a movable column of one division in readiness to move wherever ordered. This division was to show itself as threateningly as possible on the most practicable line for making an attack up the valley. I was then to effect a junction with Sherman, making my advance from the left, well toward the north end of Mission [ary] Ridge, and moving as near simultaneously with Sherman as possible. The junction once formed and the Ridge carried, communications would be at once established between the two armies by roads running on the south bank of the river. Further movements to depend on those of the enemy.

Lookout Valley was to be held by [John W.] Geary's division of the Twelfth Corps, and the two brigades of the Fourth Corps ordered to co-operate with him; the whole under command of Major-General Hooker.

Howard's corps was to be held in readiness to act either with my troops at Chattanooga or with General Sherman's and was ordered to take up a position on Friday night [the 20th] on the north side of the Tennessee near the first pontoon bridge, and there held in readiness for such orders as might become necessary.

General Smith commenced at once to collect his pontoons and materials for bridges in the North Chickamauga Creek, preparatory to the crossing of Sherman's troops, proper precautions being taken that the enemy should not discover the movement. General Sherman then returned to Bridgeport to direct the movements of his troops. Colonel [Eli] Long (Fourth Ohio Cavalry), commanding Second Brigade, Second Division Cavalry, was ordered on the 16th to report at Chattanooga on Saturday, the 21st, by noon; the intention being for him to follow up the left flank of Sherman's troops, and if not required by General Sherman, he was to cross the Chickamauga, make a raid upon the enemy's communications, and do as much damage as possible. Owing to a heavy rain-storm, commencing on Friday (20th), and lasting all of the 21st, General Sherman was not enabled to get his troops in position in time to commence operations on Saturday morning, as he expected.

Learning that the enemy had discovered Sherman's movements across Lookout Valley, it was thought best that General Howard should cross over into Chattanooga, thus attracting the attention of the enemy, with the intention of leading him to suppose that those troops he had observed moving were re-enforcing Chattanooga, and thereby concealing the real movements of Sherman. Accordingly, Howard's corps was crossed into Chattanooga on Sunday [the 22d], and took up a position in full view of the enemy. In consequence of the bad condition of the roads General Sherman's troops were occupied all of Sunday in getting into position. In the meantime, the river having risen, both pontoon bridges were broken by rafts sent down the river by the enemy, cutting off Osterhaus' division from the balance of Sherman's troops. It was thought this would delay us another day, but during the night of the 22d, two deserters reported Bragg had fallen back, and that there was only a strong picket line in our front. Early on the morning of the 23d, I received a note from Major-General Grant, directing me to ascertain by a demonstration the truth or falsity of this report.

Orders were accordingly given to General [Gordon] Granger, commanding the Fourth Corps, to form his troops and to advance directly in front of Fort Wood, and thus develop the strength of the enemy. General Palmer, commanding the Fourteenth Corps, was directed to support General Granger's right, with Baird's division refused and en echelon. Johnson's division, Fourteenth Corps, to be held in readiness, under arms, in the intrenchments, to re-enforce at any point. Howard's corps was formed en masse behind the center of Granger's corps. The two divisions of Granger's corps (Sheridan's and Wood's) were formed in front of Fort Wood; Sheridan on the right, Wood on the left, with his left extending nearly to Citico Creek. The formation being completed about 2 p.m. the troops were advanced steadily and with rapidity directly to the front, driving before them first the rebel pickets, then their reserves, and falling upon their grand guards stationed in their first line of rifle-pits, captured something over 200 men, and secured themselves in their new positions before the enemy had sufficiently recovered from his surprise to attempt to send re-enforcements from his main camp. Orders were then given to General Granger to make his position secure by constructing temporary breastworks and throwing out strong pickets to his front. Howard's corps was moved up on the left of Granger, with the same instructions, and Bridges' (Illinois) battery was placed in position on Orchard Knob. The troops remained in that position for the night.

The Tennessee River having risen considerably from the effect of the previous heavy rain-storm, it was found difficult to rebuild the pontoon bridge at Brown's Ferry. Therefore it was determined that General Hooker should take Osterhaus' division, which was still in Lookout Valley, and Geary's division, [Walter C.] Whitaker's and Grose's brigades, of the First Division, Fourth Corps, under Brigadier-General Cruft, and make a strong demonstration on the western slope of Lookout

Mountain, for the purpose of attracting the enemy's attention in that direction and thus withdrawing him from Sherman [front] while crossing the river at the mouth of the South Chickamauga.

General Hooker was instructed that in making this demonstration, if he discovered the position and strength of the enemy would justify him in attempting to carry the point of the mountain, to do so. By 4 a.m. on the morning of the 24th, General Hooker reported his troops in position and ready to advance.

Finding Lookout Creek so much swollen as to be impassable, he sent Geary's division, supported by Cruft's two brigades, to cross the creek at Wauhatchie, and work down on the right bank, while he employed the remainder of his force in constructing temporary bridges across the creek on the main road. The enemy, being attracted by the force on the road, did not observe the movements of Geary until his column was directly on their left and threatened their rear. Hooker's movements were facilitated by the heavy mist which overhung the mountain, enabling Geary to get into position without attracting attention.

Finding himself vigorously pushed by a strong column on his left and rear, the enemy began to fall back with rapidity, but his resistance was obstinate, and the entire point of the mountain was not gained until about 2 p.m., when General Hooker reported by telegraph that he had carried the mountain as far as the road from Chattanooga Valley to the white [Cravens'] house. Soon after, his main column coming up, his line was extended to the foot of the mountain, near the mouth of Chattanooga Creek. His right, being still strongly resisted by the enemy, was re-enforced by [William P.] Carlin's brigade, First Division, Fourteenth Corps, which arrived at the white [Cravens'] house about 5 p.m., in time to take part in the contest still going on at that point. Continuous and heavy skirmishing was kept up in Hooker's front until 10 at night, after which there was an unusual quietness along our whole front.

With the aid of the steamer *Dunbar*, which had been put in condition and sent up the river at daylight of the 24th, General Sherman by 11 a.m. had crossed three divisions of the Fifteenth Corps, and was ready to advance as soon as Davis' division of the Fourteenth Corps commenced crossing [the

Tennessee]. Colonel Long (Fourth Ohio Cavalry), commanding Second Brigade, Second Division Cavalry, was then ordered to move up at once, follow Sherman's advance closely, and to proceed to carry out his instructions of the day before, if not required by General Sherman to support his left flank.

Howard's corps moved to the left about 9 a. m., and communicated with Sherman about noon. Instructions were sent to General Hooker to be ready to advance on the morning of the 25th from his position on the point of Lookout Mountain to the Summertown road, and endeavor to intercept the enemy's retreat, if he had not already withdrawn, which he was to ascertain by pushing a reconnaissance to the top of Lookout Mountain.

The reconnaissance was made as directed, and having ascertained that the enemy had evacuated during the night, General Hooker was then directed to move on the Rossville road with the troops under his command (except Carlin's brigade, which was to rejoin its division), carry the pass at Rossville, and operate upon the enemy's left and rear. Palmer's and Granger's troops were held in readiness to advance directly on the rifle-pits in their front as soon as Hooker could get into position at Rossville. In retiring on the night of the 24th, the enemy had destroyed the bridges over Chattanooga Creek on the road leading from Lookout Mountain to Rossville, and, in consequence, General Hooker was delayed until after 2 p. m. in effecting the crossing of the creek.

About noon, General Sherman becoming heavily engaged by the enemy, they having massed a strong force in his front, orders were given for General Baird to march his division within supporting distance of General Sherman. Moving his command promptly in the direction indicated, he was placed in position to the left of Wood's division of Granger's corps.

Owing to the difficulties of the ground, his troops did not get in line with Granger's until about 2:30 p. m. Orders were then given him, however, to move forward on Granger's left, and within supporting distance, against the enemy's rifle-pits on the slope and at the foot of Missionary Ridge. The whole line then advanced against the breastworks, and soon became warmly engaged with the enemy's skirmishers; these, giving way, retired upon their reserves, posted within their works. Our troops advancing steadily in a continuous line, the enemy, seized with panic, abandoned the works at the foot of the hill and retreated precipitately to the crest, where they were closely followed by our troops, who, apparently inspired by the impulse of victory, carried the hill simultaneously at six different points, and so closely upon the heels of the enemy that many of them were taken prisoners in the trenches. We captured all their cannon and ammunition before they could be removed or destroyed.[77]

General Grant, himself, cannot be given credit for this remarkable assault. It must be remembered that the troops who accomplished the feat were those belonging to Thomas, and it is to Thomas' credit that his troops showed so much of his own daring and fortitude. If these forces had not carried Missionary Ridge, all of Bragg's army would have been between Sherman and Hooker forming a formidable barrier almost impossible to cross.

Thomas' report continued:

After halting for a few moments to reorganize the troops, who had become somewhat scattered in the assault of the hill, General Sheridan pushed forward in the pursuit, and drove those in his front who escaped capture across Chickamauga Creek. Generals Wood and Baird, being obstinately resisted by re-enforcements from the enemy's extreme right, continued fighting until darkness set in, slowly but steadily driving the enemy before them. In moving upon Rossville, General Hooker encountered [A. P.] Stewart's [Rebel] division and other troops. Finding his left flank threatened, Stewart attempted to escape by retreating toward Graysville, but some of his force, finding their retreat threatened from that quarter, retired in disorder toward their right, along the crest of the ridge, when they were met by another portion of General Hooker's command, and were driven by these troops in the face of Johnson's division of Palmer's corps, by whom they were nearly all made prisoners.

It will be perceived from the above report that the original plan of operations was somewhat modified to meet and take the best advantage of emergencies, which necessitated material modifications of that plan. It is believed, however, that the original plan, had it been carried out, could not possibly have led to more successful results.

The alacrity displayed by officers in executing their orders,

77. OR, I, XXXI, pt. II, pp. 92-6.

the enthusiasm and spirit displayed by the men who did the work, cannot be too highly appreciated by the nation, for the defense of which they have on so many other memorable occasions nobly and patriotically exposed their lives in battle. Howard's corps (Eleventh) having joined Sherman on the 24th, his operations from that date will be included in Sherman's report; also those of Brig. Gen. J. C. Davis' division, of the Fourteenth Corps, who reported for duty to General Sherman on the 21st. General Granger's command returned to Chattanooga, with instructions to prepare and hold themselves in readiness for orders to re-enforce General Burnside at Knoxville.

On the 26th, the enemy were pursued by Hooker's and Palmer's commands, surprising a portion of their rear guard near Graysville after nightfall, capturing three pieces of artillery and several hundred prisoners. The pursuit was continued on the 27th, capturing an additional piece of artillery at Graysville. Hooker's advance encountered the enemy [Cleburne's division] posted in the [Ringgold Gap] pass through Taylor's Ridge, who, after an obstinate resistance of an hour, were driven from the pass with considerable loss in killed, wounded, and prisoners. Our loss was also heavy. A large quantity of forage and some additional caissons and ammunition were captured at Ringgold.

On the 28th, Colonel Long (Fourth Ohio Cavalry) returned to Chattanooga from his expedition, and reported verbally that on the 24th he reached Tyner's Station, destroying the enemy's forage and rations at that place, also some cars, and doing considerable injury to the railroad. He then proceeded to Ooltewah, where he captured and destroyed some trains loaded with forage. From thence he proceeded to Cleveland, remaining there one day, destroyed their copper rolling mill and a large depot of commissary and ordnance stores. Being informed that a train of the enemy's wagons was near Charleston, on the Hiwassee, and was probably unable to cross the river on account of the break in their pontoon bridge, after a few hours' rest he pushed forward with a hope of being able to destroy them, but found, on reaching Charleston, that the enemy had repaired their bridge and had crossed their trains safely, and were prepared to defend the crossing with one or two pieces of artillery, supported by an infantry force on the north bank. He then returned to Cleveland and damaged the

Accompanying Thomas' report was a return listing the army's casualties in the three-day battle:

*Report of Casualties, Department of the Cumberland, during the battle of Chattanooga, November, 1863.*

| Command | Killed | | | Wounded | | | Missing | | | Aggregate |
| --- | --- | --- | --- | --- | --- | --- | --- | --- | --- | --- |
| | Officers | Enlisted Men | Total | Officers | Enlisted Men | Total | Officers | Enlisted Men | Total | |
| **4th Army Corps.** Major-General Granger. | | | | | | | | | | |
| 1st Division, Major-General Stanley. | 1 | 18 | 19 | 5 | 80 | 85 | .. | .. | .. | 104 |
| 2d Division, Major-General Sheridan. | 12 | 123 | 135 | 105 | 1,046 | 1,151 | .. | .. | .. | 1,286 |
| 3d Division, Brigadier-General Wood. | 14 | 136 | 150 | 59 | 792 | 851 | .. | .. | .. | 1,001 |
| Total | 27 | 277 | 304 | 169 | 1,918 | 2,087 | .. | .. | (a) | 2,391 |
| **14th Army Corps. b** Major-General Palmer. | | | | | | | | | | |
| 1st Division, Brigadier-General Johnson. c | .. | .. | 46 | .. | .. | 258 | .. | .. | .. | 304 |
| 2d Division, Brigadier-General Davis. | .. | .. | .. | .. | .. | .. | .. | .. | .. | (d) |
| 3d Division, Brigadier-General Baird. | .. | .. | 97 | .. | .. | 461 | .. | .. | 7 | 565 |
| Total | .. | .. | 143 | .. | .. | 719 | .. | .. | 7 | 869 |
| **11th Army Corps.** Major-General Howard. | | | | | | | | | | |
| 2d Division, Brigadier-General von Steinwehr. | 3 | 22 | 25 | 14 | 162 | 176 | 8 | 116 | 124 | 325 |
| 3d Division, Major-General Schurz. | .. | 1 | 1 | 1 | 13 | 14 | .. | 10 | 10 | 25 |
| Total | 3 | 23 | 26 | 15 | 175 | 190 | 8 | 126 | 134 | 350 |
| **12th Army Corps.** Major-General Slocum. | | | | | | | | | | |
| 1st Division, Brigadier-General Williams. e | .. | .. | .. | .. | .. | .. | .. | .. | .. | .. |
| 2d Division, Brigadier-General Geary. | 7 | 49 | 56 | 33 | 252 | 285 | .. | 4 | 4 | 345 |
| Total | 7 | 49 | 56 | 33 | 252 | 285 | .. | 4 | 4 | 345 |
| Grand Total | 37 | 349 | 529 | 217 | 2,345 | 3,281 | 8 | 130 | 145 | 3,955 |

a   Number missing included in sub-report.
b   Officers and enlisted men reported in same column in sub-report.
c   Third Brigade not included in sub-report.
d   No report from Second Division.
e   First Division not engaged.[78]

78. *Ibid.*, p. 98.

railroad for 5 or 6 miles in the direction of Dalton, and then returned to Chattanooga.

On the 28th, General Hooker was ordered by General Grant to remain at Ringgold until the 30th, and so employ his troops as to cover the movements of General Sherman, who had received orders to march his force to the relief of Burnside by way of Cleveland and Loudon. Palmer's corps was detached from the force under General Hooker and returned to Chattanooga.

I am, general, very respectfully, your obedient servant,

George H. Thomas,
*Major-General, U. S. Vols., Commanding.*
Brig.-Gen. Lorenzo Thomas,
*Adjutant-General, U. S. Army.*[79]

While Hooker pursued Bragg's battered army beyond Ringgold, General Sherman's columns, reinforced by Howard's and Granger's corps, marched to the relief of General Burnside's 12,000-man army holed-up in the Knoxville defenses. On November 29, Burnside's soldiers had repulsed a savage lunge by General Longstreet's Confederates at Fort Sanders. In the face of Sherman's rapid approach, Longstreet lifted the siege of Knoxville and retired northeastward through Bulls Gap to Morristown. Sherman and his vanguard entered Knoxville on Sunday, December 6. Responding to a message from General Grant that he hound Longstreet into Virginia, Sherman replied, "A stern chase is a long one."[80]

There would be no relentless pursuit of Longstreet. Burnside was left to confront Longstreet in northeast Tennessee, and Sherman's columns recalled: Generals Howard's and Granger's corps to camp in and around Chattanooga, while Sherman's 15th Corps went into winter quarters at Bridgeport and Huntsville, Alabama.

Unlike General Sherman, who secured a leave and returned to Ohio for the Christmas season, General Thomas remained at Chattanooga with his Army of the Cumberland. When General Howard suggested that Thomas take a brief leave, Thomas declined, stating, "Something is sure to get out of order if I go

79. *Ibid.*, pp. 96-7.
80. Lewis, p. 328.

away. It was always so, even when I commanded a post."[81]

Thomas was therefore at the front when he prepared his report for December, detailing operations for which he was responsible. It read:

Headquarters Department of the Cumberland.

*Chattanooga, January* 15, 1864.

General: I have the honor to report the operations of my command from December 1 to 31, 1863, as follows:

December 1, General Hooker returned to Chattanooga from Ringgold with Geary's division, of the Twelfth Corps, and Osterhaus' division, of the Fifteenth Corps. Cruft's two brigades, of the First Division, Fourth Corps, were ordered to proceed to Chickamauga battle-field and bury such of our dead as still remained unburied by the rebels. This duty finished, they were to return to their former positions on the Nashville and Chattanooga Railroad, between Whiteside's and Bridgeport. General Hooker, on evacuating Ringgold, destroyed the railroad depot and other buildings, as well as such captured property as could not be removed. General Granger's corps marched to the relief of Knoxville, acting in connection with General Sherman's command, which was also moving toward that place. Third Brigade, First Division of Cavalry, Colonel [L. D.] Watkins, of the Sixth Kentucky, commanding, was stationed at Rossville, with an infantry support of two regiments, to guard our south front. General Elliott, with the First Cavalry Division, was ordered to proceed from his position, in the vicinity of Sparta, to Kingston, East Tennessee. He received later instructions, to the effect that in case he did not reach that place in time to participate in the pursuit of Longstreet, he was to establish his headquarters at Athens, and throw out posts as far as possible to the southeast to observe the movements of the enemy in that direction.

Information given by deserters from the enemy places the rebel army in our front as follows: Cleburne's division is at Tunnel Hill, and the balance of the army is stationed between there and Dalton. They state that the troops are very much demoralized, the men being very much scattered from their

81. Oliver O. Howard, *Autobiography*, 2 Vols. (New York: Baker & Taylor Co., 1907), I, 495-6.

195

regiments, and desertions are numerous. Buckner's corps was not in the battles in front of Chattanooga, it having gone to the assistance of Longstreet seven or eight days previous.

December 3, Col. George P. Buell, Fifty-eighth Indiana Volunteers, commanding Pioneer Brigade, commenced constructing a double-track wagon road over the nose of Lookout Mountain.

December 13, [Brig.] General [Alvan C.] Gillem reports from Nashville that he had just returned to that place from the Tennessee River. The work on the Northwestern railroad was progressing. Guerrillas between the Cumberland and Duck Rivers broken up. Perkins and Ray were disposed of, the former having been killed and the latter captured. Refugees and conscripts from the south side of the [Tennessee] river report that [Nathan Bedford] Forrest and [Gideon J.] Pillow are at Jackson, West Tennessee, with about 4,000 men, 1,000 of whom are well mounted and organized.

December 15, a small party of rebels, under Maj. Joe Fontaine, Roddey's adjutant, was captured by General [Grenville M.] Dodge near Pulaski. They had been on a reconnaissance along the Nashville and Chattanooga Railroad and the Nashville and Decatur Railroad. Measures were immediately taken to guard against an attack on either railroad.

On the 17th, Howard's corps returned to Chattanooga from Knoxville; also Davis' division, of the Fourteenth Corps. The latter was posted along Spring Creek, south of Missionary Ridge, and the former returned to its position in Lookout Valley.

Through scouts we learn that the enemy is strengthening his position between Tunnel Hill and Dalton; also at Resaca, near the Coosa River, and at Allatoona Mountains, the last named place being a formidable position. Information from various sources leads to the belief that [Lt. Gen. William J.] Hardee is making the Oostenaula River his front, defended by rifle-pits and fortifications; also the Etowah River. All deserters and scouts agree in their statements that the rebels in our front are disheartened and demoralized. President Lincoln's amnesty proclamation [of December 9] was having a good effect in encouraging desertions, and movements have been taken to circulate it quite extensively within the enemy's lines. The cavalry command, under General Elliott, having been detained by General [John G.] Foster [who had succeeded Burnside] for duty in his department, Col. Eli Long, Fourth Ohio Cavalry, commanding Second Brigade, Second Division Cavalry, was stationed at Calhoun, on the Hiwassee River, for the purpose of watching the movements of the enemy in that vicinity. The balance of the Second Division, under command of General Crook, was ordered by General Grant, on the 20th, to move from Huntsville, where it then was, to Prospect, with a view to operate against Forrest.

General W. . . . [Sooy] Smith, chief of cavalry of the Military Division of the Mississippi, with the Third, Fifth, and Seventh Kentucky, Second and Fourth Tennessee, and Eighth Iowa Cavalry Regiments, started for Savannah on the 20th, to cross the Tennessee, and operate on the flank and rear of Forrest and drive him from West Tennessee.

The operations of the cavalry have been quite brilliant during the month. Col. L. D. Watkins, commanding Third Brigade, First Division, from his position at Rossville, has made several successful raids into the enemy's lines. On the 5th, a reconnaissance sent by him proceeded as far as Ringgold without finding any signs of the enemy, except stragglers and deserters. Again on the 14th, with detachments of the Fourth and Sixth Kentucky Cavalry, numbering about 250 men, he made a reconnaissance toward La Fayette, surprised that town, capturing a colonel of the Georgia Home Guards, 6 officers of the rebel signal corps, and about 38 horses and mules; our loss, none. On the 23d he sent out a scout of 150 men from Fourth and Sixth Kentucky Regiments, under command of Major [George] Welling, of the Fourth Kentucky, which proceeded as far as La Fayette, capturing at that place 1 commissioned officer, 16 non-commissioned [officers] and privates, 10 citizens (said to be violent rebels), and 38 horses and mules.

On the 22d, a party of Wheeler's cavalry, numbering about 75 men, attacked a small party of the Fourth Michigan Cavalry, stationed at Cleveland. Our loss was 1 or 2 captured, some property lost, consisting of overcoats, saddles, etc., but the enemy were finally driven off.

On the 23d, Geary's division, of the Twelfth Corps, left their camp at Lookout Valley to take up a position along the Nashville and Chattanooga Railroad, one brigade to be stationed at Bridgeport and the other at Stevenson.

On the 28th, Colonel Bernard Laiboldt, Second Missouri

Infantry, in charge of a train and escort, principally of convalescents belonging to the Fourth Corps, proceeding from Chattanooga to Knoxville, was attacked by a force of Wheeler's cavalry, numbering between 1,200 and 1,500, as he was crossing the Hiwassee River at Charleston. He immediately formed his guard in line of battle on the south side of the river, succeeded in crossing all his train in safety, and then charged the astonished rebels and drove them in confusion. He then called upon Col. Eli Long for cavalry co-operation, who sent all the force he then had in camp, numbering 150 men. With this small force Colonel Long charged the enemy with sabers and drove him 5 miles, capturing 130 prisoners, including 5 commissioned officers. Our loss was 2 killed and 15 wounded. The enemy left his dead and wounded, as well as quite a number of small-arms, etc., upon the field. Both Colonels Laiboldt and Long are entitled to great credit for the manner in which they repelled this attack. I earnestly recommend them to favorable consideration for promotion; Colonel Laiboldt, for his executive ability and efficiency as a brigade commander of the Second Division, Twelfth Army Corps; Col. Eli Long, for the valuable service he rendered during the recent battles in front of Chattanooga and for many instances of previous good conduct.

Provost-Marshal-General William M. Wiles reports that 1,080 deserters from the enemy have come into the lines of this army between the 19th of October and December 31.

I am, general, very respectfully, your obedient servant,

GEO. H. THOMAS,
*Major-General, U. S. Vols., Commanding.*

Brig. Gen Lorenzo Thomas,
*Adjutant-General U. S. Army.*[82]

82. OR, I, XXXI, pt. II, pp. 124-27.

Border designed by John P. Chapin
Photographed by George N. Barnard
Entered according to Act of Congress
AD 1885 by J. C. Buttre in the Clerk's Office of the
District Court of the U. S. for the Southern District
of New York
ENGRAVED AND PUBLISHED BY J. C. BUTTRE
48 Franklin Street, New York
REPUBLISHED BY PAUL B. VICTORIUS
Charlottesville, Virginia
From the author's collection

From the author's collection
This original military "escutcheon" or coat-of-arms, hand-painted in full color in oils on canvas, depicts the ranks, regiments, battle service, and flags and medals of General George H. Thomas. The escutcheon was painted by Captain J. C. Reynolds who served during the Civil War with the 19th Regiment, Massachusetts Volunteers. After the war, Captain Reynolds devoted himself exclusively to painting items of this nature for officers and enlisted men on special order. He maintained his home and studio in Salem, Massachusetts.

From the author's collection

$5 Treasury Note               B2616138               Series of 1891
                                              Washington,  D. C.

W. S. Rosecrans,                          E. H. Nebeker,
Register of the Treasury          Treasurer of the United States

From the author's collection    General Grant and his Staff upper right
## BATTLE OF SHILOH • APRIL 6, 1862
"The McCormick Machines come victoriously out of
every contest, and without a scratch."
Presented with compliments of McCormick Harvesting Machine Co.
Cosack & Co., Lith. Buffalo & Chicago
Entered according to Act of Congress in the year 1885 by the
McCormick Harvesting Machine Company in the office
of the Librarian of Congress at Washington.

The view at center is from the "Hornet's Nest," a landmark and natural fortress which was so named by the Confederates. The McCormick reaper is seen at lower left. In the center, the troops of Union General Benjamin Prentiss are defending the Hornet's Nest from the sunken road. This entire scene was copied by special permission from the Battle of Shiloh Panorama painting which was exhibited in Chicago in 1885. The specially-constructed circular exhibition building was located on South Michigan Ave., between East Madison and East Monroe Sts. The original oil painting on canvas from which this chromolithograph print was executed was destroyed by fire. This beautiful print is extremely rare.

## BATTLE OF SHILOH
### or
### Pittsburg Landing
### (Tennessee)
### April 6-7, 1862

Of the forces engaged in this battle, historian Thomas Leonard Livermore estimated that there were 62,682 Union soldiers and 40,335 Confederate troops. General Albert Sidney Johnston was severely wounded and died on the battlefield April 6 to be succeeded by General Pierre Gustave Toutant Beauregard who then took command of the Confederate Army. On the second day of fighting, General Grant, reinforced by the troops of General Don Carlos Buell, drove Beauregard into retreat to Corinth, Mississippi.

## BATTLE OF STONES RIVER

or

Murfreesboro, Tennessee

December 31, 1862–January 2, 1863

The Confederate forces under General Braxton Bragg were repulsed by the forces of General William S. Rosecrans' Army of the Cumberland. On the evening of January 4, 1863, Bragg's troops evacuated their lines and moved on to Tullahoma, Tennessee. A day later, Rosecrans' army crossed Stones River and occupied Murfreesboro. Both sides incurred heavy casualties. Historian Thomas L. Livermore (Colonel of the 18th New Hampshire Regiment at the war's end) estimated that there were 41,000 Federals engaged in this battle, 12,906 of whom were killed, wounded, or captured. The Confederates lost 11,739 men out of a force of 34,732.

From the author's collection                    Kurz & Allison
## THE BATTLE OF LOOKOUT MOUNTAIN
### Tennessee
### Tuesday, November 24, 1863

The battle of Lookout Mountain, popularly known as "the Battle Above The Clouds," was not fought at the top of the mountain as the latter name implies. The fighting took place several hundred feet below the mountain's crest in a mist which was rising from the Tennessee River. General Joseph Hooker ("Fighting Joe Hooker") won this battle by driving General Bragg's forces off Lookout Mountain.

## BATTLE OF MISSIONARY RIDGE
### Tennessee
### November 25, 1863

It was here that General Sherman's main attack on the outnumbered forces of Confederate General Patrick Ronayne Cleburne failed. Cleburne's troops were entrenched on Missionary Ridge which was accessible only by a steep and strenuous climb. Sherman with his divisions was not able to dislodge Cleburne's reinforced division. General Thomas' troops were in the center of General Grant's line at the foot of the ridge when Grant ordered Thomas to occupy the trenches at the foot. Instead, Thomas' men pushed forward and up this steep hill, sweeping the defenders before them in flight. The following day the Federals pursued the rebels, but Cleburne's division was able to check this pursuit, thus permitting the remaining Confederate forces to escape. Missionary Ridge obtained its name from the Cherokee mission school and chapel located there.

## THE BATTLE OF RESACA
### Georgia
### Saturday and Sunday, May 14 and 15, 1864

Sherman's objective at Resaca was to assault the Rebel perimeter guarding the Oostanaula bridges and to capture the village. Johnston relied heavily for his supply line on the railroad which ran south from Dalton, Georgia, to Atlanta. As Sherman and Thomas closed on Resaca in the Atlanta campaign, Johnston decided that continued occupation of Resaca was too hazardous and chose to abandon the area. This and other retreats by General Johnston were contributory factors in the South's losing Atlanta.

## THE BATTLE OF KENNESAW MOUNTAIN
### Georgia
### Monday, June 27, 1864

In this battle, General Sherman departed from his previous strategy of flanking movements to launch a direct assault on the Confederate forces. Very little was gained from this maneuver which was opposed by Thomas. The bloody repulse cost the Union 3,000 unnecessary casualties, while the rebel losses were less than 600.

From the author's collection                    Kurz & Allison

## THE BATTLE OF ATLANTA
### Georgia
### Friday, July 22, 1864

Without Atlanta, which was of utmost importance to the South as a major communications center, the Confederacy would be sorely hindered in its war effort. General Sherman's objective was to destroy General Joseph E. Johnston's armies and to seize the city. Under Sherman's command were Thomas' Army of the Cumberland, McPherson's Army of the Tennessee, and Schofield's Army of the Ohio, totalling about 110,000 men. Because of Johnston's continued retreats he was relieved of his command by General John Bell Hood on the orders of President Jefferson Davis on July 17, 1864. The death of General McPherson is depicted in the foreground.

## BATTLE OF NASHVILLE
Tennessee
December 15-16, 1864

Charge of the 5th and 9th Regiments of Minnesota troops under the command of Colonel Lucius Frederick Hubbard on Shy's Hill during the Battle of Nashville on Friday, December 16.

Courtesy of the Minnesota Historical Society

In 1967, the Historical Commission of Metropolitan Nashville erected a plaque at the foot of Shy's Hill, Davidson County, which reads:

On this hill was fought the decisive encounter of the battle of Nashville December 16, 1864. At 4:15 P. M. a Federal assault at the angle on top of the hill broke the Confederate line. Lt. Col. W. M. Shy, 20th Tennessee Infantry, was killed and General Thomas B. Smith was captured. The Confederates retreated over the Overton Hills to the Franklin Pike.

From the author's collection                    Kurz & Allison

## BATTLE OF NASHVILLE
### Tennessee
### DECEMBER 15 and 16, 1864

The Battle of Nashville was one of the decisive battles of the Civil War. General Thomas' Army of the Cumberland mauled Confederate General John Bell Hood's Army of Tennessee, thus helping to seal the fate of the Confederacy.

From the author's collection

Drawn by F. O. C. Darley, N. A.          Engraved by A. H. Ritchie

Entered according to Act of Congress in the year of 1868 by L. Stebbins in the Clerk's Office of the District Court of the United States for the District of Connecticut.

Published by L. Stebbins, Hartford, Ct.

Sherman's soldiers proved themselves specialists in destroying the railroads along the route of his unopposed "March to the Sea."

Courtesy of the Chicago Public Library
Civil War Museum Collection in
the G.A.R. Memorial Hall

Sash and belt of Major General
George H. Thomas, U. S. A.

From the author's collection

This blanket trunk was presented to
Mrs. Thomas by W. J. Stevens, Chief of
the U. S. Military Railroad in Nashville.



Courtesy of the
Chicago Public Library
Bronze statuette of
Major General
George H. Thomas,
U. S. A.
was cast in 1897 by
A. C. McClurg & Co.,
Chicago, Illinois.

Photograph Courtesy of
Norm Flayderman
( N. Flayderman & Co., Inc. )
New Milford, Conn.

This gem-studded
sword and scabbard was
presented to General
Thomas by the enlisted
men of the Fourth
Kentucky Volunteer
Infantry in honor of
Thomas' victory at Mill
Springs, Kentucky,
January 19, 1862.

From the Library of Congress

George H. Thomas
Major General, U. S. A.
The Rock of Chickamauga.

From the collection of Norm Flayderman

**George H. Thomas**
**Major General, U. S. A.**

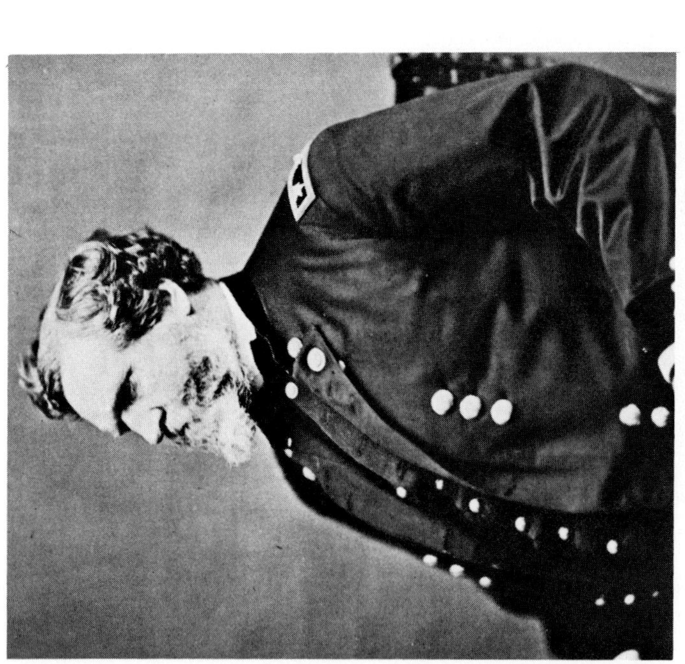

U. S. Signal Corps photo (Brady Collection)
in the National Archives

George H. Thomas
Major General, U. S. A.

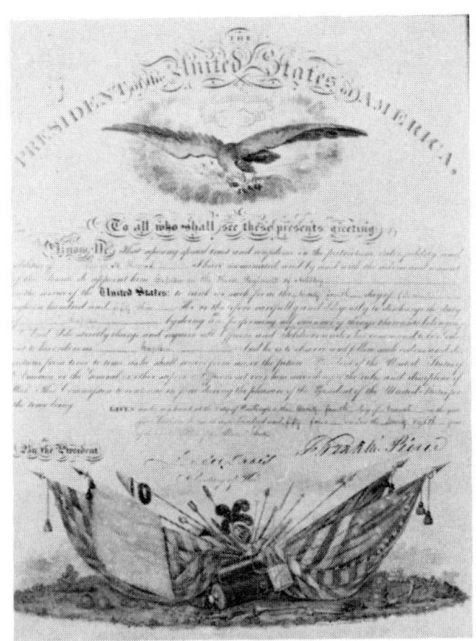

From the author's collection

George H. Thomas,
Captain 3rd Reg., U. S. Artillery
24th December 1853.

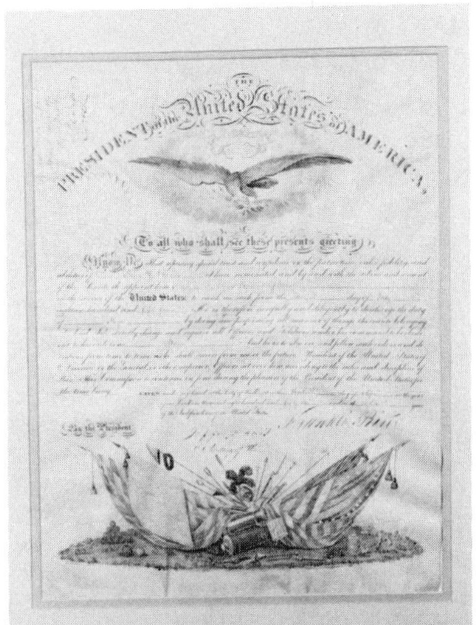

From the author's collection

George H. Thomas
Major 2nd Reg., U. S. Cavalry
12th May, 1855.

From the author's collection

George H. Thomas
Brigadier General of Volunteers
7th August 1861.

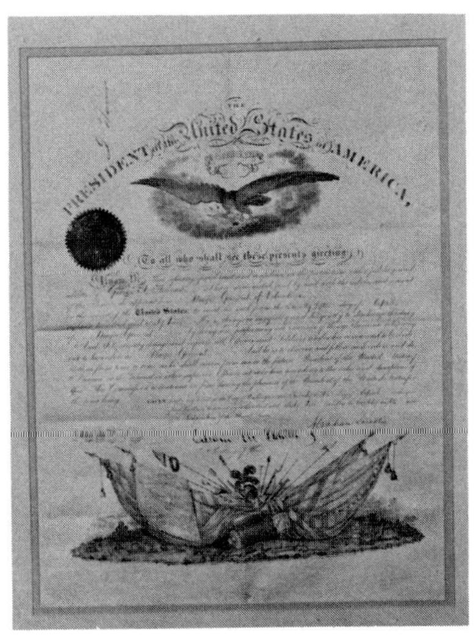

From the author's collection

George H. Thomas
Major General of Volunteers
25th April 1862.

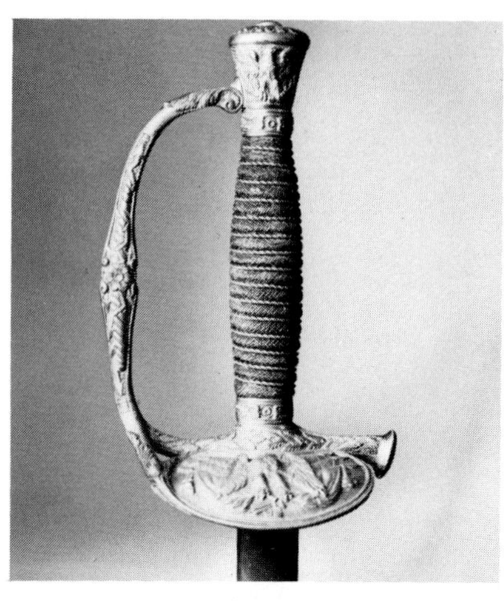



This sword was carried and used by General Thomas during the Civil War War mostly on dress occasions.

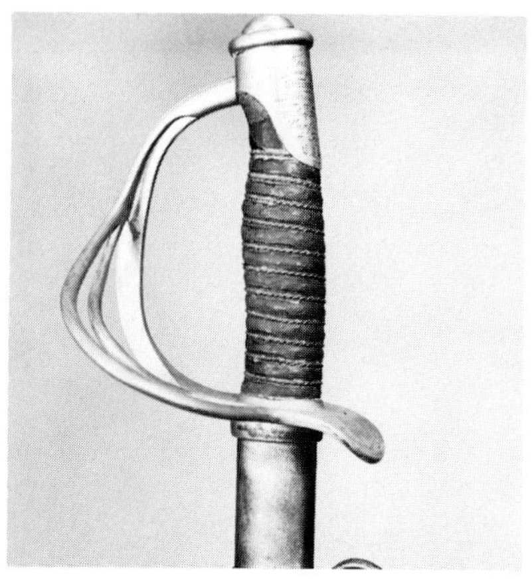



This is a standard issue Cavalry saber used by and carried by General Thomas during the campaigns of the Civil War.

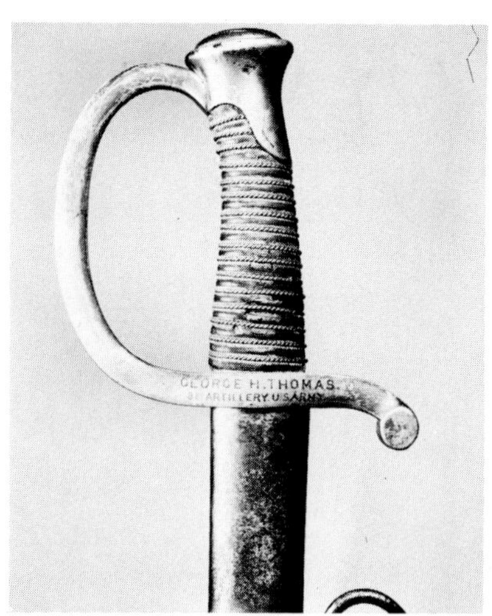



Sword used by Thomas during the occupation of Texas and the Mexican War.

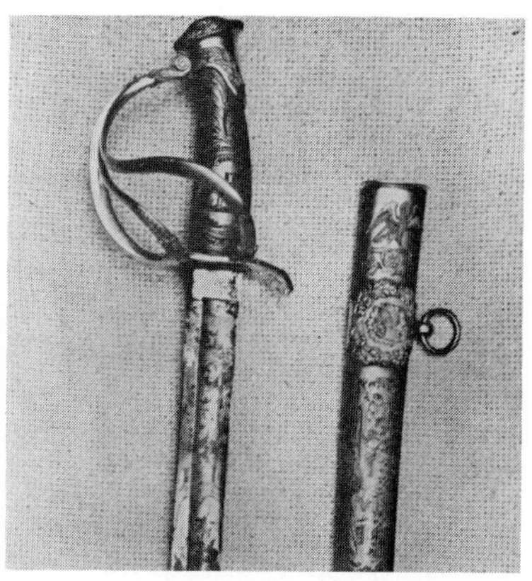



The sword and scabbard presented to Thomas for his services in the Mexican War by the citizens of Southampton County, Virginia, is on display at the Virginia Historical Society, Richmond, Virginia.

The medals of General George H. Thomas, from left to right: Civil War Union League medal, Fourteenth Army Corps medal, Army of the Cumberland medal, Army of the Cumberland special diamond-studded presentation medal, French Medal received at a later date, The Loyal Legion medal.

Each of these solid gold medals is an extra fancy specimen of the military decorations of Thomas' era. The center one is studded with small diamonds. All three medals bear inscriptions on their reverse sides from Thomas' staff-officers in the Army of the Cumberland.

Naval Observatory photo in the National Archives

This photo has been identified as Gen. George H. Thomas, (seated, center) surrounded by his officers, Council of War, Camp Ringgold, Georgia. The photo is from the collection of Capt. W. C. Margedaut, Chief of Topographical Engineers under Gen. Rosencrans.

Public Buildings Service photo in the National Archives
George H. Thomas
Major General, U. S. A.

P-22

From the author's collection
Painted by Henry A. Ogden
Thomas at Chickamauga
September 18—20, 1863.

This reproduction is from a color lithograph by Gilbert Gaul
General Thomas' Bivouac After The Second Day's Battle.
Battle of Chickamauga, Georgia
September 18-20, 1863.

P-23

From the Library of Congress
Painted by T. De Thulstrap, lithograph by
L. Prang & Co., 1886

The Battle of Missionary Ridge
Wednesday, November 25, 1863.

Photograph by Van Arnam, Troy, New York
George H. Thomas
Major General, U. S. Army.
The final resting place of General Thomas is in the Kellogg family
burial ground in the Oakwood Cemetery, Troy, New York.
The monument was designed by the distinguished sculptor, Robert
Eberhardt Launtiz of New York and was erected October 26, 1870.

The only monument erected to Thomas' memory, this impressive bronze equestrian statue of General Thomas stands at Thomas Circle, 14th and Vermont Avenue, N.W., in Washington, D. C. The sculpture is the work of John Quincy Adams Ward and was commissioned by the general's comrades in 1879.

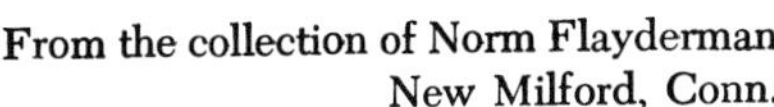

From the collection of Norm Flayderman
New Milford, Conn.

George Henry Thomas Lambert
Born at 1514 North Street
Philadelphia, Pa., July 31, 1877
George Henry Thomas Lambert, about 7 at the time he stood for this photograph, was the son of Major William Harrison Lambert who served in the Civil War. The senior Lambert amassed one of the finest and most complete collections of written and published material on General Thomas.

The George Cunningham home on High Street (presently 6th Avenue), Nashville, Tennessee, in 1864. This building was the headquarters of General George H. Thomas during the Nashville Campaign.

General Robert E. Lee
Confederate States of America.

P-27

Cook Collection, Valentine Museum,
Richmond, Virginia
John Bell Hood
General
Confederate States of America.

U. S. Signal Corps photo (Brady Collection)
in the National Archives
James Longstreet
Lieutenant General, C. S. A.

From the National Archives

Braxton Bragg
General, C. S. A.

From the Library of Congress

John Cabell Breckinridge
Major General, C. S. A.

From the Library of Congress
Felix Kirk Zollicoffer
Brigadier General, C. S. A.

From the Library of Congress
John Stuart Williams
Brigadier General, C.S.A.

Signal Corps photo (Brady Collection)
in the National Archives
David Emmanuel Twiggs
Major General, C. S. A.

First Major Union Victory at the Battle of Mill Springs, Kentucky on Sunday, January 19, 1862.
(Reproduced from *Frank Leslie's Pictorial History of the War of 1861*.)

Death of Confederate Brigadier General Felix Kirk Zollicoffer at the Battle of Mill Springs, Kentucky.
January 19, 1862.

Conveying the body of Confederate General Zollicoffer from the field of battle at Mill Springs to Somerset, Kentucky.

From the Library of Congress
Robert Anderson
Brigadier General, U. S. A.

Editor, *The Freeport Daily Journal,*
Freeport, Illinois
Smith Dykins Atkins
Colonel,
U. S. Volunteers
1835-1913

U. S. Signal Corps photo (Brady Collection) in the National Archives
Don Carlos Buell
Major General, U. S. Volunteers

From the Library of Congress
Stephen Gano Burbridge
Brigadier General,
U. S. Volunteers

From the Library of Congress
James Lowry Donaldson
Colonel, U. S. A.

Donaldson served as General
Thomas' Chief Quartermaster
from November 10, 1863
to June 12, 1865.

From the Library of Congress
Speed Smith Fry
Brigadier General,
U. S. Volunteers.

U. S. Signal Corps photo (Brady
Collection) in the National Archives
James Abram Garfield
Major General, U. S. Volunteers.

From the Library of Congress
Gordon Granger
Major General, U. S. Volunteers.

Ulysses S. Grant, General, U. S. A.

From the Library of Congress
Alvan Cullem Gillem
Brigadier General,
U. S. Volunteers.

From the Brady Collection in
the Library of Congress
Alexander Caldwell McClurg
Colonel,
U. S. Volunteers

From the Library of Congress
Henry Wager Halleck
Major General, U. S. A.

From the Library of Congress
John Franklin Miller
Brigadier General,
U. S. Volunteers.

From the Library of Congress
(Brady Collection)
the Library of Congress
Thomas Jefferson Morgan, Col.,
14th U. S. Colored Infantry.

U. S. Signal Corps Photo (Brady
Collection) in the National Archives
William Starke Rosecrans*
Major General, U. S. A.
* This name means a wreath of
roses.

From the Brady Collection in
the Library of Congress
John McAuley Palmer
Major General, U. S. Volunteers

U. S. Signal Corps Photo (Brady
Collection) in the National Archives
Lovell Harrison Rousseau
Major General, U. S. Volunteers.

U. S. Signal Corps Photo (Brady
Collection) in the National Archives
Albin Francisco Schoepf
Brigadier General,
U.S. Volunteers.

From the Library of Congress
Andrew Jackson Smith
Major General, U. S. Volunteers.

U. S. Signal Corps Photo (Brady
Collection) in the National Archives
John McAllister Schofield
Lieutenant General, U. S. A.

From the Library of Congress,
James Blair Steedman
Major General, U. S. Volunteers.

From the Library of Congress

Hon. William Henry Seward,
Secretary of State of the United States.

U. S. Signal Corps photo (Brady Collection) in the National Archives
William Tecumseh "Cump" Sherman,
General, U. S. A.

Edwin McMasters Stanton
Secretary of War, U. S. A.

From the Library of Congress, photo
from the Brady-Handy Collection
George Stoneman,
Major General, U. S. Volunteers.

U. S. Signal Corps photo (Brady
Collection) in the National Archives
Zealous Bates Tower,
Brigadier General,
U. S. Volunteers.

From the Library of Congress
photo by Brady Studio
Charles Robinson Thompson
Colonel, 12th U. S.
Colored Infantry.

U. S. Signal Corps photo (Brady
Collection) in the National Archives
Stewart Van Vliet,
Brigadier General,
U. S. Volunteers.

U. S. Signal Corps photo (Brady
Collection) in the National Archives
John Thomas Wilder,
Colonel, U. S. Volunteers.

U. S. Signal Corps photo (Brady
Collection) in the National Archives
James Harrison Wilson,
Major General, U. S. A.

From the Library of Congress
Thomas John Wood,
Major General, U. S. A.

U. S. Signal Corps photo (Brady Collection) in the National Archives
Field Pharmacy, General Thomas' Headquarters.
No date or location given.

From the Library of Congress
Photo by Geo. Barnard

The Nashville & Chattanooga passenger railroad station. During
the Civil War, the Louisville & Nashville Railroad shared its facilities
with the N & C. Nashville was considered of strategic value by the
Federals because of its importance as a railroad center.

U. S. Signal Corps photo (Brady Collection) in the National Archives

The tunnel at Tunnel Hill, Georgia, on Western & Atlantic Railroad which until late November, 1863, served as a main supply and transport artery of the Confederate Army.

From the Library of Congress

Exterior view of the Literary Department building of the University of Nashville, Tennessee, which was used as a hospital for Union soldiers in 1864.

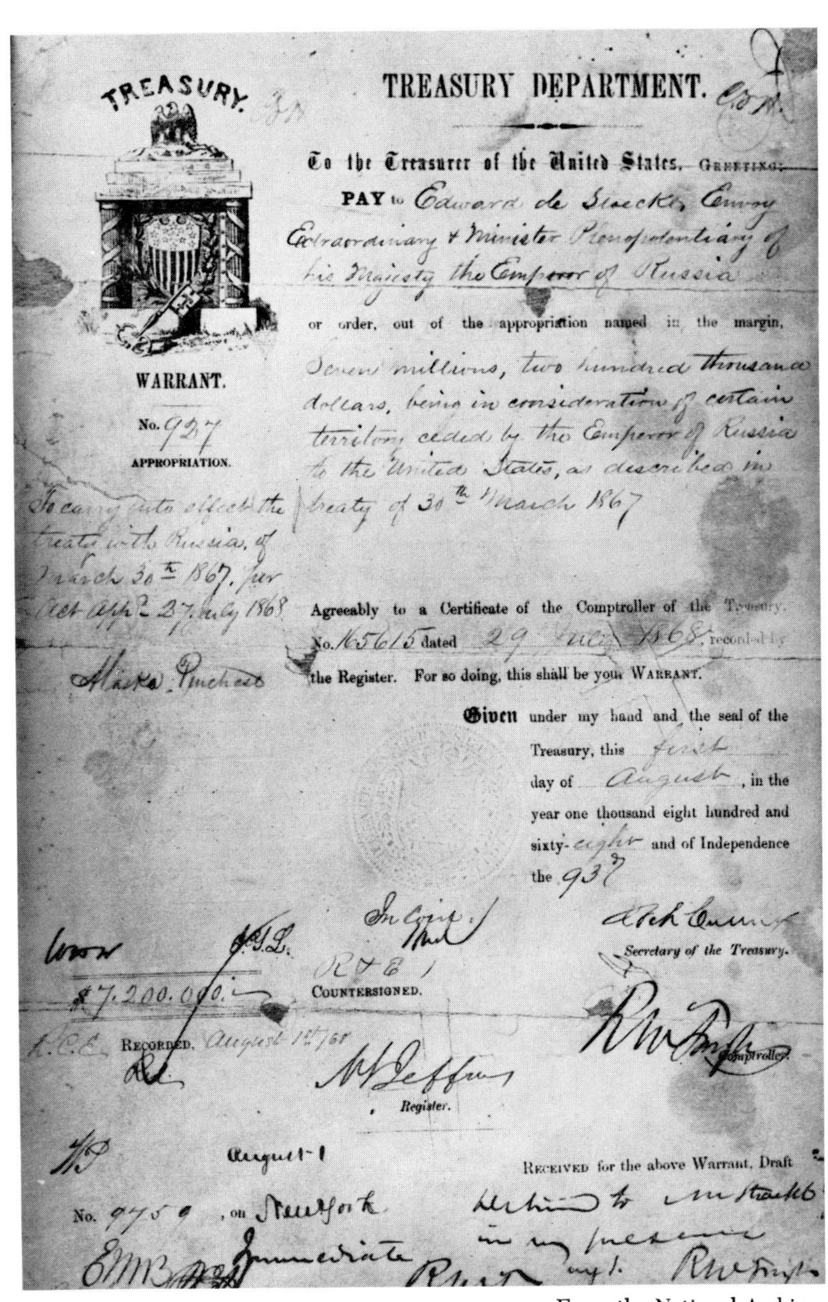

From the National Archives

Treasury Warrant No. 927 authorizing the Treasurer of the United States to issue a draft for $7,200,000 in payment for Alaska.

P-45

From the National Archives

Treasury Draft No. 9759 issued by the United States for the purchase of Alaska.

Copyright Courtesy of *Exxon Corporation*
Painted by Austin Briggs, 1964
"Old Glory Rises Over Alaska"

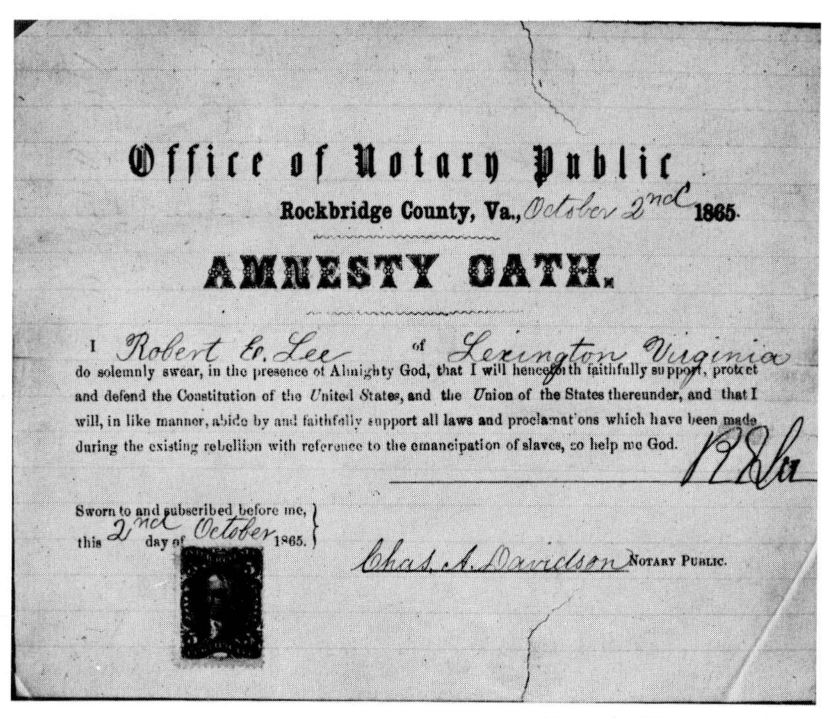



From the National Archives

The loyalty oath signed by Confederate General Robert E. Lee on Monday, October 2, 1865.

# CHAPTER SEVEN

# *Campaigning Through North Georgia*

The third winter of the war found the Army of the Cumberland scattered across Middle and East Tennessee, northeast Alabama, and northwest Georgia garrisoning key points. The core of the army camped in and around Chattanooga, where it could watch the Confederate Army of Tennessee, now led by the capable General Joseph E. Johnston. General Bragg had been replaced following the Missionary Ridge debacle. Johnston's army was in winter quarters in and around Dalton, Georgia, on the Western & Atlantic Railroad, 30 miles southeast of Chattanooga. General Thomas kept large working parties employed rebuilding railroad bridges and trestles, strengthening fortifications, and stockpiling quartermaster, commissary, and ordnance stores for the spring campaign.

During these months, Thomas had the difficult task of rationing and supplying the Armies of the Ohio and Tennessee, as well as his Cumberlanders. To underscore this problem, Major General John G. Foster, Burnside's successor as commander of the Army of the Ohio, protested that he could not move against General

Longstreet, because of the meager supplies being sent to him by General Thomas from the Chattanooga magazines. On January 13, 1864, Thomas chided Foster:

> From the condition of supplies here, I do not know how you can be supplied from this place with anything like half rations. The railroad management is unequal to the emergency, and as that management is not under my control, I cannot say how we shall succeed after the [rail] road is opened to that point. My animals are dying from starvation, too, and seeing this inevitable state of affairs, I have decided to starve with them until we can better their condition as well as our own. My only hope is that we can stand it longer than the enemy.[1]

Difficulties in repairing the damage wreaked on the single track railroads by the retreating Confederate army and Rebel raiders was the root of the supply problems. Colonel John B. Anderson had been named by General Grant railroad tsar for the Military Division. This action soon sparked a controversy. On January 8, General Thomas complained to Grant's headquarters that of the 1,200 workmen hired to repair railroads, Anderson had accepted only 500, though all were needed.[2] A series of messages were exchanged before Thomas succeeded, in mid-February, in having Daniel C. McCallum, a man enjoying his confidence, named to replace Anderson as director of military railroads in the Department of the Cumberland. The situation then improved, and, by February 15, trains were operating over the tracks of the East Tennessee & Georgia Railroad between Chattanooga and Loudon and by late March over the right-of-way of the Western & Atlantic as far as Ringgold.[3]

The new year arrived in the Union camps with cyclonic gales and ice storms, as thermometers plummeted to near zero. Ill-clad soldiers, some without great coats, tattered blankets draped over their shoulders, crowded around camp fires. Coincidentally, there was sporadic cheering from various regimental camps, signaling that a particular regiment or battery had "veteranized," as it was called when a majority of the unit's rank and file re-enlisted for

1. OR, I, XXXII, pt. I, p. 82.
2. *Ibid.*, p. 43.
3. Thomas, p. 453.

another three years, or the duration. The United States government, to induce the soldiers to re-enlist, offered 30-day furloughs. The immediate result was to severely reduce the effective force in the field of the various armies. But it secured to the colors over the long run large numbers of combat veterans, whose services would otherwise have been lost.[4]

Regiments and batteries of blacks, officered by whites, were also being organized and mustered in to further bolster the Union's numerical advantage, as the struggle had become a war of attrition. General Sherman opposed the deployment of black soldiers, but General Thomas held the opinion that the federal government had the right to use them. Stating his views, Thomas advised the War Department:

> The Confederates regard them [the blacks] as property. Therefore the Government can with propriety seize them as property and use them to assist in putting down the Rebellion. But if we have the right to use the property of our enemies, we should also have the right to use them as we would all the individuals of any other civilized nation who may choose to volunteer as soldiers in our Army. . . .
> . . . In the sudden transition from slavery to freedom it is perhaps better for the negro to become a soldier, and be gradually taught to depend on himself for support, than to be thrown upon the cold charities of the world without sympathy or assistance.[5]

Large forces in General Grant's Military Division of the Mississippi were not to be permitted to spend the winter quietly in their camps. Each of the three armies was given a task to further discomfort the Confederates and to look toward a spring campaign into north Georgia aimed at destruction of General Johnston's Army of Tennessee. Major General John M. Schofield, who had replaced General Foster as leader of the Army of the Ohio, was to expel Longstreet's forces from East Tennessee. General Thomas was to repair and guard the railroads and serve as a checkmate to Johnston's army. General Sherman was to concentrate the 16th and 17th Corps of the Army of the Tennessee at

4. Jacob D. Cox, *Atlanta* (New York: Charles Scribner's Sons, 1882), p. 16.
5. Thomas to War Dept., Nov. 18, 1863, Historical Society of Pennsylvania Library.

Vicksburg, Mississippi, preparatory to striking rapidly eastward toward Meridian, a key Confederate railroad and supply center.

Sherman marched from Vicksburg on February 3, occupied Jackson on the 7th, and pushed on across the Pearl River. General Polk's two infantry divisions, screened by Confederate cavalry, fell back in face of Sherman's thrust. On February 14, Sherman's 20,000 men occupied Meridian and Polk's army retreated into Alabama, taking position at Demopolis. At the same time, a powerful Union cavalry column led by Brigadiar General W. Sooy Smith had ridden out of the Memphis perimeter en route to join Sherman at Meridian. Smith was bluffed and turned back by General Forrest in a fight near Okolona. After destroying the Meridian magazines and the railroads, Sherman's columns returned to Vicksburg, where they arrived on March 4.

In his official report for the first two months of 1864, General Thomas detailed events in his Department of the Cumberland. As to be expected, measures taken to restore traffic over the railroads and then to protect them, along with efforts to support the Army of the Ohio in its campaign against General Longstreet northeast of Knoxville commanded considerable attention. More interesting and significant is Thomas' story of his efforts to prevent General Johnston from taking advantage of the Confederacy's interior rail system to rush reinforcements to General Polk as he retired before Sherman's advance. Thomas wrote:

Headquarters Department of the Cumberland

*Chattanooga, Tenn., March* 10, 1864.

General: I have the honor to report the operations of my command for the months of January and February, 1864, as follows:

From the 1st until as late as the 20th of January, no movements of any consequence took place. Small scouting parties of both cavalry and infantry were sent out from time to time to watch the movements of the enemy, but failed to find him in any considerable force in our immediate front.

Information gained through scouts and deserters placed Johnston's army at Dalton and vicinity, occupying the same position he had taken up after the rebel army had fallen back from Mission [ary] Ridge, November 26, 1863, and showing no disposition as yet to assume the offensive. Desertions from the enemy still continued numerous, averaging 30 per day, nearly all of whom wished to embrace the terms of the President's amnesty proclamation which, with Major-General Grant's General Orders, No. 10, [of December 12, 1863,] headquarters Military Division of the Mississippi, had been freely circulated within the rebel lines for some time previous.

On the 20th of January General G. M. Dodge, at Pulaski, Tenn., having ascertained that a force of rebel cavalry, under [Philip D.] Roddey, was constructing flat-boats, and hiding them in Little Bear Creek, Spring Creek, and Town Creek, and also that one of Roddey's regiments was foraging on the north side of the Tennessee River, he immediately informed General Grant of these movements of the enemy, who directed me to organize an expedition at once of sufficient force to drive Roddey away from where he was reported to be, and to destroy all boats and material that might in any way be used by the enemy in crossing the Tennessee River.

On the 22d information was received that [William A.] Johnson's and Morrison's brigades of Roddey's command had crossed the Tennessee somewhere between Florence [Alabama] and Clifton [Tennessee], on the 18th, intending to make a raid on our railroads. The guards along the railroads were cautioned against an attack from this party, and measures were immediately taken to drive Roddey across the river. Col. A. O. Miller, Seventy-second Indiana, commanding one expedition, reports from Blue Water (26th), via Pulaski (27th), that he engaged Johnson's brigade near Florence, routed them, killed 15, and wounded quite a number, taking them prisoners; among them 3 commissioned officers. Our loss, 10 wounded.

Brigadier-General Gillem also reports having sent out parties from along the line of the Northwestern Railroad, and their having returned with Lieutenant-Colonel Brewer, 2 captains, 3 lieutenants, and 20 men as prisoners.

A party of guerrillas, numbering about 150 men, attacked Tracy City on the 20th, and, after having three times summoned the garrison to surrender, were handsomely repulsed by our forces.

Col. T. J. Harrison, Thirty-ninth Indiana (mounted infantry), reports from Cedar Grove . . . [the 14th] that he had sent an expedition of 200 men to Sparta, to look after the guerrillas in that vicinity. They divided into five parties, concentrating at Sparta. Having passed over the localities of [Joe] Carter's, Champ Ferguson's, [Willis S.] Bledsoe's, and [Thomas B.] Murray's guerrillas, his (Harrison's) force remained on the Calf-killer five days, and during that time killed 4, wounded 5 or 6, and captured 15, including a captain and lieutenant, 30 horses, and 20 stands of arms.

The Nashville and Chattanooga Railroad having been completed on the 14th instant, and trains running regularly from Nashville to this point [Chattanooga], steps were immediately taken to commence repairing the East Tennessee and Georgia Railroad. The First Division of the Fourth Corps, Maj. Gen. D. S. Stanley commanding, was ordered on the 24th to take up a position north [east] of Chattanooga, between Chickamauga Depot and the Hiwassee River, to protect the repairs on the railroad. General Hooker, commanding Eleventh and Twelfth Corps, was ordered to relieve Stanley's division, then stationed on the Nashville and Chattanooga Railroad between Whiteside's and Bridgeport.

January 28, Maj. Gen. John M. Palmer, commanding Fourteenth Army Corps, with a portion of his command, made a reconnaissance toward the enemy's position on Tunnel Hill [8 miles northwest of Dalton]. He found him still in force at that point, and the object of the movement having been fully accomplished, General Palmer returned to Chattanooga.

February 7, Col. William B. Stokes, Fifth Tennessee Cavalry, reports from Alexandria, Tenn., that, in pursuance to orders, he had recently scouted in the vicinity of Sparta after certain bands of guerrillas infesting that neighborhood, and had succeeded in killing 17 and capturing 12, besides 20 horses and mules. Another force, under Colonel [Henry K.] McConnell, succeeded in killing 23 and capturing 40 of the same gang. Colonel Stokes ascertained that, when concentrated, the guerrillas in that section of the country will number 600 men, finely mounted. A scout also brought me information of an attack by Roddey, with a heavy force, upon our troops stationed at Lebanon, De Kalb County, Ala., on the 3d instant. The rebels were repulsed and driven in confusion toward Gadsden, when, learning that Roddey was being re-enforced by [General] Wheeler, our troops withdrew to Sand Mountain, taking possession of [a] saltpeter cave, near Fort Payne.

About the 10th instant, various reports having been received that the enemy under Johnston had weakened his force by sending re-enforcements to Polk, then opposing the advance of our forces under General Sherman; also that he had sent troops to aid Longstreet, in East Tennessee, and it being the desire of the commanding general [General Grant] of the military division effectually to clear out the rebel army directly opposed to our forces at Knoxville, I received orders on the 10th instant to prepare to start for Knoxville on the 13th with such force as could safely be spared from the protection of Chattanooga and its communications, to co-operate with the Army of the Ohio in driving Longstreet from East Tennessee.

The army at this period had been very much weakened by the absence of many regiments, who had gone to the respective States to reorganize as veteran volunteers . . . , so that in making my preparations I found but a small force available. My transportation was in a very poor condition, notwithstanding all the efforts made to replace the animals lost by starvation during the close investment of Chattanooga by the enemy, and for want of horses scarcely any of the artillery could be moved.

On the 13th the East Tennessee and Georgia Railroad was in running order to Loudon. The same day [Brig. Gen. Charles L.] Matthies' brigade, of the Fifteenth Corps (Army of the Tennessee), arrived at Chattanooga from Huntsville, in pursuance to orders from General Grant, and was immediately placed in position at Cleveland, in reserve. On the 14th I received a communication from General Grant, countermanding the orders he had given me on the 10th to proceed with a force from my command to East Tennessee, and stating that from a conversation he had had with General Foster, he (General Grant) was convinced that all that could be accomplished by the proposed campaign would not compensate for the hardships upon our men, and the disqualifying effects it would have upon them and our war material for a spring campaign. He then went on to say, that as I had been preparing for a move, he deemed it advisable to make one to my immediate front, the object being to gain possession of Dalton and as far south of that as possible.

In accordance with the above instructions, everything being in readiness, Johnson's and Baird's divisions moved out from Chattanooga and occupied Ringgold, Ga., on the 22d, taking up a position on the ridge west of East Chickamauga Creek, with two regiments of mounted infantry (Colonel [W. P.] Boone's Twenty-eighth Kentucky and Colonel [Thomas J.] Harrison's Thirty-ninth Indiana), on the east side of the creek, the former on the right flank and the latter on the left. Carlin's brigade, of Johnson's division, was stationed about midway between the main line and Taylor's Ridge.

Cruft's division of the Fourth Corps moved on the 22d from Blue Springs, near Cleveland, to Red Clay. Long's brigade of cavalry co-operated with Cruft's column, Long's instructions being to establish communication with Cruft at Red Clay, and then push on as far as possible toward Dalton, on the Spring Place road, observing well the movements of the enemy, so as to give timely warning of any attempt to turn Cruft's left flank, and should the enemy retire, to notify Cruft, so that the latter might advance from Red Clay. During the evening of the 22d General Palmer notified me, from Ringgold, that he had reliable information that Johnston had dispatched Cheatham's and Cleburne's divisions [General Hardee, accompanied by Cleburne's and Cheatham's divisions, had entrained at Dalton on February 18.] to the relief of Polk in Alabama, who was falling back before General Sherman's column.

On the 23d Davis' division of the Fourteenth Corps closed up on the balance of General Palmer's command at Ringgold. Brigadier-General Matthies, commanding a brigade of the Fifteenth Corps stationed at Cleveland in reserve, was directed to send six regiments from his command to re-enforce General Cruft at Red Clay [16 miles north of Dalton]. Colonel Long, having established communication with Cruft the evening before, advanced with his brigade of cavalry along the Spring Place road, driving in the enemy's vedettes when within 4 miles of Dalton, attacking a regiment of rebel infantry which was encamped 1 mile beyond, driving them from their camp and capturing some prisoners. The enemy then formed, and Long withdrew his command to Russell's Mills, 4 miles east of Varnell's Station, on the Cleveland and Dalton Railroad, and encamped there for the night. Cruft, by instructions from General Palmer, took position on the 23d at Lee's house, situated at the cross-roads on the road leading from Red Clay to Tunnel Hill. The command being at this time well concentrated in the vicinity of Ringgold, and having reconnoitered thoroughly on both flanks, General Palmer advanced to feel the enemy in his position at Tunnel Hill, skirmished with him 3 or 4 miles, and, finally, drove him from his position entirely, to a point about 1 mile beyond Tunnel Hill, where he formed line and opened on us with his battery.

The main force then withdrew and went into camp about 3 miles northwest of Tunnel Hill, and on the morning of the 24th the line stood as follows: Baird's division south of Taylor's Ridge, near Ringgold, with Cruft's division at Lee's house, Johnson's and Davis' divisions in advance, toward Tunnel Hill, with Boone's and Harrison's regiments of mounted infantry (the former on the left), and Harrison's men leading the advance toward Tunnel Hill, Long's brigade of cavalry at Varnell's Station, on the Cleveland and Dalton Railroad supported by Grose's brigade of Cruft's division. An advance was made in three columns. After the right and left columns had moved out some distance, the center, with the mounted infantry in advance, pushed forward and met with a fire at long range from a battery of Parrott guns, the enemy's practice being excellent and succeeding in checking the column. The right and left columns were then set in motion and succeeded in flanking the enemy's battery, forcing it to retire. Davis' division of the Fourteenth Corps was started in pursuit, and came up with a heavy force of rebels at Buzzard Roost [4 miles northwest of Dalton], a pass through what is called Rocky Face Ridge, which, as its name would suggest, is very precipitous and is a very strong position. Johnson's division of the Fourteenth Corps was advanced to the support of Davis' position on the evening of the 24th; Davis confronting the enemy at Buzzard Roost, supported by Johnson's division posted a short distance west of Tunnel Hill; Cruft on his left; Cruft's headquarters at Lee's house.

Baird's division of the Fourteenth Corps started from Tunnel Hill at 3 a.m. on the morning of the 25th to join General Cruft on the road leading from Lee's house to Dalton, with instructions to move, in conjunction with Cruft and Long's cavalry, down the eastern side of Rocky Face Ridge, and endeavor to force the enemy out of his position in the pass [Buzzard Roost] by threatening his right and rear, while Davis, supported by Johnson, attacked him in front. In the mean time, Harrison's regiment of mounted infantry (Thirty-ninth Indiana) occupied a gap [Dug] in Rocky Face Ridge, 6 miles south of Buzzard Roost and nearly opposite to Dalton, his instructions being to hold it as long as possible. Baird and Cruft found the enemy east of the ridge in heavy force and very strongly posted, skirmished heavily with him until nightfall, when both divisions were withdrawn, ascertaining before leaving that the enemy was in much stronger force than was supposed, and that in consequence of late movements on our part he had been obliged to order back to Dalton the re-enforcements he had sent to relieve Polk in Alabama.

[Brig. Gen. H. B. Granbury's brigade of] Cleburne's division (one of those reported to have gone south) attacked Colonel Harrison's mounted infantry command at daylight, on the morning of the 26th, and forced him to retire from . . . [Dug] gap. Being convinced that the rebel army at Dalton largely outnumbered the strength of the four divisions I had opposed to it, and the movement against Johnston being a complete success, insomuch as it caused the recalling of re-enforcements sent to oppose General Sherman's expedition against Meridian, I concluded to withdraw my troops to the position they had occupied previous to the reconnaissance.

Baird's division was to fall back on the evening of the 25th to Lee's farm, and on the 26th take position on a line of hills about a mile north of the town of Tunnel Hill, to cover the retirement of Johnson's and Davis' divisions from Buzzard Roost; Davis being ordered to take post at his old camp in front of Rossville, leaving one brigade to support Baird (ordered to take post of Ringgold), until General Baird had sufficient time to establish his picket-lines. Johnson was ordered to take post at Tyner's Station with two brigades of his command, sending one brigade to Graysville, and placing a strong guard in Parker's Gap, northeast of Ringgold, to protect Baird's left flank. Cruft was ordered to take up his old position at Ooltewah, and at Blue Springs (near Cleveland), sending a depot guard to protect his supplies at Cleveland. Long's brigade of cavalry ordered to take post at Cleveland, and keep the left flank well patrolled. Colonel Harrison, commanding Thirty-ninth Indiana Mounted Infantry, with the

Twenty-eighth Kentucky Mounted Infantry, Col. W. P. Boone commanding, was posted at Leet's Tan-yard, with instructions to patrol the country in the direction of La Fayette, and to picket strongly all the roads leading from Leet's in the direction of La Fayette, Resaca, and Dalton. In accordance with these instructions, Johnson withdrew on the night of the 26th to Catoosa Platform, Davis, Baird, and Harrison to Ringgold, and on the 27th they all took up the positions indicated above. Cruft and Long's cavalry also fell back to Catoosa Platform on the night of the 26th, and there took up the positions assigned them.

I am, general, very respectfully, your obedient servant,

GEO. H. THOMAS,

*Major-General, U. S. Volunteers, Commanding.*

Brig. Gen. L. Thomas,

*Adjutant-General, Washington, D. C.*[6]

On February 27, coincident with the retrograde from Rocky Face, General Thomas received a telegram from General Grant's Nashville headquarters. Grant emphasized the importance of pinning down Johnston's army at Dalton until news was received about the fate of Sherman's columns, then returning from Meridian to the Vicksburg enclave. To supply his army as it advanced beyond Ringgold, Grant gratuituously advised Thomas to keep his "trains running between Chattanooga and your position."[7]

Thomas, having already accomplished his mission by compelling Johnston to recall Hardee's divisions, let his orders stand and his troops pressed on to their designated destinations. This did not represent the characteristic response of a junior to his superior. Although Thomas was correct in his evaluation of the situation, his actions undoubtedly raised questions at Grant's headquarters.

Events in Washington soon overtook those in the field, and General Grant would not personally direct the spring campaign against the Confederates in northwest Georgia. On February 29, President Lincoln approved an act passed by Congress reviving the rank of lieutenant general. Grant was called to Washington and, on March 9, was promoted to that rank and given responsi-

6. OR, I, XXXII, pt. I, pp. 6-12.
7. OR, I, XXXII, pt. II, p. 480.

bility for direction of all the United States armies. Grant, in accepting this awesome responsibility, determined to maintain his headquarters in the field adjacent to those of Major General George G. Meade, the commander of the Army of the Potomac. There, he would be near Washington and in a position to personally oversee the forthcoming campaign aimed at destruction of Robert E. Lee's Army of North Virginia and capture of Richmond, the capital of the Confederacy.

To succeed to his position as commander of the Military Division of the Mississippi, Grant selected General Sherman, the officer-in-charge of the Department of the Tennessee, rather than General Thomas. Although Sherman at this stage of the war had yet to win a battle or a campaign and was his junior in rank in the volunteer service, Thomas kept his disappointment to himself.

Grant returned to the west, in mid-March, to discuss with Sherman the role proposed for his western "army group" and to wrap up loose ends at his former Nashville headquarters. Both Sherman and Thomas had had previous correspondence with Grant on this subject. On February 28, Thomas had written, "I believe if I can commence the campaign with the Fourteenth and Fourth Corps in front, and with Howard's corps in reserve, that I can move along the line of the railroad and overcome all opposition as far, at least, as Atlanta."[8] Sherman had written Grant, in a confident mien, "From the west, when our task is done, we will make short work of Charleston and Richmond and the impoverished coast of the Atlantic."[9]

Grant and Sherman met in Nashville on March 17 and Grant formally placed Sherman in command of the Military Division. Sherman was to command an "army group" to include General Thomas' Army of the Cumberland, the Army of the Tennessee to which Major General James B. McPherson had succeeded to command on Sherman's promotion, and the Army of the Ohio led by Major General John M. Schofield, who had replaced General Foster on February 9.

The plan of campaign outlined by Grant was simple and called for the North to concentrate its strength and to focus its resources

8. Joint Committee on the Conduct of the War, *Supplemental Report*, I, p. 197.
9. Cox, *Atlanta*, p. 19.

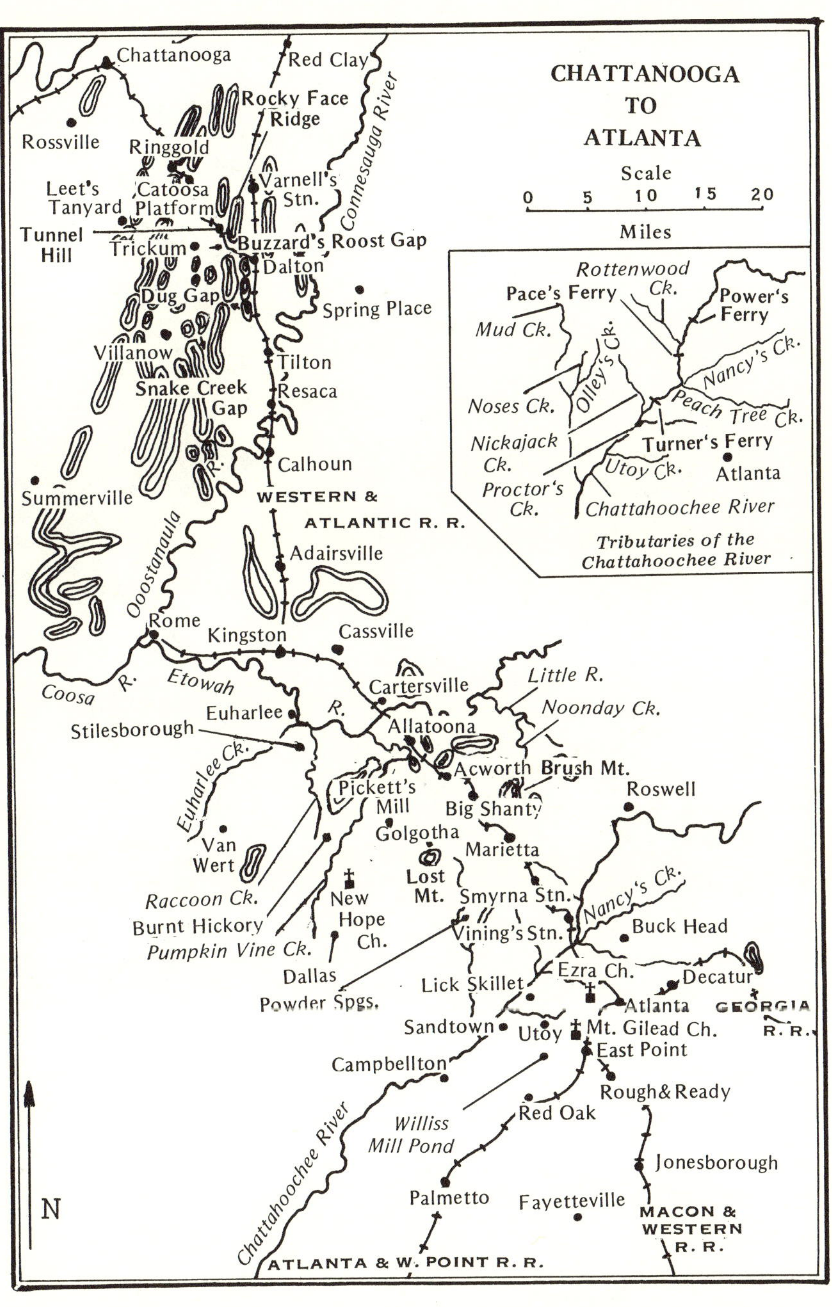

CHATTANOOGA
TO
ATLANTA
Scale
0    5    10    15    20
Miles
Chattanooga
Red Clay
Rocky Face Ridge
Connesauga River
Rossville
Ringgold
Leet's Tanyard
Catoosa Platform
Varnell's Stn.
Tunnel Hill
Trickum
Buzzard's Roost Gap
Dalton
Dug Gap
Spring Place
Villanow
Tilton
Snake Creek Gap
Resaca
R.
Calhoun
Summerville
WESTERN &
ATLANTIC R. R.
Ooostanaula
Adairsville
Rome
Kingston
Cassville
Coosa
R.
Etowah
R.
Cartersville
Little R.
Noonday Ck.
Euharlee
Stilesborough
Allatoona
Euharlee Ck.
Acworth
Brush Mt.
Pickett's Mill
Big Shanty
Roswell
Van Wert
Golgotha
Marietta
Raccoon Ck.
Lost Mt.
Smyrna Stn.
Nancy's Ck.
Burnt Hickory
New Hope Ch.
Vining's Stn.
Buck Head
Pumpkin Vine Ck.
Dallas
Lick Skillet
Ezra Ch.
Decatur
Powder Spgs.
Atlanta
GEORGIA
Sandtown
Utoy
Mt. Gilead Ch.
R. R.
Campbellton
East Point
Williss Mill Pond
Red Oak
Rough & Ready
Palmetto
Fayetteville
Jonesborough
MACON & WESTERN R. R.
ATLANTA & W. POINT R. R.
N
Rottenwood Ck.
Pace's Ferry
Power's Ferry
Mud Ck.
Olley's Ck.
Nancy's Ck.
Noses Ck.
Peach Tree Ck.
Nickajack Ck.
Turner's Ferry
Utoy Ck.
Atlanta
Proctor's Ck.
Chattahoochee River
Tributaries of the Chattahoochee River
Chattahoochee River

to insure the annihilation of the two major Confederate armies. General Grant would oversee the operations aimed at wrecking Lee's Army of Northern Virginia, while Sherman advanced on Atlanta, a key Confederate communication center, compelling General Johnston's Army of Tennessee to engage him in a war of attrition. Coincidentally, Major General Nathaniel P. Banks, upon the conclusion of his Red River Expedition, was to assemble a 25,000-man army in and around New Orleans and move on Mobile.

During the next seven weeks, Thomas' energy was engrossed preparing his Cumberlanders for the spring campaign. Railroads had to be guarded and repaired, warehouses built, supplies brought forward and stockpiled, and the troops trained and reorganized. He paid particular attention to the mustering in, organization, and training of the black regiments. On April 5, Thomas reported six black infantry regiments on duty in the department, and three more organizing, along with an artillery battery.[10]

General Thomas' reports for this period detail his activities and the trials and tribulations of his Cumberlanders, as his troops were beginning to refer to themselves. On April 5, Thomas wrote:

> Headquarters Department of the Cumberland,
> *Chattanooga, Tenn., April 5, 1864.*
> Major: I have the honor to report as follows the operations of my command during the month of March:
> On the 1st the positions of the different divisions remained nearly as mentioned in my last report [for January and February]: viz: Johnson's division, of the Fourteenth Army Corps (Palmer's), at Tyner's Station, except [John H.] King's brigade, which was at Graysville; Davis' division, Fourteenth Corps, at Shallow Ford, near Rossville; Baird's division, Fourteenth Corps, at Ringgold; Stanley's division, Fourth Corps (Granger's), at Blue Springs, near Cleveland; the balance of Granger's command being still on duty [in East Tennessee] with the Army of the Ohio. Long's brigade of cavalry was at or near Calhoun, picketing toward Columbus and Benton. The Thirty-ninth Indiana Mounted Infantry, Col. T. J. Harri-

10. Van Horne, *Life*, p. 213.

son commanding, was stationed at Leet's farm, on the road leading from [Lee and] Gordon's Mills to Ringgold and La Fayette, covering Baird's right flank. The Eleventh and Twelfth Corps, Maj. Gen. Joseph Hooker commanding, were guarding the railroad from Nashville to this point.

March 1 General Matthies and his command were ordered to rejoin the Fifteenth Corps at Huntsville, their services being no longer required; Long's brigade of cavalry was ordered to take position at Cleveland; Colonel [William P.] Innes, with eight companies of the First Michigan Engineers and Mechanics, and two regiments of colored troops, ordered to commence the construction of block-houses and other defenses along the Nashville and Chattanooga Railroad, the First Missouri Engineers and Mechanics being detailed for similar duty along the Nashville and Decatur Railroad.

On the 3d General Gordon Granger, commanding Fourth Army Corps, was directed to send one brigade of his command to Calhoun, with instructions to picket the approaches from Dalton, at Columbus and Benton; [George D.] Wagner's brigade, of Sheridan's division, accordingly took position at that place; Col. A. P. Campbell, commanding First Brigade, First Division of Cavalry, having reported the arrival of his command at Calhoun, was ordered on the 4th to proceed to Cleveland, and remain at that place for the present. Maj. Gen. Gordon Granger sent the following information from Loudon, on the 5th:

> Longstreet's cavalry is said to be making its way to join Johnston, via Marshall, Quallatown, and Murphy, thence to Benton. It was expected at Murphy to-night.

On the 5th Col. Daniel McCook, commanding Third Brigade, Davis' division, Fourteenth Army Corps, was ordered to move his brigade to Lee and Gordon's Mills, on Chickamauga Creek; Col. T. J. Harrison, commanding Thirty-ninth Indiana Mounted Infantry, stationed at Leet's Tan-yard, was driven from his position by a heavy force of rebel cavalry [from Wheeler's command], which, as was subsequently ascertained through a deserter, amounted to two brigades. They attempted to gain Harrison's rear, but failing to do so, retired by the same way they came.

Information was received from a reliable source that Johnston was being re-enforced by infantry and Roddey's cavalry;

Col. Edward McCook, commanding First Division of Cavalry, was instructed on the 8th to place his command in camp at Cleveland, and endeavor to recruit his animals as much as possible, sending out scouting parties along our front.

This division had been serving with the Army of the Ohio since the withdrawal of Longstreet from before Knoxville, and with long marches, together with the difficulty of procuring forage, the horses and transportation of the command were in poor condition. On the 8th Colonel Harrison was directed to remove his command from Lee and Gordon's Mills to a position on the road leading from the mills to Ringgold, throwing out pickets to Leet's Tan-yard and to Wood's Gap. Col. W. P. Boone, commanding Twenty-eighth Kentucky Mounted Infantry, ordered to move his command to Lee and Gordon's Mills, and report to Col. Daniel McCook, commanding the brigade at that place.

On the 9th Colonel Harrison reconnoitered the gaps in Taylor's Ridge and found the enemy in larger force than they were previous to the demonstration [by Wheeler] of the 5th. On the 13th Long's brigade of cavalry left Cleveland for Ringgold. The Western and Atlantic Railroad was in running order to Graysville the same day. During the evening Colonel McCook reported, by signal, from Lee and Gordon's Mills, that Colonel Boone had just returned from beyond La Fayette, and that he found no rebels at the gaps.

On the 16th the following information was received direct from Dalton, and from a reliable source:

Rebel force 45,000, comprising Hood's four divisions: [Carter L.] Stevenson, on the left, southeast of Dalton, 6,000; Breckinridge, on the left center, 4,000; Stewart on the right center and Hindman on the right. Hardee's four divisions: Cleburne's on the left, east of Dalton, 5,000 strong; Cheatham's on the right, and two others on the railroad. Roddey's cavalry was near Varnell's Station, numbering 2,000 men; Wheeler was in front with 11,000 men; total cavalry, 12,000 to 14,000.

March 18 the balance of Johnson's division, Fourteenth Corps, reached Graysville from Tyner's Station and went into camp at that place.

On the 20th the Western and Atlantic Railroad was in running order to Ringgold. About this time information was sent me from Dalton confirmatory of the report received from General Gordon Granger, on the 5th, to the effect that a part of Longstreet's cavalry was re-enforcing Johnston, said to be [William T.] Martin's division. Brig. Gen. G. M. Dodge, of the Army of the Tennessee, reported from Athens [Alabama] on the 23d, by telegraph, that he had pushed down both sides of the Tennessee River and found the enemy very strong on the south side, and that he had no doubt they were preparing for a raid. He could not tell whether it was the whole of [Nathan Bedford] Forrest's force or not. Brig. Gen. Kenner Garrard, Commanding the Second Cavalry Division, at Huntsville, was instructed to move his force to the support of General Dodge. In a second dispatch General Dodge said his troops struck the enemy [Col. William A. Johnson's brigade] 3 miles south of Moulton, and after a sharp fight fell back with a loss of 4 killed and 10 wounded, the enemy following for a distance of 14 miles. A number of the enemy were killed and wounded, and our force took several prisoners, among them a captain of artillery belonging to Forrest's command. Information from various sources went to show a concentration of a heavy force of cavalry in Northern Alabama, parties of rebels showing themselves in the vicinity of Caperton's Ferry on the south side of the Tennessee, and extending nearly as far west as Tuscumbia.

Col. William B. Stokes, commanding Fifth Tennessee Cavalry, reports on the 29th from Sparta, Tenn., the operations of his command against the guerrillas in that vicinity, having had several engagements with them in the space of a fortnight, in which he succeeded in completely routing and scattering them, killing and wounding a number, among them two of their most active leaders, Bledsoe and Champ Ferguson.

There had returned to the army from [veterans'] furlough up to March 31 thirty-three regiments of infantry, five of cavalry, and ten batteries of artillery, with 5,429 recruits. . . .

I am, very respectfully, your obedient servant,

GEO. H. THOMAS,

*Major-General, U. S. Volunteers, Commanding.*

Maj. R. M. Sawyer,

*Assistant Adjutant-General.*[11]

11. OR, I, XXXII, pt. I, pp. 14-16.

Thomas' report for April 1864 read:

Headquarters Department of the Cumberland,
*Chattanooga, Tenn., May* 2, 1864.

Colonel: I have the honor to report the operations of my command for the month of April as follows, viz:

On the 2d instant a force of rebels [Wheeler's], said to be 1,500 strong, made a demonstration in the direction of Cleveland and Charleston, E. Tenn., approaching to within 8 miles of Cleveland, when they divided into parties; one going out in the direction of Ducktown, through the mountains, the other remaining and falling back toward Dalton on the appearance of a force of our cavalry sent out from Cleveland in command of Colonel [Oscar H.] La Grange, of the First Wisconsin. A scout, who arrived at Cleveland on the 3d, reported that the above movement on the part of the enemy was for the purpose of covering the approach of a force from Longstreet's army which was on its way to re-enforce Johnston by way of Murphy, N. C. This was afterward ascertained to be [William T.] Martin's division of cavalry.

On the 5th the following changes were ordered in the organization of the Army of the Cumberland: The Eleventh and Twelfth Army Corps to be consolidated and known as the Twentieth Army Corps, commanded by Maj. Gen. Joseph Hooker; Maj. Gen. Gordon Granger relieved of the command of the Fourth Army Corps and Maj. Gen. O. O. Howard (formerly commanding the Eleventh Army Corps) in his stead.

Maj. Gen. P. H. Sheridan having been relieved from the command of the Second Division, Fourth Army Corps [and ordered to command the Army of the Potomac's cavalry], Maj. Gen. John Newton was assigned to that command, and ordered to report to Major-General Howard.

On the 10th Brig. Gen. J. W. Geary, commanding Second Division, Twentieth Army Corps, stationed along the railroad from Bridgeport to Stevenson, was ordered to organize an expedition, consisting of two regiments, with ten days' rations, and embark on the steamer *Chickamauga*, taking one piece of artillery to protect the boat, and then proceed down the Tennessee River as far as Decatur, Ala., examining carefully the south bank of the river, and all streams emptying into it from the south side; destroying all boats of whatever

215

kind he might find, and notifying the inhabitants that no more boats would be permitted to be used or built, except with the permission of the commanding officer. On returning, General Geary was to examine the north bank in the same manner, and destroy all boats he might find, except such as Major-General McPherson, commanding Army of the Tennessee, should need, and the boats at Decatur or Larkin's Ferry, which will be the only points at which communication across the river will be permitted, notifying the inhabitants of the same.

April 11 the cavalry command of the army was reorganized, forming four divisions, of three brigades each, averaging three regiments to a brigade.

Brigadier-General Geary returned to Bridgeport on the 15th, reporting the result of his expedition down the Tennessee to be that he proceeded as far as Triana, Ala., where he came upon the enemy [units from Brig. Gens. James H. Clanton's and Philip D. Roddey's commands] in heavy force on both sides of the river; that deeming it advisable to proceed no farther, General Geary returned, having destroyed a considerable number of boats both going and coming.

Information gained from deserters and others estimate the strength of the rebel army at Dalton to be 45,000 infantry and about 12,000 cavalry. The enemy has two brigades of cavalry at Tunnel Hill, watching our movements at Ringgold and the gaps through Taylor's Ridge, and one brigade on the road leading from Dalton to Cleveland, picketing the approaches from that direction.

The Fourth Army Corps, Maj. Gen. O. O. Howard commanding, having been relieved from duty with the Army of the Ohio, was concentrated at Cleveland on the 22d, and camped at that place and vicinity. The First Division of Cavalry, Col. Edward M. McCook commanding, was still at that point picketing and patrolling the country.

Frequent skirmishes have taken place during the month all along our front, between our own and the enemy's cavalry. In quite a sharp little affair near Leet's farm, on the 23d, we lost 5 killed and 10 wounded, besides 1 officer and 12 men taken prisoners; the enemy [Wheeler's cavalry] having had an overwhelming force, succeeded in gaining our rear. A scout, who left Dalton on the 16th, reports that two divisions from Hardee's corps were to be sent to re-enforce Lee in Virginia; this force to be replaced by [William W.] Loring's division from Mississippi. This man passed through the enemy's defenses at Buzzard Roost, and reports them very strong.

On the 29th a reconnaissance was made toward Tunnel Hill from Ringgold, composed of 300 cavalry under [Judson] Kilpatrick and [Ferdinand] Van Derveer's brigade of infantry. They advanced to within a short distance of Tunnel Hill, driving the enemy before them until they developed a largely superior force, when the expedition returned to Ringgold. About this time preparations were commenced for the proposed advance on Dalton in May. The Second Division of Cavalry, Brig. Gen. Kenner Garrard commanding, started from Columbia, Tenn., under instructions to report to General McPherson for further orders.

The Twentieth Army Corps, Major-General Hooker commanding, was directed to concentrate in Lookout Valley. General Rousseau's division, of that command, to garrison the blockhouses and other points along the line of the Nashville and Chattanooga Railroad; the balance of the corps to be placed in marching order immediately.

The Fourteenth Corps, Maj. Gen. J. M. Palmer commanding, was to concentrate at Ringgold, Ga., as soon as possible; and the Fourth Corps was in readiness to move from Cleveland as soon as ordered.

Garrard's division of cavalry being under orders to report to General McPherson for duty, McCook's division (First) was to move on Howard's left, and Kilpatrick's (Third) to operate with Palmer's corps from Ringgold.

Reliable information was received on the 30th from Atlanta (27th) that heavy re-enforcements to Johnston had been passing that point since the 20th, said to be from Mobile, estimated at 10,000 [This report was untrue.] The same person reports from Rome (28th) that part of Polk's corps was there, numbering about 5,000, and still more arriving. [There was no truth to this report. At this time Polk's infantry was in Alabama—Loring's Division at Montevallo and French's Division at Tuscaloosa.] Two trains with artillery, fourteen pieces, had arrived that day. Martin's cavalry division was also there, about 4,000 men; also, part of Polk's corps had reached Dalton the same day (28th).

A reliable scout, sent to Dalton from Chattanooga, reaching Dalton on the 25th, returned on the 30th, reporting that the whole of Hood's corps had been moved to the front from its old position in the immediate vicinity of Dalton. He went to Atlanta on the 27th, but learned nothing of importance there. At Resaca he saw the camps of . . . [Brig. Gen. John H. Kelly's] division of cavalry, and at Rome he learned that Loring's and another division had arrived from Mississippi [The latter report was in error.], thus corroborating information received from a different source.

During the month there have returned to this army from furlough, as veteran volunteers, eighteen regiments of infantry, one of cavalry, and four batteries of artillery, with an aggregate of 2,697 recruits gained while absent.

The quartermaster's department has been particularly active constructing store-houses, etc., at Chattanooga.

I am, very respectfully, your obedient servant,

GEO. H. THOMAS,

*Major-General, U. S. Volunteers, Commanding.*

Lieut. Col. R. M. Sawyer,

*A. A. G., Military Division of the Mississippi.*[12]

General Sherman, to prevent the Confederates from again employing their interior position to the disadvantage of the Union as they had in the summer of 1862 to steal a march on General Buell in the race for Chattanooga and in September 1863 to insure the defeat of General Rosecrans at Chickamauga, would coordinate his movements with those of the Federal armies in Virginia—the Army of the Potomac, the Army of the James, and lesser forces led by Major General Franz Sigel and Brigadier General George Crook.

In April, Sherman personally visited his three army commanders. He discussed with them the proposed campaign, and directed the assembly of McPherson's Army of the Tennessee and Schofield's Army of the Ohio in forward staging areas near the respective flanks of Thomas' Army of the Cumberland. May 5 was designated as the day that the columns were to march.

The concentration of the Army of the Ohio at Cleveland had

12. *Ibid.*, pp. 18-20.

been facilitated by the return of General Longstreet and his two divisions to the Army of Northern Virginia. Breaking camp on May 4, Schofield's troops, moving via the old Federal road, crossed into Georgia and took position at Red Clay on the Army of the Cumberland's left. Simultanously, McPherson's Army of the Tennessee, marching by way of Chattanooga, halted at Lee and Gordon's Mills on Thomas' right. Sherman was at the center with Thomas, and his "army group" was braced and anxious to come to grips with the foe. The distance from McPherson on the right to Schofield on the left was 16 air line miles, and Thomas, whose army was nearly equal numerically to Johnston's, was thrust somewhat forward of the wings.

Sherman began the campaign with an effective force of about 100,000 soldiers and 254 cannon. Of these, Thomas' Cumberlanders numbered 60,000 men and 130 guns; the Army of the Tennessee 25,000 men and 96 field pieces; and the Army of the Ohio 14,000 men and 28 cannon.[13]

In April, at a meeting in Chattanooga, Thomas and Sherman had discussed grand strategy. Familiar with the region's geography, Thomas called Sherman's attention to Snake Creek Gap, a route by which Resaca or Calhoun—stations on the Western & Atlantic—could be gained by a flanking column and the Confederates' position anchored on Buzzard Roost and Rocky Face turned. He offered to lead his Cumberlanders through this defile, while McPherson's Army of the Tennessee and Schofield's Army of the Ohio focused General Johnston's attention to his front. The camps then occupied by his armies, and his desire to deploy the greater numerical strength of the Army of the Cumberland at the center to cover his base and supply line, caused Sherman to modify Thomas' proposal while accepting the plan. In doing so, Sherman told Thomas, "The Army of the Tennessee are better marchers than the Army of the Cumberland and I am going to send McPherson," and his two corps through Snake Creek Gap. Whereupon, Thomas returned to his quarters, remarking to a confidant, "for I saw the game was up."[14]

13. Cox, *Atlanta*, pp. 24-25.
14. *Ibid.*, p. 31; John Watts De Peyster, "George H. Thomas," in Augustus C. Rogers, *Sketches of Representative Men North and South* (New York, 1873), pp. 569-70.

General Thomas described the troop movements of what is known as the Atlanta Campaign in four comprehensive reports. The first of these, submitted on June 5, details the marches and battles that saw Sherman's "army group" employ its superior numbers to outflank a succession of strongholds taken up by General Johnston's Confederates on a relentless 90-mile advance that carried it from the approaches to Chattanooga to the Dallas-New Hope line, 30 miles northwest of Atlanta. Thomas' initial report read:

Headquarters Army of the Cumberland,<br>
In the Field, near Dallas, Ga., June 5, 1864.

Colonel: I have the honor to report the operations of my command for the month of May as follows:

In obedience to instructions from the major-general [Sherman] commanding the military division, I got my command in readiness for a forward movement on Dalton, Ga., and was fully prepared to move on the 2d of May, as directed. Major-General Hooker, commanding Twentieth Army Corps, was directed to move from Lookout Valley, via Lee and Gordon's Mills, on East Chickamauga Creek, to Leet's farm, on the road leading from the mills to Nickajack Gap, the movement to commence on the 2d. Major-General Palmer, commanding the Fourteenth Army Corps, was to concentrate his command at Ringgold, Ga., and Major-General Howard, commanding the Fourth Army Corps, was to move from Cleveland, East Tennessee, on the 3d, and concentrate his command in the vicinity of Catoosa Springs, about three miles east of Ringgold; [Edward M.] McCook's division of cavalry to move on Howard's left; Kilpatrick's division of cavalry was stationed at Ringgold, picketing toward Tunnel Hill, and patrolling on Palmer's right flank; [Kenner] Garrard's division was detached and operating under instructions from Major-General McPherson, commanding the Army of the Tennessee. The army got into position by the 5th, and stood as above directed, communication having been fully established from the right to the left of the whole command.

According to instructions given on the 6th, the army moved on Tunnel Hill at daylight on the 7th in three columns—Palmer's corps on the direct road from Ringgold, Howard's via Lee's house, and Hooker's via Nickajack Gap and

220

Trickum. The enemy made some show of resistance in Palmer's front, but evacuated Tunnel Hill on the appearance of Howard's column on his flank, and fled toward Buzzard Roost, our troops occupying Tunnel Hill Ridge. Palmer's command was then moved forward and took position on Howard's right along the ridge, and both corps remained there for the night. Hooker's column reached Trickum Post-Office about 4 p. m. and camped for the night, picketing strongly the roads leading from Buzzard Roost and Dalton, as well as the approaches from the direction of Villanow. General Kilpatrick's division of cavalry took post at or near Gordon's Spring to be in readiness to establish communication with the Army of the Tennessee, which was expected at Villanow on the 8th.

On the morning of the 8th Harker's brigade, of Newton's division, Howard's corps, was pushed along the crest of Rocky Face Ridge to within half a mile of the rebels' signal station, where it came upon obstructions of too formidable character to admit of farther progress, except with very severe loss; it was instructed to hold the position. Wood's division, of the Fourth Corps; Davis' division, of the Fourteenth Corps, and [Daniel] Butterfield's division, of the Twentieth Corps, then pushed forward a line of skirmishers and drove the enemy to his intrenchments, our men occupying the mouth of Buzzard Roost. Geary's division, of the Twentieth Corps, made a reconnaissance well up the side of Chattoogator Mountain (a high and precipitous ridge running due south from Buzzard Roost). Geary's men fought their way well up to the enemy's intrenchments on the crest, but with considerable loss and without being able to gain possession of Mill Gap. The troops were then withdrawn to a position in the valley out of reach of the enemy's guns; Kilpatrick's communicated with General McPherson's command at Villanow, and then returned to Trickum. Brig. Gen. Ed. McCook was ordered to concentrate his cavalry division and take post on the left of General Schofield until General [George] Stoneman's [Army of the Ohio] cavalry could arrive and relieve him. From a prisoner captured at Buzzard Roost we learned that the force defending the passage of the gap amounted to 11,000 men, comprising [A. P.] Stewart's and [William B.] Bate's divisions, being supported by [Thomas C.] Hindman's and [Carter L.] Stevenson's divisions, numbering 10,000 more. They had considerable artillery, but none heavier than 10-pounder caliber. The enemy was fortifying all night of the 7th and had masked batteries at points all through the pass. Heavy skirmishing was kept up along the whole line during the 9th and 10th with considerable loss in wounded, and but few killed.

General Hooker was directed on the 10th to send one division from his command to the support of General McPherson at Snake Creek Gap, to enable the latter to operate more freely from danger to his rear.[15] Kilpatrick's cavalry was also ordered to report to General McPherson. McCook's division of cavalry, posted on the left of General Schofield's command, had a heavy skirmish with three brigades of the enemy's [Wheeler's] cavalry on the road leading to Varnell's Station, resulting in our driving the rebels to their intrenchments on Poplar Creek Hill, where they opened on McCook's troops with two pieces of artillery. Our loss was 136 men and 15 officers killed, wounded, and missing; among the latter Colonel La Grange, of the First Wisconsin, who was captured. The enemy's loss was greater than ours. General Hooker was directed to send another division from his command to Snake Creek Gap, with instructions to repair the road through the gap so as to facilitate the passage of infantry and wagons.

On the 11th it was decided to leave one corps (Howard's), supported by Stoneman's and McCook's divisions of cavalry, and move to Snake Creek Gap with the balance of the army, attacking the enemy in force from that quarter, while Howard was keeping up the impression of a direct attack on Buzzard Roost. This movement was to commence on the 12th. Instructions were given to corps commanders to provide their commands with ten days' rations and a good supply of ammunition, sending all surplus wagons back to Ringgold.

At 9 a. m. on the 13th General Howard's command occupied Dalton, it having been evacuated by the enemy on the evening of the 12th, concentrating his troops in Dalton.

15. OR, I, XXXVIII, pt. I, pp. 139-40. On May 9, McPherson's Army of the Tennessee passed through Snake Creek Gap and closed on the fortifications guarding the approaches to Resaca from the west. McPherson then lost his nerve and pulled back, taking up a strong position at the southern mouth of the gap, from where he could keep open the route he had pioneered for the "army group" and notified Sherman. The latter was keenly disappointed, and when they met, Sherman told McPherson he had missed a great opportunity. Cox, *Atlanta*, pp. 36-37.

General Howard pursued the enemy along the [Western & Atlantic] railroad in the direction of Resaca, capturing a considerable number of prisoners.

The concentration of the balance of the army in Snake Creek Gap having been completed by the night of the 12th, at 8 a. m. on the 13th Hooker's corps, preceded by Kilpatrick's cavalry, moved out on the Resaca road in support of McPherson's troops, threatening Resaca. Palmer's corps moved out of Snake Creek Gap two miles northeast of Hooker, and then took a course parallel with the Resaca road, with orders to proceed as far as the [Western & Atlantic] railroad. On reaching the neighborhood of the railroad his skirmishers encountered those of the enemy strongly posted on the hills [overlooking Camp Creek] immediately west of the railroad, and continued a fierce skirmish with them until night-fall. Butterfield's division, of Hooker's corps, moved up in support of Palmer's right.

About noon of the 14th Schofield's and Palmer's corps attacked the enemy's position on the hills bordering the railroad, meeting with very heavy resistance. General Schofield's left being threatened, and he having called on me for support, I directed Newton's division, of Howard's corps, which had just arrived from Dalton, to move to Schofield's assistance, and subsequently the whole of Howard's corps took post on the left of Schofield. During the afternoon Hooker's corps, which had been acting as support to General McPherson, was shifted to the left of Howard's command, and [Alpheus S.] Williams' division reached the position assigned him just in time to meet and repel a fierce attack of the enemy [by Stewart's and Stevenson's divisions of Hood's corps] who was endeavoring to turn Howard's left flank. McCook's division of cavalry took post on the left of Hooker to guard against any further attempt of the enemy in that direction. The fighting in Schofield's and Howard's front was very severe, but we drove the enemy from the hills he had occupied and forced him into his intrenchments beyond. From prisoners captured we learned that Johnston's entire army was confronting us.

At daylight on the morning of the 15th our line stood nearly as follows: Palmer's corps on the right, connecting with the left of McPherson's line, then Schofield, Howard, and Hooker, with McCook's cavalry on our extreme left.

Orders were issued during the night of the 14th for the whole line to advance at daylight on the 15th, provision being made for the retirement of Schofield's troops from the position they then occupied, and directions having been given them to take post on the left, where they properly belonged, as soon as crowded out from the center of my line by the advance of Palmer and Howard. About 11 a. m. General Butterfield's division, of Hooker's corps, supported by Williams' and Geary's, of the same command, attacked and carried a series of hills strongly occupied by the enemy on the eastern road leading from Tilton to Resaca. The rebels [Stevenson's division] were driven for nearly a mile and a half, our forces capturing 4 guns and a number of prisoners.

Information was received by daylight on the 16th that Johnston had evacuated Resaca, and directions were immediately given for the whole army to start in pursuit. Our troops occupied the town about 9 a. m. and commenced repairing the bridge over the Oostenaula, which had been partially burned by the enemy: a pontoon bridge was also thrown across above the railroad bridge, so that by night Howard's corps had got across, and marched on Calhoun. Hooker's command crossed the Connesauga at Fite's Ferry and at a ford in its vicinity, thence marching south across the Coosawattee toward Adairsville. Palmer's command was to follow after Howard's, except Davis' division, which was detached and sent toward Rome to the support of Garrard's cavalry, then acting under special instructions from the major-general [Sherman] commanding the military division.

On the 17th our advance skirmished with the enemy nearly the whole distance from Calhoun to within two miles of Adairsville, when a fierce skirmish ensued, completely checking our farther progress, and occasioning considerable loss in wounded. Information was brought in about dark that the whole of Johnston's army was at Adairsville.

The column was again set in motion on the morning of the 18th, the enemy having left during the night. Howard's and Palmer's commands moved on the direct road and along the railroad toward Kingston, camping at a point three miles north of the latter place. Hooker's corps moved on a road running southeast from Adairsville, his instruction being to proceed as far as Cassville, and there await further orders. General Davis' division, of the Fourteenth Corps, occupied Rome, capturing a large amount of commissary and quartermaster stores, hospital supplies, etc., and all sorts of ammunition, enough to supply his command for two weeks. The enemy tried to destroy the valuable iron-works at this place, but failed to do them much injury.

Howard's troops entered Kingston about 8 a. m. on the 19th, skirmishing with the enemy [Hardee's rear guard] on the southeastern side of the town. The column started again about 11 a. m. and came up with what was reported to be Cheatham's and another division [Cleburne's] in line of battle on a hill about half way between Kingston and Cassville. Howard's troops shelled the enemy from this position, pushing on after him to within two miles of Cassville, skirmishing with his rear guard until dark, when the command halted for the night. Baird's division, of Palmer's corps, was posted on the right of Howard's corps. Hooker's troops engaged the enemy on the road, leading direct from Adairsville to Cassville, skirmishing with him and driving him into his works at the latter place. [During the day, General Johnston had ordered an attack on Hooker's corps. Hood was to trigger the action, but instead of advancing he retired after receiving an erroneous report placing the Federals on his right and rear. Johnston accordingly assumed a defensive stance south and east of Cassville. When two—Hood and Polk—of his three corps commanders questioned their ability to hold the Cassville line, Johnston abandoned the position and crossed to the south side of the Etowah.]

At 10 p. m. General Hooker reported the town [Cassville] in possession of his troops. A deserter came into our lines with the information that Johnston received a re-enforcement of 6,000 men on the 19th, and that his army was now estimated at 70,000 strong. [General Polk with Major General William W. Loring's division had arrived from Alabama and had reported to Johnston at Resaca on the 11th. Two of Major General Samuel G. French's infantry brigades and Brigadier General William H. Jackson's cavalry division had joined Johnston at Adairsville on the 16th, while Brigadier General Francis M. Cockrill's brigade of French's division had reported to Polk at Kingston on the 18th.][16]

By direction of the major-general commanding [Sherman] . . . the whole command rested until the morning of the 23d. In the mean time, the railroad having been placed in running order as far as Cassville Depot, twenty days' rations and forage were issued to the troops. Resaca was directed to be strongly held and made a depot of supplies, only such stores and provisions to be brought forward to Kingston and Rome as could be moved by the wagons present with the army. [To outflank Johnston's formidable position centered on Allatoona Hills, Sherman's columns left the line of the Western & Atlantic, crossed the Etowah well downstream from Cartersville, and struck out toward Dallas. If successful, the Federal armies would again outflank Johnston, compelling him to abandon a fortified stronghold.] My directions were to move my army at daylight on the morning of the 23d on Dallas, by Euharlee and Stilesborough; the division of Brig. Gen. Jeff. C. Davis, at Rome, as soon as relieved by troops from General McPherson's army, to march direct on Dallas, by way of Van Wert. The advance guard of McCook's division of cavalry [having crossed the Etowah] reached Stilesborough on the afternoon of the 23d, and found the place occupied by a strong force of the enemy's cavalry, supported by infantry, which resisted his farther advance, skirmishing with him until dark. The commands of Major-Generals Hooker, Howard, and Palmer [crossed the Etowah and] camped on the south side of Euharlee Creek, in accordance with my directions.

General Hooker was directed to send one division of his command at daylight on the morning of the 24th to push the enemy across Raccoon Creek toward Allatoona, on the Alabama road, and hold him in that position until relieved by the Army of the Ohio, covering the movements of the balance of the Twentieth Corps, directly through Stilesborough, upon Burnt Hickory, at which latter place his whole command was to encamp. McCook's division of cavalry was to precede the Twentieth Corps in the movement upon Burnt Hickory, and then take up a position toward Allatoona, picketing the roads strongly, and covering the movements of the army. The Fourth Corps followed the Twentieth Corps, camping on its right, and the Fourteenth Corps, not being able to reach Burnt Hickory

16. OR, I, XXXVIII, pt. I, pp. 140-42; Cox, *Atlanta*, pp. 54-55.

on account of the crowded state of the roads and the difficult nature of the ground passed over, camped at a point on Allatoona Ridge, about half way between Stilesborough and Burnt Hickory.

McCook reached Burnt Hickory about 2 p. m., after skirmishing with the enemy about four miles. He captured a rebel courier, bearing a dispatch to the rebel General [William H.] Jackson, commanding a division of cavalry, with instructions from General Johnston to observe our movements toward Burnt Hickory, and stating that Johnston was moving in the direction of Dallas and Powder Springs. General Garrard, commanding Second Cavalry Division, informed me that he was camped on Pumpkin Vine Creek, about three miles from Dallas, and that in moving on that place, and when within a quarter of a mile from it, he was attacked by what was reported by prisoners to be Bate's division, the advance of Hardee's corps. Garrard repulsed this force and drove it back toward Dallas.

On the 25th the First Division of Cavalry (McCook's) moved on the road leading to Golgotha, preceding Butterfield's division, of the Twentieth Corps. The balance of General Hooker's command advanced on the road leading to Dallas running south of the one used by Butterfield's division. Howard's corps followed Hooker's, and in rear of Howard, Palmer's. About 11 a. m. General Geary's division, of the Twentieth Corps, being in advance, came upon the enemy in considerable force at a point about four and a half miles from Dallas, the country on both sides of the road being thickly wooded and covered with undergrowth. Geary skirmished heavily with the enemy [the 32d and 58th Alabama and Austin's Sharpshooters] slowly driving him, until Butterfield's and Williams' divisions came up and relieved Geary's troops. Soon after the arrival of Williams, about 3 p. m., the column was again put in motion, Williams' division in advance, and, although heavily engaged, drove the enemy steadily before it into his intrenchments [at New Hope Church]. Our loss was heavy, but it is believed that the loss of the enemy was much greater. Shortly after 3 p. m. the head of Howard's column got within supporting distance of Hooker's corps, and Newton's division was placed in position on Hooker's left about

6 p. m., and by morning the whole of Howard's corps was in position on the left of Hooker.[17]

On May 24, General Johnston had moved to counter Sherman's plans. He abandoned his Allatoona Pass stronghold and sent his army streaming toward Dallas by way of New Hope Church. It was a race to checkmate Sherman's bold gamble. Johnston's grim fighters marched faster and Hood's troops reached New Hope Church ahead of Hooker's Cumberlanders. In deploying his Army of Tennessee, Johnston had Hood's corps on the right, Polk's in the center, and Hardee's on the left.

"The roads were so full of wagons," Thomas continued:
> that Palmer's corps could not get into position by night of the 25th, but on the morning of the 26th Johnson's division, of the Fourteenth Corps, was moved up to within a short distance of Hooker's and Howard's commands, and was posted in reserve. Davis' division, Fourteenth Corps, which had reported back to its command (it having been relieved at Rome by troops from the Army of the Tennessee), was sent by General Palmer to move on Dallas by the most direct road from where he then was to support General McPherson's command, and communicate with the right of General Hooker. Baird's division, of the Fourteenth Corps, was left at Burnt Hickory to protect the trains at that point and the rear of the army.
>
> McCook's division of cavalry met the enemy's cavalry on the road leading from Burnt Hickory to Marietta near its intersection with the lower Dallas and Allatoona road. McCook's troops skirmished heavily with the force opposing them, inflicting on them considerable loss and capturing 52 prisoners, from whom it was ascertained that the whole of Wheeler's cavalry was posted on the right of the rebel army.
>
> The left of General Howard's corps was swung around to the right, occupying a line of hills running nearly perpendicular to the line occupied by Hooker on the 25th, thereby threatening the enemy's right. The Twenty-third Army Corps, Major-General Schofield commanding, was posted on the left of my command, Schofield's left extending to and covering the road leading from Allatoona to Dallas, via New Hope Church.

17. OR, I, XXXVIII, pt. I, pp. 142-43.

There was light skirmishing all day while Howard and Schofield were working into position, and at dark on the 26th Howard's left connected with Schofield's right. In the mean time trains were brought up and rations and ammunition issued where practicable. Strong breast-works were thrown up all along the line, the men working cheerfully and prepared to resist any attack the enemy might see fit to make.

On the 27th, in accordance with instructions given by the major-general [Sherman] commanding, the Military Division of the Mississippi, Hooker's and Howard's corps pressed the enemy, supported by considerable artillery firing. Wood's division, of Howard's corps, supported by Johnson's division, of Palmer's corps, was moved to the left of Schofield's line and swung around toward the right, attacking the enemy's right flank [at Pickett's Mill] and driving him into his rifle-pits, with considerable loss, however, to our troops. Our men had to contend with an almost hidden foe, the ground being cut up into ravines and covered by a dense forest filled with undergrowth; but notwithstanding all the difficulties of the country both officers and men did their work nobly, and having assumed a position were not to be moved from it. The enemy [Cleburne's and Hindman's divisions] came out of his works in front of Newton's division, of Howard's corps, attacking [George D.] Wagner's and [Nathan] Kimball's brigades, but was driven back after a short and warm contest.

General Davis occupied Dallas with his division on the afternoon of the 27th, skirmishing with the enemy and driving him as far as he could without losing his connection with General McPherson. Davis reported that after skirmishing all the afternoon he developed the enemy in force and strongly posted in front of his (Davis') left, with a battery in position on a hill commanding the road between him and General Hooker. Davis had, however, cut a road through the forest to his rear, by which he could communicate safely with Hooker. During the night of the 27th the enemy attacked Davis and was repulsed after a sharp fight, leaving behind him a few wounded and 27 prisoners, belonging mostly to Polk's corps. By this time it had been ascertained beyond a doubt that Johnston had his whole army with him, strengthened by Polk's command and detachments sent from various points to re-enforce him. He had taken up a strong position, which he was steadily strengthening with earth-works, evidently with the determination to make a firm stand where he then was.

On the 28th our line stood as follows: Hooker's corps (Twentieth) on the right, with Davis' division, of Palmer's corps, still on his right, but acting as a support to the Army of the Tennessee; two divisions of Howard's corps (Fourth) on the left of Hooker; then the Army of the Ohio, Major-General Schofield commanding. Wood's division, of Howard's corps, on the left of Schofield's command, with Johnson's division, of Palmer's corps, on the left of Wood; Stoneman's division of cavalry holding a hill to the left of Johnson, and then McCook's division of cavalry holding the road leading from Burnt Church to Marietta, via Golgotha, and guarding the left of the army. During the 28th there was considerable artillery firing, with skirmishing at intervals during the day and night.[18]

On the afternoon of the 28th, General Bate's division of Hardee's corps undertook a forced reconnaissance of McPherson's right, east and southeast of Dallas. The Confederates were badly mauled by the men of Logan's and Dodge's corps.

"During the night of the 29th," Thomas continued:
the enemy felt our line at several points, without making a serious attack at any one place. They found our men vigilant and fully prepared for them. Owing to the close proximity of the enemy's lines to the right of ours, neither McPherson nor Davis could withdraw from their positions without being attacked and forced to return, so that the project of using their commands to relieve Hooker, Howard, and Schofield, allowing these latter to take post on the left of the line, could not be carried out, although three attempts at a withdrawal were made by McPherson and Davis on the nights of the 29th, 30th, and 31st. In the meanwhile, the position of the army remained unchanged up to the 31st, our skirmishers and those of the enemy exchanging occasional shots.

The detailed reports of the subordinate commanders will be forwarded as soon as handed in.

I have the honor to forward herewith a consolidated return of casualties for the month. . . .

18. *Ibid.*, pp. 143-44.

I am, colonel, very respectfully, your obedient servant,
GEO. H. THOMAS,
*Major-General, U. S. Volunteers, Commanding.*
Lieut. Col. R. M. Sawyer,
*Asst. Adjt. Gen., Mil. Div. of the Mississippi.*

(Inclosure No. 1)
*List of casualties in the Army of the Cumberland during the month of May.*

| Corps | Killed | | Wounded | | Missing | | Aggregate |
|---|---|---|---|---|---|---|---|
| | Officers | Men | Officers | Men | Officers | Men | |
| 14th Army Corps | 14 | 210 | 54 | 1,100 | 2 | 75 | 1,455 |
| 20th Army Corps | 22 | 387 | 127 | 2,880 | 2 | 499 | 3,917 |
| 4th Army Corps | 30 | 493 | 120 | 2,471 | 4 | 284 | 3,402 |
| Total | 66 | 1,090 | 301 | 6,451 | 8 | 858 | 8,774[19] |

On June 1, General Stoneman's cavalry occupied Allatoona Pass without firing a shot, and from there covered repair of the railroad from Kingston to the Etowah. The next day, the 2d, Sherman vigorously resumed his flanking movements that had become and were to continue to characterize the Atlanta Campaign. During June, Sherman employed his superior numbers to successively maneuver Johnston out from behind three formidable defense lines—the New Hope Church-Dallas, the Lost Mountain-Pine Mountain-Brush Mountain, and the Brush Mountain-Noonday Creek-Mud Creek line.

Johnston's management of his retrograde was equally skillful. Each time the Federals compelled him to abandon a fortified line, he anticipated them. Seemingly at the last moment, the Confederates would pull out of their rifle-pits and artillery emplacements, leave their abatis, and fall back to a new and apparently stronger position previously selected by their engineers. This

19. *Ibid.*, p. 144.

deadly contest in which spades were trump engrossed the men in blue and gray. To compound the hardships, rains drenched the region, turning the roads into ribbons of reddish mud and normally shallow streams into raging torrents.

In a report filed on July 16, General Thomas detailed the campaigning of his Cumberlanders:

Headquarters Department of the Cumberland,
*In the Field, July 16, 1864.*

Colonel: I have the honor to report the operations of my command for the month of June, as follows:

June 1, Hooker's, Howard's, and Palmer's corps were confronting the enemy's position at New Hope Church, near Dallas, Ga., with McCook's division of cavalry on the left of the army guarding the approaches from the direction of Acworth and Marietta.

June 2, General Hooker's corps having been relieved in the position it occupied on the right of my army by General McPherson's troops, moved in support of the Army of the Ohio, Major-General Schofield commanding, and occupied the hills on the extreme left of my line which had been previously held by Stoneman's and McCook's divisions of cavalry, McCook taking post on the left of Schofield on the Dallas and Acworth road. Baird's division, of Palmer's corps, moved up from Burnt Hickory, and took up a position in reserve behind Johnson's division, of the same corps. Davis' division, of Palmer's corps, relieved General Schofield's troops at the same time that General Hooker was relieved by General McPherson's command. As soon as the troops got into their new position, Schofield's and Hooker's corps, and Baird's division, of Palmer's corps, swung round toward the right, skirmishing with the enemy as they advanced, gaining some ground, which they immediately prepared to hold. Howard's corps, on the right of my line, occupied the enemy's attention, and was held in readiness to follow the general movement against the enemy's right.

June 3, General Palmer advanced Baird's division about a mile in a southeasterly direction, and General Hooker moved Butterfield's and Geary's divisions toward the Acworth and Dallas road, sending one brigade to take possession of and

232

hold the bridge across Allatoona Creek, four miles southwest from Allatoona. General E. M. McCook, with his division of cavalry, took position on the direct road from Dallas to Acworth at the crossing of Allatoona Creek, one and a half miles south of and above the crossing held by General Hooker's troops. Scouts were sent into Acworth [a station on the Western & Atlantic, 5 miles southeast of Allatoona Pass], reaching there at 11 a. m., finding the town nearly deserted. They captured a few of the enemy's vedettes. On reaching the new position the troops were immediately set to work strengthening them by breast-works of logs, while continual skirmishing was being kept up by the enemy.

During the night of the 4th the enemy [abandoning the New Hope Church-Dallas line] fell back from our front, his works being found completely evacuated on the morning of the 5th. After a careful reconnaissance of the ground lately occupied by him, the conclusion was that he had fallen back in the direction of Big Shanty, a point on the railroad about six miles from Marietta. [Johnston's new line anchored its left on Lost Mountain, its center on Pine Mountain, and its right on Brush Mountain, southeast of Big Shanty.]

June 6, General Hooker moved his command to the vicinity of McLean's house, on the Sandtown road, near its intersection with the Burnt Hickory and Marietta road, and about three miles southwest from Acworth. General Palmer's corps was posted on General Hooker's left, Palmer's left resting on Proctor's Creek; General Howard's corps in the vicinity of Durham's house. By direction of the major-general commanding the military division [Sherman], the whole command remained in the above position until the morning of the 10th instant. In the mean time the railroad was completed through to Acworth, and rations and ammunition were replenished.

June 9, General E. M. McCook, commanding First Division of Cavalry, made a reconnaissance toward the enemy's position in our front. After passing two miles beyond the pickets of the Twentieth Army Corps, he came upon those of the enemy on the Marietta side of Allatoona Creek, and drove them in upon a heavier line about a mile beyond, coming in view of the enemy's camp on Pine . . . [Mountain] where they appeared to be in force.

June 10, Palmer's corps moved out of camp on a road running in a southeasterly direction, passing by Owen's house, and found the enemy [Bate's division] strongly posted on Pine . . . [Mountain], skirmishing with him until dark. Howard's corps moved on the Burnt Hickory and Marietta road and took post on the right of Palmer in front of Pine . . . [Mountain]. Hooker's corps moved on the same road with General Howard's command.

June 11, the commands of Generals Palmer and Howard moved to the left and slightly in advance of their position of yesterday, General Palmer's left resting on the railroad and connecting with General McPherson's army. The enemy was found to be strongly posted on a line of hills running west from . . . [Brush] Mountain to Lost Mountain, with a strong advanced work on Pine . . . [Mountain]. The approaches to this position were over a very broken and thickly wooded country which two days of rain had rendered almost impassable.

June 14, Palmer's corps and the left of Howard's pushed forward to a position about a mile in advance of their line established on the 11th, Howard's right being already in close proximity to the enemy's position on Pine . . . [Mountain. During the day, while observing Howard's movements from the Pine Mountain observation station, Confederate General Polk was killed by a projectile from one of Howard's batteries.]

June 15, the enemy [Bate's troops] having evacuated Pine . . . [Mountain] during the night, it was occupied by General Howard's troops early in the day. About noon General Hooker's corps, on the right of Pine . . . [Mountain], advanced against the enemy's position directly in his front, driving him to his main works after very heavy skirmishing and considerable loss. Howard's corps also moved against the enemy on the left of Pine . . . [Mountain] and succeeded in driving him to his main fortifications. Both Hooker and Howard established themselves within 100 yards of the enemy's main line, and immediately secured the position gained. The right of Palmer's corps moved in connection with General Howard's left.

June 16, Hooker and Howard remained in the positions taken up by them yesterday, their skirmishers being close up to those of the enemy, keeping up a steady firing all day. Palmer advanced his center division a short distance toward the enemy's works, shortening and more nearly perfecting the line established by yesterday's operations. Batteries were placed at commanding points along the entire line, and kept up a continuous fire on the enemy's works and camps.

June 17, having ascertained during the night that the enemy [Johnston, satisfied that Hardee's line on his left had become untenable in face of gains made by Schofield's Army of the Ohio, advancing on Hooker's right, swung back Hardee's corps. Hardee's troops by daybreak on the 17th had occupied and entrenched a line on the ridges east of and commanding Mud Creek.] had evacuated his main line of works, the Fourth and Twentieth Corps were advanced early in the morning, passing over the fortifications lately occupied by the enemy, and swinging around toward the southeast, proceeded until their skirmishers came upon those of the enemy, whose main force was posted on a line of hills bordering Mud Creek, on the Marietta side of it, running nearly perpendicular to their earth-works lately abandoned, and in a southwesterly direction from . . . [Brush] Mountain. The right of Palmer moved in conformity with Howard's corps, keeping up the connection with the left of it, while Palmer's left still rested on the railroad in front of . . . [Kennesaw], connecting at that point with the right of the Army of the Tennessee. Hooker's right rested at and a little in advance of Darby's house on the Sandtown road, nearly five miles due west from Marietta. Part of General Howard's troops, in the center, under the fire of a heavy cannonading previously ordered, charged the enemy's rifle-pits and effected a lodgment in the woods close up to his main line. During the night the enemy made two attacks upon this force and was repulsed each time. General McCook's division of cavalry [spearheading the advance of Schofield's army] turned the enemy's left during the afternoon, driving his [Jackson's] cavalry across Mud Creek, on the Dallas and Marietta road, to within six miles of Marietta, and capturing 2 hospitals containing 5 officers and 35 enlisted men, 14 nurses, and 2 surgeons.

June 18, at 4 a. m. Wood's division, of Howard's corps, pressed up close to the enemy's works, finding him still in force. Shortly after, the right of Howard's skirmishers, strongly supported, advanced suddenly and carried an intrenched line of rebel works, capturing about 50 prisoners. The enemy tried hard to regain the ground, but failed in every attempt they made. Howard's men pressed the enemy so closely that he could not throw out skirmishers from his works, while our pickets, and at some points our main line, kept up such a well-directed fire of musketry that the rebels could not use their artillery. During the day and night batteries were worked into positions from which the enemy's works could be enfiladed, should he remain in them by morning.[20]

General Johnston, in view of the Federal successes on the 18th (the occupation by Schofield's army of the Mud Creek-Noses Creek watershed on Hooker's left and the gains of Howard's corps), evacuated the Brush Mountain-Noonday Creek-Mud Creek line. The new Confederate main line of resistance shielding Marietta centered on Big and Little Kennesaw Mountains defended by Polk's corps now commanded by General Loring. Hood's corps held the Confederate right east of the Western & Atlantic and north of Marietta, and Hardee's corps on the left was posted on the crest of the ridge covering the approaches from flooded Noses Creek.[21]

Thomas' report continued:

June 19, at 5 a. m. each of my corps commanders notified me that the rebels had fallen back from our front, and an advance of the whole line was immediately ordered. Howard's troops came up with the enemy at 7 a. m. on the Burnt Hickory and Marietta road, finding him posted on a line of ridges just west of Marietta, and apparently in strong force. Skirmishing with him heavily all day, capturing 250 prisoners, among whom were 14 commissioned officers. General Palmer formed his corps on the left of Howard's, close up to the base of . . . [Kennesaw] Mountain. General Hooker came up with the enemy across . . . [Noses] Creek, on the Dallas and Marietta road, strongly posted on a line of ridges, evidently a continuation of those in General Howard's front. Skirmishing was kept up along the line until dark, the troops in the mean time getting well into position.

June 20, Wood's and Newton's divisions, of Howard's corps, were moved to the right to relieve Williams' and Geary's divisions, of Hooker's corps, posted across the Dallas and Marietta

20. *Ibid.,* pp. 147-50.
21. *Ibid.,* pp. 150-51.

road, near Guess' house; the movement being made in order to enable General Hooker to operate more strongly against the enemy's left flank, and at the same time cooperate with and support General Schofield's army, which was nearly two miles distant on the Sandtown road, endeavoring to cross . . . [Noses] Creek, the enemy disputing his passage. Stanley's division, of Howard's corps, carried a hill to the right of the Burnt Hickory and Marietta road, driving the enemy from his skirmish rifle-pits and into his main works. The position gained was immediately strengthened by earth-works, which were scarcely completed when the enemy in strong force assaulted Stanley and was quickly repulsed with severe loss. He made a second attempt in less than half an hour afterward, and was again driven off, our men capturing about 20 prisoners. At dark the right of Palmer connected with General Howard's left.

June 21, General Howard's troops carried a hill about 700 yards in advance of the position gained the night before; his main line was moved up about 500 yards, fortifying the position, under a terrible artillery fire from the enemy, our skirmishers taking possession of an intrenched line lately occupied by the enemy. A number of prisoners were captured, and the conduct of the troops was admirable. General Hooker's troops carried and occupied a prominent hill [on Kolb's farm] about 500 yards in advance of his old line, and then connected his left with General Howard's right.

June 22, Williams' division, of Hooker's corps, skirmished itself into position on the right of Geary's division, the right of Williams' resting at Kolb's house, on the Powder Springs and Marietta road. About 4 p. m. the enemy [Hood's corps on the night of June 21 had been pulled out of the rifle-pits north of Marietta and posted on the Powder Springs road near Zion Church, one mile northeast of Kolb's farm. Hood's attack, spearheaded by Hindman's and Stevenson's divisions, fell on Schofield's Army of the Ohio, as well as Hooker's Cumberlanders.] in heavy force attacked [Joseph F.] Knipe's brigade in its advanced position before his men had time to throw up any works, and persisted in the assault until sundown, when they withdrew, their ranks hopelessly broken, each assault having been repelled with heavy loss. While this attack on Hooker was in progress the enemy opened heavily with artillery along our whole line, to which we answered fully to his satisfaction, our practice being very fine. After dark General

Howard's left division ([David S.] Stanley's) was relieved by King's division, of the Fourteenth Corps, Stanley in turn relieving the left division of Hooker's corps, which was transferred farther to the right.

June 23, it having been found desirable to gain possession of a prominent hill a short distance in advance of Stanley's position on Howard's right, directions were given to the latter to advance a strong skirmish line toward the enemy's works in front of Stanley's and Newton's divisions, and if found practicable, without too much sacrifice, to carry the hill by assault. This movement was preceded by a heavy cannonade from Howard's batteries and part of Hooker's, lasting fifteen minutes. Stanley's skirmishers carried the enemy's skirmish rifle-pits, capturing a number of prisoners, but could not gain the main works on the crest of the hill. They held the ground gained until after nightfall, when, being attacked in front and flank by a greatly superior force, Stanley was obliged to fall back to the position he occupied in the afternoon previous to the advance. On the center and left of Howard the advanced line secured themselves in their positions and were able to hold them.

June 25, Davis' division, of Palmer's corps, being on the extreme left of my army, was relieved by troops from General McPherson's army, and moved to a position in reserve, behind the right of Howard's line. This change was effected after dark, and by daylight on the 26th Davis' troops had reached the position assigned them. Baird's division, of Palmer's corps (being relieved by troops from the Army of the Tennessee), was also withdrawn from its position in line in front of . . . [Kennesaw] Mountain and moved during the night of the 26th to a position in reserve near that occupied by Davis' troops.

Sherman now decided to forego the flanking movements that had heretofore compelled Johnston to evacuate seven strongly and skillfully fortified positions. Rather than shift McPherson's Army of the Tennessee from his left to his right, Sherman determined to make a bold frontal attack designed to sunder Johnston's Kennesaw line. On doing so, he rejected a suggestion that the "army group" seek to reach the Rebel earthworks by sapping. Sherman vetoed this suggestion, remarking that when and if that slow process carried one line, experience had demonstrated that the foe employed this time to ready two or three equally strong lines farther to the rear.[22]

On June 18, from his Big Shanty headquarters, Sherman had written Grant:

> My chief source of trouble is with the Army of the Cumberland which is dreadfully slow. A fresh furrow in a plowed field will stop the entire column, all begin to entrench. I have again and again tried to impress on Thomas that we must assail and not defend . . . and yet it seems that the whole Army of the Cumberland is so habituated to be on the defensive that . . . I cannot get it out of their heads.[23]

The die was now cast—McPherson's Army of the Tennessee would assail the Confederates of Loring's corps posted on Little Kennesaw and Pigeon Hill. Thomas' Cumberlanders were to rush Cleburne's and Cheatham's bold fighters defending Cheatham's Hill, while Schofield's men extended the Union right south of Olley Creek.

Thomas tersely described the fight for Cheatham's Hill:

> June 27, at 8 a. m. the enemy's works were assaulted at two points, one in front of Newton's division, of Howard's corps, and the other in front of Davis's division, of Palmer's corps, Davis having relieved the right division (Stanley's) of General Howard's line. Stanley moved his command a short distance to the left, and acted as a support to Newton's division in its assault upon the works, Wood's division being in reserve. Davis' assault was supported by Baird's division, of Palmer's corps, on the right, and Hooker's whole corps was held in readiness to support the movement of Palmer's and Howard's commands. Although the troops were enabled to drive the enemy into his main works [at the Dead Angle] and reached that point with their main line, they were unable to carry the positions on account of the heavy fire of musketry and canister brought to bear upon them at short range, but held the ground gained. Our loss was 1,580 killed [including Generals Harker

22. Cox, *Atlanta*, p. 118.
23. Piatt, *Thomas*, p. 534.

and Dan McCook], wounded, and missing, some of our men being shot while on the parapets of the enemy's works. We took 130 prisoners. General Davis immediately commenced fortifying his advanced position at the distance of about seventy-five yards from the enemy's fortifications, covering the working parties with such a heavy and well-directed fire of musketry that the enemy could not molest them in their operations. [McPherson's thrust was likewise blunted with the loss of 80 killed, 506 wounded, and 17 missing. On the Union right, Schofield's troops crossed Olley Creek, driving General Jackson's cavalry before them, and reached and fortified a hill overlooking Nickajack Creek.]

About midnight on the 29th the enemy attacked Davis, overwhelming his skirmishers and driving them back, when they rallied and drove the rebels back again to their works.

During the 29th and 30th all remained comparatively quiet along the line, the skirmishers in the most advanced positions only exchanging occasional shots with the enemy.

Throughout the month the enemy's cavalry in small parties, assisted by guerrillas and disloyal citizens, have been prowling along the railroad between Chattanooga and the points occupied by the main army. On a few occasions they succeeded in burning one or two unimportant bridges and attacked several trains passing over the road, burning a few cars. The troops along the railroad were always on the alert, rendering it difficult for any very serious damage to be perpetrated. All breaks or interferences to travel were speedily removed by the well-organized construction party under the immediate superintendence of Col. W. W. Wright (Forty-fourth U. S. Colored), chief engineer military railroads of the military division.

I have the honor to annex hereto a consolidated list of casualties for the month. . . .

The detailed reports of the subordinate commanders will be forwarded as soon as handed in.

I am, very respectfully, your obedient servant,

GEO. H. THOMAS,

*Major-General, U. S. Volunteers, Commanding.*

Lieut. Col. R. M. Sawyer,
*Asst. Adjt. Gen., Mil. Div. of the Mississippi.*

*List of casualties in the Army of the Cumberland during the month of June, 1864.*

| Corps | Killed | | Wounded | | Missing | | Aggregate |
|---|---|---|---|---|---|---|---|
| | Officers | Men | Officers | Men | Officers | Men | |
| Fourteenth Corps | 19 | 289 | 49 | 1,067 | 2 | 43 | 1,469 |
| Fourth Corps | 40 | 406 | 127 | 2,027 | 3 | 115 | 2,718 |
| Twentieth Corps | 8 | 178 | 83 | 1,206 | 3 | 82 | 1,560 |
| Total | 67 | 873 | 259 | 4,300 | 8 | 240 | 5,747 |

Southard Hoffman,

*Assistant Adjutant General.*

*Hdqrs. Department of the Cumberland,*
*Near Kenesaw Mountain, July 2, 1864.*[24]

General Sherman refused to admit that the June 27 attacks on Johnston's Kennesaw line were an error. In his official report describing the campaign, filed in mid-September, Sherman wrote, "Failure as it was . . . I yet claim it produced good fruits as it demonstrated to General Johnston that I would assault, and that boldly."[25]

Sherman lost no time in mourning his dead and useless regrets over his failure to shatter Johnston's line. He promptly returned to the strategy of employing superior numbers to outflank the Confederates. This time, he moved to exploit the Army of the Ohio's crossing of Olley Creek and occupation of commanding ground on the watershed separating Olley and Nickajack Creeks.[26]

Consequently, General Thomas, when he submitted his report for July, wrote:

24. OR, I, XXXVIII, pt. I, pp. 151-52.
25. OR, I, XXXVIII, pt. IV, p. 60.
26. Cox, *Atlanta*, pp. 130-31.

Headquarters Department of the Cumberland,<br>*August 17, 1864.*

Colonel: I have the honor to report the operations of my command for the month of July, as follows:

The position of the Army of the Cumberland on the morning of the 1st of July remained as established immediately after the assault on the enemy's works on the 27th of June—Hooker's corps on the right, his right connecting with the left of the Army of the Ohio, near Kolb's house, on the Powder Springs and Marietta road; Palmer's corps in the center, except King's division, which occupied the works on the left of Howard's corps, and connected with the Army of the Tennessee at the Burnt Hickory and Marietta road, in advance of York's house; the First Division of Cavalry, Brig. Gen. E. M. McCook commanding, was operating on the right of the Army of the Ohio and protecting that flank; the Second Division of Cavalry, Brig. Gen. K. Garrard commanding, was still detached from my army and operating under instructions from the commanding general [Sherman] of the Military Division of the Mississippi, and the Third Division, Col. W. W. Lowe [Lowe had relieved Kilpatrick as division commander on May 22.] commanding, was stationed on the [Western & Atlantic] railroad between Cartersville and Dalton, scouting the country thoroughly between those two points.

The troops of Generals Hooker, Howard, and Palmer had worked themselves at considerable cost of life and labor into position close up to the enemy's fortifications, at some points within a hundred yards, and everywhere so near that they could advance no farther without making a direct assault on almost impregnable works. It was then decided by the major-general [Sherman] commanding military division to leave my command where it then was, to hold the enemy in check, carefully watching his movements, while the Army of the Tennessee would be withdrawn from my left and transferred to the right of the Army of the Ohio, with a view to turn the enemy's left flank and force him from the strong position he held to the southwest of . . . [Kennesaw] Mountain. This movement was in process of execution during the night of the 2d, when about daylight of the 3d each of my corps commanders notified me that the enemy had left their respective fronts and that our skirmishers were in possession of his works.

242

[General Johnston, realizing that Sherman's people by their shift to the right were making his Kennesaw line untenable, had turned the Georgia militia and large numbers of impressed slaves to fortifying two additional lines north of the Chattahoochee. The first of these crossed the Western & Atlantic at Smyrna on the ridge separating the Nickajack and Rottenwood drainages and ran from northeast to southwest. Its left flank was covered by Nickajack Creek. The second line was close to the Chattahoochee, shielded only about two miles of bridgehead on either side of the railroad. To the northeast, this defense line was fronted by the deep ravines of Rottenwood Creek and on the southwest by Nickajack Creek.][27]

A pursuit was immediately ordered by different routes, the concentration to be at Marietta, which place was entered by my troops about 9 a. m. After a short delay the columns were again set in motion, Palmer's corps moving along the railroad by the main Marietta and Atlanta road, with Hooker's command on his right and Howard's on his left; all three within supporting distance of each other. About four miles out from Marietta they came up with the enemy's rear guard, and skirmished with him to near Ruff's Station, where he was found strongly posted in earth-works, which had evidently been finished some time previous with a view to his being obliged to make his present retrograde movement toward the Chattahoochee. The lines were formed, and by night-fall the three corps had skirmished themselves into position close up to the enemy's works, having fully developed their situation and strength. Quite a number of prisoners and stragglers were picked up during the day, about 500 being reported.

The next morning, July 4, the line of battle was readjusted, and during the afternoon the enemy's skirmishers were driven into his main works [at Smyrna] and our main line was advanced a short distance, our skirmishers intrenching themselves on the line formerly occupied by those of the enemy.

At 4 a. m. on the 5th information was received that the enemy [threatened on the extreme right, by the advance of McPherson's Army of the Tennessee which had placed these troops nearer Atlanta than Johnston's army], had evacuated his fortifications, and our troops were in possession of them.

27. *Ibid.*, p. 131; OR, I, XXXVIII, I, pp. 153-54.

A pursuit was ordered and made in three columns, Howard's corps, on the left, coming up with the enemy near Pace's Ferry [three miles upstream from the railroad bridge], over the Chattahoochee, just as he had safely effected a crossing of the river at that point and had cut loose the pontoon bridge on which he had crossed. Our skirmishers advanced to the bank of the stream, and batteries were placed in position on the high ground behind, from which they kept up a vigorous shelling of the opposite shore. Palmer's corps got to within a mile of the river, when he found the enemy strongly posted on a commanding hill and occupying a strong earth-work at the northern extremity of the railroad bridge. This force was ascertained to be Hardee's corps. General Hooker [on the right] found considerable difficulty in crossing Nickajack Creek, not having effected it at night-fall. The railroad and telegraph were repaired and placed in running order to Vining's Station, eight miles south of Marietta.

On the 6th Hooker's corps crossed to the east side of Nickajack Creek, the commands of Generals Palmer and Howard remaining in the same position as yesterday. McCook's cavalry took possession of Powers' Ferry, about five miles above Pace's Ferry. The corps commanders were directed to remain as at present posted, camping their commands in the shade as much as possible, and resting the men all they could. In the mean time details were directed to be sent to the rear to procure clothing, etc., of which the troops stood sorely in need.

In accordance with instructions given, a strong skirmish line was advanced on the 9th to feel the enemy's position and to ascertain if he were still in force on the Marietta side of the river at the railroad bridge. His position was found to be unchanged since the 5th instant. General Howard sent Newton's division of his command to the support of Garrard's division of cavalry, which had seized Roswell Factory [upstream from Power's Ferry] and the fords in its vicinity; Newton to be relieved by troops from the Army of the Tennessee, then moving toward Roswell via Marietta. [On the 8th, Schofield's Army of the Ohio had marched from Smyrna toward Sope Creek, and, during the afternoon, his troops forced their way across the Chattahoochee at Phillips Ferry. Confederate efforts to crush the bridgehead were too little and too late. The next day, the 9th, Sherman ordered General

Dodge's 16th Corps of McPherson's army and Newton's Cumberlanders to Roswell to support and reinforce Schofield.][28]

On the 10th the enemy [The Federals across the Chattahoochee in force, General Johnston, on the night of July 9-10, withdrew his three infantry corps from the bridgehead. Until the last moment, Johnston's troops maintained a bold front, resisting the probes of hordes of skirmishers thrown forward by Thomas and McPherson.] evacuated his fortifications on our side of the river and fell back toward Atlanta, destroying in his retreat the railroad and wagon bridges. The corps commanders were directed to throw forward a line of skirmishers and occupy the abandoned works. General Howard was directed to move to the left with the remaining two divisions of his corps and take post within supporting distance of the Army of the Ohio near the mouth of . . . [Sope] Creek.

On the 12th Howard's corps crossed the Chattahoochee at Power's Ferry and advanced to Abernathy's house, where he formed on the right of the Army of the Ohio, which had crossed at Phillips' Ferry a few days previous [on the 8th and 9th].

A deserter belonging to [William H. T.] Walker's division, Hardee's corps, who came into our lines on the 13th, stated that Johnston's army was stationed around Atlanta within a circuit of four miles, and that the fortifications of that place were being rapidly strengthened. In the mean time the citizens were leaving for "farther south" and the Government property was being removed.

McCook's division of cavalry moved on the 15th to a position near Vining's Station and went into camp, his instructions being to post his command along the north bank of the river, between Pace's and Turner's Ferries, as soon as the balance of the troops had crossed, and guard the rear of the army.

On the 17th, according to instructions given the night previous, General Howard sent Wood's division of his corps down along the south bank of the river to a position across Pace's Ferry road, leading to Atlanta, to cover the laying of a pontoon bridge at the ferry. As soon as Wood's troops had brushed away the enemy's pickets lining the south bank, the pontoon train, under charge of Col. G. P. Buell, Fifty-eighth

28. OR, I, XXXVIII, pt. I, pp. 154-55; Cox, *Atlanta*, pp. 137-41.

Indiana Volunteers, was moved forward to the river and a bridge laid with remarkable celerity and precision by 11 a. m., and shortly afterward a second. As soon as the first bridge was completed Palmer's corps commenced crossing and immediately after Palmer's General Hooker's command went over. Palmer's advanced division (Davis') relieved Wood's division, of Howard's command, and the latter immediately proceeded to rejoin the balance of its corps at Abernathy's house. About a mile beyond the river Davis' division came upon the enemy in some force posted among the turnings of the hills, who fired upon his advance, and, after some show of resistance, fell back toward Nancy's Creek. The column was again set in motion, and proceeded to near Kyle's Bridge, over Nancy's Creek, where line was formed by Palmer's corps, with Hooker's corps on its left, Palmer's skirmishers being pushed out from his right toward the junction of Nancy's and Peach Tree Creeks. Light skirmishing continued until dark.[29]

On the 17th, President Jefferson Davis sacked General Johnston as commander of the Army of Tennessee. Time had run out on Johnston's strategy of selling space for time in expectation of taking advantage of a blunder on Sherman's part, when Johnston permitted himself to be outmaneuvered on July 8, as Schofield's army slipped across the Chattahoochee. Johnston was replaced by John Bell Hood, one of his corps commanders, with a reputation as a savage fighter.

As Sherman's "army group" closed on Atlanta on the 18th, Thomas' Cumberlanders were on the right, Schofield's Army of the Ohio in the center, and McPherson's Army of the Tennessee on the left.

Continuing, Thomas wrote, "On the morning of the 18th":

the whole command crossed Nancy's Creek, and, driving the enemy before it in its advance, pushed forward to a position in front of the old Peach Tree road, leading from Turner's Ferry to Decatur, Palmer's right resting near the junction of Nancy's and Peach Tree Creeks, with Hooker's corps on his left, Hooker's left connecting with Howard's corps at Buck Head.

The advance of Howard's corps, moving down the main

29. OR, I, XXXVIII, pt. I, pp. 155-56.

road leading from Buck Head to Atlanta, reached the crossing of Peach Tree Creek at 6:30 a. m. on the 19th, finding the bridge destroyed and a pretty fair infantry work constructed as a bridge-head, just beyond, manned with infantry. During the afternoon a crossing was forced by Wood's division a short distance below the Buck Head and Atlanta road, and by Stanley's above, both divisions effecting a lodgment on the south side by dark, the enemy stubbornly resisting their advance. By direction of the major-general [Sherman] commanding the military division, Stanley's and Wood's divisions, of Howard's command, were closed to the left on the Army of the Ohio, which was moving on a road leading to Decatur, leaving Newton's division, of Howard's corps, to the right of the Buck Head and Atlanta road. During the afternoon of the 19th parts of Hooker's and Palmer's corps were crossed over to the south side of Peach Tree Creek, the latter meeting with considerable resistance.

The whole command was across at an early hour on the 20th and the line was adjusted. The left and center advanced to feel the enemy during the afternoon, and while on open ground and unprotected by any works, were assaulted furiously by [Hardee's corps], the attack falling first on Newton's division, which gallantly stood its ground, repelling charge after charge, although his left was very much exposed throughout the contest; thence sweeping toward the right they [Stewart's corps, formerly Loring's] assaulted Hooker's corps and the left brigade [Anson] (McCook's) of Johnson's division, of Palmer's corps. Each assault of the enemy was met gallantly by the whole line and hurled back, our men not yielding a foot of ground. The fighting continued throughout the afternoon till sundown, when the enemy, repulsed at all points, fell back to his works. Our loss [in the battle of Peachtree Creek] was severe, numbering 1,600 in killed and wounded, but judging from the number of the enemy's dead left on the field and buried by us (200 being found in Newton's front alone) his loss must have been much greater. We captured 360 prisoners, of whom 122 were wounded, besides several stand of colors, small arms, etc. Wood's and Stanley's divisions, of Howard's corps, drove the enemy from two lines of outer works, capturing some prisoners, and developed a strong line of works still farther on and within three miles of Atlanta.

During the 21st there was considerable skirmishing along the entire line, our forces in the mean time crowding up to the rebel main line of works, which were quite formidable. During the night of the 21st the enemy fell back to the for- tifications immediately encircling the city of Atlanta, and at an early hour on the 22d I had disposed my troops con- fronting the new line of defenses taken up by him. Palmer's corps still held the right of my line, with his left resting near the Western and Atlantic Railroad, two and a half miles northwest of Atlanta, connecting at that point with General Hooker's corps, which later continued the line around to the main Buck Head and Atlanta road, where Howard's corps took it up, Howard's left connecting with General Schofield's army near Colonel Howard's house, on a road leading to Atlanta about one and a half miles southeast of the main Buck Head road. The position chosen by us was a strong one, and by night-fall of the 22d had been greatly strengthened by earth-works, and it having been ascertained that from several points Atlanta could be reached with rifled artillery, orders were given to keep up a steady fire upon the town night and day. McCook's division of cavalry was crossed to the east side of the river and posted on the right of my army, along Proctor's Creek, extending over toward Mason and Turner's Ferry, on the Chattahoochee.[30]

On the 22d, to the southeast of Thomas' army, raged the terrible conflict known as the battle of Atlanta. General Hood again came out from behind the defenses, hurling Hardee's four divisions against the exposed left flank of McPherson's Army of the Tennessee. At the same time, General Cheatham leading Hood's former corps assailed the Army of the Tennessee's 15th Corps and Schofield's Army of the Ohio. In the desperate fighting that ensued, in which the Confederates scored some successes before being hurled back with frightful losses, General McPherson was killed.[31]

"From the 22d to the 28th of the month," Thomas' report con- tinued, "the position of my troops remained unchanged, with the exception that at some points ground was gained to the front,

30. *Ibid.*, pp. 156-57.
31. Cox, *Atlanta*, pp. 161-78.

and the general line shortened. Good, permanent bridges were constructed across the Chattahoochee at Pace's Ferry, and at the railroad crossing, the pontoon bridges at those two points being taken up and placed in condition for future movements."[32]

General Hood, on the 28th, despite the battering his army had taken at Peachtree Creek on the 20th and at the battle of Atlanta two days later, sent Lieutenant General S. D. Lee, who had replaced Cheatham as corps commander, to attack the Army of the Tennessee now led by General Howard. The latter army, on the 27th, had been shifted from the "army group's" left to the right. Passing to the rear of the Cumberlanders, Howard's soldiers took position on Palmer's right, covering the Lick Skillet Road. In this fight, known as the battle of Ezra Church, the Confederates were again thrown back by the Federals fighting from behind hastily thrown up breastworks.[33]

> "On the 29th," Thomas wrote:
>
> Davis' division, of Palmer's corps (Fourteenth), supported by Ward's [W. T. Ward had relieved Dan Butterfield as division commander on June 29.] division, of the Twentieth, was sent to take post on the extreme right of the army, beyond the Army of the Tennessee, with directions to push out toward the Macon and Western Railroad, and endeavor to reach it, if possible to do so, without bringing on a general engagement. Davis' skirmishers had not proceeded very far beyond the Green's Ferry road when they came upon those of the enemy intrenched. Line was then formed in front of the road, and connection established with the right of the Army of the Tennessee. In this position the troops remained for the night.
>
> By a reconnaissance made on the 31st by Davis' division it was ascertained that the enemy was in force between him and the railroad, and posted in earth-works, from which they opened on him with canister. After having developed the enemy's position, the division returned to its former position along the Green's Ferry road.
>
> The Third Division of Cavalry, Brig. Gen. Judson Kilpatrick [Kilpatrick had returned to duty July 23.] commanding, stationed along the [Western & Atlantic] railroad between Car-


32. OR, I, XXXVIII, pt. I, p. 156.
33. Cox, *Atlanta*, pp. 181-87.

tersville and Resaca, has been particularly active throughout
the month, patrolling and scouting the country thoroughly and

*Report of casualties in Army of the Cumberland during the
month of July, 1864.*

| Command | Killed | | Wounded | | Missing | | Aggregate |
| --- | --- | --- | --- | --- | --- | --- | --- |
| | Officers | Men | Officers | Men | Officers | Men | |
| 14th Army Corps: | | | | | | | |
| 1st Division | 6 | 68 | 18 | 368 | 1 | 13 | 474 |
| 2d Division | 8 | 83 | 17 | 243 | 5 | 115 | 471 |
| 3d Division | 2 | 15 | 14 | 107 | | 1 | 139 |
| Artillery | | | 1 | 19 | | | 20 |
| Total | 16 | 166 | 50 | 737 | 6 | 129 | 1,104 |
| 20th Army Corps: | | | | | | | |
| Headquarters | | | | 2 | | | 2 |
| 1st Division | 11 | 125 | 37 | 576 | | 34 | 783 |
| 2d Division | 5 | 90 | 24 | 317 | 9 | 157 | 602 |
| 3d Division | 4 | 95 | 25 | 485 | | 11 | 620 |
| Total | 20 | 310 | 86 | 1,380 | 9 | 202 | 2,007 |
| 4th Army Corps: | | | | | | | |
| 1st Division | 3 | 18 | 10 | 175 | 1 | 2 | 209 |
| 2d Division | 1 | 27 | 9 | 152 | | 7 | 196 |
| 3d Division | | 26 | 14 | 148 | 1 | 4 | 193 |
| Total | 4 | 71 | 33 | 475 | 2 | 13 | 598 |
| Grand Total | 40 | 547 | 169 | 2,592 | 17 | 344 | 3,709[34] |

34. OR, I, XXXVIII, pt. I, pp. 158-59.

guarding the railroad. The First [McCook's] and Second [Garrard's] Divisions of Cavalry, acting under instructions direct from the major-general [Sherman] commanding the military division, were absent on a movement against the enemy's communications toward Macon at the close of the month.

I have the honor to forward herewith a consolidated return of casualties. . . .

I am, colonel, very respectfully, your obedient servant,

GEO. H. THOMAS,

*Major-General, U. S. Volunteers, Commanding.*

Lieut. Col. R. M. Sawyer,

*Asst. Adjt. Gen., Mil. Div. of the Mississippi.*

General McPherson's death triggered a shuffling in the hierarchy of Sherman's "army group." On July 23, the day after McPherson was killed, Sherman and Thomas met at General Wood's command post. There, they discussed who should succeed the fallen leader as commander of the Army of the Tennessee. Major General John A. Logan (a former Democratic congressman from Illinois and not a professional soldier), the Army of the Tennessee's senior corps commander, had taken command on McPherson's death. Thomas was unimpressed with Logan, and bluntly told Sherman, Logan "is brave enough and a good officer but if he had an army I am afraid he would edge over on both sides and annoy Schofield and me. Even as a corps commander, he is given to edging out beyond his jurisdiction."[35]

General Howard's, the leader of Thomas' Fourth Corps, qualifications for the assignment were next reviewed. He was a professional soldier, a graduate of West Point. Consequently, Sherman, on July 27, named Howard to lead the Army of the Tennessee, which Sherman referred to as his "whiplash."

General Hooker, leader of Thomas' Twentieth Corps, was incensed by Howard's selection. Not only did he rank Howard, but he held Howard, whose Eleventh Corps had been routed on May 2 at Chancellorsville, as responsible for his defeat in that great battle. Hooker therefore asked to be relieved on the grounds that his "rank and service had been ignored." Thomas endorsed Hooker's request, as "approved and heartily recommended," and

35. Cleaves, p. 134.

on July 28 Hooker turned over leadership of his corps to his senior division commander, Brigadier General Alpheus S. Williams. Coincidentally, David S. Stanley, also a West Pointer, replaced Howard as leader of the Fourth Corps.

Then, in early August, Thomas lost General Palmer, the commander of his Fourteenth Corps. On the 3d, Sherman, believing that the right wing of his "army group" should take position nearer the Atlanta & West Point Railroad, moved to provide for better cooperation in that sector. Orders were issued directing General Palmer to report to Schofield and to act under Schofield's orders for the time being. This raised the question of rank, because Palmer's commission as a major general predated Schofield, though both took effect on the same day, and Schofield was senior in their previous grade. Sherman decided in favor of Schofield. Palmer protested, and asked to be relieved of his corps command. General Thomas and others vainly sought to persuade Palmer to reconsider, but, after suffering through two days of indecision that hindered troop movements in that sector, Palmer, on August 6, was relieved at Thomas' request and returned to his home in Illinois. His temporary replacement as leader of the Fourteenth Corps was Brigadier General R. W. Johnson. Then, on August 22, Jefferson C. Davis, promoted to brevet major general, assumed command of the corps.[36]

Throughout most of August, Union and Confederate soldiers confronted each other on the approaches to Atlanta. Spades remained trumps, as the troops sheltered themselves behind formidable earthworks. There were daily artillery duels, and sharpshooters made life hazardous for the careless. The weather was torrid, and the numbers reporting at sick call soared.

In an effort to compel General Hood to evacuate partially invested Atlanta, General Sherman sent cavalry columns deep into central Georgia to break up the railroads over which the Confederates supplied Hood's army. Coincidentally, Wheeler's cavalry rode north with the mission of destroying the Western & Atlantic, Sherman's lifeline.

General Thomas' report for August also covered the first eight days of September. It began:

36. Cox, *Atlanta,* pp. 189-90.

Headquarters Department of the Cumberland,<br>
Atlanta, Ga., September 13, 1864.

Colonel: I have the honor to report as follows the operations of my command during the month of August, 1864:

On the 1st instant the Army of the Cumberland was in position as heretofore reported, viz. Palmer's corps (Fourteenth) on the right, posted between the Turner's Ferry road and the Western and Atlantic Railroad, facing a little south of east; Williams' corps (Twentieth) in the center, extending from the railroad around to the Buck Head road; Stanley's corps (Fourth) on the left, between the Buck Head road and Howard's house, on roads leading from Buck Head and Decatur to Atlanta, Stanley's left being refused so as to cover the Buck Head road; Garrard's division of cavalry took post on the left of Stanley's corps with instructions to patrol the approaches to the left of the army from Decatur and Roswell Factory; Kilpatrick's division of cavalry was ordered to take post on the railroad between Marietta and the bridge over the Chattahoochee. The Army of the Cumberland held the left of the grand line investing Atlanta, besides sending two divisions (Ward's of the Twentieth and Davis' of the Fourteenth Corps) to the support of the troops of other commands operating on the extreme right of the grand army.

Major-General Palmer was directed on the 2d to move with the two remaining divisions of his corps to a position in reserve in rear of the Army of the Ohio, then operating on the extreme right toward East Point. Brigadier-General Williams, commanding the Twentieth Corps, was directed to occupy the works vacated by the troops of General Palmer's command on his right, by extending his line in that direction, and Ward's division was recalled from the support of the Army of the Ohio to enable General Williams more fully to carry out the above instructions. The withdrawal of Palmer's corps left me with the Fourth and Twentieth Corps to hold a line of works nearly five miles in length, approaching at some points to within 300 yards of the enemy's fortifications.

On the 3d Major-General Stanley pushed forward a strong line of skirmishers and succeeded in carrying the enemy's picket-line on the whole corps' front, excepting on the extreme right of his line, where his men were met by a very destructive fire of musketry and canister—the enemy opened from at least

253

twenty pieces of artillery. Our loss was about 30 killed and wounded, but we captured quite a number of prisoners, besides gaining considerable information regarding the positions of the enemy's troops and fortifications.

Both Stanley's and Williams' skirmishers again pressed those of the enemy during the afternoon of the 5th, with a view of diverting his attention from the movements of the Armies of the Tennessee and of the Ohio on our right. Palmer's corps, which had been placed in position on the right of the Army of the Ohio by direction of Major-General Sherman, pushed out from along . . . [Utoy] Creek and pressed close up to the enemy's works, capturing a strong line of rifle-pits vigorously defended. Our loss was considerable, but we took 150 prisoners and gained an advantageous position. At the close of the engagement the skirmishers of the enemy and our own were only thirty yards apart. Our main line was moved up to within 400 yards of that of the enemy.

On the morning of the 6th the enemy felt our line at various points from right to left, seemingly persistent in his efforts to find a weak point in the latter direction, on the line of Stanley's corps. From information gained by us through various sources more or less reliable, we learned the enemy had posted his militia, supported by one division of his veterans, on that part of his line immediately confronting the Fourth and Twentieth Corps, and that he used the balance of his army in extending his line to the left toward East Point, as our movements in the same direction threatened his possession of the railroads. Although this necessitated his holding a large extent of ground, he formed his troops on very advantageous ridges, strengthened by works of a most impregnable character, rendering an assault on our part unjustifiable from the useless sacrifice of life it would entail. While the enemy was busily engaged fortifying, our troops were not idle. Our position was also soon rendered impregnable to assault, and a constant shelling of the enemy's fortifications and the city of Atlanta was kept up day and night. In the meanwhile supplies of rations and clothing were being rapidly accumulated at the front, and our men enjoyed a season of rest—such rest as is to be found in the trenches. On the 6th, Maj. Gen. John M. Palmer having been relieved from the command of the Fourteenth Army Corps at his own request, Brig. Gen. R. W. Johnson, the senior division commander took command of the corps.

On the 7th, under General Johnson's direction, the corps advanced upon the enemy's works in his front, and moving rapidly carried the first line of rifle-pits, capturing 172 prisoners from [Hardee's corps] and driving the enemy to their main works. The entire line of the Fourteenth Corps was then advanced and fortified. Our loss during the 6th and 7th in the Fourteenth Corps was 70 killed and 413 wounded, including 17 officers.[37]

Schofield's right at Willis' mill pond had inched to within three miles of East Point, where the Atlanta & West Point and Macon & Western Railroads converged to continue on into Atlanta five miles to the northeast over a single track. Sherman, although close to his objective, felt that he had now stretched his "army group" as far as he safely could. He now determined to employ his artillery to soften Hood's defenses and to terrorize the civilians. At the same time, his men, employing siegecraft, a strategy Sherman vetoed in front of Kennesaw, by use of saps and parallels clawed their way toward the Rebel entrenchments.[38]

General McCook and the Army of the Cumberland's Second Cavalry Division had moved out on July 27. They rode down the west side of the Chattahoochee, crossed the river near Campbelltown, and struck the Atlanta & West Point Railroad near Palmetto Station. The Union horse soldiers wrecked two and one-half miles of track and cut the telegraph. McCook then pushed on to Lovejoy's Station, 30 miles south of Atlanta on the Macon & Western, where his men tore up an equal amount of rails and mangled five miles of telegraph wire. In and around Lovejoy's, the raiders captured and burned more than 500 wagons and took more than 700 prisoners. McCook planned to rendezvous near Lovejoy's with General Stoneman's mounted column which had moved out from the "army group's" left flank. Stoneman, however, had run into disaster, and he and about 700 of his men had been captured near Clinton. The rest of his command straggled back to the Union lines.[39]

37. OR, I, XXXVIII, pt. I, pp. 160-61.
38. Cox, *Atlanta,* p. 196.
39. *Ibid.,* pp. 188-89.

General Thomas detailed McCook's return from Lovejoy's:

. . . it was only when the command started on its return that General McCook ascertained that the enemy's cavalry was between him and McDonough, at which latter place he had expected to form a junction with General Stoneman's expedition. Finding the enemy across his road in that direction, and being burdened with a good many prisoners and considerable captured property, General McCook turned toward the Chattahoochee River by way of Newnan, on the West Point Railroad, and while on the way to that place was attacked by Jackson's division of cavalry, which he repulsed. Near Newnan the railroad was cut in three places. Between there and the [Chattahoochee] river he was surrounded by an overwhelming force of the enemy's cavalry, supported by a large infantry force. These troops he attacked in the hope of cutting his way through them, and in doing so broke the whole right of their line, riding over [Lawrence S.] Ross' (Texas) cavalry brigade [of Jackson's division] and making General Ross and his staff prisoners. The enemy sent fresh troops to supply the place of those shattered by McCook's charge, when the latter, finding he could not break their line permanently, directed his brigade commanders to cut their way out with their commands and endeavor to cross the Chattahoochee by detachments. In this they were successful, but with the loss of their artillery. The latter, however, was deliberately destroyed before being abandoned. All the prisoners captured by us (about 400 in number) were also turned loose. General McCook's loss in killed, wounded, and missing [more than 600], as well as in material, is great, but that of the enemy is considered much greater proportionately, and is even so acknowledged by themselves.

About the 10th information reached me that the enemy's entire cavalry force was concentrating in the neighborhood of Monticello and on the Ocmulgee River. Refugees and deserters from the enemy stated that it was intended to send this large concentration of cavalry under Wheeler on a raid into Tennessee against our communications.

On the afternoon of the 14th the enemy's cavalry [Wheeler's], said to be 6,000 strong, attacked Dalton. Colonel [Bernard] Laiboldt, Second Missouri Infantry, commanding that post, occupied the fort with a small command, and bravely defended his position until re-enforced.

Early on the morning of the 15th Major-General [James B.] Steedman, with two regiments of white and six companies of colored troops, arrived at Dalton from Chattanooga and immediately attacked the enemy, driving him off toward Spring Place after four hours' fighting. The enemy's loss was heavy— he left his dead and wounded on the field. Our loss was 40 killed and 55 wounded. We captured about 50 wounded and 2 surgeons. [Wheeler's columns then headed off into East Tennessee, where he could have no effect on the operations in front of Atlanta.]

Before appearing in front of Dalton, Wheeler's men had destroyed about two miles of track on the [Western & Atlantic] railroad south of Dalton, but by noon of the 17th the road was again in running order. Believing General Steedman to have sufficient troops at his disposal to beat off any further attack on the railroad, our whole attention was directed to the reduction of Atlanta, and at the same time it was determined to take advantage of the absence of the enemy's cavalry to make one more effort to break the Macon & Western Railroad. Accordingly on the 18th Brig. Gen. J. Kilpatrick, commanding Third Cavalry Division, was directed to attack and destroy both railroads, and for this purpose he was re-enforced by two brigades taken from Garrard's cavalry division, stationed on the left of the army. With this force, numbering in all about 4,000 men and two batteries of artillery, General Kilpatrick moved out from Sandtown on the evening of the 18th. He met the enemy's cavalry pickets when only a short distance out from Sandtown on the Chattahoochee, and skirmished with them to Jonesborough on the Macon railroad, driving them through that place. For six hours the command was engaged destroying the track, etc., until near midnight of the 19th, when part of his command was attacked one mile below the town and driven in, but subsequently the enemy was repulsed.

Toward daylight of the 20th he [Kilpatrick] moved in the direction of McDonough, and thence across country back to the railroad near Lovejoy's Station, reaching that point at about 11 a. m. on the 20th. There he met a brigade of infantry, and although repulsed at first, finally checked the advantage being gained by the enemy and drove him back with heavy loss. While thus engaged fighting infantry, a heavy force of cavalry with artillery came up in his rear, and he found he was completely enveloped. Determining at once to break the enemy's line and extricate his command from its delicate position, he decided to ride over the enemy's cavalry and retire on McDonough. The movement was successfully made and resulted in a complete rout of Jackson's cavalry division, numbering 4,000 men, leaving in our hands 4 guns, 3 battleflags, and all his wagons. Some prisoners were taken and the enemy's loss in killed and wounded is known to be large. Reforming his command, Kilpatrick fought the enemy's infantry for an hour longer, when finding his men running out of ammunition, he retired in the direction of Latimer's and Decatur without further molestation, reaching the latter place on the afternoon of the 22d.[40]

Although Kilpatrick had ridden around Hood's army and Atlanta, no permanent interruption of the Atlanta & West Point and Macon & Western had been effected. Workmen made necessary repairs, and within a day or two of Kilpatrick's return, locomotives and cars were again running into the city.

Thomas' report continues:

Pending the above movements to break the enemy's railroad communications, the troops in front of the city kept up a constant shelling of the fortifications and buildings of Atlanta, and, as refugees informed us, with marked effect. The heavy cavalry force under Wheeler still continued to threaten our railroad in Northern Georgia and East Tennessee without seriously interrupting communication with Chattanooga and Nashville. This, however, gave us no uneasiness, as we had a good accumulation of supplies within safe proximity to the main army. A considerable force of the enemy under [Philip D.] Roddey had made its appearance in Northern Alabama, threatening to cross the Tennessee River near Decatur, with a view of destroying the railroad between that place and Nashville. Again in the vicinity of Clarksville, Tenn., and Fort Donelson, the enemy had become troublesome, although without doing very material damage.

40. OR, I, XXXVIII, pt. I, pp. 162-63.

To the discretion and good judgment of Major-Generals Rousseau and Steedman, commanding respectively the Districts of the Tennessee and the Etowah, and to Brig. Gen. R. S. Granger, commanding the District of Northern Alabama, was left the disposal of the troops and the defense of our communications with our depots at the north.

In compliance with the directions contained in Special Field Orders, No. 57, headquarters Military Division of the Mississippi, promulgated to my corps commanders on the 16th of August, everything was placed in readiness for the execution of the contemplated movements by the time mentioned. The major-general [Sherman] commanding the military division having, however, decided to await the return of General Kilpatrick's expedition, the Army of the Cumberland did not withdraw from its works until after dark on the night of the 25th. Stanley's corps, as directed from my headquarters, commenced the movement by withdrawing from the position he then held on the left of the army, to a line of ridges and high ground beyond, and to the rear of the position where the right of the Twentieth Corps rested. Here he remained and covered the withdrawal of the Twentieth Corps, the latter having been ordered to take post on the Chattahoochee, at the railroad bridge, [and] Pace's and Turner's Ferries. Garrard's division of cavalry covered the movements of the . . . [Fourth] and Twentieth Corps, then crossed the Chattahoochee at Pace's Ferry on the 26th, and recrossing at the bridge at Sandtown on the 27th, took post on Stanley's left, picketing Utoy Creek from Utoy Post-Office to Sandtown. The above movements were successfully executed, both corps being in the positions indicated at an early hour on the morning of the 26th. At 9 a. m. of the same day Stanley withdrew still farther to a point along Utoy Creek, posting his command on some ridges facing the creek and across the Sandtown road.

The Fourteenth Corps, then commanded by Bvt. Maj. Gen. J. C. Davis [Davis had relieved Johnson on August 22.] drew out from the position it had last held on the right of the Army of the Tennessee, and moving across Utoy Creek, took post on the right of Stanley's corps. Garrard's division of cavalry was directed to operate on the left and rear of the army, while Kilpatrick's division was similarly employed on the right.

On the 27th Stanley's corps moved to Mount Gilead Church and formed line of battle along the road leading to Fairburn, skirmishing lightly with the enemy's cavalry. The Fourteenth Corps (Davis') moved as far as Holbrook's house, on the Campbellton road, advancing one brigade to Patterson's house, about a mile beyond, to cover the wagon trains of the corps. The Twentieth Corps was securely in position on the Chattahoochee River, guarding the crossing and protecting the depots at Marietta. Maj. Gen. H. W. Slocum [arrived from Vicksburg, relieved General Williams, and] assumed command of the corps, by virtue of General Orders, No. (238), War Department.[41]

By the evening of the 27th, Sherman had pulled his troops out of the investment lines north and west of Atlanta. All the corps, except the 20th—guarding the railroad bridge and Pace's and Turner's ferries—were marshaled to the city's southwest, between Atlanta and Sandtown, echeloned along the Sandtown road. Hood had not interfered with these movements, limiting his response to shadowing the Federals with light cavalry patrols. These horsemen pinpointed the Union forces, but Hood, letting his hopes get the better of his judgment, concluded that Wheeler's raid on the Western & Atlantic had been successful, and that Sherman's "army group," short of supplies, was withdrawing to the northside of the Chattahoochee via the Sandtown road. To add to his initial error in interpretation, Hood, despite warnings by Generals Hardee and S. D. Lee, stubbornly held to this view for another 48 hours. By then it was too late to redeploy his forces and keep Sherman's infantry from reaching the Atlanta & West Point Railroad.[42]

"At daylight on the 28th," General Thomas wrote:

Davis' corps moved from its encampment near Holbrook's house to Mount Gilead Church, thence past the left of Stanley's corps, taking the road leading from Redwine's house to Red Oak, on the West Point railroad. Davis reached the railroad at 4 p. m. and posted his corps on the right of it

41. *Ibid.*, pp. 163-65.
42. Cox, *Atlanta*, pp. 197-98.

facing toward East Point [7 miles to the northeast]. Stanley's command came up immediately after Davis' and formed line on the left of the road. In this position the command remained for the night. [Howard's Army of the Tennessee, advancing on Thomas' right, had gained the railroad at Fairburn, five miles to the southwest. On the 29th, Schofield's Army of the Ohio marched from near Mount Gilead and took position on Stanley's left].

Shortly after dark orders were issued to destroy the road by burning the ties and twisting the rails after heating. The work of destruction was continued throughout the night of the 28th and during part of the 29th, and when completed the railroad had been thoroughly dismantled for a distance of two miles north of my line and a little over a mile south of it.

About 6 a. m. on the 30th the Fourteenth and Fourth Corps moved from Red Oak toward the Macon railroad. The Fourteenth Corps (Davis') concentrated at Flat Shoal Church about 9 a. m., and after resting for an hour moved on in an easterly direction toward Couch's house, on the Decatur and Fayetteville road, at which point line was formed, and the command went into camp. Communication was opened with the Army of the Tennessee at Renfroe's house, two miles south of Couch's. The Fourth Corps formed on the left of the Fourteenth, its left extending beyond Mann's house, the line of the corps running in a northwesterly direction from Couch's. The advanced divisions of both corps skirmished with the enemy's infantry and cavalry during the day, and by sundown it was ascertained that the enemy was in force at Morrow's Mill, on Crooked Creek, about three-fourths of a mile distant from the left of Stanley's corps.

[On the 30th, Hood, finally realizing that the enemy was not retreating, rushed General Hardee with two corps—his own under Cleburne and Lee's—to Jonesboro. Upon reaching that area, Hardee was to assail the flank of Sherman's "army group" as it approached the Macon & Western, the last railroad into Atlanta. Hood with his third corps—Stewart's—and the Georgia militia continued to hold the Atlanta lines.]

Up to dark [on the 30th] no communication had been established [by Thomas' troops] with the Army of the Ohio.

Garrard's cavalry was in the neighborhood of Red Oak guarding the left and rear of the army.

On the morning of the 31st Stanley's corps moved to Morrow's Mill, where it found the enemy in intrenchments very well finished, but occupied only by dismounted cavalry. These were driven out. The Army of the Ohio having come up, both commands pushed out for the railroad, which was reached at the Big Bend, between Rough and Ready and Jonesborough. General Stanley posted his corps between the railroad and Crooked Creek, and in that position remained for the night. Part of the Fourteenth Corps, under Brigadier-General Baird, made a reconnaissance and demonstration in front of Couch's house and reached the Macon and Western Railroad about two miles north of Jonesborough [east of the Flint River] with the advance brigade, and destroyed about one mile of the track during the afternoon and night, although constantly annoyed by the enemy's cavalry. While in this position a heavy column of the enemy's infantry was seen moving in a southerly direction on a road still to the eastward of the one then held by them. Some stragglers belonging to this column were picked up by our skirmishers, and from them it was ascertained that the troops we saw moving were Hardee's and Lee's corps. Up to this period the enemy had evidently been deceived as to the nature and strength of our movement on his communications, and only at this late hour had he detached any considerable force from the army in Atlanta. During the afternoon of the 31st, the Army of the Tennessee being heavily attacked [by Lee's corps] in the position it had taken up the night before near Jonesborough, and General Howard having asked for re-enforcements, General Davis was instructed to send one division from his corps to its support. Kilpatrick's division of cavalry, stationed on the right of the Army of the Tennessee, . . . [forced] a passage across Flint River, and drove the enemy's pickets to within one-half mile of Jonesborough. He was then attacked in turn by a heavy force of infantry [Cleburne's] and forced to withdraw.[43]

Hood now compounded his errors. Word reached him late on the afternoon of the 31st that a strong force of Yankees (one of Schofield's divisions) had advanced and occupied Rough and

43. OR, I, XXXVIII, pt. I, pp. 165-66.

Ready. This information led to a belief by Hood that this presaged an attack on the Atlanta lines and that the thrust toward Jonesboro was a diversion. Orders were issued by Hood recalling Lee's corps and Hardee was left with only one corps to contain Sherman's powerful "army group" as it converged on Jonesboro the next day.[44]

On September 1, Thomas continued:

> . . . at an early hour the remainder of the Fourteenth Corps moved from Renfroe's house, on the Decatur and Fayetteville road, to rejoin that part of the command which had advanced the day before to the Rough and Ready and Jonesborough road. The junction formed, the corps moved south toward Jonesborough and reached the pickets of the Army of the Tennessee about two and a half miles from the point of concentration. A reconnaissance [by I. R. Edie's brigade] was then sent out toward the railroad, which drove in the enemy's skirmishers and gained possession of a ridge on the north side of Mill Creek with but small loss. Later in the afternoon two divisions [J. D. Morgan's and W. P. Carlin's] of Davis' corps (Fourteenth) were formed on the ridge and artillery was opened on the enemy's works with good effect. The line of battle being finally adjusted the command moved forward, attacking the enemy vigorously and driving him several hundred yards to his main works. An assault was then handsomely made on the works, which were carried along the entire line of Davis' command after very heavy fighting and a loss of over 1,200 men. Two field batteries of four guns each were captured in the enemy's fortifications, together with about 1,000 prisoners (including 1 general officer [Brig. Gen. Daniel C. Govan] and several field officers) and a number of small arms and battle-flags. The enemy's loss in killed and wounded was very severe. During this time the Fourth Corps (Stanley's) was moving from near Rough and Ready toward Jonesborough along the railroad, destroying it as the troops advanced. Arriving near Jonesborough the column was deployed with a view to advance against the enemy's right flank, but it being already quite late, darkness came on and prevented any extensive movement. The line of Stanley's corps was on the left

44. Cox, *Atlanta*, pp. 202-03.

of the railroad facing southwest. Davis' corps passed the night in the enemy's works, the left of the line connecting with Stanley's right at the railroad.

During the night the enemy fell back from Jonesborough, retreating toward Lovejoy's Station, where he was followed on the morning of the 2d by the Fourth Corps and the Armies of the Tennessee and of the Ohio. [Coincidentally, Hood, discovering that he had been outgeneraled, evacuated Atlanta, and on the 2d concentrated his Army of Tennessee at Lovejoy's Station.] Davis' corps was directed to remain at Jonesborough to bury the dead and collect captured property. Stanley's corps moved along the railroad and to the left of it, coming up with the enemy just north of Lovejoy's Station about noon. Line of battle was formed and preparations made to advance against the enemy, in conjunction with the Army of the Tennessee on the right. It was only at a late hour, however, that the assault was made and darkness prevented any decisive movement. Part of Stanley's troops gained the enemy's works and carried a small portion of them, but could not hold possession of the ground for want of co-operation on the part of the balance of the line. During the night information reached us that at 11 a. m. on the 2d the mayor and authorities of Atlanta had surrendered the city to a force of the Twentieth Corps, Major-General Slocum commanding, which in obedience to instructions previously given had been sent out from the Chattahoochee to feel the enemy's strength. The city had been evacuated the night previous, . . . [Hood's] army destroying in its retreat public property of considerable value, including eighty carloads of ammunition. Fourteen pieces of artillery and several thousand stand of small-arms were found.

On the 3d the major-general commanding [Sherman] the military division issued orders to the effect that the campaign was ended, and that the grand army would return to Atlanta and vicinity until a new plan could be considered regarding future movements. Directions were at the same time given for the withdrawal of the troops. Corps commanders were instructed to send to the rear all surplus wagons and whatever material that could obstruct the movements of the troops. The enemy still remained intrenched at Lovejoy's, although he was discovered to be moving his trains toward Griffin with the supposed intention of withdrawing his main army to that point or still farther.

At 8 p. m. on the 5th, in conjunction with the rest of the army, the Fourth Corps quietly withdrew from its position and fell back to Jonesborough, reaching that place at daylight on the 6th. The withdrawal was admirably conducted and executed with complete success, although much impeded by a rain-storm and consequent bad condition of the roads.

Both corps (Stanley's and Davis') remained quietly at Jonesborough during the 6th, although Davis' rear guard was attacked by the enemy as it was moving through the town to join the balance of the corps in position north of it. The enemy occupied Jonesborough during the afternoon with a cavalry advance guard, but contented himself with exchanging a few shots with our skirmishers.

On the 7th at 7 a. m. the Fourth Corps withdrew from its camps near Jonesborough, moved along the railroad to near Sykes' house, northeast of Rough and Ready, and took up a position for the night. The Fourteenth Corps fell back simultaneously with Stanley's command, marching on the main road leading to Rough and Ready from Jonesborough, and was posted on the right of the Fourth Corps, north of Rough and Ready. The enemy showed no disposition to follow the movements of either command.

The Army of the Cumberland reached Atlanta on the 8th, and was posted on the outskirts of the town—Davis' corps on the right, across the Campbellton road, Slocum's corps in the center, and Stanley's on the left. The pickets of all three corps were thrown out well to the front, and occupied commanding positions.

In concluding this report, I take the greatest pleasure in calling attention to the uniform gallantry displayed by the officers and troops of the Army of the Cumberland in all the battles in which they participated, and in their unwavering constancy and devotion to duty at all times during the entire campaign, commencing with the contests at Rocky Face Ridge and around Dalton and ending with the operations at Jonesborough and vicinity, which forced the enemy to evacuate Atlanta. During these four months of active campaign hardly a day has passed that some portion of this army was not engaged either in skirmishing or in actual battle with the enemy, and on every occasion behaving with that self-reliance which is the sure prestige of success. All may be justly proud of their par-

Along with his report, General Thomas submitted several enclosures. The one focusing on battle casualties read:

*Consolidated report of casualties in Army of the Cumberland for August, 1864.*

| Command | Killed | | | Wounded | | | Missing | | | Aggregate | | |
|---|---|---|---|---|---|---|---|---|---|---|---|---|
| | Officers | Men | Total | Officers | Men | Total | Officers | Men | Total | Officers | Men | Total |
| Fourth Army Corps | 5 | 33 | 38 | 4 | 174 | 178 | 3 | 27 | 30 | 12 | 234 | 246 |
| Fourteenth Army Corps | 8 | 151 | 159 | 27 | 793 | 820 | | 22 | 22 | 35 | 966 | 1,001 |
| Twentieth Army Corps | 1 | 39 | 40 | 8 | 181 | 189 | | 11 | 11 | 9 | 231 | 290 |
| Cavalry Command | 4 | 15 | 19 | 12 | 185 | 197 | 10 | 227 | 237 | 26 | 427 | 453 |
| TOTAL | 18 | 238 | 256 | 51 | 1,333 | 1,384 | 13 | 287 | 300 | 82 | 1,858 | 1,940 |

GEO. H. THOMAS,
*Major-General, U. S. Volunteers, Commanding.*
Hdqrs. Department of the Cumberland,
*Atlanta, Ga., September 19, 1864.* [45]

45. OR, I, XXXVIII, pt. I, pp. 166-68.

ticipation in the campaign against Atlanta.

Among the many gallant and lamented dead who have given their lives to sustain and defend the honor of their country and Government we must enumerate Brig. Gen. C. G. Harker and Col. Dan. McCook, Fifty-Second Ohio Volunteer Infantry, who were mortally wounded leading their respective brigades in the assault on the enemy's intrenchments near . . . [Kennesaw] Mountain, June 27. They were both skillful, brave, and accomplished officers.

The members of my staff were at all times efficient and active in the discharge of their various duties.

I am, colonel, very respectfully, your obedient servant,
GEO. H. THOMAS,
*Major-General, U. S. Volunteers, Commanding.*
Lieut. Col. R. M. Sawyer,
*Asst. Adjt. Gen., Mil. Div. of the Mississippi.*

While Thomas had properly given credit to his Cumberlanders for their successes in the late campaign, the actions of this modest and unassuming general earned for him a respect and admiration accorded to no other Union general, including Grant, Sherman, and Sheridan. Captain Henry Stone of Thomas' staff spoke for many in a paper he presented before the Military Historical Society of Massachusetts in 1895, titled, "Critical Sketches of Some Federal and Confederate Military Leaders":

One secret not only of Thomas's unvarying success but of his wonderful hold upon the confidence and affections of his army is the fact that everyone in it was to him a man and a soldier. . . . He was unremitting in his effort that they should be well supplied, well looked after, and always brought to the right place at the right time. . . . When every day brought at least a skirmish he invariably made his way to the head of the column . . . where he often dismounted and walked to the outer skirmish line to reconnoiter. . . . His woodcraft was almost unerring. He could make his way through the thickest forest and come out at the spot he aimed for. When under fire, his movements . . . were as deliberate as at any time. . . . He was never seen riding up and down his lines waving his sword, shouting, or going through ceremonies. . . . Whenever and wherever his soldiers saw him they knew that all was right, and they read in his fixed countenance the . . . harbinger of victory. On the march nobody ever saw him, with an escort trailing, dashing past a moving column of troops, throwing up dust or mud and compelling them to leave the road. If any had the right of way, it was they. He would break through the woods or flounder across a swamp rather than force his men from the road and wear them out by needless fatigue.

He sometimes had terrific outbursts of temper. It was usually under complete control but when it did break out it was volcanic. He once so alarmed a teamster who, when his mules were stalled, was beating them over the head with the butt of his whip, that the poor fellow took to the woods to escape he knew not what fate. Again when the servants and orderlies about his headquarters were chasing a stray goose and making a great shouting and disturbance he flamed out so that everybody ran and hid from his wrath while the poor goose, after a short circling flight, lighted at his feet as if for protection and safety. To all dumb animals he was a friend and protector. . . . It was exhibitions of meanness and cruelty to those who could not defend themselves, rather than any great faults or crimes, which chiefly stirred his passion. He . . . liked as he sat by the campfire to hear the droll anecdotes and adventures of his soldiers. . . . He liked to occupy himself with some mechanical work for which he had great fondness and aptitude, or with the study of science, history or philosophy . . . . He was well versed in constitutional law, or rather, perhaps in the Constitution itself.[46]

46. Henry Stone, "Critical Sketches of Some Federal and Confederate Military Leaders," *Military Historical Society of Massachusetts*, Vol. X, pp. 195-97.

# CHAPTER EIGHT

# *Thomas Routs Hood's Army of Tennessee*

When the Federals occupied Atlanta on September 2, 1864, General Sherman had accomplished only part of his mission. The city now belonged to Sherman, but the Army of Tennessee, some 40,000 seasoned veterans had escaped. Sherman, pleased with the immediate outcome of his campaign, seemed at the moment to take no further interest in Hood's army, although it is conceivable that a renewed Federal offensive at this time might have crushed and scattered these Confederate troops once and for all.

In an unprecedented display of military ruthlessness, the Yankee commander decided to evacuate the civilian population of Atlanta, demonstrating a callous disregard of the hardships this tactic would impose on the refugees. Hood's forces were allowed to assist the unfortunate citizenry to sanctuary within Confederate territory during the short truce agreed upon for that purpose.

The Atlanta campaign had proved costly to both armies. Starting with a force approaching 50,000 men when he succeeded General Joseph E. Johnston on July 18 as commander of the Army of Tennessee, Hood by September 20 had lost twenty percent of his strength, but not all of it because of casualties or desertions.

On September 10, Georgia Governor Joseph E. Brown, disillusioned with the Confederate cause and seeking some sort of reapproachment with the Federal authorities, withdrew his state troops from active duty with the Rebel army under the pretense of allowing them furloughs. Sherman's forces had also dwindled proportionately, his losses totalling about 24,000 men, down from a strength of 106,000 on July 1.[1]

On September 21, having first secured the transfer of thousands of Federal prisoners from the infamous Andersonville stockades to newly established prison pens at Florence, South Carolina, and Millen, Georgia, to prevent their release by Yankee raids into that area of Georgia, General Hood marched his army from Lovejoy's Station on the Macon & Western 25 miles westward to Palmetto on the Atlanta & West Point Railroad. Here he began refitting his command in preparation for an attack on Sherman's line of communications.

While Hood's Army of Tennessee was stationed at Palmetto, Confederate President Jefferson Davis visited the camps, having been requested to do so by Hood himself. Hood hoped that the appearance here of Davis would boost the morale of troops still chafing over the loss of a revered commander, General Johnston, whom Hood had replaced, and of the city of Atlanta, the capture of which was a severe blow to Confederate pride and to fading prospects for a Southern victory.

In his speech before the troops, Davis charged General Johnston and Georgia Governor Brown with responsibility for Atlanta's fall and for Sherman's success. He then went on to confide to his soldiers the outline of a new strategy he had devised to ruin and destroy Sherman's "army group."

Davis' address was characterized by the naivete and fatuousness which imbued some Southern leaders. In an attempt to inspire these unhappy and despondent men, Davis forgot discretion and freely revealed future movements planned by the Army of Tennessee against Sherman. Hood's forces, he said, could soon look forward to joining Bedford Forrest in Middle Tennessee from where they would drive the Federals back to the Ohio River.

1. Stanley F. Horn, *The Army of Tennessee* (Indianapolis: Bobbs-Merrill, 1941), p. 368.

Sherman learned of Davis' speech through a Yankee spy who was present at the camp, as well as through newspaper accounts of the incident. Years later Sherman wrote in his *Memoirs*, "He [Davis] made no concealment of these vainglorious boasts, and thus gave us the full key to his future designs. To be forewarned was to be forearmed, and I think we took full advantage of the occasion."

With a Tennessee campaign now an alternative to resuming the baiting of Sherman on the Atlanta approaches, Hood, on September 29 and 30, recrossed the Chattahoochee River, and by October 3 was camped near Lost Mountain, west of Marietta, from where Stewart's corps was sent to break up the Western & Atlantic between Big Shanty and the Etowah. The immediate result of this maneuver was that Sherman, with a large force, marched out of Atlanta to ward off this new threat from Hood. Sherman was bewildered as to Hood's intentions and movements. The latter was weaving his troops into the Georgia countryside near the railroad line to strike repeatedly at Sherman's highly sensitive line of supply—the Western & Atlantic. Hood continued to march northward, alarming Sherman and the entire North with his increasing nearness to Tennessee. Sherman had no choice but to continue to pursue the wily Confederate leader. General George Thomas, who had been sent to Middle Tennessee, was ordered to start preparing for a possible confrontation with Hood.

By mid-October, Hood's army was again in the vicinity of La Fayette, some 25 miles south of Chattanooga, and nearer yet to the Chickamauga battlefield of grim memories. Here Hood was faced with the option of allowing Sherman's much larger army to catch up and do battle, an option he felt entailed too great a risk, or to embark now on the much-discussed invasion of Tennessee. Indifferent now as to whether or not Sherman followed him out of Georgia, Hood looked to a Tennessee Campaign as the first of a series of brilliant strategic maneuvers designed not only to rout the defending armies and capture the city of Nashville, but also eventually to bring the Army of Tennessee through Kentucky and into Virginia, where Hood and Lee would join forces against General Grant, thereby allowing General Lee "in command of our combined armies, to march upon Washington, or turn upon and annihilate Sherman."[2]

On October 16, Hood turned his infantry columns south and then west toward Gadsden, Alabama, where he arrived on the 20th. There, during the next two days, General Hood met and discussed with his immediate superior, General P. G. T. Beauregard, his plan to push on, cross the Tennessee River at Guntersville, and strike into Middle Tennessee. Beauregard approved the proposal.

Five days later, Hood's march for Tennessee began in earnest. On Wednesday, October 26, Sherman, headquartered temporarily at Gaylesville, Alabama, discovered that Hood's army had left Gadsden and was now at or near Decatur, 75 miles to the northwest. Only Wheeler's cavalry had been left behind, expressly "to watch and harass Sherman."

It was at this point that Sherman decided General Thomas could take care of Hood in the "barrens of Tennessee," while he himself, with his "army group," would undertake a march southeastward through the state of Georgia to the Atlantic coast. Thomas had been in Nashville since early October, having been assigned there by General Sherman to cope with Forrest's cavalry whose slashing raids were causing havoc in Middle and West Tennessee.

It had been General Grant's intention that Sherman attack and destroy Hood's army before beginning his march to Savannah. As late as November 1, 1864, Grant still entertained some doubts as to the propriety of the movement.

The following telegram clearly demonstrates Grant's desire that Sherman deal with Hood before beginning a march to the sea:

*City Point, November* 1, 1864—6 p. m.

Major-General Sherman:

Do you not think it advisable, now that Hood has gone so far north, to entirely ruin him before starting on your proposed campaign? With Hood's army destroyed, you can go where you please with impunity. I believed, and still believe, if you had started south while Hood was in the neighborhood of you, he would have been forced to go after you. Now that he is far away he might look upon the chase as useless, and he will go in one direction while you are pushing in the other.

2. Horn, p. 379.

If you can see a chance of destroying Hood's army, attend to that first, and make your other move secondary.

U. S. Grant, Lieutenant-General.[3]

Sherman vigorously defended his proposed march by return wire:

*Kingston, Georgia, November* 2, 1864.

Lieutenant-General U. S. Grant, City Point, Virginia:

If I turn back, the whole effect of my campaign will be lost. By my movements I have thrown Beauregard (Hood) well to the west, and Thomas will have ample time and sufficient troops to hold him until the reenforcements from Missouri reach him. We have now ample supplies at Chattanooga and Atlanta, and can stand a month's interruption to our communications. I do not believe the Confederate army can reach our railroad-lines except by cavalry-raids, and [Major General James H.] Wilson will have cavalry enough to checkmate them. I am clearly of the opinion that the best results will follow my contemplated movement through Georgia.[4]

Grant allowed himself to be persuaded of the primacy of Sherman's mission and finally acceded to Sherman's demands that the latter be permitted to march through Georgia from Atlanta to Savannah, leaving Hood to Thomas. General Grant sent the following message to Sherman, giving authorization for the march:

*City Point, Virginia, November* 2, 1864—11:30 a. m.

Major-General Sherman:

Your dispatch of 9 a. m. yesterday is just received. I dispatched you the same day, advising that Hood's army, now that it had worked so far north, ought to be looked upon now as the "object." With the force, however, that you left with General Thomas, he must be able to take care of Hood and destroy him.

I do not see that you can withdraw from where you are to follow Hood, without giving up all that we have gained in territory. I say, then, go on as you propose.

U. S. Grant, Lieutenant-General.[5]

3. Sherman, II, 164.
4. *Ibid.*, p. 165.
5. *Ibid.*, p. 166.

With 62,000 hand-picked officers and men, 5,500 cavalry, 62 pieces of field artillery, more than adequate ammunition, and forty days' rations of most staples, Sherman could now embark on his campaign. Thomas was left with a small force of some 30,000 widely scattered troops to face Hood's superior army.

Sherman left himself open to severe criticism for his abandonment of Thomas, whose force, depleted by casualties during the summer campaign, was unequipped for major battle. Inasmuch as Sherman had no enemy at his front, there was little danger, and he could have accomplished his purpose with half the men. Critics of Sherman later claimed that Thomas made, at Nashville, Sherman's march to the sea a success.

Sherman succeeded in obtaining Grant's approval of the venture only after misleading the commander-in-chief as to the strength of Thomas' army. Grant could not know the actual circumstances in the field and therefore relied heavily on Sherman's communications for his information. But Grant, for reasons of his own, had always favored Sherman over Thomas. Grant "disliked and distrusted Thomas." Although the latter's experience, achievements, and seniority in military service were superior to Sherman's, Grant had, in March, 1864, passed over Thomas to name Sherman his successor as commander of the Military Division of the Mississippi.[6]

Sherman had hastened back to Atlanta from Gaylesville, breaking up the Western & Atlanta from the Etowah to the Chattahoochee. Atlanta was torched, and in the early morning hours of Wednesday, November 16, Sherman moved out with his army on the Decatur road in a southeasterly direction to begin his famous "March to the Sea." When the columns passed near the site of the bloody battle of Atlanta fought July 22, 1864, Sherman was moved to tears at the memory of his fallen comrade, General James B. McPherson, who had lost his life in that fatal fight.

When Sherman reached the outskirts of Atlanta, he paused to look back on the city. In his later life, he recalled this moment:

Behind us lay Atlanta, smoldering and in ruins, the black

6. Robert R. McCormick, *Ulysses S. Grant: The Great Soldier of America* (New York: Bond Wheelright, 1950), p. 219.

smoke rising high in air, and hanging like a pall over the ruined city. . . .

Then we turned our horses' heads to the east; Atlanta was soon behind the screen of trees and became a thing of the past. Around it clings many a thought of desperate battle, of hope and fear, that now seem like the memory of a dream; and I have never seen the place since.[7]

One of the celebrated expeditions in the annals of warfare, Sherman's March to the Sea gained him fame and ill fame both during and long after the Civil War, although his campaign from Chattanooga to Atlanta remains his greatest achievement.

In his *Memoirs*, Sherman perceived the fall of Atlanta as heralding the beginning of the end of the Confederacy: "Atlanta was known as the 'Gate-City of the South,' was full of foundries, arsenals, and machine-shops, and I knew that its capture would be the death-knell of the Southern Confederacy."[8] Atlanta was the real prize; the march southeastward to the coastal city of Savannah was of secondary importance. Sherman places the two events in their proper perspective in this excerpt from his writings:

> I only regarded the march from Atlanta to Savannah as a "shift of base," as the transfer of a strong army, which had no opponent, and had finished its then work, from the interior to a point on the sea-coast, from which it could achieve other important results. I considered this march as a means to an end, and not as an essential act of war. Still, then, as now, the march to the sea was generally regarded as something extraordinary, something anomalous, something out of the usual order of events; whereas, in fact, I simply moved from Atlanta to Savannah, as one step in the direction of Richmond, a movement that had to be met and defeated, or the war was necessarily at an end.[9]

If turning his back on Thomas and Hood seemed reckless of Sherman, this was not exactly true. The selection of Thomas for so bold an enterprise as defeating Hood's army was made not without considerable deliberation. Unlike Grant, Sherman held

7. Sherman, II, 178-79.
8. *Ibid.*, p. 99.
9. *Ibid.*, pp. 220-21.

Thomas' military capabilities in high esteem and had the greatest confidence in Thomas to get the job done.

And, although Thomas' forces were numerically inferior to those of Hood when Sherman set out from Atlanta, Sherman was counting on Thomas to build-up at Nashville a formidable army to deal with the Confederate general by the time Hood could penetrate deep into Middle Tennessee.

Sherman had provided Thomas with a sturdy and tested core— Stanley's 4th Corps and Schofield's 23d Corps—around which to form a powerful army. General Wilson, a trusted and proven cavalry leader, had been detached from the eastern armies and ordered to Middle Tennessee with the mission of making Thomas' mounted arm a force to reckon with. A. J. Smith's two divisions of the Sixteenth Corps were en route from western Missouri. Including the approximately 9,000 armed troops already in Nashville, plus an equal number of men in the Quartermaster Corps there, Thomas was expected to organize and deploy a force of approximately 70,000 soldiers. The additional troops were, however, far-flung, from the 5,000 men under James Steedman in and around Chattanooga to General Smith's 14,000 soldiers now with General Rosecrans in Missouri.[10]

When Hood left Gadsden in late October, he had planned to join with Forrest at Guntersville and there cross the Tennessee River. But Forrest was delayed and Hood was compelled to move farther west to effect a joint crossing. At each successive stop— Decatur, then Courtland, and then Tuscumbia—Hood was barred from crossing for one reason or another. At Tuscumbia, Hood expected to equip his army with the necessary supplies and provisions for the arduous campaign ahead and then to cross easily into Tennessee. But here he was subjected to further infuriating delays because a section of the railroad on which he was depending to bring up supplies had been destroyed and inclement weather slowed the repair work.[11]

In all more than three weeks were lost between the time Hood set out from Gadsden on October 22 and the day he crossed to the north bank of the Tennessee River to establish his head-

10. Horn, pp. 381-82.
11. *Ibid.*, pp. 380-82.

quarters at Florence, Alabama, on November 13.

At Florence, Hood was again delayed waiting for General Forrest, who reported on the 14th, and for the army's three corps—now led by Generals S. D. Lee, Cheatham, and Stewart—to cross the rain-swollen river. It was another week before the combined forces, 45,000 strong, broke camp. When the army left Florence on November 21, the heads of the columns were pointed toward Tennessee. Hood's goal was to interpose between General Schofield's army then at Pulaski and Nashville.

While Hood impatiently suffered the myriad obstacles preventing him from putting his bold plan into immediate operation, a scheme in which time was of the essence, General Thomas was busy at Nashville squeezing every possible advantage out of this unexpected reprieve from an increasingly imminent confrontation with the Army of Tennessee. Thomas now had additional time to consolidate his scattered forces and to strengthen the city's already imposing defense system.

When the Federals first occupied Nashville in late February, 1862, the city soon became a vast depot for supplies, as well as a center of mass transportation and communications. Several months after the troops arrived, Captain James St. Clair Morton of the United States Corps of Engineers was ordered to Nashville to select and survey the best sites for the protection of the city. This measure was taken to ensure that all roads giving access to Nashville would be well defended.

Captain Morton was also directed by General Buell, then commanding the Department of the Ohio, to consult with Andrew Johnson, military governor of Tennessee, to determine what defenses were needed around the capitol in Nashville. Anxious about the possibility of raids upon the capitol by Rebel forces, Governor Johnson was relieved when Captain Morton laid out and fatigue parties built the necessary parapets and breastworks surrounding the edifice which were later to be manned by Federal infantry and artillery units. When Hood's intentions first became known, it was decided that the fortifications begun by Captain Morton in 1862 must be strengthened and extended. This task was assigned to Brigadier General Zealous B. Tower.

At Nashville, Tower not only completed the defenses that Captain Morton had commenced, but with the aid of Thomas' men also built additional forts which were designed to give support to the entrenchments around the city. Thomas had organized the employees of the Quartermaster Department into a corps, placing in command the Chief Quartermaster, James L. Donaldson, under the direct supervision of General Tower. After finishing this assignment, Tower remained in Nashville to fight against Hood.

In a comprehensive report, dated January 20, 1865, General Thomas, with the advantage of hindsight, detailed the events of the period—September 7-November 14—as they unfolded:

Headquarters Department of the Cumberland,<br>
Eastport, Miss., January 20, 1865.

Colonel: I have the honor to report the operations of my command from the date of the occupation of Atlanta, Ga., as follows:

From the 7th to the 30th of September the Fourth, Fourteenth, and Twentieth Army Corps, composing the Army of the Cumberland, remained quietly in camp around the city of Atlanta. The enemy was reported posted in the neighborhood of Jonesborough. During the greater portion of the above-mentioned period an armistice existed between the two armies for the purpose of exchanging prisoners captured on both sides during the preceding campaign.

About the 20th of September the enemy's cavalry, under Forrest, crossed the Tennessee River near Waterloo, Ala., and appeared in front of Athens, Ala., on the 23d, after having destroyed a portion of the railroad between the latter place and Decatur, Ala. Considerable skirmishing took place, and the garrison, Colonel [Wallace] Campbell, One Hundred and tenth U. S. Colored Troops, commanding, withdrew into the fort. By night-fall the town was completely invested, and the quarter-master and commissary buildings destroyed by the enemy. On the morning of the 24th the enemy opened on the fort with a 12-pounder battery, firing from two directions, north and west, which was answered by the artillery of the garrison. Later two flags of truce were received demanding a surrender, which was declined by Colonel Campbell, when he was requested to grant Major-General Forrest a personal interview, and complied with the request. At this interview Colonel Campbell allowed himself to become convinced by

278

the rebel commander that it was useless to contend against the largely superior force of the enemy confronting him, and was induced to surrender his command. The garrison, at the time, consisted of 450 men belonging to the One Hundred and sixth, One Hundred and tenth, and One Hundred and eleventh U. S. Colored Troops, and about 150 men of the Third Tennessee Cavalry.

Thirty minutes after the evacuation of the fort re-enforcements, consisting of the Eighteenth Michigan and One Hundred and second Ohio Regiments, arrived, and after a severe fight were also forced to yield. Forrest then moved toward Pulaski, destroying the [Tennessee & Alabama] railroad as he advanced, captured the garrison at the Sulphur Branch trestle, and skirmished heavily all day of the 27th with the garrison of Pulaski, but withdrew toward night-fall. Major-General Rousseau was present at Pulaski during the engagement, having collected such troops as he could spare from other points of his command to assist in staying the progress of the enemy in the destruction of our railroad communications.

On the 29th Forrest withdrew from the immediate vicinity of the railroad after having thoroughly destroyed it from Athens to within five miles of Pulaski, and on the same day the Nashville & Chattanooga Railroad was cut near Tullahoma and Decherd by small parties from his command, sent out for the purpose; but the road was again in running order on the 30th.

As Forrest changed the scene of his operations from the . . . [Tennessee & Alabama] railroad over to the one leading to Chattanooga, General Rousseau moved rapidly by rail around through Nashville to Tullahoma, and prepared for his reception. On the same day (29th of September) 5,000 men from the District of the Etowah, Maj. Gen. J. B. Steedman commanding, crossed to the north of the Tennessee River to check Forrest's movements and protect and keep open the communication by rail with Chattanooga. Newton's division, Fourth Corps, was ordered from Atlanta September 26, and replaced Steedman's command at Chattanooga on the 28th. Morgan's division, of the Fourteenth Corps, started from Atlanta for the same purpose on the 29th of September, and to re-enforce the troops operating against Forrest.

In compliance with verbal instructions from Major-General

Sherman, I left Atlanta with Morgan's division [on September 29] to take immediate charge of affairs in Tennessee, and reached Nashville October 3.

On the withdrawal of Forrest's troops from Athens a garrison was sent out to reoccupy the post by Brig. Gen. R. S. Granger, commanding District of Northern Alabama, who also sent a scouting party from Huntsville toward Fayetteville to locate the enemy. This party ascertained that Forrest passed through Fayetteville on the night of the 29th, and moved toward Decherd. After passing Fayetteville, however, he divided his forces, part going south through New Market toward Huntsville [Alabama], and the remainder, under Forrest in person, moved through Lynchburg toward Columbia. The first column, 4,000 strong, under [Abraham] Buford, appeared in front of Huntsville during the evening of the 30th, and immediately sent in a summons to the garrison to surrender, which the latter refused to do. The enemy remained throughout the night in the vicinity of the town, and repeated the demand for its surrender on the morning of October 1, and, meeting with an answer similar to the one received on the night previous, he [Buford] moved off in the direction of Athens, which place was attacked by him at about 3 p. m. without effect, the garrison holding its own nobly. The second column (under Forrest in person, and estimated at 3,000 men) made its appearance near Columbia on the morning of the 1st, but did not attack that place.

During these operations of Forrest in Middle Tennessee small parties of the enemy made their appearance in the neighborhood of McMinnville and Liberty, but made no serious demonstrations.

Morgan's division, of the Fourteenth Army Corps, which started from Atlanta on the 29th of September, reached Stevenson [Alabama] during the morning of the 1st of October, and pushed on toward Huntsville immediately, reaching that place during the night, and set out for Athens at an early hour on the morning of the 2d, repairing the railroad as it advanced. The enemy, under Buford, resumed the attack on Athens on the 2d, but was again handsomely repulsed by the garrison, consisting of the Seventy-third Indiana, Lieutenant-Colonel [Alfred B.] Wade commanding. Failing in this second attempt, Buford moved off toward Elk River, pursued by a small force of our cavalry belonging to General Granger's command. The other column, under Forrest, started from near Columbia on the morning of the 3d, and moved off in the direction of Mount Pleasant, paroling all his prisoners before his departure. During his stay in the neighborhood he destroyed about five miles of [Tennessee & Alabama] railroad between Carter's Creek and Spring Hill, including three bridges.

The enemy's intention to make good his escape to the south side of the Tennessee River being now evident, directions were given to General Morgan, at Athens, to move with his division toward Bainbridge and endeavor to secure the crossing at that place in advance of Forrest, whilst General Rousseau, already on the way to Columbia from Nashville with a force of 4,000 mounted men, hastily collected together, was to push after the enemy through Mount Pleasant, and press him in the rear. [John T.] Croxton's brigade of cavalry started from Farmington, and, moving through Lewisburg, pursued a southwesterly course toward Lawrenceburg. The above was the position of the troops on the morning of October 3. On the same day information reached me that Major-General [Cadwallader C.] Washburn, with 3,000 cavalry and 1,500 infantry, was moving up the Tennessee River to participate in the operations against Forrest. Directions were sent to him on the 4th to leave his infantry at Johnsonville, move with his cavalry by water to Clifton, and thence across the country toward Pulaski, joining General Rousseau's column at that point. Lieutenant-Commander [Moreau] Forrest, U. S. Navy, commanding the naval force on the upper Tennessee, was requested to send some gun-boats down the river to Florence, Ala., and endeavor to prevent the enemy crossing in that vicinity, if the high stage of water then prevailing in the Tennessee would admit of his crossing the upper shoals with his gun-boats.

Morgan's division reached Rogersville during the evening of the 4th, having been delayed in crossing the Elk River, and on the same night Forrest passed through Lawrenceburg. A report was received that Buford's command succeeded in crossing the Tennessee River at Brown's Ferry on the 3d instant. On the 6th General Washburn reached Waynesborough, still moving eastward, and on the same day came up with the enemy's rear guard at Shoal Creek bridge and skirmished with it slightly, but still not in time to prevent the main body of the enemy [under Forrest] from safely effecting a crossing of the Tennessee at Bainbridge. Thus both columns of the enemy succeeded in escaping, although closely pursued by our forces. On . . . [October] 8th directions were sent to General Rousseau to destroy all ferry-boats and other means of crossing the river, and then move his command below Florence to await further orders. At the same time General Morgan was directed to return to Athens.

Pending these operations in Tennessee the whole aspect of affairs about Atlanta had undergone a change. Hood [on September 29] had crossed the Chattahoochee River, and had sent one corps [Stewart's] of his army to destroy the railroad between . . . [Marietta and the Etowah], which he had effectually accomplished for a distance of over twenty miles, interrupting all communications between the forces in Tennessee and the main army with General Sherman in Georgia. He then moved around south of Rome to the west side of the Coosa River, and, taking a northeasterly course, marched toward Summerville and La Fayette, threatening Chattanooga and Bridgeport.

The following dispositions were made on the 11th: [John T.] Croxton's cavalry brigade was to move to some point sufficiently near his supplies at Athens, and not too far removed from the Tennessee River to protect the crossings from Decatur down as far as Eastport; Morgan's division, of the Fourteenth Corps, to move without delay from Athens to Chattanooga by rail, and Steedman's command following Morgan's from Decatur to Bridgeport. General Rousseau's troops were recalled from below Florence, and ordered to concentrate at Athens without delay. The District of Northern Alabama, comprising the posts of Decatur, Huntsville, Stevenson, and intermediate points, was left with its ordinary garrisons, and our whole attention turned toward Hood's movements in Northern Georgia.

On the 12th the enemy's cavalry attacked Resaca, but the place was resolutely held by [D. D.] Watkins' brigade of cavalry, and the railroad bridges saved from destruction. The same day Brigadier-General [George D.] Wagner reported from Chattanooga the enemy's cavalry, 250 strong, had occupied La Fayette, Ga.; whereupon instructions were sent him to call in the detachments at Tunnel Hill, Ringgold, and intermediate points along the railroad between there and

Chattanooga, and quietly make preparations to defend his post.

On the 13th one corps of Hood's army appeared in front of Dalton, and a summons to surrender, signed by Hood in person, was sent in to Colonel [Lewis] Johnson, Forty-fourth U. S. Colored Troops, commanding the garrison. Colonel Johnson, being convinced of the uselessness of contending against so overwhelming a force of the enemy [Stewart's Corps]; and knowing there was no succor at hand, complied with the demand.

On the 14th Morgan's division reached Chattanooga, and General Steedman's command arrived at Bridgeport, where he received orders to proceed to Chattanooga. After remaining at Dalton one day, during which he destroyed about five miles of railroad, the enemy [Stewart's Corps] moved off to the westward, through Nickajack Gap, to rejoin the remainder of Hood's army near Summerville, to which point he had been followed by General Sherman with the Fourth, Fourteenth, Fifteenth, and Seventeenth Army Corps, the Twentieth Corps having been left behind at Atlanta to hold the place. In compliance with instructions from Major-General Sherman, Morgan's division, of the Fourteenth Corps, and Wagner's, of the Fourth, were sent from Chattanooga to rejoin their respective commands at Summerville. A force of 1,500 men was set to work, under the direction of Col. W. W. Wright, chief engineer U. S. military railroads, to repair the railroads south of Chattanooga, there being twenty-four miles of rails and ties totally destroyed, besides several important bridges carried away by high water; yet, with characteristic energy on the part of Colonel Wright and Capt. J. C. Van Duzer, superintendent of military telegraph, the repairs were rapidly carried forward.

Telegraphic communication with Atlanta was restored on the 21st, and trains commenced running regularly on the 28th [of October]. On the . . . [former] date the enemy was at Gadsden, Ala., whilst General Sherman's forces were at Gaylesville, both armies remaining inactive and watchful of the other's movements. Whilst at the latter place Special Field Orders, No. 105, Military Division of the Mississippi, was issued by General Sherman, and the substance of it sent to me by telegraph, as follows:

In the event of military movements or the accidents of war separating the general in command from his military division, Maj. Gen. George H. Thomas, commanding the Department of the Cumberland, will exercise command over all the troops and garrisons not absolutely in the presence of the general-in-chief.

A written communication, received a few days previous, in which I was instructed to remain in Tennessee and defend the line of the Tennessee River, gave a detailed account of his plans for a campaign into the heart of Georgia. The Fourteenth and Twentieth Corps of my command were to go with General Sherman, the Fourth Corps [Stanley's] remaining with me in Tennessee. My instructions were to pursue the enemy if he followed General Sherman's column, but, in any event, to hold Tennessee.

On the 26th [of October] the enemy's infantry made its appearance in strong force in front of Decatur, Ala., and during the afternoon attacked the garrison, but not vigorously, and without effect. Re-enforcements, amounting to two full regiments, were sent from Chattanooga to General [Robert S.] Granger at that point, and he was directed to hold his post at all hazards. On the 27th the enemy commenced intrenching his position around Decatur, working steadily throughout the day, and skirmishing continually, but no artillery was used. At night their campfires showed a heavy force. Under cover of the darkness, and with a strong force, the enemy drove in our pickets and established a line of rifle-pits within 500 yards of the town. On the 28th a sortie was made by a part of the garrison, which advanced under cover of the guns of the fort down the river bank and around to the rear of the enemy's pits, clearing them of their occupants and capturing 120 prisoners belonging to Cheatham's . . . [corps], besides killing and wounding a number. The same day the Fourteenth U. S. Colored Troops, Colonel [Thomas J.] Morgan commanding, carried one of the enemy's batteries up the river, after driving off the supports; the guns were spiked, and the command returned to Decatur. Our loss was 3 officers killed, and several officers and men wounded. General Granger estimated the force opposing him at one corps [Cheatham's], and his scouts informed him there was also a corps at Warrenton, Ala., with [Robert M.] Russell's brigade of cavalry at Guntersville, on the river; Roddey's division of cavalry was picketing the south side of the Tennessee from Decatur to Tuscumbia, and Forrest, with the main force, was reported at Corinth, Miss., with outposts at Eastport and along the west bank of the Tennessee.

On the 29th General Granger reported the enemy in his front to be withdrawing from Decatur toward Courtland. The same day General Croxton, commanding the brigade of cavalry picketing the north bank of the Tennessee River, reported the enemy crossing at the mouth of Cypress Creek, two miles below Florence, stating at the same time that he would move with all the force he could spare to drive the enemy back. Directions were sent to General [Edward] Hatch, commanding division of cavalry, at Clifton, on the east bank of the Tennessee, to move to the support of Croxton at Florence, impressing upon both commanders the necessity of keeping the enemy from crossing to the north side of the river until the Fourth Corps, already on its way from General Sherman in Georgia, could arrive and get into position to meet him.

Hood's plans had now become evident, and from information gained through prisoners, deserters, and other sources, his intention was to cross into Middle Tennessee. To enable him to supply his army he had been repairing the Mobile and Ohio Railroad for some time previous, and trains were now running as far north as Corinth and thence east [over the Memphis & Charleston] to Cherokee Station, bringing his supplies by that route from Selma and Montgomery. The advance division [Thomas J.] (Wood's) of the Fourth Corps reached Athens on the 31st, the other two divisions of the corps following along rapidly. The Twenty-third Corps, Maj. Gen. J. M. Schofield commanding, having been ordered by Major-General Sherman to take post at Resaca and report to me for orders, was immediately ordered by me to Pulaski (as soon as I learned Hood had appeared in force on the south side of the Tennessee), and was also on its way to Tennessee, moving in rear of the Fourth Corps. The enemy effected a lodgment for his infantry on the north side of the Tennessee, about three miles above Florence, on the 31st, notwithstanding Croxton's endeavors to drive him back, and his cavalry, in large force, pressed Croxton across Shoal Creek to its east bank. Orders were immediately sent to General Stanley to concentrate the Fourth Corps at Pulaski and await further instructions.

In the mean time Forrest was moving . . . [north] ward from Corinth, Miss., and [then eastward] from Paris, Tenn., making his appearance on the 28th at Fort Heiman, an earthwork on the west bank of the Tennessee, about seventy-five miles from Paducah, where he captured gun-boat No. 55 [*Undine*] and two transports on the 31st, having previously burned the steamer *Empress*. His force was composed of seventeen regiments of cavalry, with nine pieces of artillery.

On the 2d of November he had succeeded in planting batteries above and below Johnsonville (one of our bases of supplies on the Tennessee River, and the western terminus of the Northwestern railroad), completely blockading the river and isolating at that place three gun-boats, eight transports, and about a dozen barges. The garrison was composed of about 1,000 men of the Forty-third Wisconsin, Twelfth U. S. Colored Troops, and a detachment of the Eleventh Tennessee Cavalry, all under command of Col. C. R. Thompson, Twelfth U. S. Colored Troops. The naval forces, under command of Lieut. E. M. King, attacked the enemy's batteries below Johnsonville, but were repulsed after a severe contest, but not before they recaptured from the enemy one of the transports above mentioned, having on board two 20-pounder Parrott guns, and a considerable quantity of quartermaster's stores, and forcing the enemy to destroy the gun-boat No. 55, captured on the 31st of October. On the 4th the enemy opened on the gun-boats [*Key West, Towah,* and *Elfin*], transports, and on the town from batteries posted on the opposite bank of the river, to which the artillery of the garrison and the gun-boats gave a brisk response. The latter becoming disabled, and as great fears were entertained of their being seized by the enemy, it was resolved to fire them, as also the transports, to prevent their falling into his hands. In carrying this into operation, the flames spread to the buildings of the commissary and quartermaster's departments, and also to a large amount of stores on the levee, soon converting the whole into a mass of ruins. The loss to the Government, as far as estimated, is set down at $1,500,000, of which about $300,000 belong to the subsistence department, and the remainder to the quartermaster's department. I believe that there was no cause to apprehend that the enemy could effect a crossing at Johnsonville, and the destruction of property was consequently unnecessary.

On the morning of the 5th the enemy again opened fire on the garrison, and after a furious cannonade of more than an hour's duration withdrew from his position across the river and disappeared. He crossed the Tennessee above Johnsonville by means of two large flat-boats constructed by his men and two small boats belonging to one of the gun-boats, and then moved off in the direction of Clifton.

Major-General Schofield, with the advance of the Twenty-third Corps, arrived in Nashville on the 5th, and was immediately started toward Johnsonville by rail, reaching that place the same night, and found the enemy had already retreated. Directions were then sent General Schofield to leave a sufficiently strong force for the defense of that point, and with the balance of his command proceed to carry out the instructions already given him, viz, to join the Fourth Corps at Pulaski, and assume command of all the troops in the vicinity, watch the movements of Hood, and retard his advance into Tennessee as much as possible, without risking a general engagement, until Maj. Gen. A. J. Smith's command could arrive from Missouri, and Maj. Gen. J. H. Wilson could have time to remount the cavalry regiments dismounted to furnish horses for Kilpatrick's division, which was to accompany General Sherman in his march through Georgia.

At this time I found myself confronted by the army which, under General J. E. Johnston, had so skillfully resisted the advance of the whole active army of the Military Division of the Mississippi from Dalton to the Chattahoochee, re-enforced by a well-equipped and enthusiastic cavalry command of over 12,000 men, led by [Nathan Bedford Forrest] one of the boldest and most successful commanders in the rebel army. My information from all sources confirmed the reported strength of Hood's army to be from 40,000 to 45,000 infantry, and from 12,000 to 15,000 cavalry. My effective force at this time consisted of the Fourth Corps, about 12,000, under Maj. Gen. D. S. Stanley; the Twenty-third Corps, about 10,000, under Maj. Gen. J. M. Schofield; Hatch's division of cavalry, about 4,000; Croxton's brigade, 2,500, and [Horace] Capron's brigade of about 1,200. The balance of my force was distributed along the railroad, and posted at Murfreesborough, Stevenson, Bridgeport, Huntsville, Decatur, and Chattanooga, to keep open our communications, and hold the posts above named if attacked, until they could be re-enforced, as up to this time it was impossible to determine which course Hood would take—advance on Nashville or turn toward Huntsville. Under these circumstances it was manifestly best to act on the defensive until sufficiently re-enforced to justify taking the offensive. My plans and wishes were fully explained to General Schofield, and, as subsequent events will show, properly appreciated and executed by him.

From the 1st to the 10th of November the enemy's position at Florence [and Tuscumbia] had remained materially unchanged. He had laid a pontoon bridge by mooring it to the piers of the old railroad bridge, at that place, and had crossed over one corps of infantry (S. D. Lee's) and two divisions of cavalry; the other two corps (Stewart's and Cheatham's) were still on the south side of the river. His cavalry had pushed out to Shoal Creek, skirmishing continually with Hatch's and Croxton's commands along the line of that stream, but showing no disposition to advance beyond.

General Sherman's uncertain position at Kingston, Ga., where he still remained in camp, had much to do with detaining the enemy, doubtless causing considerable speculation as to his future movements. On the 12th of November communication with General Sherman was severed, the last dispatch from him leaving Cartersville, Ga., at 2.25 p. m. on that date. He had started on his great expedition from Atlanta to the sea-board, leaving me to guard Tennessee or to pursue the enemy if he followed the commanding general's column. It was therefore with considerable anxiety that we watched the forces at Florence, to discover what course they would pursue with regard to General Sherman's movements, determining thereby whether the troops under my command, numbering less than half those under Hood, were to act on the defensive in Tennessee, or take the offensive in Alabama.

I have the honor to be, colonel, very respectfully, your obedient servant,

Geo. H. Thomas,
*Major-General, Commanding.*

Lieut. Col. R. M. Sawyer,
*Asst. Adjt. Gen., Military Division of the Mississippi.*[12]

General Hood, upon leaving his Florence bridgehead, directed his army toward Columbia, some 45 miles south of Nashville. More importantly, Columbia was about midway between Nashville and Pulaski, where Thomas' field army under General Scho-

12. OR, I, XXXIX, pt. I, pp. 584-91.

field had been posted awaiting Hood's advance. Schofield's force, consisting of the Fourth and Twenty-third Corps plus three cavalry brigades under General Hatch, numbered about 30,000 men, approximately three-fifths the force Hood commanded, Therefore, Thomas instructed Schofield that, if the Confederates should make any forward progress, he was to avoid a confrontation and instead move with caution toward Nashville.

As Hood's army swept into Tennessee, Cheatham's corps marched in a northerly direction toward Waynesboro, Stewart's corps headed northeast to Lawrenceburg, and Stephen D. Lee's corps worked its way north between these two columns on the Chisholm Road. Operating in advance of the infantry were Nathan Bedford Forrest's horse soldiers. As the Confederates pushed forward into Tennessee, Forrest's corps skirmished frequently with the troopers of Union cavalrymen Horace Capron, John T. Croxton, and Edward Hatch whom Schofield had deployed to retard Hood's march.

Hood's immediate goal was to place his army between Schofield at Pulaski and Thomas at Nashville. By this movement, Hood hoped to prevent Schofield from joining Thomas, then to attack an isolated Schofield and, finally, unimpeded, to advance against Thomas at Nashville.

On Sunday, November 20, General Hatch had informed Schofield that the Confederates were coming. On the 22d when the Confederate forces entered Lawrenceburg, barely 20 miles west of Pulaski, Schofield hurriedly put his troops in motion toward Duck River. Columbia is on the south bank of the east to west flowing Duck River. The race was on by the two armies for the Duck River crossings.

It was imperative that Schofield prevent the enemy from getting in his rear, thereby cutting off any chance of his uniting with Thomas in Nashville. He pushed his men hard, never stopping long enough to let the weary troops rest and, on November 24, arrived in Columbia, fortuitously just as Forrest's cavalry was attempting to seize the Duck River crossings. General Wilson, who had arrived during the retrograde, took command of the Union mounted arm and was directed to cover Schofield's left flank. He deployed most of his cavalry in and around the countryside toward Lewisburg and Shelbyville, at the same time keeping a sharp lookout for the enemy at the fords and crossings of the river upstream from Columbia. The two armies skirmished, Forrest was driven off, and Schofield immediately set up his defenses south of the city to engage Hood's forces if attacked.

Meanwhile, Brigadier General Joseph A. Cooper, commanding the First Brigade of the Second Division of the Twenty-Third Army Corps stationed at fire-gutted Johnsonville on the east bank of the Tennessee River, 50 miles west of Nashville, was ordered by General Thomas to proceed to Centerville about 25 miles northwest of Columbia to protect Schofield's right flank.

When the rest of Hood's forces approached Columbia on the morning of Saturday, November 26, Schofield, realizing he was in grave danger, withdrew his command the following evening, the 27th, to the north bank of Duck River. This retreat involved destruction of the railway and pontoon bridges, thus preventing the enemy from making use of them.

Hood did not attack Schofield at Columbia as expected. Instead, he allowed the Federal troops to slip across the river. Undaunted, Hood now put another scheme into action. Early on the 29th, leaving General Stephen D. Lee to feint with two divisions in front of Schofield on the river's south bank to divert Schofield's attention from what was happening behind him, Hood crossed Duck River with seven infantry divisions well to the east. He then moved them north through the countryside toward Spring Hill, eleven miles away. With Lee in his front and Stewart and Cheatham on his flank and rear, Schofield would be placed in a perilous situation and Hood would succeed in his objective of preventing Schofield and Thomas from joining forces at Nashville.

Schofield had assured Thomas that he would delay Hood as long as was practicable. But, in the early morning hours of the 29th, General Wilson sent messages to both Thomas and Schofield warning them that Hood's infantry was crossing Duck River upstream. The Rebel infantry had been preceded by Forrest's cavalry. Wilson advised Schofield to withdraw to Spring Hill, while he and his cavalry delayed the enemy's advance. At the same time, Schofield received peremptory orders from Thomas "to fall back from Columbia and to take up your position at Franklin, leaving a sufficient force at Spring Hill to contest the enemy's progress until you are securely posted at Franklin."[13]

Schofield hurried General Stanley with Brigadier Generals George D. Wagner's and Nathan Kimball's divisions north from Columbia along the Franklin Pike to secure Spring Hill, sending his guns and trains with them. The rest of his force remained at the river, protecting the crossings. En route to Spring Hill, Stanley detached Kimball's force, which was ordered to stand guard on the north side of Rutherford's Creek, six miles north of Columbia. Generals Stanley and Wagner had barely arrived at Spring Hill when Forrest's cavalry appeared. The two forces engaged in a minor affray. Forrest's people, repulsed by the Federals, retreated three miles north to Thompson's Station. Stanley then formed Wagner's men in a defensive stance east of the village.

In his efforts to repel Hood's army, Schofield had dispersed his troops, and the scattered divisions were now vulnerable to assault by the numerically-superior Confederate forces. Hood, as he pushed ahead on a narrow road, halted more than half of his men at Rutherford's Creek, well east of the Franklin Pike and ordered Cheatham's corps forward to assail the Spring Hill Federals.

The attack began about 3 p. m., but was neither executed properly nor made with full force—Stewart's reinforced corps had been halted earlier and was not sent to reinforce Cheatham until evening—and Wagner's division, whose skillful use of artillery fire kept the enemy at bay, was not brushed aside.

Toward sunset, Schofield, who had remained with Jacob D. Cox's Twenty-third Corps division at Duck River, started the last of his men toward Spring Hill. On reaching the Franklin Pike, the head of his column was fired upon by an enemy brigade but was able to proceed undisturbed when the attackers pulled back. Thus it was that "the whole army was safely concentrated in Spring Hill"—with one division (Thomas H. Ruger's) at Thompson's Station from where it had dislodged Forrest's cavalry—"by the early morning hours."[14] General Schofield held Spring Hill, keeping the road open to the north of the village for the withdrawal of his main column and numerous wagon trains.

13. Thomas, p. 527.
14. Horn, p. 389.

Undaunted by their failure to dislodge Wagner's division and seize the road in a grip of steel earlier in the day, the Confederates bivouacked on the hillsides and in the hollows east of the Franklin Pike, confident that they would have a second chance to rout Schofield's army in the morning.

Poor communications and misunderstood orders among the Confederate leaders at Spring Hill, compounded by an inept deployment of overwhelming number had combined to snatch victory from Hood's army. But if Confederate blunders before and shortly after sunset that day gave the Federals cause to give thanks and the Southerners reason for exasperation, how much more would the events of that night provoke agonizing retrospection among Hood and his commanders as to the glory that might have been. In the words of one of Thomas' staff officers, "A single Confederate brigade . . . planted squarely across the pike, either north or south of Spring Hill, would have effectually prevented Schofield's retreat, and daylight would have found his whole force cut off from every avenue of escape by more than twice its numbers, to assault whom would have been madness and to avoid whom would have been impossible."[15]

As a precautionary measure, Major General Edward Johnson's division of S. D. Lee's corps, which had reinforced Bate's division of Cheatham's corps, was stationed near the pike to forestall any nocturnal passage by the Federals. Despite reports of some scattered movements along the pike, and seemingly unmindful of Hoods's orders to Cheatham to "cut off anything that might be passing," the officers Cheatham subsequently assigned to reconnoiter the area sent back word that all was calm. Consequently, Johnson's division did not attack.

But the fact remains "that Schofield, apparently caught in a trap, in some unexplained fashion escaped and got away. That there was some sort of tragic bungling in the handling of the Confederate forces is inescapable. . . . Whose fault it was is a question upon which there has never been agreement, but that it was the greatest of all the lost opportunities of the Confederate armies is almost universally conceded."[16]

15. *Ibid.*
16. *Ibid.*, p. 386.

One of Hood's biographers, John P. Dyer, denounced both Hood and Cheatham for the Spring Hill fiasco. Twice it was that Cheatham unwittingly called off his troops just as their continued attacks would almost certainly have wrought havoc on the Federal army.

When nightfall came, the fighting ceased, and "the Confederate Army slept, but not even one regiment stacked its arms in the turnpike."[17] Hood, having deployed Forrest's corps north of the town, judged this force sufficient to prevent Schofield fleeing Spring Hill during the night, and allegedly shrugged off the afternoon's dreadful blunders with the comment, "It makes no difference now. General Forrest will hold the turnpike north of Spring Hill and will stop the enemy if he tries to pass toward Franklin. In the morning we will have a surrender without a fight. We can sleep quiet tonight."[18]

In truth, only one of Forrest's three divisions (Jackson's) had sufficient ammunition to even attempt to block Schofield's retreat, and one division could not hold in check Schofield's army.[19]

Schofield's retreating columns withdrew in view of Hood's sleeping forces. As they marched rapidly toward Franklin, Schofield's van under Cox encountered Ross' brigade of Jackson's division but easily broke the roadblock, thus clearing the way for the Union army.

When toward midnight, Hood was roused and told of Yankee movements along the pike (Schofield's main force, finding the road open, was brazenly "quick-stepping" it to Franklin, passing "within a hundred yards of the bivouacked Confederates."), he gave the order for attack, but imprudently settled back to sleep without first making sure that his orders were implemented. The weary Hood, who was sorely in need of respite from the often agonizing pain of old battle wounds which had previously claimed a leg and withered an arm, did not trouble to bestir himself to investigate a matter that most certainly deserved his personal attention. It was later whispered that Hood's laxity at Spring Hill might be attributable to an alcoholic stupor or too much lauda-

17. John P. Dyer, *The Gallant Hood* (Indianapolis: Bobbs-Merrill, 1950), p. 287.
18. *Ibid.*, p. 288.
19. Horn, p. 393.

num, but this is conjecture.[20]

The enigma is that while Cheatham admitted that he did indeed receive the order to attack through Hood's emissary and assistant adjutant general, Major A. P. Mason, Cheatham's admission is contradicted by Mason's testimony that he "never sent [Cheatham] the order . . . [but] fell asleep again before writing it."[21]

Apparently Hood was never informed of Mason's unpardonable lapse and was furious at Cheatham for "his failure to make the night attack." Hood and Cheatham subsequently reconciled and, according to accounts of Hood's contemporaries, Hood absolved Cheatham of blame and even went so far as to apologize for censuring him.[22]

By dawn of Wednesday, November 30, Schofield's vanguard had reached Franklin and was immediately posted in the entrenchments built by the Federals during a previous occupation. The first line of defense was established within a radius of half a mile from the junction of the Carter's Creek and Columbia pikes, southwest of the town. Schofield ordered his engineers to improve the one ford available for crossing the river, to plank the railway bridge, and to replace a burned-out highway bridge. As soon as it was practicable, the wagon trains were rushed under cover of darkness across the Big Harpeth River and on toward Nashville, protected from the enemy by General Wood's division which was posted on the high ground north of the river.

Schofield did not expect to fight at Franklin. His major concern was to get his men and trains to Nashville as quickly as possible. He had already notified his soldiers to continue the retreat toward Nashville by 6 p. m. if Hood had made no move by then. But if forced to give battle, he was prepared to take a stand. All morning long, his weary regiments had been arriving at Franklin, brigade after brigade. By noon, the last of his forces had made their appearance and three of his five infantry divisions were posted in front of the town, entrenched on a perimeter with its flanks anchored on the Big Harpeth River. Wagner's division

20. *Ibid.*
21. *Ibid.*, p. 390.
22. *Ibid.*, pp. 390-91.

was positioned on either side of the Columbia Pike, about one-half mile in front of the center of the main line of resistance.

When the Confederate camps wakened early that morning, Spring Hill had been evacuated by Schofield's army. Schofield's rear guard, Wagner's division, was already several miles away as it screened the army's retreat. Hood's rage and humiliation knew no bounds when he learned of Schofield's escape. "The best move in my career as a soldier I was thus destined to behold come to naught" was his bitter lament. As Stanley Horn concedes in his *Army of Tennessee*, Hood's overall strategy at Spring Hill was indeed "brilliant," failing only because of "amazingly poor tactical work."[23]

Cognizant of this painful irony, Hood verbally excoriated several of his senior commanders, too shaken to grasp the agonizing truth—that he and he alone was ultimately responsible for the triumphs or failures of his army.

No wonder that the morale of the leaders and soldiers of this once-proud army was less than jubilant as they hurried after Schofield, sure of nothing now except that "the chance to get between Schofield and Thomas had been irretrievably lost."[24] Such was the mood of these men that they were consumed with the single-minded desire to even the score. It was a yearning for revenge that drove them forward to Franklin that morning and into the afternoon.

There, from Winstead's Hill, about three miles south of Franklin and which, from its crest, afforded a sweeping view of the rustic Big Harpeth Valley, Hood studied the Federal fortifications through his field glasses. Then, against the sage advice of his most seasoned generals, against any reasonable hope of victory, he ordered his ill-prepared army to form for a "direct frontal attack."

Meanwhile, Schofield, still hopeful of avoiding battle with Hood until he could secure his men and trains behind the fortifications of Nashville, was communicating his uneasiness to his immediate superior:

*Franklin, November 30, 1864, 3 p. m.*

Major-General Thomas, Nashville:

23. *Ibid.*, p. 394.
24. *Ibid.*

I have just received your dispatch asking whether I can hold Hood here three days. I do not believe I can. I can doubtless hold him one day, but will hazard something in doing that. He now has a large force, probably two corps, in my front, and seems prepared to cross the river above and below. I think he can effect a crossing tomorrow in spite of all my efforts, and probably to-night, if he attempts it. A worse position than this for an inferior force could hardly be found. I will refer your question to General Wilson this evening. I think he can do very little. I have no doubt Forrest will be in my rear tomorrow, or doing some greater mischief. It appears to me that I ought to take position at Brentwood [about eight miles north of Franklin] at once. If A. J. Smith's division and the Murfreesborough garrison join me there, I ought to be able to hold Hood in check for some time. I have just learned that the enemy's cavalry [Jackson's division] is already crossing three miles . . . above. I will have lively times with my trains again.

J. M. Schofield, Major-General.[25]

In response, General Thomas directed Schofield to send his wagon trains immediately to Nashville:

*Nashville, November 30, 1864.*
Major-General Schofield, Franklin:
Your despatch of 3 p. m. is received. Send back your trains to this place at once, and hold your troops in readiness to march to Brentwood, and thence to this place as soon as your trains are fairly on the way, so disposing your force as to cover the wagon trains. Have all R. R. trains sent back immediately. Notify General Wilson of my instructions. He will govern himself accordingly. Relieve all garrisons in block-houses, and send back by railroad trains last over the road.
Acknowledge receipt.

Geo. H. Thomas,
*Major-General U. S. Vols., Commd'g.*[26]

In anticipation of needing additional men and ammunition in the morning, whatever the outcome of the 30th, Schofield telegraphed Thomas for reinforcements:

25. Jacob D. Cox, *The March to the Sea* (New York: Charles Scribner's Sons, 1883) pp. 237-38.
26. *Ibid.*, p. 238.

> Headquarters, Army of the Ohio
> *Franklin, Tenn.    November 30, 1864.*
> Major-General Geo. H. Thomas, Nashville, Tenn.:
> General — — Please send A. J. Smith's division to Brentwood
> early tomorrow morning. Also please send to Brentwood to-
> morrow morning one million rounds of infantry ammunition,
> 2,000 rounds three-inch and 1,000 rounds light twelve artillery.
> J. M. Schofield, Major-General.[27]

Although the lateness of the hour that the Confederate army arrived on the southern approaches to Franklin argued for postponing any attempt at battle that day, the volatile Hood, too impatient to wait even for all of his men or for all of his artillery to catch up, issued the orders for battle. Thus it was that "as soon as Stewart and Cheatham announced that their lines had been formed and adjusted to each other . . . at four o'clock they went forward under the declining autumn sun, their bayonets flashing, their tattered flags flying in the November breeze. In the whole history of war there was never such an imposing military spectacle as was here presented—eighteen brigades of infantry, with their cavalry support, marching in a straight line across an open field, in full view of their commanding general and of the entrenched enemy."[28]

Brave indeed were these soldiers and so inspired by the righteousness of their cause and a passion for vengeance that they pressed forward lustily and soon enveloped and routed the two brigades of Wagner's division positioned across the Columbia Pike, one-half mile in front of the Federal entrenchments. The fury of the attack sent Wagner's panic-stricken men backwards through the main works, closely pursued by the Rebels. Only by an almost superhuman counterattack was the Confederate surge blunted and in savage fighting turned back. The bitter struggle continued until long after dark. Repeated attempts to storm the works were made by the desperate Southerners, each one adding to the already grim toll of dead and wounded, and each vigorously and successfully repulsed by the defending forces.

27. *Ibid.*
28. Horn, p. 399.

When the fighting ceased that night, hours after the sun had gone down, the battlefield was strewn with Confederate dead, many of whom had intrepidly charged across an open field against a foe ensconced behind breastworks and backed by superior artillery. The Federals who had about 22,000 engaged against a Confederate force of 20,000 suffered 2,320 casualties of whom 1,104 were missing and probably taken prisoner, an additional 1,033 were wounded, and only 189 were killed.[29]

Hood's losses were staggering. His casualties amounted to 6,252, with 1,750 killed, 702 missing, and 3,800 wounded.[30] Six Confederate generals died in or as a result of the action at Franklin—Patrick R. Cleburne, States Rights Gist, Hiram B. Granbury, Otho F. Strahl, and John Adams—all killed on the battlefield. John C. Carter, mortally wounded, died ten days later. Five other generals —John C. Brown, Francis Marion Cockrell, Arthur M. Manigault, William A. Quarles, and Thomas M. Scott—suffered disabling wounds, and another general, George W. Gordon, was taken prisoner.

Schofield exulted in his report to Thomas that evening:

> *Franklin, November 30th, 7:10 p.m.*
> Major-General Thomas, Nashville:
> The enemy made a heavy and persistent attack with about two corps, commencing at 4 p.m. and lasting until after dark. He was repulsed at all points, with very heavy loss—probably 5,000 or 6,000 men. Our loss is probably not more than one-fourth that number. We have captured about 1,000 prisoners, including one brigadier general. Your despatch of this p.m. is received. I had already given the orders you direct, and am executing them.
>
> J. M. Schofield, Major-General.[31]

Thomas telegraphed his congratulations, but at the same time warned Schofield to continue to be wary of Hood.

29. *Ibid.*, pp. 403-404.
30. Thomas L. Livermore, *Numbers and Losses in the Civil War In America: 1861-1865* (Bloomington: Indiana University Press, 1957), p. 132.
31. Cox, *March to the Sea*, p. 238.

Nashville, November 30, 1864.

Major-General Schofield, Franklin:

Your telegram is just received. It is glorious news, and I congratulate you and the brave men of your command. But you must look out that the enemy does not still persist. The courier you sent to General Cooper at Widow Dean's could not reach there, and reports that he was chased by rebel cavalry on the whole route, and finally came into this place. Major General Steedman, with five thousand men, should be here in the morning. When he arrives, I will start General A. J. Smith's command and General Steedman's troops to your assistance at Brentwood.

Geo. H. Thomas,<br>Major General, U. S. Vols., Comd'g.[32]

Schofield's forces had evacuated Franklin before midnight. In his haste to rendezvous with Thomas at Nashville, Schofield abandoned his dead and seriously wounded on the battlefield. Union surgeon Charles S. Frink, with the aid of a well-organized ambulance corps, removed the ambulatory wounded. Others who could not be found in the darkness sought shelter in whatever buildings were available.

When the sun rose on that "ghastly scene," the morning of December 1, the Confederates were occupied gathering up the wounded to take to the field hospitals or to other facilities in the town. The bodies of the dead, many piled corpse upon corpse in the rifle-pits and breastworks, were buried, with the blue and gray being separately interred. Then, heedless of the terrific punishment it had so recently undergone, the battered, decimated Army of Tennessee was soon in motion for Nashville and toward its destiny.

No matter that the Confederate force "was now at great disadvantage, strategically and numerically,"[33] Hood was still confident that the phoenix of victory would rise from the ashes of his thus far disastrous Middle Tennessee campaign.

By now Schofield had crossed the Big Harpeth without further difficulty and had drawn back into the Nashville defenses. There,

32. *Ibid.*
33. Horn, p. 405.

Thomas welcomed him, and the Union army, now swelling rapidly with the promised reinforcements, prepared to meet the foe.

Two lines of defense guarded the southern approaches to Nashville. Thomas posted his combat troops in the "outer line," while he assigned to the employees of the Quartermaster's Corps the responsibility of defending the "inner line." The inner perimeter shielded the city proper, while the outer line about a mile southeast, south, and southwest of the city, was approximately seven miles in extent.

General Thomas, to guard the railroad leading from Nashville to Chattanooga, had deployed detachments at strategic points along the line at Murfreesboro, Decherd, Stevenson, Bridgeport, and Whitesides. At Murfreesboro 8,000 men under Major General Lovell H. Rousseau were posted.

Barely two weeks previously Sherman had turned his back on Thomas and had headed for the sea at Savannah, leaving Thomas with a small but rapidly growing army to face Hood while Sherman marched through Georgia, opposed only by Wheeler's cavalry and the Georgia Militia. It now became the responsibility of Thomas to defend the Tennessee heartland and to prevent Hood from crossing the Ohio River and striking eastward to unite with General Lee.

It was under these conditions and circumstances that Thomas had begun the almost superhuman exertions of organizing and refitting an army. His success in this venture depended greatly on the loyal assistance and co-operation he received from his officers and soldiers, a devotion such as had never before been exhibited during the war.

Refusing to be intimidated by the proddings he received from the authorities in Washington and by the growing impatience of General Grant, Thomas stubbornly determined to ensure that his bases of supplies and lines of communications were well-established before attacking Hood. Thomas "looked upon the lives of his soldiers as a sacred trust, not to be carelessly imperiled"; for this reason he would not be badgered into premature battle. The historian Gamaliel Bradford observed that "to fight under Thomas was like having a wall at your back or a great battery to cover you."

It has been noted that Sherman moved faster and got farther

than Thomas, because Sherman learned from Grant how to cut loose from fixed bases of supplies in the mid-stages of the war. But whereas Thomas "never lost a battle or a movement," of Sherman it could only be said that he "never won a battle or lost a campaign." Thomas stood firm, remaining calm and unyielding in the face of tremendous pressure from Washington. He waited for the most opportune moment to attack the entrenched forces of Hood and thereby succeeded in achieving one of the masterful strokes of the Civil War.

On leaving Franklin, Hood headed for Nashville where he hoped to defeat Thomas and to seize the city. On the morning of December 4, the Army of Tennessee closed to within 600 yards of Thomas' outer defenses, preceded by a colorful array of flags such as are usually displayed only in drills. Hood posted his infantry and artillery and strengthened his position. Coincidentally, Hood sent Nathan Bedford Forrest with two divisions of cavalry and a strong force of infantry to break up the Nashville & Chattanooga Railroad. Bridges were burned, track torn up, and blockhouses captured. But, when Forrest closed in on Murfreesboro on the 7th, his men were mauled by the Federals in the battle of the Cedars.

Hood did not plan to move against the overwhelming defenses that confronted him in and around the city; instead, he would lure Thomas outside his fortifications and attack him there.

While the Confederates were busy constructing their breastworks during the first week of December, 1864, Thomas, too, was caught up in the final stages of preparation for the forthcoming battle. An experienced cavalry officer, Thomas insisted that all of General Wilson's cavalry be mounted before he would move against Hood. Defying direct orders from Grant to begin the attack, Thomas, in stubborn righteousness, demurred and resumed his efforts to first properly equip his soldiers. With President Lincoln and Secretary of War Stanton badgering him, demanding immediate action from Thomas, Grant issued peremptory orders for an assault on December 6. Again, Thomas procrastinated. The condition of his army, which was not yet outfitted to his satisfaction, persuaded him that he could not fight a battle at this time with the results he desired.

Thomas' recalcitrance at Nashville almost cost him his command. With the Army of Tennessee partially investing the city, and Forrest in control of the area between Nashville and Murfreesboro, Grant was under the impression that the opposing forces there were more nearly equal than they were. Grant at once took steps to have Thomas replaced, first by General Schofield, and subsequently by Major General John A. Logan.

On Thursday, December 8, the weather at Nashville, which had been unseasonably mild for more than a week, suddenly changed. A severe winter storm poured freezing rain upon the armies. The ground was soon covered with snow and ice and the horses and men slid and sprawled upon the glassy surface. The freezing storm transformed the hills and hollows about Nashville into slopes of slippery ice, and it was humanly impossible to move an army under these adverse conditions.

Advised of this unexpected turn of events, Grant rescinded his first order to replace Thomas. But, when four days later Thomas still had not attacked despite again being ordered to do so, Grant sent General Logan to assume command at Nashville.

In September of 1864, General Logan of Illinois had been urged to take a leave of absence from Sherman's "army group" at Atlanta to go north to campaign for the Lincoln administration during the weeks immediately preceding the November presidential election. Logan left Atlanta and his beloved Fifteenth Corps before the march to the sea began. Then, before his leave of absence expired, he was called to Washington by Secretary of War Stanton to report for duty and, once there, was ordered to Nashville to relieve General Thomas who at that time was preparing for battle with Hood. Upon reaching Louisville, Kentucky, Logan was informed that Thomas was successfully holding his own against Hood's army. Logan immediately telegraphed Grant that progress was being made at Nashville and that he therefore felt it was unnecessary for him to supersede Thomas at this time. Grant concurred in this judgment and furthermore permitted Logan to return to his former command in Sherman's army, which by now had reached Savannah. It was not until some time afterwards that Thomas learned of Logan's self-sacrificing behavior.

The concern evoked in Washington by what seemed like interminable dallying on Thomas' part precipitated the following interchange which is here presented to demonstrate the depth of anxiety felt by Grant and his superiors pending the outcome of the perilous situation before Nashville. The source in every case is the *Official Records of the War of the Rebellion,* the standard multi-volumed compendium of the Civil War, set forth through the documents of leaders on both sides who participated in it. Unfortunately, it is no longer widely available in public libraries.

## No. 1

On December 1, Thomas telegraphed Chief-of-Staff Henry Halleck a terse account of the circumstances at Nashville, making it clear that his first priority was to outfit General James H. Wilson's cavalry corps before engaging Hood:

*Nashville, December 1, 1864, 9:30 p. m.*

Major-General Halleck,
       Washington, D. C.:

After General Schofield's fight [at Franklin] of yesterday, feeling convinced that the enemy very far outnumbered him, both in infantry and cavalry, I determined to retire to the fortifications around Nashville, until General Wilson can get his cavalry equipped. He has now about one-fourth the number of the enemy, and consequently is no match for him. I have two iron-clads [*Carondelet* and *Neosho*] here, with several gun-boats, and Commodore [Le Roy] Fitch assures me that Hood can neither cross the Cumberland, nor blockade it. I therefore think it best to wait here until Wilson can equip all his cavalry. If Hood attacks me here, he will be more seriously damaged than he was yesterday; if he remains until Wilson gets equipped, I can whip him, and will move against him at once. I have Murfreesborough strongly held, and therefore feel easy in regard to its safety. Chattanooga, Bridgeport, Stevenson, and Elk River bridges also have strong garrisons.

Geo. H. Thomas,
*Major-General U.S.V. Commanding.*[34]

## No. 2

The situation at Nashville was called to General Grant's atten-

34. OR, I, XLV, pt. II, p. 3.

tion by the following dispatch:

> War Department,
> *Washington, December 2, 1864, 10.30 a. m.*
> Lieutenant-General Grant,
>  City Point:
> The President feels solicitous about the disposition of General Thomas to lay in fortifications for an indefinite period "until Wilson gets equipments." This looks like the [George B.] McClellan and [William S.] Rosecrans strategy of do nothing and let the rebels raid the country. The President wishes you to consider the matter.
>
> > E. M. Stanton,
> > *Secretary of War.*[35]

## No. 3

Upon receiving Stanton's dispatch, General Grant telegraphed General Thomas:

> *City Point, Va., December 2, 1864, 11 a. m.*
> Major-General Thomas,
>  Nashville, Tenn.:
> If Hood is permitted to remain quietly about Nashville, you will lose all the [rail] road back to Chattanooga, and possibly have to abandon the line of the Tennessee. Should he attack you it is all well, but if he does not you should attack him before he fortifies. Arm and put in the trenches your quartermaster employes, citizens, etc.
>
> > U. S. Grant,
> > *Lieutenant-General.*[36]

## No. 4

Two and a half hours later, following receipt of the preceding from the War Department, a dispatch of the same meaning, but more definite, was sent by Grant to Thomas:

> *City Point, Va., December 2, 1864, 1.30 p. m.*
> Major-General Thomas,
>  Nashville, Tenn.:
> With your citizen employees armed, you can move out of

35. *Ibid.,* pp. 15-16.
36. *Ibid.,* p. 17.

Nashville with all your army and force the enemy to retire or fight upon ground of your own choosing. After the repulse of Hood at Franklin, it looks to me that instead of falling back to Nashville, we should have taken the offensive against the enemy where he was. At this distance, however, I may err as to the best method of dealing with the enemy. You will now suffer incalculable injury upon your railroads, if Hood is not speedily disposed of. Put forth, therefore, every possible exertion to attain this end. Should you get him to retreating, give him no peace.

U. S. Grant,
*Lieutenant-General.*[37]

### No. 5

Grant's impatience is evident in his two previous dispatches to Thomas received on December 2, at 11 a. m., and 1.30 p. m. They prompted Thomas to reply on the same day, giving his reasons for being cautious:

*Nashville, December 2, 1864, 10 p. m.*
(Received 1.15 a. m. 3d.)

Lieutenant-General U. S. Grant,
    City Point:
Your two telegrams of 11 a. m. and 1.30 p. m. to-day are received. At the time that Hood was whipped at Franklin, I had at this place but about 5,000 men [and two divisions] of General [A. J.] Smith's command, which added to the force under General Schofield would not have given me more than 25,000 men; besides General Schofield felt convinced that he could not hold the enemy at Franklin until 5,000 could reach him. As General Wilson's cavalry force also numbered only about one-fourth that of Forrest, I thought it best to draw the troops back to Nashville and await the arrival of the remainder of General Smith's force, and also a force of about 5,000 commanded by Major General [James] Steedman, which I had ordered up from Chattanooga.

The divisions of General Smith arrived yesterday morning, and General Steedman's troops arrived last night. I now have infantry enough to assume the offensive, if I had more cavalry,

37. *Ibid.*

305

and will take the field anyhow as soon as the remainder of General [Edward] McCook's division of cavalry reaches here, which I hope will do in two or three days. We can neither get re-enforcements or equipments at this great distance from the North very easily; and it must be remembered that my command was made up of the two weakest corps [the Fourth and Twenty-third] of General Sherman's army [group] and all the dismounted cavalry except one brigade, and the task of reorganizing and equipping has met with many delays, which have enabled Hood to take advantage of my crippled condition. I earnestly hope, however, that in a few more days I shall be able to give him a fight.

Geo. H. Thomas,
*Major-General, U. S. Volunteers, Commanding.*[38]

## No. 6

*City Point, December 5, 1864, 8 p. m.*

Major-General Thomas,
    Nashville, Tenn.:

Is there not danger of Forrest moving down the . . . [Cumberland] to where he can cross it? It seems to me whilst you should be getting up your cavalry as rapidly as possible to look after Forrest, Hood should be attacked where he is. Time strengthens him, in all probability, as much as it does you.

U. S. Grant,
*Lieutenant-General.*[39]

## No. 7

*Nashville, Tenn., December 5, 1864, 10 p. m.*

Major-General H. W. Halleck,
    Washington, D. C.:

I have been along my entire line to-day. The enemy has not advanced at all since the 3d instant. If I can perfect my arrangements I shall move against the advanced position of the enemy on the 7th instant. I have heard from Chattanooga this evening that the wires were working north as far as Murfreesborough, though I have not heard anything from General Rousseau. Prisoners we have taken yesterday and to-day report

38. *Ibid.*, pp. 17-18.
39. *Ibid.*, p. 55.

306

that Hood has to draw his supplies from the Memphis and Charleston Railroad, wagoning from Cherokee Station. If an expedition could be started from Memphis against the Mobile and Ohio Railroad, and thus cut off Hood's means of supply, he will run the risk of losing his whole army, if I am successful in pushing him back.

Geo. H. Thomas,<br>
*Major-General, U. S. Volunteers, Commanding.*[40]

No. 8

On Tuesday, December 6, General Thomas received a dispatch from General Grant with orders to attack at once, and not to wait any longer for remounting Wilson's cavalry:

*City Point, Va., December 6, 1864, 4 p. m.*

Major-General G. H. Thomas,
      Nashville, Tenn.:

Attack Hood at once, and wait no longer for a remount of your cavalry. There is great danger of delay resulting in a campaign back to the Ohio River.

U. S. Grant,<br>
*Lieutenant-General.*[41]

No. 9

It was on Monday, the 5th, that Grant first emphasized to Thomas that he should not delay his attack on Hood. In his reply, General Thomas stated that he needed three more days' time in which to mount an adequate force of cavalry to cover his flanks against Forrest's superior numbers of horse soldiers:

*Nashville, December 6, 1864, 8 p. m.*

Lieutenant-General U. S. Grant,
      City Point:

Your telegram of 6.30 p. m. December 5 is just received. As soon as I can get up a respectable force of cavalry I will march against Hood. General Wilson has parties out now pressing horses, and I hope to have some 6,000 or 8,000 cavalry

40. *Ibid.*
41. *Ibid.*

307

mounted in three days from this time. General Wilson has just left me, having received instructions to hurry the cavalry re-mount as rapidly as possible. I do not think it prudent to attack Hood with less than 6,000 cavalry to cover my flanks, because he has, under Forrest, at least 12,000. I have no doubt Forrest will attempt to cross the [Cumberland] river, but I am in hopes the gun-boats will be able to prevent him. The enemy has made no new developments to-day. [Major General John C.] Breckinridge is reported at Lebanon, Tennessee, with 6,000 men, but I cannot believe it possible. [Thomas was correct, the Breckinridge story was a wild rumor.]

Geo. H. Thomas,<br>
Major-General, U. S. Volunteers, Commanding.[42]

## No. 10

Nashville, Tenn., December 6, 1864, 9 p. m.<br>
(Received 12.25 a.m. 7th.)

Lieutenant-General U. S. Grant,
    City Point:

Your telegram of 4 p. m. this day is just received. I will make the necessary dispositions and attack Hood at once, agreeable to your orders, though I believe it will be hazardous with the small force of cavalry now at my service.

Geo. H. Thomas,<br>
Major-General, U. S. Volunteers, Commanding.[43]

## No. 11

War Department,<br>
Washington, December 7, 1864, 10.20 a. m.

Lieutenant-General Grant:

You remember that when [Frederick] Steele was relieved [as commander of the Department of Arkansas] by [Major General E. R. S.] Canby, he was ordered to Cairo [Illinois] to report to this Department. What shall be done with him? The order superseding Rosecrans [as commander of the Department of Missouri] by [Major General Grenville M.] Dodge has been issued. Thomas seems unwilling to attack because it is hazardous, if all war was anything but hazardous. If he

42. *Ibid.*
43. *Ibid.*

308

waits for Wilson to get ready, Gabriel will be blowing his last
horn.

Edwin M. Stanton.[44]

## No. 12

*Nashville, Tenn., December 7, 1864, 9 p. m.*

Major-General H. W. Halleck:

Washington, D. C.:

The enemy has not increased his force in our front. Have
sent gun-boats up the river above Carthage; one returned to-
day and reported no signs of the enemy on the river-bank from
forty miles above Carthage to this place. Captain Fitch, U. S.
Navy, started down the river yesterday with a convoy of transport steamers, but was unable to get them down, the enemy
[Brig. Gen. James R. Chalmers] having planted three batteries
on a bend of the river [opposite Bell's Mills] between this and
Clarksville. Captain Fitch was unable to silence all three of
the batteries yesterday, and will return again tomorrow morning, and, with the assistance of the [ironclad] *Cincinnati*, now
at Clarksville, I am in hopes will now be able to clear them out.
So far the enemy have not materially injured the Nashville and
Chattanooga Railroad.

Geo. H. Thomas,

*Major-General, U. S. Volunteers, Commanding.*[45]

## No. 13

*City Point, Va., December 8, 1864, 4 p. m.*

(Received 5.30 p. m.)

Major-General Halleck, Washington:

Please direct General Dodge to send all the troops he can
spare to General Thomas. With such an order he may be relied
on to send all that can properly go. They had probably better
be sent to Louisville, for I fear either Hood or Breckinridge will
get to the Ohio River. I will submit whether it is not advisable
to call on Ohio, Indiana and Illinois for 60,000 men for thirty
days. If Thomas has not struck yet, he ought to be ordered
to hand over his command to Schofield. There is no better man

44. *Ibid.,* p. 84.
45. *Ibid.,* p. 85.

to repel an attack than Thomas, but I fear he is too cautious to ever take the initiative.

U. S. Grant,
*Lieutenant-General.*[46]

## No. 14

*City Point, Va., December 8, 1864, 8.30 p. m.*
Major-General Thomas,
      Nashville, Tenn.:

Your dispatch of yesterday received. It looks to me evident the enemy are trying to cross the Cumberland River and are scattered. Why not attack at once? By all means avoid the contingency of a foot race to see which, you or Hood, can beat to the Ohio. If you think necessary, call on the Governors of States to send a force into Louisville to meet the enemy if he should cross the [Cumberland] river. You clearly never should cross except in the rear of the enemy. Now is one of the finest opportunities ever presented of destroying one of the three armies of the enemy. If destroyed, he never can replace it. Use the means at your command, and you can do this and cause a rejoicing that will sound from one end of the land to another.

U. S. Grant,
*Lieutenant-General.*[47]

## No. 15

*Nashville, Tenn. December 8, 1864, 9.30 p. m.*
Lieutenant-General Grant, City Point:

If you wish General Thomas relieved from command, give the order. No one here will, I think, interfere. The responsibility, however, will be yours, as no one here, so far as I am informed, wishes General Thomas' removal.

H. W. Halleck,
*Major-General and Chief-of-Staff*[48]

## No. 16

*Nashville, Tenn., December 8, 1864, 9.30 p. m.*

46. *Ibid.*, p. 96.
47. *Ibid.*, p. 97.
48. *Ibid.*, p. 96.

310

Major-General H. W. Halleck,
    Washington, D. C.:
No material change has been discovered in the enemy's position to-day. He attempted to advance his picket-line on the Franklin road, but was driven back. With every exertion on the part of General Wilson, he will not be able to get his force of cavalry in condition to move before Sunday [the 11th]. I have a report from the river as high up as Carthage; no body of the enemy can be seen or heard of. I also have information that there is no enemy between Carthage and Albany, Ky.

There are two iron-clads [*Carondelet* and *Neosho*] above Harpeth Shoals, on the Cumberland River, and [Rear] Admiral [S. Phillips] Lee is at Clarksville with the [ironclad] *Cincinnati*. I have requested him to patrol the river from Clarksville to Harpeth, so as to discover and effectually prevent any attempt [by] the enemy to cross below.

> Geo. H. Thomas,
> *Major-General, U. S. Volunteers, Commanding.*[49]

## No. 17

*City Point, Va., December* 8, 1864, 10 p. m.

Major-General Halleck, Washington:
Your dispatch of 9 p. m. just received. I want General Thomas reminded of the importance of immediate action. I sent him a dispatch this evening which will probably urge him on. I would not say relieve him until I hear further from him.

> U. S. Grant,
> *Lieutenant-General.*[50]

## No. 18

*Washington, D. C.,*
*December* 9, 1864, 10.30 a. m.

Major-General Thomas,
    Nashville, Tenn.:
General Grant expresses much dissatisfaction at your delay in attacking the enemy. If you wait till General Wilson mounts all his cavalry you will wait till doomsday, for the waste equals the supply. Moreover, you will soon be in the same condition

49. *Ibid.,* p. 97.
50. *Ibid.,* p. 96.

that Rosecrans was last year—with so many animals that you cannot feed them. Reports already come in of a scarcity of forage.

H. W. Halleck,
*Major-General and Chief-of-Staff.*[51]

## No. 19

*Nashville, December* 9, 1864, 11.30 p.m.
(Received 10th.)

Lieutenant-General U. S. Grant, City Point, Va.:

Your dispatch 7.30 p. m. is just received. I can only say in further explanation why I have not attacked Hood that I could not concentrate my troops and get transportation in order in shorter time than it has been done, and am satisfied I have made every effort that was possible to complete the task.

Geo. H. Thomas,
*Major-General, U. S. Volunteers, Commanding.*[52]

## No. 20

*City Point, Va., December* 9, 1864, 11 a.m.
(Received 1.45 p. m.)

Major-General Halleck,
Washington, D. C.:

Dispatch of 8 p. m. last evening from Nashville shows the enemy scattered for more than seventy miles down the river, and no attack yet made by Thomas. Please telegraph orders relieving him at once and placing Schofield in command. Thomas should be directed to turn over all orders and dispatches received since the battle of Franklin to Schofield.

U. S. Grant,
*Lieutenant-General.*[53]

## No. 21

*War Dept., Adjt. General's Office,
Washington, D. C., December* 9, 1864.

General Orders,
        No.—.

51. *Ibid.*, p. 114.
52. *Ibid.*, p. 115.
53. *Ibid.*, pp. 115-16.

In accordance with the following dispatch from Lieutenant General Grant, viz.:

Please telegraph order relieving him (General Thomas) at once and placing Schofield in command. Thomas should be directed to turn all dispatches received since the battle of Franklin to Schofield.

U. S. Grant,<br>
Lieutenant-General.

The President orders:

I. That Major-General J. M. Schofield assume command of all troops in the Departments of the Cumberland, the Ohio, and the Tennessee.

II. That Major-General George H. Thomas report to General Schofield for duty and turn over to him all orders and dispatches received by him, as specified above.

By order of the Secretary of War:

E. D. Townsend,<br>
Assistant Adjutant General.[54]

### No. 22

Nashville, Tenn., December 9, 1864, 2 p. m.

Major-General H. W. Halleck,

Washington, D. C.:

Your dispatch of 10.30 a. m. this date received. I regret that General Grant should feel dissatisfaction at my delay in attacking the enemy. I feel conscious that I have done everything in my power to prepare, and that the troops could not have been gotten ready before this, and if he should order me to be relieved I will submit without a murmur. A terrible storm of freezing rain has come on since daylight, which will render an attack impossible until it breaks.

Geo. H. Thomas,<br>
Major-General, U. S. Volunteers, Commanding.[55]

### No. 23

Nashville, December 9, 1864, 1 p. m.

Lieutenant-General U. S. Grant, City Point, Va.:

Your dispatch of 8.30 p. m. of the 8th is just received. I had

54. *Ibid.*, p. 114.
55. *Ibid.*

nearly completed my preparations to attack the enemy to-morrow morning, but a terrible storm of freezing rain has come
on to-day, which will make it impossible for our men to fight
to any advantage. I am, therefore, compelled to wait for the
storm to break and make the attack immediately after. Admiral Lee is patrolling the river above and below the city, and
I believe will be able to prevent the enemy from crossing. There
is no doubt but that Hood's forces are considerably scattered
along the river with the view of attempting a crossing, but it
has been impossible for me to organize and equip the troops
for an attack at an earlier time. Major General Halleck informs
me that you are very much dissatisfied with my delay in attacking. I can only say I have done all in my power to prepare,
and if you should deem it necessary to relieve me I shall submit
without a murmur.

Geo. H. Thomas,
*Major-General, U. S. Volunteers, Commanding.*[56]

No. 24

*Washington, December* 9, 1864, 4.10 p. m.
Lieutenant-General Grant,
    City Point, Va.:
Orders relieving General Thomas had been made out when
his telegram of this p. m. was received. If you still wish these
orders telegraphed to Nashville they will be forwarded.

H. W. Halleck,
*Major-General and Chief-of-Staff.*[57]

No. 25

*City Point, Va., December* 9, 1864, 5.30 p. m.
( Received 6 p. m. )

Major-General Halleck,
    Washington:

56. *Ibid.*, p. 115. July 1862 found Samuel Phillips Lee in command of the North
Atlantic Blockade Squadron. Then, in the summer of 1864, he was assigned
to the Mississippi Squadron patroling the Mississippi and its major tributaries
to keep them open. When General Thomas needed help in patroling the
rivers, he called upon Admiral Lee to watch the Cumberland River above
and below Nashville to prevent Hood's forces from crossing the river.
Admiral Lee was so effective in patroling the river with his gunboats that
an enemy crossing in force was impossible.
57. *Ibid.*, p. 116.

314

General Thomas had been urged in every way possible to attack the enemy, even to the giving the positive order. He did say he thought he would be able to attack on the 7th, but didn't do so, nor has he given a reason for not doing it. I am very unwilling to do injustice to an officer who has done as much good service as General Thomas has, however, and will, therefore, suspend the order relieving him until it is seen whether he will do anything.

U. S. Grant,
*Lieutenant-General.*[58]

## No. 26

*City Point, Va., December* 9, 1864, 7.30 p. m.
Major-General Thomas,
    Nashville, Tenn.:

Your dispatch of 1 p. m. received. I have as much confidence in your conducting a battle rightly as I have in any other officer; but it has seemed to me that you have been slow, and I have had no explanation of affairs to convince me otherwise. Receiving your dispatch of 2 p. m. from General Halleck, before I did the one to me, I telegraphed to suspend the order relieving you until we should hear further. I hope most sincerely that there will be no necessity of repeating the orders, and that the facts will show that you have been right all the time.

U. S. Grant,
*Lieutenant-General.*[59]

## No. 27

General Thomas meanwhile had dispatched the following message to his principal subordinates:

Headquarters Department of the Cumberland.
*December* 9, 1864.
Major-General John M. Schofield,
    Commanding Twenty-third Army Corps:
Owing to the severity of the storm raging to-day it is found necessary to postpone the operations designed for to-morrow

58. *Ibid.*
59. *Ibid.*, p. 115.

morning until the breaking up of the storm. I desire, however, that everything be put in condition to carry out the plan contemplated as soon as the weather will permit it to be done, so that we can act instantly when the storm clears away. Acknowledge receipt.

Geo. H. Thomas,
*Major-General, U. S. Volunteers, Commanding.*
(Same to Major-General A. J. Smith, commanding Detachment Army of the Tennessee; Major-General J. B. Steedman, commanding District of the Etowah; Brigadier-General Thomas J. Wood, commanding Fourth Army Corps).[60]

## No. 28

Headquarters Department of the Cumberland.
*December* 9, 1864.
Major-General John M. Schofield,
Commanding Twenty-third Army Corps:
What news have you of the position this morning, and have the enemy's lines been changed or any movement on his part been discovered?

Geo. H. Thomas,
*Major-General, U. S. Volunteers, Commanding.*
(Same to Major-General A. J. Smith, commanding Detachment Army of the Tennessee; Brigadier-General Thomas J. Wood, commanding Fourth Army Corps; Major-General James B. Steedman, commanding District of the Etowah.)[61]

## No. 29

Headquarters Department of the Cumberland.
*December* 10, 1864.
Brigadier-General Thomas J. Wood,
Commanding Fourth Army Corps:
What is the condition of the ground between the enemy's line and your own? Is it practicable for men to move about on it with facility? I would like your opinion about it.

Geo. H. Thomas,
*Major-General, U. S. Volunteers, Commanding.*[62]

60. *Ibid.*, p. 118.
61. *Ibid.*
62. *Ibid.*, p. 132.

No. 30

Headquarters Fourth Army Corps.<br>
Near Nashville, December 10, 1864, 3 p. m.

Major-General George H. Thomas,
> Commanding:

The ground between the enemy's lines and my own is covered with heavy sleet, which would make the handling of troops very difficult, if not impracticable. I am confident troops cannot move with facility. From the condition of the ground an offensive movement would necessarily be feeble, and feebleness of movement would almost certainly result in failure. I will send you, as soon as I can prepare it, a more full report of certain facts in writing, and will probably call at your headquarters this evening.

Th. J. Wood,<br>
Brigadier-General of Volunteers, Commanding.[63]

## No. 31

Here, again, we see General Grant's impatience regarding Thomas' hesitation in attacking the enemy when the surrounding countryside was covered with sleet. It is hard to believe that Grant did not realize how hazardous the terrain then was. Late in the afternoon of Sunday, December 11, Grant sent the following dispatch to General Thomas:

City Point, Va., December 11, 1864, 4 p. m.

Major-General Thomas,
> Nashville, Tenn.:

If you delay attack longer the mortifying spectacle will be witnessed of a rebel army moving for the Ohio River, and you will be forced to act, accepting such weather as you find. Let there be no further delay. Hood cannot stand even a drawn battle so far from his supplies of ordnance stores. If he retreats and you follow, he must lose his material and much of his army. I am in hopes of receiving a dispatch from you to-day announcing that you have moved. Delay no longer for weather or reenforcements.

U. S. Grant,<br>
Lieutenant-General.[64]

63. *Ibid.*, pp. 132-33.
64. *Ibid.*, p. 143.

317

No. 32

*Nashville, Tenn., December* 11, 1864, 10.30 p. m.
Lieutenant-General U. S. Grant,
    City Point:

Your dispatch of 4 p. m. this day is just received. I will obey the order as promptly as possible, however, much I may regret it, as the attack will have to be made under every disadvantage. The whole country is covered with a perfect sheet of ice and sleet, and it is with difficulty the troops are able to move about on level ground. It was my intention to attack Hood as soon as the ice melted, and would have done so yesterday had it not been for the storm.

Geo. H. Thomas,<br>
Major-General, U. S. Volunteers, Commanding.[65]

No. 33

Thomas called his principal subordinates together to consult with them relative to the imperative orders he had received from General Grant to place his army into a position for attack. This directive, they agreed, was impossible to honor until the ice "melted sufficiently to enable the men to march." On Monday, the 12th, General Thomas telegraphed General Halleck:

*Nashville, Tenn., December* 12, 1864, 10.30 p. m.
Major-General H. W. Halleck,
    Washington, D. C.:

I have the troops ready to make the attack on the enemy as soon as the sleet which now covers the ground has melted sufficiently to enable the men to march. As the whole country is now covered with a sheet of ice so hard and slippery it is utterly impossible for troops to ascend the slopes, or even move over level ground in anything like order. It has taken the entire day to place my cavalry in position, and it has only been finally effected with imminent risk and many serious accidents, resulting from the number of horses falling with their riders on the roads. Under these circumstances I believe an attack at this time would only result in a useless sacrifice of life.

Geo. H. Thomas,<br>
Major-General, U. S. Volunteers, Commanding.[66]

65. *Ibid.*
66. *Ibid.*, p. 155.

318

In spite of General Grant being continuously advised by Thomas of the impossibility of attacking Hood's forces during the inclement weather, nothing could alter Grant's opinion of the situation at Nashville. So, on December 13, General Grant ordered General Logan to Nashville to take over the command of the army under Thomas, provided Thomas had not attacked the enemy. On Thursday, the 15th, General Grant left his City Point, Virginia, headquarters for Nashville. While on their way, Grant and his party learned that the battle had started on the 15th. At that time, Logan was in Louisville and Grant in Washington, D. C.

It is evident that Grant's request for urgency in Thomas' immediate attack had reasons which were not related to the situation at Nashville. On the 14th, General Halleck had sent the following dispatch to Thomas:

No. 34

*Washington, D. C., December* 14, 1864, 12.30 p. m.
Major-General Thomas,
   Nashville:
It has been seriously apprehended that while Hood, with a part of his forces, held you in check near Nashville, he would have time to operate against other important points left only partially protected. Hence, General Grant was anxious that you should attack the rebel force in your front, and expressed great dissatisfaction that his orders had not been carried out. Moreover, so long as Hood occupies a threatening position in Tennessee, General Canby is obliged to keep large forces upon the Mississippi River, to protect its navigation and to hold Memphis, Vicksburg, etc., although General Grant had directed a part of these forces to co-operate with General Sherman. Every day's delay on your part, therefore, seriously interferes with General Grant's plans.

H. W. Halleck,<br>
*Major-General and Chief-of-Staff.*[67]

No. 35

*Nashville, Tenn., December* 14, 1864, 8 p. m.
Major-General H. W. Halleck,
   Washington, D. C.:

67. *Ibid.,* p. 180.

319

Your telegram of 12.30 p. m. to-day is received. The ice having melted away to-day, the enemy will be attacked to-morrow morning. Much as I regret the apparent delay in attacking the enemy, it could not have been done before with any reasonable hope of success.

Geo. H. Thomas,
*Major-General, U. S. Volunteers, Commanding.*[68]

The preceding dispatches were given to show how a commander may be forced to fight front and rear at one and at the same time. There can be no doubt of the sincere intentions of those in authority more than five hundred miles away. Had General Thomas, however, been rushed foolishly against Hood in obeying outside pressure, his army may have been defeated, and Hood could have continued his march toward the Ohio River. Thomas would not be pushed into a premature movement against the enemy until his preparations were completed.

Thomas was a good organizer and was called on to display this talent in integrating the various units, among them the right wing (formerly of the Sixteenth Army Corps) under the command of General Andrew J. Smith, into a powerful striking force. General Smith's troops, since the winter of 1863-64, had so often moved from one theatre of the war to another under various army commanders to meet emergencies as they occurred that they referred to themselves as the "lost tribes of Israel."

In the reorganization of the cavalry, General Thomas gave full support and personal assistance to General Wilson in his efforts to collect and remount his dismounted horse soldiers and to prepare them for the field. The government remount corrals lacked sufficient horses. Apprised of Wilson's need, Secretary of War Stanton authorized General Thomas to employ force, if necessary, to impress all the suitable horses he could locate in Tennessee and Kentucky. This was rather an unusual method to pursue, but it got results. Street railways, livery stables, stage lines, private owners, farmers, and circuses were called upon. Early in December, General Thomas had received from Secretary of War Stanton authority to "seize and impress" all horses available for his cavalry.

68. *Ibid.*

No. 36

War Department,<br>
December 1 [2?], 1864, 9.30 p. m.

Major General Thomas,
  Nashville:

You are authorized to seize and impress horses and every other species of property needed for the military service in your command. You should not hesitate an hour about exercising this power at Nashville and Louisville, and wherever property can be had. Horses and equipments enough for Wilson might thus be procured immediately. Receipts may be given for the property by the seizing officer, designating the property and its value.

Edwin M. Stanton,<br>
Secretary of War.[69]

By December 10, Wilson was able to mount 12,000 cavalry, many armed with the Spencer "seven-shot" repeating carbine. The mounted arm had a vital role in the battle of Nashville, but is seldom given just recognition for its excellent performance. As Donn Piatt has written, "The part played by the cavalry in our great battles was often concealed or minimized, while the infantry operations filled the public eye and for the time dimmed the credit due the cavalry arm. The history of the war does not afford another case where the cavalry formed the determining factor, and, notwithstanding this, where it was so largely overlooked in the distribution of honors."

When General Thomas received orders from General Grant on December 11 to march out and give battle, whether or not his cavalry was mounted, he would not permit himself to be driven into action as long as his preparations were incomplete. Thomas called a meeting of his commanders to inform them of this order. The wintry sleet storm had punished the area. The country in and around Nashville was covered with snow and ice, and it was impossible for either cavalry or infantry to march or maneuver. When the senior officers assembled, the consensus was not to fight at this time under such adverse conditions.

69. *Ibid.,* p. 18.

321

General Wilson was the first to speak. It was his opinion that to operate efficiently under these conditions was out of the question, unless his horses were properly rough-shod. To prepare 10,000 horses would require several days. A victory could not be relied upon unless there was proper coordination between the cavalry and infantry. General Wood, leader of the Fourth Army Corps, formerly a cavalry officer, was next to speak. He seconded General Wilson's opinion. General Steedman also agreed. The consensus was to wait until the weather became favorable. When the meeting adjourned, Thomas asked General Wilson to remain after the others had left. Thomas then said in a tone of sincerity, "Wilson, they treat me at Washington and at Grant's headquarters as though I were a boy! They do not seem to think that I have sense enough to plan a campaign or fight a battle, but if they will only let me alone a few days, I will show them that they are mistaken. I am sure we will whip Hood and destroy his army, if we go at them under favorable instead of unfavorable conditions."[70]

The nagging and prodding that General Thomas received from General Grant's headquarters at City Point and from Washington was, as historian Piatt has written, such "as no officer in command of an army had [had] before, and Thomas was treated day by day as if he needed tutelage." General Thomas vowed he would not commit the same blunder that occurred in the earlier days of the war when the pressures exerted from Washington with "On to Richmond" sent Brigadier General Irwin McDowell to defeat at First Manassas (Bull Run).

On Wednesday, December 14, 1864, the weather moderated and the ice began to melt. A fog blanked the area the next morning. Reveille sounded at four on the morning of the 15th in the Union camps, and some 55,000 men were turned out. General Hood mustered an army of approximately 38,000. While the battle lines were formed, the generals anxiously waited for the fog to lift. About nine o'clock the signal was given, and the lines moved forward. General Wilson's Cavalry Corps was on the right; Smith's Corps on Wilson's left; General Wood (temporarily in command of the Fourth Corps), was on Smith's left; and General Steedman's "provisional detachment," District of the Eto-

70. Piatt, *Thomas*, p. 585.

wah was on the extreme left of the Union line. General Schofield's Twenty-third Corps was in reserve. Brigadier General John F. Miller was in command of the troops garrisoning Nashville, and General Donaldson commanded the quartermaster's department employees. General Wood's corps, in the center, forced the Confederates from their advanced Montgomery Hill entrenchments, while Generals Schofield, Smith, and Wilson swept back the Rebel left, and overwhelmed the Confederates of Stewart's Corps posted in Redoubts Nos. 1-5 and behind the stone wall paralleling the Hillsboro Pike. Pulling back, the Confederates took up a new position with their right anchored on Peach Orchard Hill and their left on Shy's Hill. Finally, Thomas was able to send the dispatch that Halleck and Grant were so eager to read:

### No. 37

*Nashville, Tenn., December* 15, 1864, 9 p. m.
(Received 11.25 p. m.)

Major-General H. W. Halleck,
      Washington, D. C.:

I attacked the enemy's left this morning and drove it from the river below the city, very nearly to the Franklin pike, a distance about eight miles. Have captured General Chalmers' headquarters and train, and a second train of about 20 wagons, with between 800 and 1,000 prisoners and 16 pieces of artillery. The troops behaved splendidly, all taking their share in assaulting and carrying the enemy's breastworks. I shall attack the enemy again to-morrow, if he stands to fight, and, if he retreats during the night, will pursue him, throwing a heavy cavalry force in his rear, to destroy his trains, if possible.

Geo. H. Thomas,
*Major-General, U. S. Volunteers, Commanding.*[71]

The conflict resumed the next day and decisively ended that evening. The Confederates, routed from Shy's Hill and compelled to abandon Peach Orchard Hill, fell back in confused retreat down the Franklin Pike. General Thomas with his staff on horseback approached the crest of Peach Orchard Hill. Observing the Rebel retreat, the general raised his hat in joy and

71. OR, I, XLV, pt. II, p. 194.

exclaimed, "Oh, what a grand army I have! God bless each member of it."

Units of General Hood's Army of Tennessee had fought with distinction from Fort Donelson and Shiloh to Atlanta and Nashville. They had been at Stones River, Lookout Mountain, and Missionary Ridge. But now the impact of the well-equipped Union forces was too much. Compelled to flee in confusion, Hood's army saw its combat effectiveness sapped as Thomas relentlessly hounded it beyond the Tennessee River.

During the war there had been many bloody battles—Shiloh, Atlanta, Chickamauga, Missionary Ridge, Stones River, Chancellorsville, Cold Harbor, Fredericksburg, and Gettysburg—which had cost the lives of thousands of soldiers, but none had been as conclusive as Nashville.

Had Confederate General Hood been able to capture Nashville, the Federals would have had their problems in Kentucky, because the Army of Tennessee would have been able to invade that state, thus increasing war weariness in the Northern States. Continued warfare could have caused difficulty in floating more war credits and might have reinforced the "peace at any price" movement in the North that had lost much of its strength and credibility as a result of the capture of Atlanta, Sheridan's victory at Cedar Creek, and Lincoln's reelection.

Union General Schofield gave credit to General Thomas for the decisiveness of the battle of Nashville, stating that the defeat and practical destruction of General Hood's army paved the way to the speedy termination of the war with the defeat of General Lee's Army of Northern Virginia and its surrender at Appomattox Court House. It was Thomas' victory at Nashville and not Sherman's march to the sea that settled the war in the West. This was a major contributing factor that decided the Civil War. Had the Confederates taken Nashville, Sherman would have been powerless to stop General Hood and his troops from marching on to the Ohio River and relieving pressure on General Lee at Petersburg and Richmond. Thomas' victory at Nashville was one of the most skillful and decisive of the Civil War.

## No. 38

General Thomas telegraphed his wife, informing her of his

success on the first day at Nashville:

Nashville, December 15, 1864.

Mrs. F. L. Thomas,
New York Hotel, New York:
We have whipped the enemy, taken many prisoners and considerable artillery.

Geo. H. Thomas,<br>Major-General, U. S. Volunteers, Commanding.[72]

General Thomas gave credit to his forces, not the least to General Steedman's black troops—the 1st Brigade under Colonel Thomas J. Morgan and the 2d Brigade under Colonel Charles R. Thompson, both of whom performed gallantly at the battle of Nashville. As General Thomas rode over the battlefield in the Peach Orchard Hill area, he saw their dead mingled with the bodies of the white soldiers, and he observed, "This proves the manhood of the negro."

On January 4, 1876, Watts De Peyster addressed the New-York Historical Society on "Nashville—the Decisive Battle of the Rebellion." After describing the battle, he quoted what he declared to be General Thomas' words regarding black troops, "It will take time for the regeneration of the Negro, but he will come out purified by the terrible ordeal to which he has been subjected and assume an honorable position in the ranks of humanity. That which is too weak to stand the protracted trial will perish; that which is too thoroughly infected with the poisonous influence of slavery will slough off; but the remnant will be found to be men and discharge their duties as citizens in our midst."

In striking contrast to the dispatches received before the battle, General Thomas was handed the following messages during the night of December 15, and on the morning of the 16th:

## No. 39

Washington, D. C., December 15, 1864, 11.30 p. m.

Major-General Thomas,
Nashville, Tenn.:
I was just on my way to Nashville, but receiving a dispatch

72. *Ibid.*

from [John C.] Van Duzer, detailing your splendid success of
to-day, I shall go no farther. Push the enemy now, and give
him no rest until he is entirely destroyed. Your army will
cheerfully endure many privations to break up Hood's army
and render it useless for future operations. Do not stop for
trains or supplies, but take them from the country, as the
enemy have done. Much is now expected.

U. S. Grant,
*Lieutenant-General.*[73]

## No. 40

*Washington, D. C., December* 15, 1864, 11.45 p. m.
Major-General Thomas,
    Nashville, Tenn.:
Your dispatch of this evening [No. 38] just received. I congratulate you and the army under your command for to-day's
operations, and feel a conviction that to-morrow will add more
fruits to your victory.

U. S. Grant,
*Lieutenant-General.*[74]

## No. 41

*War Department,*
*Washington, December* 15, 1864, 12 midnight.
(Sent 12.05 a.m. 16th)
Major-General Thomas,
    Nashville:
I rejoice in tendering to you and the gallant officers and
soldiers of your command the thanks of this Department for
the brilliant achievements of this day, and hope that it is the
harbinger of a decisive victory, that will crown you and your
army with honor and do much toward closing the war. We
shall give you a hundred guns in the morning.

Edwin M. Stanton,
*Secretary of War.*[75]

## No. 42

*Washington, D. C., December* 16, 1864.
(Sent 11.25 a.m.)

73. *Ibid.,* p. 195.
74. *Ibid.*
75. *Ibid.*

Major-General Thomas,
    Nashville, Tenn.:

Please accept for yourself, officers, and men the nation's thanks for your good work of yesterday. You made a magnificent beginning. A grand consummation is within your easy reach. Do not let it slip.

*A. Lincoln.*[76]

Receiving the many congratulatory telegrams, Thomas permitted himself to contemplate his victory and, characteristically, to pay tribute to the gallantry of his troops:

## No. 43

*Headquarters Department of the Cumberland.*
*Eight Miles from Nashville, December 16, 1864, 6 p. m.*
                    (Received Washington 5.30 a.m. 17th)

The President of the United States,
Honorable E. M. Stanton,
Lieut. Gen. U. S. Grant, and
Governor Andrew Johnson, Nashville:

This army thanks you for your approbation of its conduct yesterday, and to assure you that it is not misplaced. I have the honor to report that the enemy has been pressed at all points to-day on his line of retreat to the Brentwood Hills, and Brigadier-General [Edward] Hatch, of Wilson's corps of cavalry, on the right, turned the enemy's left, and captured a large number of prisoners, number not yet reported. Major-General Schofield's troops, next on the left of cavalry, carried several heights, captured many prisoners and six pieces of artillery. Brevet Major-General Smith, next on the left of Major-General Schofield, carried the salient point [Shy's Hill], of enemy's line with [William L.] McMillen's brigade, of [John] McArthur's division, capturing 16 pieces of artillery, 2 brigadier generals, and about 2,000 prisoners. Brigadier-General [Kenner] Garrard's division, of Smith's command, next on the left of McArthur's division, carried the enemy's intrenchments, capturing all the artillery and troops of the enemy on the line. Brigadier General Wood's corps, on the Franklin pike, took up the assault, carrying the enemy's intrenchments [on Peach Orchard Hill] in his front, captured 8 pieces of artillery, some-

76. *Ibid.*, p. 210.

thing over 600 prisoners, and drove the enemy within one mile of Brentwood Pass. Major General Steedman, commanding detachments of the different armies of the Military Division of the Mississippi, most nobly supported General Wood's left, and bore a most honorable part in the operations of the day.

I have ordered the pursuit to be continued in the morning at daylight, although the troops are very much fatigued. The greatest enthusiasm prevails. I must not forget to report the operations of Brigadier-General [Richard W.] Johnson, in successfully driving the enemy, with the co-operation of the gunboats, under Lieutenant Commander Fitch, from their established batteries on the Cumberland River below the city of Nashville, and of the services of Brigadier-General [John T.] Croxton's brigade, in covering and relieving our right and rear, in the operations of yesterday and to-day. Although I have no report of the number of prisoners captured by Johnson's and Croxton's commands, I know they have made a large number. I am glad to be able to state that the number of prisoners captured yesterday greatly exceeds the number reported by me last evening. The roads, fields, and intrenchments are strewn with the enemy's small-arms, abandoned in their retreat. In conclusion, I am happy to state that all this has been effected with but a very small loss to us. Our loss does not probably exceed 3,000; very few killed.

Geo. H. Thomas,<br>
Major-General, U. S. Volunteers, Commanding.[77]

## No. 44

*Washington City, December* 18, 1864, 12.20 p. m.
Major-General Thomas,
  Nashville, Tenn.:

The armies operating against Richmond [and Petersburg] have fired 200 guns in honor of your great victory. Sherman has fully established his base on Ossabaw Sound, with Savannah fully invested. I hope to be able to fire a salute to-morrow in honor of the fall of Savannah. In all your operations we hear nothing of Forrest. Great precautions should be taken to prevent him crossing the Cumberland or Tennessee below Eastport. After Hood is driven as far as it is possible to follow

77. *Ibid.,* pp. 210-11.

him, you want to reoccupy Decatur and all other abandoned
points.

U. S. Grant,<br>
*Lieutenant-General.*[78]

But, after the congratulations, the prodding from Thomas'
superiors began anew:

No. 45

*Washington, December* 21, 1864, 12 m.<br>
(Via Nashville, Tenn.)

Major-General Thomas:

Permit me, general, to urge the vast importance of a hot
pursuit of Hood's army. Every possible sacrifice should be
made, and your men for a few days will submit to any hardship and privation to accomplish the great result. If you can
capture or destroy Hood's army Sherman can entirely crush
out the rebel military force in all the Southern states. He begins
a new campaign about the 1st of January, which will have the
most important results, if Hood's army can now be used up. A
most vigorous pursuit on your part is therefore of vital importance to Sherman's plans. No sacrifice must be spared to
attain so important an object.

H. W. Halleck,<br>
*Major-General and Chief-of-Staff.*[79]

General Thomas responded to his prodders from City Point
and Washington with a crushing statement after their series of
needling telegrams:

No. 46

*Headquarters Department of the Cumberland.*<br>
*In the Field, December* 21, 1864.

Major-General H. W. Halleck,
Washington, D. C.:

Your dispatch of 12 m. this day is received. General Hood's
army is being pursued as rapidly and as vigorously as it is
possible for one army to pursue another. We cannot control
the elements, and you must remember that to resist Hood's

78. *Ibid.,* p. 248.
79. *Ibid.,* p. 295.

329

advance into Tennessee I had to reorganize and almost thoroughly equip the force now under my command. I fought the battles of the 15th and 16th instant with the troops but partially equipped, and, notwithstanding the inclemency of the weather and the partial equipment, have been enabled to drive the enemy beyond Duck River, crossing two streams [the Big Harpeth River and Rutherford's Creek] with my troops, and driving the enemy from position to position, without the aid of pontoons, and with but little transportation to bring up supplies of provisions and ammunition.

I am doing all in my power to crush Hood's army, and, if it be possible, will destroy it; but pursuing an enemy through an exhausted country, over mud roads, completely sogged with heavy rains, is no child's play, and cannot be accomplished as quickly as thought of. I hope, in urging me to push the enemy, the Department remembers that General Sherman took with him the complete organization of the Military Division of the Mississippi, well equipped in every respect as regards ammunition, supplies, and transportation, leaving me only two corps, partially stripped of their transportation to accommodate the force taken with him, to oppose the advance into Tennessee of that army which had resisted the advance of the Army of the Military Division of the Mississippi on Atlanta, from the commencement of the campaign until its close, and which is now, in addition, aided by Forrest's cavalry.

Although my progress may appear slow, I feel assured that Hood's army can be driven from Tennessee, and eventually driven to the wall, by the force under my command; but too much must not be expected of troops which have to be reorganized, especially when they have the task of destroying a force in a winter's campaign which was able to make an obstinate resistance to twice its numbers in spring and summer. In conclusion, I can safely state that the army is willing to submit to any sacrifice to oust Hood's army, or to strike any other blow which would contribute to the destruction of the rebellion.

Geo. H. Thomas,<br>
*Major-General.*[80]

The following day Thomas received two dispatches of congratu-

80. *Ibid.*, pp. 295-96.

lations, one from Secretary Stanton and the other from General Grant:

No. 47

*City Point, Va., December 22, 1864.*

Major-General Thomas,
      Nashville, Tenn.:

You have the congratulations of the public for the energy with which you are pushing Hood. I hope you will succeed in reaching his pontoon bridge at Tuscumbia before he gets there. Should you do it, it looks to me that Hood is cut off. If you succeed in destroying Hood's army, there will be but one army [the Army of Northern Virginia] left to the so-called Confederacy capable of doing us harm. I will take care of that and try to draw the sting from it, so that in the spring we shall have easy sailing. You now have a big opportunity, which I know you are availing yourself of. Let us push and do all we can before the enemy can derive benefit either from the raising of Negro troops or the concentration of white troops now in the field.

U. S. Grant,<br>*Lieutenant-General.*[81]

No. 48

*War Department,*<br>*Washington, December 22, 1864, 9 p. m.*

Major-General Thomas,
      In the Field:

I have seen to-day General Halleck's dispatch of yesterday and your reply. It is proper for me to assure you that this Department has the most unbounded confidence in your skill, vigor, and determination to employ to the best advantage all the means in your power to pursue and destroy the enemy. No Department could be inspired with more profound admiration and thankfulness for the great deeds you have already performed, or more confiding faith that human effort could accomplish no more than will be done by you and the gallant officers and soldiers of your command.

Edwin M. Stanton,<br>*Secretary of War.*[82]

81. *Ibid.,* p. 307.
82. *Ibid.*

331

To this General Thomas replied with deep appreciation for a friendly compliment that had come down from one in authority:

### No. 49

*Columbia, Tenn., December 23, 1864, 8 p. m.*
(Received 1 a. m. 25th)

Honorable E. M. Stanton,
Secretary of War, Washington, D. C.:

Your two dispatches [only one reproduced above] of 9 p. m. 22d instant are received. I am profoundly thankful for the hearty expression of your confidence in my determination and desire to do all in my power to destroy the enemy and put down the rebellion, and, in the name of this army, I thank you for the complimentary notice you have taken of all connected with it for the deeds of valor they have performed. I will forward the list of meritorious officers to-morrow or next day.

Geo. H. Thomas,
*Major-General, U. S. Volunteers, Commanding.*[83]

General Thomas, on the conclusion of the campaign, issued an order commending his troops. It read:

### No. 50

*Hdqrs. Dept. of the Cumberland.*
*Pulaski, Tenn., December 29, 1864.*

General Orders,
No. 169.

Soldiers: The major-general commanding announces to you that the rear guard of the flying and dispirited enemy was driven across the Tennessee River on the night of the 27th instant. The impassable state of the roads and consequently impossibility to supply the army compels a closing of the campaign for the present.

Although short, it has been brilliant in its achievements and unsurpassed in its results by any other of this war, and is one of which all who participated therein may be justly proud. That veteran rebel army which, though driven from position

83. *Ibid.*, p. 319.

to position, opposed a stubborn resistance to much superior numbers during the whole of the Atlanta campaign, taking advantage of the absence of the largest portion of the army which had been opposed to it in Georgia, invaded Tennessee, buoyant with hope, expecting Nashville, Murfreesborough, and the whole of Tennessee and Kentucky to fall into its power an easy prey, and scarcely fixing a limit to its conquests, after having received the most terrible check at Franklin, on the 30th of November, that any army has received during this war, and later met [on December 7] with a signal repulse from the brave garrison of Murfreesborough in its attempt to capture that place, was finally attacked at Nashville, and although your forces were inferior to it in numbers, it was hurled back from the coveted prize upon which it had only been permitted to look from a distance, and finally sent flying, dismayed and dis-ordered, whence it came, impelled by the instinct of self-preservation, and thinking only how it could relieve itself for short intervals from your persistent and harrassing pursuit, by burning the bridges over the swollen streams as it passed them, until finally it had placed the broad waters of the Tennessee River between you and its shattered, diminished, and dis-comfited columns, leaving its artillery and battle-flags in your victorious hands, lasting trophies of your noble daring and lasting mementoes of the enemy's disgrace and defeat.

You have diminished the forces of the rebel army, since it crossed the Tennessee River to invade the State, at the least estimate, 15,000 men, among whom were killed, wounded, or captured 18 general officers.

Your captures from the enemy, as far as reported, amount to 68 pieces of artillery, 10,000 prisoners, as many stands of small-arms, several thousand of which have been gathered in, and the remainder strew the route of the enemy's retreat, and between 30 and 40 flags, besides compelling him to destroy much ammunition and abandon many wagons, and, unless he is mad, he must forever relinquish all hope of bringing Ten-nessee again within the lines of the accursed rebellion.

A short time will now be given you to prepare to continue the work so nobly begun.

By command of Major-General Thomas:

Wm. D. Whipple,<br>Assistant Adjutant General.[84]

84. OR, I, XLV, pt. I, pp. 50-51.

Then, on January 20, 1865, General Thomas submitted a report detailing military operations for which he was responsible during the preceding nine weeks. It read:

Headquarters Department of the Cumberland.<br>
Eastport, Miss., January 20,1865.

Colonel:

On the 12th of November communication with General Sherman was severed, the last dispatch from him leaving Cartersville, Ga., at 2.25 p. m. on that date. He had started on his great expedition from Atlanta to the Seaboard, leaving me to guard Tennessee or to pursue the enemy if he followed the commanding general's column. It was therefore with considerable anxiety that we watched the forces at Florence, to discover what course they would pursue with regard to General Sherman's movements, determining thereby whether the troops under my command, numbering less than half those under Hood, were to act on the defensive in Tennessee, or take the offensive in Alabama.

The enemy's position at Florence remained unchanged up to the 17th of November, when he moved Cheatham's corps to the north side of the river, with Stewart's corps preparing to follow. The same day part of the enemy's infantry, said to be Lee's corps, moved up the Lawrenceburg road to Bough's Mill, on Shoal Creek, skirmishing at that point with Hatch's cavalry, and then fell back a short distance to some bluffs, where it went into camp.

The possibility of Hood's forces following General Sherman was now at an end, and I quietly took measures to act on the defensive. Two divisions of infantry, under Maj. Gen. A. J. Smith, were reported on their way to join me, from Missouri, which, with several one-year regiments then arriving in the department, and detachments collected from points of minor importance, would swell my command, when concentrated, to an army nearly as large as that of the enemy. Had the enemy delayed his advance a week or ten days longer, I would have been ready to meet him at some point south of Duck River, but Hood commenced his advance on the 19th [On the 20th, S. D. Lee's corps marched and on the 21st Hood followed with his other two infantry corps.] moving on parallel roads from

Florence toward Waynesborough, and shelled Hatch's cavalry out of Lawrenceburg on the 22d. My only resource then was to retire slowly toward my re-enforcements, delaying the enemy's progress as much as possible, to gain time for re-enforcements to arrive and concentrate.

General Schofield commenced removing the public property from Pulaski preparatory to falling back toward Columbia. Two divisions . . . [Wagner's of the Fourth Corps and Cox's of the Twenty-third Corps] had already reached Lynnville, a point fifteen miles north of Pulaski, to cover the passage of the wagons and protect the [Tennessee & Alabama] railroad. Capron's brigade of cavalry was at Mount Pleasant, covering the approach to Columbia from that direction; and, in addition to the regular garrison, there was at Columbia a brigade [Strickland's] of Ruger's division, Twenty-third Army Corps. I directed the two remaining brigades of Ruger's division, then at Johnsonville, to move—one [Moore's] by railroad around through Nashville to Columbia, the other [Cooper's] by road via Waverly to Centerville—and occupy the crossings of Duck River near Columbia, Williamsport, Gordon's Ferry, and Centerville.

Since the departure of General Sherman about 7,000 men belonging to his column had collected at Chattanooga, comprising convalescents returning to their commands and men returning from furlough. These men had been organized into brigades, to be made available at such points as they might be needed. My command had also been re-enforced by twenty new one-year regiments, most of which, however, were absorbed in replacing old regiments whose terms of service had expired.

On the 23d, in accordance with directions previous given him, General [Robert S.] Granger commenced withdrawing the garrisons from Athens, Decatur, and Huntsville, Ala., and moved off toward Stevenson, sending five new regiments of that force to Murfreesborough, and retaining at Stevenson the original troops of his command. This movement was rapidly made by railroad, without opposition on the part of the enemy. That same night General Schofield evacuated Pulaski and moved toward Columbia, reporting himself in position at that place on the 24th. The commanding officer at Johnsonville [Brigadier General William D. Whipple] was directed to evacuate that post, after removing all public property, and retire to Fort Donelson, on the Cumberland, and thence to Clarksville. During the 24th and 25th the enemy skirmished with General Schofield's troops at Columbia, but showed nothing but dismounted cavalry until the morning of the 26th, when his infantry came up and pressed our line strongly during that day and the 27th, but without assaulting. As the enemy's movements showed an undoubted intention to cross above or below the town, General Schofield withdrew to the north bank of Duck River during the night of the 27th and took up a new position, where the command remained during the 28th, undisturbed. Two divisions of the Twenty-third Corps [Cox's and Ruger's] were placed in line in front of the town, holding all the crossings in its vicinity, while Stanley's corps, posted in reserve on the Franklin pike, was held in readiness to repel any vigorous attempt the enemy should make to force a crossing; the cavalry, under command of Brevet Major-General Wilson, held the crossings above those guarded by the infantry.

About 2 a. m. on the 29th the enemy [Forrest's cavalry having crossed Duck River at Huey's Mills on the afternoon of the 28th] succeeded in pressing back General Wilson's cavalry, and effected a crossing on the Lewisburg pike; at a later hour part of his infantry crossed at Huey's Mills, six miles above Columbia. Communication with the cavalry having been interrupted and the line of retreat toward Franklin being threatened, General Schofield made preparations to withdraw to Franklin. General Stanley, with one division of infantry [Wagner's] was sent to Spring Hill, about fifteen miles north of Columbia, to cover the trains and hold the road open for the passage of the main force, and dispositions were made preparatory to a withdrawal and to meet any attack coming from the direction of Huey's Mills. General Stanley reached Spring Hill just in time to drive off the enemy's cavalry [part of Forrest's command] and save the trains; but later he was attacked by the enemy's infantry [Cheatham's corps] and cavalry combined, who engaged him heavily and nearly succeeded in dislodging him from the position, the engagement lasting until dark.

Although not attacked from the direction of Huey's Mills, General Schofield was busily occupied all day at Columbia resisting the enemy's attempts to cross Duck River, which he successfully accomplished, repulsing the enemy many times, with heavy loss. Giving directions for the withdrawal of the troops as soon as covered by the darkness, at a late hour in the afternoon General Schofield, with Ruger's division, started to the relief of General Stanley, at Spring Hill, and when near that place he came upon the enemy's cavalry, but they were easily driven off. At Spring Hill the enemy was found bivouacking within 800 yards of the road. Posting a brigade to hold the pike at this point, General Schofield, with Ruger's division, pushed on to Thompson's Station, three miles beyond, where he found the enemy's camp-fires still burning, a cavalry force [Ross' Texas Brigade] having occupied the place at dark, but had disappeared on the arrival of our troops. General Ruger then quietly took possession of the cross-roads.

The withdrawal of the main force from in front of Columbia was safely effected after dark on the 29th; Spring Hill was passed without molestation about midnight, and making a night march of twenty-five miles, the whole command got into position at Franklin at an early hour on the morning of the 30th; the cavalry moved on the Lewisburg pike, on the right or east of the infantry.

At Franklin General Schofield formed line of battle on the southern edge of the town to await the coming of the enemy, and in the meanwhile hastened the crossing of the trains to the north of [Big] Harpeth River.

On the evacuation of Columbia orders were sent to Major-General [Robert S.] Milroy, at Tullahoma, to abandon that post and retire to Murfreesborough, joining forces with General Rousseau at the latter place. General Milroy was instructed, however, to maintain the garrison in the block-house at Elk River bridge. Nashville was placed in a state of defense and the fortifications manned by the garrison, re-enforced by a volunteer force, which had been previously organized into a division, under Bvt. Brig. Gen. J. L. Donaldson, from the employees of the quartermaster's and commissary departments. This latter force, aided by railroad employees, the whole under the direction of Brigadier-General Tower, worked assiduously to construct additional defenses. Major-General Steedman, with a command numbering 5,000 composed of detachments belonging to General Sherman's column, left behind at Chattanooga (of which mention has heretofore been made), and also . . . [two brigades] of colored troops, started from Chattanooga by rail on the 29th of November, and reached Cowan on the morning of the 30th, where orders were sent him to proceed direct to Nashville. At an early hour on the morning of the 30th the advance of Maj. Gen. A. J. Smith's command reached Nashville by transports from Saint Louis. My infantry force was now nearly equal to that of the enemy, although he still outnumbered me very greatly in effective cavalry; but as soon as a few thousand of the latter arm could be mounted I should be in a condition to take the field offensively and dispute the possession of Tennessee with Hood's army.

The enemy followed closely after General Schofield's rear guard in the retreat to Franklin, and upon coming up with the main force, formed rapidly and advanced to assault our works, repeating attack after attack during the entire afternoon, and as late as 10 p. m. his efforts to break our line were continued. General Schofield's position was excellently chosen, with both flanks resting upon the [Big Harpeth] river, and the men firmly held their ground against an overwhelming enemy, who was repulsed in every assault along the whole line. Our loss, as given by General Schofield in his report transmitted herewith (and to which I respectfully refer), is, 189 killed, 1,033 wounded, and 1,104 missing, making an aggregate of 2,326. We captured and sent to Nashville 702 prisoners, including 1 general officer [George W. Gordon] and 33 stand of colors. Maj. Gen. D. S. Stanley, commanding Fourth Corps, was severely wounded at Franklin whilst engaged in rallying a portion of his command [two of Wagner's brigades] which had been temporarily overpowered by an overwhelming attack of the enemy.

At the time of the battle the enemy's loss was known to be severe, and was estimated at 5,000. The exact figures were only obtained, however, on the reoccupation of Franklin by our forces, after the battles of December 15 and 16, at Brentwood Hills, near Nashville, and are given as follows: Buried upon the field, 1,750; disabled and placed in hospital at Franklin, 3,800, which with the 702 prisoners already reported, makes an aggregate loss to Hood's army of 6,252, among whom were 6 general officers killed, 6 wounded, and 1 captured. The important results of the signal victory cannot be too highly appreciated, for it not only seriously checked the enemy's advance, and gave General Schofield time to remove his troops and all his property to Nashville, but it also caused deep depression among the men of Hood's army, making them doubly cautious in their subsequent movements.

Not willing to risk a renewal of the battle on the morrow, and having accomplished the object of the day's operations, viz, to cover the withdrawal of his trains, General Schofield, by my advice and direction, fell back during the night to Nashville, in front of which city line of battle was formed by noon of the 1st of December, on the heights immediately surrounding Nashville, with Maj. Gen. A. J. Smith's command occupying the right, his right resting on the Cumberland River, below the city; the Fourth Corps (Brig. Gen. T. J. Wood temporarily in command) in the center; and General Schofield's troops (Twenty-third Army Corps) on the left, extending to Nolensville pike. The cavalry, under General Wilson, was directed to take post on the left of General Schofield, which would make secure the interval between his left and the [Cumberland] river above the city.

General Steedman's troops reached Nashville about dark on the evening of the 1st of December, taking up a position about a mile in advance of the left center of the main line, and on the left of the Nolensville pike. This position being regarded as too much exposed, was changed on the 3d, when, the cavalry having been directed to take post on the north side of the [Cumberland] river at Edgefield, General Steedman occupied the space on the left of the line vacated by its withdrawal. During the afternoon of the 2d the enemy's cavalry, in small parties, engaged our skirmishers, but it was only on the afternoon of the 3d that his infantry made its appearance, when, crowding in our skirmishers, he commenced to establish his main line, which, on the morning of the 4th, we found he had succeeded in doing, with his salient on the summit of Montgomery Hill, within 600 yards of our center, his main line occupying the high ground on the southeast side of Brown's Creek, and extending from the Nolensville pike—his extreme right—across the Franklin and Granny White pikes, in a westerly direction, to the hills south and southwest of Richland Creek, and down that creek to the Hillsborough pike, with cavalry extending from both his flanks to the river. Artillery was opened on him from several points on the line, without eliciting any response.

The block-house  at the [Nashville & Chattanooga] railroad

crossing of Overall's Creek, five miles north of Murfreesborough, was attacked by [William] Bate's division, of Cheatham's corps, on the 4th, but held out until assistance reached
it from the garrison at Murfreesborough. The enemy used
artillery to reduce the block-house, but although seventy-four
shots were fired at it, no material injury was done. General
Milroy coming up with three regiments of infantry, four companies of the Thirteenth Indiana Cavalry, and a section of
artillery, attacked the enemy and drove him off. During the
5th, 6th, and 7th Bate's division, re-enforced by a division
[Sears' brigade of Stewart's corps and Palmer's brigade from
Lee's corps] . . . and 2,500 of Forrest's cavalry, demonstrated
heavily against Fortress Rosecrans, at Murfreesborough, garrisoned by about 8,000 men, under command of General Rousseau. The enemy showing an unwillingness to make a direct
assault, General Milroy, with seven regiments of infantry, was
sent out on the . . . [7th] to engage him. He was found a short
distance from the place on the Wilkinson pike, posted behind
rail breast-works, was attacked and routed [in a fight known
as the battle of the Cedars], our troops capturing 207 prisoners and two guns, with a loss of 30 killed and 175 wounded. On
the same day Buford's cavalry entered the town of Murfreesborough, after having shelled it vigorously, but he was speedily
driven out by a regiment of infantry and a section of artillery.

On retiring from before Murfreesborough the enemy's cavalry
moved northward to Lebanon and along the bank of the Cumberland in that vicinity, threatening to cross to the north side
of the river and interrupt our railroad communication with
Louisville, at that time our only source of supplies, the enemy
[Chalmers' division] having blockaded the river below Nashville by batteries along the shore. The Navy Department was
requested to patrol the Cumberland above and below Nashville
with the gun-boats then in the river, to prevent the enemy from
crossing, which request was cordially and effectually complied
with by Lieut. Commander Le Roy Fitch, commanding
Eleventh Division, Mississippi Squadron. At the same time
General Wilson sent a cavalry force [J. H. Hammond's brigade]
to Gallatin to guard the country in that vicinity.

The position of Hood's army around Nashville remained unchanged, and, with the exception of occasional picket-firing,
nothing of importance occurred from the 3d to the 15th of
December. In the meanwhile I was preparing to take the

offensive without delay; the cavalry was being remounted, under the direction of General Wilson, as rapidly as possible, and new transportation furnished where it was required.

During these operations in Middle Tennessee the enemy, under [John C.] Breckinridge, [Basil] Duke, and [John] Vaughn, was operating in the eastern portion of the state against Generals [Jacob] Ammen and [Alvan C.] Gillem. On the 13th of November, at midnight, Breckinridge, with a force estimated at 3,000, attacked General Gillem near Morristown, routing him and capturing his artillery, besides taking several hundred prisoners; the remainder of the command, about 1,000 in number, escaped to Strawberry Plains, and thence to Knoxville. General Gillem's force consisted of 1,500 men, comprising three regiments of Tennessee cavalry, and six guns, belonging formerly to the Fourth Division of Cavalry, Army of the Cumberland, but had been detached from my command at the insistance of Governor Andrew Johnson, and were then operating independently under Brigadier-General Gillem. From a want of co-operation between the officers directly under my control and General Gillem may be attributed, in a great measure, the cause of the latter's misfortune.

Following up his success, Breckinridge continued moving southward through Strawberry Plains to the immediate vicinity of Knoxville, but on the 18th withdrew as rapidly as he had advanced. General Ammen's troops, re-enforced by 1,500 men from Chattanooga, reoccupied Strawberry Plains on that day.

About that period Major-General [George] Stoneman (left at Louisville by General Schofield to take charge of the Department of the Ohio during his absence with the army in the field) started for Knoxville, to take general direction of affairs in that section, having previously ordered Brevet Major-General [Stephen G.] Burbridge to march with all his available force in Kentucky, by way of Cumberland Gap, to Gillem's relief. On his way through Nashville General Stoneman received instructions from me to concentrate as large a force as he could get in East Tennessee against Breckinridge, and either destroy his force or drive it into Virginia, and, if possible, destroy the salt-works at Saltville and the [Virginia & Tennessee] railroad from the Tennessee line as far into Virginia as he could go without endangering his command.

November 23, General Stoneman telegraphed from Knoxville that the main force of the enemy was at New Market, eight

341

miles north of Strawberry Plains, and General Burbridge was moving on Cumberland Gap from the interior of Kentucky, his advance expecting to reach Barbourville that night. On the 6th of December, having received information from East Tennessee that Breckinridge was falling back toward Virginia, General Stoneman was again directed to pursue him, and destroy the railroad as far across the state line as possible—say, twenty-five miles.

Leaving him to carry out these instructions, I will return to the position at Nashville.

Both armies were ice-bound for a week previous to the 14th of December, when the weather moderated. Being prepared to move, I called a meeting of the corps commanders on the afternoon of that day, and having discussed the plan of attack until thoroughly understood, the following Special Field Order, No. 342, was issued:

> Paragraph IV. As soon as the state of the weather will admit of offensive operations the troops will move against the enemy's position in the following order:
>
> Maj. Gen. A. J. Smith, commanding Detachment of the Army of the Tennessee, after forming his troops on and near the Hardin Pike, in front of his present position, will make a vigorous assault on the enemy's left.
>
> Major-General Wilson, commanding the Cavalry Corps, Military Division of the Mississippi, with three divisions, will move on and support General Smith's right, assisting, as far as possible, in carrying the left of the enemy's position, and be in readiness to throw his force upon the enemy the moment a favorable opportunity occurs. Major-General Wilson will also send one division on the Charlotte pike to clear that road of the enemy and observe in the direction of Bell's Landing, to protect our right rear until the enemy's position is fairly turned, when it will rejoin the main force.
>
> Brig. Gen. T. J. Wood, commanding the Fourth Army Corps, after leaving a strong skirmish line in his works from Laurens' Hill to his extreme right, will form the remainder of the Fourth Corps on the Hillsborough pike, to support General Smith's left, and

operate on the left and rear of the enemy's advanced position on . . . Montgomery Hill.

Major-General Schofield, commanding Twenty-third Army Corps, will replace Brigadier-General [Nathan] Kimball's division, of the Fourth Corps, with his troops, and occupy the trenches from Fort Negley to Laurens' Hill with a strong skirmish line. He will move with the remainder of his force in front of the works and co-operate with General Wood, protecting the latter's left flank against an attack by the enemy.

Major-General Steedman, commanding District of the Etowah, will occupy the interior line in rear of his present position, stretching from the reservoir on the Cumberland River to Fort Negley, with a strong skirmish line, and mass the remainder of his force in its present position, to act according to the exigencies which may arise during these operations.

Brigadier-General [John F.] Miller, with the troops forming the garrison of Nashville, will occupy the interior line from the battery on Hill 210 to the extreme right, including the inclosed work on the Hyde's Ferry road.

The quartermaster's troops, under command of Brigadier-General Donaldson, will, if necessary, be posted on the interior line from Fort Morton to the battery on Hill 210.

The troops occupying the interior line will be under the direction of Major-General Steedman, who is charged with the immediate defense of Nashville during the operations around the city.

Should the weather permit the troops will be formed (in time) to commence operations at 6 a. m. on the 15th, or as soon thereafter as practicable.

On the morning of the 15th of December, the weather being favorable, the army was formed and ready at an early hour to carry out the plan of battle promulgated in the special field order of the 14th. The formation of the troops was partially concealed from the enemy by the broken nature of the ground, as also by a dense fog, which only lifted toward noon. The enemy was apparently totally unaware of any intention on our part to attack his position, and more especially did he seem not to expect any movement against his left flank.

To divert his attention still further from our real intentions, Major-General Steedman had, on the evening of the 14th, received orders to make a heavy demonstration with his command against the enemy's right, east of the Nolensville pike, which he accomplished with great success and some loss, succeeding, however, in attracting the enemy's attention to that part of his lines, and inducing him to draw re-enforcements from toward his center and left. At soon as General Steedman had completed his movement, the commands of Generals Smith and Wilson moved out along the Hardin pike and commenced the grand movement of the day, by wheeling to the left and advancing against the enemy's position across the Hardin and Hillsborough pikes. A division of cavalry [Johnson's] was sent at the same time to look after a battery of the enemy's on the Cumberland River at Bell's Landing, eight miles below Nashville. General Johnson did not get into position until late in the afternoon, when, in conjunction with the gun-boats under Lieut. Commander Le Roy Fitch, the enemy's battery was engaged until after night-fall, and the place was found evacuated on the morning of the 16th.

The remainder of General Wilson's command, Hatch's division leading and [Joseph F.] Knipe in reserve, moving on the right of General A. J. Smith's troops, first struck the enemy along Richland Creek, near Hardin's house, and drove him back rapidly, capturing a number of prisoners, wagons, etc., and continuing to advance, whilst slightly swinging to the left, came upon a redoubt [No. 5] containing four guns, which was splendidly carried by assault, at 1 p. m., by a portion of Hatch's division, dismounted, and the captured guns turned upon the enemy. A second redoubt, [No. 4] stronger than the first, was next assailed and carried by the same troops that captured the first position, taking 4 more guns and about 300 prisoners. The infantry, [John] McArthur's division, of General A. J. Smith's command, on the left of the cavalry, participated in both of the assaults; and, indeed, the dismounted cavalry seemed to vie with the infantry who should first gain the works; as they reached the position nearly simultaneously, both lay claim to the artillery and prisoners captured.

Finding General Smith had not taken as much distance to the right as I expected he would have done, I directed General Schofield to move his command (the Twenty-third Corps)

from the position in reserve to which it had been assigned
over to the right of General Smith, enabling the cavalry thereby
to operate more freely on the enemy's rear. This was rapidly
accomplished by General Schofield, and his troops participated in the closing operations of the day.

The Fourth Corps, Brig. Gen. T. J. Wood commanding,
formed on the left of General A. J. Smith's command, and as
soon as the latter had struck the enemy's flank, assaulted . . .
Montgomery Hill, Hood's most advanced position, at 1 p. m.,
which was most gallantly executed by the . . . [Second] Brigade
. . . [General Samuel Beatty's] Division, Col. P. Sidney Post,
Fifty-ninth Illinois, commanding, capturing a considerable
number of prisoners. Connecting with the left of Smith's troops
(Brigadier-General Garrard's division), the Fourth Corps continued to advance, and carried by assault the enemy's entire
line in its front and captured several pieces of artillery, about
500 prisoners, some stands of colors, and other material. The
enemy was driven out of his original line of works and forced
back to a new position along the base of Harpeth Hills, still
holding his line of retreat to Franklin—by the main pike,
through Brentwood, and by the Granny White pike. Our line
at nightfall was readjusted, running parallel to and east of the
Hillsborough pike—Schofield's command on the right, Smith's
in the center, and Wood's on the left, with the cavalry on the
right of Schofield; Steedman holding the position he had gained
early in the morning.

The total result of the day's operations was the capture of
sixteen pieces of artillery and 1,200 prisoners, besides several
hundred stand of small-arms and about forty wagons. The
enemy had been forced back at all points, with heavy loss; our
casualties were unusually light. The behavior of the troops was
unsurpassed for steadiness and alacrity in every movement, and
the original plan of battle, with but few alterations, strictly
adhered to.

The whole command bivouacked in line of battle during the
night on the ground occupied at dark, whilst preparations were
made to renew the battle at an early hour on the morrow.

At 6 a. m. on the 16th Wood's corps pressed back the enemy's
skirmishers across the Franklin pike to the eastward of it, and
then swinging slightly to the right, advanced due south from
Nashville, driving the enemy before him until he came upon
his new main line of works, constructed during the night, on

what is called Overton's Hill [Peach Orchard Hill] about five miles south of the city and east of the Franklin pike. General Steedman moved out from Nashville by the Nolensville pike, and formed his command on the left of General Wood, effectually securing the latter's left flank, and made preparations to co-operate in the operations of the day. General A. J. Smith's command moved on the right of the Fourth Corps (Wood's), and establishing connection with General Wood's right, completed the new line of battle. General Schofield's troops remained in the position taken up by them at dark on the day previous, facing eastward and toward the enemy's left flank, the line of the corps running perpendicular to General Smith's troops. General Wilson's cavalry, which had rested for the night at the six-mile post on the Hillsborough pike, was dismounted and formed on the right of Schofield's command, and by noon of the 16th had succeeded in gaining the enemy's rear, and stretched across the Granny White pike, one of his two outlets toward Franklin.

As soon as the above dispositions were completed, and having visited the different commands, I gave directions that the movement against the enemy's left flank should be continued. Our entire line approached to within 600 yards of the enemy's at all points. His center was weak, as compared with either his right, at . . . [Peach Orchard] Hill or his left, on the hills [one of which was Shy's Hill] bordering the Granny White pike; still I had hopes of gaining his rear and cutting off his retreat from Franklin.

About 3 p. m. Post's brigade, of Wood's corps, supported by [Abel D.] Streight's brigade, of the same command, was ordered by General Wood to assault . . . [Peach Orchard] Hill. This intention was communicated to General Steedman, who ordered the brigade of colored troops commanded by Colonel Morgan, Fourteenth U. S. Colored Troops, to cooperate in the movement. The ground on which the two assaulting columns formed being open and exposed to the enemy's view, he, readily perceiving our intention, drew re-enforcements from his left and center to the threatened point. This movement of troops on the part of the enemy was communicated along the line from left to right.

The assault was made, and received by the enemy with a tremendous fire of grape [sic] and canister and musketry; our men moved steadily onward up the hill until near the crest, when the reserve of the enemy rose and poured into the assaulting column a most destructive fire, causing the men first to waver and then to fall back, leaving their dead and wounded—black and white indiscriminately mingled—lying amid the abatis, the gallant Colonel Post among the wounded. General Wood readily reformed his command in the position it had previously occupied, preparatory to a renewal of the assault.

Immediately following the effort of the Fourth Corps, Generals Smith's and Schofield's commands moved against the enemy's works in their respective fronts, carrying all before them, irreparably breaking his line in a dozen places, [storming Shy's Hill] and capturing all his artillery and thousands of prisoners, among the latter . . . [three] general officers [Edward Johnson, Henry R. Jackson, and Thomas B. Smith]. Our loss was remarkably small, scarcely mentionable. All of the enemy that did escape were pursued over the tops of Brentwood and Harpeth Hills.

General Wilson's cavalry, dismounted, attacked the enemy simultaneously with Schofield and Smith, striking him in reverse, and gaining firm possession of the Granny White pike, cut off his retreat by that route.

Wood's and Steedman's troops, hearing the shouts of victory coming from the right, rushed impetuously forward, renewing the assault on . . . [Peach Orchard] Hill, and although meeting a very heavy fire, the onset was irresistible, artillery and innumerable prisoners falling into our hands. The enemy, hopelessly broken, fled in confusion through the Brentwood Pass, the Fourth Corps in a close pursuit, which was continued for several miles. when darkness closed the scene and the troops rested from their labors.

As the Fourth Corps pursued the enemy on the Franklin pike, General Wilson hastily mounted Knipe's and Hatch's divisions of his command, and directed them to pursue along the Granny White pike and endeavor to reach Franklin in advance of the enemy. After proceeding about a mile they came upon the enemy's cavalry, under Chalmers, posted across the road and behind barricades. The position was charged by the Twelfth Tennessee Cavalry, Colonel [George] Spalding commanding, and the enemy's lines broken, scattering him in all directions and capturing quite a number of prisoners, among them Brig. Gen. E. W. Rucker.

During the two days' operations there were 4,462 prisoners

captured, including 287 officers of all grades from that of major-general, 53 pieces of artillery, and thousands of small arms. The enemy abandoned on the field all his dead and wounded.

Leaving directions for the collection of the captured property and for the care of the wounded left on the battle-field, the pursuit was continued at daylight on the 17th. The Fourth Corps pushed on toward Franklin by the direct pike, whilst the cavalry moved by the Granny White pike to its intersection with the Franklin pike, and then took the advance.

Johnson's division of cavalry was sent by General Wilson direct to [the Big] Harpeth River, on the Hillsborough pike, with directions to cross and move rapidly toward Franklin. The main cavalry column, with Knipe's division in advance, came up with the enemy's rear guard strongly posted at Hollow Tree Gap, four miles north of Franklin; the position was charged in front and in flank simultaneously, and handsomely carried, capturing 413 prisoners and 3 colors. The enemy then fell back rapidly to Franklin, and endeavored to defend the crossing of [Big] Harpeth River at that place; but Johnson's division coming up from below on the south side of the stream, forced him to retire from the river-bank, and our cavalry took possession of the town, capturing the enemy's hospital, containing over 2,000 wounded, of whom about 200 were our own men.

The pursuit was immediately continued, by Wilson, toward Columbia, the enemy's rear guard slowly retiring before him to a distance of about five miles south of Franklin, where the enemy made a stand in some open fields just north of West Harpeth River, and seemed to await our coming. Deploying Knipe's division as skirmishers, with Hatch's in close support, General Wilson ordered his body guard—the Fourth U. S. Cavalry, Lieutenant [Joseph] Hedges commanding—to charge the enemy. Forming on the pike in column of fours, the gallant little command charged, with sabers drawn, breaking the enemy's center, whilst Knipe's and Hatch's men pressed back the flanks, scattering the whole command and causing them to abandon their artillery. Darkness coming on during the engagement enabled a great many to escape, and put an end to the day's operations.

The Fourth Corps, under General Wood, followed immediately in rear of the cavalry as far as [the Big] Harpeth River, where it found the bridges destroyed and too much water on the fords for infantry to cross. A trestle bridge was hastily constructed from such materials as lay at hand, but could not be made available before night-fall. General Steedman's command moved in rear of General Wood, and camped near him on the banks of the [Big] Harpeth. Generals Smith and Schofield marched their corps along the Granny White pike, and camped for the night at the intersection with the Franklin pike. The trains moved with their respective commands, carrying ten days' supplies and 100 rounds of ammunition [per man].

On the 18th the pursuit of the enemy was continued by General Wilson, who pushed on as far as Rutherford's Creek, three miles from Columbia. Wood's corps crossed to the south side of [the Big] Harpeth River and closed up with the cavalry. The enemy did not offer to make a stand during the day. On arriving at Rutherford's Creek the stream was found to be impassable on account of high water, and running a perfect torrent. A pontoon bridge, hastily constructed at Nashville during the presence of the army at that place, was on its way to the front, but the bad condition of the roads, together with the incompleteness of the train itself, had retarded its arrival. I would here remark that the splendid pontoon train properly belonging to my command, with its trained corps of pontoniers, was absent with General Sherman.

During the 19th several unsuccessful efforts were made by the advanced troops to cross Rutherford's Creek, although General Hatch succeeded in lodging a few skirmishers on the south bank. The heavy rains of the preceding few days had inundated the whole country and rendered the roads almost impassable. Smith's and Schofield's commands crossed to the south side of [the Big] Harpeth River, General Smith advancing to Spring Hill, whilst General Schofield encamped at Franklin. On the morning of the 20th General Hatch constructed a floating bridge from the debris of the old railroad bridge over Rutherford's Creek, and crossing his entire division pushed out for Columbia, but found, on reaching Duck River, the enemy had succeeded the night before in getting everything across, and had already removed his pontoon bridge; Duck River was very much swollen and impassable without a bridge. During the day General Wood improvised a foot bridge over Rutherford's Creek, at the old road bridge, and by night-fall had succeeded in crossing his infantry entire, and one or two of his batteries, and moved forward to Duck River.

The pontoon train coming up to Rutherford's Creek about noon of the 21st, a bridge was laid during the afternoon and General Smith's troops were enabled to cross. The weather had changed from dismal rain to bitter cold, very materially retarding the work in laying the bridge, as the regiment of colored troops to whom that duty was intrusted seemed to become unmanned by the cold and totally unequal to the occasion. On the completion of the bridge at Rutherford's Creek sufficient material for a bridge over Duck River was hastily pushed forward to that point, and the bridge constructed in time to enable Wood to cross late in the afternoon of the 22d and get into position on the Pulaski road, about two miles south of Columbia. The water in the river fell rapidly during the construction of the bridge, necessitating frequent alterations and causing much delay. The enemy, in his hasty retreat, had thrown into the stream several fine pieces of artillery, which were rapidly becoming uncovered, and were subsequently removed.

Notwithstanding the many delays to which the command had been subjected, I determined to continue the pursuit of Hood's shattered forces; and for this purpose decided to use General Wilson's cavalry and General Wood's corps of infantry, directing the infantry to move on the pike, whilst the cavalry marched on its either flank across the fields; the remainder of the command, Smith's and Schofield's corps, to move along more leisurely, and to be used as the occasion demanded.

Forrest and his cavalry, and such other detachments as had been sent off from his main army whilst besieging Nashville, had rejoined Hood at [Franklin and] Columbia. He had formed a powerful rear guard, made up of . . . all his organized force, Walthall [the hardcore elements from eight infantry brigades], and all his available cavalry, under Forrest. With the exception of his rear guard, his army had become a disheartened and disorganized rabble of half-armed and barefooted men, who sought every opportunity to fall out by the wayside and desert their cause to put an end to their sufferings. The rear guard, however, was undaunted and firm, and did its work bravely to the last.

During the 23d General Wilson was occupied crossing his command over Duck River, but took the advance on the 24th, supported by General Wood, and came up with the enemy just south of Lynnville, and also at Buford's Station, at both of which places the enemy made a short stand, but was speedily dislodged, with a loss in killed, wounded, and prisoners. Our advance was so rapid as to prevent the destruction of the bridges over Richland Creek. Christmas morning, the 25th, the enemy, with our cavalry at his heels, evacuated Pulaski, and was pursued toward Lamb's Ferry over an almost impracticable road and through a country devoid of subsistence for man or beast. During the afternoon [Thomas J.] Harrison's brigade found the enemy strongly intrenched at the head of a heavily wooded and deep ravine, through which ran the road, and into which Colonel Harrison drove the enemy's skirmishers; he then waited for the remainder of the cavalry to close up before attacking; but before this could be accomplished the enemy [led by Forrest], with something of his former boldness, sallied from his breast-works and drove back Harrison's skirmishers, capturing and carrying off one gun belonging to Battery I, Fourth U. S. Artillery, which was not recovered by us, notwithstanding the ground lost was almost immediately regained. By night-fall the enemy was driven from his position, with a loss of about 50 prisoners.

The cavalry had moved so rapidly as to out-distance the trains, and both men and animals were suffering greatly in consequence, although they continued uncomplainingly to pursue the enemy. General Wood's corps kept well closed up on the cavalry, camping on the night of December 25 six miles out from Pulaski, on the Lamb's Ferry road, and pursuing the same route as the cavalry, reached Lexington, Ala., thirty miles from Pulaski, on the 28th, on which date, having definitely ascertained that the enemy had made good his escape across the Tennessee at Bainbridge, I directed farther pursuit to cease. At Pulaski the enemy's hospital, containing about 200 patients, fell into our hands, and four guns were found in Richland Creek. About a mile south of . . . [Pulaski] he destroyed twenty wagons loaded with ammunition, belonging to Cheatham's corps, taking the animals belonging to the train to help pull his pontoons. The road from Pulaski to Bainbridge, and indeed back to Nashville, was strewn with abandoned wagons, limbers, small-arms, blankets, etc., showing most conclusively the disorder of the enemy's retreat.

During the foregoing operations with the advance Smith's

and Schofield's troops were in motion toward the front, General Smith's command reaching Pulaski on the 27th, whilst General Schofield was directed to remain at Columbia for the time being.

On our arrival at Franklin, on the 18th, I gave directions to General Steedman to move with his command across the country from that point to Murfreesborough, on the Chattanooga railroad, from whence he was to proceed by rail to Decatur, Ala., via Stevenson, being joined at Stevenson by Brig. Gen. R. S. Granger and the troops composing the garrisons of Huntsville, Athens, and Decatur. Taking general direction of the whole force, his instructions were to reoccupy the points in Northern Alabama evacuated at the period of Hood's advance, then cross the Tennessee with the balance of his force and threaten the enemy's railroad communications west of Florence.

General Steedman reoccupied Decatur on the 27th, and proceeded to carry out the second portion of his instructions, finding, however, that the enemy had already made good his escape to the south side of the Tennessee, and any movement on his railroad would be useless.

On announcing the result of the battles to Rear-Admiral S. P. Lee, commanding Mississippi Squadron, I requested him to send as much of his force as he could spare around to Florence, on the Tennessee River, and endeavor to prevent Hood's army from crossing at that point; which request was most cordially and promptly complied with. He arrived at Chickasaw, . . . [Ala.], on the 24th, destroyed there a rebel battery, and captured two guns with caissons at Florence Landing. He also announced the arrival at the latter place of several transports with provisions.

Immediately upon learning of the presence at Chickasaw, Miss., of the gun-boats and transports with provisions, I directed General Smith to march over from Pulaski to Clifton, via Lawrenceburg and Waynesborough, and take post at Eastport, Miss. General Smith started for his destination on December 29.

On the 30th of December I announced to the army the successful completion of the campaign, and gave directions for the disposition of the command, as follows: Smith's corps to take post at Eastport, Miss.; Wood's corps to be concentrated at Huntsville and Athens, Ala.; Schofield's corps to proceed to Dalton, Ga.; and Wilson's cavalry, after sending one division to Eastport, Miss., to concentrate balance at or near Huntsville. On reaching the several positions assigned to them the different commands were to go into winter quarters and recuperate for the spring campaign.

The above not meeting the views of the general-in-chief [U. S. Grant], and being notified by Major-General Halleck, chief of staff, U. S. Army, that it was not intended for the army in Tennessee to go into winter quarters, orders were issued on the 31st of December for Generals Schofield, Smith, and Wilson to concentrate their commands at Eastport, Miss., and that of General Wood at Huntsville, Ala., preparatory to a renewal of the campaign against the enemy in Mississippi and Alabama.

During the active operations of the main army in Middle Tennessee General Stoneman's forces in the northeastern portion of the State were also very actively engaged in operating against Breckinridge, Duke, and Vaughn. Having quietly concentrated the commands of Generals Burbridge and Gillem at Bean's Station, on the 12th of December General Stoneman started for Bristol, his advance under General Gillem striking the enemy, under Duke, at Kingsport, on the North Fork of the Holston River, killing, capturing, or dispersing the whole command. General Stoneman then sent General Burbridge to Bristol, where he came upon the enemy, under Vaughn, and skirmished with him until the remainder of the troops—Gillem's column—came up, when Burbridge was pushed on to Abingdon, with instructions to send a force to cut the [Virginia & Tennessee] railroad at some point between Saltville and Wytheville, in order to prevent re-enforcements coming from Lynchburg to the salt-works. Gillem also reached Abingdon on the 15th, the enemy under Vaughn following on a road running parallel to the one used by our forces.

Having decided merely to make a demonstration against the salt-works and to push on with the main force after Vaughn, General Gillem struck the enemy at Marion [Virginia] early on the 16th, and after completely routing him, pursued him to Wytheville, Va., capturing all his artillery and trains and 198 prisoners. Wytheville, with its stores and supplies, was destroyed, as also the extensive lead-works near the town and the railroad bridges over Reedy Creek. General Stoneman then turned his attention toward Saltville, with its important salt-works. The garrison of that place, re-enforced by [Henry L.] Giltner's, [George B.] Cosby's, and [Vincent A.] Witcher's commands and the remnant of Duke's, all under the command of Breckinridge in person, followed our troops as they moved on Wytheville, and on returning General Stoneman met them at Marion, where he made preparations to give Breckinridge battle, and disposed his command so as to effectually assault the enemy in the morning, but Breckinridge retreated during the night, and was pursued a short distance into North Carolina, our troops capturing some of his wagons and caissons.

General Stoneman then moved on Saltville with his entire command, capturing at that place 8 pieces of artillery and a large amount of ammunition of all kinds, 2 locomotives, and quite a number of horses and mules. The extensive salt-works were destroyed by breaking the kettles, filling the wells with rubbish, and burning the buildings. His work accomplished, General Stoneman returned to Knoxville, accompanied by General Gillem's command, General Burbridge's proceeding to Kentucky by way of Cumberland Gap. The country marched over was laid waste to prevent its being used again by the enemy—all mills, factories, bridges, etc., being destroyed. The command had everything to contend with as far as the weather and roads were concerned, yet the troops bore up cheerfully throughout, and made each twenty-four hours an average march of forty-two miles and a half.

The pursuit of Hood's retreating army was discontinued by my main forces on the 29th of December, on reaching the Tennessee River; however, a force of cavalry, numbering 600 men, made up from detachments of the Fifteenth Pennsylvania, Second Michigan, Tenth, Twelfth, and Thirteenth Indiana Regiments, under command of Col. William J. Palmer, Fifteenth Pennsylvania, operating with Steedman's column, started from Decatur, Ala., in the direction of Hood's line of retreat in Mississippi. The enemy's cavalry, under [Philip D.] Roddey, was met at Leighton, with whom Colonel Palmer skirmished and pressed back in small squads toward the mountains. Here it was ascertained that Hood's trains passed through Leighton on the 28th of December and moved off toward Columbus, Miss. Avoiding the enemy's cavalry, Colonel Palmer left Leighton on the 31st of December, moved rapidly via La Grange and Russellville and by the Cotton-gin road, and overtook the enemy's pontoon train, consisting of 200 wagons and 78 pontoon boats, when ten miles out from Russellville [Alabama]. This he destroyed.

Having learned of a large supply train on its way to Tuscaloosa, Colonel Palmer started on the 1st of January toward Aberdeen, Miss., with a view of cutting it off, and succeeded in surprising it about 10 p. m. on the same evening, just over the line in Mississippi. The train consisted of 110 wagons and 500 mules, the former of which were burned, and the latter sabered or shot. Returning via Toll-gate, Ala., and on the old military and Hacksburg roads, the enemy, under Roddey, [Jacob] Biffle, and [Alfred A.] Russell, was met near Russellville and along Bear Creek, whilst another force, under [Frank] Armstrong, was reported to be in pursuit of our forces. Evading the force in his front, by moving off to the right under cover of the darkness, Colonel Palmer pushed for Moulton, coming upon Russell when within twelve miles of Moulton, and near Thorn Hill attacked him unexpectedly, utterly routing him, and capturing some prisoners, besides burning five wagons. The command then proceeded to Decatur without molestation, and reached that place on the 6th of January, after a march of over 250 miles. One hundred and fifty prisoners were captured and nearly 1,000 stand of arms destroyed. Colonel Palmer's loss was 1 killed and 2 wounded.

General Hood, while investing Nashville, had sent into Kentucky a force of cavalry numbering about 800 men and two guns, under the command of Brigadier-General [Hylan B.] Lyon, with instructions to operate against our railroad communications with Louisville. McCook's division of cavalry was detached on the 14th of December and sent to Bowling Green and Franklin to protect the [Louisville & Nashville rail] road. After capturing Hopkinsville, Lyon was met by [Oscar H.] La Grange's brigade near Greensburg, and after a sharp fight was thrown into confusion, losing one gun, some prisoners, and wagons; the enemy succeeded, however, by making a wide detour via Elizabethtown and Glasgow, in reaching the Cumberland River and crossing at Burkesville, from whence General Lyon proceeded, via McMinnville and Winchester, Tenn., to Larkinsville, Ala., on the Memphis and Charleston Railroad, and attacked the little garrison at Scottsborough on the 10th of January. Lyon was here again repulsed and his command scattered, our troops pursuing him toward the Tennessee River, which, however, he, with about 200 of his men and his remaining piece of artillery, succeeded in crossing; the rest of his command scattered in squads among the mountains.

Col. W. J. Palmer, commanding Fifteenth Pennsylvania Cavalry, with 150 men, crossed the river at Paint Rock and pursued Lyon to near Red Hill, on the road from Warrenton to Tuscaloosa, at which place he surprised his camp during the night of the 14th of January, capturing Lyon himself, his one piece of artillery, and about 100 of his men, with their horses. Lyon being in bed at the time of his capture, asked his guard to permit him to dress himself, which was acceded to, when, watching his opportunity, he seized a pistol, shot the sentinel dead upon the spot, and escaped in the darkness. This was the only casualty during the expedition.

To Colonel Palmer and his command is accorded the credit of giving Hood's army the last blow of the campaign, at a distance of over 200 miles from where we first struck the enemy on the 15th of December, near Nashville.

To all of my sub-commanders—Major-Generals Schofield, Stanley, Rousseau, Steedman, Smith, and Wilson, and Brig. Gen. T. J. Wood—their officers and men, I give expression of my thanks and gratitude for their generous self-sacrifice and manly endurance under the most trying circumstances and in all instances. Too much praise cannot be accorded to an army which, hastily made up from the fragments of three separate commands, can successfully contend against a force numerically greater than itself and of more thoroughly solid organization, inflicting on it a most crushing defeat—almost an annihilation.

Receiving instructions unexpectedly from General Sherman, in September, to repair to Tennessee and assume general control of the defenses of our line of communication in the rear of the Army of the Mississippi, and not anticipating a separation from my immediate command, the greater number of my staff officers were left behind at Atlanta and did not have an opportunity to join me after General Sherman determined on making his march through Georgia, before the communications were cut. I had with me Brig. Gen. W. D. Whipple, my chief of staff; Surgeon G. E. Cooper, medical director; Capts. Henry Stone, Henry M. Cist, and Robert H. Ramsey, assistant adjutants-general; E. C. Beman, acting chief commissary; Capts. John P. Willard and S. C. Kellogg, aides-de-camp; and Lieut. M. J. Kelly, chief of couriers; all of whom rendered important services during the battles of the 15th and 16th, and during the pursuit. I cordially commend their services to favorable consideration.

There were captured from the enemy during the various actions of which the foregoing report treats, 13,189 prisoners of war, including 7 general officers and nearly 1,000 other officers of all grades, 72 pieces of serviceable artillery, and — battle flags. During the same period over 2,000 deserters from the enemy were received, to whom the oath was administered. Our own loss will not exceed 10,000 in killed, wounded, and missing.

I have the honor to transmit herewith a consolidated return of casualties . . . .

I have the honor to be, colonel, very respectfully, your obedient servant,

Geo. H. Thomas,<br>
Major-General, Commanding.

Lieut. Col. R. M. Sawyer,
 *Asst. Adjt. Gen., Military Division of the Mississippi.*

Report of casualties of the Army of the Cumberland

| Command | Killed | Wounded | Missing | Aggregate |
|---|---|---|---|---|
| Twenty-third Army Corps: | | | | |
|  Battle of Franklin | 189 | 1,033 | 1,104 | 2,326 |
|  Battle of Nashville | 9 | 154 | .... | 163 |
| Fourth Army Corps: (a) | | | | |
| Detachment Army of the Tennessee | | | | |
|  (Maj. Gen. A. J. Smith commanding: | | | | |
| Battle of Nashville | 77 | 665 | 2 | 744 |
| Cavalry Corps (Bvt. Maj. Gen. J. H. Wilson commanding): | | | | |
| Battles of Franklin & Nashville | 88 | 437 | 91 | 616 |
|  Total | 363 | 2,289 | 1,197 | 3,849 |

(a) No report received.

Southard Hoffman,<br>
Assistant Adjutant-General[85]

85. *Ibid.*, pp. 32-47.

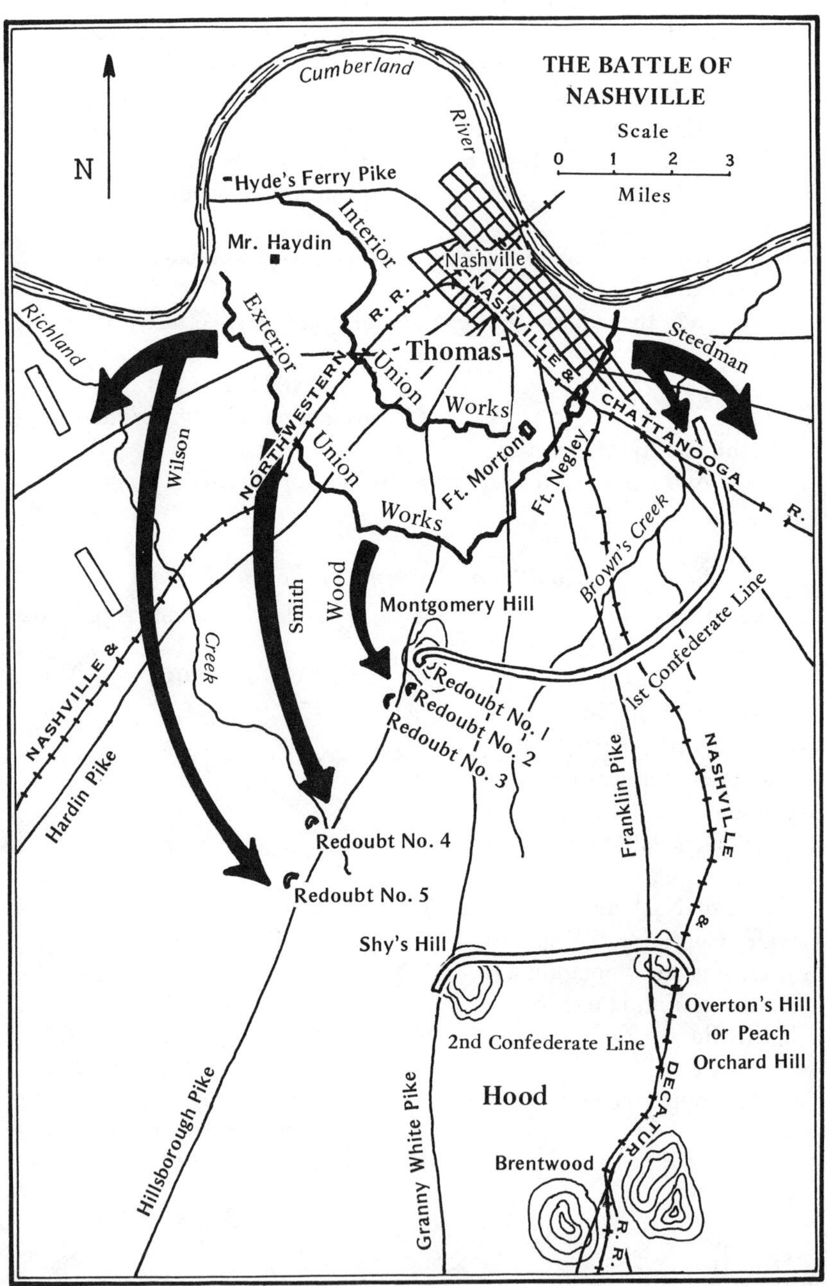

THE BATTLE OF
NASHVILLE
Scale
0  1  2  3
Miles
N
Cumberland
River
Hyde's Ferry Pike
Interior
Mr. Haydin
Nashville
NASHVILLE &
Thomas
R. R.
Richland
Exterior
Union
Works
Steedman
Wilson
NORTHWESTERN
Union
Ft. Morton
Ft. Negley
CHATTANOOGA
R.
Smith
Wood
Works
Brown's Creek
Creek
Montgomery Hill
1st Confederate Line
Redoubt No. 1
Redoubt No. 2
Redoubt No. 3
Franklin Pike
NASHVILLE &
Hardin Pike
Redoubt No. 4
Redoubt No. 5
Shy's Hill
Overton's Hill
or Peach
Orchard Hill
Hillsborough Pike
2nd Confederate Line
Granny White Pike
Hood
DECATUR
Brentwood
R. R.

## CHAPTER NINE

# *Winding Down the War*

General Thomas' role in the final months of the war focused on administration and supply rather than leading troops in the field. Coincident with the end of the pursuit of General Hood's shattered army, Thomas ordered his troops into winter quarters and redefined the limits of military rule in his department. Writing Governor Andrew Johnson of Tennessee, Thomas suggested that the governor reinstitute civil rule. "All should certainly now feel that the establishment of rebel authority in the State of Tennessee is hopeless," he reminded Johnson.[1]

Johnson was agreeable and moved promptly to implement Thomas' suggestion. General Grant, however, had different ideas in respect to warfare—there would no longer be a period of relative peace and quiet during the winter months. On the last day of 1864, Thomas was handed a telegram from General Halleck reading, "Lieutenant-General Grant does not intend that your army should go into winter quarters. All must be ready for active operations in the field."[2] This, however, did not mean that Thomas would again be campaigning at the head of a mighty

1. Van Horne, *Life*, pp. 369-70.
2. *Ibid.*, p. 376.

359

host. General Sherman even suggested that the Army of the Cumberland carry the war into Alabama's fertile Black Prairie region, as yet unravaged by the conflict, capture the industrial center of Selma, and Montgomery, where the now tottering government of the Confederacy had been organized less than four years before. Thomas was agreeable to such a campaign in the spring. Grant, however, had his doubts. Contacting Sherman, Grant observed, Thomas "is too ponderous in his preparations and equipments to move through a country rapidly enough to live off it."[3]

Grant was not ready to give Thomas the opportunity to adjust to the new mode of warfare as characterized by Sherman's March to the Sea and to be further underscored by Sherman's campaign through the Carolinas. Instead, Thomas would be called upon to reinforce Sherman in North Carolina and to bolster the army Major General Edward R. S. Canby was organizing for a hard-hitting attack aimed at capturing Mobile. Thus, during what was to be the last winter of the war, Thomas' most effective infantry and artillery units were sent to other theatres of the conflict. Then, as winter merged into spring, General Thomas employed his cavalry to penetrate deeply into the rapidly shrinking Confederate heartland.

Major General George Stoneman was alerted to ready his mounted force for a sweep through East Tennessee and into western North Carolina to wreck railroads and wreak havoc to the west of and rear of the hodge-podge Confederate forces confronting Sherman's march. Simultaneously, Major General James H. Wilson was to strike southward into Alabama, carrying the fire and sword to the Black Prairie region. This situation confounded General Wilson, one of Grant's young protégés, who with the advantage of hindsight wrote:

> Just what they counted upon or expected from Thomas, whom they had promoted to major general of the regular army . . . was never made clear. They sent Schofield with one army corps to the east, Smith with another to Alabama, and Wood to Huntsville. In other words, they scattered their in-

3. Piatt, *Thomas*, p. 578.

fantry around as well as the splendid body of cavalry I had got together with so much trouble.[4]

On June 1, 1865, General Thomas submitted a report summarizing operations in the department for which he was responsible. It began:

Headquarters Department of the Cumberland,<br>
*Nashville, June* 1, 1865.

General: I have the honor to report the operations of my command from the date of the last report made by me, January 20, as follows:

General A. J. Smith's corps, at that period, was with me at Eastport, Miss.; four divisions of General Wilson's cavalry were encamped on the opposite or north bank of the Tennessee River, at Waterloo and Gravelly Springs, Ala., and the Fourth Corps, Major-General Stanley commanding, was stationed at Huntsville, Ala. This, with the ordinary garrisons of the country, composed my command. The General-in-Chief of the Army [Grant] having given up the intention of my continuing the campaign against the enemy in Mississippi and Alabama, I received a order by telegraph from Major-General Halleck, chief of staff, to send General A. J. Smith's command and 5,000 of General Wilson's cavalry by river, to report to Major-General Canby, at New Orleans, for the purpose of taking part in an expedition at that time preparing to operate against Mobile. Smith's corps started from Eastport on the 6th of February, and Knipe's division of cavalry left Nashville on the 12th.[5]

Upon receipt of General Grant's orders to resume the campaign, Thomas had also ordered General Schofield to mass the Twenty-third Corps (the Army of the Ohio) at Eastport. Schofield accordingly marched his troops from Columbia to Clifton, on the Tennessee, preparatory to taking boats up the river, but at Clifton, on January 14, orders were received by Schofield from the War Department detaching his Twenty-third Corps from Thomas' command and ordering it eastward for duty on the Atlantic seaboard. After arriving in the Washington, D. C., area, Schofield's command was sent to the North Carolina

4. Wilson, *Under the Old Flag*, Vol. II, p. 180.
5. OR, I, XLIX, pt. I, p. 342.

361

Sounds. There, on March 23, it rendezvoused with Sherman's columns near Goldsboro.[6]

"About the period of the departure of Smith's corps," Thomas continued,

> information was received, through various sources, to the effect that part of the shattered remnants of Hood's army, viz, Cheatham's and Lee's corps, were on their way from Mississippi to South Carolina, moving via Selma and Montgomery, Ala., to re-enforce that portion of the enemy's army operating against General Sherman. There remained in Central Mississippi, under [Lieutenant] General [Richard] Taylor, but one corps of the enemy's infantry, and about 7,000 of Forrest's cavalry, the headquarters of the command being at Meridian, Miss.[7]

The news reaching Thomas regarding the movements of Hood's battered Army of Tennessee was distorted. Hood had been relieved as army commander on January 23, and arrangements perfected to shift most of the army from Tupelo to the Carolinas. S. D. Lee's corps, now commanded by Carter L. Stevenson, left immediately. It was followed by Cheatham's corps on the 25th, and by Stewart's on January 30. Some 4,000 officers and men from the army were retained in the west and sent to bolster the Confederate forces being gathered for the defense of Mobile.[8]

On February 6, General Thomas wrote:

> a communication was received from Lieutenant-General Grant, directing an expedition, commanded by General Stoneman, to be sent from East Tennessee to penetrate North Carolina, and well down toward Columbia, S. C., to destroy the enemy's railroads and military resources in that section, and visit a portion of the State beyond the control or reach of General Sherman's column. As the movement was to be merely for the purpose of destruction, directions were given General Stoneman to evade any heavy engagements with the enemy's forces.

6. Cox, *March to the Sea,* pp. 129, 147.
7. OR, I, XLIX, pt. I, p. 342.
8. Horn, pp. 422-23.

Again, on the 13th of February, General Grant telegraphed me to prepare a cavalry expedition, about 10,000 strong, to penetrate Northern Alabama, acting as a co-operative force to the movement on Mobile by General Canby. Before leaving Eastport, Miss. [to return to Nashville], I had directed General Wilson to get his command in readiness for just such a campaign, of which the above was simply an outline, my instructions being for him to move on Tuscaloosa, Selma, and Montgomery, Ala., and to capture those places if possible, after accomplishing which he was to operate against any of the enemy's forces in the direction of Mississippi, Mobile, or Macon, as circumstances might demand.[9]

By the beginning of March, reinforcements, despite the loss of Knipe's division, had raised the strength of Wilson's cavalry corps to more than 27,000, of whom 20,000 were mounted and 15,000 armed with either Spencer seven-shot rifles or carbines. Wilson proudly referred to his command as "the largest body of cavalry ever collected on the American continent."

Wilson was fearful that he might not be permitted to employ the maximum force. One day as he and Thomas met on a steamboat, while en route to review the corps, Wilson argued persuasively that a "demonstration" would be a useless waste of strength and energy. "If permitted to employ his entire available command," Wilson promised the defeat of Nathan Bedford Forrest's cavalry corps, as well as the capture of Selma, Montgomery, and Columbus. After the cavalry had passed in review, Thomas reassured Wilson that he could make his raid. Grant, on being apprised of the situation, agreed, provided that Wilson was allowed "all the latitude of an independent commander."[10]

Thomas continued:

The bad state of the roads, combined with the condition of the horses of . . . [Wilson's] command after completing the severe campaign in pursuit of Hood, prevented any movement for the time being, and it was only on the 22d of March that General Wilson, with [Emory D.] Upton's, [Eli] Long's, and

9. OR, I, XLIX, pt. I, p. 342.
10. Wilson, *Under the Old Flag*, Vol. II, pp. 165, 180.

[Edward] McCook's divisions, could leave Chickasaw, Ala. Hatch's division remained at Eastport, Miss., and R. W. Johnson's at Pulaski, Tenn., it not being possible to mount them fully, to hold the country and prevent guerrilla depredations. When General Sherman was organizing his army for its march to the Atlantic sea-board, in November, he issued an order directing me to assume control of all the forces of the Military Division of the Mississippi not present with him and the main army in Georgia. Based on that order, all the operations of the troops within the limits of the above-mentioned military division have, during the interval, been made under my immediate direction, and I have been held responsible for their faithful execution.

On the 30th of March General Wilson's cavalry reached Elyton [today's Birmingham], after an extremely difficult, toilsome, and exhausting march, on account of bad roads, swollen streams, and the rough nature of the country, which had also been almost entirely stripped of all subsistence for man or beast. At Elyton Croxton's brigade, of McCook's division, was detached and sent to capture and destroy Tuscaloosa, and then march to rejoin the main body near Selma. With the remainder of his command, General Wilson pushed rapidly forward to Montevallo, where he destroyed five extensive iron-works, and other valuable property. On the outskirts of the town the enemy's cavalry [under Philip D. Roddey and Wirt Adams] was found in force, attacked, routed, and pursued through Plantersville, leaving in our possession three pieces of artillery and several hundred prisoners.

At 3 p. m. on the 2d of April General Wilson reached the immediate vicinity of Selma, and rapidly formed Upton's and Long's divisions to attack the defenses of the town—Long attacking on the Summerfield road, and Upton across a swamp deemed impassable by the enemy. Dismounting two regiments from each of the brigades of Colonels [J. K.] Miller and [Robert H. G.] Minty, General Long and those two officers gallantly leading their men in person, charged across an open field, 500 yards wide, over a stockade, which they tore up as they passed, through the ditch and over the enemy's parapets, sweeping everything before them. Our loss was 46 killed and 200 wounded; Colonel [George W.] Dobb, Fourth Ohio, among the former, and General Long and Colonels Miller and [Charles C.] McCormick among the latter. General Upton met with less resistance than Long—entered the enemy's works and the town, capturing many prisoners. In the darkness and confusion following the assault Generals Forrest, Buford, Adams, [Frank] Armstrong, and others made their escape. Lieut. Gen. Dick Taylor had left earlier in the afternoon. As the fruits of the victory, however, there remained 26 guns and 2,700 prisoners, besides large amounts of ordnance and other property of great value. Twenty-five thousand bales of cotton had already been destroyed by the enemy.

General Wilson remained at Selma from the 2d to the 10th of April, resting his command and completing the destruction of the immense workshops, arsenals, and foundries, and waiting for Croxton to rejoin from his expedition to Tuscaloosa, it having been ascertained, through the enemy, that he [had] captured Tuscaloosa and was moving to Selma via Eutaw.

On the 10th General Wilson crossed the Alabama River and moved toward Montgomery, receiving the surrender of that town, without a contest, on the 12th. The enemy burned 85,000 bales of cotton before evacuating. At Montgomery five steamboats, several locomotives, one armory, and several foundries were destroyed. On the 14th operations were resumed by Upton's division moving through Mount Meigs and Tuskegee toward Columbus, Ga., and Colonel La Grange, with three regiments of his brigade, of McCook's division, marching along the railroad to West Point via Opelika. On the 16th General Upton, with about 400 dismounted men, assaulted and carried the breast-works of Columbus, saving, by the impetuosity of his attacks, the bridges over the Chattahoochee, and capturing 52 field guns in position, besides 1,200 prisoners. The rebel ram *Jackson*, nearly ready for sea, and carrying an armament of six 7-inch guns, fell in to our hands and was destroyed, as well as the navy-yard, foundries, the arsenal and the armory, sword and pistol factory, accouterments, shops, papermills, 4 cotton factories, 15 locomotives, 200 cars, and an immense amount of cotton, all of which were burned. The same day, the 16th of April, La Grange captured Fort Tyler, at West Point, above Columbus on the Chattahoochee, after assaulting it on three sides, the defense being stubborn. Three hundred prisoners, 3 guns, and several battle-flags were taken, besides a large quantity of supplies.

On the 18th the march toward Macon [Georgia] was resumed, Minty's (late Long's) division leading. By a forced march the bridges across Flint River, fifty-four miles from Columbus, were secured, compelling the abandonment by the enemy of five field guns and a large amount of machinery; 40 prisoners were captured and 2 cotton factories destroyed. At 6 p. m. on the 20th of April the authorities of Macon, under protest, surrendered the city to the Seventeenth Indiana, Colonel Minty's advance regiment, claiming, under the provisions of an armistice then reported existing between the forces of Generals Sherman and Johnston, that the capture was contrary to the usages of war. General Wilson, not being at hand when the surrender was made, when the case was reported to him, with admirable good judgment declined to recognize the validity of the claim asserted, as the city had been taken possession of by one of his subordinates before he (General Wilson) could be advised of the existence of an armistice, and he therefore held, as prisoners of war, Maj. Gens. Howell Cobb and G. W. Smith, and Brigadier-Generals [William W.] Mackall, [Felix H.] Robertson, and [Hugh] Mercer. On the 21st General Wilson was notified by General Sherman, from Raleigh, N. C., over the enemy's telegraph wires and through the headquarters of General Joseph E. Johnston, that the reported armistice was a reality and that he was to cease further operations.[11]

Time was rapidly running out on the Confederacy. On April 2, the same day that Wilson's men seized Selma, General Lee's Army of Northern Virginia abandoned its Petersburg lines and President Jefferson Davis and his government fled Richmond. News that Union troops had entered Richmond reached General Thomas on Monday, the 3d, and he ordered a 100-gun salute fired from the cannons on Nashville's capitol hill. It was an exciting day in the city for the soldiers and those loyal to the Union cause.

Then, on April 7, as Thomas stood by, William G. "Parson" Brownlow was inaugurated governor of Tennessee, Andrew Johnson having become Vice President of the United States. Three days later, on the 10th, news that General Lee had surrendered his army to General Grant at Appomattox Court House on the previous day caused "great rejoicing." Thomas tele-

11. OR, I, XLIX, pt. I, pp. 342-44.

graphed the Union commanders at Chattanooga, Knoxville, Memphis, and Murfreesboro, directing 200-gun salutes to be fired "at meridian tomorrow at each point in your command."

Mobile was occupied by General Canby's forces on the 12th, and, on the 15th, General Thomas was stunned to learn that President Lincoln had been assassinated. Nashville was plunged into mourning, as flags were half-masted. Then, on the 17th, Generals Sherman and Joseph E. Johnston, meeting near Durham Station, North Carolina, signed a memorandum of agreement calling for an armistice by all armies in the field. On April 24, Sherman was notified that President Johnson had disapproved Sherman's agreement with Johnston. This was followed on Wednesday, April 26, by the surrender of the troops of Johnston's command on the same terms as those given to General Lee's at Appomattox.[12]

Meanwhile, General Thomas continued:

> To return to General Stoneman's expedition from East Tennessee. Owing to the difficulty of procuring animals for his command and the bad conditions of the roads, General Stoneman was only enabled to start from Knoxville about the 20th of March, simultaneously with General Wilson's departure from Chickasaw, Ala. In the meantime General Sherman [on February 17] had captured Columbia, S. C., and was moving northward into North Carolina. About this period reports reached me of the possibility of the evacuation of Lee's army at Richmond and Petersburg, Va., and in that event of his forcing a passage through East Tennessee, via Lynchburg and Knoxville. To guard against that contingency, Stoneman was sent toward Lynchburg to destroy the railroad and military resources of that section and of Western North Carolina. The Fourth Army Corps was ordered to move from Huntsville, Ala., as far up into East Tennessee as it could supply itself, repairing the railroad as it advanced, forming, in conjunction with [Davis] Tillson's division of infantry, a strong support for General Stoneman's cavalry column in case it should find more of the enemy than it could conveniently handle and be obliged to fall back.
>
> With three brigades, [Simeon B.] Brown's, [John K.] Miller's,

12. Cleaves, pp. 280-81.

and [William J.] Palmer's, commanded by General Gillem, General Stoneman moved, via Morristown, Bull's Gap, and thence eastward up the Watauga and across Iron Mountain, to Boone, N. C., which he entered on . . . [March 28], after killing or capturing about seventy-five home guards. From Boone he crossed the Blue Ridge and went to Wilkesborough, on the Yadkin, where supplies were obtained in abundance, after which he changed his course toward Southwestern Virginia. A detachment was sent to Wytheville [Virginia] and another to Salem [Virginia] to destroy the enemy's depots at those places and the railroad, whilst the main body marched on Christianburg and captured the place. The [Virginia & Tennessee] railroad to the eastward and westward of the town was destroyed for a considerable distance. The party sent to Wytheville captured that place after some fighting and burned the [Virginia & Tennessee] railroad bridges over New River and several creeks, as well as the depots of supplies. The detachment sent to Salem did the same, and proceeded to within four miles of Lynchburg, destroying as they advanced. A railroad was never more thoroughly dismantled than was the . . . [Virginia & Tennessee] Railroad from Wytheville to near Lynchburg.

Concentrating his command General Stoneman returned to North Carolina, via Jacksonville and Taylorsville, and went to Germantown, where Palmer's brigade was sent to Salem, N. C., to destroy the large cotton factories located there and burn the bridges on the [Piedmont] railroad between Greensborough and Danville and between Greensborough and the Yadkin River, which was most thoroughly accomplished, after some fighting, by which we captured about 400 prisoners. At Salem 7,000 bales of cotton were burned by our forces. From Germantown the main body moved south to Salisbury, where they found about 3,000 of the enemy [led by W. M. Gardner] defending the place, and drawn up in line of battle behind Grant's Creek to await Stoneman's attack. Without hesitation a general charge was made by our men, resulting in the capture of all the enemy's artillery—14 pieces—and 1,364 prisoners. The remainder scattered and were pursued. During the two days following the troops were engaged destroying the immense depots of supplies of all kinds in Salisbury, and burning all the bridges for several miles on all the railroads leading out of the town.

On the afternoon of April 13 the command moved westward to Statesville and Lenoir, at which latter point General Stoneman left the troops to be disposed of by General Gillem, and proceeded with the prisoners and captured artillery to East Tennessee, reporting his arrival, on the 19th, at Greeneville, and detailing the disposition of his troops, which was as follows: Palmer's brigade, with headquarters at Lincolnton, N. C., to scout down the Catawba River, toward Charlotte; Brown's brigade, with headquarters at Morganton, to connect with Palmer down the Catawba; and Miller's brigade, with General Gillem, was to take post at Asheville, with directions to open up communication through to Greeneville, East Tenn; the object in leaving the cavalry on the other side of the mountains being to obstruct, intercept, or disperse any troops of the enemy going south, and to capture trains.

General Gillem followed the directions given him, and marched on Asheville, with Miller's brigade, but was opposed at Swannanoa Gap by a considerable force of the enemy. Leaving sufficient of his force to amuse them, with the balance he moved by way of Howard's Gap, gained the enemy's rear, and surprised and captured his artillery; after which he made his appearance in front of Asheville, where he was met by a flag of truce on the 23d, with the intelligence of the truce existing between Generals Sherman and Johnston, and bearing an order from General Sherman to General Stoneman for the latter to go to the railroad station at Durham's, or Hillsborough, nearly 200 miles distant, whereas the distance to Greeneville, East Tenn., was but sixty. Coming to the conclusion that the order was issued by General Sherman under the impression that the Cavalry Division was still at Salisbury or Statesville, General Gillem determined to move to Greeneville. The rebel General [James G.] Martin, with whom he communicated under the flag of truce, demanded the rendition of the artillery captured, which, of course, could not be granted, and in return General Gillem requested the rebel commander to furnish his troops with three days' rations, as by the terms of the armistice they were required to withdraw. Had it not been for this, Asheville and its garrison would have fallen into our hands.

Up to that period I had not been officially notified of the existence of any armistice between the forces of Generals Sherman and Johnston, and the information only reached me through my sub-commanders, Generals Wilson and Stoneman, from Macon, Ga., and Greeneville, East Tenn., almost simultaneously. The question naturally arose in my mind, whether the troops acting under my direction by virtue of General Sherman's Special Field Orders, No. 105, series of 1864, directing me to assume control of all the forces of the Military Division of the Mississippi "not absolutely in the presence of the general-in-chief," were to be bound by an armistice or agreement made at a distance of several hundred miles from where those troops were operating, and of which they were advised through an enemy then in such straightened circumstances that any ruse, honorable at least in war, was likely to be practiced by him to relieve himself from his difficult position.

Then, again, General Sherman was operating with a movable column beyond the limits of his territorial command, viz, the Military Division of the Mississippi, and far away from all direct communication with it, whereas "the troops not absolutely in the presence of the general-in-chief" were operating under special instructions, and not even in co-operation with General Sherman against Johnston; but, on the contrary, General Stoneman was dismantling the country to obstruct Lee's retreat, and General Wilson was moving independently in Georgia or co-operating with General Canby. Before I could come to any conclusion how I should proceed under the circumstances and without disrespect to my superior officer, General Sherman, Mr. Secretary Stanton telegraphed to me from Washington on the 27th of April, and through me to my sub-commanders, to disregard all orders except those coming from General Grant or myself, and to resume hostilities at once, sparing no pains to press the enemy firmly, at the same time notifying me that General Sherman's negotiations with Johnston had been disapproved.

Based on that notification the following dispositions were made with a view of capturing President Davis and party, who, on the cessation of the armistice, had started south from Charlotte, N. C., with an escort variously estimated at from 500 to 2,000 picked cavalry, to endeavor to make his way to the Trans-Mississippi. General Stoneman was directed to send the brigades of Miller, Brown, and Palmer, then in Western North Carolina, to concentrate at Anderson, S. C., and scout down the Savannah River to Augusta, Ga., if possible, in search of the fugitives. General Gillem being absent, Colonel Palmer,

Fifteenth Pennsylvania Cavalry, took command of the expedition. By rapid marching they succeeded in reaching and crossing the Savannah River in advance of Davis, and so disposed the command as to effectually cut off his retreat toward Mississippi, and forced him to alter his route toward the Atlantic coast. General Wilson, at Macon, Ga., was also notified of the action taken at Washington on General Sherman's negotiations with Johnston, and he was directed to resume hostilities at once—especially to endeavor to intercept Davis.

Scarcely were the above orders issued and in process of execution, when notification reached me of the surrender by Johnston of all the enemy's forces east of the Chattahoochee River. General Wilson received similar notification from General Sherman, direct through the enemy's territory, and immediately took measures to receive the surrender of the enemy's establishments at Atlanta and Augusta, and to occupy those points, detailing for that purpose Brevet Major-General Upton with his division. General McCook was sent with a force to occupy Tallahassee, Fla., and to receive the surrender of the troops in that vicinity. Thus a cordon of cavalry, more or less continuous, was extended across the State of Georgia from northwest to southeast, and communication established through the late so-called Southern Confederacy. With characteristic energy, Generals Wilson and Palmer had handbills printed and profusely circulated in all directions throughout the country, offering the President's reward for the apprehension of Davis, and nothing could exceed the watchfulness exhibited by their commands.

On the 3d of May, Davis dismissed his escort at Washington, Ga., and accompanied by about half a dozen followers, set out to endeavor to pass our lines. Nothing definite was learned of the whereabouts of the fugitives until on the evening of the 7th of May, the First Wisconsin Cavalry, Lieut. Col. Henry Harnden commanding, with 150 men, ascertained at Dublin, on the Oconee River, fifty-five miles southeast from Macon, that Davis and party had crossed the river at that point during the day, and had moved out on the Jacksonville road. At daylight on the 8th Colonel Harnden continued the pursuit, finding the camp occupied by Davis on the evening previous, between the forks of Alligator Creek, which was reached just four hours after it had been vacated. The trail was pursued as far as the ford over Gum Swamp Creek, Pulaski County, when darkness rendered it too indistinct to follow, and the command encamped for the night, having marched forty miles that day.

On the 9th Colonel Harnden pushed on to the Ocmulgee River, crossed at Brown's Ferry, and went to Abbeville, where he ascertained Davis' train had left that place at 1 a. m. that same day, and had gone toward Irwinville, in Irwin County. With this information Colonel Harnden moved rapidly on toward the latter town, halting within a short distance of it to wait for daylight, in order to make certain of the capture. Before leaving Abbeville, Colonel Harnden, learning of the approach from the direction of Hawkinsville of the Fourth Michigan Cavalry, Colonel [Benjamin D.] Pritchard commanding, went to meet that officer and informed him of his close pursuit of Davis; Colonel Pritchard stating in reply that he had been sent to Abbeville also to watch for Davis. After Colonel Harnden's departure, Colonel Pritchard, with part of his command, started for Irwinville by a more direct route than that used by the detachment of the First Wisconsin, arriving at Irwinville at 2 a. m. on the 10th, where, on inquiry, it was ascertained that there was a camp about a mile from town on the other road leading to Abbeville. Approaching cautiously, for fear it might be our own men, Colonel Pritchard sent a dismounted party to interpose between it and Abbeville, and then waited for daylight to move forward and surprise the occupants. Daylight appearing, a rapid advance was made and the encampment surprised, resulting in the capture of Jefferson Davis and family, John H. Reagan, Postmaster-General of the so-called Confederacy, 2 aides-de-camp, the private secretary [Harrison Burton] of Davis, 4 other officers, and 11 enlisted men.

Almost immediately after the completion of the above movement, Colonel Harnden's men coming down the Abbeville road were hailed by the party sent out during the night by Colonel Pritchard to secure the capture of the camp, and on being challenged answered "friends," but fell back, under the impression they had come upon an enemy; whereupon shots were exchanged before the real position of affairs could be ascertained, resulting in the loss on one side of 2 men killed and 1 wounded, and of 3 wounded on the other. Considerable [ill] feeling was caused by the manner in which the Fourth Michigan effected the apprehension of Davis, to the detriment of Colonel Harnden's party, but great credit is justly due and should be given to the First Wisconsin Cavalry for the persistency of its pursuit, and it is only to be regretted they did not arrive on the ground in time to reap the benefit of their labors. For the full particulars of the operations of both detachments I have the pleasure of referring you to the reports of Lieutenant-Colonel Harnden, First Wisconsin, and Captain [John C.] Hathaway, Fourth Michigan.

With the surrender of Johnston's army to General Sherman all the detachments of the Confederate armies east of the Chattahoochee signified their willingness to surrender, except a few guerrilla bands who were outlawed, special directions being given to grant all such no quarter. On the 7th of May notification was received by me via Eastport and Meridian, Miss., of the surrender of General Taylor's army to General Canby, at Citronelle, Ala., on the 4th. No armed force of the enemy east of the Mississippi remaining to interfere, I gave orders for the occupation by my forces of such portions of the reclaimed territory as it was necessary to hold whilst telegraphic and railroad communication was being restored, to the accomplishment of which the people of the country zealously gave their assistance.

May 16 General Grant, through his chief of staff, General Rawlins, directed me to order to some point north of the Tennessee River all of Wilson's cavalry except 4,000 veterans, who are to remain at Macon, Augusta, and Atlanta, Ga.; those returning to be concentrated at some convenient point in Tennessee or Kentucky, preparatory to being mustered out or otherwise disposed of. All convalescents and others about the hospitals throughout my command not requiring medical treatment have, by virtue of General Orders, No. 77, been mustered out of service. The quartermaster, commissary, and ordnance departments have all been reduced to the smallest scale consistent with the demands of the service. During the past three months [March through May] the defenses of all the posts within my command have been thoroughly inspected by Brigadier-General Tower, inspector of fortifications Military Division of the Mississippi. . . . For detailed accounts of the operations of the commands of Generals Stoneman and Wilson I invite the attention of the lieutenant-general commanding [Grant] to the reports of those officers, as well as to those of their subordinates, Generals Gillem, Palmer, and others. They have brought the cavalry arm of the service to a state of efficiency unequaled in any other army for long and difficult marches through the enemy's country, and particularly for self-reliance and fortitude in assaulting strong positions which might well cause hesitation in veteran infantry.

I am, general, respectfully, your obedient servant,

Geo. H. Thomas,

*Major-General, U. S. Army, Commanding.*

Brig. Gen. J. A. Rawlins,

*Chief of Staff, U. S. Army.*[13]

The capture of President Davis was followed by the surrender, on May 26, of the Confederate forces in the Trans-Mississippi. On May 9, the day before the capture of Davis and his party, General Thomas had bid farewell to the veteran Fourth Corps, Army of the Cumberland. Recalled from East Tennessee, regiments and batteries, some of which had campaigned from Bowling Green and Mill Springs to Nashville and beyond, were being redeployed to Texas. From a reviewing stand erected on the city's fringes, General Thomas and his party watched as the regiments and batteries, some of the former numbering scarcely 100-strong, passed. "Reverently and affectionately they saluted the old hero as they reached the reviewing stand," wrote one who marched. "Thousands of soldiers . . . never looked upon that strong and kindly face again," he added.[14]

In his office next morning, Thomas penned a soldierly farewell to the corps:

> The General Commanding the Department takes pride in conveying to the Fourth Army corps the expression of his admiration, excited by their brilliant and martial display at the Review yesterday.
>
> As the battalions of your magnificent corps swept successively before the eye, the coldest heart must have warmed with interest in contemplation of these men, who had passed through the varied and shifting scenes of this great, modern tragedy, who had stemmed with unyielding breasts the Rebel tide threatening to engulph the landmarks of Freedom; and who,

13. OR, I, XLIX, pt. I, pp. 344-47.
14. W. W. Gist, "The Battle of Franklin," *Tennessee Historical Magazine,* Vol. VI (October, 1920), p. 262.

bearing on their bronzed and furrowed brows the ennobling marks of the years of hardship, suffering and privation, undergone in defense of freedom and the integrity of the Union, could still preserve the light step and wear the cheerful expressions of youth.[15]

General Thomas was called to Washington in the third week of May to attend the Grand Review. President Johnson and General Grant and thousands watched on the 23d as General Meade's Army of the Potomac marched along Pennsylvania Avenue and passed in review. The next day, the parade featured the men of the West, including the veterans of Thomas' Fourteenth Corps, the men who had stood tall at Stones River and Chickamauga. Sherman's troops were more ragged, more loose in their tred, more rough-cut than Meade's soldiers. The Army of the Cumberland, as a unit, did not participate, but Thomas knew that the trials and tribulations of the marches, camps, and battles bound them together in an undying brotherhood, and their sacrifices would be commemorated long after the last Cumberlander had answered the last post. The big parade over, Thomas held a reunion with the officers and men of his old corps.[16]

15. *Army and Navy Journal,* June 3, 1865.
16. Richard O'Connor, *Thomas: Rock of Chickamauga* (New York: Prentice-Hall, 1948), p. 335.

# CHAPTER TEN

# *Final Years*

At the end of the war, General Thomas was appointed commander of the Military Division of the Tennessee, embracing the States of Kentucky, Tennessee, Georgia, Alabama, and Mississippi, with headquarters at Nashville, Tennessee. He held this command from June 27, 1865, to August 13, 1866. In this difficult position Thomas administered the affairs of the district with admirable skill and patriotism. His next assignment was as commander of the Department of the Tennessee, including the same states, from August 13, 1866, to March 11, 1867, with headquarters at Nashville, until November 1, 1866, and at Louisville, Kentucky, until March 11, 1867, when he was assigned to the command of the 3d Military District, which was composed of the States of Alabama, Georgia, and Florida. Shortly thereafter he requested to be relieved from this district, and reassignment was granted to him on March 15, 1867. He was next placed in charge of the Department of the Cumberland to include the states of Kentucky, Tennessee, and West Virginia from March 16, 1867, to January 5, 1869. His last assignment was in command of the Division of the Pacific from June 1869 to his death on March 28, 1870.

On Monday, June 12, 1865, the General Assembly of the State of Tennessee adopted the following Joint Resolutions:[1]

Whereas, the pleasing intelligence has reached us, that the distinguished soldier and commander, Major General G. H. Thomas, has been assigned to this military division:

Resolved, by the General Assembly of the State of Tennessee, That we do most heartily congratulate our citizens upon the appointment of this model soldier, possessing as we do the most unbounded confidence in his ability and judgment, and believing that under his rule, early peace and quiet and Unionism will prevail in every section of our State.

Resolved further: That we tender to the President and War Department, our special thanks for their assignment of General Thomas over this military division, and, with his consent, we propose to adopt him as a Tennesseean, General Thomas having endeared himself to us, both by distinguished services, and by many acts of noble and unostentatious kindness.[1]

Although Thomas was born in Virginia, he accepted the honor of becoming a citizen of the State of Tennessee which he expressed in the following letter:

Headquarters, Department of the Cumberland,
*Nashville, June 28, 1865.*

Honorable A. J. Fletcher,
    Secretary of the State of Tennessee.

Sir:—I have the honor to acknowledge the receipt of a copy of Joint Resolutions of the General Assembly of the State of Tennessee, conferring on me the distinguished honor of adopting me as a citizen of the State. For this magnanimous and courteous act of the General Assembly words cannot express my profound appreciation.

With the sincere hope that their patriotic efforts may inspire public confidence and restore the State to a state of peace and prosperity.

I remain, dear sir, very respectfully,
    Your ob't serv't,

Geo. H. Thomas,
*Major General, U.S.A.*[2]

1. Van Horne, *Life*, p. 414.
2. *Ibid.*

Then, on Saturday, September 2, 1865, the Tennessee legislators adopted this resolution:

Resolved, by the General Assembly of the State of Tennessee, That the thanks of the people of the State of Tennessee, be presented to Major General George H. Thomas, and the officers and soldiers under his command, for his wise and spirited, and their brave and patriotic conduct in the battle of Nashville, in defense of the capital of the State, in December, 1864, and that a gold medal be struck in commemoration of the great and decisive event, and be presented to him.

That the medal exhibit on the one side, a head of Major General Thomas in profile, with inscription around it, "To Major General George H. Thomas, from the State of Tennessee," and on the other side, the capitol and other appropriate inscriptions.

That the Governor of the State of Tennessee cause and procure the gold medal to be struck at as early a day as practicable, and present the same to Major General Thomas, with a letter of thanks, in the name of this General Assembly, and of the people of the State of Tennessee.[3]

This gold medal was ordered from Tiffany's in New York City. On December 15, 1866, the second anniversary of the battle of Nashville, Governor Brownlow presented the gold medal to General Thomas with these inspiring remarks:

The pleasant duty devolves on me, of presenting to you on this interesting occasion the elegant gold medal voted to you something like a year ago, by the General Assembly of Tennessee, whose members—Senators and Representatives—now surround you. And although this medal is the finest article of the kind yet executed in America, its value to you does not consist in the amount of the precious metal it contains, nor yet, in the exquisite workmanship of the artist, but in the motives which prompted the gift, and the patriotic source it originates from. It is intended to express the high regard in which you are held by a loyal Tennessee legislature, as a military chieftan, a tried and devoted partiot, and a modest unassuming gentleman.

3. *Ibid.*, p. 415.

General, in no spirit of flattery, I must be permitted to say, that in the great struggle of four years, which recently convulsed the Nation, of all military commanders, you are perhaps the only one that never lost a battle, and in the government of armies and departments never made a mistake.

There is something very appropriate in the presentation of this medal to-day, and in this capitol, the anniversary of the battle of Nashville. Two years ago to-day, at the head of a gallant army, you were engaged in a deadly conflict with the enemies of our country around this city; and two years ago to-morrow you closed out that conflict, saving this city from ruins, and sending the cohorts of treason howling into Dixie, —"away down South in Dixie." A portion of the enemy remained to receive their long lost rights—the only rights that traitors are entitled to—Funeral Rights.

Trusting that you may never have occasion to command another army on the field of carnage, and that you may live long to enjoy the fruits of the victories you have contributed to achieve, I hand this medal over to one who will never dishonor it.[4]

## General Thomas replied:

Governor Brownlow, and Gentlemen of the Senate and House of Representatives of the Legislature of Tennessee:

Profoundly sensible of the high honors you have this day conferred on me, I confess myself totally unable to thank you in appropriate terms. Be assured, however, of my sincere appreciation of these honors, and particularly of the compliments which you have paid to the officers and soldiers who participated with me in defeating the enemy two years ago to-day at Nashville.

Some thirty years ago I received my diploma at the Military Academy, and soon after a commission in the Army.

On receiving that commission I took an oath to sustain the Constitution of the United States, and the Government, and to obey all officers of the Government placed over me. I have faithfully endeavored to keep that oath. I did not regard it so much an oath, as a solemn pledge on my part to return the Government some little service for the great benefit I had received in obtaining my education at the Academy.

4. *Ibid.*, pp. 415-16.

While I cannot venture to speak of myself, without fear of being accused of egotism, I can, with pleasure, sincerity, and pride, speak of the brave soldiers and officers who, at the commencement of the late war, voluntarily came forth from the private walks of life, and devoted their lives to the defense of the Government established by our fathers.

It has been my pleasure, on all occasions, to witness the devotion of our army, and I, to-day, take pride in saying, that no other country on earth ever produced such another army as that which assembled to put down the rebellion.[5]

After General Thomas recited the circumstances for making the success of the campaign possible in Tennessee, and, after giving a brief narration of the operations south of Nashville, he briefly described the battle before that city:

On that day [December 15] General Steedman commenced the battle on the left and so occupied the attention of the enemy, that he appeared entirely to forget the other portions of his line, and concentrated heavily at that point, evidently expecting a battle there.

This was expected in my programme, and after General Steedman had opened the battle and been engaged about half an hour, the troops were moved on their respective positions, and, almost like men in review, took post after post, and drove the enemy to the hills.

The next day, by the skillful maneuver of the cavalry commander [General Wilson], the enemy's left was entirely turned; and then, by one of the most gallant assaults I have ever witnessed, the entire line of the enemy was swept from left to right. And so ended one of the strongest and most daring armies the enemy ever equipped.

It is with the greatest pleasure that I avail myself to-day of the opportunity of speaking in praise of those gallant men and officers then under my command.[6]

In February of 1868, General Thomas learned that President Andrew Johnson (who was having his troubles with the radical wing of the Republican Party while at the same time "he was not

5. *Ibid.*, pp. 416-17.
6. *Ibid.*, p. 417.

satisfied with the course of General Grant") had sent Thomas'
name to the Senate for nomination as a brevet lieutenant general
and brevet general, under which rank he undoubtedly would have
served as General of the Army. Thereupon Thomas promptly sent
the following telegram to an influential senator, Benjamin F.
Wade of Ohio:

*Louisville, February 22, 1868, 2.30 p. m.*

Hon. B. F. Wade,
President United States Senate:
The morning papers of Louisville announce officially that
my name was yesterday sent to the Senate for confirmation as
brevet lieutenant general and brevet general.

For the battle of Nashville I was appointed major general
in the United States Army. My services since the war do not
merit so high a compliment, and it is now too late to be
regarded as a compliment, if conferred for service during
the war.

I, therefore, earnestly request that the Senate will not confirm the nomination.

Geo. H. Thomas,
*Major-General.*[7]

On the next day Thomas sent this dispatch to President
Johnson:

*Nashville, Tenn., February 23, 1868.*

To The President Of The United States.
The Washington dispatch to the *Louisville Journal* of yesterday says my name has been sent to the Senate recommended
for the brevet rank of lieutenant general and general.

Whilst sincerely thanking you for the proposed compliment,
I earnestly request you to recall the recommendation. I have
done no service since the war to deserve so high a compliment,
and it is now too late to be regarded as a compliment, if
conferred for services during the war.

George H. Thomas,
*Major-General.*[8]

Thomas was averse to this as he felt that he was being used

7. *Ibid.,* p. 420.
8. *Ibid.,* pp. 420-21.

as an instrument by those opposing the Radical Reconstructionists in Congress for displacing General U. S. Grant in command of the Army.

In the same year General Thomas was touted as a candidate for the Presidency of the United States. He received numerous letters from "politicians all over the North," but he refused to allow his name to be used. He further stated that, "I will have nothing to do with politics. I am a soldier, and I know my duty; as a politician, I would be lost. No sir; not even if I were elected unanimously would I accept. I want to die with a fair record, and this I will do if I keep out of the sea of politics and cling to my proper profession."[9]

In April of 1867, he had written a letter to his friend J. Watts de Peyster in which he expressed his opinion about being a candidate for any political office, "I have too much regard for my own self-respect to voluntarily place myself in a position where my personal and private character can be assailed with impunity by newspaper-men, and scurrilous political pettifoggers and demagogues."[10]

Near the close of the war, Thomas had learned that his friends and admirers in Louisville and Cincinnati were raising money as a gift for him in recognition of his untiring devotion to duty during the conflict. Upon learning of this movement, he stated in a letter to the editor of the *Cincinnati Gazette* on Tuesday, January 17, 1865, "I would greatly prefer, and, if not premature, request that any sum which may be raised for that purpose may be devoted to the founding of a fund for the relief of disabled soldiers and of the indigent widows and orphans of officers and soldiers who have lost their lives during the war. I am amply rewarded when assured that my humble services have met with the approbation of the Government and the people."[11] In the same manner he courteously, but decidedly, refused to accept all presents.

In the fall of 1868, Colonel Alfred L. Hough, aide-de-camp to General Thomas, accompanied him to Washington, where he served on a lengthy court of inquiry to investigate the official conduct of Brigadier General Alexander B. Dyer, Chief of

9. Johnson, p. 234.
10. Van Horne, *Life,* p. 422.
11. Johnson, pp. 233-34.

Ordnance. The court convened in Washington November 9, 1868, and was dissolved May 15, 1869, its findings and opinions having been approved and confirmed by President Grant. While there in early 1869, soon after Grant had been elected Eighteenth President, General Thomas and his aide called upon Grant. Their talk was of a general nature until President-elect Grant changed the conversation to a subject which had been on his mind since having been elected President. He said, "Thomas, there has got to be a change on the Pacific coast, and either you or Sheridan will have to go there; how would you like it?" For a moment General Thomas paused, then he replied, "As for myself I would have no objection to serving there, but on Mrs. Thomas' account I would not want to take her any further away from her friends in the East." This was a reasonable request made by General Thomas. Before President-elect Grant could respond, Mrs. Grant interrupted and said, "Your having a wife is one reason why you should go there instead of Sheridan, as he ought to stay here, where he can get one." Grant changed the conversation and nothing more was said about it.

When General Thomas and Colonel Hough left for the evening, he turned to his aide and said in a very solemn tone, "Hough, we are going to California, that was settled to-night." General Thomas would rather have stayed in the Department of the Cumberland in Louisville than go to the Pacific, "but would rather go than have his rank degraded."[12]

On June 1, 1869, Thomas was assigned to the command of the Military Division of the Pacific headquartered in San Francisco at 204 Sutter Street, relieving General Halleck of that command. President Grant had previously planned to assign General Schofield to this important command. Schofield was then Thomas' junior in rank, and Thomas became so upset about this that he protested. Grant then reversed his decision in favor of Thomas. Thomas held this command until his death. Included in this Military Division were the States of California, Oregon and Nevada, and the territories of Arizona, Idaho and Washington. His military supervision of this vast region was of the same admirable character that he had before displayed, winning the respect

12. Van Horne, *Life*, pp. 433-34.

of all good citizens and effecting a salutary restraint upon all "evil-doers."

Soon after General Thomas arrived in San Francisco, he met his long time friend Major General Erasmus D. Keyes, who was surprised to see a drastic change in Thomas' pallid complexion. Keyes saw that the expression on his face showed the effects of the war, that his eyes had lost their usual sparkle, and that his lips were drawn. General Keyes added that, "although a mortal malady had entrenched itself in his vitals, he made no complaint, but applied himself with his customary strictness of duty." Thomas was at Keyes' home to attend the wedding of Keyes' daughter Caroline, and in his conversation with Thomas on that occasion Keyes said, "Thomas, I notice no change in our social relations now from when in Florida, New Orleans, and Charleston I used to order you to go and drill the company." Thomas replied in a dignified and courteous manner, "There is none and why should there be?"[13]

In the summer of 1869, Thomas embarked with his aide-de-camp, Colonel Hough, on a tour of inspection of the interior military posts which constituted the Military Division of the Pacific. Their journey took them from Nevada northward into Idaho, Oregon, and the Washington Territory. They traveled down the Columbia River to Portland, Oregon, where they boarded a small steamer and continued on to the Alaskan posts. The two men spent three months and covered some 8,000 miles inspecting Thomas' command before returning to San Francisco on September 16.

Following this extensive tour, Thomas detailed the results of his inspection of the military forces in Alaska to General Sherman, who had succeeded Grant as commander of the United States Army:

> Western Union Telegraph
> War Dept.
> 9:15 a.m., Sept. 21, 1869
>
> By Telegraph from San Francisco, Cal.
> To Gen. W. T. Sherman
> Com'd'g. Army U S
> I would not change the troops now stationed in Alaska until

13. Keyes, *Fifty Years*, p. 167.

Congress has passed laws regulating the killing of fur bearing animals and intercourse with the natives. The posts now established are necessary and have done good already in preventing illicit trade in whiskey between unscrupulous whites and natives. I do not perceive that there is any immediate prospect of immigration to Alaska. There is the greatest abundance of lumber in all the islands forming the southern strip of territory, but there is no probability that any one will undertake to get it out as long as there is such an abundance of the same kind, equally good, in Oregon, Washington Territory and British Columbia. The only fear of any collusion with the natives is through the unscrupulous whiskey traders and persons prospecting for gold.

Up to this time the gold hunters have had friendly intercourse with the natives, but should important discoveries of gold be made, there will be a rush of adventurers to the Territory and the usual depredations will soon follow. If it is desirable to perpetuate the fur seal and seal otters, it will be necessary for Congress to pass laws regulating the manner of killing these animals. Indiscriminate killing and injudicious hunting will drive them away in one or two seasons. I will explain more fully in my report.

The Aleutians are a civilized race, very industrious, docile and amiable. They have a weakness for whiskey, and already the whiskey dealers have demoralized all to whom they have access. There was a marked difference between the natives of St. George and St. Paul Islands and those at Unalaska and Kodiak. The latter are mostly diseased and indolent, brought about in the short time the Territory has been in our possession by coming in contact with the reckless men visiting the country. I do not believe Alaska can ever become an agricultural country; there are some tracts of meadow land, however, that may be made available for grazing, unless the climate proves to be too rigorous to graze during the winter. Hay cannot be made in any quantity because of the frequent and heavy rains in all seasons. There were many valuable banks along the southern coast of the Aleutian peninsula also in Bering Sea for cod, halibut, and other fish, and in all the streams salmon of fine quality can be taken in almost incredible quantities. Coal is found in a great many places. It is of fair quality and may be deeper in the veins. The coal may be mined with profit when the demand increases. Professor Davidson of the Coast

Survey reports a very large district in the Chilcot River country rich in iron ore conveniently situated for mining and smelting. Gold has been found on the Sticksene and Tarkon Rivers but as yet in no very large quantities.

> Geo. H. Thomas
> *Maj. Genl*
> *USA*
> *Commanding*[14]

The Alaskan territory which General Thomas had visited represented one of the most interesting and valuable territorial acquisitions made by the United States in the 19th century. For the trifling sum of $7,200,000, about $12.28 per square mile or less than two pennies an acre, the United States came into possession of 586,400 square miles of land that has since proved invaluable both as a source of natural resources and as a base for the defense of our western shores.

Congress did not make any official provision for the governing of Alaska until seventeen years after the purchase. In the interim, the territory was administered successively by the United States Army, the Department of the Treasury, and the Department of the Navy.

While General Thomas was in Chicago in the fall of 1869, he described his tour of inspection to his friend, Colonel Daniel H. Rucker, with the comment that "it was fast traveling for a slow man."[15]

General Thomas had gone East to Washington to give his report to the War Department. Upon his return to San Francisco in November of 1869, his aides, being concerned about his health, were happy to see him and were delighted to see that his gracious wife had accompanied him. The long wear and tear on his body and mind, however, was too much for his health, and it had taken its toll.[16]

When General Thomas had first arrived in San Francisco, a banquet was given in his honor by General Halleck whom he was succeeding. During the evening's conversation with Halleck, he

14. Adjutant General's Office, Old Military Branch, Military Archives Division, National Archives, Washington, D. C.
15. Van Horne, *Life*, p. 437.
16. Cleaves, p. 304.

learned for the first time that it was General Schofield who had been first selected to replace him before the battle of Nashville. Thomas had suspected this, and, becoming very upset with this information, he said, "I knew it. I knew he was the man."[17] It was because of General Halleck's delay, as Halleck explained it to Thomas, that Thomas' relief was not completed when first ordered. It was during this period of delay that Thomas had telegraphed Halleck from Nashville informing him that it was necessary to postpone immediate action against the enemy because of the December sleet storm. When the second plan for replacing Thomas by General Logan was being implemented, the weather moderated and the sweeping victory was won by Thomas' Army of the Cumberland.

Thomas had had the feeling that there was an enemy in his camp when he first learned that the overly ambitious Schofield was being sent to him by General Sherman, and he had feared that an effort would be made to remove him. The plan had fallen through, but Schofield never forgot. On March 12, 1870, a communication appeared in the *New York Daily Tribune* signed, "One who fought at Nashville," and severely criticised Thomas' conduct of the Middle Tennessee Campaign. Thomas suspected that Schofield was the author of the article, considered it as an attack upon him, and "as another manifestation of Schofield's enmity."[18] He determined to answer it, but he was sure that many of his former soldiers would answer also.

This article, addressed to the Editor, with the heading "Secrets of History—The Battle of Nashville—Was Grant's Order a Blunder?" gave the impression that the Nashville Campaign was won at Franklin, Tennessee, where "the enemy had been whipped until there was very little in him, and there was not the remotest possibility of his attacking Nashville." Its tone and claims indeed astonished many former soldiers of Thomas' Army of the Cumberland.

Then, on March 19, 1870, there appeared another article in the *New York Daily Tribune* defending the hero of Nashville and signed, "Another Man." It read:

17. Van Horne, *Life,* p. 440.
18. *Ibid.,* p. 439.

The letter in your issue of the 12th, by "One Who Fought at Nashville," is so wide of the facts in a variety of ways that it would be hardly worth while to reply to it, if the excathedra manner in which the statements are made did not convey the idea that the writer is a competent witness in the case at issue both as to fact and opinions. . . . So well was [the Nashville strategy] planned and so scientifically and thoroughly was the plan carried out, that to-day it is made a study at the Military Academy among the great battles in history. Nobody who knows what that army was, and what its failings were, will dare dispute the fact that Thomas' removal would have proved a great, if not a fatal error, and that a very large part of the enthusiam, vim, and heartiness with which the battle of Nashville was fought was due to the fact that—in the current words of the men in the ranks—"This is old Pap's fight, and we're going to win it for him."

Thomas was understandably distressed by this unwarranted controversy. Shortly after nine, on March 28, he left his home in the Lick House for his 204 Sutter Street headquarters. On the way to his office he was greeted by his neighbors and was very cheerful in spirit. He arrived at his office about 9:30 a. m., and beginning his usual duties, conversed with his aide, Colonel Hough. It was during this conversation that they discussed the recent article which had so bothered Thomas. As Hough recalled, Thomas said:

The criticism ["Secrets of History"] upon my plan is really funny reading. I am only astonished that the letter should have been published, for some of its statements are easily refuted, and others show an insubordination and intrigue that will astonish the public. The answer to it is a good and just one, and whoever wrote it has my thanks. I am now satisfied that what I have suspected for some time is true, that is, that General Schofield intrigued for my removal, to enable him to get my command. I have long known that he asked to be sent back to me from Atlanta to Nashville, which always surprised me, as there was apparently at this time a much greater opportunity for gaining distinction with General Sherman than with me, and now I can understand it. Now that he is piqued, that the order placing him in command is called a blunder, he is endeavoring to right himself before the public by attacking me, who have nothing to do with this discussion; but it will fail, for plenty of my old officers will answer him, as I am assured by letters now. I say him, because the article was directly inspired by him. I am assured of this on the authority of a friend in St. Louis.

It is an outrageous article, and as a military criticism is ridiculous, and easily answered, as it is in this first reply to it; it will create much indignation among the officers who fought at Nashville, who will be astonished at some of the statements. At one statement, though, I am amazed, and it convinces me of Schofield's duplicity, and that is that he, one of my subordinates, should have applied, in his letter of December 26, 1864, to General Grant, without my knowledge, to be transferred with his command to the Atlantic; this is the first time I ever heard of this application. What will reflecting people say after hearing of this letter? If a subordinate officer can presume to ask that his commander be weakened to the extent to which this article states General Schofield did, is it not also reasonable to suppose that he had written letters previously to General Grant, so commenting on affairs at Nashville as to suggest to him the propriety of substituting Schofield for me, and thereby have originated the causes for his present disagreeable situation? In the matter of winter quarters; suppose I had been permitted by General Grant to place my troops in winter quarters in accordance with my order, and after hearing of Sherman's successful march to the sea and intention to move in the direction of Richmond to join Grant, he does not see that I could have cooperated with Sherman by moving through the northern part of Georgia, Western North Carolina, and East Tennessee towards the same objective point, thus aiding somewhat towards the final triumph of our forces in Virginia. This, or whatever was necessary, would have [been] done by me, if my plans had not been upset by this letter of Schofield of December 26, now for the first time known to me.[19]

Colonel Hough then left General Thomas alone in his office to write a reply to the anonymous letter supposedly written by General Schofield. When Hough returned to the general's office

19. *Ibid.*, pp. 440-42.

about 1:45 p. m., he found Thomas unconscious and the letter unfinished. Hough summoned Army doctors Charles McCormick and Robert Murray, who administered medication. He rallied slightly from his attack, which was thought to be caused by indigestion. He seemed to get better, but he complained about a pain in his right temple. One of the doctors told Hough that this was a bad sign, diagnosing it as apoplexy. His condition gradually worsened until 7:25 p. m., at which time he passed away.[20] Thomas died at the early age of 53 years, 7 months, and 28 days.

His death is said to have resulted from ailments "incurred from long service and exposure in the line of duty in the Army of the United States." With him at the time of his death were his wife; her sister, Miss Julia Kellogg; Army Surgeons Charles McCormick and Robert Murray; Colonels John P. Willard, Sanford C. Kellogg, and Alfred L. Hough of his personal staff; and several other officers. The body was embalmed that evening and the next day was taken to the Lick House where he had resided. On the afternoon of March 30, private Episcopal services were conducted in the Lick House by the Right Reverend Bishop W. Ingraham Kip. As soon as practicable after private religious services, the remains, in charge of Colonel Willard, were borne to Troy, New York, for burial.[21]

In the Louisville *Courier-Journal* for April 2, 1870, appeared the following dispatch received by General Philip H. Sheridan from General Sherman:

To Gen. P. H. Sheridan, Commanding Military
    Division of Missouri:
I have telegraphed Colonel Willard, in charge of General Thomas' remains, to consult with Mrs. Thomas and to determine as to some of the details of the funeral. The funeral party should reach Troy, New York, by Thursday of next week, and, if the burial is to be there, then Friday will be the proper day, as you must be at Philadelphia on Saturday, and the President also. If the body is properly prepared, it could be taken from Troy to West Point on Monday, April 11th, and the funeral take place on Tuesday, the 12th. Please have someone

20. *Ibid.*, p. 443.
21. *Ibid.*

well out on the road at Bridger, or Fort Sanders, to see Colonel Willard and get an answer on these points, that I may announce the day of the ceremonies to the general public.

W. T. Sherman,<br>General.

It was the wish of Sherman and some of the military leaders that Thomas' body be interred at West Point, but Mrs. Thomas declined the request. In her letter to Sherman, on April 2, she expressed her desire:

> I regret that I cannot yield to the desire of having the burial at West Point. As Troy will be my future home, I feel that I must bury General Thomas in my family lot at the cemetery there. I will leave to you the arrangements for a military funeral at Troy. On the arrival of the remains there, they will be deposited temporarily in the receiving vault. Colonel Willard knows my wishes. Private services have already been held here. Sincere thanks for your attention.
>
> Frances L. Thomas.[22]

As the Commander-in-Chief of the Army, Sherman, a classmate of General Thomas' at West Point, had announced his death to the Army as a tribute to the memory of this gallant soldier:

Headquarters of the Army,<br>Adjutant General's Office,<br>Washington, March 29, 1870.

General Orders
No. 34,

It has become the painful duty of the General to announce to the Army the death of one of our most exalted generals, George H. Thomas, who expired last evening, at half-past seven, in San Francisco, California.

There is no need to turn to the archives to search for his history, for it is recorded in almost every page during the past ten years; but his classmate and comrade owes him a personal tribute, in which he knows every member of the Army shares. General Thomas entered the Military Academy in the class of 1836; graduated in 1840, and was commissioned as a Second

22. Thomas, pp. 621-22.

Lieutenant, Third Artillery, and sent to Florida. He served
with his regiment continuously until December 24, 1853, when
he became a Captain, having been particularly distinguished
at Monterey and Buena Vista, Mexico. On the 12th of May,
1855, he was appointed to the Second Cavalry as Major, and
served with that regiment continuously until he became its
Colonel on the 3d of May, 1861. The great civil war found
him at his post, true and firm, amidst the terrible pressure he
encountered by reason of his birthplace—Virginia, and President Lincoln commissioned him as a Brigadier General of
Volunteers, and sent him to Kentucky. There, too, his services
were constant and eminent in the highest degree. He won the
first battle in the West, at Mill Spring[s], Kentucky, and, from
first to last, without a day's or an hour's intermission, he was
at his post of duty, rising steadily and irresistibly through all
the grades to the one he held as Major General of the Regular
Army at the time of his death. At Shiloh, Corinth, Perryville,
Stone[s] River, Chickamauga, Chattanooga, Atlanta, and Nashville, he fulfilled the proudest hopes of his ardent friends, and,
at the close of the war, General George H. Thomas stood in
the very front rank of our war generals.

The General has known General Thomas intimately since
they sat as boys on the same bench, and the quality in him,
which he holds up for the admiration and example of the
young, is his complete and entire devotion to duty. Though
sent to Florida, to Mexico, to Texas, and Arizona, when duty
there was absolute banishment, he went cheerfully, and never
asked a personal favor, exemption, or leave of absence. In
battle he never wavered. Firm, and of full faith in his cause,
he knew it would prevail, and he never sought advancement
of rank, or honor at the expense of any one. Whatever he
earned of these were his own, and no one disputes his fame.
The very impersonation of honesty, integrity, and honor, he
will stand to us as the beau ideal of the soldier and gentleman.

Though he leaves no child to bear his name, the Old Army
of the Cumberland, numbered by tens of thousands, called him
father, and will weep for him in tears of manly grief.

His wife, who cheered him with her messages of love in
the darkest hours of war, will mourn him now in sadness,
chastened by the sympathy of a whole country.

The last sad rites due him as a man and a soldier will be
paid at Troy, New York, on the arrival of his remains, and all

of his family and all his old comrades who can be present are
invited there to share in the obsequies.

At all military posts and stations the flag will be placed at
half staff, and fifteen minute-guns fired on the day after the
receipt of this order; and the usual badges of mourning will
be worn for thirty days.

By command of General Sherman:

E. D. Townsend,<br>
Adjutant General[23].

Final military arrangements for the funeral were set forth in
the following General Order from Sherman's headquarters.

Headquarters of the Army<br>
Adjutant General's Office<br>
Washington, April 3, 1870.

General Orders
No. 37

The body of Major General George H. Thomas will be buried
at Troy, New York, on Friday, April 8th, at 12 o'clock noon,
and the ceremonies will be conducted in military order, under
the supervision of Major General George G. Meade, Commanding Military Division of the Atlantic. The escort will be
a battalion of eight companies; and General Meade is authorized to use two of the companies of the Engineer battalion
from Willett's Point, two companies of the general recruits
from Governor's Island, and the band from West Point.

All officers of the Army who can be spared from duty, all
civil officers of the General and State Governments, members
of the Volunteer Armies, Civic Societies, and citizens generally
are invited to be present to manifest their respect to the memory of him who holds a sacred place in the heart of every
American.

By command of General Sherman:

E. D. Townsend,<br>
Adjutant General.[24]

The funeral ceremonies and services were impressive. Out of
respect to General Thomas, all Troy business and public build-

23. Van Horne, *Life*, pp. 446-47; Johnson, pp. 257-59.
24. Van Horne, *Thomas*, p. 447.

394

ings were draped in mourning, and business was suspended for part of the day. He was buried from St. Paul's Episcopal Church at noon on Friday, April 8. The funeral services were conducted in the church by the Right Reverend Bishop William C. Doane of the Protestant Diocese of Albany. President Grant and four members of his Cabinet, as well as members of Congress, and New York Governor John T. Hoffman attended the funeral. Also in attendance was Major General Irwin McDowell who commanded the military detachments of regulars, which consisted of two companies of Engineers from Willett's Point (now Fort Totten, N. Y.), one company of the First Artillery from Fort Hamilton, N. Y. (at New York Harbor's Narrows), one company of the First Artillery from Fort Schuyler (Rome, N. Y.), and two companies from Fort Columbus, Governor's Island. Officers of the Navy, representatives from the Society of the Army of the Cumberland, prominent officials from municipal governments from nearby cities, and many people in all walks of life joined in the services.[25].

The pallbearers were his most distinguished Civil War comrades: Generals George G. Meade, William S. Rosecrans, John M. Schofield, Joseph Hooker, John Newton, William B. Hazen, Gordon Granger, and Andrew J. McKay. A large military escort under the command of General Henry D. Wallen led the military and civil funeral procession that extended for a mile.

The remains of General Thomas were interred in the Kellogg family lot in Troy's Oakwood Cemetery on the Hudson River. Mrs. Thomas had an impressive monument erected in the form of a sarcophagus of white marble, surmounted by a finely sculptured American eagle grasping in its talons an accurate representation of the sword used by the general during the war.[26] The monument designed by the well known sculptor, Robert Eberhardt Launitz of New York City, was erected on October 26, 1870.

On the front, the inscription is in raised letters, his name encircled by a wreath of oak and laurel:

25. *New York Times*, April 9, 1870; Van Horne, *Life*, p. 448.
26. Van Horne, *Life*, p. 448.

## GEORGE H. THOMAS,
Major General U. S. Army.

Born Southampton County, Va. July 31, 1816.

Died San Francisco, Cal. March 28, 1870.

Two members of the general's family refused to attend the services. His sisters, Misses Judith E. and Frances Thomas, told their neighbors, "Our brother died to us in 1861." An historian observed, "So intense was their feeling against their brother that they turned his picture to the wall, and unto death, would have nothing to do with him."

A meeting of the Society of the Army of the Cumberland was held in Troy, New York, for the purpose of extending an invitation to General James A. Garfield to be its principal speaker at their next annual reunion to be held in Cleveland, Ohio, on November 25, 1870. The request was for a eulogy to be given by Garfield on the life and character of Thomas. At the time of Thomas' death, Garfield was President of the Society, which had been founded in February of 1868. At the Society's first meeting after Thomas' decease, the following resolution was passed:

> Resolved, That it is vain by words to attempt to express our loss, or to describe the grief which pervades this society in view of this sad event.
>
> Resolved, That the banners of this society be draped in mourning and that an appropriate memorial page be inscribed upon its records.
>
> Resolved, That some fitting monument should be erected by his countrymen to mark the spot where the remains of our beloved commander rest, and that this society shall take the initiatory steps for its erection, and to that end a committee of one from each State represented in the society be now appointed, to arrange some method to procure the necessary funds, and to provide a design, specifications and estimates therefor, and to report at the next meeting.
>
> Resolved, That the president shall appoint some comrade to prepare a biography of General Thomas, and collate and arrange the obituary proceedings of the various States and

396

associations in honor of his memory with a view to future publication by this society.[27]

The Committee met from time to time, until almost ten years had elapsed before the "fitting monument," an impressive bronze equestrian statue of Thomas, was erected in Thomas Circle, in a picturesque open space at the intersection of Rhode Island, Massachusetts, and Vermont Avenues, and Fourteenth and M Streets in Washington, D. C. The statue, by John Quincy Adams Ward, a sculptor of renown, was dedicated on November 19, 1879. Stanley Matthews, Senator from Ohio, made an eloquent presentation address, and the statue was received for the nation by Rutherford B. Hayes, President of the United States. It is the only monument to his memory. And it does not, of course, "mark the spot where the remains" lie.

At the unveiling of the statue, General Sherman, speaking for a delegation of veterans, predicted that the day would come when Southerners "would make pilgrimages to this splendid monument in memory of a great and noble man." "Brave George Thomas," said Sherman, "will become the ideal of the South." But this has not come to pass.

General Thomas' estate was settled under the laws of Tennessee, to the benefit of Mrs. Thomas thus preventing any other heirs from making any claims. From the records of the Surrogate's Court in the County of Rensselaer, Troy, New York, General Thomas died intestate. A Decree of Settlement of his estate was entered in that court on April 10, 1872, in accordance with the laws of the domicile of the deceased, being the State of Tennessee, and since General Thomas died without children the entire estate was granted to his widow, Frances L. Thomas, who was also named Administratrix of his estate. Considerable for the time and for a soldier with little opportunity to mind his personal affairs, it amounted to more than thirty-four thousand dollars.

In an admirable address given before the Annual Meeting of the New-York Historical Society on January 4, 1876, titled, "The Decisive Battle of the Rebellion," John Watts De Peyster, in praising General Thomas for his achievements, offered this tribute:

27. *Ibid.*, pp. 449-50.

When the propitious moment arrived, when the first hour of success, but of unequalled triumph struck, Thomas struck, and the most perfectly ordered attack of the war was delivered, and the most decisive defeat of the war was achieved. . . .

Turned, baffled and breached on every side, [General] Hood was tumbled into utter ruin. The irresistible flood of victory burst upon him and swept him away, rolling along with it the bodies of his men and horses, and the material of his host dissolved into nothingness.

De Peyster further called attention to "the torture which was applied to Thomas to compel him to override his own common sense and fight this battle before he was properly prepared. Halleck was at him; Stanton was at him; Grant was at him; Sherman was at him; and even Lincoln, innocent of any intention to do so, was dragged in to assist in applying the pressure."

In May of 1890, when Thomas L. James of Utica, New York, and his wife were returning by train from a trip to Cleveland for the dedication of the Garfield Memorial, they found themselves in company of a fellow traveler, General Sherman. During this trip General Sherman conversed freely with them about Union and Confederate commanders he had known. After paying the highest respect to these generals, he placed Generals Longstreet and Joseph E. Johnston at the head of the Confederates. After he had cited Grant, McPherson, Sheridan, and others, he noted that "after all, in many respects Thomas was a typical soldier." "Old Tom," he said, "as we always called him, was a classmate of mine at West Point, and was always a thorough gentleman, thoughtful and respectful of other people's feelings, and who knew not only how to command but how to obey." Then General Sherman told the story how Thomas was made a brigadier general:

Mr. Lincoln, in the early part of the war, sent for me to come to Washington. While there he did me the honor to consult me regarding the names of those he intended to nominate to the Senate for brigadier generals. After hearing the proposed list I said to him, "Why don't you nominate old Thomas?" His reply was that Thomas was born in Virginia, and there were doubts as to his loyalty. In my most earnest manner I protested indignantly against this most cruel accusation. I said: "Mr. President, Old Tom is as loyal as I am and as a soldier he is superior to all on your list." Mr. Lincoln said, "Will you be responsible for him?" and I unhesitating replied, "With the greatest pleasure."

The President instantly sent his name among others to the Senate. In the afternoon of that day I went to the Senate Chambers to see my brother, John Sherman, of Ohio, and he told me of the names on the list of brigadier generals that had been sent to the Senate, and said they had all been confirmed, Thomas with the rest. I then began to recollect that I had not seen Thomas for twenty years, and I had become responsible for him. It was a hot day, and the thing so worried me that I went to the War Department and asked where Colonel Thomas, now brigadier general, was to be found. I was told, in Maryland, some eight or ten miles from the city. So I ordered a carriage and started at once, my anxiety to see him impelling me to urge the driver to make as rapid time as he could. When I arrived at the place I inquired where Colonel Thomas was; and the sergeant of the guard went with me to Thomas' tent, and found that he was in the saddle superintending some movement of the troops. Controlling my impatience, I waited in no easy frame of mind, that sultry day, for his return, and as there is an end to everything, Thomas came back at last and we greeted one another heartily.

"Tom," said I, "you are a brigadier general." "I don't know of any one that I would rather hear such news from than you," he replied. "But," I said, "Tom, there are some stories about your loyalty. How are you going?" "Billy," he replied, "I am going South." "My God!" I exclaimed, "Tom, you have put me in an awful position; I have become responsible for your loyalty." "How so?" said he. So I related to him the conversation between President Lincoln and myself, when he leaned back, and remarked, "Give yourself no trouble, Billy; I am going South, but at the head of my men." And so he did, and no nobler man, no braver, better soldier, and no more courteous gentleman ever lived.

General Sherman then gave a very thrilling description of the battle of Nashville, which he said itself alone proved Thomas to possess all the qualities of a great commander. Mrs. James then asked him where he placed Hood as a soldier— if he ranked anywhere near Johnston and Longstreet. "No, madam," energetically replied General Sherman, "I don't; still he always gave me a great deal of trouble and annoyance when he was in front of me. For, madam, there is no telling what such a fellow will do."[28]

Thomas guarded his personal life to such a degree that, even after his death, his wife would not reveal his personal papers. Naturally there are fewer intimate stories regarding his life than about the lives of other military heroes. His reticent shyness was probably due to many instances in which he experienced hurt feelings. There are, however, many testimonies to Thomas' character. Colonel Theodore A. Dodge once said of him:

> He was essentially cast in a large mold, in mind and body; so modest that he shrunk from command, to which he was peculiarly fitted; with courage of the stamp that ignores self; possessing steadfastness in greater measure than audacity, he yet lacked none of that ability which can deal heavy blows; while no antagonist was ever able to shake his foothold. Honesty in thought, word, and deed was constitutional with him. A thorough military training, added to a passionate love of his profession and great natural powers, made him peer of any soldier. Sedate in mind and physically slow in movement, he yet aroused great enthusiasm.[29]

On Friday, March 3, 1865, General Thomas had received the Thanks of Congress for his victory at the battles of Franklin and Nashville. (He was one of fifteen army officers so honored during the Civil War.) Writing of that occasion, General Richard W. Johnson, who had been associated with General Thomas for some thirteen years, said of him:

> Looking back at the achievements of Thomas he is seen in his true character—an incorruptible patriot, a brave, wise, and skillful soldier. And as years pass by and the bitter wounds engendered by the war have been healed, his honored name will be more and more venerated by the people of America, as they will see in his life those noble traits of character which

28. Coppée, pp. 319-20.
29. Francis Trevelyan Miller, ed., *The Photographic History of the Civil War,* 10 Vols. (New York: Review of Reviews, 1912), IX, 103.

distinguished him, in an eminent degree, in every period of his manhood. Let the young study his character and strive to imitate his noble example. No better model can be placed before them than that completely rounded, skillful, judicious, modest soldier, that wise, calm, self-poised, steadfast chieftain, the hero of Chickamauga and Nashville, the able commander of the Army of the Cumberland.[30]

Charles A. Dana, who as an Assistant Secretary of War and who had recommended to the government that General William S. Rosecrans be replaced by Thomas in October, 1863, made these comments about General Thomas in his *Recollections of the Civil War:*

> He was certainly an officer of the very highest qualities, soldierly and personally. He was a man of the greatest dignity of character. He had more the character of George Washington than any other man I ever knew. At the same time he was a delightful man to be with; there was no artificial dignity about Thomas. He was a West Point graduate, and very well educated. He was very set in his opinions, yet he was not impatient with anybody—a noble character.[31]

Perhaps the most comprehensive of all tributes to the character and achievement of Thomas (as well as the most ornate) is that by William Swinton found in his *Twelve Decisive Battles of the War:*

> When the Rebellion opened, Major Thomas was a soldier of twenty years' experience, during which he had not only not turned aside to the attractions of civil life, but had accepted only . . . [three] furloughs. It was during his latter leave of absence that the insurrection broke out, and Thomas received the colonelcy of his regiment, now styled the Fifth Cavalry.
>
> From this time the fame of General Thomas becomes national. His complete and admirable victory at Mill Springs was the first triumph of magnitude for the North since the disaster at Bull Run [First Manassas], and brought back a needed

30. Johnson, p. 30.
31. Suzanne Colton Wilson, *Column South* (Flagstaff, Ariz.: Colton, 1960), pp. 356-57.

401

prestige to the Union army. As commander of the Fourteenth Army Corps, under Rosecrans, he was conspicuous in the marching and fighting which preceded Murfreesboro [Stones River], and all-glorious in that decisive battle. Him, Rosecrans then portrayed as "true and prudent, distinguished in council and celebrated on many battle-fields for his courage." It was he who, alone and unaided, saved the Army of the Cumberland at Chickamauga, when the example of all around him might have excused him for flying from the lost field.

And again, accordingly, the enthusiastic tribute of praise comes up in the report of Rosecrans: "To Major General Thomas, the true soldier, the prudent and undaunted commander, the modest and incorruptible patriot, the thanks and gratitude of the country are due for his conduct at the battle of Chickamauga." It was Thomas, whose troops, "forming on the plain below with the precision of parade," made the wonderful charge on Missionary Ridge which threw Bragg back into Georgia. It was he who in the grand Atlanta campaign commanded, under Sherman, more than three-fifths of that army, and who delivered the opening battle at Buzzard's Roost and the closing battle at Lovejoy's. It was Thomas, in fine, who set the seal of success on the Georgia campaign, three hundred miles away in Nashville.

Imposing in stature, massive in thew and limb, the face and figure of General Thomas consort well with the impression made by his character, the firm mouth, the square jaw, the steady blue eye, the grave expression habitual on the impassive countenance being indices to well-known traits. The war showed that his gifts, like his qualities, were, in the main, of that more solid and substantial sort which gain less immediate applause than what is specious and glittering, but which lead on to enduring fame. Yet there was noticeable in him a rare felicitous union of qualities which do not often appear with full vigor in the same organization. Cautious in undertaking, yet, once resolved, he was bold in execution; deliberate in forming his plan and patiently waiting for events to mature, yet when the fixed hour struck he leaped into great activity. Discretion in him was obviously spurred on by earnestness, and earnestness tempered by discretion. Prudent by nature, not boastful, reticent, he was not the less free from the weakness of will and tameness of spirit which are as fatal to success as rashness. He was, in short, one of those "whose blood and judgment are so well commingled that they are not a pipe for Fortune's finger to sound what stop she pleases."

Of his complete mastery of his profession in all its details, of his consummate skill as a general, the best monument is the story of his battles; for he never lost a campaign or a field, he never met his enemy without giving him cause to grieve for the *rencontre*, and he culled laurels from the fields on which brother-officers were covered with disgrace, and more than once pucked up drowning honor by the locks, as at Chickamauga. As he did not himself fail, so he did not suffer himself to be ruined by incompetency in superiors, much less in subordinates, for he was accustomed to consider beforehand such possibilities and to guard against them. His successes were won by art, not tossed to him by fortune; and whenever victory came to him he was conscious of having earned it. Such successes indicate temperaments at once solid and acute, and in which wisdom and valor concur, Nestor of the council and Hector of the field.

He was a soldier who conned his maps before he marched his army, who planned his campaign before he fought it, who would not hurry, who would not learn by thoughtless experiments what study could teach, who believed in the duty of a general to organize victory at each step. He was a lover of system, and was nothing if not systematic. He approved what was regular, and required proof of what was irregular; had that fondness for routine which does not ill become an old army officer; and even in exigencies desired everything to proceed duly and in order. He was not a slave to method, but naturally distrusted what was unmethodical; and that he invariably won battles by virtue of time-honored principles, and in accordance with the rules of the art of war, was, besides its value to the country, a truth invaluable to military science in the land, whose teachings had been somewhat unjustly cast into contempt by the conduct of other successful soldiers. His Nashville campaign gave more than one instance of the trait just noted. Superiors were vexed at his constant retreat from the Tennessee, at his flight behind the parapets of Nashville, at his delay to attack the investing force; but neither this vexation nor the danger of removal which threatened him could avail with Thomas, for that soldier would not be badgered into premature battle. Soon after the wisdom of Thomas in delaying attack in order to mount his cavalry approved itself, for never before in the war had grand victory been so energetically followed by pursuit. In the battle itself, too, spectators fancied that he was pausing too long before engaging his right flank, but he held that wing poised, as it were, in the air till the fit moment, when he swung it like a mighty sledge upon the Confederate and smote him to the dust.

The best justification of his system was its success, for if discreet he was safe; if slow, sure. He provided for dilemmas and obstacles, he suffered no surprises, made no disastrous experiments at the sacrifice of position, of prestige, or of the lives of his troops, and, indeed, he was wont to make the enemy pay dearly for the privilege of defeat, and usually lost fewer troops in action than his adversary, whether pursuing the offensive or the defensive. Thus, if the processes of his thought were slow of evolution, they at least attained to their goal.

His natural impulse would seem to be to stand *inebranlable* on the defensive, and, having taken manfully his enemy's blows till the assailant was exhausted, then to turn upon him in furious aggression; so it was with his first national victory at Mill Springs, and so with his latest at Nashville, while his fight at bay at Chickamauga is immortal. A fine analyzer of character might perhaps trace a sympathy between this military method, on the one hand, and the well-known personal traits of the soldier on the other: his modesty, his unassuming, unpretending spirit, his absence of self-assertion and habit of remaining in the background, and, therewith, his vigor when aroused and his bold championship of any cause entrusted to him. At all events, the fame of his persistency, of his firmness, almost amounting to obstinacy, of the unyielding grip with which he held his antagonist, became worldwide. When Grant hurried to the relief of beleaguered Chattanooga, there to supplant Rosecrans, he telegraphed to Thomas, then in command, "Hold on to Chattanooga at all hazards"; to which message came the sententious response: "Have no fear. Will hold the town till we starve." When steadfast he stood . . . [on Snodgrass Hill], on the field of Chickamauga, after the columns on both of his flanks had given way, the torrent of Bragg's onset, the hail of fire that swept the Union ranks moved him not a jot from his firm base, and the billow that swamped the rest of the field recoiled from him. "The rain descended, and the floods came and beat upon that house, and it fell not: for it was founded upon a rock." Thereafter the soldiers of the Army of the

Cumberland were wont to call him "The Rock of Chicka-mauga."

Grave and wise at the council board, yet it is on the well-contested field that Thomas shines most conspicuous. In the ordinary tide of battle he is emphatically the imperturbable, calm, poised, entirely cool, self-possessed one, on whom the shifting fortunes of the day have only a subdued effect, and whose equanimity even success cannot dangerously disturb. But he is greatest in extremity, that "trier of spirits." In the supreme moment of exigency, which demands a great soul to grasp it—such a one as came to overtasked Hooker at Chancellorsville—Thomas shines out pre-eminent and asserts his superiority. Phlegmatic at most hours, the desperate crises of battle are alone sufficient to stir his temperament into fullest action, and then his quiet, steady eyes flame a little with battle-fire.

He had the great quality of inspiring in his troops perfect confidence and great devotion. Indeed, his soldierly skill was well set off by the air and manner of a soldier: unaffected, manly, far from the pettiness bred by long pampering in the drawing-room, but with a simplicity, robustness, and hardiness of character like that of his own physique, the inheritance of thirty years in field and garrison. Dignified and decorous, his brother-officers found him free from show and pretence, frank, open, and magnanimous; while to his troops he was kindly and amiable. He excited no envy or jealousy in his rivals, who found him straightforward and conscientious; and his men had cause to know that he was observant of merit and rewarded it. His reputation was without reproach, his controlled temper superior to the vicissitudes of camp and battle, and joined to them was a courage which set life at a pin's fee. A Virginian, and of such social ties as might well have made him "a Pharisee of the Pharisees," he had proved at the outset the quality of the allegiance he bore to the republic by casting in his lot with the Union arms. His loyalty was disinterested and the result of conviction, not of political aspiration.

The progress of the war, too, gave him, as it did so many officers, a chance to show the quality and stability of his patriotism. Even while the country resounded with the glories of Chickamauga and Missionary Ridge, Sherman, his junior in experience, in length of service, and in years, and his equal only in rank, was appointed over him to the command vacated by

General Grant. Without murmur, perhaps without thought of injury, Thomas took his place under Sherman with the cheerful obedience of a true soldier. On the eve of Nashville he was to have been relieved of command, but desired, for the sake of the country, that he might execute a long-formed plan, after which he would be at such disposal as might seem fit.

Such was General Thomas, the completely rounded, skillful, judicious, modest soldier, a man compact, of genuine stuff, a trustworthy man:

"Rich in saving common sense,

and, as the greatest only are,

In his simplicity sublime."[32]

32. Johnson, pp. 247-53.

# APPENDICES

## APPENDIX A

### Mrs. Frances Thomas' Pension

In 1879, Mrs. Thomas was 58 years of age when she applied for a widow's pension. She was granted a monthly stipend of $30.00. At that time she was living at 3 Park Place in Troy, New York. Then, by an Act of Congress, on February 20, 1885, she was granted an increase to $2,000.00 per annum under Certificate No. 183243, from the U. S. Pension Agency. The following is a transcript of the Act:

Private—No. 102.

AN ACT granting an increase of pension to Mrs. Frances L. Thomas, widow of Major General George H. Thomas.

Be it enacted by the Senate and House of Representatives of the United States of America in Congress assembled, That the Secretary of the Interior be, and he is hereby, authorized and directed to increase the pension of thirty dollars a month now received by Mrs. Frances L. Thomas, widow of Major General George H. Thomas, to two thousand dollars per annum, to take effect from and after the passage of this act.

Approved, February 20th, 1885.*

*Copy of document dated March 16, 1885, by the Department of State is in the author's possession.

## APPENDIX B

### General Thomas' Unfinished Letter
### of March 28, 1870

General Thomas' unfinished reply to the anonymous letter supposedly written by General Schofield printed in the *New York Tribune* of March 12, 1870. General Thomas was preparing this letter when he was stricken with his fatal attack of apoplexy:

The article in the *Tribune* was evidently brought out by the assertions in the *Gazette* correspondence that [General] Grant would have committed a serious blunder had he relieved Thomas by Schofield, who as appears by the article, claims the battle of Franklin was fought under his immediate supervision, and was so eminently successful, that he consequently was as acceptable to the army as General Thomas. (That may or may not be.) It is hoped that the troops would have done their duty under any commander; but [Generals] Wood and Stanley and many other officers of rank, who participated prominently in that battle, know the peculiar situation of affairs that rendered it necessary, General Thomas should remain in Nashville to receive the reenforcements which were arriving daily, supervising and expediting their equipment (the cavalry sent back by General Sherman being all dismounted, the new regiments arriving from the States needing camp equipage, etc., to enable them to take the field), and that Schofield happened to command the troops immediately opposing the advancing enemy, by virtue of his position as an army commander, (he commanded the army of the Ohio).

The criticisms on the plan of battle and point of attack (referring to Nashville) are too unimportant to notice. With regard to the mistake of not using 10,000 to great advantage, the original position of the 10,000 men. (Schofield's Army of the Ohio, Twenty-third corps, in reserve), being central, rendered them available for promptly reenforcing Steedman, should the enemy concentrate so heavily on him as to endanger his position, when he made his demonstration on the enemy's right, to draw attention from the real point of attack.

Steedman having reported early in the morning that he could not be driven from his position, this reserve was no longer needed where it then was, and was ordered to form in support of [A. J.] Smith, and support him in his advance on the enemy's left. Smith's advance leaving an internal between his right, and the left of the cavalry, the 10,000 men were ordered to fill up the gap, and became engaged toward the close of the day's operations. It is therefore left to candid minds to judge, whether the 10,000 men were advantageously posted originally and afterwards used to advantage, or not.

It is believed that no other officer of high rank in the army, except the writer of the *Tribune* article, will say that General

Thomas was so fully convinced that the enemy had retreated at the close of the first day of the battle, that he gave no orders to continue operations the next day, but ordered a pursuit. The blunder of the pontoon train is admitted in so far, that the staff officer who wrote the order to the commander of the train, by mistake wrote Murfreesboro pike, instead of Nolensville pike, and the train had gone a mile or two on that pike before the mistake was discovered, but it was promptly rectified before it had gone four miles out of the way, and then joined the army, and got to the front perhaps as quickly as it could have done by the Franklin pike, as it marched across the country by a free and practicable road. It could not have reached Franklin, under any circumstances, in time to place a bridge for the crossing of the troops when the infantry reached that point.

It was always supposed, too, that every officer of high rank, who fought in the battle of Nashville, knew that until Duck River was crossed, the enemy could be pursued with any prospect of success, only by the main road. [Big] Harpeth River, Rutherford['s] Creek, and Duck River, were all then rendered impassable by high water, in consequence of the thaw, the day before the battle, and heavy rains during the battle. All bridges over those streams, for twenty or thirty miles on either side of the main road, had been destroyed. All practicable roads to Duck River, emerged from the main road, and consequently troops following them would have been soon separated from the main column, and [have been] placed beyond supporting distance. The report of General Thomas explains the difficulties in laying a pontoon bridge across Rutherford['s] Creek, and accounts for the delay at that stream, and also at Duck River. After Duck River was crossed at Columbia, the Waynesboro and Lawrenceburg roads might have been taken by a part of the force, which in all probability could not have reached thereby the flank of the enemy in time to have inflicted any serious damage, because Hood had by that time placed his main column south of Richland Creek, and within a day's march of the point on the Tennessee River, when his pontoon bridges had been in position for several weeks. The above sufficiently accounts for the statement in the *Tribune* article, that a corps frequently did not march [more] than its length in three days.

The infantry were at all events on the main road, where they could have [been] made available in case there was any necessity for using them, while the Fourth corps closely following up the cavalry, enabled General Wilson to do exactly what "One who fought at Nashville" says might have [been] done if the infantry had been marched along the main road with three days' rations in haversacks.

Wilson's cavalry was constantly harassing the enemy's flanks, whenever the condition of the roads and streams would admit of his doing so; and it was this vigorous conduct of the cavalry which caused the enemy to retreat with such haste, as to get beyond the reach of the main column before all the infantry could cross Duck River.

The writer virtually admits that General Schofield believed there was no further necessity for pursuit after the enemy had crossed Richland Creek at Pulaski, as he says on the 26th of December he wrote to General Grant that Hood's army was then used up, that there was no further need of his troops in Tennessee, and asked to be ordered to the Army of the Potomac.

Here there is a little discrepancy between the *Tribune* article and the actual facts. The writer says after the escape of Hood, General Thomas published an order placing the troops in winter quarters, and commenced planning a campaign for the next spring and summer against Corinth, etc. By reference to General Thomas' report, it will be seen that the order was issued on the 30th of December. Schofield says on the 26th. Perhaps General Schofield was not aware of the reasons for this objectionable order.

The report of General Sherman to the Committee on the Conduct of the War will explain it, as it will there be seen that General Thomas was expected to take care of Tennessee, until Sherman reached the sea and gave further instructions. (Smith's corps was to go to Eastport, Mississippi; Wood's corps to Huntsville and Athens; Schofield's corps to Dalton; Wilson's cavalry between Huntsville and Eastport, along the Tennessee River).

If, when General Thomas was sent back to Nashville, his army had been sent with him . . . the Fourteenth and Fourth corps, there would have been no cause for the present newspaper contest about the battle of Nashville. There is ample proof already published that Thomas had at his command when Hood commenced his movement against Sherman's communication, only a small division of troops stationed along the two lines of communication between Nashville and Chattanooga to protect them against small raiding parties. When he reported the situation to General Sherman, and applied for reenforcements to meet the advance of Hood, the Fourth corps and dismounted cavalry were first sent, and General Thomas was informed that he would get reenforcements by several new regiments then on their way to join Sherman's army. Afterwards Thomas was informed that A. J. Smith's command would be ordered to join him from Missouri.

Thomas then urged that additional reenforcements should be sent him, as most of the convalescent troops at Chattanooga belonged to different corps and different armies, and could not be relied upon from want of effective organization to more than defend that place. Schofield was then ordered to report to Thomas.

With the exception of the Fourth and Twenty-third corps, Croxton's, Hatch's and Capron's brigades of cavalry, all the troops sent by Sherman had to be equipped for field service, including transportation. To attend to the equipping of this force, as well as to be able to correspond with General Sherman, Thomas was compelled to remain in Nashville, whilst he placed Schofield in immediate charge of the troops engaged in watching the movement of Hood, and retarding his advance on Nashville. This necessity existing until the army fell back to Nashville, gave Schofield the opportunity to fight the battle of Franklin. This was a very brilliant battle, most disastrous to the enemy, and as the writer in the *Tribune* says, no doubt contributed materially to the crowning success at Nashville . . . .

Colonel Sanford Kellogg added, "A few blurred and disconnected lines follow as the angel of death hovered near him, and then General Thomas fell to the floor of his office unconscious."

APPENDIX C

A Military Outline of General Thomas' Military Service as Adapted and Expanded from George W. Cullum *Biographical Register Of The Officers And Graduates Of The U. S. Military Academy at West Point, New York* (New York: Van Nostrand, 1868), 33-40.

Thomas was a cadet at the United States Military Academy at West Point, New York, from July 1, 1836, to July 1, 1840. He was 12th in a class of 42. Upon graduation he was promoted in the army to:

Second Lieutenant, Third Artillery, July 1, 1840.<br>
Company D, Third Artillery, July 1, 1840, to<br>
December 31, 1843.

He was on graduating leave to September 30, 1840.

Served on garrison duty at Fort Columbus [on Governor's Island], New York, to November 23, 1840.

Participated in the Second Seminole War, from December 9, 1840, to February 6, 1842. Saw service with Major Richard D. Wade in the expedition against the Seminoles, capturing 70 Indians, on November 6, 1841.

Was Breveted First Lieutenant, November 6, 1841,<br>
for Gallantry and Good Conduct in the War against<br>
the Seminole Indians.

On garrison duty at New Orleans Barracks, Louisiana, to June 30, 1842; Fort Moultrie [on Sullivan's Island, in Charleston Harbor], South Carolina, to December 5, 1843; Fort McHenry [at Baltimore], Maryland, to October 19, 1844.

Assigned to<br>
Company C, Third Artillery, December 31, 1843,<br>
to July 29, 1844, stationed at Fort McHenry.<br>
First Lieutenant, Third Artillery, April 30, 1844.

Thomas joined Company E, Third Artillery, July 29, 1844, to August 6, 1845, at Fort Moultrie.

He was assigned to recruiting service at Charleston, South Carolina, to March 15, 1845.

Served in the Military Occupation of Texas, from 1845 to 1846.

412

He and his company left Fort Moultrie on June 26, 1845, on orders to report to General Zachary Taylor at New Orleans, Louisiana, and on July 24, sailed for Texas, under command of General Taylor, arriving at Corpus Christi, Texas, [first U. S. troops to occupy soil of Texas]. Saw service in the Mexican War, from 1846 to 1848. Participated in the defense of Fort Texas [at Brownsville], Texas, from May 3 to 9, 1846.

Breveted Captain, September 23, 1846, for
Gallant and Meritorious Conduct in several
conflicts at Monterrey, Mexico.

The Battle of Monterrey, September 21 to 23, 1846; the Battle of Buena Vista, February 22 to 23, 1847.

Breveted Major, February 23, 1847, for
Gallant and Meitorious Conduct in the
Battle of Buena Vista, Mexico.

On garrison duty at the mouth of the Rio Grande, Texas, from 1848 to 1849; at Brazos Santiago, Texas, from August 9, 1848, to February 1, 1849, in charge of the commissary depot; was on leave of absence to August 1, 1849; with regiment at Fort Adams, Rhode Island [on Brentons Point near Newport], to September 12, 1849.

Company B, Third Artillery, from August 6, 1849,
to December 24, 1853.

Hostilities against the Seminole Indians in Florida, from 1849 to 1850; on garrison duty at Fort Independence [on Castle Island in Boston Harbor], Massachusetts, to March 28, 1851.

On detached service as an Instructor of Artillery and Cavalry at the United States Military Academy at West Point, New York, from April 2, 1851, to May 1, 1854.

Captain, Third Artillery, December 24, 1853.
Company A, Third Artillery, December 24, 1853,
to May 12, 1855.

On frontier duty, with regiment on the march to Benicia Barracks and Arsenal, at Benicia, California, commanding the Third Artillery Battalion in May of 1854; in June Thomas commanded a battalion of the First and Third Artillery and was en route to Fort Yuma [on the Colorado River, opposite mouth of the Gila], California, arriving there on July 14, 1854, commanding the post at that place to July 21, 1855.

413

Major, Second Cavalry, May 12, 1855.

On garrison duty at Jefferson Barracks [10 miles south of St. Louis], Missouri, serving with the Second Cavalry from September 25 to October 27, 1855. On court martial duty at Fort Washita [near False Washita River, 25 miles above its mouth], Indian Territory, serving to January of 1856. On recruiting service in New York, to May, 1856. With regiment on frontier duty and commanding Fort Mason [on Comanche Creek, near the Llano River], Texas, to September 8, 1856.

Assigned to court martial duty in Texas, to April 6, 1857, and again at Fort Mason, Texas, with regiment and commanding to November 8, 1857; was in command of regiment from October 21, 1857, to November 12, 1860, and commanded post of San Antonio, Texas, to December 9, 1857; Fort Mason, Texas, to June 26, 1858; Fort Belknap [on the Red Fork of the Brazos River], Texas, to February 23, 1859; and Camp Cooper [five miles east of the mouth of the Ateys Creek, in Throckmorton County], Texas, to November, 1860.

Thomas commanded an escort of Texas Indians to their new home in the Indian Territory, from July 30 to August 21, 1859.

Leading the expedition to the headwaters of the Red and Canadian Rivers in the Red River Country, from 1859 to 1860.

While engaged in a Kiowa Expedition in 1860, in a skirmish with Indians near the head of Clear Fork of the Brazos River on August 26, 1860, he was wounded in the face by an arrow.

Thomas was granted a leave of absence, from November 12, 1860, to April 11, 1861.

Served during the Civil War from 1861 to 1865. In command of a regiment until June 3, engaged in reorganizing and equipping his regiment at Carlisle Barracks, Pennsylvania, from April 14 to May 27, 1861, excepting from April 21 to 25, when he was with four companies at Harrisburg and York, Pennsylvania.

Lieutenant Colonel Second Cavalry, April 25, 1861.

Colonel Second Cavalry, May 3, 1861,

[later became the Fifth Cavalry,

by an Act of Congress, August 3, 1861].

Participated in operations in the Shenandoah Valley, from June 1, to August 26, 1861, was in command of a brigade while engaged in the action of Falling Waters [or Hoke's Run], Virginia,

414

July 2, 1861; Action at Martinsburg, Virginia, July 3, 1861; and Skirmish at Bunker Hill, Virginia, July 15, 1861.

Brigadier General, U. S. Volunteers, August 17, 1861.

Duty in the Department of the Cumberland, at Louisville, Kentucky, from September 6 to November 30, 1861; in command of Camp Dick Robinson, Kentucky, from September 18 to October 28, 1861, organizing and mustering Kentucky and Tennessee Volunteers.

In advance on Crab Orchard and Lebanon, Kentucky, in command of the 1st Division, Army of the Ohio, from October 28 to November 30, 1861.

Also commanded a division [Army of the Ohio], November 30, 1861, to March 19, 1862, being in command and successfully engaged in the Battle of Mill Springs [also known as Logan Cross Roads], Kentucky, January 19 and 20, 1862.

Movement on Nashville, Tennessee, by way of Somerset, Lebanon, and Louisville, Kentucky, from February 15 to March 4, 1862.

Engaged in the Tennessee and Mississippi Campaign from March 19 to June 26, 1862. Participated in the march to Pittsburg Landing, Tennessee, leading his division, a reserve of the Army of the Ohio, from March 19 to April 9, 1862.

Commanded the Right Wing [Army of the Tennessee] during the advance to and Siege of Corinth, Mississippi, from April 9 to May 30, 1862.

Major General, U. S. Volunteers, April 25, 1862.

In command at Corinth, Mississippi, from June 5 to 22, 1862.

Service with the Army of the Ohio, under Major General Don Carlos Buell, and campaigning in Northern Alabama, Tennessee, and Kentucky, from June 26 to November 7, 1863.

On duty at Tuscumbia, Alabama, guarding the Memphis & Charleston Railroad from June 26 to July 25, 1862. In command at Decherd, Tennessee, from August 5 to 15; McMinnville, Tennessee, from August 19 to September 3; and Nashville, Tennessee, from September 7 to 14, 1862.

En route to Kentucky and pursuit of the enemy from Prewitt's Knob, Kentucky, and to Louisville, Kentucky, from September 20 to 26, 1862.

Was second in command of the Army of the Ohio, in advance

415

into Kentucky, from September 30 to November 7, 1862, being present near the Battle of Perryville (Chaplin Hills), on October 8, 1862, in command of the Right Wing of the Army of the Ohio, and in pursuit of the enemy to Barbourville, Kentucky.

Commanding the Centre of the Fourteenth Army Corps, Army of the Cumberland, in Major General William S. Rosecrans' Tennessee Campaign from November 7, 1862, to October 19, 1863.

Engaged in the Battle of Stones River [or Murfreesboro], from December 31, 1862, to January 2, 1863.

Advance on Tullahoma, Tennessee, from June 24 to July 4, 1863. Action at Hoover's Gap, Tennessee, June 26, 1863; Spring Gay, July 1, 1863; and crossing of the Elk River, July 3.

Chickamauga Campaign from August 16 to September 22, 1863, and the Battle of Chickamauga, September 18 and 20, 1863, and Rossville, Georgia, September 21, 1863.

Checked the enemy's advance upon Chattanooga and vicinity, September 21, 1863, into which he retired and commenced fortifying.

In command of the Department and the Army of the Cumberland, relieving General William S. Rosecrans on October 19, 1863, being engaged in the operations for opening communications by the Tennessee River and Lookout Valley, from October 27 to November 24, 1863.

Brigadier General, U. S. Army, October 27, 1863.

Operations about Chattanooga, Tennessee, November 23-26, 1863; Battle of Orchard Knob, Tennessee, November 23, 1863; storming of Missionary Ridge, Tennessee, was the decisive battle on November 25, 1863. Pursuit of the enemy and combat near Ringgold, Georgia, November 26, 1863.

Reorganizing his Army of the Cumberland from December 1, 1863, to May 6, 1864. Forced reconnaissance of Rocky Face, February 22-29, 1864.

Atlanta Campaign: Invasion of northwest Georgia, from May 7 to September 7, 1864, commanding the Army of the Cumberland [the Fourth, Fourteenth, and Twentieth Army Corps, and three cavalry divisions]. Engaged in the operations about Dalton, Georgia, from May 7 to 13, 1864.

Demonstrations against Resaca, Georgia, from May 13, until occupied on May 16, 1864; advance to and action at Cassville,

Georgia, from May 17 to 19, 1864; and occupation of Rome, Georgia, by Davis' Division of the Fourteenth Army Corps, May 18, 1864.

Battles of New Hope Church, Pumpkin Vine Creek, Picketts' Mill, and Burned Hickory, from May 25 to 28, 1864.

Actions about Pine Mountain, with daily constant engagements, from June 5-20, 1864.

Battles of Kolb's Farm [June 22] and Kennesaw Mountain [June 27], and action along the Kennesaw lines June 20-July 2, 1864. Action at Ruff's Station, Georgia, July 4, 1864.

Crossing of the Chattahoochee River, Georgia, from July 12 to 17, 1864.

Battle of Peach Tree Creek ["Hood's First Sortie"], Georgia, July 20, 1864.

Siege of Atlanta, from July 22 to September 2, 1864.

Assault on the enemy's entrenchments at Jonesboro, Georgia, on September 1, 1864.

Reorganizing the Army of the Cumberland and the defense of Tennessee against the Rebel invasion of Confederate General John Bell Hood, from October to December, 1864, at Nashville, Tennessee; Battle of Nashville, on Thursday and Friday, December 15 and 16, 1864, where the Confederate Army of the Tennessee was routed, and driven beyond the Tennessee River, with enormous loss of men and material.

President Lincoln promoted Thomas for his success at Nashville:

Major General, U.S. Army, December 15, 1864.

On March 3, 1865, General Thomas, his officers, and soldiers received a vote of thanks by the Congress of the United States of America for the defeat of the Rebel Army of Tennessee under General Hood.

Then the General Assembly of the State of Tennessee "Resolved," on November 2, 1865, their appreciation in the name of the people of the State of Tennessee, for Thomas' success in the Battle of Nashville, in defense of the Capital of the State.

Thomas was in command of the Military Division of the Tennessee, with headquarters in Nashville from June 27, 1865, to August 13, 1866. It included the States of Kentucky, Tennessee, Georgia, Alabama, and Mississippi.

417

He was a member of the Board for Recommendations for Brevets to grades of brigadier and major generals in the Regular Army, from March 14 to 24, 1866.

Thomas was commander of the Department of the Tennessee, embracing the States of Kentucky, Tennessee, Georgia, Alabama, and Mississippi, from August 13, 1866, to March 11, 1867, with headquarters at Nashville, Tennessee, until November 1, 1866, and at Louisville, Kentucky, until March 11, 1867.

He was assigned to the command of the Third Military District, comprising the States of Georgia, Florida, and Alabama, from March 11 to 15, 1867, from which he requested to be relieved, and was appointed to command the Department of the Cumberland, embracing Kentucky, Tennessee, and West Virginia, with headquarters at Louisville, Kentucky to May 15, 1869.

On August 17, 1867, General Thomas was assigned by President Andrew Johnson to take command of the Fifth Military District comprising the States of Louisiana and Texas, but was relieved from this command on August 27, because of poor health.

General Thomas was appointed President of the Court of Inquiry on September 10, 1868, to investigate the official conduct of Brigadier General Alexander B. Dyer, U. S. Army, Chief of Ordnance. The court convened in Washington, D. C., on November 9, 1868, and terminated on May 15, 1869. President Grant approved and confirmed the findings and opinions of this hearing.

Thomas commanded the Military Division of the Pacific, with headquarters at San Francisco, California, from June 1, 1869 to March 28, 1870.

General Thomas died at San Francisco, California, on March 28, 1870, aged 53 years, 7 months, and 28 days.

# Appendix D—Biographical Sketches

## BREVET MAJOR GENERAL SMITH D. ATKINS
### U. S. VOLUNTEERS

Smith D. Atkins was born near Elmira (Horseheads), Chemung County, New York, on June 9, 1835. He was the son of Adna Stanley and Sarah Dykins Atkins. In 1848, he came to Illinois with his parents at the age of thirteen years, living on a farm until 1850. His education began as he entered the printing-office of the *Prairie Democrat,* to learn the printer's trade. The *Prairie Democrat* was Freeport's first newspaper published and founded in November of 1847. While there he would study in his spare time. He continued his studies at "Old Sandstone," Rock River Seminary, Mount Morris, Illinois. In the fall of 1853 while a student of law, he became associated with Hiram Bright in Freeport. He was admitted to practice law on June 27, 1855.

In the latter part of 1855, he went to Chicago, Illinois, to continue to read law. There he entered the office of Goodrich & Scoville until September 1, 1856, when he returned to Freeport to enter private law practice. In 1860, when Abraham Lincoln was a candidate to the Presidency, Atkins became active during the campaign giving his full support to the election of Lincoln. In the same year he was elected State's Attorney for the Fourteenth Judicial Circuit for the State of Illinois, encompassing Jo Daviess, Stephenson, and Winnebago Counties. While he was trying a criminal case in Stephenson Circuit Court, he received a telegram stating that, inasmuch as Fort Sumter, in Charleston Harbor, South Carolina, had been fired upon by the Confederate forces on Friday, April 12, 1861, President Lincoln had issued his first call for 75,000 volunteers for three months' service on Monday, April 15, 1861, in order to subdue the rebellion of the Confederacy. While he was in the midst of this case, Atkins was so disturbed by the rebellious attitude of the South that he obtained permission from the Court to resign his office as prosecuting attorney. His request was granted and the Court appointed another lawyer to continue with the trial. He drafted an enlistment roll. His name being at the head of the list, he was the first citizen to enlist as a private volunteer in Stephenson County. At the end of the day he had enlisted 100 men from Freeport to the roll thus organizing a company choosing him as their captain. He and his companions proceeded to Springfield, Illinois where they were mustered in as Company A, 11th Illinois Volunteer Infantry. At the expiration of his three months' service, Atkins re-enlisted for the next three years as a private, at Bird's Point, Missouri. Again on April 30, 1861, he was selected captain of

Co. A, 11th Illinois Infantry Volunteers. On March 21, 1862, he was promoted to major of the 11th Regiment by War Governor Yates of Illinois for his extra-ordinary bravery in the Battle of Fort Donelson, Tennessee (February 13-16, 1862). Then on September 4, 1862, Governor Yates promoted Major Atkins to the colonelcy of the 92d Regiment Illinois Infantry Volunteers. With this regiment ,Col. Atkins played an important part in the Battle of Chickamauga, Georgia (September 18-20, 1863).

On June 17, 1863, Colonel Atkins commanded the 2d Brigade, 3d Division, Army of Kentucky, Department of Ohio. When the 92d Illinois Regiment was assigned to the Department of the Cumberland, he was placed in the 1st Division of the Reserve Corps as commander of the 1st Brigade. Later the regiment was mounted and furnished with the famous Spencer "seven-shooter" repeating rifles (which were an answer to Lincoln's prayers) and was transferred to Wilder's Lightning Brigade of Mounted Infantry. He accompanied and commanded the regiment until it was transferred to General Hugh Judson Kilpatrick's Cavalry Division. In the meantime, General Kilpatrick reorganized his division in preparation to accompany General Sherman's march to the sea from Atlanta to Savannah, Georgia, and through the Carolinas. Kilpatrick assigned the command of the Second Brigade to Colonel Atkins for the purpose of deceiving and holding the enemy while Sherman was making his movement through Georgia. Atkins' mission was successful. In all of his capacities as an officer, he was popular among his men. He was a strict disciplinarian, but very compassionate with the men who served under him. He was courageous with a keen sense of judgment as a strategist. His men placed their their confidence in him and did not hesitate to follow him in battle.

On Thursday, January 12, 1865, Colonel Atkins was breveted brigadier general of volunteers and on Monday, March 13, 1865, major general of volunteers by President Lincoln for gallantry and meritorious and distinguished service during the Civil War. At the close of the war he was honorably mustered out of service on Wednesday, June 21, 1865, from Concord, North Carolina.

On Wednesday, August 23, 1865, he married Miss Eleanor Hope Swain at Chapel Hill, North Carolina. The service was performed by Dr. F. M. Hubbard. Miss Swain was the youngest daughter of Governor David L. Swain of North Carolina. Two daughters and a son were born of this marriage.

He was 5 feet 10 inches in height, weighed 194 lbs., had a light complexion, blue eyes, brown hair, and his occupation was attorney-at-law.

After the war, General Atkins returned to his home in Freeport. He also returned to the newspaper business, his love, and for a number of years was editor and owner of the *Freeport Journal*. He was active in the public affairs of his community. He also served as the City's Postmaster for more than nineteen years.

On December 10, 1906, at the age of 71, he made an application for a veteran's pension. He was placed on the pension rolls of the United States, receiving a pension of $30.00 a month.

He died at his home, 44 Prospect Terrace, on Thursday evening, March 27, 1913, at the age of 77. He is buried in the city cemetery by the side of his mother and father.[1]

1. The History of Stephenson County, Illinois (Chicago: Western Historical Company, 1880), pp. 612, 613 and 614; Portrait and Biographical Album of Stephenson County, Illinois (Chicago: Chapman Brothers, 1888), pp. 189, 190 and 191; Addison L. Fulwider, A.M., History of Stephenson County, Illinois (Chicago: The S. J. Clarke Publishing Company, 1910), Vol. II, pp. 5, 6, and 7.


## ALDEN F. BROOKS

Alden Finney Brooks, the artist who executed the painting of General George H. Thomas in 1873, in Chicago, Illinois, is considered to be one of the finest portrait painters in the nation. The Thomas portrait is on permanent display in the G.A.R. Memorial Hall of the Chicago Public Library.

Brooks was born in West Williamsfield, Ashtabula County, Ohio, on April 3, 1840. As a boy, he had the desire to become an artist. In 1856, when he was sixteen his family moved to Platteville, Wisconsin. Here he grew to adulthood, a young man standing 5 feet 8½ inches tall, with a fair complexion, blue eyes and auburn hair.

In 1859, he decided to make a trip to California afoot which took him six months to complete. Along the way he made several sketches, and when he reached the coast he painted several portraits. The experience he gained from this was much more valuable to him than any monetary returns. He was in the town of Grass Valley, California, when the news of the Civil War reached him. Hearing the call to arms across the continent, he decided to return to his native state of Ohio by the way of South America to volunteer. On Wednesday, August 13, 1862, Brooks volunteered as a private in Co. I of the 105th Regiment, Ohio Infantry. In his first battle, he was wounded in action at Perryville, Kentucky, on Wednesday, October 8, 1862. Shortly after he became corporal of his company and on Friday, April 1, 1864, he was promoted to the rank of 1st lieutenant of Co. G by Governor John Brough of Ohio.

His gift for drawing became an asset to him during his services in the war, especially for drawing maps and topographical sketching. He was recognized for this talent and was assigned to the office of brigade topographical engineer. For his outstanding services at the battle of Hoover's Gap, Tennessee, June 26, 1863, he acquired a very responsible position as topographical engineer on the staff of

General Joseph J. Reynolds. During the last year of the war, Brooks became assistant topographical engineer on the staff of General George H. Thomas.

However, in spite of his busy schedule, he also found time for romance. The following is a letter written by Lt. Brooks to Brigadier General Wm. D. Whipple requesting that he be granted a leave-of-absence for the purpose of getting married:

> Head Qr. Top. Engr. Office DC
> Atlanta, Georgia
> Sept. 25th, 1864

Brig. Genl Wm. D. Whipple
    A.A.G. and Chief of Staff
        Sir

Having been working night and day for several days on the campaign map for Maj.-Gen. Sherman I would most respectfully request a leave of absence for 25 days for the express purpose of getting married also to attend to some business respecting to National Cemetery at Chattanooga.

> I have the honor to be
> Your most obt. Servant.
> /signed/          A. F. Brooks
> 1st Lt. 105th O.V.I.

His request was granted. Brooks was married to Miss Ellen Theresa Woodworth on Saturday, October 8, 1864, in West Williamsfield, Ohio, by Rev. Franklin L. Arnold. Four children were born of this marriage. They were Bessie I. (Mrs. G. W. Maher), Frances M. (Mrs. Arthur Wyld), Carol Louise (Mrs. Herman A. MacNeil) and Merle Thompson Brooks.

Brooks was honorably discharged at Cleveland, Ohio, on Wednesday, June 28, 1865. At the close of the war he laid down his engineer's pencil and took up his palette to continue his art in Chicago (1870) and became the pupil of Edwin White, a noted historical and portrait painter. (In 1850, White studied art in Dusseldorf, Paris, Rome, and Florence, spending some eight years abroad. His works were exhibited at the National Pennsylvania Academies, the American Art-Union, the Boston Athenaeum, and the Washington Art Association.) Brooks soon became identified with the art life of Chicago, a reputation he enjoyed for more than twenty years. At one time he lived at 4357 St. Lawrence Avenue. He opened his first studio there and was just getting comfortably settled when he was burned out in the Chicago Fire of 1871. Most of his sketches made during the Civil War and also more than a thousand dollars worth of paintings were lost. In 1881, he further expanded his studies in art and went to Paris, France, to study under the renowned Carolus-Duran and exhibited his works in the salon there in 1882. He is best known for his portraiture. In 1892, he was awarded the Yerkes prize in Chicago. In 1895, he was honored by the Illinois State Fair for his outstanding work. Among his many paintings were: "Governor John R. Tanner," of Illinois; "Judge Kirk Hawes," The Chicago Public Library; "Boys Fishing," Union League Club of Chicago; "Isaac Elwood" (1917), and "Joseph Glidden" (1889), Northern Illinois University, De Kalb, Illinois.

Brooks passed away on Monday, June 13, 1932, at the advanced age of 92 years, 2 months, and 10 days, having died at his home from pneumonia resulting from an automobile collision in Winnetka, Illinois, which occurred on June 10. He suffered a fractured collar bone and basal skull fracture. He was a widower residing at 518 Elder Lane in the North Shore suburb. At that time his granddaughter, Miss Violet Wyld lived with him. He was buried at Oakwoods Cemetery in Chicago, Illinois, on Wednesday, June 15, 1932.

The following is quoted from the obituary column of the *Chicago Daily News* appearing in the issue on Tuesday, June 14, 1932:

A. F. Brooks, Painter,
93, Crash Victim, Dies

Alden F. Brooks, 518 Elder Lane, Winnetka, Civil War veteran and a former portrait painter, died yesterday at his home of pneumonia. It resulted from a fractured collar bone suffered June 10 in an automobile collision at Elder Lane and Woodlawn avenue in the suburb. Mr. Brooks, who was 93 years old, once had President McKinley sit for him.

At the time of the accident he was riding with his granddaughter, Miss Violet Wyld, who lived with him, and his daughter, Mrs. George Maher of Kenilworth.

The obituary of his death also appeared in the *Chicago Daily Tribune* June 14, 1932.[2]

2. American Art Annual (Washington, D. C.: The American Federation of Arts, 1933), Vol. XXX, p. 444; The Graphic (Chicago: The Graphic Company, 1891), Vol. No. 14, p. 335; Department of the Interior, Bureau of Pensions (Washington: Jan. 2, 1915); Hdqrs., 105th, Ohio Vol., (Ringgold, Ga., April 8, 1864), Lt. Col. George T. Perkins, Commanding Reg't.


## GEORGE DURY

George Dury, artist, painted the full length portrait of General George H. Thomas. The painting now hangs in the Tennessee State Library and Archives in Nashville, Tennessee.

He was born in Munich, Germany, in 1817. He received his early training from the best artists in Munich, a city known for its art. His work attracted the attention of Louis I, of Bavaria. He became the King's protege and was given the privilege of copying the paintings of his choice in the Royal Galleries.

In 1849, Dury came to America, locating in Nashville, Tennessee. Here he established a favorable reputation and was considered the best portrait painter in the South.

His portrait of President James K. Polk's wife is deemed one of "the finest expressions of his genius." The painting has a distinguished setting in the White House.

Any number of his paintings can be found among the old families of the South. He painted several portraits of General Robert E. Lee. One of these is considered one of his finest pieces of work.

Dury died in 1894 at the age of 77.[3]

3. Will T. Hale and Dixon L. Merritt, A History of Tennessee and Tennesseans (Chicago and New York: The Lewis Publishing Company, 1913), Vol. III, pp. 741-742.


## ROBERT EBERHARDT SCHMIDT VON DER LAUNITZ

Robert E. Launitz, a talented sculptor, was born in Riga, Russia, on November 4, 1806. He came from a well-bred family. Launitz emigrated to the United States about 1828 at the age of 22. In his early youth, he was educated in the classics and in the field of military science. In lieu of this training and because of his propensity toward art, he decided to become a sculptor. To further his study in sculpturing, he decided to go to Rome, Italy, where an uncle maintained a studio, and where he spent some time learning the basic fundamentals. To further continue his study, he spent four years in the studio of Albert Bertel Thorvaldsen, a Danish sculptor, (who in 1793 was awarded a gold medal at the Academy at Copenhagen).

Launitz developed to be one of the finest sculptors in America. Later he found employment in John Frazee's marble yard in New York City. Frazee was a pioneer sculptor. In 1831, Launitz and Frazee formed a partnership. Besides being versed in his native tongue, Launitz could speak several foreign languages, such as French, German, Italian and Spanish. He was able to employ and train the very best of foreign stone carvers. This became an asset to their firm. Launitz was responsible for developing the carving industry in America. In 1833, he was invited to become a member of the National Academy of Design for his outstanding work. He wrote a book on tombstone design, which was later used and copied by other stone-cutters with limited skills. In 1839, his partner, Frazee, was commissioned to design the New York Custom House. This left Launitz in charge of the operation of their studio. One of Launitz's first achievements was completed in 1845, and was the portrait statue of Charlotte Canda in Greenwood Cemetery. This brought him fame. In 1848, the Kentucky legislature commissioned him to design and execute a monument (Battle Monument) "to those who had fallen in defense of their country." This monument was placed in the State Cemetery at Frankfort, Kentucky. One of his last monuments was the statue of Pulaski, erected in Savannah, Georgia, in 1854. One of his finest masterpieces was the designing and carving of the beautiful white marble monument to General George H. Thomas which was erected on October 26, 1870, in the Kellogg family burial ground in Oakwood Cemetery, Troy, New York. At the close of the Civil War, Launitz was confronted with the competition of "ready-made" memorials and "cast-iron" statues and his business declined. He died in New York City on December 13, 1870.[4]

4. Dumas Malone, Dictionary of American Biography (New York: Charles Scribner's Sons, 1933), Vol. XI, p. 31; Albert TenEyck Gardner, Yankee Stone-cutters (New York: Columbia University Press, 1945), p. 68; Margaret Farrand Thorp, The Literary Sculptors (Durham, N. C.: Duke University Press, 1965), p. 192.

## ALEXANDER C. McCLURG
### BREVET BRIGADIER GENERAL, U. S. VOLS.

Alexander Caldwell McClurg was born in Philadelphia, Pennsylvania, on September 9, 1832. He was the son of Alexander and Sarah (Trevor) McClurg. His ancestors were of Scotch-Irish descent. Receiving his early education in Pittsburgh, when he was seventeen years old he entered Miami University at Oxford, Ohio, and was graduated four years later. After graduation he entered the law office of Walter H. Lowrie, who was Chief Justice of the Pennsylvania Supreme Court. Because of his failing health and his loss of interest in the legal profession, McClurg abandoned the legal profession after one year.

In 1859, he went to Chicago seeking employment in some other field. He was employed as a clerk with the largest bookstore in the West, the firm of S. C. Griggs & Company. This firm was organized in 1847 as Griggs and Brothers.

Shortly after the outbreak of the Civil War, with others he was influential in organizing the Crosby Guards in Chicago which was mustered into the Federal service on Thursday, August 21, 1862. On August 27, he became a captain heading Company H of the 88th Illinois Infantry Volunteers. On Monday, February 29, 1864, he was made Captain, Asst. Adj. Gen. of Vols., then Lt. Col. Asst. Adj. Gen. assigned from October 3, 1864 to August 1, 1865.

On Wednesday, October 8, 1862, his regiment participated at the battle of Perryville, Kentucky, their first active engagement. In this engagement he demonstrated the ability of an officer that attracted the attention of his corps commander, General Alexander M. McCook. For his extraordinary conduct in the field and his ability to lead men, General Thomas, appointed McClurg as Acting Assistant

Adjutant-General of the Fourteenth Army Corps in May of 1863. He saw action in the Chickamauga campaign from August 16, 1863 to September 20, 1863. McClurg's daring deeds in the army became predominant when he acquired a reputation for fearlessness. His most distinguished performance was delivering a message to General Mc-Cook's corps on the eve of the battle of Chickamauga. He was successful in his mission by passing through the enemy's territory, delivering the order, and in leading General McCook to safety. He again served with great distinction, and was considered one of the most competent staff officers in the Western Army. Brigadier General Jefferson C. Davis recommended McClurg for promotion to the rank of lieutenant colonel (Asst. Adj. Gen. assigned from October 3, 1864 to August 1, 1865) for his distinguished gallantry and good conduct at the battle of Jonesboro, Georgia, September 1, 1864, and so McClurg was made chief of his staff. McClurg continued in this capacity, participating in the campaigns of General Sherman's army on the March to the Sea, ending his services after the battle of Bentonville, North Carolina, on March 19, 1865. He was breveted colonel of volunteers on June 7, 1865, and brigadier general, U. S. volunteers on September 18, 1865, for his distinguished war service. He was honorably discharged in St. Paul, Minnesota, on September 19, 1865.

General McClurg was urged by General Thomas to enter the Regular Army which he declined. Instead he returned to Chicago to his former occupation.

In April of 1866, McClurg, along with F. B. Smith and D. B. Cook, were taken into the firm of S. C. Griggs & Company. After the disastrous Chicago fire of 1871 (which started on the evening of Sunday, October 8 and lasted through the morning of Tuesday, October 10), Mr. S. C. Griggs sold his interest to his partners. General McClurg, Messrs. F. B. Smith, and E. L. Jensen became the principal owners, and the company became known as Jensen, McClurg & Co. In 1886 McClurg became the sole owner of the firm. Shortly after, A. C. McClurg & Co. was formed in February of 1899; it was at Madison Street and Wabash Avenue in Chicago. Later it was again destroyed by fire. The company relocated in a new building on Wabash Avenue south of Adams Street.

On April 17, 1877, General McClurg married Miss Eleanor Wheeler, daughter of Judge Nelson Knox Wheeler of New York City. Two sons were born of this marriage. He and his family resided at 60 Lake Shore Drive until 1893, when he built a residence at 125 Lake Shore Drive (Chicago). He died in St. Augustine, Florida, of Bright's disease on April 15, 1901 at the age of 68.

General McClurg was Vice President of The Chicago Historical Society from 1884 to 1898 and was President from 1898 to 1899. He was a trustee of The Newberry Library (Chicago) from 1892 to 1901.[5]

5. Dumas Malone, Dictionary of American Biography (New York: Charles Scribner's Sons, 1933), Vol. XI, pp. 595-596.

## JOHN M. PALMER
### Major General, U. S. Vols.

John McAuley Palmer was born in Scott County, Kentucky, on September 13, 1817. He was the son of Louis D. and Ann Hansford (Tutt) Palmer. His grandparents, the Thomas Palmers, emigrated to Virginia from England in the early part of the eighteenth century. His father, a prominent farmer and a "Jacksonian Democrat," left Kentucky with his family for Illinois in 1831 because of his anti-slavery sympathies. The family settled in Alton, and in 1834 John Palmer entered Shurtleff College and spent two years there. His family moved to Carlinville in 1839, and it was there he began to study law in the office of John S. Greathouse, being admitted to the bar in December of that year. His political career began in 1840, when he gave his support to President Martin Van Buren.

On December 20, 1842, he married Miss Malinda Ann, daughter of James Neely of Carlinville. Ten children were born of this marriage. His wife died in 1885.

In 1843, he was elected Probate Judge of Macoupin County; in 1847, he was elected as a member of the convention to amend the State Constitution. In 1843, he was reelected Probate Judge, then in November of the same year, he was elected County Judge, the office created by the new State Constitution, which he held until 1852. In 1852, he was elected to the State Senate to fill a vacancy and held this office until 1854.

In 1854, he opposed the Kansas-Nebraska Bill which was sponsored by Senator Stephen A. Douglas. Palmer favored the Missouri Compromise and the Compromise measures of 1850.

On Wednesday, May 1, 1861, he began his military career and on the 25th was elected colonel of the 14th Regiment of Illinois Infantry in Jacksonville, Illinois. On Friday, December 20, 1861, he received the rank of brigadier general of volunteers. He saw service in Missouri, participating in the engagements of Point Pleasant, Friday, March 7, 1862. He was in command of a division under General John Pope during the engagements of New Madrid, Friday, March 14, 1862, and Island No. 10, Tuesday, April 6-8, 1862, on the Mississippi River.

Later in 1862, he became commander of the 1st Division in the Army of the Mississippi, he fought superbly at the battles of Stones River (or Murfreesboro), Tennessee, from Wednesday, December 31, 1862, to Friday, January 2, 1863, and at Chickamauga, on Friday and Saturday, September 19-20, 1863. For his fine display of gallantry in the former engagements, he was commissioned major general of volunteers to rank from, November 29, 1862.

In October of 1863, he was made commander of the Fourteenth Army Corps; he participated in the battles around Chattanooga, such as Missionary Ridge, November 25, 1863; in 1864 he continued to command the Fourteenth Corps on the Atlanta Campaign. He served with General William T. Sherman until August of 1864 when he requested to be relieved of his command because of a dispute he had with Sherman when he refused to take orders from General Schofield. General Palmer claimed that Schofield was his junior in rank. His request was granted, and in turn, he was given the command of the Military Department of Kentucky. Palmer served in this command from February, 1865, to May 1, 1866, when he requested to be relieved of his post. He was mustered out of the service on September 1, 1866.

In 1867, he became affiliated with Milton Hay, practicing law in Springfield, Illinois. In 1868, General Palmer was elected governor of the State of Illinois on the Republican ticket, serving a four-year term from 1868 to 1872. During the disastrous Chicago fire of 1871, when the people were left destitute, he immediately sent money and supplies to their aid.

General Palmer re-married on April 4, 1888, to Hannah (Lamb) Kimball, daughter of James Lamb and the widow of L. R. Kimball. In 1891, General Palmer was elected United States Senator as a Democrat. He died in Springfield, on September 25, 1900, and was buried in Carlinville, Illinois.

The widow of General Palmer, Hannah L., received a widow's pension under Certificate No. 508,886 at the rate of fifty (50) dollars per month, which was approved on February 20, 1901. She died on August 22, 1927.[6]

6. Dumas Malone, Dictionary of American Biography (New York: Charles Scribner's Sons, 1934), Vol. XIV, pp. 187-188; U. S. Senate, Bill (S. 5091) granting a pension to Mrs. Hannah L. Palmer (copy on file with the author).


## REV. JOHN PIERPONT

John Pierpont was born on April 6, 1785, in Litchfield, Connecticut. He was graduated from Yale College in 1804 and was a classmate of John Caldwell Calhoun (a Southern statesman). Later, he studied law in the Litchfield Law School. Pierpont married his fourth cousin, Miss Mary Sheldon Lord, on Sept. 23, 1810. Six children were born of this marriage — three sons and three daughters.

In 1812, he practiced law in Newburyport, Mass., but soon gave this up due to lack of clients. In his spare time, he did some writing, composing "The Portrait, a poem surcharged with Federal sentiment, which he declaimed Oct. 27, 1812, before the Washington Benevolent

Society of Newburyport." For this he became famous, but it was not successful financially. Then in 1814, he tried his hand in a business venture with his brother-in-law (in Boston, with a branch in Baltimore), and in 1815 the business failed.

While he was still in Baltimore, he successfully published "his beautiful executed Airs of Palestime (Baltimore, 1816), which was reprinted twice in Boston in 1817, and which put him for the time being in the front rank of American poets." His other works were, "two later volumes, Airs of Palestime and Other Poems" (1840) and "The Anti-Slavery Poems of John Pierpont" (1843). He became an accomplished poet.

In October of 1818, he was graduated from Harvard Divinity School and on April 14, 1819 was ordained a minister. He became the pastor of the Hollis Street Church in Boston.

He followed his ministry. Later he became a pastor of the First Unitarian Society of Troy, New York, serving from 1845 to 1849. Then in 1849 to 1858, he served in the First Congregational Unitarian Church of West Medford, Mass. His first wife died August 23, 1855. He remarried Harriet Louise (Campbell) Fowler of Pawling, New York, on December 8, 1857, who survived him.

At the outbreak of the Civil War, he obtained from Governor John A. Andrew of Massachusetts (known as one of the "war governors"), a commission as chaplain in the 22d Mass. Volunteer Infantry Regiment. Although he was 76 years old, he marched with the regiment from Boston, enrolling at Springfield, Mass. on Sept. 20, 1861, for 3 years' service. He was mustered into service on Oct. 21, 1861, at Halls Hill, Virginia, with the Army of the Potomac. Two weeks later, on Tuesday, November 5, 1861, he tendered his resignation as chaplain because he felt it was too strenuous for his age and received an honorable discharge. He died Aug. 27, 1866, at the age of 81.[7]

7. Charles Brooks and James M. Usher, History of the Town of Medford, Mass., (Boston: Rand, Avery, & Company, 1886), pp. 257-258 and 259; Dumas Malone, Dictionary of American Biography (New York: Charles Scribner's Sons, 1934), Vol. XIV, pp. 586-587.


## KATE BROWNLEE SHERWOOD

In preparing the selection of poetry and prose material for the commemoration volume of the Semi-Centennial Memorial of The Photographic History of The Civil War (Volume Nine), Poetry and Eloquence, Dr. Dudley H. Miles, Editor, in one of the "In Memoriam" sections of this volume selected eleven subjects. One of which was

Thomas at Chickamauga

by

Kate Brownlee Sherwood.


Katherine Brownlee Sherwood was born in Poland, Mahoming County, Ohio, on September 24, 1841. She was the daughter of Judge James Brownlee. Her paternal forebears were Scotch, and her maternal ancestors were Irish and Dutch. She was educated in one of the first educational institutions in Ohio at the Poland Union Seminary. For some twenty years, Mrs. Sherwood was engaged in journalistic, literary, and philanthropic work. In 1872, while active in a woman's club, she took an interest in the National Council of Women. During and after the Civil War, she became a favorite among the Union soldiers at their annual reunions. She also received recognition from the ex-Confederate soldiers.

On April 6, 1887, she wrote a poem for the unveiling ceremonies of the equestrian statue of Confederate General Albert Sidney Johnston at New Orleans, Louisiana, and also the one about Thomas at Chickamauga. In 1882, Mrs. Sherwood became the editor of the Woman's Department of the *National Tribune*, a newspaper published in Washington, D. C., "in the interest of the Union soldiers, and while serving in this capacity," she helped organize the Woman's Relief Corps, a national organization which raised and spent $500,000, "for the needy veterans and their families," and established and maintained the homes for soldiers, widows, and orphans. She was also responsible for the establishment of the National Relief Corps House at Madison, Ohio, "for the care of indigent army nurses and the widows and mothers of soldiers," and "was an energetic and active worker in all philanthropic works that come in her way."[8]

8. The National Cyclopaedia of American Biography—History of the United States (New York: James T. White & Company, 1899), Vol. II, p. 201.


## W. J. STEVENS

W. J. Stevens was general superintendent of the United States Military Railroads, Division of the Mississippi, in Nashville, Tennessee. Soon after the battle of Nashville (Dec. of 1864), Stevens presented a large blanket chest to Mrs. Thomas. It was hand-made by the men under his command. In the center of the cover of the chest, there is a large inlaid brass presentation plaque with the following inscription:

Presented To Mrs. Gen'l George H. Thomas By
W. J. Stevens, U. S. M. R. R.—Nashville 1865.

Stevens served under Colonel Daniel C McCallum. McCallum was appointed Director and Superintendent of the United States Military Railroads by Secretary of War Edwin M. Stanton on Tuesday, February 11, 1862.

While Stevens served as general superintendent, his division, (Mississippi) used 3,383 cars in transporting corps and armies with all their artillery, equipments, and material, 97,544 feet of bridges were built or repaired, and 433 miles of tracks were laid or relaid. The total expenditures of this operation for his division during the Civil War was:

| | |
|---|---|
| Labor | $16,792,193.05 |
| Materials | 12,870,588.06 |
| Total Expenditures | $29,662,781.11 |

On Thursday, January 31, 1862, the Federal Government passed an act settng up an agency for the purpose of controlling seized Southern railroads.

When Colonel McCallum was appointed to direct the railroads in the United States, he was given authority without any interference so that he could operate his vast assignment to its greatest efficiency. At first, the commanders were somewhat slow in accepting this type of transportation. Prior to this time the railroads were operated in the war zones and controlled by the army commanders in charge of an affected area. But they soon learned how important and effective this new mode of transportation was by utilizing the rails for the movement of supplies, troops, and wounded. McCallum was most fortunate to be surrounded by men of capabilities when he once said, "that the Government was peculiarly fortunate in securing the services of civilian officers of great nerve, honesty, and capability, to whom the whole country owes a debt of gratitude." McCallum was breveted brigadier general of U. S. Vols. on Sept. 24, 1864, and major general, U. S. Vols. on Monday, March 13, 1865. Then on Sunday, January 1, 1865, he was promoted to Director and General Manager of the United States Military Railroads.

Credit also should go to General Herman Haupt (graduate of West Point, Class of 1831) for the success of the entire operation. Both McCallum and Haupt worked amiably. Haupt in the field in charge of construction and McCallum in the office.

On Tuesday, August 8, 1865, the United States Military Railroads were returned to the owners by an Executive Order.[9]

* Mrs. Thomas' trunk is in the author's collection.

9. George B. Abdill, Civil War Railroads (Seattle, Washington: Superior Publishing Company, Bonanza Books, Div., of Crown Publishers, Inc., 1961), pp. 9-11; Official Records of the War of the Rebellion (Washington, D. C., 1900), Series III, Vol. V, pp. 1004-1005.

# JOHN QUINCY ADAMS WARD

John Quincy Adams Ward, sculptor of renown, was born near Urbana, Champaign County, Ohio, on the family homestead on June 29, 1830. He was the son of John Adams and Eleanor (Macbeth) Ward. His ancestors emigrated to Jamestown, Virginia, from Norfolk, England, in the early part of the seventeenth century. In addition to attending the schools in Urbana, Ward was also taught by private tutors. As a boy, he often visited the village potter to learn how to work with clay in modeling farm animals and men on horseback. At the age of sixteen, his parents put him to work on the farm milking cows and doing other chores. He was displeased with farm chores, preferring to model horses out of clay. His Presbyterian parents wished that he would become a minister or a doctor. Ward studied medicine for awhile but soon gave this up. At the age of nineteen he paid a visit to his married sister in Brooklyn, New York.

This trip was the turning point in his life. His sister, knowing his love for clay modeling, suggested that he visit the studio of Henry Kirke Brown, a renowned sculptor. The training under Brown a genial, "broad-minded" master is what Ward needed. He practiced every skill used in sculpturing—first working in clay, then in plaster, graduating to marble, and finally working in bronze. He remained with his master for seven years learning all the techniques necessary to become an accomplished sculptor. In 1854, Brown while working on the equestrian statue of Washington, considered one of the finest pieces of sculpture in the nation, carved "J. Q. A. Ward, Asst." on the base of the statue. This pleased young Ward for being recognized by his master. On several occasions Brown complemented his young protege by saying, "Ward has more than Greenough, Crawford Powers and all the other American sculptors combined."

Ward spent two winters in Washington, D. C., from 1857 to 1859 where he executed busts of Hannibal Hamlin (Lincoln's Vice-President), Joshua R. Gaddings, John P. Hale, and other notable statesman. Then in 1861, he opened a studio in New York City, New York, where he practiced his profession and lived for half a century.

One of the first statues to grace New York's Central Park, and one of the finest to be found there, was Ward's "Indian Hunter," which he completed in 1868. He originally conceived the idea of his statue as a statuette in 1857. Ward spent several months among the Indians of the Northwest to get his inspiration for this famous statue. Then in 1861, he created his popular statuette in full-length, "The Freedman," which he cast in bronze in 1865. It was "an authentic figure of a Negro, seated, looking very quietly at the schackles from which he had been released." From his childhood days Ward was well acquainted with both the Indian and Black types. In 1867, both the "Indian Hunter," and the "Freedman" were on exhibit at the Paris Exposition.

Ward's statue of General John F. Reynolds was unveiled at Gettysburg, Pennsylvania, in 1872. Then in 1869 he completed the bronze figure of a Civil War soldier on a high granite pedestal, called the 7th Regiment Memorial, which was placed in Central Park in 1873.

Among some of his famous works were: General James A. Garfield monument in Washington, D. C.; Henry Ward Beecher monument in Brooklyn, New York; the Soldiers and Sailors monument in Syracuse, N. Y.; and General Sheridan equestrian in Albany. N. Y.

His masterpiece is his equestrian statue of Major General George H. Thomas, the "Rock of Chickamauga" which was unveiled in Washington, D. C., in 1878.

As one critic stated, "Ward is a sculptor who has, one might say, a truly pagan affection for the beautiful; who seeks nature because he loves her; who selects from a broad field what best will suit his purpose; and who possesses withal that dramatic instinct and training by which outward things are made to enter into himself, to become transformed by the mixture with them of his own personality, and to be reproduced fresh, living and sparkling. . . . He is possessed by an intellectual seriousness which never allows him to waste his strength upon commonplace, paltry, or merely pretty subjects, or to make use of tricks and artifices, conventional or individual; in the next place, his aesthetic instincts are keen, and he does not fail to please, to attract, to reach. . . . Again, he has an impassioned love for the free-prairie, the Indian, the free social life of cities, the free republic of letters and of citizens. Still further, he is learned in his art, not often at a loss for the mechanical means necessary to the interpretation of human thought and emotion; and finally, he has listened, as Herakleitos would say, to the voice of the sibyl, "'who teaches what mere learning can never teach.'"

He was a member of the following organizations:
Ward was Vice-President of the Fine Arts Federation; President of the National Sculpture Society; a trustee of the Metropolitan Museum of Art and of the American Academy in Rome; an honorary member of the National Institute of Architects; a member of the Architectural League; Vice-President of the Century Club; and member of the Union League Club and of the Ohio Society.

In 1858, he married Miss Anna Bannan, the daughter of John and Rebecca (Noyes) Bannan. She died in 1870. Ward remarried in 1878 to Miss Julia Valentine, daughter of Charles and Julia (Devens) Valentine, but she died a year later. In 1906 he married Mrs. Rachel Smith, a widow, daughter of Simon and Jane (Lefevre) Ostrander of Newburg, New York. He died on May 1, 1910, at his home in New York at the advanced age of seventy-nine, leaving a widow. No children were born of this marriage. He is buried in his home town of Urbana, Ohio, where is grave is marked with a replica of the "Indian Hunter."[10]

10. The National Cyclopaedia of American Biography (New York: James T. White & Company, 1899), Vol. II, pp. 364-365; Dictionary of American Biography, (N. Y., Charles Scribner's Sons, 1936), Vol. XIV, pp. 427-428-429.


## ELIHU B. WASHBURNE

Elihu Benjamin Washburne, General Grant's sponsor, was born in Livermore, Maine, on September 23, 1816. Leaving home at the age of fourteen to embark on a career, he changed his name by adding an "e" to it in imitation of his English ancestors. He studied law at Harvard Law School, passing the bar examination in 1840 and soon after was permitted to practice law. He was married to Miss Adele Gratiot on July 31, 1845. Seven children were born of this marriage.

Washburne foresaw the opportunities in the West and went to Illinois, settling in Galena. It was here Washburne first became acquainted with Ulysses Simpson Grant. Washburne served sixteen years as a congressman from Illinois. He was responsible for the establishment of our national cemeteries. Physical disabilities prevented him from military duty during the Civl War. However, Washburne watched the career of Grant, and it was to his influence that Grant owed his first promotions. Serving as a member of President Grant's first cabinet, Washburne was appointed Secretary of State and was confirmed by the Senate on March 15, 1869. Because of ill health he resigned the office in less than a week. Shortly thereafter, he was appointed to the important position of Minister to France which he served with distinction. He resigned this office in 1877 and returned to the United States. After a successful career in politics he retired. In 1884, he became President of the Chicago Historical Society and served in this capacity to 1887. He passed the latter part of his life in reading, studying, and lecturing before literary institutions. During his lifetime, Washburne collected paintings, manuscripts, and autographs. At the time of his death he desired to leave all of his collection to the Chicago Historical Society. He died in Chicago, Illinois, on October 22, 1887.[11]


11. The National Cyclopaedia of American Biography (New York: James T. White & Company, 1897), Vol. IV, pp. 14-15; Dictionary of American Biography, Troye-Wentworth (New York: Charles Scribner's Sons, 1936), Vol. XIX, pp. 504-505-506.

# Bibliography


* Abdill, Geo. B. *Civil War Railroads.* New York: Bonanza Books, Division of Crown Publishers, Inc. 1961.
* *Battles and Leaders of the Civil War.* New York: The Century Co., 1884-1888. 4 vols.
* Boynton, Henry V., Bvt. Brig. Gen., U. S. V. *Was General Thomas Slow At Nashville?* New York: Francis P. Harper, 1896.
* Catton, Bruce. *Never Call Retreat.* The Centennial History of the Civil War. Garden City, New York: Doubleday & Company, Inc., 1965. Volume Three.
* Cist, Henry M., Bvt. Brig. Gen. U.S.V. *The Army of the Cumberland.* New York: Charles Scribner's Sons, 1882. vol. VII.
* Cleaves, Freeman. *Rock of Chickamauga, The Life of General George H. Thomas.* Norman: University of Oklahoma Press, 1948.
* Commager, Henry Steele. *The Blue and the Gray.* Indianapolis - New York: The Bobbs-Merrill Company, Inc., 1950. vols. I and II.
* Connolly, James A. *Three Years in the Army of the Cumberland.* (Edited by Paul M. Angle.) Bloomington: Indiana University Press, 1959.
* Coppée, Henry. LL.D. *General Thomas.* New York: D. Appleton and Company, 1893.
* Cox, Jacob D. (Late Maj.-Gen. Commanding Twenty-Third Army Corps). *Atlanta.* New York: Charles Scribner's Sons, 1882, 1885. vol. IX.
* ... ................ *The March to the Sea—Franklin and Nashville.* New York: Charles Scribner's Sons, 1882, 1885. Vol. X.
* Cullum, George W., Bvt. Maj. Gen. Colonel U.S. Army Engineers, Retired. *Biographical Register of the Officers and Graduates of the United States Military Academy, at West Point, New York.* Cambridge, Mass.: The Riverside Press, 1901. vol. IV.
* ................ Boston and New York: Houghton, Mifflin and Company, 1891. vol. II.
* Deaderick, Barron. *Strategy in The Civil War.* Harrisburg, Pa.. The Military Publishing Company, 1946.
* DePeyster, Gen. John Watts. *Major-General George H. Thomas, The Annual Address Delivered Before the New-York Historical Society,* Tuesday Evening, January 5, 1875. Published by Atlantic Publishing Co., New York, 1875.
* ................ New York, January 4, 1876.
* Drewry, William Sidney. *The Southampton Insurrection.* Washington, D. C.: The Neale Company, 1900. Reprinted by Johnson Publishing Company, Murfreesboro, N. C., 1968.

* Dyer, John P. *The Gallant Hood.* Indianapolis-New York: The Bobbs-Merrill Company, Inc., 1950.

French, Samuel G. *Two Wars.* Nashville, 1901.

* Gardner, Charles K. *Dictionary of the Army of the United States.* New York: D. Van Nostrand, 1860.

* Gorham, George C. *Life and Public Services of Edwin M. Stanton.* Boston and New York: Houghton, Mifflin and Company, 1899. vols. I, II.

* Gracie, Archibald. *The Truth About Chickamauga.* Boston and New York: Houghton, Mifflin and Company, 1911.

* Grant, Ulysses S. *Personal Memoirs.* New York: Charles L. Webster & Company, 1885. 2 Vols.

* Heitman, Francis B. *Historical Register and Dictionary of the United States Army,* (From its organization, Sept. 29, 1789 to March 2, 1903.) Washington, D. C.: Government Printing Office, 1903. vols. 1 and 2.

Hood, John B. *Advance and Retreat—Personal Experiences in the United States and Confederate States Armies.* (New Orleans, 1880). Published for the Hood Orphan Memorial Fund.

* Horn, Stanley F. *The Decisive Battle of Nashville.* Baton Rouge: Louisiana State University Press, 1956.

* ................ *The Army of Tennessee.* Indianapolis: The Bobbs-Merrill Company, 1941. Norman: Assigned to the University of Oklahoma Press, 1952.

* Johnson, Richard W., Brig.-Gen. U.S.A. (Retired). *Memoir of Maj.-Gen. George H. Thomas.* Philadelphia: J. B. Lippincott & Co., 1881.

* Johnston, William Preston. *The Life of Gen. Albert Sidney Johnston.* New York: D. Appleton and Company, 1878.

* Lee, Captain Robert E. Lee (son of Gen. Lee). *Recollections and Letters of General Robert E. Lee.* Garden City, New York: Garden City Publishing Company, 1926.

Leslie, Frank. *Pictorial History of the American Civil War.* Edited by Hon. E. G. Squier. New York: Published by Frank Leslie, 1862. vol. I.

* McElroy, Joseph C. *Chickamauga—Record of the Ohio Chickamauga and Chattanooga National Park Commission.* Cincinnati: Earhart & Richardson, Printers and Engravers, 1896.

* McKinney, Francis F. *Education in Violence.* The Life of George H. Thomas and The History of the Army of the Cumberland. Detroit: Wayne State University Press, 1961.

* Mitchell, Joseph B. *The Battle of Chickamauga, Battles of the Civil War, 1861-1865, A Pictorial Presentation.* Little Rock, Arkansas: Pioneer Press, Civil War Publication, Inc., 1960.

Morison, Samuel Eliot and Commager, Henry Steele. *The Growth of the American Republic.* New York: Oxford University Press, 1962. Vols. One & Two.

* O'Connor, Richard. *Thomas: Rock of Chickamauga.* New York: Prentice-Hall, Inc., 1948.

*Official Records of the War of the Rebellion.* 128 vols. Washington, D. C., 1880-1901. (30 volumes are in the author's collection.)

* Okun, S. B. *The Russian-American Company.* Cambridge, Mass.: Harvard University Press, 1951.

* Phisterer, Frederick, Capt. U.S.A. *Association of Survivors—Army of the Cumberland.* Historical Sketch. Columbus, Ohio: Press of John L. Trauger, 1898.

* *Photographic History of the Civil War, The.* Francis Trevelyan Miller, Editor-in-Chief. New York: The Review of Reviews Co., 1912. 10 vols.

* Piatt, Donn. Major-General George H. Thomas. *Memories of the Men Who Saved the Union.* New York and Chicago: Belford, Clarke & Company, 1887.

* .................. *General George H. Thomas.* A Critical Biography, With Concluding Chapters by Henry V. Boynton. Cincinnati: Robert Clarke & Co., 1893.

* Powell, William H., Major 22d Infantry, U.S.A. *Powell's Records of Living Officers of the United States Army.* Philadelphia: L. R. Hamersly & Co., 1890.

* Reynolds, Donald E. *Editors Make War—Southern Newspapers in the Secession Crisis.* Nashville: Vanderbilt University Press, 1966, 1970.

* Shanks, William F. G. *Personal Recollections of Distinguished Generals.* New York: Harper & Brothers, Publishers, 1866.

* Sherman, William T. *The Memoirs of General William T. Sherman.* New York: Charles L. Webster & Co., 1891. 2 vols.

* .................. *The Sherman Letters.* Edited by Rachel Sherman Thorndike. New York: Charles Scribner's Sons. 1894.

* Shiels, Archie W. *The Purchase of Alaska.* College, Alaska, U.S.A.: The University of Alaska Press, 1967.

* Smith, Justin H. *The War With Mexico.* Gloucester, Mass.: Peter Smith, 1963. 2 Vols.

* *Society of the Army of the Cumberland Yearbook.* Thirty-Third Reunion, Chattanooga, Tennessee, September 18, 19, and 20, 1905. Cincinnati: The Robert Clarke Company, 1906.

* Thomas, Benjamin P. and Hyman, Harold M. *Stanton: The Life and Times of Lincoln's Secretary of War.* New York: Alfred A. Knopf, 1962.

* Thomas, Wilbur. *General George H. Thomas, The Indomitable Warrior.* New York: Exposition Press, Inc., 1964.

* Tucker, Glenn. *Chickamauga: Bloody Battle in the West.* Indianap-

olis, New York: The Bobbs-Merrill Company, Inc., 1961.

Van Horne, Thomas B. *History of the Army of the Cumberland.* Cincinnati: Robert Clarke & Co., 1875. 2 Vols. and Atlas.

* . ................ *The Life of Major General George H. Thomas.* New York: Charles Scribner's Sons, 1882.

* Warner, Ezra J. *Generals in Blue.* Baton Rouge: Louisiana State University Press, 1964.

* . ................ *Generals in Gray.* Baton Rouge: Louisiana State University Press, 1959.

*Welles, Gideon. *Diary of Gideon Welles.* Edited by Howard K. Beale. Assisted by Alan W. Brownsword. New York: W. W. Norton & Company, Inc., 1960. 3 vols. (Originally published in Boston, 1911.)

* Wilson, Suzanne Colton. *Column South.* Flagstaff, Arizona: J. F. Colton and Co., 1960.

* Books in the author's library.


## NEWSPAPERS

*The Chicago Daily News,* Tuesday, June 14, 1932, Page 5, Col. 5.
Obituary Notice — Alden Finney Brooks, Artist.

*The Chicago Daily Tribune,* Tuesday, June 14, 1932, Page 26, Col. 6.
Obituary Notice — Alden Finney Brooks, Artist.

*The Chicago Daily Tribune,* Tuesday, April 16, 1901. Page 3, Cols. 2, 3, and 4.
Obituary Notice—General A. C. McClurg.

*The Louisville Courier-Journal.*
Obituary Notice — General George H. Thomas
Wednesday, March 30, 1870.
Friday, April 1, 1870, Page 1.
Wednesday, April 6, 1870, Page 4.

*The New York Daily Tribune*
Secrets Of History
The Battle Of Nashville, signed by,
"One Who Fought At Nashville."
Saturday, March 12, 1870, Page 1.
also, signed by, "Another Man."
Saturday, March 19, 1870, Page 1.

*The New York Times,* Wednesday, March 30, 1870, Page 5, Cols. 2 and 3.
Obituary Notice — General George H. Thomas
also, Saturday, April 9, 1870, Page 1, Cols. 4, 5, and 6.


## MISCELLANEOUS

American Biography, Dictionary of. *John Frazes.* Edited by Allen Johnson and Dumas Malone. New York: Charles Scribner's Sons, 1931, vol. VII.

American Biography, Dictionary of. *Robert Everhardt Schmidt von der*

*Launtiz.* Edited by Dumas Malone. New York: Charles Scribner's Sons, 1933, vol. XI.

American Biography, Dictionary of. *General Alexander Caldwell Mc-Clurg.* Edited by Dumas Malone. New York: Charles Scribner's Sons, 1933, vol. XI.

American Biography, Dictionary of. *General John McAuley Palmer.* Edited by Dumas Malone. New York: Charles Scribner's Sons, 1934, vol. XIV.

American Biography, Dictionary of. *John Pierpont.* Edited by Dumas Malone. New York: Charles Scribner's Sons, 1934, vol. XIV.

American Biography, Dictionary of. *George Henry Thomas.* Edited by Dumas Malone. New York: Charles Scribner's Sons, 1936, vol. XVIII.

American Biography, Dictionary of. *John Quincy Adams Ward.* Edited by Dumas Malone. New York: Charles Scribner's Sons, 1936, vol. XIX.

American Biography, The National Cyclopaedia of. *Mrs. Katherine Brownlee Sherwood.* New York: James T. White & Company, 1899, Vol. II.

American Biography, The National Cyclopaedia of. *Elihu Benjamin Washburne.* New York: James T. White & Company, 1897, vol. IV.

American Heritage, The Picture History of The Civil War. New York: American Heritage Publishing Co., Inc., 1960, vol. II.

American History, Dictionary of. *The Mexican War.* Edited by James Truslow Adams. New York: Charles Scribner's Sons, 1940, vol. III.

Army, Department of the—Headquarters, United States Army, Alaska. *The U.S. Army in Alaska.* July, 1972, USARAL Pamphlet No. 360-5.

Certified copy of Certificate of Death of General Thomas from the Dept. of Public Health, City and County of San Francisco, California, as entered in Book 2, Page 42 for the year 1870, File No. 901. Copy of this certificate is in the author's possession dated Feb. 23, 1968.

Cyclopaedia, The New Century. *Albert Bertel Thorvaldsen.* Edited by Clarence L. Barnhart. New York: Appleton-Century-Crafts, Inc., vol. Three.

Goodridge, Wilson. Smyth County History and Traditions. Published in connection with the Centennial Celebration of Smyth County, Virginia, 1932.

*Huguenot Emigration, History of the, to America.* Charles W. Baird. New York: Dodd, Mead & Company, 1885, vol. I.

*Kentucky. A History of the State.* Edited by W. H. Perrin, J. H. Battle and G. C. Kniffin. Louisville, Kentucky and Chicago, Illinois: F. A. Battey and Company, 1887.

Lambert, Major William H. He delivered an Oration on (Major General) George Henry Thomas, given before the Society of the Army of the Cumberland at Rochester, New York, on September 17, 1884. Philadelphia: Pennypacker & Rogers, 1884. (only sixty-five copies printed for private distribution.)

National Archives and the Library of Congress. Sources of photographs of commanders of Union and Confederate Armies. Sources of photographs, of Military Civil War Records, and of letters referring to Major General George H. Thomas.

Pendleton, Wm. C. *History of Tazewell County and Southwest Virginia. Richmond, Virginia:* W. C. Hill Printing Company, 1920.

Southampton County, Clerk of the Circuit Court of., Courtland, Virginia. Will of Mrs. Elizabeth Thomas, mother of General Thomas.

State of New York, Troy., Clerk of Surrogate's Court, County of Rensselaer. Decree of Settlement of the Estate of General George H. Thomas. Dated and Recorded April 10, 1872. Certified copy of the Decree of Settlement in the author's possession.

# INDEX

Augusta, Ga., 370, 371, 373
Austin, Texas, 65
Austin's Sharpshooters, 227

B

Backus, Capt. E, 26, 30
Bailey's Crossroads, Ga., 151
Bainbridge, Ala., 281, 351
Bainbridge, Capt. H., 26, 28, 31
Baird, Brig. Gen. Absolam, 141, 150,
    151, 152, 155, 156, 157, 158, 159,
    162, 164, 165, 166, 183, 184, 190,
    191, 193, 208, 209, 212, 262
Baird's Division, 141, 150, 151, 152,
    153, 154, 155, 156, 157, 162, 163,
    164, 177, 183, 188, 206, 207, 208,
    211, 225, 228, 232, 238, 239
Baltimore and Washington Battalion,
    27, 29
Baltimore Harbor, Md., 16
Banks, Maj. Gen. Nathanial P., 211
Barbour, Bvt. Maj., 26, 30
Barbourville, Ky., 342
Barbourville Bridge, 75
Bardstown, Ky., 104, 114
Barker, Capt. J. D., 125, 161, 165
Barnes, Col. Sidney M., 158
Barnes' Brigade, 158
Barrell, Surg. H. C., 165
Bate, Maj. Gen. William B., 221, 230,
    234, 293, 340
Bate's Division, 221, 227, 230, 340
Battery H, Fifth Artillery, 156
Battery I, 4th Artillery, 351
Battle Creek, Ala./Tenn., 111, 150
Battle of the Cedars, Tenn., 301
Battle of Ezra Church, Ga., 249
Battle of Peachtree Creek, Ga., 247
Beall, Brig. Gen. William N. R., 53
Bean's Station, Tenn., 353
Bear Creek, Ala., 355
Beatty, John, 121, 123, 127, 132, 150,
    158, 159, 160, 165
Beatty, Brig. Gen. Samuel, 122, 345
Beatty's Brigade, 121, 123, 158, 160
Beatty's Division, 122, 150, 345
Beauregard, Gen. P. G. T., 67, 68,
    105, 106, 109, 111, 272, 273
Beebe, Surg. G. D., 125
Beech Grove, Tenn., 81, 131
Beech Grove camp, 84
Beersheba Springs, 185
Belknap, Col. William G., 41
Bell Buckle, Tenn., 128
Bell's Landing, Tenn., 341

Bell's Mills, 309
Belmont, Mo., 76
Beman, E. C., 356
Benton, Tenn., 211, 212
Bering Sea, 386
Bethpage Bridge, Tenn., 129
Biffle, Col. Jacob, 355
Big Bend, Ga., 262
Big Harpeth River, Tenn., 294, 299,
    330, 337, 338, 349
Big Kennesaw Mountain, Ga., 236
Big Shanty, Ga., 239, 271
Big Spring, Tenn., 130
Bird's Mill, Ga., 154
Birmingham, Ala., (See Elyton, Ala.)
Bissell, Col. William H., 34, 37, 44
Bissell's Regt., (See Second Illinois
    Regt.)
Black Fort (Monterrey, Mexico), 29
Black Prairie Region, Ala., 360
Bledsoe, Willie S. (guerrilla), 204,
    214
Bliss, Capt. W. W., 23, 28
Blue Bird Gap, Ga., 153
Blue Grass Region, 111, 115
Blue Ridge Mountains, 368
Blue Springs, Tenn., 206, 208, 211
Blue Water, Tenn., 203
Bobo's Cross-Roads, Tenn., 132, 133
Bolivar Springs, Ala., 150
Boone, N. C., 368
Boone, Col. W. P., 206, 209, 213
Boone's Regt., 207
Border State Conference, 72
Boston Harbor, Mass., 50
Bough's Mill, Ala., 334
Bowles, Col. William A., 34, 37, 43
Bowling Green, Ky., 75, 76, 103, 115,
    116, 117, 355, 374
Boyle, Brig. Gen. Jeremiah T., 101
Bradford, Gamaliel, 300
Bradyville, Tenn., 128
Bragg, Gen. Braxton, 16, 19, 20, 24,
    25, 26, 27, 28, 29, 32, 37, 38, 40,
    43, 44, 45, 52, 53, 105, 111, 112,
    113, 114, 117, 126, 128, 129, 136,
    137, 138, 140, 146, 167, 169, 172,
    179, 180, 181, 182, 194, 402, 404
Bragg's Army, 114, 118, 128, 129, 149,
    152, 153, 168, 170, 171, 183, 191
Bragg's Battery, 26, 27, 28, 31, 32, 37
Bragg's Cavalry, 129
Bragg's Horse-Artillery, 25
Bragg's troops, 114, 137
Brakefield Point, Tenn., 134
Bramlette, Col. Thomas E., 79

442

Department of the Treasury, 387
De Peyster, John Watts, 325, 383, 397, 398
Deputy Clerk, Southampton Co., 5
Dillon, Capt. Boston, 80
Dilworth, Lt. R., 26
District of Louisiana, 65
District of Northern Alabama, 280, 282
District of the Etowah, 259, 279, 316, 322, 343
Division of the Mississippi, 175
District of the Tennessee, 259
Dixie, 380
Dloss (Indian Guide), 55
Doane, Bishop William C., 395
Dobb, Col. George W., 364
Dodge, Maj. Gen. Grenville M., 196, 203, 214, 245, 308, 309
Dodge's Corps, 230, 245
Dodge, Col. Theodore A., 400
Donaldson, Bvt. Brig. Gen. J. L., 278, 323, 337, 343
Donaldson, Lt. James S., 39, 143
Dry Valley Rd., Ga., 162, 163
Dublin, Ga., 371
Duck River, Tenn., 104, 196, 289, 290, 330, 334, 335, 336, 349, 350
Ducktown, Tenn., 215
Dug Gap, Ga., 151, 152, 153, 208
Duke, Brig. Gen. Basil, 341, 353, 354
*Dunbar* (steamboat), 189
Duncan, Blanton, 72
Durham's house, 233
Durham Station, N. C., 367, 369
Dutton, C., 10
Dutton, William, 10
Dyer, Brig. Gen. Alexander B., 383
Dyer, John P., 293
Dyer's House, 157

### E

Easley's Farm, Ga., 151, 152
East Chickamauga Creek, Ga., 206, 220
East Point, Ga., 253, 254, 255, 261
Eastport, Miss., 110, 278, 282, 285, 328, 334, 352, 353, 361, 363, 364, 373
East Tenn., 73, 101, 112, 115, 136, 201, 205, 211, 220, 257, 258, 341, 342, 360, 362, 367, 369, 390
East Tennessee & Ga. Railroad, 200, 204, 205
Eastern Ky., 84
Edgefield, Tenn., 339

Edict of Nantes, 3
Edie, Col. I. R., 263
Edie's Brigade, 263
*Editors Make War*, 60
Eighteenth Ind. Battery, 167
Eighteenth Michigan Inf., 279
Eighteenth Ohio Inf., 150, 177
Eighteenth Tennessee Inf., 153
Eighteenth U. S. Infantry, 85, 91, 94, 121
Eighth Iowa Cavalry, 197
Eleventh Army Corps, 173, 177, 178, 180, 192, 193, 204, 212, 215, 251
Eleventh Michigan Inf., 165
Eleventh Tenn. Cavalry, 286
*Elfin* (gunboat), 286
Elizabethtown, Ky., 75, 355
Elliott, Ga., 196
Elliott, Brig. Gen. Washington L., 184, 195
Elk River, Tenn., 129, 134, 280, 281, 303, 337
Elk River Railroad Bridge, 129
Elyton (Birmingham), Ala., 364
Emerson, Asst. Surg. John, 13, 14, 15
Emory, Brig. Gen. William H., 52, 53
*Empress* (steamer), 286
Encarnacion (See Hacienda of Encarnacion)
Engerman, Stanley L., 61
Engineer Battalion, 394
England, 3
Etowah River, Ga., 196, 225, 226, 231, 271, 274, 282
Euharlee, Ga., 226
Euharlee Creek, Ga., 226
Eutaw, Ala., 365
Evans, Brig. Gen. Nathan G., 53
Everett, Capt. T. S., 81
Everglades, Fla., 16
Ezra Church, Battle of, 249

### F

Fairburn, Ga., 260, 261
Fairfield, Tenn., 130, 131, 132
Fairfield Rd., 131
Fairfax and Manchester Rd., 132
Falling Waters, Va., 71
Farmington, Miss., 106, 281
Fayetteville, Tenn., 280
Featherstone's house, 134
Federals, the, 81, 89, 105, 110, 112, 129, 138, 142, 143, 146, 225, 231, 245, 269, 270, 277, 291, 292, 294, 295, 298, 301, 324

Federal armies, 66, 218, 226, 293
Federal Cavalry, 81
Federal Constitution, 64
Federal Government, 64, 72
Federal troops, 290
Ferguson, Champ (guerrilla), 185,
 204, 214
Field, Maj. Gen. Charles W., 53
Field, Capt. G. P., 26, 29, 31
Fifteenth Army Corps, 186, 189, 194,
 195, 205, 206, 212, 248, 283, 302
Fifteenth Mississippi Inf., 95, 96
Fifteenth Pennsylvania Cav., 356, 371
Fifth Cavalry, 53, 71, 74, 401
Fifth Ky. Cav., 197
Fifteenth Pennsylvania Cav., 354
Fifth Tennessee Cav., 204, 214
Fifty-eighth Alabama Inf., 227
Fifty-eighth Indiana Inf., 196, 246
Fifty-second Ohio Vol. Infantry, 267
Fire Island, Tenn., 169
First Artillery, 41, 43, 44, 395
First Bull Run, 322
First Dragoons, 38, 39, 43
First East Tenn. Regt., 85, 184
First Illinois Inf., 37, 40
First Infantry, 24, 25, 26, 27, 28, 29,
 30, 34
First Kentucky Cav., 79, 81, 84, 95
First Manassas, 322, 401
First Michigan Engineers & Mechanics,
 177, 212
First Middle Tenn. Inf., 185
First Mississippi Rifles, 40, 43
First Missouri Engineers & Mechanics,
 212
First Ohio Artillery, 165
First Ohio Cavalry, 125, 165
First Tennessee Regt. Inf. (Union), 91
First U.S. Cavalry, 53, 63, 67
First Wisconsin Cavalry, 215, 222, 371,
 372, 373
Fishing Creek, Ky., 80, 81, 83, 84
Fishing Creek Ford, 83
Fitch, Commodore Le Roy, 303, 309,
 327, 340, 344
Fite's Ferry, Ga., 224
Fitz Gibbon, Maj. Thomas C., 185
Flat Shoal Church, Ga., 261
Fletcher, A. J., 378
Flint Ridge, Tenn., 184
Flint River, Ga., 262, 366
Florence, Ala., 110, 203, 270, 276, 281,
 282, 285, 288, 334, 335, 352
Florida, 10, 13, 47, 48, 50, 57, 60, 144,
 377, 385, 393

Florida Indians, 15
Florida peninsula, 16
Flynt, Maj. G. E., 94, 125, 165
Fogel, Robert W., 61
Fogg, Maj. H. M. R., 88
Fontaine, Maj. Joe, 196
Forrest, Lt. Commander Moreau, 281
Forrest, Lt. Gen. Nathan B., 132, 139,
 140, 153, 170, 196, 197, 202, 214,
 270, 276, 277, 278, 279, 280, 281,
 282, 285, 287, 289, 290, 293, 301,
 302, 305, 306, 308, 328, 350, 351,
 362, 363, 365
Forrest's Cavalry, 139, 153, 156, 169,
 272, 280, 289, 290, 291, 293, 330,
 336, 340, 362, 363
Forrest's Command, 132, 214, 293
Fort Adams, Rhode Island, 50
Fort Belknap, Texas, 54
Fort Brooke, Fla., 16
Fort Brown, Texas, 48, 65
Fort Columbus, N.Y. Harbor, 12, 13,
 395
Fort de la Teneria, Mexico, 27, 30
Fort Diablo, Monterrey, Mexico, 26
Fort Donelson, Tenn., 103, 104, 258,
 324, 336
Fort Hamilton, N.Y., 395
Fort Heiman, Ky., 286
Fort Henry, Tenn., 103, 104
Fort Independence, Mass., 50
Fort Lauderdale, Fla., 13, 14, 15
Fort McHenry, Md., 16
Fort Mason, Texas, 54
Fort Morton, Tenn., 343
Fort Moultrie, S.C., 16, 68, 179
Fort Negley, Tenn., 343
Fort Payne, Ala., 205
Fort Pillow, Tenn., 109
Fort Sanders, Tenn., 194, 392
Fort Schuyler, N.Y., 395
Fort Sumter, S.C., 67, 68, 69, 70, 73
Fort Texas, 17, 23, 24
Fort Texas siege, 18
Fort Totten, N.Y., 395
Fortress Rosecrans, Tenn., 340
Fort Tyler, Ga., 365
Fort Wood, Tenn., 181, 188
Forty-fourth U.S. Colored Inf., 240,
 283
Forty-second Indiana Inf., 123
Forty-third Wisconsin Inf., 286
Foster, Maj. Gen. John G., 196, 199,
 201, 205, 210
Fosterville, Tenn., 129
Fourteenth Army Corps, 117, 118, 124,

126, 129, 135, 149, 150, 163, 165, 166, 167, 177, 181, 183, 188, 189, 192, 196, 206, 210, 211, 212, 217, 220, 221, 225, 228, 231, 238, 241, 249, 250, 253, 254, 255, 259, 260, 261, 262, 263, 265, 266, 278, 280, 282, 283, 284, 375, 402

Fourteenth Michigan Inf., 185

Fourteenth Ohio Inf., 85, 90, 91, 93

Fourteenth U.S. Colored Troops, 284, 346

Fourth Army Corps, 173, 177, 180, 183, 187, 188, 190, 193, 195, 198, 204, 206, 207, 210, 211, 212, 215, 216, 217, 220, 221, 226, 230, 231, 235, 241, 250, 251, 252, 253, 254, 259, 261, 263, 264, 265, 266, 276, 279, 283, 284, 285, 287, 289, 306, 316, 317, 322, 335, 338, 339, 342, 343, 345, 346, 347, 357, 361, 367, 383

Fourth Artillery (Washington Bat.), 34, 42, 43

Fourth Kentucky Regt. Inf., 85, 86, 87, 91, 92, 94, 95, 99, 164, 197

Fourth Michigan Inf., 197, 372, 373, 382

Fourth Ohio Cav., 187, 192, 197, 364

Fourth Tenn. Cav. Regt., 197

4th U.S. Infantry Regt., 16, 25, 26, 27, 30, 31, 32

Fox Capt. P. V., 177

Frankfort, Ky., 77, 113

*Frank Leslie's Magazine*, 96, 97

Franklin, Tenn., 290, 291, 293, 294, 295, 296, 297, 298, 299, 301, 303, 305, 312, 313, 333, 336, 337, 338, 339, 345, 346, 349, 350, 352, 357, 388, 400

Franklin Pike, 119, 291, 292, 323, 327, 336, 339, 345, 346, 347, 349, 355

Franklin Rd., 311

Fredericksburg, battle of, 324

French, Maj. Gen. Samuel G., 10, 27, 32, 43, 45, 225

French's Division, 217, 225

Frink, U. Surgeon Charles S., 299

Fry, Maj. Cary H., 44

Fry, Col. James B., 115

Fry, Col. Speed S., 87, 88, 89, 91, 94, 97, 99

Fry's Division, 117, 118, 119, 122

Fullerton, Bvt. Brig. Gen. J. S., 143

G

Gadsden, Ala., 204, 272, 276, 283

Gallatin, Tenn., 117, 118, 185, 340

Galt House, 113

Gardner, W. M., 368

Garfield, Brig. Gen. James A., 135, 142, 144, 145, 160, 162, 166, 174, 175, 396

Garfield Memorial (Cleveland, Ohio), 398

Garland, Lt. Col. John, 24, 25, 26, 28, 29, 32

Garnett, Brig. Gen. Robert S., 53

Garrard, Brig. Gen. Kenner, 53, 214, 217, 220, 227, 247, 327

Garrards' Cavalry, 224, 257, 262

Garrard's Division of Cavalry, 244, 251, 253, 259, 327, 345

"Gate-City of the South", 275

"Gateway City", 136

"Gateway to the deep South", 135

Gaw, Capt. W. B., 158, 159, 161, 165

Gaylesville, Ala., 272, 274, 283

Geary, Brig. Gen. John W., 187, 188, 189, 193, 215, 216, 221, 236

Geary's Division, 187, 188, 189, 195, 197, 221, 224, 227, 237

Georgia, 57, 60, 137, 199, 201, 209, 219, 252, 270, 271, 272, 273, 282, 284, 285, 287, 300, 333, 364, 370, 371, 377, 390, 402

Georgia Campaign, 402

Georgia Home Guards, 197

Georgia Militia, 243, 261, 300

Georgians, 64

Germantown, N. C., 368

Gettysburg, battle of, 324

Gibraltar of the West, 103

Gilbert, Brig. Gen. Charles C., 114

Gilham, Maj. William, 57

Gillem, Brig. Gen. Alvan G., 94, 196, 203, 341, 353, 354, 368, 369, 370, 373

Gillem's Command, 354

Giltner, Col. Henry L., 353

Gist, Brig. Gen. States Right, 298

Glasgow, Ky., 112, 115, 355

Goddard, Maj. C., 125

Goldsborough, N. C., 69, 362

Golgotha, Ga., 227, 230

Gordon, Brig. Gen. George W., 298, 338

Gordon's Ferry, Tenn., 335

Gordon's Mill, Ga., 150

Gordon's Spring, Ga., 221

Gorman, Brig. Gen. Willis A., 35, 38, 39

Govan, Brig. Gen. Daniel C., 263

452

Russell's Mills, 206
Russellville, Ala., 110, 354, 355
Rutherford's Creek, 291, 330, 349, 350

S

Sacket, Delos B., 53
St. George Island, 386
St. Louis, Mo., 54, 104, 338, 390
St. Paul's Island, 386
St. Paul's Episcopal Church, 51, 395
Salem, N.C., 129, 131, 368
Salisbury, 368, 369
Salt River, 76
Saltillo, Mexico, 32, 34, 35, 39, 41
Saltillo garrison, 33
Saltville, Va., 341, 353, 354
Sam (the Thomas overseer), 5
San Antonio, Texas, 54, 65
Sand Mountain, 136, 150, 204
Sandtown, 257, 259, 260
Sandtown Rd., 233, 235, 237, 259, 260
San Francisco, Calif., 1, 2, 70, 384, 385,
    387, 392, 396
San Luis Potosi, 33, 41
Santa Ana, Gen. Antonio Lopez de, 33,
    35, 39, 41
Savannah, Ga., 275, 300, 302, 328
Savannah, Tenn., 104, 105, 197, 370
Savannah River, 371
Sawyer, Lt. Col. R. M., 214, 218, 231,
    240, 251, 288, 357
Schoepf, Brig. Gen. Albin F., 79, 80,
    81, 82, 84, 85, 86, 90, 91, 93, 101,
    107
Schofield, Maj. Gen. John M., 201, 210,
    218, 219, 221, 222, 223, 224, 228,
    229, 230, 232, 234, 235, 237, 239,
    240, 245, 246, 251, 252, 255, 261,
    262, 276, 285, 287, 288, 289, 290,
    291, 292, 293, 294, 295, 296, 297,
    298, 299, 302, 303, 305, 309, 312,
    313, 315, 316, 323, 324, 335, 336,
    337, 338, 339, 341, 343, 344, 345,
    346, 347, 349, 353, 356, 360, 361,
    384, 388, 389, 390, 395
Schofield's Army, 235, 236, 237, 248,
    277, 293, 294, 295, 351
Schofield's Army of the Ohio, 244, 248
Schofield's Corps, 350
Schofield's Division, 262
Schofield's troops, 232, 327, 336, 345,
    346
Schurz, Maj. Gen., 193
Scott, F. P., 185
Scott, Capt. J. M., 26

Scottsborough, 355
Scott, Thomas M., 298
Scott, Maj. Gen. Winfield, 53, 56, 62,
    64, 65, 77, 78
Scribner, Pvt. Benjamin F., 121, 164
Scribner's Brigade, 121, 130, 156
Scully, Lt. Col. James W., 94, 185
Sears' brigade, 340
Secession Convention, 65
Second Dragoons, 28, 35
Second East Tenn. Regt., 85
Second Illinois Regt., 34, 36, 37, 40, 44
Second Indiana Cav., 160
Second Indiana Regt., 35, 36, 43
Second Infantry, 26
Second Kentucky Regt., 34, 35, 37, 40,
    44
Second Michigan Regt., 354
Second Minnesota Regt., 86, 91, 92, 93,
    95
Second Missouri Infantry, 256
Second Regt., U.S. Cavalry, 52, 54, 71,
    74
Second Seminole War, 13, 16
Second Tennessee Cav., 197
Second Tennessee Regt., 91
Second U.S. Cavalry, 53
Secretary of War, 8, 53, 67
Seddon, James A., Sec. War, 146
Sedgwick, John, 53
Selma, 285, 360, 362, 363, 364, 365,
    366
Seminole Indians, 16
Seminole War, 10
Sequatchie Valley, 111, 136, 172
Sevenmile Creek, 106, 107
Seventeenth Army Corps, 201, 283
Seventeenth Indiana Regt., 130, 366
Seventeenth Ohio Regt., 80, 83, 90, 93
Seventh Kentucky Cav., 197
Seventh U.S. Infantry, 17, 19, 20, 21,
    23
Seventy-fourth Ohio Regt., 125, 165
Seventy-second Indiana Regt., 130, 203
Seventy-third Indiana Regt., 280
Shallow Ford, 211
Shanklin, Lt. Col. James M., 123
Shanks, W. F. G., 127
Shelbyville, 123, 126, 128, 289
Shelbyville-Western Line, 128
Shellmound, 150
Shenandoah Valley, 71
Shepherd, Lt. Col. Oliver L., 121
Sheridan, Gen. Philip H., 120, 121,
    122, 132, 159, 160, 181, 188, 191,
    193, 215, 267, 324, 384, 391, 398

264, 285, 287, 336, 338, 356, 361
Stanley's (T. R.) Brigade, 158, 160, 177
Stanley's Cavalry, 123
Stanley's Corps, 259, 260, 261, 262, 263, 264, 265, 276, 284, 336
Stanley's Division, 204, 211, 237, 239, 247
Stanley, Gen. Timothy R., 158, 160, 165, 193, 237, 291, 337
Stanton, Edwin M., 68, 99, 100, 126, 173, 174, 301, 302, 304, 309, 320, 321, 326, 327, 331, 332, 370, 398
Starkweather, John C., 119, 122
Starkweather's Brigade, 119, 120, 122, 156
Starnes, Col. James W., 132
Stars and Stripes, 32
State Rd. (see LaFayette Rd.)
Statesville, 369
Steedman, Col. James B., 91, 93, 133, 143, 161, 164, 257, 259, 276, 279, 299, 305, 316, 322, 325, 327, 337, 339, 343, 344, 345, 346, 352, 354, 356, 381
Steedman's Brigade, 132, 133
Steedman's Camp, 91
Steedman's Command, 282, 283, 349
Steedman's Division, 160, 163
Steele, Gen. Frederich, 308
Steen, Capt. Enoch, 35, 43
Stephens, Alexander H., 62
Steuart, George H., 53
Steubenville, 79, 136
Stevens' Gap, 138, 150, 151, 152, 153, 170
Stevenson, Ala., 175, 197, 215, 280, 282, 287, 300, 303, 335, 352
Stevenson, Gen. Carter L., 213, 221, 362
Stevenson's Divisions (Carter L.), 221, 223, 224, 237
Stewart, Pvt., 23
Stewart, Gen. 277
Stewart, Gen. A. P., 157, 191, 221, 290, 297
Stewartsborough, 119, 120
Stewart's Corps, 247, 261, 271, 282, 283, 288, 289, 291, 323, 362
Stewart's Creek, 119, 120
Stewart's Corps, 334, 340
Stewart's Little Giant Division, 157, 221, 223
Sticksene, 387
Stilesborough, 226, 227
Stitch, Joseph, 94

Stokes' Battery, 122
Stokes, Col. William B., 204, 214
Stone, Capt. Henry, 267, 356
Stoneman, Gen. George, 53, 65, 221, 255, 256, 341, 353, 354, 360, 362, 367, 368, 369, 370, 373
Stoneman's Cavalry, 231, 367
Stoneman's Division, 222, 230, 232
Stones River, 117, 118, 120, 122, 123, 125, 126, 127, 324, 375, 393, 402
Stoughton, W. L., 165
Strahl, Otho, 298
Strawberry Plains, 341, 342
Streight, Gen. Abel D., 246
Streight's Brigade, 246
Strickland's Brigade, 335
Stringer's Ridge, 180
Stuart, Gen. James Ewell Brown "Jeb" 53
Sturgis, Gen. Samuel D., 53
Sulphur Brand, 279
Summerfield Rd., 364
Summerton Rd., 190
Summerville, 282, 283
Sumner, Edwin, 52, 53
Swannanon Gap, 369
Swinton, William, 401
Sykes' House, 265

T

Tallahassee, Fla., 371
Tampico, 32
Tampa Bay, 16
Tarkon Rivers, 387
Taylor, Lt. Gen. Richard, 362, 365
Taylor's Army, 23, 33, 373
Taylor's Ridge, 136, 192, 206, 207, 213, 216
Taylor's Store, 150
Taylorsville, 368
Taylor, Brig. Gen. Zachary, 16, 18, 23, 24, 29, 32, 33, 44, 48, 111
Tennessee, 68, 74, 75, 78, 98, 100, 103, 105, 111, 112, 129, 136, 148, 194, 199, 214, 271, 272, 276, 277, 280, 281, 282, 284, 287, 288, 289, 319, 320, 328, 330, 333, 334, 338, 341, 353, 356, 359, 366, 373, 377, 378, 379, 380, 381, 397
Tennessee & Ala. R.R., 279, 281, 335
Tennessee Campaign, 271
Tennessee River, 76, 103, 104, 105, 110. 111, 129, 135, 136, 37, 150, 167, 169, 172, 177, 180, 181, 184, 187, 188, 190, 196, 197, 203, 214,

462

215, 216, 258, 272, 276, 278, 279,
281, 282, 284, 285, 286, 287, 290,
300, 304, 324, 332, 333, 351, 352,
354, 355, 361, 373, 403
Tenth Indiana Regt., 86, 87, 89, 91,
92, 95, 354
Tenth Kentucky Regt., 85, 90, 91, 93
Tenth St. (N. Y.), 57
Terrejón, Brig. Gen. Anastasio, 40
Terrejón's Cavalry, 40
Terrett, Lt. J. C., 27, 30
Terrill, William B., 115
Texas, 16, 56, 60, 64, 65, 71, 116, 374,
393
Texas Congress, 17
Texas Rangers, 24, 65
Third Artillery, 10, 13, 15, 16, 35, 36,
43, 52, 111, 179, 393
Third Confederate Cavalry, 130
Third Indiana Regt., 37, 40, 43
Third Kentucky Cavalry, 197
Third Tennessee Cavalry, 279
Third U. S. Infantry Regt., 16, 25, 26,
27, 28, 29, 30, 31
Thirteenth Indiana Cavalry, 340, 354
Thirteenth U. S. Infantry, 125
Thirty-Eighth Indiana Regt., 164
Thirty-Eighth Ohio Infantry, 80, 83,
90, 93
Thirty-Fifth Ohio Infantry Rgt., 81,
83, 164
Thirty-First Ohio Infantry Regt. 90, 93
Thirty-Ninth Indiana Mt. Infantry, 81,
203, 206, 208, 211, 212
Thirty-Second Alabama Infantry, 227
Thomas' Army, 84, 181, 248, 288, 388
Thomas, Artillery, 32
Thomas' Battery, 33, 37
Thomas Circle (Wash., D. C.), 397
Thomas' Corps, 129, 137, 138, 139,
140, 141
Thomas, Cumberlanders, 246
Thomas' Division, 104, 111
Thomas, Elizabeth Rochelle (mother),
2, 5, 8
Thomas Family, 3
Thomas' forces, 142, 276
Thomas, Frances C. (sister), 70, 2, 49,
396
Thomas, Frances K. (wife), 51, 56, 57,
70, 324, 325, 384, 391, 392, 397,
400
Thomas, John C. (father), 2
Thomas, Judith Elvira (sister), 49, 70,
396
Thomas, Maj. Gen. George Henry, 1,

2, 3, 4, 5, 7, 8, 9, 11, 12, 13, 15,
16, 17, 23, 24, 27, 32, 33, 43, 44,
45, 47, 48, 49, 50, 51, 52, 53, 54,
56, 57, 58, 59, 63, 65, 67, 70, 71,
74, 75, 79, 80, 81, 82, 84, 85, 86,
87, 89, 90, 95, 96, 97, 99, 100, 101,
103, 104, 105, 106, 109, 110, 111,
112, 113, 114, 116, 117, 118, 125,
127, 128, 129, 135, 136, 137, 138,
139, 140, 141, 142, 144, 145, 147,
149, 150, 166, 167, 170, 171, 174,
175, 176, 177, 179, 180, 181, 182,
183, 191, 193, 194, 195, 197, 198,
199, 200, 201, 202, 209, 210, 211,
214, 215, 218, 219, 220, 228, 230,
231, 232, 236, 239, 240, 241, 245,
246, 248, 249, 251, 252, 256, 258,
260, 261, 263, 266, 267, 278, 289,
290, 292, 295, 297, 299, 300, 301,
302, 303, 304, 305, 306, 307, 308,
309, 310, 311, 312, 313, 314, 315,
316, 317, 318, 319, 320, 321, 322,
323, 324, 325, 326, 327, 328, 329,
330, 331, 332, 333, 334, 345, 357,
359, 360, 361, 362, 363, 366, 367,
374, 375, 378, 379, 380, 381, 382,
383, 384, 385, 387, 388, 389, 390,
391, 392, 393, 394, 395, 396, 397,
398, 399, 400, 401, 402, 403, 404,
405, 406
Thomas' Line, 143
Thomas, Brig. Gen. Lorenzo, 179, 194,
198, 209
"Thomaston" (Thomas homestead), 2
Thomas' troops, 261
Thompson, Pvt., 23
Thompson, Col. Charles R., 286, 325
Thompson's Station, 291, 337
Thorn Hill, 355
Thruston, Lt. Col. Gates P., 161
Tiffany's, 379
Tile, Pvt. John, 55
Tillson, Davis, 367
Tilton, 224
*Time on the Cross:* The Economics of
American Negro Slavery, 61
Toll-Gate, Ala., 355
Topographical Engineers, 31
*Towah* (gunboat), 286
Tower, Brig. Gen. Zealous B., 277,
278, 337, 373
Town Creek, 203
Townsend, E. D., 313, 394
Tracy City, 203
Trail, Maj. Xerxes, 36, 38
Trans-Mississippi, 370

Trenton, 150, 167, 178
Trenton and Lebanon Rd., 151
Triana, Ala., 216
Trickum, 221
Trickum Post-Office, 221
Triune, 129
Troy, N. Y., 51, 127, 391, 392, 393,
    394, 395, 396, 397
Tullahoma, 126, 128, 129, 132, 133,
    176, 279, 337
Tullahoma Campaign, 129, 136
Tullahoma Rd., 132
Tunnel Hill, 182, 195, 196, 204, 206,
    207, 208, 216, 217, 220, 221, 282
Tunnel Hill Ridge, 221
Tupelo, Miss., 106, 111, 362
Turchin, Gen. John, 152, 162, 165
Turchin's Brigade, 153, 162, 177
Turner, Nat, 4, 5
Turner's Ferry, 245, 246, 259, 260
Turner's Ferry Rd., 253
Tuscaloosa, Ala., 217, 355, 356, 363,
    364, 365
Tuscumbia, Ala., 110, 214, 276, 285,
    288, 331
Tuscumbia Creek, 109
Tuskegee, Ala., 365
Twelfth Army Corps, 173, 178, 180,
    187, 193, 195, 197, 198, 204, 212,
    215
Twelfth Indiana Regt., 354
Twelfth Kentucky Regt., 85, 91, 93
Twelfth Tenn. Cav., 347
Twelfth U.S. Colored Troops, 286
*Twelve Decisive Battles of the War*,
    401
Twentieth Corps, 126, 128, 132, 173,
    177, 217, 220, 226, 227, 230, 231,
    233, 235, 241, 249, 250, 251, 253,
    254, 259, 260, 264, 266, 278, 283,
    284
Twentieth Tenn. (C. S.), 95
Twenty-Eighth Ky. Mt. Inf., 206, 209,
    213
Twenty-First Corps, 126, 128, 136, 154,
    164, 173
Twenty-First Regt. Ky. Vol., 94
Twenty-Sixth Tenn. (rebel), 123
Twenty-Third Army Corps, 228, 276,
    285, 287, 289, 290, 291, 306, 315,
    316, 323, 335, 336, 339, 343, 344,
    357, 361
Twiggs, Brig. Gen. Daniel, 24, 28, 29,
    32, 65
Tyner's Station, 192, 208, 211, 213

## U

Unalaska, 386
*Undine* (gunboat), 286
Union, the, 1, 57, 59, 60, 62, 64, 65,
    70, 71, 73, 87, 148, 218
Union Armies, 105
Union Army, 53, 74, 115, 140, 141,
    293, 300, 402
Union Cavalry, 139
Union Club, 73
Union Flag, 168
Union forces, 138, 149, 181, 324
Union Home Guards, 73
Union people, 101
Union troops, 126, 128, 366
United States, 4, 16, 58, 60, 61, 65,
    98, 100, 145, 366, 383, 387
United States Army, 9, 12, 63, 64, 66,
    68, 194, 198, 210, 353, 374, 382,
    387, 395
U. S. Corps of Engineers, 277
United States Dragoons, 48
United States Flag, 68
United States Fleet, 68
United States forces, 65, 99
United States Government, 59, 70, 73,
    201
United States Military Academy, 7, 8,
    50, 51, 57
U. S. Military R.R.s, 283
United States Navy, 73, 281
United States Volunteers, 74, 106, 266,
    267, 316, 318, 323, 325
United States troops, 65
Upton, Bvt. Maj. Gen. Emory D., 363,
    365, 371
Upton's Division, 364, 365
Utica, N. Y., 398
Utoy Creek, 254, 259
Utoy Post Office, 259

## V

Valdez (a Mexican), 18
Van Cleve, Col. Horatio P., 92, 154
Van Cleve's Division, 158
Van Derveer, Ferdinand, 132, 158,
    164, 217
Van Derveer's Brigade, 132, 158
Van Dorn, Gen. Earl, 53, 103, 106,
    108
Van Duzer, Capt. John C., 283, 326
Van Vliet, Stewart, 9, 10, 11
Van Wert, 226
Varnell's Station, 206, 207, 213, 222

West's Farm, 79
Wetmore, Stephen R., 90, 93
Wetmore's Battery, 91, 93
Wheaton, Frank, 53
Wheeler, Capt. Erastus, 39
Wheeler, Maj. Gen. Joseph, 172, 204, 213, 256, 257, 258, 260
Wheeler's (Joseph) Brigade, 120
Wheeler's Cavalry, 179, 197, 198, 216, 222, 228, 252, 256, 257, 272, 300
Wheeler's Command, 212
Wheeling, W. Va., 62
Whipple, Wm. D., 333, 335, 356
Whitaker, B. G. Walter C., 143, 188
White Oak Creek, 84, 85
Whitesburg, 186
Whitesides 195, 204
Whiting, Lt. Henry M., 43
Whittemore's Bat. (H, 2nd Ill. Mounted), 185
Widow Davis' House, 152
Widow Dean's, 299
Widow Glenn's House, 154, 155, 157, 171
Widow Hoover's House, 130
Widow's Creek, 150
Wilder, Col. John H., 167, 168
Wilder, John T., 128, 130, 132, 133, 153, 154, 169
Wilder's Lightning Brigade, 128, 129, 130, 151, 154, 155, 167, 169, 170
Wiles, Provost-Marshal, Gen. William M., 198
Wilkesborough, 368
Wilkinson Cross-Roads, 120
Willard, Col. John P., 158, 161, 165, 356, 391, 392
Willett's Point, N. Y., 394, 395
William H. Horstman & Sons (mil. store), 48
Williams, ———— (guerrillas at Lawrenceburg), 185
Williams, Brig. Gen. Alpheus S., 193, 223, 227, 237, 252, 253, 254, 260
Williams' Corps, 253
Williams' Division, 224, 227, 237
Williamsport, 335
Williams, Capt. William G., 30
Willich, Gen. August, 162, 165
Willis' Mill Pond, 255
Wilson, Lt. Col. Henry, 24, 25, 28, 29, 31
Wilson, Maj. Gen. James H., 176, 273,

276, 287, 289, 296, 303, 304, 307, 308, 309, 311, 320, 321, 322, 323, 339, 340, 341, 342, 344, 347, 349, 350, 353, 356, 357, 360, 363, 365, 366, 367, 371, 373, 381
Wilson's Brigade, 25
Wilson's Cavalry, 301, 303, 305, 307, 336, 347, 350, 352, 361, 363
Wilson's Cavalry Corps, 322, 327, 364
Wilson's Command, 344, 346, 366
Winchester & Hillsborough Rd., 134
Winchester & McMinnville Rd., 134
Winchester & Manchester Pike, 134
Winchester Rd., 133, 355
Winstead's Hill, 295
Witcher, Vincent A., 353
Wolford's Cavalry, 91, 92
Women's Relief Corps, 167
Woodruff, W. E., 73
Woods, Bvt. 1st Lt. G.W.F., 26, 28, 30
Wood, Thomas J. Brig. Gen., 53, 111, 141, 158, 160, 161, 162, 164, 181, 191, 193, 230, 251, 316, 317, 322, 328, 339, 342, 343, 345, 346, 347, 349, 350, 353, 356, 360
Wood's Corps, 323, 327, 345, 346, 349, 350, 351, 352
Wood's Division, 159, 177, 181, 183, 188, 190, 221, 229, 230, 235, 236, 239, 245, 246, 247, 285
Wood's Gap, 213
Wood's Troops, 245
Wool, Brig. Gen. John E., 34, 39, 42, 44
Worth, Col. William J., 15, 20, 25, 32
Worth's Division, 25
Wright, Col. W. W., 240, 283
Wytheville, 353, 354, 368

## Y

Yadkin River, 368
Yanks, the, 89
Yankees, the, 76, 137, 262
Yell, Col. Archibald, 34, 38, 39
York's House, 242

## Z

Zion Church, 237
Zollicoffer, Brig. Gen. Felix K., 75, 78, 79, 80, 81, 82, 84, 88, 89, 94, 95, 96, 97, 98

THE MIDDLE TENNESSEE THEATER
Scale
0 5 10 15 20
Miles
N
Big
Waverly
NASHVILLE & NORTHERN R.
Johnsonville
Tennessee
TENNESSE
Duck
Buffalo
Centreville
Williamsp
Colu
Mt. Pleasant
River
Clifton
Lynnvill
Waynesborough
Purdy
Savannah
Lawrenceburg
Pulask
MOBILE
Pittsburg Landing
Phillips Creek
Monterey
Hamburg
Creek
Shoal
Bridge Ck.
Corinth
Farmington
Waterloo
Cypress Creek
Lexington
Tuscumbia
Eastport
Muscle Shoals
Florence
Rienzi
Iuka
Leighton
R.
Cherokee Station
Tuscumbia
CENTRAL
Courtland
& OHIO R. R.
MISSISSIPPI
LaGrange
Russellville
Moulton
ALAB